Laura Lemay
with revisions by Rafe Colburn

SAMS Teach Yourself Perl in 21 Days

SECOND EDITION

SAMS
800 East 96th St., Indianapolis, Indiana, 46240 USA

Sams Teach Yourself Perl in 21 Days, Second Edition

International Standard Book Number: 0-672-32035-5

Library of Congress Catalog Card Number: 00-105848

Printed in the United States of America

First Printing: June 2002

05 04 4 3 2

Trademarks

Warning and Disclaimer

Bulk Sales

Sams Publishing offers excellent discounts on this book when ordered in quantity for bulk purchases or special sales. For more information, please contact

U.S. Corporate and Government Sales
1-800-382-3419
corpsales@pearsontechgroup.com

For sales outside of the U.S., please contact

International Sales
international@pearsoned.com

Acquisitions Editors
Mark Taber
Katie Purdum

Development Editor
Scott D. Meyers

Managing Editor
Charlotte Clapp

Project Editor
Anthony Lawrence Wesley Reitz III

Production Editor
Chip Gardner

Indexer
Erika Millen

Technical Editor
Jason Pellerin

Interior Design
Gary Adair

Cover Design
Aren Howell

Layout Technicians
Rebecca Harmon
Susan Geiselman
Stacey Richwine-DeRome

Contents at a Glance

Contents

Appendixes 589

About the Authors

LAURA LEMAY is a member of the gregarious, brightly colored species of computer-book author known as *tutorialis prolificus.* Although she has been spotted writing in the wild for numerous years, more public sightings have occurred frequently since 1995, including several versions of *Sams Teach Yourself HTML, Sams Teach Yourself Java in 21 Days,* and *The Official Marimba Guide to Castanet*.

When not writing books, her primary habitat is in Northern California. Should you encounter her in person, do not make any sudden movements. Further field notes may be found at `http://www.lne.com/lemay/`.

RAFE COLBURN is a programmer and author working in North Carolina. His previous books include *Sams Teach Yourself CGI in 24 Hours* and *Special Edition Using SQL.* He also has a Web site at `http://rc3.org` that he updates often, and can be reached at `rafe@rc3.org`.

Acknowledgments

To Larry Wall, for writing Perl.

To the excellent Perl programmers who reviewed this book—J. Eric Townsend, Rafe Colburn, Chris Spurgeon, and Ian McKallen—for being so good at finding my mistakes and confusions and offering helpful suggestions for "Other Ways To Do It."

To the perl.ind conference on the WeLL—ditto.

To all the nice folks at Sams Publishing for being very patient indeed during the writing of this book.

And to Eric, for everything, not the least of which was introducing me to Perl a long, long time ago.

—Laura Lemay

I'd like to thank the staff at Sams for their patience, support, and encouragement. And, as always, I'd like to thank my wife—she's a rock.

—Rafe Colburn

Tell Us What You Think!

As the reader of this book, *you* are our most important critic and commentator. We value your opinion and want to know what we're doing right, what we could do better, what areas you'd like to see us publish in, and any other words of wisdom you're willing to pass our way.

I welcome your comments. You can e-mail or write me directly to let me know what you did or didn't like about this book—as well as what we can do to make our books stronger.

Please note that I cannot help you with technical problems related to the topic of this book, and that due to the high volume of mail I receive, I might not be able to reply to every message.

When you write, please be sure to include this book's title and author as well as your name and phone or fax number. I will carefully review your comments and share them with the author and editors who worked on the book.

E-Mail: opensource@samspublishing.com

Mail: Mark Taber
Associate Publisher
Sams Publishing
800 East 96th Street
Indianapolis, IN 46240 USA

Introduction

A long time ago at a workstation manufacturer far, far away, a young writer was learning how to program sed and awk scripts on Unix systems. This was before there was a *Sams Teach Yourself Unix,* so I learned Unix scripting the old-fashioned, time-honored way: trial and error, sketchy online documentation, copying other people's scripts, and asking a lot of questions. Particularly asking a lot of questions. Each time I got stuck I would send e-mail to my various Unix-proficient friends, and each time I would get a patient reply carefully pointing out what I was doing wrong. In addition to the advice, however, nearly every e-mail started with "You should use Perl to do that."

It seemed that no matter what I wanted to do, the answer always included "you should use Perl to do that." Eventually, I got the hint, abandoned the hodgepodge of Unix programs I was working with, and learned Perl. And now I can't imagine using anything else.

"You should use Perl to do that" could easily be the motto of the Perl language (except that it already has a number of mottoes). Perl is the duct tape of programmer tools; it might not be the best solution to any particular problem, but it's certainly capable and pretty darn useful for just about any problem. Quick to use, quick to run, quick to change, you can often hack together a solution to a problem in Perl faster than it would take a C++ IDE to start up.

And you accomplish these solutions not just on a Unix system—Perl runs on a wide variety of platforms including Windows and Mac, and is just as useful on those GUI-centric platforms as it is on a more command line–centric system such as Unix. Use the Web? Perl is one of the most popular languages (and arguably the standard) for writing CGI scripts and for maintaining Web servers.

However, before you can use Perl, you have to learn it. Perl is a mishmash of various Unix tools, shell scripting, C, and occasional object-oriented features. That's where *Sams Teach Yourself Perl in 21 Days* comes in. This book is a gentle but thorough introduction to the Perl language and how it can be used. If you're a beginning programmer, or if you have some background, you'll learn the basics and build on them as the book progresses. If you're an experienced programmer, you might find the first few chapters easy going, but there's plenty of content later to challenge even a veteran. In either case, by the time you finish this book you will have a near-complete grasp of the entirety of the Perl language and how to use it.

How This Book Is Organized

This book is split into 21 lessons and three weeks. Each week covers a variety of topics, growing in complexity, and building on the lessons before it.

Each lesson describes a topic and contains two or three examples that illustrate each topic. At the end of each lesson, you get a chance to apply what you've learned with quizzes and exercises (and the answers to those quizzes also appear at the end of each lesson). On the final day of each week, we'll pause for a day to explore some longer, more useful examples in Perl, to review what you've learned in the previous week and show how larger scripts can be built.

The lessons in *Sams Teach Yourself Perl in 21 Days* include the following:

Day 1, "An Introduction to Perl," is the basic background to what Perl is, what it does, how it works, and how to get started using it.

Day 2, "Working with Strings and Numbers (Scalar Data)," introduces *scalar data*, the basic building blocks in the language, and some simple operators for using them.

Day 3, "More Scalar Data and Operators," finishes up what we started on Day 2, with more detail on the various ways you can manipulate numbers and strings. You'll also get a basic introduction to input and output in this lesson.

Day 4, "Working with Lists and Arrays," shows how to create and manipulate groups of data.

Day 5, "Working with Hashes," expands on the information from the last lesson with an exploration of hashes (also called *associative arrays* or *keyed lists*).

Day 6, "Conditionals and Loops," moves from the subject of data to program flow. This chapter covers conditionals (`if` statements) and loops (`while` and `for`) as well as similar constructs.

Day 7, "Exploring a Few Longer Examples," is the first of our longer-example lessons. Here, we'll look at three examples that make use of what you've learned so far.

Day 8, "Manipulating Lists and Strings," explores some of the various ways in which Perl can be used to manipulate data stored in either a list (an array or hash) or in a string. This includes searching, sorting, extracting, or adding elements, or processing all the elements in some way.

Day 9, "Pattern Matching with Regular Expressions," is the first of two chapters exploring one of Perl's most powerful features, *regular expressions*, which allow you to create and match patterns of characters in data.

Day 10, "Doing More with Regular Expressions," expands on what you learned the day before with more detail about extracting and replacing data matched by patterns, as well as building more complex patterns.

Day 11, "Creating and Using Subroutines," delves into creating subroutines (sometimes called *functions* or *procedures*) to allow reusable code.

Chapter 12, "Debugging Perl," is a bit of a sideline from the description of the core language. In this chapter we'll look at the source-level debugger that can help you track down subtle problems in your code.

Chapter 13, "Scope, Modules, and Importing Code," collects several issues surrounding global and local variables, compile-time versus runtime execution, and the use of code libraries, called modules.

Chapter 14, "Exploring a Few Longer Examples," is the second of the longer example chapters.

Day 15, "Working with Files and I/O," expands on the simple input and output you've learned in the previous parts of the book. You explore working more directly with files on the computer's file system and doing more with getting input into a script and outputting data from that script.

Day 16, "Using Perl for CGI Scripting," explores how to use Perl specifically for creating Web server–based CGI scripts.

Day 17, "Managing Files and Directories," is an extension of the chapter on file input and output; this chapter explores how to work with file systems, including navigating directory hierarchies and renaming and moving files.

Day 18, "Perl and the Operating System," explores several features of Perl that are specific to particular platforms. Much of Perl was developed for Unix and continues to be Unix-centric; the Windows version of Perl has libraries that take advantage of specific features of the platform. This lesson explores those platform-specific features.

Day 19, "Working with References," explores one of the more advanced features of Perl—the use of references, which allow more efficient data management and more complex nested data structures.

Day 20, "Odds and Ends," finishes up the book with a summary of the few features of Perl that weren't covered in the rest of the book.

Day 21, "Exploring a Few Longer Examples," is the last of the longer example chapters.

Conventions Used in This Book

Any word or term that appears on your screen is presented in a monospaced font to mimic the way it looks on your screen:

```
it will look like this
```

Text that you should type is presented in a bold monospaced font:

`type in text that looks like this`

Placeholders for variables and expressions are presented in *`monospaced italic`* type.

Note

A Note presents interesting, sometimes technical pieces of information related to the surrounding discussion.

Tip

A Tip offers advice or offers an easier way to do something.

Caution

A Caution advises you of potential problems and helps you steer clear of disaster.

WEEK 1

Getting Started

WEEK 1

DAY 1

An Introduction to Perl

Greetings and welcome to *Sams Teach Yourself Perl in 21 Days*! Today, and for the next 20 days, I'll be your guide to all things Perl. By the time you finish this book—or at least by the time you put it down—you should know enough Perl to accomplish just about anything you'd like to do, and to converse intelligently with other Perl programmers.

Today we're going to start with some basic information to ease you into working with Perl. Today's lesson is kind of short; just enough to give you a little background and to get you started with some simple Perl scripts. In particular, you will

- Learn some background on Perl: what it is, who created it, who's working on it now.
- Find out why you should learn Perl (reasons besides "my boss told me to.")
- Explore some actual Perl code, so you can get an idea about how Perl is written and run (and be prepared for the rest of this week's lessons).

And so, without further ado, let's get started. Week one, Chapter one, section one—Onward!

What Is Perl and Where Did It Come From?

Perl is not a typo for *pearl*. Perl is an acronym. It stands for *P*ractical *E*xtraction and *R*eport *L*anguage, which is a pretty good description of what Perl does particularly well. *Extraction* for looking at files and pulling out the important parts (for example, the actual text data from an HTML file, or the user or hostnames from a networking log file); and *report* for generating output and, well, reports, based on the information that was extracted. It's a *practical* language because it's much easier to write these sorts of programs quickly in Perl than it would be in a language such as C.

Perl was created in 1987 by Larry Wall, who at the time was already well known in the Unix-software world for having written the freely available `patch` program as well as the Usenet newsreader `rn`. The story goes that Larry was working on a task for which the Unix program `awk` (the popular extraction and report language of the time) wasn't powerful enough, but he realized the task would take a whole lot of work to accomplish in a language such as C. So Perl was created as a scripting language that borrows bits from various other Unix tools and languages, such as `sed`, `grep`, `awk`, shell scripting, and, yes, C. Also, as with `patch` and `rn`, Perl was released for free to the Unix community. And the Unix community approved.

For many years, Perl was the language of choice for Unix system administrators and other Unix programmers who needed a flexible, quick-to-program language to accomplish tasks for which a language such as C would be overkill (or take too much work), or for tasks that were too complex for shell scripting. It was because of its existing popularity as a Unix language that Perl became popular as a Web language for creating CGI scripts. CGI (*C*ommon *G*ateway *I*nterface), originally developed on Unix for Unix Web servers, allowed programs and scripts to be run on Web servers in response to HTML forms or other input from Web pages. Perl fit neatly into that niche, and as the Web and CGI grew more popular, so did Perl. As Web servers and tools spread to systems other than Unix, so did Perl, and these days you can get Perl for just about any computer or operating system out there, for use with Web development or as a general-purpose programming language. Larry Wall originally "owned" Perl and was responsible for keeping it updated and incorporating new changes. These days, with Perl a much larger program and much harder to maintain, the task of updating and maintaining Perl now falls to a close-knit group of volunteer programmers. These programmers, including Larry Wall, maintain the core Perl source, port the source to platforms other than Unix, coordinate bug fixes, and establish the "standard" Perl release (the Authors file in the standard Perl distribution lists the primary *dramatis personae* of Perl). No single organization owns Perl; like the GNU tools (GNU emacs, GCC, GDB, and so on) and the Linux operating system; Perl is defined and managed on a volunteer, goodwill basis. It's also available free of charge; all you have to do is download and install it.

The current major version of Perl is Perl 5, and it is the version this book covers. All Perl releases also have minor versions with various numbers and letters, which most commonly fix bugs that were found in the original release (although some new features do creep into the minor version releases). The current Unix and Windows version of Perl as I write this book is 5.6.1. If you are running Mac OS X Perl 5.6 is included as a standard component.

These minor numbers might have changed by the time you read this, as work is ongoing on all the Perl ports (and at any time, there might be separate releases for less stable beta versions as well as the current "official" version). For the most part, however, the minor version is less important than making sure you have some version of Perl 5 installed.

> If you are running Mac OS X, you are running a flavor of Unix and Perl that behaves as if it were running on a Unix system. Follow along with the Unix directions using the command promt from the Terminal.app.

Why Learn Perl?

There are an enormous number of programming languages available on the market today, all of which seem to claim to be able to solve all your problems in half the time, at a quarter of the cost, and then bring about world peace, too. So why learn Perl over another one of those vaunted languages?

The best reason is that different tools work best for different tasks, and Perl is particularly good at a number of common tasks. But there are a number of other good reasons to learn and use Perl.

Perl Is Useful

How's that for a good reason? Perl is probably the language for you if any of the following profiles describe you.

- You're a system administrator looking for a general-purpose scripting language
- You're a Web programmer with a dozen CGI programs that your Web designers want you to write
- You're a fairly well-versed Unix user looking to expand your knowledge
- You're a programmer looking to quickly prototype a more complicated program
- You just want a language that will enable you to hack around with stuff

You can do real work in Perl, and you can get it done right away.

Perl Doesn't Need Any Fancy Software

To use Perl, you do not need to buy a nifty shrink-wrapped Perl program. You don't need a Perl compiler or an integrated Perl development environment. You don't need a browser that supports Perl or a computer that says "Perl Inside." All you need is one thing: the standard Perl interpreter. You can get that for free, simply by downloading it. Okay, there is one other thing you need: You must have a text editor in which to write your Perl scripts. One of these comes with every system you can run Perl on, so you're still safe.

You Can Program Perl Quickly

Perl is a scripting language, which means that your Perl scripts are just text files, and they're executed on the fly when Perl runs them. You don't have to use a compiler to convert your code to some other format like an executable or a bytecode file, as you would for a language such as C or Java. This makes Perl quicker to get running for initial programs, makes the debugging process faster, and also allows you to modify your Perl scripts quicker and easier than in C.

Note

Scripting languages are often called *interpreted languages* in Computer Science parlance. Although Perl might appear to be an interpreted language because its programs are scripts and the Perl interpreter runs those scripts, Perl is actually *both* a compiled and interpreted language.

When it operates on a script, Perl reads in the whole thing, parses it for syntax, compiles it, and then executes the result. Although this gives Perl scripts the *appearance* of being interpreted, and you can modify and rerun Perl scripts right away as you can with an interpreted language, it also gives you some measure of control over the compilation process. Perl also runs faster than a pure interpreted language does (although not as fast as a compiled language).

Perl Is Portable

Because Perl is a scripting language, a Perl script is a Perl script is a Perl script regardless of which platform you run it on. Although there are differences in Perl on different platforms, and features that only work on some platforms (I'll point those out as we run across them), in many cases moving a script from one platform to another can be done without modifying the script in any way whatsoever—without having to laboriously port to a new operating system, without even having to recompile your source code.

Perl Is Powerful

Perl was designed to be a superset of many fairly complex Unix tools. It's also got all the features you'd expect in a high-level language (and many you wouldn't). Most everything you can do in a sophisticated language such as C, you can do in Perl, although there are, of course, tasks for which C would be better than Perl, and vice versa. You can do simple top-to-bottom scripts in Perl. You can do structured programming in Perl. You can do advanced data structures in Perl. You can do object-oriented programming in Perl. It's all there.

If Perl alone isn't good enough for you, there are also extensive archives of various tools and libraries (called *modules*) to do various common tasks in Perl. Modules to do database interaction, networking, encryption, ties to other languages—just about everything you can think of—are available in these archives. In many cases, if you think, "I need to do *X* in Perl," someone has already done *X* and put their code in the archives for you to use. Perl's cooperative nature means that there are an enormous number of resources for you to take advantage of.

Perl Is Flexible

One of the mottoes of Perl is "There's more than one way to do it." (This is commonly referred to by Perl folk as the acronym TMTOWTDI). Remember this phrase, because I'll be coming back to it throughout the book. The Perl language was designed around the idea that different programmers have different ways of approaching and solving problems. So instead of you having to learn how to adapt your thinking to a small set of commands and syntactical constructs (as in C or Java), the Perl language has an enormous number of constructs and shortcuts and side effects—many of which accomplish the same thing other constructs do, but in slightly different ways.

This does make Perl a very large, complex, complicated language (when I first encountered Perl as a young and idealistic programmer, my first reaction was, "It's so UGLY!"). But Perl's size and depth of features also make it extremely flexible and fun to use. You can write a very straightforward, C-like Perl script—one that uses some of Perl's various shortcuts, while still being entirely readable—or one that relies so heavily on Perl side effects and hidden features that you can make other programmers' heads explode just trying to read it (sometimes that can be a fun way to spend a quiet afternoon). It's your choice how you want to use Perl—you don't have to modify your thinking to fit the language.

Perl Is Easy to Learn

Despite the fact that Perl is a large, complex, powerful language, with lots of features and different ways of accomplishing the same tasks, it's not a difficult language to learn. Really. Mastering *all* of Perl can be quite daunting (and there's only a handful of people who can claim to know *every* nuance of the language and remember them all immediately without looking something up). But the easy parts of Perl are very easy (particularly if you've already got a programming background), and you can learn enough Perl to do useful work very quickly. Then as you progress and become more familiar with the language you can add more features and more shortcuts as you need them.

The Perl Community Is Out There

Perl has been developed and supported on a volunteer basis for nearly ten years now, with programmers all around the world devoting their time to evolving the language and developing the tools that can be used with it. On the one hand, this might seem like a sort of communist idea—there's no company to blame when things go wrong, no tech support number to call when you can't get it to work. On the other hand, the Perl community has provided such an enormous body of helpful libraries, mounds of documentation, and FAQ files that you can get most of your questions answered and get help when you need it. You won't really get that with C, where you usually end up buying a book or two, or seven or twenty, and then you're still on your own.

Getting Started Programming in Perl

I could go on and on about why Perl is cool and why you should use it, but then you'd get bored and go buy someone else's book. So let's put aside the background and get down to work.

Installing Perl

To use Perl—to program in it and to run Perl scripts—you need to have Perl installed on your system. Fortunately, this isn't difficult. As I mentioned before, Perl is free for the downloading, so all you need is some time connected to the Internet to get it.

If you don't have Perl installed, or if you're not sure if you do or not, your first step is to fire up your Web browser and visit `http://www.perl.com/`. Put that URL into your bookmarks or favorites; it is the central repository of all things relating to Perl. You not only find the Perl interpreter package itself, but also the Comprehensive Perl Archive Network (CPAN), Perl news, Perl documentation, Perl conferences and contests, Perl jokes, and just about anything else you can think of.

The page at `http://www.perl.com/pub/a/language/info/software.html` has information about the latest versions of Perl for each platform. You can use that information, and the instructions that come with the Perl package itself, to download and install Perl on your system.

For specifics, you might also want to turn to the back of this book, to Appendixes B, and C, which have simple instructions for installing Perl for Unix and Windows, respectively.

Before continuing with this chapter, you should have Perl installed and working on your system.

Perl One-Liners and Perl Scripts

There are two ways a Perl script can be run: As a bit of code that you type and execute immediately on the command line, or as a script that is contained and executed as a separate file.

The first kind of Perl script is called a Perl one-liner because typically they are only one-line long (although sometimes, depending on the task, that line can get awfully long). Perl one-liners are often used for really simple, specialized tasks where you might only need to do something once; for example, to rename all the files in a directory, or to change all the instances of one word to some other word in those same files. One-liners are quick to write and quick to use, but because they are contained entirely on the command line they cannot be saved anywhere—if you make a mistake typing them you'll have to start all over again.

The other kind of Perl script is contained in a separate file and executed by Perl as if it were its own program. This is the most common and most powerful kind of Perl script and the one you'll use for most of the scripts in this book.

In the next section we'll start out with examples of both these types of scripts.

An Example: The Ubiquitous Hello World

A long-standing tradition in the programming world is the Hello World program. When a programmer encounters a new language or a new system, the first program they are supposed to write simply prints "Hello, World!" to the screen. Far be it for me to go against tradition, so the first Perl script we'll examine in this book will do just that. In this section, you'll run a version of Hello World as a one-liner, and then in the next section you'll run Hello World as a standalone script.

Creating the One-Liner

Hello World as a one-liner is about the simplest Perl script you can do, and it's a quick way to find out if you've got Perl installed correctly on your system.

On Unix, from a command prompt, type the following (the bold parts are the part you actually type; the percent sign is the prompt). Watch out for the quotes—there are single quotes on the outside and double quotes on the inside):

```
% perl -w -e 'print "Hello, World!\n";'
```

On Windows, open a DOS or command-prompt window (look under the Start menu), and then type this command (as in Unix, watch out for the quotes, they're all double quotes, but there are four of them):

```
C:\> perl -w -e "print \"Hello, World!\n\";"
```

What to Do if It Doesn't Work

What happens if it doesn't print Hello, World! onto your screen? If you get errors such as `Unmatched '`, `Syntax Error` or `Can't find string terminator`, make sure you typed exactly the same thing as I have given you here. Quotes are most likely to be your problem—make sure you are not confusing single quotes (') and double quotes ("). If you are working on Windows, don't mix up your backslashes (\) with your forward slashes (/).

If you get a `perl: Command Not Found` error on Unix, a `name not recognized as a command` or a `bad command or filename` error on Windows, then one of three things has occurred: Perl has not been installed on your system, you do not have access to it, or it is not in your execution path. Go back to the Appendix B for Unix or Appendix C for Windows to make sure you have Perl installed correctly.

If nothing happens—if the computer just sits there—then it is likely that you accidentally included a space between the dash and the letter of one of the options (-w or -e), or used different letters from -w or -e. You can press Control+C to get out of the script and start again.

How It Works

The Hello World one-liner has four basic parts:

- The perl command
- The -w option
- The -e option
- The script, surrounded by quotes

With the `perl` command you're calling Perl to execute your script. The -w option turns on warnings. Perl warnings are helpful for debugging. You can turn them on here or in the body of your script. We'll get into more detail about warnings in the next example.

The -e option tells Perl that there is a one-liner script coming up. Any time you use a one-liner, you'll need the -e option.

The part just after the -e is the Perl code itself, inside single quotes ('), or double quotes (") for Windows. In this case, the code inside single quotes is `print "Hello, World.\n";`. The double quotes around the Hello World part are part of the Perl code—in Windows, the outer double quotes are regular quotes, but the inner double quotes have to be backslashed (`\"`)

Another Example: Create Hello World As a Script

Now let's do the same thing, only this time we'll create Hello World as a separate file and execute the script that way. You'll need a text editor. Not a word processor, but specifically an editor just for text: emacs, vi, or pico are just fine for Unix; use Notepad or the shareware programs TextEdit or UltraEdit on Windows; you can use SimpleText BBedit or any of the mentioned Unix tools on Mac OS X.

Create Hello World as a Script

Fire up your text editor and type the two lines shown in Listing 1.1 (well, three if you count the blank one in the middle).

Listing 1.1 The `hello.pl` Script

```
#!/usr/bin/perl -w

print "Hello, World!\n";
```

Don't type the numbers at the beginning of the lines in the listings throughout this book; they're just there so I can tell you, line by line, what's going on in the script.

Also note that if you are in Windows that this version of Hello World is slightly different from the one-liner version, so don't just repeat what you did there.

If you're on Unix, you'll want to make sure you include that first line (colloquially called the "sh'bang"—or shebang—line: "sh'" for the hash (or sharp) and "bang" for the exclamation point). This line tells Unix which program to use to actually run the script. The one gotcha here is that the pathname in that line has to match the actual path to the Perl interpreter; if you installed it in `/usr/bin/perl` or somewhere else in your system, include that pathname there instead of the one in line 1 of Listing 1.1.

If you're on Windows or on the Mac, you don't usually need to include this first line at all. It won't really matter either way because the `#` at the start of the line is a comment, and Perl will ignore that line on platforms other than Unix. However, if you intend to write Perl scripts that will eventually be run on Unix, it is a good idea to get into the habit of including the shebang line, even if it's not entirely necessary.

Note

> If you're intending to use Perl on Windows for Web CGI scripting, some Web servers (notably Apache) require a shebang line in your Perl scripts (albeit one with a Windows-style path starting with C:). Yet another reason to get into the habit.

Save that file as, say, `hello.pl`. Actually, you can call it anything you want, with or without the `.pl` extension. If you're on Windows, you'll probably want to include the `.pl`, though; Windows prefers its programs to have extensions, and it'll make things work better overall.

Note

> Don't feel like typing? All the scripts you'll be exploring in this book are also contained on the Web site for this book at `http://www.typerl.com/`, so you can use the versions there instead of laboriously typing them in. However, typing in a Perl script (and fixing the errors that inevitably occur) helps you learn how Perl scripts work, so you should try typing at least these first couple scripts.

Running the Hello World Script

The next step is to use Perl to actually run your script.

On Unix, you'll need to make your script executable, and then simply type the name of the script on the command line like this:

```
% chmod +x hello.pl
% hello.pl
```

Note

> Depending on how your execution path is set up, you might have to include the current directory when you call the script, like this:
>
> `% ./hello.pl`

On Windows, open a DOS or command window and type `perl -w` and the name of the script, as shown here:

```
C:\perl\> perl -w hello.pl
```

If you're on Windows NT and have Perl set up so that `.pl` files are associated with Perl scripts (as described in Appendix B), then you should be able to just type the name of the script itself, as follows:

```
C:\perl\> hello.pl
```

> If you're on Windows 9x, you'll need to use the full `perl` command each time.

On any platform, you should see the phrase `"Hello, World!"` printed to the screen.

What to Do if the Hello World Script Doesn't Work

If you don't get "Hello, World!" printed to your screen this time, run through all the same checks you did with the one-liner to make sure that you've typed the right thing with all the right quotes. Make sure the first line starts with a hash mark (#).

If you get a `File not found` error or `Can't open perl script`, make sure you're in the same directory as your Perl script, and that you're typing the filename exactly as you did when you saved the script.

If you get a `Command not found` error on Unix, make sure the path in your shebang line matches the actual path to your Perl interpreter.

If you get `Permission denied` on Unix, make sure that you've remembered to make your script executable (use the `chmod +x` command).

How Does It Work?

So, now you've got a one-line Perl script that prints the phrase `"Hello, World!"` to the screen and a two-line file that does the same thing. It seems simple enough, but there's some basic Perlness about that script that I should describe.

First of all, although this is one of the simplest examples of a Perl script, the idea for larger Perl scripts is the same. A Perl script is a series of statements, executed one at a time starting from the top and continuing to the bottom. (There are occasionally digressions to subroutines, bits of code executed multiple times for loops, or code from programs included from separate libraries and modules, but that's the basic idea).

The first line in the Hello World script is a comment. You use comments to describe bits of Perl code to explain what they do, as well as to add reminders for things you have yet to do—basically, to annotate your script for any particular reason you'd like. Comments are ignored by Perl, so they're there exclusively for you and anyone else who might be reading your code. Adding comments to a script is considered good programming style, although generally you'll use fewer comments than actual code in your script.

This particular comment in Listing 1.1 is a special kind of comment on Unix systems, but it's a comment none the less. Perl comments start with a hash mark (`#`), and everything from the hash until the end of the line is ignored. Perl doesn't have multiline comments; if you want to use multiple lines you'll have to start them all with a hash.

Note

> Actually, Perl does have multiline comments, but those are used mostly for included Perl documentation (called PODs), and not for actual comments. Stick to hashes.

The second line of in the file (line 3 in Listing 1.1), and the only line in the one-liner, is an example of a basic Perl statement. It's a call to the built-in function `print`, which simply prints the phrase "`Hello, World!`" to the screen (well, actually, to the standard output, but that's the screen in this case. More about the standard output tomorrow). The `\n` inside the quotes prints a newline character; that is, it shifts the cursor from the end of the current line to the start of the next line. Without it your script will end with the cursor still at the end of the Hello World phrase and not neatly on the next line.

Note also the semicolon at the end of the line. Most simple Perl statements end with a semicolon, so that's important—don't forget it.

You'll learn more about all these concepts—statements, comments, functions, output, and so on, later on in this chapter and tomorrow in Day 2, "Working with Strings and Numbers (Scalar Data)."

A Note About Warnings

Turning on warnings is an extremely good idea when you're learning to write Perl scripts (and often a good idea even when you're experienced at it). Perl is very forgiving of strange and sometimes wrong code, which can mean hours spent searching for bugs and weird results in your scripts. Turning on warnings helps uncover common mistakes and strange places in your code where you might have made mistakes. Get in the habit of it and it'll save you a lot of debugging time in the long run.

There are various ways of turning on Perl warnings depending on whether you are using Perl one-liners or scripts, and sometimes depending on the platform you're running on.

- For any Perl one-liner, use -w on the command line.
- On Unix, use the `-w` option in the shebang line.
- On Windows, call your Perl scripts using the `perl` command and use -w on the command line, or, if `.pl` files are associated with Perl, use the `-w` option in the shebang line.
- In MacPerl, choose "Compiler Warnings" from the Script menu.

Another Example: Echo

Let's do another example. Here's a script that prompts you for some input, and then echoes that input to the screen, like this:

```
% echo.pl
Echo? Hi Laura
Hi Laura
%
```

Listing 1.2 shows the contents of the `echo.pl` script.

LISTING 1.2. The `echo.pl` Script

```
1: #!/usr/local/bin/perl -w
2: # echo the input to the output
3:
4: print 'Echo? ';
5: $input = <STDIN>;
6: print $input;
```

You don't have to understand all of this script right now; I'll explain all the details tomorrow on Day 2. But you should feel comfortable typing and running this script, and have a general idea of how it works. Here's a quick run-through of the code:

Lines 1 and 2 are both comments: The first for the shebang line, the second to explain what the script does.

Line 4 prompts you to type something. Note that unlike `"Hello World!\n"` there's no `\n` in this string. That's because you want the cursor to stay on the end of the line after you finish printing, so your prompt actually behaves like a prompt.

Line 5 reads a line of input from the keyboard and stores it in the variable called `$input`. You don't have to keep track of the characters that get typed, or when the end of the line occurs; Perl reads up until the user hits Return (or Enter) and considers that the line.

Finally, Line 6 prints the value of the variable `$input` back to the screen.

A Third Example: The Cookie Monster

Here's one more example, just for fun. Back in the days of text-only computer terminals, there was a practical-joke program that floated around for a while called "the cookie monster." The cookie monster program would lock up your terminal and endlessly prompt you to "Give me a cookie." (or, "I WANT A COOKIE." or some variation), and no matter what you typed, it would always insist it wanted a cookie. The only way out of the program was to actually type **`cookie`**, something that only seemed obvious after you had spent an hour trying to get out of the program.

Listing 1.3 shows a simple Perl version of the cookie monster program.

LISTING 1.3 The `cookie.pl` Script

```
#!/usr/local/bin/perl -w
#
# Cookie Monster

$cookie = "";

while ( $cookie ne 'cookie') {
  print 'Give me a cookie: ';
  chomp($cookie = <STDIN>);
}

print "Mmmm. Cookie.\n";
```

This one's slightly more complicated than either Hello World or Echo. Here's a sample of what it looks like when you run it:

```
% cookie.pl
Give me a cookie: asdf
Give me a cookie: exit
Give me a cookie: quit
Give me a cookie: stop
Give me a cookie: I mean it
```

LISTING 1.3 continued

```
Give me a cookie: @*&#@(*&@$
Give me a cookie: cookie
Mmmm.  Cookie.
%
```

> That last line is a bit of a variation on the traditional cookie monster program. Note also that this one is pretty easy to get out of; a simple Ctrl+C will break right out of it. The original program was not nearly so nice. But hey, it's only Day One; we can't get that sophisticated yet.

Here's what is going on in the Cookie script, line by line:

- Line 2 and 3 are comments (you should be able to figure that out by now).
- Line 5 initializes the `$cookie` variable to be the empty string `""`.
- Line 7 is the start of a `while` loop. As long as the test inside the parentheses is true, the code inside the curly braces will be executed. Here, the test is to see if the `$cookie` variable does not contain the word `cookie`. You'll learn more about `while` and other loops on Day 4, "Conditionals and Loops."
- Line 8 prompts for the cookie. Note that there's no newline character at the end.
- Line 9 looks really weird. The `chomp` function, which you'll learn more about tomorrow, simply strips the newline (return) character off the end of whatever it was you typed (and stored in the `$cookie` variable).

Once again, if you don't understand every line, don't panic. This is the gentle tour. All will become clear to you tomorrow.

Going Deeper

Going deeper? We've barely gone shallow! You'll find this section at the end of each lesson in this book. The idea behind these "Going Deeper" sections is that there's stuff about Perl that I don't have the time to teach you, or additional ways of doing things (remember, "there's more than one way to do it"). The Going Deeper section in each chapter will give you short overview of these features and pointers to places where you can learn more—the online Perl documentation that comes with your Perl interpreter or the information on `http://www.perl.com/`.

Getting Perl Documentation

Much of Perl's online documentation is in the form of *man pages* (*man* being Unix shorthand for *manual*). Throughout this book, I'll be referring to those man pages, for example, the `perlfunc` or `perlop` man pages. If you're on a Unix system, you can usually access these man pages using the `man` command, like this:

```
% man perlfunc
```

The contents of all the man pages are also available in *pod* format, a special form of Perl documentation that can be read on any platform or converted to plain text or HTML using conversion programs that come with Perl (*pod* stands for *p*lain *o*ld *d*ocumentation). The pod pages themselves are stored in the pod directory of your Perl distribution; you can read them on Unix or Windows using the `perldoc` command and the name of a Perl man page, like this:

```
% perldoc perlfunc
```

If you want to know about a specific Perl function such as `print` or `chomp`, use the `-f` option to `perldoc`, as follows:

```
% perldoc -f print
```

Finally, all the Perl man pages are also available on the Web at `http://www.perldoc.com/`. Often, I find it easier to read and search the Perl man pages via the Web than with the `perldoc` or `man` commands.

If you can't take any of this silly online stuff, and you must have a paper document, one the best ways to go deeper, in general, is in the book, *Programming Perl* (Wall, Christiansen and Orwant, O'Reilly, 2000), also known as the Camel book (for the camel on its cover). The camel book is the definitive reference bible for Perl, and describes Perl in almost terrifying detail—although it's also quite dense and hard to read. The goal of *Sams Teach Yourself Perl* is that you'll learn all the basics, but if you do want to explore some of the more esoteric features of the language, you'll probably find *Programming Perl* an important volume to have. (My copy is quite well-thumbed and scribbled in.)

Getting Help

In addition to the man pages with Perl and online at `www.perl.com`, there are also a number of places you can get help learning Perl from other people if you're stuck.

The Web site `http://learn.perl.org` has a number of resources for beginners, including a whole lot of articles on basics and common problems (with solutions). They also host a number of E-mail mailing lists where you can ask questions.

If you have access to Usenet news, the newsgroup `comp.lang.perl.misc` is a very high volume group, but a lot of people who are very involved with Perl monitor that group. Be forewarned that you should try to get your questions answered using resources on the Web before asking on Usenet; if your question has already been answered in an FAQ you might find the responses you get from a Usenet post to be quite abrupt.

Summary

Today was more of a "hello, how are you" day than a day of hard work. In this lesson, you learned a little bit about Perl history and background, why it's a fun language and why it might be useful for you to learn. After all that background in the first half of the lesson you got your first glimpse at what Perl scripts look like and how to get them to run on your system. You also learned the difference between Perl one-liners and scripts, some basic information about comments, Perl statements, and how Perl scripts run. At this point, you should have Perl installed on your system and ready to go—from here on, it's all code.

Q&A

Q. If Perl is so easy to learn, why do I need 21 days to learn it?

A. You probably don't. If you've got 21 days and nothing else to do, you can learn a whole lot of Perl—more Perl than many people who call themselves Perl programmers know. But chances are good that you can pick up just enough Perl to get by in the first week or two, and ignore the harder stuff until you feel more adventurous or need to do more with the language. If you've already got a strong programming background in some other language, you can probably rip through these earlier chapters quite a bit faster than at the rate of a chapter a day. One of Perl's basic tenets is that you should be able to get your job done as quickly as possible with the least amount of work. If you can get your job done after reading only a little bit of this book, by all means go for it.

Q. I have no programming background, although I've worked with HTML a lot and I know a little JavaScript. Can I learn Perl?

A. I don't see why not. Although I've written this book for people who already have a small amount of programming background, if you work slowly through the book, do all the examples and exercises and experiment on your own, you shouldn't have too much trouble. Perl's flexibility makes it a great language for learning programming. And because you already know about other Web technologies, Perl fits right in with what you already know.

Q. Is the code I write called a Perl program or a Perl script?

A. It depends on how nitpicky you want to get about semantics. One argument goes that compilers compile programs and interpreters interpret scripts. So you have C and Java programs (and C and Java compilers), but JavaScript or AppleScript scripts. Because Perl is essentially an interpreted language, the code you write is a Perl script and not a Perl program. Another argument is that because what you're doing is Perl programming, you're creating a program as part of that process. A third argument is that it really doesn't matter. I like that last argument, but my editor wants me to be consistent, so I'll stick to that first argument and call them scripts.

Q. I typed in the Hello World one-liner and I can't get it to work! Help!

A. Are you sure you have Perl installed on your system? Getting Perl installed and working is the major task to do for today. If you flip to the back of the book, to the Appendixes, you'll find instructions on getting Perl installed and working on your system (assuming that you're on Unix, Windows, or a Mac). In addition, the docs that come with your distribution can go a long way toward helping you get everything working.

Q. I'm on Windows. When I double-click my `hello.pl` script, a window comes up really quickly and then vanishes. I'm obviously doing something wrong, but what?

A. You should be running these scripts from a command or DOS prompt, not from an Explorer window. Start a command-prompt window first, CD to the appropriate directory, and then try running your script using the examples earlier in this chapter. For Windows 2000 you'd usually just type the name of your script. For Windows ME type `perl -w` and the name of your script. Here's a simple example:

```
C:\> cd ..\scripts
C:\scripts> perl -w hello.pl
```

Q. I'm on Windows. You mention that the `#!` ("shebang") line at the start of the file is a Unix thing. Why do I have to include it if I'm not on Unix and don't intend to ever be on Unix?

A. You don't, if you don't expect your Perl scripts to ever need to run on Unix (although watch out, some Web servers might require it for Perl scripting). Because the shebang line starts with a hash, it's actually a Perl comment, so it's ignored by the Windows Perl interpreter. You don't need to include it. But it's a good habit to get into, should you ever need to write Perl scripts on Unix, or worse, convert everything you've ever written on Windows to Unix.

Q. In your examples, some of your print commands use double-quotes, and others use single quotes. Why?

A. Good catch! There's a specific reason for that, involving whether or not you use `\n` or variable names inside the thing you're printing. You'll learn about the difference tomorrow.

Workshop

The workshop section, part of each chapter, has two parts:

- A Quiz, to make sure you've understood the concepts I covered in this chapter
- Exercises, so you can work with Perl on your own and gain experience actually using what you've learned.

Answers to both the quiz and exercise questions are shown below.

Quiz

1. What does Perl stand for? What does it mean?
2. Who wrote Perl originally? Who maintains it now?
3. What's the most recent version of Perl?
4. What are the basic differences between compiled and interpreted languages? Which one is Perl? Why is this useful?
5. Which statement best describes Perl?
   - Perl is a small, powerful, tightly defined language with a minimum of constructs to learn and use.
   - Perl is a large, powerful, flexible language with lots of different ways of doing different things.
6. What's on the `http://www.perl.com/` Web site?
7. What's the difference between a Perl one-liner and a Perl script?
8. What do the -w and -e parts of a Perl one-liner do?
9. What does the shebang line in a Perl script do?
10. How do you create comments in Perl?
11. What are Perl warnings? How do you turn them on for one-liners? For scripts on your platform? Why are they useful?

Exercises

1. Try modifying the `hello.pl`, `echo.pl`, and `cookie.pl` scripts in various small ways. Don't get carried away and try to develop an operating system or anything, just try small things.

   See what kind of errors you get if you try to introduce various errors into the script (for example, try typing comments without the leading `#`, removing closing quote marks, or forgetting a semicolon). Become familiar with the sorts of errors that Perl complains about when you forget parts of a statement.
2. Modify the Hello World script to print the greeting twice.
3. Modify the Hello World script to print the greeting twice—on the same line.
4. BUG BUSTER: What's wrong with this script?

   ```
   !/usr/local/bin/perl -w
   print "Hello, World!\n";
   ```
5. BUG BUSTER: What's wrong with this one? (Hint: there are two errors)

   ```
   #!/usr/local/bin/perl -w
   print 'Enter your name: '
   # save the data $inputline = <STDIN>;
   print $inputline;
   ```
6. (Extra Credit) Combine the Hello World and Cookie examples so that the script prompts you for your name and then says hello to you, repeatedly, until you type **`goodbye`**. Here's some sample output from this script:

   ```
   Enter your name: Laura
   Hello Laura!
   Enter your name: Anastasia
   Hello Anastasia!
   Enter your name: Turok the Almighty
   Hello Turok the Almighty!
   Enter your name:  goodbye
   hello goodbye!
   %
   ```

Answers

Here are the answers to the Workshop questions in the previous section.

Quiz Answers

1. Perl stands for Practical Extraction and Report Language. That means it's a language for extracting things from files and creating reports on those things. The *practical* part means it's a useful language for these sorts of tasks.

2. Larry Wall is the original author of Perl and continues to be intimately involved with its development. Perl is maintained and supported primarily by a group of volunteer developers.
3. The exact answer to this question will vary depending on the version of Perl you have installed. The major current version, however, is Perl 5.6.
4. Compiled languages use a compiler program to convert the program source code into machine code or bytecode. You then run that final version to execute the program. With interpreted languages, however, the source code is the final code, and the interpreter program reads the source file and executes it as is.

   Perl is a combination of a compiled and an interpreted language. It behaves like an interpreted language in that it's fast to create, fast to change, and portable across different platforms; but it also compiles the source before running it and, therefore, has the speed and error-correcting features of a compiled language.
5. The second statement best describes Perl:
   - Perl is a large, powerful, flexible language with lots of different ways of doing different things.
6. The `http://www.perl.com/` Web site is the central repository of all things Perl: it's the place to look for the most recent version of Perl, the Comprehensive Perl Archive Network (tools, modules, and utilities relating to Perl), documentation, frequently asked questions, and more information—just about anything you could want that relates to Perl.
7. A Perl one-liner is a usually short (often one-line) script run directly from the command line (or, on the Mac, run from the One Liner dialog box). A Perl script is usually a longer script contained in a separate file.
8. The -w option turns on Perl warnings. The -e indicates the next bit of text, inside quotes, is a line of Perl code.
9. The shebang line is used on Unix to tell Unix which program to execute for a given script. It contains the path name to the Perl interpreter on your platform.

   On platforms other than Unix, the shebang line looks just like a regular comment and is usually ignored.
10. Comments in Perl start with a `#`. Everything from the `#` to the end of the line is ignored.
11. Perl warnings are special diagnostic messages that can help fix common errors and point out places where you might be doing something that will result in behavior you might not expect. Beginning Perl programmers are advised to turn on warnings as you learn; to help understand how Perl behaves in different unusual situations.

To turn on warnings for Perl one-liners, use the `-w` option on the Perl command line.

To turn on warnings on Unix, use the `-w` option in the shebang line.

To turn on warnings on Windows, use the `-w` option on the Perl command line.

Exercise Answers

1. No answers to Exercise 1.
2. Here's one way to do it:

```
#!/usr/ bin/perl -w

print "Hello, World!\n";
print "Hello, World!\n";
```

3. Here's one way to do it:

```
#!/usr/ bin/perl -w

print "Hello, World! Hello, World!\n";
```

   Here's another way:

```
print "Hello, World!";
print "Hello, World!\n";
```

4. There's a hash mark missing from the first line of that script. That line will produce an error (or, on Unix, the script probably won't run at all).
5. There are two errors:
   - The first `print` statement is missing a semicolon at the end of the line.
   - The line just after that starts with a comment—all the text after the hash mark is considered a comment and is ignored.
6. Here's one way to do it (given what you've learned today):

```
#!/usr/ bin/perl -w

$name = "";

while ( $name ne 'goodbye') {
  print 'Enter your name: ';
  chomp($name = <STDIN>);
  print "Hello, ";
  print $name;
  print "!\n";
}
```

DAY 2

Working with Strings and Numbers (Scalar Data)

Scalar data is a fancy Perl term that means data consisting of a single thing. Numbers and strings are both forms of scalar data. In this chapter, you'll learn about scalar data, scalar variables, and various operators and functions that operate on scalar data. All these things are the basic building blocks that you will use in just about any Perl script you write.

Today's topics include

- Using numbers and strings
- Scalar variables: defining, using, and assigning values to them
- Simple arithmetic
- Comparisons and tests

Scalar Data and Scalar Variables

Perl, for the most part, has a flexible concept of data types. Unlike languages such as C or Java, which have distinct types for integers, characters, floating-point numbers, and so on (and strict rules for using and converting between types), Perl only distinguishes between two general kinds of data. The first type is *scalar data*, for single things such as numbers and strings of characters; and the second is *list data*, for collective things such as arrays. The distinction is not academic; Perl has both scalar and list variables to keep track of, and different constructs in Perl might behave differently depending on whether they operate on scalar or list data, or the context—scalar or list context— in which they are operating. You'll learn about all these things as the book progresses. For today, however, let's keep things simple and stick to only numbers and strings and the variables that can hold them. We'll leave list data for later on in the book.

Although today I'll refer exclusively to numbers and strings as scalar data, there's actually a third form: references are also a form of scalar data. But you don't need to know about references this early in your Perl education, so I'll ignore them for now. You'll learn about references much later, on Day 19, "Working with References."

Numbers

Numbers in the text of your Perl scripts can be used just about any way you'd like to type them. All the of following are valid numbers in Perl:

```
4
3.2
.23434234
5.
1_123_456
10E2
45e-4
0xbeef
012
```

Integers are represented by whole numbers, and floating-point numbers with an integer and decimal part. Floating points less than 1 can start with the decimal itself (as in `.23434234`), or can contain a decimal with no actual decimal part (`5.`). Commas are not allowed; the underscores in `1_123_456` are an optional way of expressing a longer number so that it's more readable (they're removed from the number when it's been evaluated). You indicate exponents using an uppercase or lowercase `e` and a positive or negative number (for a positive or negative exponent). Hexadecimal and octal numbers are represented by a leading `0x` or a leading `0`, respectively.

Perl does not differentiate between integers and floats, signed and unsigned, or short and long numbers. A number is simply a type of scalar data and Perl converts between number types as needed in your scripts.

Strings

In other languages, such as C, strings are considered a collection of characters and are stored in collective arrays, but in Perl a string is a singular thing and is simply another form of scalar data.

Strings can be represented in two ways: as zero or more characters surrounded by single quotes (`' '`) or by double quotes (`" "`). For example, all of the following are strings:

```
'this is a string'
"this is also a string"
""
"$fahr degrees Fahrenheit is $cel degrees Celsius"
"Hello, world!\n"
```

Strings can contain any kind of ASCII data, including binary data (both high and low ASCII characters). However, text strings typically contain only low ASCII characters (regular characters, no accents, or special characters). Strings also have no size limits; they can contain any amount of data, limited only by the amount of memory in your machine. Although reading the complete works of Shakespeare or a ten-megabyte Unix kernel into a single Perl string might take a while and eat up a whole lot of memory, you could certainly do it.

There are two differences between using single quotes and double quotes for strings. The first is that a double-quoted string will perform *variable interpolation* on its contents, that is, any variable references inside the quotes (such as `$fahr` and `$cel` in the previous example) will be replaced by the actual values of those variables. A string with single quotes, such as `'$fahr degrees Fahrenheit is $cel degrees Celsius'`, will print just like you see it here with the dollar signs and variable names in place. (If you want an actual dollar sign in a double-quoted string you'll have to put a backslash in front of the dollar sign: `"that apple costs \$14 dollars"`.) I'll discuss variables more in a bit.

Note

> Variable interpolation also works with strings that contain list variables. You'll learn more about this on Day 4, "Working with Lists and Arrays."

The second difference between single and double-quoted strings is that double-quoted strings can contain the escape characters shown in Table 2.1. These will look familiar to you if you know C, but there are a number of other escapes special to Perl. In single-quoted strings, escape sequences are, for the most part, printed as typed, so `'Hello World!\n'` will print as `Hello World\n`, instead of including a newline at the end. There are two exceptions to that rule: `\'` and `\\` will enable you to put quotes and backslashes, respectively, into single-quoted strings.

```
'This is Laura\'s script'          # prints This is Laura's script
'Find the input in C:\\files\\input' # prints Find the input in C:\files\input'
```

TABLE 2.1 Perl Escape Characters for Strings

Character	*Meaning*
`\n`	Newline
`\r`	Carriage return
`\t`	Tab
`\f`	Formfeed
`\b`	Backspace
`\a`	Bell
`\e`	Escape
`\0`*nn*	Octal (where *nn* are digits)
`\x`*nn*	Hexadecimal (where *nn* are digits, `a-f` or `A-F`)
`\c`*C*	Control characters, where *C* is any character (for example, `\cC` is equivalent to Control-C)
`\u`	Make next letter uppercase
`\l`	Make next letter lowercase
`\U`	Make all following letters uppercase
`\L`	Make all following letter lowercase
`\Q`	Do not match patterns (regular expressions only)
`\E`	End `\U`, `\L` or `\Q` sequences

Note We'll look at `\u`, `\l`, `\U`, `\L`, and `\E` in "Going Deeper" at the end of this chapter. `\Q` will be covered as part of regular expressions on Day 9, "Pattern Matching with Regular Expressions."

Empty strings, that is, strings with no characters, are represented simply with quotes and no characters. Note that the empty string `""` is not the same as a string with a space (`" "`).

So which should you use, double- or single-quoted strings? It depends on what you need the string for. If you need escapes and variable interpolation, use a double-quoted string. If you've got a string with a lot of dollar signs in it (actual dollar amounts, for example); then you might use a single-quoted string instead.

Converting Between Numbers and Strings

Because both numbers and strings are scalar data, you don't have to explicitly convert between them; they're interchangeable. Depending on the context, Perl will automatically convert a string to a number or vice versa. So, for example, the string `"14"` could be added to the number 5 and you'd get the number 19 as a result.

This might sound kind of weird, at first, but it does make things like input and output very easy. Need a number entered at the keyboard? You can just read what was typed and then use it as a string. There's no need to use `special` functions or procedures to convert everything back and forth. Perl does it for you.

Perl will even attempt to do the right thing with seemingly nonsensical statements such as `"foo" + 5` or `"23skidoo" + 5`. In the former, a string without any numbers (`"foo"`) will convert to 0, so `"foo" + 5` evaluates to 5. For the latter, and a numeric string with extra trailing characters `"23skidoo"` will just lose the extra characters, so, `"23skidoo" + 5` evaluates to 28. If you use Perl warnings (via the `-w` option or by choosing Scripts, Compiler Warnings in MacPerl), Perl will complain about these sorts of operations, as well it should.

There's one exception to the automatic conversion in Perl, and that's with strings that appear to contain octal and hexadecimal numbers. See "Going Deeper" later in this chapter for details.

Scalar Variables

To store a piece of scalar data, you use a scalar variable. Scalar variables in Perl start with a dollar sign (`$`) and are followed by one or more alphanumeric characters or underscores, like this:

```
$i
$length
$interest_compounded_yearly
$max
$a56434
```

The rules for picking a name for your variable (any Perl variables, not just scalar variables) are

- Variable names should start with a letter or underscore (after the initial `$`, of course). Other numbers or characters such as `%`, `*`, and so on are usually reserved for special Perl variables.
- After the first character, variable names can contain any other letters, numbers, or underscores.
- Variable names are sensitive to upper and lowercase—that is, `$var` is a different variable from `$VAR` and from `$Var`.
- Variables that start with a letter or an underscore cannot be longer than 255 characters (I personally get a headache trying to imagine variable names that long, but hey, knock yourself out).

You don't have to declare or initialize variables in Perl; you can use them as you need them. Scalar variables without initial values will have the undefined value. You don't have to worry about the undefined value—it'll always show up as either an empty string or a 0 value, depending on where you use them (that interchangeability feature again). You really should initialize your variables explicitly to something, however, and if you have warnings turned on in Perl, you'll get warnings that let you know when you're trying to use an undefined variable.

Note

I'm glossing over the undefined value here. At this point, you don't have to know much about it although later on in this book (on Day 4, "Working with Lists and Arrays," specifically), you'll learn more about how to test for it (using the `defined` function) or undefine a variable (using the `undef` function).

To assign a value to a variable, use an assignment operator. The most common one is the equal sign (`=`). This assignment operator simply assigns a value to a variable, with the variable reference on the left and the value on the right, as follows:

```
$i = 1;
```

The assignment operator returns the value of the thing assigned, and assignment expressions evaluate from right to left, so you can "cascade" assignments like this (where `$b` is assigned the value 4, and then `$a` gets the value of that expression (also 4):

```
$a = $b = 4;
```

Perl also has a number of shortcut assignment operators that I'll discuss tomorrow in "More Scalar Data and Operators."

If you've used other languages, you know that variables are usually considered to have a global or local scope. Perl variables are no different: A variable used in the main body of a Perl script—as we're using it here, and as we'll be using it for the time being—is global in scope to that script (it's available to all parts of the script).

Perl also allows you to create local variables inside subroutines and loops, and also allows global variable namespace management across scripts via packages, but you have to declare and use those variables in a special way to prevent them from being global. You'll learn more about local variables on Day 11, "Creating and Using Subroutines," and more about scope on Day 13, "Scope, Modules, and Importing Code," but for now we'll stick with simple global variables.

Constructing Perl Scripts

In yesterday's lesson, I explained a little bit about what a Perl script actually looks like, and we looked at both a Perl one-liner and a Perl script. Let's pause in this discussion about data to go into a little more detail about that, and about the general ground rules for combining data, variables, and other operations into Perl statements, and Perl statements into Perl scripts.

Perl scripts, whether they are executed as one-liners or in separate files, consist of one or more statements, usually executed in order. Perl statements can be simple statements, such as variable assignment or the expressions you'll learn about later today, or they can be more complex statements like conditionals and loops, which you'll learn about on Day 6, "Conditionals and Loops." Simple statements must end with a semicolon.

Beyond that semicolon rule, Perl doesn't care a lot about whitespace (spaces, tabs, returns) as long as it can figure out what you're trying to do. You can write an entire Perl script of multiple statements on a single line, all lumped together. Sometimes when Perl programmers are showing off they will write Perl one-liners that are like this; technically one-liners because they're run on the Perl command line, but made up of dozens or even hundreds of Perl statements all lumped together (and therefore nearly unreadable).

Generally, however, Perl scripts are written on multiple lines, one statement per line, with some form of indentation to improve readability. What form of indentation style you use is up to you, although Perl programmers tend to conform to a C-like indentation style. (The `perlstyle` man page contains further suggestions for how Larry Wall prefers to format his code, and is worth a read even if you prefer a different formatting style).

Perl statements can also contain expressions, where an expression is simply something that results in a value. `1 + 1` is an expression (that evaluates to 2). Variable assignment (`$a = 1`, for example) is an expression that evaluates to the value of the thing assigned. Perl expressions can often be used anywhere a value is expected, including inside other expressions.

Arithmetic Operators

Operators are not the most thrilling of Perl topics to read about, but you need them to build expressions. Perl has a fairly robust set of operators for building expressions with scalars. You'll learn about some of these operators today, and most of the remainder of them tomorrow in Day 3, "More Scalar Data and Operators."

We'll start with the arithmetic operators, which perform arithmetic operations on numeric data. Strings are converted to numbers as needed. Perl includes the operators shown in Table 2.2 for basic arithmetic operations, with the operands usually appearing on either side of the operator, as you'd expect.

TABLE 2.2 Arithmetic Operators

Operator	*What it Does*	*For Example*	*Results In*
`+`	Addition	`3 + 4`	`7`
`-`	Subtraction (2 operands)	`4 - 2`	`2`
	Negation (1 operand)	`-5`	`-5`
`*`	Multiplication	`5 * 5`	`25`
`/`	Floating-point division	`15 / 4`	`3.75`
`**`	Exponent	`4**5`	`1024`
`%`	Modulus (remainder)	`15 % 4`	`3`

Little of this should be a surprise to you, although the exponent operator might be new. For exponents, the left-side operand is the base, and the right side is the exponent, so `10**3` is the same as 10^3 and evaluates to 1000.

Operator precedence—the order in which operators are calculated, if there are more than one in a single expression, is for arithmetic as you learned it in Ninth grade: multiplication, division, and modulus are performed first, then addition and subtraction. However, negation (unary `-`, as it's sometimes called) has a higher precedence than multiplication, and the exponent operator has an even higher precedence than that (higher precedence means that those expressions are evaluated first). You'll learn more about operator precedence tomorrow on Day 3, "More Scalar Data and Operators."

Arithmetic and Decimal Precision

All arithmetic in Perl is done using floating-point numbers. Although this is convenient for doing simple math (no worrying about converting between integers and floats), there are a number of gotchas surrounding floating-point math that you might need to watch out for.

First is that the division operator always uses floating-point division. The expression `15 / 4` results in 3.75, not 3 as it would be in integer division (and what you would expect if you're coming from C). If you really want an integer result, you can use the `int` function to remove the decimal part, like this:

```
$result_as_int = int 15 / 4;   # result will be 3
```

Another side effect of floating-point division is that sometimes you end up with way more precision than you want. For example, take the simple expression:

```
print 10 / 3;
```

This expression results in the number `3.33333333333333`. This is fine if you want the number `3.33333333333333`, but not if all you want is, say, `3.33` or just `3.3`.

Perl has no built-in mathematical rounding functions, but you can use its printing functions to accomplish the same thing. The `printf` and `sprintf` functions, borrowed from C, are used to format a numerical value inside a string. The `printf` function, like `print`, prints the value to the screen, whereas `sprintf` just returns a string that you can assign to a variable or use inside some other expression. Because Perl converts happily between numbers and strings, you can use either of these functions to control rounding. For example, to print `3.33333333333` to the screen as a value with only two decimal places, use this expression:

```
printf("%.2f", 10/3);
```

The `%.2f` part of this expression is the important part; it says print a floating-point value (`f`) with 2 decimal places after the decimal point (.2).

To convert a value to a rounded-off equivalent inside your Perl script, without printing anything, use `sprintf` instead of `printf`:

```
$value = sprintf("%.2f", $value); # round $value to 2 decimals
```

You'll learn a little more about `printf` and `sprintf` tomorrow.

The final gotcha to note about floating-point arithmetic is in what's called a rounding-off error. Because of the way floating-point numbers are stored, sometimes very simple floating-point arithmetic might result in values that are extremely close to, but not quite, what you'd expect. For example, a simple operation such as `4.5 + 5.7` might actually result in the number `10.199999999999999`, rather than `10.2` as you might expect. Most of the time this isn't a problem, as Perl can keep track of the numbers internally, and `print` will cover up very small inaccuracies like this when you actually print the numbers. One particular place it will show up is if you attempt to compare the value of an expression like this to a constant—a test to see if the expression `4.5 + 5.7` is equal to 10.2 might return false. Keep this rounding-off error in mind as you work with Perl—and particularly watch out for it if you start getting results you don't expect.

One-Liners: Simple Calculator

Ever needed to do a little math really quick, the sort of thing that's too complex to do in your head? I normally keep a calculator around for just these reasons, but my desk is really messy (one of the occupational hazards of being a writer), and I'm lucky if I can find stuff I really need. My computer, like all computers, comes with an online calculator, but because I'm often sitting working with Perl at a command line I can type faster than I can pull down a menu.

With one-liners, Perl enables your computer to become the most complicated basic calculator in the world.

```
% perl -e 'print 154/7'
22
```

Note: Don't forget, on Windows, use double quotes, not single quotes after the `-e`.

This isn't a very elegant one-liner. I left off the `-w` option, because we're not doing anything here that requires warnings. I also left off the double quotes on the item we're printing (the math being calculated) because they're not necessary here—but it also means that there isn't a newline, so the next command prompt will show up right next to the result (you'll have to figure out what is result and what is prompt). Finally, I also left off the semicolon because there's a loophole in Perl that says that if there's only one statement in the script you don't need the semicolon. And yet, it still works. If I wanted to make this pretty and proper, it would look more like this:

```
% perl -w -e 'print "154/7\n";'
```

This would give you roughly the same result, but it would take a lot more characters, and, therefore more opportunities to mistype. Sometimes with Perl it's just fine to be lazy and ugly (well, in your scripts, at least. Perl doesn't care about your personal habits).

An Example: Converting Fahrenheit to Celsius

With numbers, strings, and scalar variables under your belt, you can now start to write simple Perl scripts. Here's a script that prompts you for a Fahrenheit number and then converts it to Celsius. Here's what it looks like when it's run:

```
% temperature.pl
Enter a temperature in Fahrenheit: 212
212 degrees Fahrenheit is equivalent to 100 degrees Celsius
%
```

Listing 2.1 shows the Perl code for this script:

LISTING 2.1 The `temperature.pl` Script

```
1:  #!/usr/local/bin/perl -w
2:
3:  $fahr = 0;
4:  $cel = 0;
5:
6:  print 'Enter a temperature in Fahrenheit: ';
7:  chomp ($fahr = <STDIN>);
8:  $cel = ($fahr - 32) * 5 / 9;
9:  print "$fahr degrees Fahrenheit is equivalent to ";
10: printf("%.0f degrees Celsius\n", $cel);
```

This script is quite similar to the `echo.pl` script you did yesterday, but let's go over it, line by line, based on what you've learned so far today about scalars, numbers, strings, and variables.

Lines 3 and 4 initialize the variables we'll use in this script: `$fahr` for a Fahrenheit value, and `$cel` for a Celsius one. Although we could have written this script without initializing the variables, when it's done this way we have a nice list of all the variables we use in the script and what they do.

Line 6 prints the prompt. Here I used a single-quoted string because there are no variables or escapes here to worry about; just characters.

Line 7 gets a line of input from the keyboard and stores that string in the scalar variable `$fahr`. The `chomp` function pulls the newline off the response. This line is probably still kind of puzzling, but stay tuned, tomorrow you'll learn how input and the `chomp` function work.

In Line 8, all the real work takes place. Here we do the conversion calculation to the value in `$fahr`, and store the result in the scalar variable `$cel`. Note that even though the data you read from the keyboard is in string form, Perl doesn't care. You can go ahead and perform calculations on that data as if it were numbers. Of course, if you enter something nonnumeric like `"philanthropic,"` Perl will squawk about it, thanks to warnings. Tomorrow, we'll learn more about verifying input; for now, let's assume that all the input we get is in the form that we expect.

Note the use of the parentheses in line 8 as well. If the order in which expressions are evaluated in an expression is not what you want, you can use parentheses to group expressions so they evaluate correctly. Here we used them to make sure `32` is subtracted from the value in `$fahr` before it's multiplied by `5` and then divided by `9`. Without the parentheses, the multiplication and division would happen first.

Finally, in lines 9 and 10, we print out the result. Line 9 uses the now familiar `print` function (note that the `$fahr` variable will be replaced with its actual value using Perl's automatic variable interpolation). In line 10, however, we're using the `printf` function to control how the Celsius temperature is printed out. If we used a regular print, the value of `$cel` would be a floating-point number—and could be a very large floating-point number, depending on how the calculation turned out. Using `printf` with a format (here, `%1.0f`, a floating-point format with no decimal places), we can limit the value of Celsius to a decimal (integer) number. Why not just use a `%d` integer format, instead? Because `%d` would simply truncate the Celsius result to the integer value—7.45 would print as 7, but so would 7.89. The floating-point format rounds the Celsius to the nearest integer instead, providing a more accurate result.

Note that although we have two print statements here (one `print`, one `printf`), the output appears on a single line. The first string to print did not end with `\n`, which means that the second string is printed on that same line.

You'll learn more about `print` and `printf` tomorrow on Day 3, "More Scalar Data and Operators."

Operators for Tests and Comparisons

Perl's comparison operators are used to test the relationship between two numbers or two strings. You can use equality tests to see if two scalars are equal, or relational operators to see if one is "larger" than another. Finally, Perl also includes logical operators for making boolean (true or false) comparisons. You'll commonly use the operators for tests as part of conditional and loop operations—`if`s and `while`s—, which we'll look at some tomorrow and in detail on Day 6, "Conditionals and Loops."

The Meaning of Truth

No, we're not going to digress into a philosophical discussion here, but before actually going through the operators, you do need to understand just what Perl means by the terms *true* and *false*.

First off, any scalar data can be tested for its truth value, which means that not only can you test to see if two numbers are equivalent, you can also determine if the number `4` or the string `"Thomas Jefferson"` is true. The simple rule is this: All forms of scalar data (all numbers, strings, and references) are true except for three things:

2

- The empty string (`""`)
- Zero (`0`), which can also be `"0"`
- The undefined value (which looks like `""` or `0` most of the time anyhow).

With these rules in mind, let's move onto the actual operators.

Equality and Relational Operators

Equality operators test whether two bits of data are the same; relational operators test to see whether one value is greater than the other. For numbers, that's easy: comparison is done in numeric order. For strings, a string is considered less than another if the first one appears earlier, alphabetically, than the other (and vice versa for greater than). Character order is determined by the ASCII character set, with lowercase letters appearing earlier than uppercase letters, and spaces count. If a string is equal to another string, it must have the same exact characters from start to finish.

Perl has two sets of equality and relational operators, one for numbers and one for strings, as listed in Table 2.3. Although their names are different, they are both used the same way, with one operand on either side. All these operators return `1` for true and `""` for false.

TABLE 2.3 Equality and Relationship Operators

Test	*Numeric Operator*	*String Operator*
equals	`==`	`eq`
not equals	`!=`	`ne`
less than	`<`	`lt`
greater than	`>`	`gt`
less than or equals	`<=`	`le`
greater than or equals	`>=`	`ge`

Here are a bunch of examples of both the number and string comparisons:

```
4 < 5               # true
4 <= 4              # true
4 < 4               # false
5 < 4 + 5           # true (addition performed first)
6 < 10 > 15         # syntax error; tests cannot be combined
'5' < 8             # true; '5' converted to 5
'add' < 'adder'     # use lt for strings; this is an error under -w
'add' lt 'adder'    # true
'add' lt 'Add'      # false; upper and lower case are different
'add' eq 'add '     # false, spaces count
```

Note that none of the equality or relational expressions can be combined with other equality or relational expressions. Although you can have an arithmetic expression `5 + 4 - 3`, which evaluates left to right, you cannot have an expression `6 < 10 > 15`; this will produce a syntax error in Perl because there's no way to evaluate it.

Be careful also to remember that `==` is the equals test, and is not to be confused with `=`, which is the assignment operator. The latter is an expression that can return true or false, so if you accidentally use `=` where you mean `==`, it can be hard to track down the error.

It might seem odd to have to worry about two sets of comparison operators when Perl can convert between numbers and strings automatically. The reason there are two sets is precisely because numbers and strings can be automatically converted; you need a way of saying "no, really, compare these as numbers, I mean it."

For example, let's say there was only one set of relationship operators in Perl, as in other languages. And say you had an expression like `'5' < 100`. What does that expression evaluate to? In other languages, you wouldn't even be able to make the comparison; it'd be an invalid expression. In Perl, because numbers and strings can be converted from one to the other, this isn't invalid altogether. But there are two equally correct ways to evaluate it. If you convert the `'5'` to a number, you get 5 < 100, which is true. If you convert `100` to a string, you get `'5' < '100'`, which is false, because in ASCII order, the character `5` appears *after* the character `1`. To avoid the ambiguity, we need two sets of operators.

Forgetting that there are two sets of comparison operators is one of the more common beginning Perl programmer mistakes (and one which can be infuriatingly difficult to figure out, given that `'this' == 'that'` converts both strings to `0` and then returns true).

However, if you turn on warnings in Perl, it will let you know when you've made this mistake (yet another good reason to keep warnings turned on in all your scripts, at least until you're feeling a bit more confident in your programming ability).

Logical Operators

Logical or boolean operators are those that test other tests and evaluate their operands based on the rules of boolean algebra. That is, for the values of x and y:

- x AND y returns true only if both x and y are also true
- x OR y returns true if either a or y (or both) are true
- NOT x returns true if x is false and vice versa

I've capitalized AND, OR, and NOT in the preceding list to differentiate the boolean algebra concepts from the actual operator names. Otherwise, things can get confusing when we start talking about how you can use `&&` or `and` to deal with and, or `||` or `or` to deal with or, and/or `not` for not (I'll try to avoid talking this way for just this reason).

In Perl's usual way of making sure you've got enough syntax choices to hang yourself, Perl has not just one set of logical comparisons, but two: one borrowed from C, and one with Perl keywords. Table 2.4 shows both these sets of operators.

TABLE 2.4 Logical Comparisons

C-Style	*Perl Style*	*What it means*
`&&`	`and`	logical AND
`||`	`or`	logical OR
`!`	`not`	logical NOT

There are also operators for logical XOR—`^` and `xor`—but they're not commonly used outside bit manipulations, so I haven't included them here.

The only difference between the two styles of operators is in precedence; the C-style operators appear higher up on the precedence hierarchy than the Perl-style operators. The Perl-style operators' very low precedence can help you avoid typing some parentheses, if that sort of thing annoys you. You'll probably see the C-style operators used more often in existing Perl code; the Perl-style operators are a newer feature, and programmers who are used to C are more likely to use C-style coding where they can.

Both styles of logical AND and NOT are short-circuiting, that is, if evaluating the left side of the expression will determine the overall result, then the right side of the expression is ignored entirely. For example, let's say you had an expression like this:

```
($x < y) && ($y < $z)
```

If the expression on the left side of the `&&` is false (if `$x` is greater than `$y`), the outcome of the right side of the expression is irrelevant. No matter what the result, the whole expression is going to be false (remember, logical AND states that both sides must be true for the expression to be true). So, to save some time, a short-circuiting operator will avoid even trying to evaluate the right side of the expression if the left side is false.

Similarly, with `||`, if the left side of the expression evaluates to true, then the whole expression returns true and the right side of the expression is never evaluated.

Both forms of logical operators return false if they're false. If they're true, however, they have the side effect of returning the last value evaluated (which, because it's a nonzero or nonempty string, still counts as true). Although this side effect would initially seem silly if all you care about is the true value of the expression, it does allow you to choose between several different options or function calls or anything else, like this:

```
$result = $a || $b || $c || $d;
```

In this example, Perl will walk down the list of variables, testing each one for "truth." The first one that comes out as true will halt the expression (because of short-circuiting), and the value of `$result` will be the value of the last variable that was checked.

Many Perl programmers like to use these logical tests as a sort of conditional, as in this next example, which you'll see a lot when you start looking at other people's Perl code:

```
open(FILE, 'inputfile') || die 'cannot open inputfile';
```

On the left side of the expression, `open` is used to open a file, and returns true if the file was opened successfully. On the right side, `die` is used to exit the script immediately with an error message. You only want to actually exit the script if the file couldn't be opened—that is, if `open` returns false. Because the `||` expression is short circuiting, the `die` on the right will only happen if the file couldn't be opened.

I'll come back to this on Day 6, when we cover other conditional statements in Perl (and you'll learn more about `open` on Day 15, "Working with Files and I/O."

Pattern Matching

One last operator I'd like to introduce today enables you to do pattern matching in Perl. Pattern matching, also called *regular expressions,* is a tremendously powerful feature in Perl that will probably form the core of a lot of scripts you write; in fact in the middle of this book, on Days 9 and 10, we'll go into pattern matching with mind-boggling detail. But pattern matching is so useful and so essential to Perl that it is worth introducing, even in a very limited capacity, way up here in Day 2.

You've already seen a test that compares two strings for equality using the `eq` operator, like this:

```
$string eq 'foo'
```

That test will only return true if the value contained in the scalar variable `$string` is exactly equal to the string `'foo'`. But what if you wanted to test to see if the value of `$string` contained `'foo'`, or if the value of `$string` contained `123`, or if it contained any digits at all, or three spaces followed by three digits, or any other pattern of letters or numbers or whitespace that you can think of? That's pattern matching. If you've used the `*` to refer to multiple filenames on a command line, it's the same idea. If you've used regular expressions in any form on Unix, it's exactly the same thing (Perl's are slightly different, but follow many of the same rules).

To construct a pattern matching expression, you need two things: a comparison operator and a pattern; like this:

```
$string =~ m/foo/
```

This expression tests to see if the value of `$string` contains the characters `foo`, and if it does, it returns true. `$string` could be exactly `'foo'` and the test would be true. `$string` could also be `'fool'`, `'buffoon'`, or `'foot-and-mouth disease'` and this test would still return true. As long as the characters `f o` and `o`, in that order, are contained somewhere inside `$string`, this test will return true.

The `=~` operator is the actual pattern match operator; it says to do pattern matching on the scalar thing on the left side of the operator with the pattern on the right side of the operator. There is also an operator for negated patterns, that is, return true if the pattern doesn't match: `!~`. In this case, the test would only return true if `$string` did *not* contain the characters `foo`.

The `m/.../` operator, to the right of the pattern matching operator, is the pattern itself. The part inside the slashes is the pattern you will match on. Here our pattern is `foo`. For now we'll stick to matching simple alphabetic and numeric characters, as we progress through the book you'll learn about special characters that match multiple kinds of things. Note that you don't have to include either single or double quotes around the characters you're looking for. If you want to include a slash in your pattern, preface it with a backslash:

```
$string =~ m/this\/that/
```

This pattern will match the characters `this/that` anywhere inside `$string`.

For these patterns, the `m` part is optional. Most of the time, you'll see patterns written without the `m`, like this:

```
$string =~ /foo/
```

There's a major catch to watch out for with patterns that match specific characters, similar to those you've learned about today: the characters you're matching are case-sensitive. This pattern, `/foo/`, will only match exactly the characters `f o` and `o`; it will not match uppercase F or O. So if `$string` contains "Foo" or "FOO" the pattern matching test will not return true. You can make the pattern case-insensitive by putting an i at the end of the pattern, which means it will search both upper and lowercase.

```
/foo/i
```

You can use case-sensitive or insensitive pattern matching depending on what you're looking for in the test.

Table 2.5 shows a summary of the pattern-related operators and expressions. We'll look more at patterns as the book progresses.

TABLE 2.5 Operators for Patterns

Operator	*What it Means*
`=~`	match test
`!~`	negated match test
`m/.../ /.../`	pattern
`m/.../i /.../i`	case insensitive pattern

Another Example: More Cookies

Let's make a simple modification to the cookie.pl script from yesterday to use pattern matching. Listing 2.2 shows `cookie.pl`, to refresh your memory:

LISTING 2.2 The `cookie.pl` Script

```
1: #!/usr/local/bin/perl -w
2: #
3: # Cookie Monster
4:
5: $cookie = "";
6:
7: while ( $cookie ne 'cookie') {
8:   print 'Give me a cookie: ';
9:   chomp($cookie = <STDIN>);
10: }
11:
12: print "Mmmm. Cookie.\n";
```

Line 7 is the important line we're interested in here. The test in line 7 includes the string comparison test `ne` (not equals), so that each time the `$cookie` variable does *not* include the string cookie, the loop will repeat. (We'll look at this kind of loop in a little more detail tomorrow and at all kinds of loops on Day 6).

When you run this example, you have to type the string "cookie" exactly to get out of it. Typing anything else will just repeat the loop.

A useful modification, then, would be to allow the user to type something that contains the word "cookie"—for example, "cookies," or "here's a cookie, now shut up," or any other phrase.

All we need to do is modify that one line, line 7, and change the `ne` comparison to a pattern match and the string to a pattern, like this:

```
while ( $cookie !~ /cookie/i) {
```

Why are we using the `!~` pattern matching operator, rather than `=~`? We need a negated comparison here; one that returns true if the comparison does *not* work. Just as the original nest was a negated comparison (`ne`, a not-equals string test), we need a negated pattern match here.

The pattern here is simply the string `cookie`. Note that in simple patterns like this one you don't need the quotes around the string, and note also I am not using the `m` part of the pattern operator (as I mentioned in the previous section, it's very commonly omitted). I've also included the `i` option at the end of the pattern so that the `cookie` won't be case sensitive—the user can type `cookie` or `Cookie` or `COOKIE` and that will be okay.

Listing 2.3 shows the final script, which I've called `cookie2.pl`:

LISTING 2.3 The `cookie2.pl` Script

```
#!/usr/local/bin/perl -w

$cookie = "";

while ( $cookie !~ /cookie/i) {
  print 'Give me a cookie: ';
  chomp($cookie = <STDIN>);
}

print "Mmmm.  Cookie.\n";
```

Going Deeper

Perl is such a wide and deep language that I can't hope to explain it all without ending up with a phonebook-sized volume. In this section, then, are the things you can do with scalar data that I haven't covered in the previous sections. Some of these things we'll explore in more detail later on in this book, but for the most part these topics are parts of the language you'll have to explore on your own.

As I mentioned yesterday, throughout this book, when I refer to the `perlop` or `perlfunc` man pages—or to any Perl man pages—you can find these pages as part of the documentation for your Perl interpreter, or on the Web at `http://www.perldoc.com/`.

Quoting Strings and Patterns

The quote characters `''` and `""` in Perl might seem like immutable requirements for creating strings, but, actually, they're not. There are a number of ways you can create strings in Perl besides using single and double quotes, some of which interpolate variables, and some of which don't. For example, instead of creating the string `'Beware the ides of March'` with single quotes, you could use the `q//` operator, like this:

```
q/Beware the ides of March/
```

Don't like quotes or slashes? No problem. You can use the `q//` operator with any non-alphanumeric or nonwhitespace character (that is, no letters, numbers, spaces, or tabs), as long as you use the same character to begin and end the string and start the whole thing with a `q`. The following examples are all equivalent in Perl:

```
'Beware the ides of March'

q/Beware the ides of March/

q#Beware the ides of March#

q(Beware the ides of March)
```

As with single quotes, the `q//` operator does not interpolate variables. For double quotes and variable interpolation, you can use the `qq//` operator in the same way:

```
"stored $num reminders"
qq/stored $num reminders/
qq^stores $num reminders^
```

You might want to use these formats if, for example, you have a string with lots of quotes in it that all need escaping. By substituting, say, a slash character for the quote, you can put quotes inside your strings without having to escape them.

See the `perlop` man page for details on the various quote-like operators.

If you're thinking `q//` and `qq//` look something like `m//`, you're right; they're both considered quoting operators: one for strings, the other for patterns. In fact, you can use `m//` in the same way, with any nonalphanumeric character substituted for the slash:

```
m?foo?
```

```
m$cookie$
```

If you do use a pattern with a character other than the slash, note that you do have to retain the `m` at the start of the pattern. If you leave it off you must use the slash.

Unquoted Strings (Barewords)

Single words in lowercase without quotes that have no other meaning in Perl are interpreted as strings. Perl calls them *barewords*, and they're generally discouraged because they make scripts very hard to read, are error-prone, and you never know when a bareword you use a lot will end up being a reserved word in a future version of the language. Avoid them. If you have Perl warnings turned on, it will complain about this sort of thing.

Upper and Lowercase Escapes

In Table 2.1, I summarized the escape characters available for interpolated (double-quoted) strings. Amongst those were escapes for upper and lowercasing strings (`\l`, `\u`, `\L`, `\U`, and `\E`). Use these escapes to force upper or lowercase values in strings.

The `\l` and `\u` escapes are used to make the next letter in the string lower or uppercase. You could use `\u`, for example, to make sure the start of a sentence was capitalized. `\L` and `\U` are used to make lower or uppercase a series of characters inside a string; they will both convert the characters that follow in the string until the end of the string or until a `\E` occurs. These escapes aren't necessarily useful in ordinary quoted strings, but they'll become useful later on when you create patterns for search-and-replace procedures.

More About Variable Interpolation in Strings

Variable interpolation is the capability of Perl to replace variable references in strings with their actual values. In some cases, however, it might be difficult for Perl to figure out where the variable ends. For example, take the following string:

```
"now reading the $valth value\n";
```

In this string, the variable to be interpolated is actually called `$val` and contains a number. But because the final string will say something like `"now reading 12th value"`, the name of the variable butts up against the `th` part and Perl looks for a variable called `$valth` instead of `$val`. There are a number of ways around this sort of problem—not the least of which is concatenating multiple strings to form the final one. But, Perl also provides syntax to get around this problem, like this:

```
"now reading the ${val}th value\n";
```

The curly braces (`{}`) in this case are simply delimiters so that Perl can figure out where the variable name starts and ends; they are not printed in the final value. Using curly braces in this way can help get around problems in variable interpolation.

Octal and Hexadecimal Numbers

The `0123` and `0xabc` formats you learned about in the section on numbers apply only to the numbers you actually type into the code for your scripts (*literals* in Computer Science parlance). Input from strings or from the keyboard in octal or hex notation will remain as strings; you can convert those strings to actual numbers using the `oct` function like this:

```
$num = '0x432';
print $num;       # prints 0x432
$hexnum = oct $num;
print $hexnum;    # prints 1074 (decimal equivalent)
$num = '0123';
print (oct $num);  # prints 83
```

The `oct` function can tell from the context whether the string is an octal or hex number; you can also use the `hex` function for hex numbers only.

Summary

Numbers and strings everywhere! Today you learned quite a lot about scalar data. Perl uses the term *scalar data* to refer to single things, and most particularly numbers and strings. Scalar variables, which start with `$`, hold scalar data.

With scalar data in hand, you can create Perl statements, perform arithmetic, compare two values, assign values to variables, change the values of variables, and convert between numbers and strings.

Today you also learned a little about pattern matching, including the pattern matching operators `=~` and `!~`, and the pattern operator `m//`.

The built-in functions you learned about today include these (we'll go into more detail about some of these tomorrow; see the `perlfunc` man page for more details about these functions):

- `print` takes a list of comma-separated values and strings to print and outputs those values to the standard output (`STDOUT`).
- `printf` takes a formatting string and any number of values, and prints those values according to the codes in the formatting string.
- `sprintf` does the same thing as `printf`, except it returns the formatted string without printing anything.
- `chomp` with a string argument removes any trailing newlines from that string and returns the number of characters it deleted.
- `int` takes a number and returns the integer part of that number (truncating any decimal part).

Q&A

Q. How do I define a variable so that it'll only contain a number?

A. You can't. Perl doesn't have strong number types the way other languages do; the closest you can get is a scalar variable, and that can contain either a number or a string.

Most of the time, this will not matter; Perl will convert strings to numbers for you and vice versa.

Q. But what if I end up with data in string form that isn't a number and I try to do something numeric with it?

A. The default behavior is as I described in the section on "Converting Between Numbers and Strings." Strings with no numeric content will become 0. Strings that start with numbers and then revert to characters will lose the characters.

If you have warnings turned on in your Perl script, then Perl will warn you when you're trying to do things to nonnumeric data so you can correct the operation of your scripts before you have this problem.

If you're worried about getting nonnumeric data from the user, you should be checking their input when they make it. We did some of this today; I'll show you more tricks for verifying input on Day 6 and Day 9.

Q. My calculations are returning floating-point numbers with way too many numbers after the decimal point. How do I round off numbers so they only have two decimal places?

A. See the section on "Arithmetic Operators," where I explain how to use `printf` and `sprintf` to do this very thing.

Q. But `printf` and `sprintf` are string functions. I want to round off numbers.

A. Both numbers and strings are forms of scalar data in Perl. What you can do to one, you can do to the other (in many cases). Use `printf` and `sprintf`. Really.

Workshop

The workshop provides quiz questions to help you solidify your understanding of the material covered, and exercises to give you experience in using what you've learned. Try and understand the quiz and exercise answers before you go on to tomorrow's lesson.

Quiz

1. What are the two types of data you can use in Perl?
2. What kinds of data make up scalar data?
3. What are the differences between double- and single-quoted strings?
4. Which of the following are valid scalar variables?

```
$count
$11foo
$_placeholder
$back2thefuture
$long_variable_to_hold_important_value_for_later
```

5. What's the difference between the `=` and `==` operators?
6. What's the difference between a statement and an expression?
7. What does this expression evaluate to: `4 + 5 / 3**2 * 6`?
8. How do you round off numbers in Perl?
9. What are the values that Perl considers false?
10. Why are there different operators for number and string comparisons?
11. Define what a *short-circuiting* logical operator does.
12. How is a pattern-matching test different from an equality test?

13. You have a pattern `/ing/`. Which of the following strings does this pattern match to?

    `'Singapore'`

    `'viking'`

    `'vainglorious'`

    `'intermingle'`

    `'Westinghouse'`

    `'Ingmar'`

Exercises

1. Modify temp.pl to convert Celsius back to Fahrenheit.
2. Write a program that prompts you for the width and length of a room, and then prints out the square footage.
3. BUG BUSTERS: What's wrong with this program?

```
print 'Enter the word Foo: ';
chomp($input = <STDIN>);
if ($input = 'foo') {
   print "Thank you!\n";
} else {
   print "That's not the word foo.\n";
}
```

4. BUG BUSTERS: How about this version?

```
print 'Enter the word foo: ';
chomp($input = <STDIN>);
if ($input == 'foo') {
   print "Thank you!\n";
} else {
   print "That's not the word foo.\n";
}
```

5. Modify Exercise 6 from yesterday (the combination of hello world and cookie) so that it will exit if you type any of the following: `goodbye`, `good-bye`, `bye-bye`, `ok bye`, or just `bye`.

Answers

Here are the answers to the Workshop questions in the previous section.

Quiz Answers

1. The two types of data you can use in Perl are scalar data, for individual things such as numbers and strings and list data, for collective things such as arrays.

2. Numbers, strings, and references. Full credit if you only said numbers and strings; we haven't talked about references yet.
3. There are two differences between single- and double-quoted strings:
   - Double-quoted strings can contain any number of special character escapes; single-quoted strings can only contain `\'` and `\\`.
   - Double-quoted strings will interpolate variables inside them (that is, replace the variables with their values).
4. All the variables in that list except for `$11foo` are valid. `$11foo` is invalid because it starts with a number (Perl does have variables that start with numbers, but they're all reserved for use by Perl).
5. The `=` operator is the assignment operator, to assign a value to a variable. The `==` operator is for testing equality between numbers.
6. A statement is a single operation in Perl. An expression is a statement that returns a value; you can often nest several expressions inside a single Perl statement.
7. 7.33333333333333, give or take a 3 or two.
8. To round off numbers without printing them, use `sprintf`. To print numbers with less precision, use `printf`.
9. Perl has three false values: 0, the empty string `""`, and the undefined value.
10. Perl has different operators for numbers and strings because of its capability to auto-convert scalar values and the differences in handling both those values.
11. Short-circuiting operators only evaluate their right-side operands when necessary. If the value of the left-side operator determines the overall value of the expression (for example, if the left side of a `&&` operator is false), the expression will stop.
12. Equality tests return true if the scalars on both sides of the operator are exactly equal. Pattern matching tests result true of the scalar on the left side of the operator contains characters that match the pattern on the right side of the operator.
13. All the given strings match the pattern `/ing/` except for the last one, `'Ingmar'`, which does not match because of the capital I. If the pattern `/ing/` had an i at the end (`/ing/i`) then it would have matched the last pattern, as well.

Exercise Answers

1. Here's one answer:

```
#!/usr/local/bin/perl -w

$cel = 0;
$fahr = 0;
```

```
print 'Enter a temperature in Celsius: ';
chomp ($cel = <STDIN>);
$fahr = $cel * 9 / 5 + 32;
print "$cel degrees Celsius is equivalent to ";
printf("%d degrees Fahrenheit \n", $fahr);
```

2. Here's one answer:

```
#!/usr/local/bin/perl -w

$width = 0;
$length = 0;
$sqft = 0;

print 'Enter the width of the room (feet): ';
chomp ($width = <STDIN>);
print 'Enter the length of the room (feet): ';
chomp ($length = <STDIN>);
$sqft = $width * $length;
print "The room is $sqft square feet.\n";
```

3. The test inside the parentheses for the `if` statement uses an assignment operator instead of an equality operator. This test will always return true.
4. This time, the test inside the parentheses has a number equality test; because this test compares strings, you need an `eq` test instead.
5. Here's one answer:

```
#!/usr/local/bin/perl -w

$name = "";

while ( $name !~ /bye/ ) {
  print 'Enter your name: ';
  chomp($name = <STDIN>);
  print "Hello, ";
  print $name;
  print "!\n";
}
```

DAY 3

More Scalar Data and Operators

Scalar data, as you learned yesterday, involves individual items such as numbers and strings. Yesterday, you learned several things you could do with scalar data; today, we'll finish up the discussion, show you more operators you can play with, and finish up with some related topics. The things you can expect to learn today are

- Various assignment operators
- String concatenation and repetition
- Operator precedence
- Pattern matching for digits
- A short overview of input and output

Assignment Operators

Yesterday, we discussed the basic assignment operator, `=`, which assigns a value to a variable. One common use of assignment is an operation to change the value of a variable based on the current value of that variable, such as:

```
$inc = $inc + 100;
```

This does exactly what you'd expect; it gets the value of `$inc`, adds 100 to it, and then stores the result back into `$inc`. This sort of operation is so common that there is a shorthand assignment operator to do just that. The variable reference goes on the left side, and the amount to change it on the right, like this:

```
$inc += 100;
```

Perl supports shorthand assignments for each of the arithmetic operators, for string operators I haven't described yet, and even for `&&` and `||`. Table 3.1 shows a few of the shorthand assignment operators. Basically, just about any operator that has two operands has a shorthand assignment version, where the general rule is that

```
variable operator= expression
```

is equivalent to

```
variable = variable operator expression
```

There's only one difference between the two: in the longhand version, the variable reference is evaluated twice, whereas in the shorthand it's only evaluated once. Most of the time, this won't affect the outcome of the expression, just keep it in mind if you start getting results you don't expect.

TABLE 3.1 Some Common Assignment Operators

Operator	*Example*	*Longhand equivalent*
`+=`	`$x += 10`	`$x = $x + 10`
`-=`	`$x -= 10`	`$x = $x - 10`
`*=`	`$x *= 10`	`$x = $x * 10`
`/=`	`$x /= 10`	`$x = $x / 10`
`%=`	`$x %= 10`	`$x = $x % 10`
`**=`	`$x **= 10`	`$x = $x**10`

Note that the pattern matching operator, `=~`, is not an assignment operator and does not belong in this group. Despite the presence of the equals sign (`=`) in the operator, pattern matching and variable assignment are entirely different things.

Increment and Decrement Operators

The `++` and `--` operators are used with a variable to increment or decrement that variable by 1 (that is, to add or subtract 1). And as with C, both operators can be used either in prefix fashion (before the variable, `++$x`) or in postfix (after the variable, `$x++`). Depending on the usage, the variable will be incremented or decremented before or after it's used.

If your reaction to the previous paragraph is "Huh?", here's a wordier explanation. The `++` and `--` operators are used with scalar variables to increment or decrement the value of that variable by 1, sort of an even shorter shorthand to the `+=` or `-=` operators. In addition, both operators can be used before the variable reference—called prefix notation, like this:

```
++$x;
```


Or, in postfix notation (after the variable), like this:

```
$x++;
```

The difference is subtle and determines when, in the process of Perl's evaluation of an expression, that the variable actually gets incremented. If you used these operators as I did in those previous two examples—alone, by themselves—then there is no difference. The variable gets incremented and Perl moves on. But, if you use these operators on the right side of another variable assignment, then whether you use prefix or postfix notation can be significant. For example, let's look at this snippet of Perl code:

```
$a = 1;
$b = 1;
$a = ++$b;
```

At the end of these statements, both `$a` and `$b` will be 2. Why? The prefix notation means that `$b` will be incremented before its value is assigned to `$a`. So, the order of evaluation in this expression is that `$b` is incremented to 2 first, and then that value is assigned to `$a`.

Now let's look at postfix:

```
$a = 1;
$b = 1;
$a = $b++;
```

In this case, `$b` still ends up getting incremented; its value at the end of these three statements is 2. But `$a`'s value stays at 1. In postfix notation, the value of `$b` is used before it's incremented. `$b` evaluates to 1, that value is assigned to `$a`, and then `$b` is incremented to 2.

Note

To be totally, rigorously correct, my ordering of how things happen here is off. For a variable assignment, everything on the right side of the `=` operator always gets evaluated before the assignment occurs, so in reality, `$a` doesn't get changed until the very last step. What actually happens is that the original value of `$b` is remembered by Perl, so that when Perl gets around to assigning a value to `$a`, it can use that actual value. But unless you're working with really complex expressions, you might as well think of it as happening before the increment.

Even though using assignment operators and increment operators in the same statement can be convenient, you should probably avoid it because it can cause confusion.

String Concatenation and Repetition

String and text management is one of Perl's biggest strengths, and quite a lot of the examples throughout this book are going to involve working with strings—finding things in them, changing things in them, getting them from files and from the keyboard, and sending them to the screen, to files, or over a network to a Web browser. Today, we started by talking about strings in general terms.

There are just a couple more things I want to mention about strings here, however, because they fit in with today's "All Operators, All the Time" theme. Perl has two operators for using strings: `.` (dot) for string concatenation, and `x` for string repetition.

To concatenate together two strings you use the `.` operator, like this:

```
'four score' . ' and seven years ago';
```

This expression results in a third string containing `'four score and seven years ago.'` It does not modify either of the original strings.

You can put together multiple concatenations, and they'll result in one single long string:

```
'this, ' . 'that, ' . 'and the ' . 'other thing.'
```

Perl also includes a concatenate-and-assign shorthand operator; similar to the operators I listed in Table 3.1:

```
$x .= "dog";
```

In this example, if `$x` contained the string "`mad`", then after this statement `$x` would contain the string `"maddog"`. As with the other shorthand assignment operators, `$x .= 'foo'` is equivalent to `$x = $x . 'foo'`.

The other string-related operator is the `x` operator (not the `X` operator; it must be a lowercase *x*). The `x` operator takes a string on one side and a number on the other (but will convert them as needed), and then creates a new string with the old string repeated the number of times given on the right. Some examples:

```
'blah' x 4;  # 'blahblahblahblah'

'*' x 3;    # '***'

10 x 5;    # '1010101010'
```

In that last example, the number `10` is converted to the string `'10'`, and then repeated five times.

3

Why is this useful? Consider having to pad a screen layout to include a certain number of spaces or filler characters, where the width of that layout can vary. Or consider, perhaps, doing some kind of ASCII art where the repetition of characters can produce specific patterns (hey, this is Perl, you're allowed—no, encouraged—to do weird stuff like that). At any rate, should you ever need to repeat a string, the `x` operator can do it for you.

Operator Precedence and Associativity

Operator precedence determines which operators in a complex expression are evaluated first. *Associativity* determines how operators that have the same precedence are evaluated (where your choices are left-to-right, right-to-left, or nonassociative for those operators where order of evaluation is either not important, not guaranteed, or not even possible). Table 3.2 shows the precedence and associativity of the various operators available in Perl, with operators of a higher precedence (evaluated first) higher up in the table than those of a lower precedence (evaluated later). You'll want to fold down the corner of this page or mark it with a sticky note; this is one of those tables you'll probably refer to over and over again as you work with Perl.

You can always change the evaluation of an expression (or just make it easier to read) by enclosing it with parentheses. Expressions inside parentheses are evaluated before those outside parentheses.

Note that there are a number of operators in this table you haven't learned about yet (and some I won't cover in this book at all). I've included lesson references for those operators I do explain later on in this book.

Table 3.2 Operator Precedence and Associativity

<table>
<tr><th>Operator</th><th>Associativity</th><th>What it means</th></tr>
<tr><td><code>-></code></td><td>left</td><td>Dereference operator (Day 19, “Working with References”</td></tr>
<tr><td><code>++ --</code></td><td>non</td><td>Increment and decrement</td></tr>
<tr><td><code>**</code></td><td>right</td><td>Exponent</td></tr>
<tr><td><code>! ~ \ + -</code></td><td>right</td><td>Logical not, bitwise not, reference (Day 19), unary +, unary -</td></tr>
<tr><td><code>=~ !~</code></td><td>left</td><td>Pattern matching</td></tr>
<tr><td><code>* / % x</code></td><td>left</td><td>Multiplication, division, modulus, string repeat</td></tr>
<tr><td><code>+ - .</code></td><td>left</td><td>Add, subtract, string concatenate</td></tr>
<tr><td><code><< >></code></td><td>left</td><td>Bitwise left shift and right shift</td></tr>
<tr><td><code>unary operators</code></td><td>non</td><td>Function-like operators (See today’s “Going Deeper” section)</td></tr>
<tr><td><code>< > <= >= lt gt le ge</code></td><td>non</td><td>Tests</td></tr>
<tr><td><code>== != <=> eq ne cmp</code></td><td>non</td><td>More tests (<code><=></code> and <code>cmp</code>, Day 8, “Data Manipulation with Lists”)</td></tr>
<tr><td><code>&</code></td><td>left</td><td>Bitwise AND</td></tr>
<tr><td><code>| ^</code></td><td>left</td><td>Bitwise OR, bitwise XOR</td></tr>
<tr><td><code>&&</code></td><td>left</td><td>C-style logical AND</td></tr>
<tr><td><code>||</code></td><td>left</td><td>C-style logical OR</td></tr>
<tr><td><code>..</code></td><td>non</td><td>Range operator (Day 4, “Working with Lists and Arrays”)</td></tr>
<tr><td><code>?:</code></td><td>right</td><td>Conditional operator (Day 6, “Conditionals and Loops”)</td></tr>
<tr><td><code>= += -= *= /=, etc.</code></td><td>right</td><td>Assignment operators</td></tr>
<tr><td><code>, =></code></td><td>left</td><td>Comma operators (Day 4)</td></tr>
<tr><td><code>list operators</code></td><td>non</td><td>list operators in list context (Day 4)</td></tr>
<tr><td><code>not</code></td><td>right</td><td>Perl logical NOT</td></tr>
<tr><td><code>and</code></td><td>left</td><td>Perl logical AND</td></tr>
<tr><td><code>or xor</code></td><td>left</td><td>Perl logical OR and XOR</td></tr>
</table>

Using Patterns to Match Digits

Yesterday I introduced you to the bare basics of pattern matching. You learned how to look for strings contained inside other strings, which gives you some flexibility in your scripts and what sort of input you can accept and test. Today, and in future days, you'll learn about new kinds of patterns you can use in the pattern operator `/.../` and how to use those to make your scripts more flexible and more powerful.

Today we'll look at patterns that are used to match digits, any digit, from 0 to 9. Using what you learned yesterday you could test for digits like this:

```
if ($input =~ /1/ or $input =~ /2/ or $input =~ /3/ or $input =~ /4/ or
   $input =~ /5/ or $input =~ /6/ or … }
```


But that would be a lot of repetitive typing, and Perl has a much better way of doing that same thing. The `\d` pattern will match any single digit character, from 0 to 9. So, the statement `$input =~ /\d/` would test `$input` to see if it contained any numbers, and return true if it did. If input contained 1, it would return true. It would return true if input contained `"23skidoo"` or `"luckynumber123"` or `"1234567"`.

Each `\d` stands for a single digit. If you want to match two digits, you can use two `\d` patterns:

```
$input =~ /\d\d/;
```

In this case `"23skidoo"` would return true, but `"number1"` would not. You need two digits in a row for the pattern to match.

You can also combine the `\d` pattern with specific characters:

```
$input =~ /\dup\d/;
```

This pattern matches, in order: any digit, the character `u`, the character `p`, and then any digit again. So "`3up4"` would match; `"comma1up1semicolon"` would match; but `"14upper13"` would not. You need the exact sequence of any number and specific characters.

You can also match any character that is *not* a digit using the `\D` pattern. `\D` matches all the letters, all the punctuation, all the whitespace, anything in the ASCII character set that isn't 0 through 9. You might use this one specifically—as we will in the next section—to test your input to see if it contains any nonnumeric characters. When you want your input to be numeric, for example, if you were going to perform arithmetic on it, or compare it to something else numeric, you want to make sure there are no other characters floating around in there. `\D` will do that:

```
$input =~ /\D/;
```

This test will return true if `$input` contains anything nonnumeric. `"foo"` is true, as is `"foo34"`, `"23skidoo"`, or `"a123"`. If the input is `"3456"` it will return false—there are only numeric characters there.

Table 3.3 shows the patterns you've learned so far.

TABLE 3.3 Patterns

Pattern	*Type*	*What it does*
`/a/`	Character	Matches `a`
`/\d/`	Any digit	Matches a single digit
`/\D/`	Any character not a digit	Matches a single character other than a digit

An Example: Simple Statistics

Here's an example called `stats.pl`, which prompts you for numbers, one at a time. When you're done entering numbers, it gives you a count of the numbers, the sum, and the average. It's a rather silly kind of statistics script, but it'll demonstrate tests, variable assignment, and pattern matching for input verification (and we'll be building on this script later on). Here's an example of what it looks like when run (including what happened when I accidentally typed an `r` in the middle of entering the numbers):

```
% stats.pl
Enter a number: 3
Enter a number: 9
Enter a number: 3
Enter a number: r
Digits only, please.
Enter a number: 7
Enter a number: 4
Enter a number: 7
Enter a number: 3
Enter a number:

Total count of numbers: 7
Total sum of numbers: 36
Average: 5.14
%
```

Listing 3.1 shows the code behind the statistics script.

LISTING 3.1 The `stats.pl` Script

```
#!/usr/local/bin/perl -w

$input = ''; # temporary input
$count = 0;  # count of numbers
$sum = 0;    # sum of numbers
$avg = 0;    # average

while () {
  print 'Enter a number: ';
  chomp ($input = <STDIN>);
  if ($input eq '') { last; }

  if ($input =~ /\D/) {
      print "Digits only, please.\n";
      next;
  }

  $count++;
  $sum += $input;
}

$avg = $sum / $count;

print "\nTotal count of numbers: $count\n";
print "Total sum of numbers: $sum\n";
printf("Average (mean): %.2f\n", $avg);
```

This script has three main sections: an initialization section, a section for getting and storing the input, and a section for computing the average and printing out the results.

Here's the initialization section (with line numbers in place):

```
$input = ''; # temporary input
$count = 0; # count of numbers
$sum = 0;   # sum of numbers
$avg = 0;   # average
```

We're using four scalar variables here: one to store the input as it comes in, one to keep track of the count of numbers, one to hold the sum, and one to hold the average.

The next section is where you prompt for the data and store it:

```
while () {
  print 'Enter a number: ';
  chomp ($input = <STDIN>);
  if ($input eq '') { last; }

  if ($input =~ /\D/) {
```

```
14:         print "Digits only, please.\n";
15:         next;
16:     }
17:
18:     $count++;
19:     $sum += $input;
20: }
```

This second part of the script uses a `while` loop and a couple `if` conditionals to read the input repeatedly until we get a blank line. And also to test the input to make sure that we didn't get anything that wasn't a number. I still haven't discussed how loops and conditionals are defined in Perl (and we won't get around to it until Day 6). So, I'm going to pause here and give you a very basic introduction so you will not be totally lost for the next few days.

A `while` loop says "while this thing is true, execute this stuff." With a `while` loop Perl executes a test, and if the test is true it executes everything inside the curly braces (here, everything in between lines 9 and 20). Then, it'll go back and try the test again, and if it's true again, it'll execute all that code again, and so on. The loop means it goes around and around and around until the test is false.

Usually, the test is contained inside the parentheses (line 8), and can be any of the tests you learned about yesterday. Here, there is no test, so this is an infinite loop; it never stops, at least not here. We'll find a way to break out of it from inside the loop.

An `if` conditional is simpler than a loop. An `if` conditional has a test, and if the test is true, Perl executes some code. If the test is false, sometimes Perl executes some other code (if the `if` conditional has a second part, called an `else`), and sometimes it just goes onto the next part of the script. So, for example, in the `if` conditional in line 11, the test is if the input is equal to the empty string `''`. If the test is true, `last` is executed. The `last` keyword is used to immediately break out of a `while` loop and stop looping. If the test is false, Perl skips over line 11 altogether and continues onto line 13.

In the `if` conditional, lines 13 through 16, the test is a pattern match. Here we're testing the `$input` to see if it contains any nondigit characters. If it does, we execute the `print` statement in line 14, and then call `next`. The `next` keyword skips to the end of the `while` loop (in this case, skipping lines 18 and 19), and restarts the next loop at the top of the `while` again. Just as with line 11, if the test in line 13 was false, Perl skips over everything in line 13 to 16 and continues onto line 18 instead.

Now that you know about `if` and `while`, let's start at the top and figure out what this bit of code actually does. It's a `while` loop with no test, so it'll keep going forever until something breaks you out of it. Inside the body of the `while`, we use line 10 to grab the actual input (and I know you're still waiting to learn what `chomp` and `<STDIN>` do; it's coming up soon). Line 11, as I mentioned, tests for an empty string, and if we got one, breaks out of the loop. The empty string in the input will only occur if the user hit return without typing anything; that is the signal to the stats program that the end of input has been reached. Note the string test (`ne`) here; a number test would convert the empty string to 0, which is not what we want. 0 is valid input for the stats program.

When you get to line 13 we know we have something in `$input`, but we want to make sure that you have valid input, that is, numeric data. You're going to be performing arithmetic on this data in lines 18 and 19, and if you end up with nonnumeric data in the input, and warnings turned on, Perl is going to complain about that data. By verifying and rejecting invalid input you can make sure your scripts do not do unfriendly things like spew errors, or crash when your users are running them.

Lines 13 through 15 are the input validation test. If the input did contain nonnumeric data, we print an error and the loop restarts by prompting for new data.

By the time we get to line 18 we now know that we have data to be handled in `$input` and that data does not contain nonnumeric characters. Now we can add that new data to our current store of data. In lines 18 and 19 we increment the `$count` variable, and modify the `$sum` variable to add the new value that was input. With these two lines we can keep a running total of the count and the sum as each new bit of input comes along, but we'll wait until all the data has been entered to calculate the average.

And, finally, we finish up by calculating the average and printing the results:

```
22: $avg = $sum / $count;
23:
24: print "\nTotal count of numbers: $count\n";
25: print "Total sum of numbers: $sum\n";
26: printf("Average (mean): %.2f\n", $avg);
```

Line 22 is a straightforward calculation, and lines 24 through 26 print the count, the sum, and the average. Note the `\n` at the beginning of the first `print` statement; this will print an extra blank line before the summary. Remember that `\n` can appear anywhere in a string, not just at the end.

In the third summary line, you'll note we're using `printf` again to format the number output. This time, we used a `printf` format for a floating-point number that prints 2 decimal places of that value (`%.2f`). You get more information about `printf` in the next section.

Input and Output

We'll finish up today with two topics that initially might not seem to fit with everything else we've talked about concerning scalar data: handling simple input and output. I've included them here essentially for one reason: so you know what's been going on in the scripts you've been writing that read input from the keyboard and print output to the screen.

In this section we'll talk about simple input and output, and as the book progresses you'll learn more about input and output to disk files, culminating on Day 15, "Working with Files and I/O."

File Handles and Standard Input and Output

First, some terminology. In the scripts you've been looking at today and yesterday, you've used Perl code to read input from the keyboard and to write output to the screen. In reality, *the keyboard* and *the screen* aren't the best terms to use because, actually, you're reading from a source called *standard input*, and writing to a destination called *standard output*. Both of these concepts are borrowed from Unix systems, where using pipes and filters and redirection are common, but if you're used to Windows or the Mac, the idea of a standard input or output might not make much sense.

In all cases, when you're reading data from a source, or writing data to a destination, you'll be working with what are called file handles. Most often, *file handles* refer to actual files on the disk, but there are instances where data might be coming from or going to an unnamed source, for example, from or to another program such as a Web server. To generalize data sources and destinations that are not actual files, Perl gives you built-in file handles for standard input and standard output called `STDIN` and `STDOUT` (there's also `STDERR`, for standard error, but we'll leave that for later). These two file handles happen to include (and, in fact, are most commonly used for) input from the keyboard and output from the screen.

Reading a Line from Standard Input with <STDIN>

In the scripts we've seen so far in this book, there's usually been a line for reading input from the keyboard that looks something like this:

```
chomp($inputline = <STDIN>);
```

You'll see that line a lot in Perl code, although often it occurs on multiple lines, something like this (the two forms are equivalent):

```
$inputline = <STDIN>;
chomp($inputline);
```

You know now that `$inputline` is a scalar variable, and that you're assigning something to it. But what?

The `STDIN` part of this line is the special built-in file handle for standard input. You don't have to do anything to open or manage this special file handle; it's there for you to use. In case you're wondering why it's in all caps; that's a Perl convention to keep from confusing file handles from other things in Perl (such as actual keywords in the language).

The angle brackets around `<STDIN>` are used to actually read input from a file handle. The `<>` characters, in fact, are often called the input operator. `<STDIN>`, therefore, means *read input from the STDIN file handle*. In this particular case, where you're assigning the `<STDIN>` expression to a scalar variable, Perl will read a line from standard input and stop when it gets to a newline character (or a carriage return on the Macintosh). Unlike in C, you don't have to loop through the output and watch every character to make sure it's a newline; Perl will keep track of that for you. All you need is `<STDIN>` and a scalar variable to store the input line in.

Note

> The definition of what a line is for `<STDIN>` is actually determined by Perl's input record separator, which is a newline character by default. On Day 9, "Pattern Matching with Regular Expressions," you'll learn how to change the input record separator. For now, just assume that the end of line character is indeed the end of a line and you'll be fine.

All this talk about input and output brings us to the somewhat amusingly named `chomp` function. When you read a line of input using `<STDIN>` and store it in a variable, you get all the input that was typed and the newline character at the end as well. Usually, you don't want that newline character there, unless you're printing the input right back out again and it's useful for formatting. The built-in Perl `chomp` function, then, takes a string as input, and if the last character is a newline, it removes that newline. Note that `chomp` modifies the original string in place (unlike string concatenation and other string-related functions, which create entire new strings and leave the old strings alone). That's why you can call `chomp` by itself on its own line without reassigning the variable that holds that string.

Note

> Previous versions of Perl used a similar function for the same purpose called `chop`. If you read older Perl code, you'll see `chop` used a lot. The difference between `chomp` and `chop` is that `chop` indiscriminately removes the last character in the string, whether it's a newline or not, whereas `chomp` is safer and doesn't remove anything unless there's a newline there. Most of the time, you'll want to use `chomp` to remove a newline from input, rather than `chop`.

Writing to Standard Output with `print`

When you get input into your Perl script with `<STDIN>`, or from a file, or from wherever, you can use Perl statements to do just about anything you like with that input. The time comes, then, when you'll want to output some kind of data as well. You've already seen the two most common ways to do that: `print` and `printf`.

Let's start with `print`. The `print` function can take any number of arguments and prints them to the standard output (usually the screen). Up to this point we've only used one argument, but you can also give it multiple arguments, separated by commas. Multiple arguments to `print`, by default, will get concatenated together before they get printed:

```
print 'take THAT!';
print 1, 2, 3;    # prints '123'
$a = 4;
print 1, ' ', $a;  # prints "1 4"
print 1, " $a";    # same thing
```

Note

I say *by default* because multiple arguments to print actually form a list, and there is a way to get Perl to print characters in between list elements. You'll learn more about this tomorrow on Day 4, "Working with Lists and Arrays."

I mentioned the `STDOUT` file handle earlier, as the way to access the standard output. You might have noticed, however, that we've been printing data to the screen all along with `print`, and we've never had to refer to `STDOUT`. That's because Perl, to save you time and keystrokes, assumes that if you use `print` without an explicit file handle, you want to use standard output. In reality, the following Perl statements do exactly the same thing:

```
print "Hello World!\n" ;

print STDOUT "Hello World!\n";
```

More about the longer version of `print` when you learn more about file handles that are attached to actual files, on Day 15.

`printf` and `sprintf`

In addition to the plain old workhorse `print`, Perl also provides the `printf` and `sprintf` functions, which are most useful in Perl for formatting and printing numbers in specific ways. They work almost identically to those same functions in C, but beware: `printf` is much less efficient than `print`, so don't just assume you can use `printf` everywhere because you're used to it. Only use `printf` when you have a specific reason to do so.

As you learned yesterday, you use the `printf` function to print formatted numbers and strings to an output stream, such as standard output. `sprintf` formats a string and then just returns that new string, so it's more useful for nesting inside other expressions (in fact, `printf` calls `sprintf` to do the actual formatting).

Both `printf` and `sprintf` take two or more arguments: the first, a string containing formatting codes, and then one or more values to plug into those codes. For example, we've seen examples of `printf` that rounded off a floating-point number to two decimal places, like this:

```
printf("Average (mean): %.2f", $avg);
```

We've seen one that truncates it to an integer, like this:

```
printf("%d degrees Celsius\n", $cel);
```

3

Yesterday, you also saw how to use `sprintf` to round a floating-point number to two digits of precision:

```
$value = sprintf("%.2f", $value);
```

The format codes follow the same rules as the C versions (although the `*` length specifier isn't supported), and can get quite complex. A simple formatting code that you might use in Perl looks like this:

```
%l.px
```

The `x` part is a code referring to the type of value; in Perl you'll be most interested in the `d` formatting code for printing integers, and the `f` formatting code for printing floating-point numbers. The `l` and the `p` in the formatting code are both optional. `l` refers to the number of characters the value should take up in the final string (padded by spaces if the value as printed is less than `l`), and `p` is the number of digit precision of a floating-point number. All numbers are rounded to the appropriate precision.

If you need to print an actual percent sign in your output, you'll need to use two of them:

```
printf("%d%% humidity \n", $hum);
```

Here are some typical examples of how either `sprintf` or `printf` might be used:

```
$val = 5.4349434;
printf("->%5d\n", $val);     # 5
printf("->%11.5f\n", $val);  # 5.43494
printf("%d\n", $val);        # 5
printf("%.3f\n", $val);      # 5.435
printf("%.1f\n", $val);      # 5.4
```

Multiple formatting codes are interpolated left to right in the string, each formatting code replaced by an argument (there should be an equal number of formatting codes and extra arguments):

```
printf("Start value : %.2f End Value: %.2f\n", $start, $end);
```

In this example, if `$start` is `1.343` and `$end` is `5.33333`, the statement will print this:

```
Start value : 1.34 End Value: 5.33
```

If you're unfamiliar with C's `printf` formatting codes, you might want to refer to the `perlfunc` man page (or the `printf` man page) for more details.

Another Example: Stocks

To cement what you've learned today, let's work through another simple example that uses assignment, `while` loops, `if` conditionals, pattern matching, input, and both `print` and `printf` statements.

This example is a stock performance tracker. All you do is enter the purchase price of your stock and its current price, and it tells you if your investment has lost money, made money, or broken even, and by what percentage:

```
% stock.pl
Enter the purchase price: 45
Enter the current price: 48
Your investment has made money.
Your return on investment is 6.7%
% stock.pl
Enter the purchase price: 45
Enter the current price: 40
Your investment has lost money.
Your return on investment is -11.1%
% stock.pl
Enter the purchase price: 45
Enter the current price: 45
Your investment has broken even.
Your return on investment is 0.0%
```

Stock prices must be entered as decimals (not fractions such as 14 5/8), and must be digits. We'll check for both of these things in the script.

Listing 3.2 shows the code for our simple stock tracker. Before reading the following description see if you can go through the code and understand what's going on here.

Listing 3.2 The `stock.pl` Script

```
#!/usr/local/bin/perl -w

$start = 0;
$end = 0;
$return = 0;

while () {
    print "Enter the purchase price: ";
    chomp ($start = <STDIN>);

    print "Enter the current price: ";
    chomp ($end = <STDIN>);

    if ($start eq ''  or $end eq '' ) {
        print "Either the purchase or current price is missing.\n";
        next;
    }

    if ($start =~ /\D/ or $end =~ /\D/ ) {
        if ($start =~ /\// or $end =~ /\//) {
            print "Please enter prices as decimal numbers.\n";
            next;
        } else {
            print "Digits only, please.\n";
            next;
        }
    }

    last;
}

$return = ($end - $start) / $start * 100;

if ($start > $end) {
    print "Your investment has lost money.\n";
} elsif ($start < $end ) {
    print "Your investment has made money.\n";
} else {
    print "Your investment has broken even.\n";
}

print "Your return on investment is ";
printf("%.1f%%\n", $return);
```


This example has three main sections: an initialization section, a section for getting and verifying input, and a section for calculating and printing the result. I'm going to skip the initialization because you've already seen a bunch of them and you know what they look like by now.

Getting and Verifying the Input

This `while` loop, in lines 7 to 30, is for getting the initial input from the user and is the most complex part of this script:

```
7:  while () {
8:      print "Enter the purchase price: ";
9:      chomp ($start = <STDIN>);
10:
11:     print "Enter the current price: ";
12:     chomp ($end = <STDIN>);
13:
14:     if ($start eq ''  or $end eq '' ) {
15:         print "Either the purchase or current price is missing.\n";
16:         next;
17:     }
18:
19:     if ($start =~ /\D/ or $end =~ /\D/ ) {
20:         if ($start =~ /\// or $end =~ /\//) {
21:             print "Please enter prices as decimal numbers.\n";
22:             next;
23:         } else {
24:             print "Digits only, please.\n";
25:             next;
26:         }
27:     }
28:
29:     last;
30: }
```

Initially this will look very similar to the `while` loop in the `stats.pl` script: same infinite loop, same `if` test with pattern matching. But there are some significant differences here.

The most important difference to note is that `stats.pl` repeats over and over again until the user is done inputting data, whereas this script only needs two pieces of correct data and then it's done. In fact, blank input here is an error, and should be tested for. The other two errors we are checking for are nondigit input, and input made in fractional format (14 5/8, for example). We could lump the latter two together because the slash character / is a nondigit character, but printing a more specific error in that specific case makes for a more user-friendly script.

Our infinite loop, then, will continue looping until we get two acceptable pieces of numeric data. Then we can break out of the loop and move on.

Lines 8 through 12 enable you to look at things line by line. They prompt for the data, and store that data in the scalar variables `$start` and `$end`. Note that we prompt for both values before testing for validity, rather than doing one at a time. (One at a time would make more sense, usability-wise, but given what you know so far about Perl we would have to duplicate a lot of code, so this way is shorter).

In lines 14 through 17 we test both `$start` and `$end` to see if they are empty, that is, if the user pressed Return without entering any data. If they did, we call next, which skips to the end of the loop and restarts again from the beginning, prompting again for the data.

In the `if` statement starting in line 19 things start getting weird. Line 19 is the same test for nondigitness you saw in the stats program; this pattern checks for any input that contains data that isn't a number. This test will trap both data that is completely nonsensical for the script, along with data that might make conceptual sense but that we can't handle—the fractional numbers that I mentioned earlier (14 5/8, 101 15/16, and so on, as stock prices are sometimes listed).

If the test in line 19 is true, the code in line 20 and onward begins executing. That code includes the test in line 20. This test is a character pattern for a single slash—we have to backslash it here because its inside the pattern matching operator. This test, then, is here to trap those fractional numbers. If this test returns true, lines 21 and 22 are executed; we print an error (a hint, actually, and next is called to skip to the end of the loop and restart again).

If the test in line 20 is not true—that is, if we have data that contains something other that a digit, but that doesn't contain a slash—then the code in lines 23 through 26 gets executed. The `else` clause is part of the `if` conditional. In an `if` conditional, if the test is true, the first block of code inside the curly braces is executed. If the test is false, Perl looks for the `else` clause, and if there is one, then that code gets executed instead. Depending on the state of the test, you'll get either one block or another—never both.

In this case, if we have nonnumeric data that doesn't contain a slash, say, `"rasberry"`, that data will return true for the test in line 19, so the block going from lines 19 to 27 will get executed. The test in line 20, however, will be false—no slash—so Perl will skip lines 20 through 22 and instead execute the `else` block in lines 23 through 26; print an error, and call next to again run through the same prompting-and-testing loop.

The `else` part of the `if` conditional is optional—if there isn't one and the test is false, Perl just goes on executing. So if the user does indeed enter the right data, then the tests in lines 14 and 19 will be false. None of the code in lines 14 through 17 or lines 19 through 27 gets executed if the data is correct. Perl just goes straight down to line 29; `last`, which breaks us out of the `while` loop to stop asking for data.

Calculating and Printing the Result

With correct data in hand, we can go ahead and perform some arithmetic without worrying that what we've actually been given is a string or some weird combination of numbers and strings. All that is behind us now. Line 32 computes the percentage return on investment and stores it in the variable `$return`.

```
32: $return = ($end - $start) / $start * 100;
```

Note that we need the parentheses around the subtraction here to change the operator precedence. Without the parentheses, the division and multiplication would have been performed first, and then the subtraction, which would not have been correct.

Lines 34 through 40 print our little report on how your investment is doing, and here you can see more `if`s and `else`s. The one in the middle—`elsif`—is just a shorthand notation for nesting `if` conditionals inside `else` statements. You'll learn more about it on Day 6.

Nested `if`s, as this structure is called, is a way of cascading different tests and results. You'll see a lot of these sorts of structures. The tests start at the top, and if a test is true, that result is printed, and the nested `if` is over. Perl skips to the bottom and doesn't do any more tests. If the test is false, another test is tried until one matches or the final else at the end is the default result.

In this case, there are only three possible results: `$start` can be less than `$end`, start can be greater than `$end`, or `$start` and `$end` can be equal. In the first two tests we check for the first two cases. The last case doesn't need a test because it's the only possible remaining outcome, so it gets caught in the final else in lines 38 through 40.

The final lines, 42 and 43, print out the percentage return on investment we calculated in line 32. Here we use a `printf` instead of a `print`, so that we can format the floating-point number to have a single digit of precision.

```
43: printf("%.1f%%\n", $return);
```

In this line, `%.1f` is the formatting code—`.1` for the single digit after the decimal point, `f` for a floating-point number. The two percents after the formatting code (`%%`) are used to print out an actual percent character in the output. `\n`, as you know, is a newline, therefore, the result looks something like this:

```
Your return on investment is 110.9%
```

A Note About Using Functions

Now that you've learned about the `print` and `chomp` functions, as well as had a glimpse of other functions such as `int` and `sprintf`, this is a good time to go over how function calls work. If you've been paying careful attention, you might have noticed that I've been calling the `print` function like this:

```
print "Hello, World!\n";
```

I've also been calling `chomp` and `printf` like this:

```
chomp($input = <STDIN>);
printf("Average (mean): %.2f", $avg);
```

One form has parentheses around the arguments to the function, the other form doesn't. Which is correct? The answer is *both*. Parentheses around the arguments to a function are optional; as long as Perl can figure out what your arguments are, either form works just fine.

In this book, I've used a smattering of both. My general rule is that if a function takes one argument—`int` or `oct` being good examples—I'll leave off the parentheses. If it takes multiple arguments or if its argument is an expression (`printf` or `chomp`), then I use parentheses. The `print` function can go either way depending on the situation.

Depending on what you're familiar with—and what looks right to you—feel free to pick your own rule for parenthesizing functions in your own scripts. I should mention, however, that the rule of parentheses being optional "as long as Perl can figure out what your arguments are," can occasionally be tricky to figure out, particularly with multiple arguments and when some of them are parenthesized expressions or lists. To make it even more complex, some of Perl's built-in functions are actually operators, and have a different precedence from actual function calls. (see the next section, "Going Deeper," for more information). There are rules of precedence to determine exactly how complex function calls are to be evaluated, but the safest solution, if Perl appears to be ignoring your arguments or producing weird results, is to include parentheses around all the arguments. Turning on Perl warnings will also help catch some of these problems.

3

Going Deeper

Had enough of strings and numbers yet? Want to learn more? No problem. This section has a number of other features to look at concerning scalar data before we forge on ahead to lists.

Operators are all discussed in the `perlop` man page, whereas functions are discussed in the `perlfunc` man page. As I mentioned before, you can get to all these pages through the use of the `perldoc` command or on the Web at `http://www.perl.com/pub/doc/manual/html/pod/`.

Useful Number and String Functions

Perl includes quite a few built-in functions for a variety of purposes. Appendix E, "Perl Functions," contains a summary of those functions, and the `perlfunc` man page also describes them in further detail. In particular, Perl includes a number of useful functions for numbers and strings, including those summarized in Table 3.4. We'll explore some of these in more detail in forthcoming chapters; others you'll have to explore on your own.

TABLE 3.4 Number and String Functions

Function	*What it does*
`abs`	Absolute value
`atan2`	Arctangent
`chr`	The character represented by a number in the ASCII character set
`cos`	Cosine
`exp`	e to the power of (use `**` for exponentiation)
`int`	Truncate decimal part of a float
`index`	Returns the position of the first occurrence of the substring in string
`lc`	Lowercase a string
`lcfirst`	Lowercase the first character in a string
`length`	Length (number of bytes)
`log`	Logarithm
`ord`	The number of a character in the ASCII character set
`rand`	Random number
`reverse`	Reverse a scalar
`rindex`	Reverse index (starts from end of string)
`sin`	Sine
`sqrt`	Square root
`substr`	Returns a substring starting at an offset of some length
`uc`	Uppercase a string
`ucfirst`	Uppercase the first letter in a string

Bitwise Operators

Perl provides the usual set of C-like operators for twiddling bits in integers: `~`, `<<`, `>>`, `&`, `|`, and `^`, as well as assignment shortcuts for those operators. See the `perlop` man page for specifics.

The `cmp` and `<=>` Operators

In addition to the relational operators I described in the section on comparisons, Perl also has the `<=>` and `cmp` operators. The former is for numbers, and the latter for strings. Both return `-1`, `0`, or `1` depending if the left operator is greater than the right, the operators are equal, or if the right operator is greater than the left, respectively. These operators are most commonly used for creating `sort` routines, which you'll learn more about on Day 8.

Functions and Function-Like Operators

Perl's built-in functions actually fall into two groups: functions that are functions, and operators that take one argument and masquerade as functions. The function-like operators fall in the middle of the precedence hierarchy and behave like operators in this respect (whereas function calls with parentheses always have the highest precedence). See the `perlop` man page under "Named Unary Operators" for a list of these functions.

Summary

Today was Part 2 of everything you ever wanted to know, and probably a whole lot you didn't, about scalar data. Today you got to look at more tables of operators, in particular operators for assigning things to variables, or changing the values of variables, and for concatenating and repeating strings. You also learned about operator precedence, which determines which operators get to go first when you have an expression with lots of them in it.

Along the way you also learned about pattern matching with digits and some about `if` and `while` (although you'll learn a whole lot more about them on Day 6).We finished today's lesson talking about input and output, and in particular using `<STDIN>` to get data into a Perl script and the various `print` functions to print it out again. You also learned a bit about calling functions with and without parentheses around their arguments.

The built-in functions you learned about today include (see the `perlfunc` man page for more details about these functions):

- `print` takes a list of comma-separated values and strings to print and outputs those values to the standard output (`STDOUT`).
- `printf` takes a formatting string and any number of values, and prints those values according to the codes in the formatting string.
- `sprintf` does the same thing as `printf`, except it returns the formatted string without printing anything.
- `chomp` with a string argument removes any trailing newlines from that string and returns the number of characters it deleted.
- `chop` is the older version of `chomp`; it removes the last character from the string and returns the character it removed.

Q&A

Q. I want to iterate over a string and count the occurrences of the letter t. How can I do this in Perl?

A. Well, you could use a `for` loop and one of the string functions to work your way through the string one character at a time, but that would be a terrible amount of overkill (and expose you as a C programmer who still thinks of strings as null-terminated arrays). Perl's good with strings, and it has built-in mechanisms for finding stuff in strings so you don't have to do perverse character-by-character comparisons. You'll learn more about this sort of pattern matching on. Don't spend a lot of time iterating over strings until you read that.

Q. I don't understand why in these scripts you are testing for nonnumeric data using `\D`, when we could be testing for numeric data using `\d`. To me it would make more sense to just test for numbers if you want numbers.

A. The problem is that both `\d` and `\D` stand for just one character. So you could test for numeric data with `\d` and your pattern would match perfectly as long as your input was 1, 2, 3, 4, and so on, through 9. But if your input was 10 or above, that would be more than a single character, and would not match the pattern, and, therefore, produce an error. Theoretically you want your test to work for *any* number: 1 should be just as acceptable as 11 or 111111. Later on you'll learn how to do a pattern that matches one or more digits. For now, matching a single nondigit character is an easy work around, the data itself can be any number of characters but all you need is one character to be the wrong thing.

Q. Can I use `printf` just like I do in C?

A. Well, you can, but you should really get used to working with `print` instead. The `print` function is more efficient, and helps cover up things like rounding-off errors in floating-point numbers. It's really a much better idea to use `print` for the vast majority of cases and only fall back on `printf` for specific reasons (like rounding).

If you do use `printf`, you can use all the formatting codes you can in the C version of `printf` except for `*`.

Q. Why is it important that some functions are functions and some functions are actually operators? Don't they all behave the same?

A. Nope. Functions and operators behave slightly different. Functions, for example, have a higher precedence. And arguments to an operator might be grouped based on precedence (giving you odd results) as well. In most cases, however, the difference between a function and an operator should not cause you to lie awake at night.

Workshop

The workshop provides quiz questions to help you solidify your understanding of the material covered and exercises to give you experience in using what you've learned. Try and understand the quiz and exercise answers before you go on to tomorrow's lesson.

Quiz

1. What's the difference between the postfix increment operator (`$x++`) and the prefix increment operator (`++$x`)?
2. What does operator precedence determine? How about associativity?
3. What is the difference between the following patterns?

   `/d/`

   `/\d/`

   `/\D/`

   `/d\d/`

4. You have the pattern `/\d\d\D/`. Which of the following strings does this pattern match to?

   `'456'`

   `'d55'`

   `'55+'`

   `'4aa'`

   `'4b'`

5. What is a file handle? Why do you need one?
6. Define standard input and output. What are they used for?
7. What does the `chomp` function do?
8. What are the differences between `print`, `printf`, and `sprintf`? When would you use each one?
9. What do the following operators do?

   ```
   .
   **
   ne
   ||
   *=
   ```

Exercises

1. Write a program that accepts any number of lines of any kind of input, ending with a Return or Enter (similarly to how the `stats.pl` program works). Return the number of lines that were entered.

3

2. BUG BUSTER: What's wrong with this bit of code?

```
while () {
 print 'Enter a name: ';
 chomp ($input = <INPUT>);
 if ($input ne '') {
   $names++;
}
 else { last; }
}
```

3. Write a program that accepts input as multiple words on different lines, and combines those words into a single string.
4. Write a program that takes a string and then centers it on the screen (assume an 80-character line, and that the string is less than 80 characters). Hint: the `length` function will give you the length in characters of a string.
5. Modify the Fahrenheit to Celsius converter program from yesterday to make sure that the input is a valid digit. If the user enters something invalid, loop until the input is valid. Watch out for negative numbers!

Answers

Here are the answers to the Workshop questions in the previous section.

Quiz Answers

1. The difference in prefix and postfix operators is when the variable reference is used and when its value is evaluated. Prefix operators increment the value before using it; postfix increments the variable afterward.
2. Operator precedence determines which parts of an expression are evaluated first given expressions that contain other expressions. Associativity determines the order in which operators that have the same precedence are evaluated.
3. The patterns are as follows:
   - `/d/` matches the single character d.
   - `/\d/` matches a single digit.
   - `\/D/` matches a single nondigit character.
   - `/d\d/` matches a d followed by a single digit.
4. The pattern `/\d\d\D/` matches two digits and one nondigit, in that order. None of the given strings match the pattern except for `'55+'`.
5. A file handle is used to read data from or write data to a source or a destination, be it a file, the keyboard, the screen, or some other device. File handles provide a common way for Perl to handle input and output with all those things.

6. Standard input and output are generic input sources and output destinations (that is, not specifically from or to files). They are most commonly used to get input from the keyboard or to print it to the screen.
7. The `chomp` function removes the newline from the end of a string. If there is no newline on the end of the string, chomp does nothing.
8. The print function is the general way of printing output to the screen or to some other output destination. The printf function prints formatted strings to some output destination; `sprintf` formats a string, but then simply returns that formatted string value instead of printing it.
9. The answers are

   `.` concatenates strings

   `**` creates exponential numbers

   `ne` "not equals" for strings

   `||` logical OR (C-style)

   `*=` Multiply and assign; same as `$x = $x * $y`

Exercise Answers

1. Here's one answer:

```
#!/usr/local/bin/perl -w

$input = ''; # temporary input
$lines = 0; # count of lines


while () {
 print 'Enter some text: ';
 chomp ($input = <STDIN>);
 if ($input ne '') {
   $lines++;
  }
 else { last; }
}

print "Total number of lines entered: $lines\n";
```

2. The file handle for standard input is `STDIN`, not `INPUT`.
3. Here's one answer:

```
#!/usr/local/bin/perl -w

$input = ''; # temporary input
$sent = ''; # final sentence;
```

```
while () {
 print 'Enter a word: ';
 chomp ($input = <STDIN>);
 if ($input ne '') {
   $sent .= $input . ' ';
  }
 else { last; }
}

print "Final sentence: $sent\n";
```

4. Here's one answer:

```
#!/usr/local/bin/perl -w

$input = ""; # temporary input
$space = 0; # space around
$length = 0 ; # length of string

print 'Enter some text: ';
chomp ($input = <STDIN>);
$length = length $input;
$space = int((80 - $length) / 2);
print ' ' x $space;
print $input;
print ' ' x $space . "\n";
print '*' x 80;
```

5. Here's one answer:

```
#!/usr/local/bin/perl -w

$fahr = 0;
$cel = 0;

while () {
    print 'Enter a temperature in Fahrenheight: ';
    chomp ($fahr = <STDIN>);

    if ($fahr =~ /\D/ and $fahr !~ /-/) {
        print "Digits only, please.\n";
        next;
    }

    last;
}

$cel = ($fahr - 32) * 5 / 9;
print "$fahr degrees Fahrenheit is equivalent to ";
printf("%.0f degrees Celsius\n", $cel);
```

WEEK 1

DAY 4

Working with Lists and Arrays

Days 2 and 3 dealt primarily with individual things. Today, we'll talk about groups of things, namely, lists and arrays, and the various operations you can do to manage (and mangle) them, including

- What arrays and lists are, and the variables for storing them
- Defining and using arrays
- List and scalar context, and why context is crucial to understanding Perl
- More about `<STDIN>` and reading input into lists
- Printing lists

List Data and Variables

If scalar data is defined as being made up of individual things, then you can think of list data as a collective thing—or, more rightly, as a collection of scalar things. Just as the term *scalar data* can include both numbers and strings, the term *list data* usually refers to one of two specific things: arrays and hashes.

We'll talk about arrays today and go deeper into hashes tomorrow on Day 5, "Working with Hashes."

An array is a collection of any number of scalar things. Each individual thing, or element, can be accessed by referring to the number of its position in the array (its index). Array indexes in Perl start from 0. Figure 4.1 shows an illustration of a simple array with some numbers and strings in it.

FIGURE 4.1.
Anatomy of an Array.

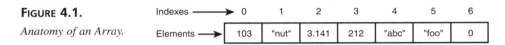

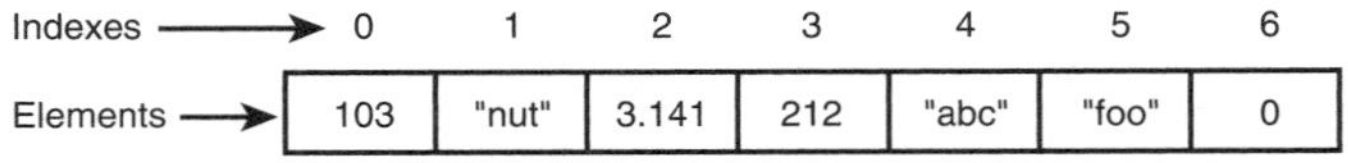

Indexes →	0	1	2	3	4	5	6
Elements →	103	"nut"	3.141	212	"abc"	"foo"	0

Arrays are ordered, which means they have a first element, last element, and all the elements in between in a specific order. You can change the order of elements in an array by sorting it, or iterate over the elements one at a time, from start to finish.

Arrays are stored in array variables, just like scalars are stored in scalar variables. An array variable starts with the at sign (`@`). Beyond the first character, array variables have the same rules as far as names go:

- Names can be up to 255 characters long, and can contain numbers, letters, and underscores.
- Names are case sensitive; upper and lowercase characters are different.
- Array variables, unlike scalar variables, can start with a number, but can then only contain other numbers.

In addition, scalar and array variable names do not conflict with each other. The scalar variable `$x` is a different variable from the array variable `@x`.

In addition to list data being stored and accessed in an array, list data also has a raw form called, appropriately, a list. A list is simply an ordered set of elements. You can assign a list to a variable, iterate over it to print each of its elements, nest it inside another list, or use it as an argument to a function. Usually, you'll use lists to create arrays and hashes, or to pass data between a list and other lists. In many cases, you can think of lists and arrays being essentially interchangeable.

Defining and Using Lists and Arrays

The care and feeding of the wily Perl array includes defining it, assigning it to an array variable, sticking elements in and taking them out, and finding out its length (the number of elements). There are also a whole lot of things you can do to manipulate arrays and their data, but let's start with the basics.

Unlike other languages, in which arrays have to be carefully set up before you can use them, arrays in Perl magically appear as you need them and happily grow and shrink to the number of elements you have in them at any given time. They can also contain any kind of scalar data: numbers, strings, or a mix of both, and as many elements as you want, limited only by the amount of memory you have available.

> Arrays can contain references, too, but you haven't learned about those yet. Be patient; all will become clear on Day 15, "Working with Files and I/O."

Creating Lists

As I mentioned earlier, a *list* refers to a general collective set of data; an *array* can be considered a list that has been stored in an array variable. In reality, you can use lists anywhere arrays are expected, and vice versa.

To create a list, type the initial elements separated with commas and surrounded by with parentheses. This list syntax provides raw list data that can be used to create an array or a hash, depending on the kind of variable the list is assigned to. Let's look at a few array examples now and we'll cover hashes tomorrow on Day 5.

Here's an example of list syntax used to create an array called `@nums`, which has four elements:

```
@nums = (1, 2, 3, 4);
```

Lists of strings work just as easily:

```
@strings = ('parsley', 'sage', 'rosemary', 'thyme');
```

List syntax can contain any mixture of strings, numbers, scalar variables, and expressions that result in scalars, and so on:

```
@stuff = ('garbonzo', 3.145, $count, 'defenestration', 4 / 7, $a++);
```

An empty list is simply a set of empty parentheses:

```
@nothing = ();
```

You can nest lists within other lists, but those sublists are not retained in the final array; all the elements are squished together in one single array with empty sublists removed:

```
@combine = (1, 4, (6, 7, 8), (), (5, 8, 3));
```

The final array in `@combine` will be `(1, 4, 6, 7, 8, 5, 8, 3)`.

Similarly, nesting array variables will do the same thing; all the elements in the subarrays will be concatenated into one larger list:

```
@nums = (1, 2, 3, 4);
@strings = ('parsley', 'sage', 'rosemary', 'thyme');
@combine2 = (@nums, @strings);
# results in (1, 2, 3, 4, 'parsley', 'sage', 'rosemary', 'thyme')

@nums = (@nums, 5); # results in  (1, 2, 3, 4, 5);
```

Say you're defining an array of one-word strings, for example, for the days of the week, or a list of names. A very common Perl trick for creating arrays of one-word strings is to use the quoting function `qw` ("quote word.") The `qw` operator lets you avoid typing all those quote marks and commas, and might actually make the array easier to read:

```
@htmlcolors = qw(
   black white red green
   blue orange purple yellow
   aqua grey silver fuchsia
   lime maroon navy olive
);
```

You don't need to surround all the words with parentheses; in fact, you can use any character you want:

```
@directions = qw/north south east west/;
@days = qw?mon tue wed thu fri sat sun?;
```

I prefer the parentheses because it reminds me that this is a list.

The `qw` operator is in the same class of operators as the `q//` and `qq//` operators that I discussed in the going deeper section on Day 2, "Working with Strings and Numbers," as well as the `m//` operator for quoting patterns. All these operators allow you to use any character to surround the text within them.

Creating Lists Using the Range Operator

Want to create a list containing numbers between 1 and 1000? It'd be pretty inefficient to do it by typing all those numbers in. It'd be much easier to use a loop of some sort to stick the numbers in one at a time, but that's still kind of kludgy. (A *kludge*, by the way, is old geek-talk for a less than optimal solution to a problem. Duct tape is a popular kludgy solution for many real-world problems. Some misguided individuals might argue that Perl itself is a kludge).

Anyhow, given any situation where you think, "There must be an easy way to do this," chances are really good that there is an easy way to do it in Perl. In this case, what you need is the range operator (..). To create an array with elements from 1 to 1000, do this:

```
@lotsonums = (1 .. 1000);
```

That's it, you're done. The `@lotsonums` array now contains 1000 elements, from 1 to 1000. The range operator works by counting from the left side operand up to the right side operand by 1 (you cannot use it to count down).

The range operator also magically works for characters:

```
@alphabet = ('a' .. 'z'); # contains 26 elements for characters
```

We'll come back to the range operator on Day 6, "Conditionals and Loops," when we go over iteration.

Assignment and Lists

Until now we've been using list syntax on the right side of assignment expression, to create a list and assign it to an array. You can also use a list of variable references on the left side of an assignment as well, and Perl will assign values to those variables based on the list on the right.

4

For example, take this expression:

```
($a, $b) = (1, 2);
```

There's a list on both sides of that expression, but the list on the left is still a valid place to put variables. What Perl does with this expression is assign the values in the list on the right to the variables in the list on the left, in the same order in which they appear. So `$a` will get 1, and `$b` will get 2. This is, of course, equivalent to putting those values on separate lines, but it is a convenient way of setting values to variables. Note that the assignments actually happen in parallel, so you can do something like this:

```
($x, $y) = ($y, $x);
```

This example swaps the values of `$x` and `$y`. Neither happens before the other, so it all works out safely.

The rule when you have list syntax on both sides of an assignment operator is that each variable on the left gets a value on the right. If there are more variables than values, then the extra variables will be assigned the undefined value. If there are more values than variables, the extra values will be ignored.

You can put array variables on the right, and that array will be expanded into its elements and then assigned as per list syntax:

```
($a, $b) = @nums;
```

You can even nest arrays within lists on both sides, and they will get expanded into their respective elements and assigned using the previous rules—with one exception:

```
($a, @more) = (10, 11, 12, 13, 14);
```

In this example, `$a` gets `10`, and `@more` gets the list `(11, 12, 13, 14)`. Array variables on the left side of a list assignment are greedy—that is, they store all remaining members of the list on the right side of the assignment. This is important when considering an example like the following:

```
($a, @more, $b) = (10, 11, 12, 13, 14);
```

In this case, `$a` gets `10`, `@more` gets the list `(11, 12, 13, 14)`, and `$b` gets the undefined value. Because arrays eat up all the remaining values on the right, there won't be any values left for `$b` to be defined to.

Accessing Array Elements

So you have an array, perhaps with some initial elements via list syntax, or perhaps it's just an empty array you're looking to fill with values later on (based on the standard input, for example).

To access any array element, use the `[]` subscript syntax with the index position of the element you want to access inside the brackets:

```
$nums[4];
```

This example will give you the value of the fifth element in the `@nums` array. The following example will change that value to `10`:

```
$nums[4] = 10;
```

Stop and look at that syntax for a bit. Does it look weird to you? It should. Here, we're referring to the fifth element of an array called `@nums`, but we're using what appears to be a scalar variable. That's not a typo—that's how the syntax works. You use `@arrayname` to refer to the entire array, and `$arrayname[index]` to access or assign a value to an element inside that array.

That doesn't mean you can't use `$arrayname` to refer to a regular scalar value; `$arrayname`, `$arrayname[]`, and `@arrayname` are all different things. The best way to remember this is to remember that the elements of arrays are always scalar values, so you need a scalar variable to access them, even if they're inside an array (and Perl warnings will catch you if you forget).

Array indexes start from 0 and each index can only be a whole number (an integer, in other words). So `$arrayname[0]` refers to the first element in an array, `$arrayname[1]` refers to the second element, and so on. You don't need to use an actual number as the array index, you can use a variable reference or any other kind of expression:

```
$array[$count]; # the element at position $count;
```

What happens if you try to access an element that doesn't exist—for example, to access position 5 of a 3-element array? If you have warnings turned on in Perl, you'll get an error. Otherwise, you'll get an undefined value (`0` or `""`, depending on the context).

Growing Arrays

An array in Perl is exactly as big as it needs to be, and no larger. If you need to add more elements to an array, you can just add them, and Perl will expand the array to fit. You can keep adding elements as long as you need to; you're only limited by the amount of memory on your computer. Perl doesn't care how many elements you need.

There are a number of ways to actually add new elements to an array. You could create a list with an array variable and the new elements, and then assign that list to the original array variable again:

```
@array = (@array, "more", "elements", "here");
```

You could just add an element to the last position in the list:

```
@array = (0, 1, 2) # has elements in positions 0, 1, and 2
$array[3] = "foo"; # array is now (0, 1, 2, "foo")
```

If you add an element beyond the last element of an array, Perl will grow the array to fit, add the new element, and set the intervening elements to be undefined. So, for example:

```
@t = (1, 2, 3);
$t[5] = 6;
```

The array `@t`, after these two lines, will contain the elements `(1, 2, 3, `*`undefined`*`, `*`undefined`*`, 6)`. If you try to access those undefined values in the middle, Perl will give you a warning (assuming you have warnings turned on). See the section, "Dealing with the Undefined Value," for how to avoid accidentally running into these values.

One of the easiest ways to add an element to an array—and the most commonly used—is to use the `push` function. The `push` function takes a list and a scalar element as arguments and sticks the element onto the end of that list.

```
@nums = (1,2,3,4);
push @nums, 5; # @nums is now (1,2,3,4,5);
```

Note that if you give push an array argument, it modifies its array in place; you don't have to reassign it back to the original variable.

Finding the Length of an Array

To get the number of elements in an array, use this statement:

```
$numelements = @arrayname;
```

Don't think about that right now, just learn it: to get the number of elements in an array, use a scalar variable and assign an array variable to it. I'll explain why this works a bit later on, in the section, "List and Scalar Context."

Sorting Lists and Arrays

In other languages, if you want to sort the contents of an array, you might have to write your own sort routine. That's not so in Perl because it has one built in. To sort an array, all you have to do is use the `sort` function:

```
@orderednums = sort @nums;
```

This assignment will sort the array `@nums`, and then assign the new list to the `@orderednums` variable. The `@nums` array still remains unsorted.

That particular simple use of `sort` sorts the contents of `@nums` in ASCII order—that is, in string order, so 5543 will appear lower in the array than 94 (because 5 comes before 9). To sort the array in numeric order, use a special comparison in the middle:

```
@orderednums = sort { $a <=> $b } @nums;
```

The part of the sort routine determines how the array will be sorted using the comparison operator `<=>`. We'll go over customizing sort routines on Day 8, "Manipulating Lists and Strings," but for now you can learn that by rote: to sort an array by number, use sort with a comparison in the middle. To sort an array by ASCII strings, use the short form without the comparison.

Processing Each Element of an Array

Say you wanted to work through an array one element at a time, and do something with each element for example, print it, double it, move it somewhere else—what you're doing doesn't matter, the goal here is to process each element at a time and do something with that element. This is often called *iterating* over a list or an array. There are a number of ways you can do this in Perl (of course). For example, because you already know how to do a `while` loop and you know how to get the number of elements in an array, you could use a temporary counter starting from 0, test it against the number of elements, and increment it every time.

```
$numelements = @array;  # get number of elements
$while ($counter < $numelements) {
   # process element $counter
   # increment #counter
   # repeat
}
```

On Day 6, you'll learn about all kinds of other loops that do the same thing, but right now there's one simple loop that provides the quickest and easiest way to do this—use a `foreach` loop, like this:

```
foreach $x (@list) {
   # do something to each element
}
```

The `foreach` loop executes once for each element in the list inside parentheses (here it's the `@list` array, but it could be a raw list, a range, or anything else that gives you a list as a result—for example, the `sort` function). For each element in the list, the value of that element is assigned to a scalar variable (here, `$x`), and the code inside the opening and closing brackets is executed. You could, for example, use a `foreach` loop to print each element of a list, to test them for some value (greater than 100? Contains nondigit characters?), or to remove undefined values.

More about `foreach` tomorrow when we talk about hashes, and on Day 6.

Finding the End of an Array

Related to finding the length of an array in Perl is finding the end of the array. The end of the array in Perl is indicated by the index number of its last element. Keep in mind at all times that array indexes in Perl start from 0, so the length of the array is not the same as its top-most index number. The end of the array is always one less than the length of the array.

You could keep track of the end of the array by keeping a counter, or by taking the length of the array and subtracting one, but Perl has syntax that gives you the index number of the last element in the array: `$#arrayname`.

With this index number it's easy to write loops that iterate from index 0 to the last element in the array:

```
$i = 0;
while ($i <= $#array) {
   print $array[$i++], "\n";
}
```

If you change the value of `$#arrayname`, you grow or truncate the length of the array. Setting `$#arrayname` to a value larger than its current value sets all the intervening elements to the undefined value. Setting it smaller will discard all the elements at the end of the array (it's generally not a good idea to change `$#arrayname` for just this reason).

I will remind you again here that the `$#arrayname` syntax is *not* the correct way to find out the length of (or number of elements in) the array. Because array indexes start from 0, the `$#array` syntax will give you *one less than the total number of elements in the array*.

Dealing with the Undefined Value

I touched on the undefined value on Day 2, when I mentioned that scalar variables without explicit values end up with the undefined value. If you do not initialize your variables before you use them, they will have the undefined value.

The undefined value is no value; it is a hole, the absence of value. Perl will treat the undefined value as a 0 or an empty string, and the undefined value is false in a test just as those other values are. But if you have warnings turned on—which is always a good idea—then the undefined values will provoke ugly warnings from Perl.

To avoid undefined values in your scalar variables, always initialize them before you use them, as we have been doing in all our examples. There are often a few smaller cases where you don't really need to initialize your variables up front—counter and loop variables, for example, where the variable is used in that one loop and then discarded.

But this is the chapter on lists and arrays, and it is probably lists and arrays where the undefined value is going to be most problematic. While looping and growing and putting together arrays, it is not unusual for some of the places within an array to end up with the undefined value. I showed you a simple example of how this might happen in the section on growing arrays:

```
@t = (1, 2, 3);
$t[5] = 6;
```

The array `@t` now contains the elements `(1, 2, 3, `*`undefined, undefined,`*` 6)`. If you then try to print the array `@t` with warnings turned on, Perl will complain about those undefined values.

To avoid the warnings, and make sure you're only dealing with actual defined values in your arrays, you can test for the existence of an undefined value using the `defined` function:

```
if (!defined $array[$index]) {
   print "Element $index is undefined.\n";
}
```

```
if (defined $array[$index]) {
   push @newarray, $array[$index];
}
```

The `undef` function can actually be used anywhere, inside or outside of array elements, to undefine any variable location. It can also be used without any arguments, in which case, it simply returns the undefined value, for example:

```
@holeinthemiddle = (1, undef, undef, undef, 5);
```

You an also use it to remove the value from a variable, like this:

```
undef $var;
```

Because of the former use of the `undef` function, as an easy way of using an undefined value, the undefined value is commonly referred to simply as `undef` (and I'll be referring to it that way throughout the rest of this book).

Deleting Elements from an Array

Perl does not have a command to take any specific array element, remove it from an array, and shorten the array by one, but there are a number of ways to accomplish roughly the same thing.

The `pop` function (the opposite of `push`) will remove the last element in an array, modifying the existing array in place:

```
pop @array;
```

Setting the `$#arrayname` variable to something less than its current value will also delete elements from the end of the list. In both these cases, the elements you want to delete must be at the end of the array, so you'll have to arrange it appropriately.

One of the easiest ways to delete an element is simply to call the `undef` function for that element and leave it in the array:

```
undef($array[$index]);
```

The array element that you undefined with `undef` will still be there in the array; it'll just hold the undefined value. Each time you process the array to print it or do something with its elements you'll have to test for undefined values (but you should probably do that anyhow):

```
if (defined $array[$index]) {
   # do something with the value
}
```

If you explicitly want to remove the `undef` values you'll have to reconstruct the array. Perl does have an explicit `delete` function:

```
delete($array[$index]);
```

As with `undef` this will set the position of the deleted element to the undefined value, but it will not move any of the other existing elements. However, `delete` works the same as `pop` and if you `delete` the last element in the array it will indeed remove that element altogether.

Testing for the Existence of an Element

You can find out if any particular array element exists using the `exists` function:

```
if (exists $array[$count]) {
   # …
}
```

Note that `exists` is different from `defined`. If an element is in the array but `undef`, for example, `defined` will return false but `exists` will return true. An element must truly not exist at all for `exists` to return false.

An Example: More Stats

Remember the script we did yesterday for simple statistics, where you entered numbers in one at a time, and the script calculated the count, sum, and average? Let's modify that script today to store the numbers that get entered into an array. Having the numbers around after the initial input means we can do more things with them, such as sorting them or finding the median (a different number from the mean).

Here's how the new version of the statistics script looks when it's run:

```
% morestats.pl
Enter a number: 4
Enter a number: 5
Enter a number: 3
(many more numbers in here that I've deleted for space)
Enter a number: 47
Enter a number: 548
Enter a number: 54
Enter a number: 5485
Enter a number:

Total count of numbers: 49
Total sum of numbers: 10430
Maximum number: 5485
Minimum number: 2
Average (mean): 212.86
Median: 45
```

There are two differences in obvious behavior between yesterday's version of the statistics script and this one:

- It calculates the maximum and minimum numbers that were entered.
- It finds the median number (the middle number in a sorted list of all the numbers).

In the code, however, there's one other significant difference between this version and the last: here we're using an array to store the input data, rather than just discarding it (when you run the script, you still end the input with a blank line). Listing 4.1 shows the code for the new listing.

LISTING 4.1 The `morestats.pl` Script

```
#!/usr/local/bin/perl -w

$input = '';   # temporary input
@nums = ();    # array of numbers;
$count = 0;    # count of numbers
$sum = 0;      # sum of numbers
$avg = 0;      # average
$med = 0;      # median

while () {
  print 'Enter a number: ';
  chomp ($input = <STDIN>);
  if ($input eq '') { last; }

  if ($input =~ /\D/) {
      print "Digits only, please.\n";
      next;
  }

  push @nums, $input;
  $count++;
  $sum += $input;
}

@nums = sort { $a <=> $b } @nums;
$avg = $sum / $count;
$med = $nums[$count / 2];

print "\nTotal count of numbers: $count\n";
print "Total sum of numbers: $sum\n";
print "Minimum number: $nums[0]\n";
print "Maximum number: $nums[$#nums]\n";
printf("Average (mean): %.2f\n", $avg);
print "Median: $med\n";
```

The `morestats.pl` version of the statistics script has four main sections: initialization, data entry, sorting the data and calculating the statistics, and, finally, printing the results.

The initialization section, lines 3 through 8, is the same as it was in the previous script, except that we've added two variables: an array variable (`@nums`) in line 4, to store the numeric inputs, and a `$med` variable in line 8 for the median. As with the other variables, we don't have to initialize the `@nums` variable, but it looks nice and groups all our variables up at the top of the script.

Lines 10 through 23 are the new `while` loop for entering in the input. If you compare this version to the version in yesterday's lesson, you'll see that there's actually not much that's new here. We're still accepting numbers one line at a time, still checking for digits only, and still incrementing the `$count` and updating the `$sum` for each number. The difference is in line 20, where for each turn of the loop we append the input to the `@nums` array using the `push` function.

With all the input in place, we move onto line 25, where we sort the `@nums` array using the special numeric sort routine I described earlier. Note that I don't have to define the `$a` or `$b` variables—these variables are local to `sort` and are discarded as soon as the sort is complete. Line 26 calculates the average (the mean), as it did in our previous version of the script, and line 27 calculates the median value.

Some points about the median—given a sorted set of data, the median is roughly defined as the value in the middle (it determines the true middle value, whereas the average can be skewed if there are especially high or low values). In statistics, if the number of values in the set is odd, the median is simply the value in the middle. If the number of values is even, then the middle value is actually the mean of the two values surrounding the actual middle. Here, I've simplified things; our median will be the middle value if the data set has an odd number of values, and the largest value of the lower half if the data set is even. That'll be close enough for our purposes.

To find the value in the middle, we need to find the array index number for the middle. The `$count` variable gives us the highest index number, so all we need to do is divide that by two and use that to index the array. Note that if there is an odd number of elements, the result of this division will be a floating-point number. This is okay; array indexes must be integers, and Perl will truncate the number before using it.

This brings us to the final summary in lines 29 to 34. Count, sum and average as the same as before, but now we've also added maximum, minimum, and median. Maximum and minimum are easy; because our array is sorted, we don't even need to calculate anything; we can just pull the first and last elements off of the array. And because we calculated the median earlier, all we need to do is print it as we have the other values.

List and Scalar Context

Before we leave arrays behind, I'd like to pause significantly to discuss the subject of context. *Context*, in Perl, is the notion that different bits of data act differently depending on what you're trying to do with them. Context can be particularly baffling to understand, and if you're confused about context you can end up with results that seem to make absolutely no sense (or bits of other people's scripts that produce results seemingly out of nowhere). On the other hand, when you understand context in Perl, and how different operations use context, you can do very complex things very quickly, which would take several lines of code in other languages.

> If you're an experienced programmer and you've been scanning the book for the important stuff up to this point, stop it right now. Take the time to read this section carefully and make sure you understand it. Context can trip up both novice and experienced Perl programmers alike.

What Is Context?

So just what does *context* mean? Let's use an analogy from English: take the word *contract*. Define it, in 25 words or fewer.

What's the definition of the word *contract*? The correct answer is; actually, "It depends on how you use it." In the sentence, "I just signed the contract," it's a noun, and the definition of *contract* as a noun is "a legal agreement between two parties." In another sentence, "Extreme cold causes the rivets to contract," it's used as a verb, and the definition is "to become smaller in size or length." Same word, same spelling, but a different meaning (and, actually a different pronunciation) depending on whether it's used in a noun context or a verb context.

"Okay," you say, "but what does this have to do with Perl?" I'm getting to that. Take the simple Perl expression `5 + 4`. What does that expression evaluate to?

"Uh, 9," you reply, wondering if there's a catch. You bet there's a catch. What if you stick that expression into a test, like this:

```
if (5 + 4) { ... )
```

Now what does `5 + 4` evaluate to? Well, it still evaluates to 9. But then, because it's being used as a test, it also evaluates to true (remember, only `0` and `""` are false). In the *context* of a test—Perl folk call it a *boolean context*—the expression `5 + 4` evaluates to a boolean value, not a number. The `if` construct expects a true or false value for the test, so Perl happily gives it one.

When numbers and strings are automatically converted from one to the other, they're converted based on context. In arithmetic, Perl expects numeric operands (a numeric context), so it converts any strings to numbers. The string operators, in turn, have a string context, so Perl converts numeric values to strings to satisfy the context.

Numeric, string, and boolean contexts are all forms of the more general scalar context. For the most part, you won't have to worry a lot about differentiating between the three because Perl can figure it out and convert it for you.

Where the complications arise is with differentiating between scalars and lists. Every operation in Perl is evaluated in either a scalar or list context. Some operations in Perl expect a scalar context, others expect lists, and you'll get errors in Perl if you try to stick the wrong kind of data where the other is expected. A third—and very common—class of operations can be evaluated in *either* a scalar or list context and might behave differently in one context than they do in the other. And, to make matters even more complex; there are no standard rules for how lists behave in a scalar context or vice versa. Each operation has its own rules, and you have to keep track of them or look them up. For every operation in Perl, then, if you're mixing lists and scalars, you should be asking yourself three questions:

- What context am I in (scalar or list)?
- What type of data am I using in that context?
- What is supposed to happen when I use that data in that context?

For the rest of this section, then, I'll discuss a few instances of when context is important. But this is definitely an area that will take further diligence on your part as you develop your skills in Perl. Keep those three questions and the Perl documentation close at hand, and you'll be fine.

Finding the Number of Elements in an Array, Revisited

You've already seen one example of how context is important. Remember how to find out the length of an array, using this line?

```
$numelements = @arrayname;
```

I told you then to just learn the rule and not worry about it. This is a classic example of where context can be confusing in Perl. The `$numelements` variable is a scalar variable, so the assignment to that variable is evaluated in a scalar context—a scalar value is expected on the right-hand side of the `=` (that's the answer to your first question: What context am I in? You're in a scalar context).

In this example, you've put a list on the right side, in a scalar context (the answer to the second question: What kind of data am I using?). So the only remaining question is, "What's supposed to happen to a list in this context?" In this case, what happens is that the number of elements in the array `@arrayname` ends up getting assigned to the `$numelements` variable. An array variable, evaluated in a scalar assignment context, results in the number of elements in the list.

Don't think of it as converting the list to a scalar; it doesn't work that way. There's no conversion going on. The list simply behaves differently in this context than it does elsewhere.

You can use this number-of-elements feature by supplying an array variable anywhere a scalar value is expected—for example, in any of these expressions:

```
$med = $arrayname[@arrayname / 2]; # median value, remember?
$tot = @arrayname + @anotherarray + @athird;
if (@arrayname > 10) { ... }
while (@arrayname) { ... }
```

If this seems confusing or difficult to read, you can always stick to the simple assignment of a scalar on one side and an array variable on the other. Or, if you're only getting the length of the array so that you can iterate over its values, you can use `$#array` as the stopping value instead of the number of elements, and avoid the whole thing.

Context and Assignment

Assignment is probably the most common case in which context becomes important—or, at least, it's one of the places where context is easiest to explain. With the left and right side of the assignment operator, you can have contexts that match (scalar = scalar, list = list), or mismatched contexts (scalar = list, list = scalar). In this section, I'll go over some of the simple rules for how context works in assignments.

Let's start with the easy cases, where the context matches. You've already learned all these. Scalar to scalar is an individual thing to an individual thing, with numbers and strings converted at will:

```
$x = 'foo'; # scalar variable, scalar value
```

You've also learned about list-to-list assignments, with list syntax and array variables on the left and right sides of the assignment operator, as well as nested inside other lists:

```
@nums = (10, 20, 30);
($x, $y, $z) = @nums;
($a, @nums2) = @nums;
```

Now let's look at the cases where the context doesn't match. Say you try to assign a scalar in a list context, as in either of these examples:

```
@array = 3.145;
```

```
($a, $b) = $c;
```

This one's easy! In these cases, the scalar value on the right is simply converted into a list and then assigned using list assignment rules. `@array` becomes a list of a single value, `3.145`, `$a` gets the value of `$c`, and `$b` becomes undefined.

The hardest case is dealing with assigning a list on the right to a scalar on the left. You've learned what happens when you assign an array variable to a scalar variable (you get the number of elements in the array):

```
$numelements = @array;
```

You'll also get the number of elements in the list if the value on the right is a raw list:

```
$numelements = sort @array;
```

When you use actual list syntax, however, the rule is different:

```
$x = (2, 4, 8, 16);
```

In this case, the rule is that all the values in the list except the *last* one are ignored. The value of `$x` here will be 16. Note that this is also a different rule from assigning the list (`$x)` to that same list, as list-to-list assignment starts from the *first* element, 2, and discards unused elements.

The most important thing to remember about these contexts is that there is no general rule for how a list behaves in a scalar context—you just have to know the rules. Keep those three questions in mind and you should be fine.

Other Contexts

There are a few other contextual situations worth touching on—things that you should be aware of as you work with lists and scalars.

First, there's boolean context, where a value is tested to see if it's true or false (as in the test for an `if` or a `while`). You've already learned how a scalar value, in boolean context, is true if it has any value except `""`, 0, or undefined.

Lists in boolean context follow a similar rule—a list with any elements, including undefined elements, is true in a boolean context. An empty list is false.

The second situation where context might be important is with functions. Some functions take a list as their argument, and all their arguments are combined and evaluated in that context. If you use functions with parentheses around their arguments, as you learned about yesterday, then there's no problem—you're giving the function a list of arguments. If you don't use parentheses, however, Perl will try and build a list from the arguments you give it. If those arguments contain lists or parenthesized expressions, however, Perl might get confused. Take this example with print, which is one of the functions that expects a list context:

```
print 4 + 5, 6, 'foo';
```

In this case, the arguments to print are evaluated as if they were the list `(9, 6, 'foo')`. With this case, however, the rule is different:

```
print (4 + 5), 6, 'foo';
```

Because of that parenthesized expression, Perl will assume that the `4 + 5` expression is its only argument, and become confused about what the `6` and the `'foo'` are doing hanging off the end. If you have Perl warnings turned on, it'll catch these (and complain about using constants in a void context). In this case, it's best to solve the problem by parenthesizing the entire list of arguments so there's no ambiguity:

```
print ((4 + 5), 6, 'foo');
```

Most of the time, Perl can figure out whether parentheses mean a function call, an expression, or a list. And, in most of the remaining cases, Perl warnings will help you figure out what's going on where there's ambiguity. But keep the differences and context in mind as you write your Perl scripts.

The `scalar` Function

Sometimes you really want to use a list in a scalar context, but it's awkward to go out of your way to create a scalar context for that operation (for example, creating a temporary scalar variable just to force the list into a scalar context). Fear not, there is a shorthand way. You can always force a list to be evaluated scalar context, using the `scalar` function. For example, take the following two statements:

```
print @nums;
print scalar(@nums);
```

The `print` function evaluates its arguments in a list context (this is why you can specify multiple arguments to print separated by commas). The first of these statements, then, expands the `@nums` array in a list context, and prints the values of that array. The second forces `@nums` to be evaluated in a scalar context which, in this case, prints the number of elements in `@nums`.

Input, Output, and Lists

We'll finish up today's lesson as we did yesterday: by talking a little more about input and output, this time with list and array context in mind. There are two topics to cover here that will help you work more with input and with files:

- Using `<STDIN>` in a list context
- Printing lists

Using <STDIN> in list context

Yesterday, you learned about `<STDIN>`, and how it's used to read data from the standard input. Up to now, we've been using it like this:

```
chomp($in = <STDIN>);
```

A close look at that line shows that you're using `<STDIN>` here in a scalar context—you're assigning it to the scalar variable `$in`. Like many other Perl operations, the input operator `<>` behaves differently in a list context than it does in a scalar one.

If you use `<STDIN>` in a scalar context, Perl reads a line of input up until the newline character. In a list context, however, `<STDIN>` reads all the input it can get, with each line stored as a separate element in the list. It only stops when it gets to an end-of-file.

That's a rather confusing explanation, given that standard input wouldn't seem to really have an end-of-file. But it does, actually. Typing a Ctrl+D (Ctrl+Z on Windows) tells Perl "this is the end of file" for standard input. If you use `<STDIN>` in a list context, then, Perl will wait until you've entered all your data and hit Ctrl+D or Ctrl+Z, put all that data into a list, and then continue with the script.

The use of input in a list context is much more useful when you're reading input from actual files, and you've got an explicit end-of-file. Generally you'll use `<STDIN>` to read individual lines of input from the keyboard in a scalar context. But it's important to realize the difference between input in a scalar context versus input from a list context; as with many other parts of Perl, there are differences in behavior between the two, and if you confuse them the bugs can get tricky.

Printing Lists

In the examples we've done in this chapter we've printed lists by using loops to examine and print each element of the list. If you just want to print the elements of a list without modifying them, however, there's an easier way: just print them using the `print` function. Given that `print` assumes its arguments are in list context, this makes it easy.

Well, sort of easy. Here's a simple list from 1 to 9:

```
@list = (1..9);
```

If you print this list with just the `print` function, you'll end up with this:

```
123456789
```

You won't even get a newline character at the end. By default, by printing a list, all the values of the list are concatenated together.

What if you want to print them with spaces in between them? You could use a `while` or `foreach` loop to do that. But there is an easier way. You can use variable interpolation for the list variable. You might remember yesterday we talked about variable interpolation inside strings, where given a string `"this is string $count"`, the `$count` variable would be replaced with its actual value. Variable interpolation also happens with array and hash variables—the contents of the array are simply printed in order, separated by a space. For example, if you include the `@list` variable inside quotes, with a newline character:

```
print "@list\n";
```

These lines will result in the list being printed with spaces in between the elements, with a newline at the end.Variable interpolation with list variables makes it easy to print out the contents of a list without resorting to loops. Note, however, that this does mean if you want to use the `@` character inside a double-quoted string, you'll often need to backslash it to prevent Perl from searching for an array that doesn't exist (and then complaining that it doesn't). Perl warnings will let you know if you're making this mistake.

Another way to control the printing of lists is to set special global Perl variables for the output field separator and output record separator. More about these special variables in today's "Going Deeper" section.

Going Deeper

We've covered a lot in this lesson, but there's still more about arrays and hashes I haven't discussed (really!). This section summarizes some of the features of lists, arrays, and hashes that I haven't covered in the body of this lesson. Feel free to explore these parts of Perl on your own.

Negative Array Indexes

In the array access expression `$array[index]`, usually the index will be the position of the element in the array, starting from 0. You can also use negative array subscripts, like this:

```
$array[-1];
```

Negative array subscripts will count back from the end of the array—so an index of `-1` refers to the last index in the array (same as `$#array)`, `-2` refers to the second to last index, and so on. You can also assign to those positions, although it might be a better idea to use syntax that's more explicit and easier to read in that instance.

More About Ranges

Earlier in this lesson, we used the range operator `..` to create a list of numeric elements. Ranges also have several features I didn't mention in that section. For example, you can use ranges with characters, and the range will generate a list of all the characters in the ASCII character set between the operands. For example, the range `'a' .. 'z'` results in a list of 26 characters from a to z.

You can also use this behavior in various magical ways, combining numbers and letters or multiple letters, and the range will happily oblige with values between the upper and lower values.

The range operator can also be used in a scalar context, and returns a boolean value. The `perlop` man page describes it as "The operator is bistable, like a flip-flop, and emulates the line-range (comma) operator of `sed`, `awk`, and various editors." I suppose if you have worked with `sed` or `awk` and understand what this means, you can use the range operator in this way. (I don't, and I haven't.) There is also a three-dot range operator (...) which more closely emulates `sed`'s behavior. See the `perlop` man page under Range Operator for more information and examples.

`chomp` and `chop` on Lists

The `chomp` and `chop` functions, to remove newlines or characters from the end of strings, also work with lists as their arguments. On lists, they work through each element in the list and remove the newline or the last character from each element. This could be useful for removing all the newline characters from input you read from a file into a list.

See the `perlfunc` man page for more information on `chomp` and `chop`.

Output Field, Record and List Separators

Part of Perl's built-in library is a set of global variables that can be used to modify Perl's behavior in many situations. You'll learn about many of these variables as this book progresses, or you can see the `perlvar` man page for a list of them all.

Relevant to the discussion today are the output-field, output-record, and list-separator variables. These three global variables can be set to change the default way that Perl prints lists. Table 4.1 defines these variables.

TABLE 4.1 Output Global Variables

Variable Name	*What it does*
`$,`	Output field separator; the characters to print in between list elements. Empty by default.
`$\`	Output record separator; the characters to print at the end of a list. Empty by default.
`$"`	Same as the output field separator, except only for list variables interpolated inside strings. A single space by default.

As you learned in the section "Printing Lists," when you print a bare list, Perl will concatenate all the values in the list together:

```
print (1,2,3);  # prints "123";
```

In reality, Perl actually prints the elements of the list with the value of the output field separator between the elements and the output record separator at the end. Because both those variables are empty by default, you get the previous behavior. You could set those variables to get different printing behavior:

```
$, = '*';
$\ = "\n";
print (1,2,3);  # prints "1*2*3\n"
```

The list field separator behaves similarly to the output field separator, but only when you use a list variable inside a string. By default the list field separator contains a string—and that's the default printing behavior for list variables interpolated into strings. Change the list field separator to change the printing behavior for array variables inside strings.

Void Context

In addition to list, scalar, and boolean context, Perl also has a void context, which is defined as simply a place where Perl doesn't expect anything. You'll most likely see this in warnings and errors when you included something where Perl didn't expect it—"unexpected constant in void context," for example.

Summary

Today was list day. As you learned, a list is just a bunch of scalars, separated by commas and surrounded by parentheses. Assign it to an array variable `@array`, and you can then get at the individual elements of that array using array access notation `$array[index]`. You also learned about finding the last index in the array (`$#array`), and the number of elements in the array (`$elements = @array`). We finished up that section with a couple of notes on list syntax and assignment, which allows you to assign variables to values in parallel in lists on either side of an assignment expression.

After arrays, we tackled context, which allows Perl to evaluate different things differently in either scalar or list context. You learned the three questions for figuring out context: What context is expected in an expression? What data have you given it? What is that data supposed to do in that context?

Finally, we finished up with more information about simple input and output using lists. Tomorrow, we'll complete your basic list education by talking about hashes. (Actually, way up on Day 19, "Working with References," we'll get into more advanced data structures, so we're not completely done with lists yet, but lists, arrays, and hashes will get you quite a lot for your Perl repertoire).

The built-in functions you learned about today (see the `perlfunc` man page for more details about these functions) include

- `qw` takes a list of strings, separated by spaces, and returns a list of individual string elements. `qw` allows you to avoid typing a lot of quote marks and commas when you have a long list of strings to define.
- `push` and `pop` add and delete elements from the end of a list or array, respectively.
- `defined` takes a variable or list location and returns true if that location has a value other than the undefined value.
- `undef` takes a variable or list location and assigns it the undefined value. With no arguments, `undef` simply returns the undefined value, which means it can be used to refer to that value.
- `delete` undefines an element in an array, or, if that element is the last element in the array, deleted it altogether.
- `exists` tests for the existence of an element.
- `sort` takes a list as an argument and sorts that list in ASCII order, returning the sorted list. Sort in numeric order with the statement `{ $a <=> $b }` just before the list.
- `scalar` evaluates a list in a scalar context.

Q&A

Q. What's the difference between the undefined value and `undef`?

A. Not a whole lot. The undefined value is what gets put in variables, or in array or hash value locations when there isn't an actual value—if you use one without initializing it, or if you add elements to an array past the boundaries of that array. If you want to explicitly use the undefined value, for example, to undefine a variable or to include that value in an array, you use the `undef` function. Because of the close relationship between the undefined value and `undef`, it's very common to see `undef` used to mean the undefined value (as in "the last three elements of that array are `undef`"). In real code, if you use `undef` anywhere you want an undefined value, you won't go wrong.

Q. I want to create an array of arrays.

A. You can't do that. Well, not right now. To create arrays of arrays, or arrays of hashes, or any kind of nested data structures, you need to use references. You won't learn about references for a while yet, so just sit tight for now. We'll cover references in Chapter 19.

Q. Why, when you delete an element from an array using `delete`, does it just `undef` the element? Why doesn't it delete it and reconstruct the array? Delete means delete, doesn't it?

A. Not necessarily. Array elements are indexed by number, and the relationship between an element and its index might be important. By deleting an element, you'd end up renumbering all the elements in the farther down in the array, which might not be what you want to do. The delete function does the safe thing and just adds an `undef` placeholder (except if the element to be deleted is the last element, in which case it's considered safe to remove it). You can always reconstruct the array if you really want those elements deleted.

Q. Augh! I don't understand list and scalar context. If different operations can do different things, and there are no rules for how lists and scalars behave in each other's contexts, doesn't that mean I have to remember what every operation does for every context?

A. Uh, well, yes. No. Kind of. If list versus scalar context is totally abhorrent to you, in any given script, you can usually avoid most of the more esoteric instances of context. Remember how to use the few that are important (getting the length of an array, for example), and look up the rest when something doesn't work right.

If you end up having to read other people's Perl code, however, chances are good you'll end up needing to keep context in mind and watch out for sneaky contexts.

Q. I want to find the number of elements in a list, so I did "length @array..."

A. Hold it right there! The `length` function is a fine function—for strings and numbers. To find the number of elements in a list, you should be using the array variable in a scalar context: `$numelements = @array`.

Q. How do I search an array for a specific element?

A. One way would be to iterate over the array using a `foreach` or `while` loop, and test each element of that array in turn. Perl also has a function called `grep` (after the Unix search command) which will do this for you. You'll learn more about `grep` on Day 11, "Creating and Using Subroutines."

Workshop

The workshop provides quiz questions to help you solidify your understanding of the material covered and exercises to give you experience in using what you've learned. Try and understand the quiz and exercise answers before you go on to tomorrow's lesson.

Quiz

1. Define the differences between lists and arrays.
2. What do each of these variables refer to?

```
$foo
@foo
$foo[1]
```

3. What's the result of this list:

```
@list = (1, (), (4, 3), $foo, ((), 10, 5 + 4), (), (''));
```

4. What are the results of the following Perl statements? Why does each expression evaluate to the result it does?

```
($x, $y, $z) = ('a', 'b');
($u, @more, $v) = (1 .. 10);
$nums[4] = (1, 2, 3);  # @nums previously contained (10,9,8)
undef $nums[4];
$nums[$#nums];
$foo = @nums;
@more = 4;
```

5. What's the rule for converting a list into a scalar?
6. How do you sort an array?
7. What's the difference between using `<STDIN>` in a scalar context and using it in a list context? Why is this important?

Exercises

1. Write a script that reads in numbers, one line at a time (similar to the stats program), and stores them in an array. Then write a loop that prints out those same numbers, one on each line.
2. Write a script that prompts the user for two numbers and then creates an array of numbers between the lower and higher bound (make sure the user can enter either the lower or higher number first).
3. You have an array with the following values:

   ```
   ("foo", 1, undef, 45, undef, undef, "atlas", undef, 101, undef)
   ```

   Write a script that iterates over that array and changes all the undefined values to the string `'*zot!*'`.
4. BUG BUSTER: What's wrong with this script? (Hint: there might be more than one error!)

   ```
   print 'Enter list of numbers: ';
   chomp($in = <STDIN>);
   @nums = split(" ", $in);

   @sorted = sort @nums;
   print "Numbers: @sorted\n";

   $totalnums = $#nums;
   print "Total number of numbers: $totalnums\n";
   ```

4

Answers

Here are the answers to the Workshop questions in the previous section.

Quiz Answers

1. A list is simply a collection of scalar elements. An array is an ordered list indexed by position.
2. The answers are

   `$foo` is a scalar variable

   `@foo` is an array variable

   `$foo[1]` is the second element in the array @foo
3. The result of the list is: `(1, 4, 3, $foo, 10, 9, '')`. Actually, `$foo` will be expanded into whatever the value of `$foo` actually is.

4. The answers are

    a. `$x` gets `'a'`, `$y` gets `'b'`, `$z` gets undefined. Assignment to lists on the left side happens in parallel, each value on the right assigned to each variable on the left.

    b. `$u` gets 1, `@more` gets `(2,3,4,5,6,7,8,9,10)`, and `$v` gets undefined. Array variables on the left side of a list assignment eat up all remaining values on the right.

    c. `$nums[4]` gets 3. Assignment of list syntax to a scalar assigns only the last value in the list and ignores all the previous values.

       If the previous value of `@nums` was `(10,9,8)`, the new value of `@nums` is `(10,9,8,undef,3)`. Assigning a raw list to a scalar ignores all but the last value in the list.

    d. `$nums[4]` will be set to the undefined value (it was previously 3).

    e. `$nums[$#nums]` refers to the value at the last index in the list.

    f. `$foo` gets the number of elements in the `@nums` array.

    g. The 4 will be "promoted" to a list, and `@more` will be the list of one element: `(4)`.

5. Trick question! There is no rule for converting a list into a scalar. You can't even convert a list into a scalar. Lists behave differently in a scalar context depending on how you use them.

6. Sort an array using the sort function:

    ```
    @sorted = sort @array;
    ```

7. Using `<STDIN>` in a scalar context reads one line of input up until the user hits Return and stores it in a scalar variable. Using `<STDIN>` in a list context reads all the lines of input in the standard input up until end-of-file, and stores each line as a separate element in the list. The difference is important because it changes the way your program behaves and how you get input into that program.

Exercises

1. Here's one answer:

    ```
    #!/usr/local/bin/perl -w

    $input = '';  # temporary input
    @nums = ();  # array of data (doesn't have to be nums)

    while () {
      print 'Enter data: ';
      chomp ($input = <STDIN>);
      if ($input eq '') { last; }
    ```

```
  if ($input =~ /\D/) {
      print "Digits only, please.\n";
      next;
  }

  push @nums, $input;
}

foreach $key (@nums) {
    print "$key\n";
}
```

2. Here's one answer:

```
#!/usr/local/bin/perl -w

$one = 0;
$two = 0;

while () {
    print 'Enter a range boundary: ';
    chomp ($one = <STDIN>);
    print 'Enter the other range boundary: ';
    chomp ($two = <STDIN>);

    if ($one eq ''  or $two eq '' ) {
        print "Either the beginning or ending boundary is missing.\n";
        next;
    }

    if ($one =~ /\D/ or $two =~ /\D/ ) {
        print "Digits only, please.\n";
        next;
    }

    last;
}

if ($one < $two) {
    @array = ($one .. $two);
} else {
    @array = ($two .. $one);
}

print "@array\n";
```

3. Here's one way to do it:

```
#!/usr/local/bin/perl -w

@array = ("foo", 1, undef, 45, undef, undef, "atlas", undef, 101, undef);
@newarray = (); # new array;
```

4

```
foreach $key (@array) {
    if (!defined $key) {
        push @newarray, "*zot!*";
    } else {
        push @newarray, $key;
    }
}

print "@newarray\n";
```

4. There is only one error in the line $totalnums = $#nums. The assumption here is that $#nums contains the total number of elements, which it doesn't (it contains the highest index, which is one less than the total number of elements). Use $totalnums = @nums instead, or $totalnums = $#nums+1.

   Another assumption that could possibly be an error is that this script refers to numbers repeatedly, prompting for numbers, sorting them in an array called `@nums`, and so on, but the sorting routine in the middle of the script is an ASCII sort, not a numeric sort. This could produce some interesting and not expected results if an actual numeric sort was what was intended.

DAY 5

Working with Hashes

Arrays and lists provide a basic way of grouping together scalars, but they're pretty basic as far as data structures go. Perl provides a second form of list data (or a third, if you count raw lists) called hashes. In many situations—depending on the data you've got and what you want to do with it—hashes are better than arrays for storing and accessing data.

Today, then, we'll cover hashes. You'll learn all about

- How hashes are different from arrays
- Defining hashes
- Accessing hash elements
- Hashes and context
- Using `split` to split a string into a list (or hash).
- Still more patterns

Hashes Versus Arrays and Lists

You learned yesterday that a list is a collection of scalars, and that an array is an ordered list, indexed by element. A hash is also a way of expressing a collection of data, but the way the data is stored is different.

A hash is an unordered collection of pairs of scalars, often called keys and values (See Figure 5.1). You access an element (a value) in a hash by referring to it by its key. Neither the keys or the values are in any kind of order; you cannot refer to the first or last element in a hash, nor can you numerically iterate over the elements in that hash, like you can an array (although you can get a list of the hash's keys, of its values, or of both in pairs, and access all a hash's elements that way). Hashes are more useful than arrays in many ways, most typically because it's easier to keep track of elements in named slots (keys in hashes) rather than by numbers (indexes in arrays).

FIGURE 5.1
Hashes.

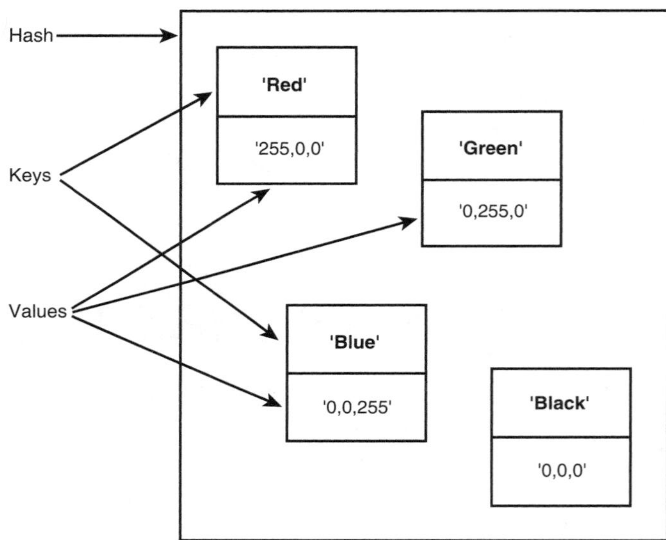

Note

Hashes are sometimes called associative arrays, which is actually a better description of what they do (the keys are associated with their values). In fact, associative arrays are the original name for hashes, but today's Perl programmers prefer to call them by the much shorter and less awkward name hash.

As with arrays, hashes have their own variables with their own symbol at the beginning. Hash variables start with a percent (`%`), and follow all the same rules as array variables do. As with all variables, the hash variable `%x` is a different thing than the array variable `@x` or the scalar variable `$x`.

Defining and Using Hashes

Arrays and hashes can be created and used in many of the same ways. Hashes, however, do have some peculiarities and extra features that result from the way data is stored in a hash. For example, when you put data into a hash, you'll have to keep track of two scalars for each element (the key and the value). Because hashes are unordered, you'll have to do extra work to extract values from the hash, as well as to sort them and print them. In addition, hashes perform differently than arrays in a scalar context. Read on to learn about all these things.

List Syntax and Hashes

List syntax—enclosing the elements of a list inside parentheses, separated by commas—works to create a hash just as well as it does an array. Just stick a hash variable on the left side of the assignment, rather than an array variable, like this:

```
%pairs = ('red', 255, 'green', 150, 'blue', 0);
```

With an array variable on the left side of the assignment, this statement would create an array of six elements. With a hash variable (`%pairs`), the elements are added to hash in pairs, with the first element a key and the second its value, the third element the second key, and the fourth element its value, and so on down the line. If there are an odd number of elements in the list, the last element will be a key in the hash, and its value will be `undef`. If you have Perl warnings turned on, you'll also get a warning about this ("Odd number of elements in hash assignment").

5

With this kind of formatting, it's sort of difficult to figure out at a glance what parts of the list are the keys and which are the values, or if you do indeed have an odd number of elements without counting them. (It only gets worse the larger the lists get.) Many Perl programmers format list syntax for hashes like this, with the keys and values on their own lines:

```
%temps = (
   'Boston', 32,
   'New York', 24,
   'Miami', 78,
   'Portland', 45,
    # and so on...
);
```

Even better is the `=>` operator, which behaves exactly the same way as the comma, but makes it easier to see the link between the keys and the values. So that first example up there with the colors would look like this:

```
%pairs = ('red'=>255, 'green'=>150, 'blue'=>0);
```

And the second, with the cities:

```
%temps = (
   'Boston' => 32,
   'New York' => 24,
   'Miami' => 78,
   'Portland' => 45,
    # and so on...
);
```

One other shortcut you can use for hashes: Perl expects the key part of each hash element to be a string, so you can leave the quotes off the key to save yourself some typing and Perl will figure out what you mean. If the key contains a space, however, you'll have to leave the quotes in place (Perl isn't *that* smart):

```
%pairs = (red=>255, green=>150, blue=>0);
```

In an array or list, any of your elements can be duplicates of any others because the elements are ordered.You can also use the index number to look up those values in the array. With hashes, however, because your keys are used to look up values in the hash, it is important that you use unique keys, with no duplicates. In fact, Perl won't allow you to use duplicate keys, the value of the key farther in the list will overwrite the value closer to the beginning, and there will only be one key/value pair for each unique key:

```
%temps = (
   'Boston' => 32,
   'New York' => 24,
   'Miami' => 78,
   'Portland' => 45,
   'Boston' -> 30,  # this value will overwrite 32
    # and so on...
};
```

Keys must be unique, but values, on the other hand, are entirely independent of each other and can contain as many duplicates as you need.

As with lists, `()` assigned to a hash variable creates an empty hash:

```
%hash = ();  # no keys or values
```

Converting Between Arrays, Lists, and Hashes

A second way to create a hash is to use an array or a list for its initial elements. Because both hashes and arrays use lists as their raw form, you can copy them back and forth between each other with no problems:

```
@stuff = ('one', 1, 'two', 2);
%pairsostuff = @stuff;
```

In this example, assigning the array `@stuff` to the hash `%pairsostuff` causes the array elements to be expanded into a list, and then paired off into two key/value pairs in the hash. It behaves just the same as if you had typed all the elements in list syntax. Watch out for those odd-numbered elements, however; you'll end up with a key whose value is `undef` (Perl warnings will let you know if this is happening. You might want to test an array before assigning it to a hash to make sure that it contains an even number of elements to avoid printing a warning).

What about converting a hash back into a list? Here's an example where you're assigning a hash to an array:

@stuff = %pairsostuff;When you put a hash on the right side of a list assignment, or in fact use it in any situation where a raw list is expected, Perl will "unwind" the hash into its component elements (key, value, key, value, and so on). The expanded list is then assigned to the array `@stuff`.

There is a catch to this nifty unwinding behavior: because hashes are not ordered, the key/value pairs you get out of a hash will not necessarily be in the same order you put them in, or in any kind of sorted order. Hash elements are stored in an internal format that makes them very fast to access, and are unwound in that internal order. If you must create a list from a hash in a certain order, you'll have to build a loop to extract them in a specific order (more about this later).

Accessing Hash Elements

To get at or assign a value to a hash, you need to know the name of the key. Unlike arrays, which just have bare values in a numeric order, hashes have key value pairs. When you know the key, however, you can then use curly braces ({}) to refer to a hash value, like this:

```
print $temps{'Portland'};
$temps{'Portland'} = 50;
```

Note that this syntax is similar to the array access syntax `$array[]`—you use a scalar variable `$` to get at a scalar value inside a hash, but here you use curly braces `{}` surrounding the key name, as opposed to brackets. The thing inside the braces should be a string (here we used a single-quoted string), although Perl will convert numbers to strings for you. Also, if the key only contains a single word, you can leave off the quotes and Perl will know what you mean:

```
$temps{Portland} = 50; # same as $temps{'Portland');
```

5

As with arrays, the variable name in the hash access syntax doesn't interfere with scalar variables of the same name. All the following refer to different things, even though the variable name is the same:

```
$name          # a scalar

@name          # an entire array

%name          # an entire hash

$name[$index] # a scalar value contained in the array name at $index

$name{key}     # a scalar value contained in the hash name at the key 'key'
```

Also, as with arrays (sensing the trend, here?), you can assign values to individual hash elements using that same hash element-access syntax with an assignment statement, and the old value at that key is replaced with the new value:

```
%hash{key} = $newvalue;
```

If you assign a value to a key that does not exist, that key/value pair is automatically created for you.

Deleting Hash Elements

Use the `delete` function to delete elements, both keys and values, from a hash. Unlike with arrays, where `delete` did roughly the same thing as `undef`—simply undefining a value but leaving it there—with hashes, `delete` actually does delete every trace of the element from the hash.

The `delete` function takes a reference to a hash element (commonly just the hash access expression such as `$hashname{'key'}`) and deletes both that key and value, returning the value that was deleted. So, for example, to move an element from one hash to another (deleting it from one hash and adding it to another), you could use syntax something like this:

```
$hash2{$key} = delete $hash{$key};
```

As with arrays, you can also test to see if a particular key/value pair exists in a hash using the `exists` function. The `exists` function tests to see if a given hash value exists in a hash and returns the value if it does (note that the value attached to that key could very well be undefined; `exists` only tests for the actual existence of the key). Use `exists` like this:

```
if (exists $hashname{$key})  { $hashname{$key}++; }
```

This particular statement tests to see if the value at the key `$key` exists, and if it does, it increments the value at that key (assuming, of course, that the value is a number).

Processing All the Values in a Hash

To process all the elements in an array, you use a `foreach` or a `while` loop to iterate over all the values, testing each one for some feature and then doing something to that value if the test was true. But how do you do that for hashes? Hashes are unordered, so you can't just start from key zero and go on until the end. There is no key zero, and no end (well, there is, internally, but you can't get at that order).

The most commonly used answer to this problem is to use one of two functions: `keys` or `values`. These functions both take a hash as an argument, and then return, respectively, a raw list of all the keys in the hash, or a raw list of all the values in the hash. With either of these lists, you can use `foreach` or another loop to process each element of the hash without worrying about missing any.

So, for example, let's say you had a hash containing a list of temperatures indexed by city name (as we had in a previous example in this section) and you wanted to print a list of those cities and temperatures, in alphabetical order. You could use `keys` to get a list of all the keys, `sort` to sort those keys, and then a `foreach` loop to print the value of each of those keys, like this:

```
foreach $city (sort keys %temps) {
    print "$city: $temps{$city} degrees\n";
}
```

This loop works by working through the list of elements and assigning each one to the `$city` variable in turn (or any variable you pick). You can then use that variable in the body of the loop as the key into the hash to get the value of the current element. This is an extremely common group of lines for accessing and processing hash elements; you'll see this a lot as we write examples over the next few days.

5

Hashes and Context

Let's return to context and go over how hashes behave in the various contexts. For the most part, hashes behave just like lists, and the same rules apply, with a couple of wrinkles.

You've seen how to create a hash from list syntax, where the hash will match keys to pairs, like this:

```
%pairs = (red=>255, green=>150, blue=>0);
```

In the reverse case, where you use a hash where a list is expected, the hash will unwind back into its component parts (in some undetermined order), and then follow the same rules for any list.

```
@colors = %pairs;       # results in an array of all elements
```

```
($x, $y, $z) = %pairs; # first three elements of unwound hash assigned to vars,
                       # remaining elements ignored
print %pairs;          # prints unwound hash elements concatenated together
```

In all these instances, if you use a hash in a list context—for example, on the right side of an assignment—then the hash will be "unwound" back into individual items, and then the list behaves as it does in any list or scalar context. The one peculiar case is this one:

```
$x = %pairs;
```

At first glance, this would seem to be the hash equivalent of the way to get the number of elements out of an array (`$x = @array`). However, Perl behaves differently with this one than it does with arrays—the result in `$x` will end up being a description of the internal state of the hash table (something like 3/8 or 4/100), which in 99% of cases is probably not what you want. To get the number of elements (key/value pairs) in a hash, use the `keys` function and then assign it to a scalar variable instead:

```
$x = keys %pairs;
```

The `keys` function returns a list of the keys in the hash, which is then evaluated in a scalar context, and gives the number of elements.

Note

Curious about just what I mean by "a description of the internal state of the hash?" Okay, then. The result of assigning a hash variable in a scalar context gives you two numbers, separated by a slash. The second is the number of slots that have been allocated for the internal hash table (often called "buckets"), and the first is the number of slots actually used by the data. There's nothing you can do with this number, so if you see it, you've probably done something wrong (probably you're trying to get the number of keys in your hash, and what you really wanted was to use `%x = keys %hash` instead of `$x = %hash`.

An Example: Frequencies in the Statistics Program

Let's modify our statistics script again, this time to add a feature that keeps track of the number of times each number appears in the input data. We'll use this feature to print out a histogram of the frequencies of each bit of data. Here's an example of what that histogram will look like (other than the histogram, the output the script produces is the same as it was before, so I'm not going to duplicate that here):

```
Frequency of Values:
1  | *****
2  | *************
3  | *******************
4  | ****************
5  | ***********
6  | ****
43 | *
62 | *
```

To keep track of each number's frequency in our script, we use a hash, with the keys being the actual numbers in the data and the values being the number of times that number occurs in the data. The histogram part then loops over that hash and prints out a graphical representation of the number of times the data occurs. Easy!

Listing 5.1 shows the Perl code for our new script.

LISTING 5.1 stillmorestats.pl

```
#!/usr/local/bin/perl -w

$input = '';  # temporary input
@nums = ();   # array of numbers;
%freq = ();   # hash of number frequencies
$count = 0;   # count of numbers
$sum = 0;     # sum of numbers
$avg = 0;     # average
$med = 0;     # median
$maxspace = 0;# max space for histogram

while () {
  print 'Enter a number: ';
  chomp ($input = <STDIN>);
  if ($input eq '') { last; }

  if ($input =~ /\D/) {
      print "Digits only, please.\n";
      next;
  }

  push @nums, $input;
  $freq{$input}++;
  $count++;
  $sum += $input;
}

@nums = sort { $a <=> $b } @nums;
$avg = $sum / $count;
$med = $nums[$count / 2];

```

LISTING 5.1 continued

```
32: print "\nTotal count of numbers: $count\n";
33: print "Total sum of numbers: $sum\n";
34: print "Minimum number: $nums[0]\n";
35: print "Maximum number: $nums[$#nums]\n";
36: printf("Average (mean): %.2f\n", $avg);
37: print "Median: $med\n\n";
38: print "Frequency of Values:\n";
39:
40: $maxspace = (length $nums[$#nums]) + 1;
41:
42: foreach $key (sort { $a <=> $b } keys %freq) {
43:   print $key;
44:   print ' ' x ($maxspace - length $key);
45:   print '| ', '*' x $freq{$key}, "\n";
46: }
```

This script hasn't changed much from the previous one; the only changes are in lines 5, 10, line 23, and the section at the end, in lines 38 to 46. You might look over those lines now to see how they fit into the rest of the script that we've already written.

Lines 5 and 10 are easy. These are just new variables that we'll use later on in the script: the `%freq` hash, which will store the frequency of the data; and `$maxspace`, which will hold a temporary space variable for formatting the histogram (more about this when we go over how the histogram is built).

Line 23 is much more interesting. This line is inside the loop where we're reading the input; line 22 is where we push the current input onto the array of values. In line 23, what we're doing is looking up the input number as a key in the frequencies hash, and then incrementing the value referred to by that key by 1 (using the `++` operator).

The key is the number itself, whereas the value is the number of times that number appears in the data. If the number that was input doesn't yet appear as a key in the hash, then this line will add it and increment the value to `1`. Each time after that, it then just keeps incrementing the frequency as the same number appears in the data.

At the end of the input loop, then, you'll end up with a hash that contains, as keys, all the unique values in the data set, and as values, the number of times each value appears. All that's left now is to print the usual sum, average and median, and a histogram of that data.

Instead of going over lines 38 through 46 line by line as I've done in past examples, I'd like to show you how I built this loop when I wrote the script itself, so you can see my thinking in how this loop came out. This will actually give you a better idea of why I did what I did.

My first pass at this loop was just an attempt to get the values to print in the right order. I started with a `foreach` loop not unlike the one I described in "Processing All the Values in a Hash" earlier in this lesson:

```
foreach $key (sort { $a <=> $b } keys %freq) {
  print "Key: $key Value: $freq{$key}\n";
}
```

In this loop, I use `foreach` to loop over each key in the hash. The order in which the elements are presented, however, is controlled by the list in parentheses on the first line. The `keys %freq` part extracts all the keys from the hash, `sort` sorts them (remember, `sort` by default sorts in ASCII order, adding `$a <=> $b` forces a numeric sort). This results in the hash being processed in order from lowest key to highest.

Inside the loop, then, all I have to do is print the keys and the values. Here's the output of the loop when I add some simple data to `%freq`:

```
Key: 2 Value: 4
Key: 3 Value: 5
Key: 4 Value: 3
Key: 5 Value: 1
```

That's a good printout of the values of the `%freq` hash, but it's not a histogram. My second pass changes the `print` statement to use the string repetition operator `x` (you learned about it on Day 3) to print out the appropriate number of asterisks for the frequency of numbers:

```
foreach $key (sort { $a <=> $b } keys %freq) {
  print "$key |", '*' x $freq{$key}, "\n";
}
```


This is closer; it produces output like this:

```
2 | ****
3 | *****
4 | ***
5 | *
```

The problem comes when the input data is larger than 9. Depending on the number of characters in the key, the formatting of the histogram can get really screwed up. Here's what the histogram looked like when I input numbers of one, two and three digits:

```
2 | ****
3 | *****
4 | ***
5 | *
13 | **
24 | *
45 | ***
2345 | *
```

So the thing to do here is to make sure there are the appropriate number of spaces before the pipe character (|) to make sure everything in the histogram lines up correctly. I did this with the `length` function, which returns the number of characters (bytes, actually), in a scalar value, and that `x` operator again.

We start by finding out the maximum amount of space we'll need to allow for. I got that number from the largest value in the data set (because the data set is sorted, the largest value is the last value), and I added 1 to it to include a space at the end:

```
$maxspace = (length $nums[$#nums]) + 1;
```

Then, inside the loop, we can add some `print` statements: The first one prints just the key. The second one will pad out the smaller numbers to the largest number's width by adding an appropriate number of spaces. The third one prints the pipe and the stars for the histogram:

```
foreach $key (sort { $a <=> $b } keys %freq) {
  print $key;                           # print the key
  print ' ' x ($maxspace - length $key); # pad to largest width
  print '| ', '*' x $freq{$key}, "\n";    # print the stars
}
```

This last version of the histogram is the version I ended up with in Listing 5.1.

Note

The way I did the formatting here is kind of a hack, and I don't recommend this method for anything more substantial than the few characters we're dealing with in this example. Perl has a set of procedures specifically for formatting data on ASCII screens (remember, it's the Practical Extraction and *Report* Language). In this age of HTML and Web-based reports, Perl ASCII formatting isn't as commonly used, but you can get a taste for it from the `perlform` man page.

Extracting Data into Arrays or Hashes Using the `split` Function

When you read input from the keyboard, often that data is in a convenient form so that you can just test it a little, assign it to a variable and then do whatever else you want to with it. But a lot of the input you'll deal with—particularly from files—is not often in a form that's so easy to process. What if the input you're getting has ten numbers per line? What if it came from Excel or a database and it's in comma-separated text? What if there's one part in the middle of the line you're interested in, but you don't care about the rest of it?

Often, the input you get to a Perl script will be in some sort of raw form, and then it's your job to extract and save the things you're interested in. Fortunately, Perl makes this very easy. One way to extract data out of a string is to split that string into multiple elements, and save those elements as an array or a hash. Then you can manipulate the elements in the array or hash individually. A built-in function, called `split`, does just this.

Let's take the simplest and most common example: your input data is a single string of elements, separated by spaces:

```
$stringofnums = '34 23 56 34 78 38 90';
```

To split this string into an array of elements, you would use `split` with two arguments:

A string of one space, and the string you want to split. The `split` function will return a list, so usually you'll want to assign the list to something (like an array):

```
@nums = split(' ', $stringofnums);
```

The result of this statement is an array of seven elements, split from the original string: `(34, 23, 56, 34, 78, 38, 90)`.

Or you could assign it to a set of variables:

```
($x, $y, $z, undef, @remainder) = split(' ', $stringofnums);
```

In this case, the first three numbers in the string get assigned to the first three variables, the fourth (`34`) gets thrown away (`undef`), and the last three are stored in `@remainder`.

This form of `split`, with a single-space argument, is actually a special case. The single space tells `split` to split the string on any white space characters, including spaces or tabs, to skip over multiple whitespace characters, and to ignore any leading or trailing whitespace as well. It does it all for you, automatically.In fact, this form of split is so common you could ignore the space argument altogether and just call split with the string argument and it would automatically split on whitespace:

5

```
@nums = split $stringofnums;
```

I will use the `string` argument in all my examples to remind you what `split` is splitting on.

If you want to split a string on anything other than whitespace; for example, if your data is separated by commas, by pipe characters (|), or by anything else, you must use a pattern. These are the same regular expression patterns you have seen before. Here's an example that splits on commas:

```
$commasep = "45,32,56,123,hike!";
@stuff = split(/,/, $commasep);
```

Another Example: Alphabetical Lists of Names

For another example, let's put together hashes and `split` into a simple example that reads a list of names, puts those names into a hash keyed by last name, and then prints out the list in alphabetical order, last name first. Here's an example of what it looks like:

```
Enter a name (first and last): Umberto Eco
Enter a name (first and last): Isaac Asimov
Enter a name (first and last): Fyodor Dostoyevski
Enter a name (first and last): Albert Camus
Enter a name (first and last): Bram Stoker
Enter a name (first and last): George Orwell
Enter a name (first and last):
Asimov, Isaac
Camus, Albert
Dostoyevski, Fyodor
Eco, Umberto
Orwell, George
Stoker, Bram
```

Listing 5.2 shows our short little script to read and adjust the data.

LISTING 5.2 The `names.pl` Script

```
#!/usr/local/bin/perl -w

$in = '';       # temporary input
%names = ();    # hash of names
$fn = '';       # temp firstname
$ln = '';       # temp lastname

while () {
    print 'Enter a name (first and last): ';
    chomp($in = <STDIN>);
    if ($in eq '') { last; }

    ($fn, $ln) = split(' ', $in);
    $names{$ln} = $fn;
}

foreach $lastname (sort keys %names) {
    print "$lastname, $names{$lastname}\n";
}
```

This script has three basic sections: initialize the variables, read in the data, and print it back out again. I'll skip the initialization part because that should be obvious by now.

Lines 8 through 15 read the data in a way that should look familiar from the statistics script, using a `while` loop, an `if` to test for an empty entry, and `<STDIN>` in a scalar context. Unlike `stats`, where we put the elements into an array, line 13 uses `split` to separate the name input into two temporary scalar variables, `$fn` and `$ln`. Then in line 14, we add that first and last name pair to the `$names` hash, with the last name as the key.

With the hash all set up with the data, we can go ahead and print it. Again, you've seen this syntax before, most recently in the histogram example previously in this lesson. Here, we're sorting the keys in alphabetical order, so we can use the simpler form of sort here. And, finally, the `print` statement in line 18 uses the `$lastname` variable (which contains the current key) and the hash lookup for that key to print out the first and last names.

A Few More Patterns

To finish up—because we have a little space left over today—I'd like to tuck a couple more patterns into your regular expressions repertoire, so that you can keep building on what you've learned (and so that I can use them in the last example you're about to work through).

So far you've learned about patterns with individual characters:

```
/abc/
```

Patterns with digits:

```
/\d/
```

And patterns with nondigits:

```
/\D/
```

Here's another one: `\s` is a whitespace character. Whitespace in Perl is a space, a tab, a newline, a carriage return, or a formfeed. The `\s` pattern counts as any of these. Just as with `\d`, however, `\s` only means a *single* whitespace character, so the pattern `/\s/` will match one and only one space, tab, newline, and so on. Grouping all the whitespace characters together under one special character allows you to not worry about whether your user is typing spaces or tabs, or whether the system your running on is using newlines or carriage returns or both. It's just whitespace. The general rule is if its whitespace, use `\s` in your pattern.

`\S` is the opposite of `\s`. Its any character that isn't whitespace: any number or letter or punctuation; anything that isn't a space, a tab, a newline, and so on.

5

The problem with the `\d`, `\D`, `\s` and `\S` characters, as I've mentioned, is that they match only a single character. Sometimes it would be useful to be able to match one or more of these characters, so your pattern would be true if you had one digit or eight, or one space or four. Either way would work. The pattern would be much more flexible that way.

You can do that by adding a `+` to the pattern. The `+` applies to the character just before it. So this pattern matches one or more digits:

```
/\d+/
```

This pattern matches one or more whitespace characters:

```
/\s+/
```

But this pattern matches a single whitespace character, followed by one or more digits:

```
/\s\d+/
```

The `+` only applies to the pattern just before it. It can also apply to any pattern, not just the `\s` or `\d` special patterns. This pattern, for example, matches one or more m's:

```
/m+/
```

Table 5.1 shows our pattern summary so far.

TABLE 5.1 Patterns

Pattern	*Type*	*What it does*
`/a/`	Character	Matches `a`
`/\d/`	Any digit	Matches a single digit
`/\D/`	Any character not a digit	Matches a single character other than a digit
`/\s/`	Any whitespace	Matches a single space, tab, newline, carriage return or formfeed
`/\S/`	Any character not whitespace	Matches a single character other than whitespace
`+`	One or more	Matches one or more of the pattern just before it

Yet Another Example: Stock Price Converter

This final example uses split and patterns. The script in Listing 5.3 is a bit of an enhancement to the stock script on Day 3—the script where you typed in the beginning and ending prices of a stock, and it calculated the return on your investment. In that version of the script, you weren't allowed to enter stocks in the old-style format of fractional prices (14 5/8); we tested for that using regular expressions and printed an error.

This script isn't really a stock script; instead it's more of a price-checking and fixing script. It allows prices in plain numeric format. It checks for nondecimal characters and prints an error, as before. But if you enter in a price in a fractional format, it converts that price to a decimal format, rounding off to two decimal places. Pressing return with no input exits the script:

```
% checkprice.pl
Enter a stock price: 14
Price: 14
Enter a stock price: 14.5
Price: 14.5
Enter a stock price: zbf
Digits only, please.
Enter a stock price: 14 7/8
Price: 14.88
Enter a stock price: 14 1/2
Price: 14.50
Enter a stock price: 14 15/16
Price: 14.94
Enter a stock price:
%
```

Listing 5.3 shows the code for this script.

LISTING 5.3 The `checkprice.pl` Script


```
#!/usr/local/bin/perl -w

$price = 0;  # stock price
$whole  = 0; # temp whole number
$frac = "";  # temp fractional num
$numer = 0;  # numerator
$denom = 0;  # denominator

while () {
    print "Enter a stock price: ";
    chomp ($price  = <STDIN>);
    if ($price eq '') { last; }

    if ($price =~ /\//) {  # process fractions
        if ($price =~ /\d\s+/) { # "14 5/8" (numbers with whole part)
            ($whole, $frac) = split(' ', $price);
        } else { # "5/8" (no whole part)
            $whole = 0;
            $frac = $price;
        }
```

LISTING 5.3 continued

```
21:
22:         ($numer, $denom) = split(/\//,$frac);
23:         $price = $whole + ($numer / $denom);
24:         $price = sprintf("%.2f", $price);
25:     }
26:
27:     if ($price =~ /\D/ and $price !~ /\./ ) {
28:         print "Digits only, please.\n";
29:         next;
30:     }
31:
32:     print "Price: $price\n";
33: }
```

A lot of this structurewill look familiar to you. The `while` loop, the tests for the empty string in line 12, and the nondigits tests in lines 27 through line 30 are all borrowed from earlier examples. The part I want to focus on here is the big if test in lines 14 through 25. This is where we check for fractional numbers, and if we find them, convert them to decimal numbers.

The first test is the pattern in line 14, which tests for the slash in the fraction. This is the same test we've used before. Note once again that the slash character is a special character in patterns, so we have to backslash it to escape it.

Fractional numbers could be entered in two forms: with a whole number part (for example, "12 1/2"), or as just the fraction, with no whole number ("15/16"). Because we'll treat both cases slightly different, there's another test in line 15 to break them apart. The test we use is one for the whitespace in between the whole number and the fraction. But be careful here. I started out just testing for the whitespace and thought that was enough:

```
if ($price =~ /\s+/)
```

This pattern, as you just learned, tests for one or more whitespace characters. I figured that would get the space in between the whole number and the fractional number, which it did. But it also matched if I typed a space and then a fractional number with no whole number at all. That was a bug.

So what I really want to match is some number, then some whitespace. I added a digit to the pattern as you see in line 15, and this works better.

Given input with a whole number and a fractional part, the first thing to do is to split the two into a list. Here our list is actually two scalar variables, `$whole` and `$frac`, and we're splitting on whitespace.

If the input does not have a whole part, we drop to the `else` clause of the `if` (line 17), and here the `$whole` variable gets set to 0, and `$frac` can contain the entire value of `$price`. No splitting is needed. We'll need these variables later, so this first block initializes them from the data we've been given.

Line 22 is another split, this time of the fraction itself. Here we're splitting the fraction into a numerator and a denominator, an upper part and a lower part. The character we're splitting on is the slash, so we'll put that into a split pattern, and once again the two parts are assigned to scalar variables `$numer` and `$denom`.

Finally, with all the parts of the equation extracted from the input, we can do some math in line 23. Divide the numerator by the denominator, and add it to the whole number to get the decimal equivalent.

Note

> If this script was truly robust we should probably check to make sure `$denom` did not contain 0, or that the fraction contained a smaller numerator than denominator, but this is good enough for now. Later on, in the lessons on patterns, you'll learn how to do this same operation using just patterns.

And finally, the result of our math is usually a floating-point number, and sometimes a rather long floating-point number. Stock prices are usually quoted in decimal numbers with only two numbers after the decimal points, so we'll use a call to `sprintf` to round off our numbers.

Going Deeper

Hashes have a lot of similarities to arrays and lists, so actually we don't need to go much deeper for this lesson. Hashes use one other function that might be useful: `each`.

The `keys` function takes a hash as an argument and returns a list of the hash's keys. The `values` function does the same thing with the values in the hash. The `each` function does both: with a hash as an argument, it returns a list of two elements—the first a key and the second a value. Calling `each` multiple times works through all the hash's elements. As with all hash elements, the pairs you get out of the hash are in some undetermined order. After all the elements have been exhausted, `each` returns an empty list `()`. You can learn more about `each` in the `perlfunc` man page.

Summary

Today, we completed your background in list data with a discussion of hashes, which are similar to arrays and lists except that they arrange data into keys and values as opposed to simply storing elements in a numeric order. You learned about the hash variable `%hash`, and how to look up a value using hash access `$hash{'key'}`. You also learned how to delete keys from the hash, and how to process each element of a hash using a `foreach` loop and the `keys` function. We finished up with some discussion about the `split` function, and you learned about a few more patterns for pattern matching.

The built-in functions you learned about today include (see the `perlfunc` man page for more details about these functions):

- `delete` takes a hash key as an argument and deletes that key and value from the hash. Unlike `undef`, which undefines a value in a hash or an array but preserves the location, `delete` removes the key/value pair altogether.
- `exists` takes a hash key and returns true if the hash key exists (the corresponding value might be undefined (`undef`)).
- `keys` takes a hash and returns a list of all the keys in that hash.
- `values` takes a hash and returns a list of all the values in that hash.
- `split` splits a string into a list of elements. The first argument to split can be a pattern, a string of one character, or be omitted altogether. In the latter two cases, `split` splits on whitespace.

Q&A

Q. All these different variable characters! How can I keep them straight!

A. The more you use them, the easier it'll be to remember which one is used where. If it helps, you can think of the scalar variable character `$` as a dollar sign—dollars are numbers, and are scalar. The at sign (`@`) is a sort of A character—A stands for array. And the percent sign (`%`) for hashes has a slash with two dots—one dot for the key, and one for the value. In array and hash element accesses, think of what you want the result of the expression to be: if you want a single element, use `$`.

Q. Hashes are just plain associative arrays, aren't they? They aren't actual hash tables?

A. Hashes are indeed sometimes called associative arrays, and were called that in previous versions of Perl (the term *hashes* became popular because *associative arrays* was kind of unwieldy to say and too many characters to type). They're called *hashes*, as opposed to *keyed lists* or *associative arrays*, because internally they are indeed implemented as real hash tables, and have all the speed advantages of a hash table over a more basic keyed collection, particularly for really huge collections.

Q. All the examples you showed for hashes used a key to get a value. If you have a value is there any way to get at its corresponding key?

A. Nope. Well, there isn't a function to do it. You could use a `foreach` loop and the `keys` function, and then test each key to see if it matched the value you have. But keep in mind that although hashes require unique keys, different keys can all have the same value, so even though you have a value there's no guarantee that only one key will match with it. There isn't the same correspondence between a value and its key as there is the key to its value.

Q. You can print an array just with `print "@array\n"`. can you print a hash with `print "%hash\n"`?

A. No, hash variables do not interpolate inside double quotes the way scalar and array variables do. You will have to use a `foreach` loop and the `keys` function to iterate over the hash and print each element.

Q. When I was running the `names.pl` script, I typed in two people with the same last name (Ernest Hemingway and Fred Hemingway). Ernest Hemingway disappeared! What's going on here?

A. Hashes require unique keys. The `names.pl` script is keyed by last name. When you entered Hemingway, Ernest, the key for Hemingway was created. But when you entered Hemingway, Fred, the value for the Hemingway key was changed, and Ernest was erased. I've included an exercise in the workshop so you can play with methods for working around this little problem.

Workshop

The workshop provides quiz questions to help you solidify your understanding of the material covered and exercises to give you experience in using what you've learned. Try and understand the quiz and exercise answers before you go on to tomorrow's lesson.

Quiz

1. Define the differences between lists, arrays, and hashes.
2. What do each of these variables refer to?

```
$foo
@foo
%foo
```

```
$foo{'key'}
$foo[$key]
$foo{$key}
```

3. What are the results of the following Perl statements? Why does each expression evaluate to the result it does?

```
%stuff = qw(1 one 2 two 3 three 4 four);
@nums = %stuff
$foo = %stuff;
$foo = keys %stuff;
```

4. What happens if you use a hash in a list context? In a scalar context?
5. How do you sort a hash?
6. Define the differences between the `keys`, `values`, and `each` functions.
7. What's `split` good for?

Exercises

1. Modify stats so that the user can enter numbers all on one line.
2. Write a script that prompts you for a sentence, tells you the number of characters in the sentence, the number of words, and prints the sentence in reverse word order. (Hint: use the `length`, `split`, and `reverse` functions).
3. Modify the `names.pl` script to accept (and handle) names with middle names or initials (for example, Percy Bysshe Shelley or William S. Burroughs).
4. A hash only works with unique keys. But the `names` script would be more useful if it could store names with multiple duplicate last names (for example, Charlotte Bronte, Emily Bronte, and Anne Bronte). How might you modify the `names.pl` script to accommodate this?

Answers

Here are the answers to the Workshop questions in the previous section.

Quiz Answers

1. A list is just a collection of scalars; an array is an ordered list, indexed by position; and a hash is an unordered list of key/value pairs, indexed by the keys.
2. The answers are

   `$foo` is a scalar variable

   `@foo` is an array variable

   `%foo` is a hash variable

`$foo{'key'}` is the value that matches ‘key’ in the hash `%foo`.

`$foo[$key]` is the value at the index `$key` in the array `@foo`.

`$foo{$key}` is the value that matches `$key` in the hash `%foo` (which might not be the same value as `$foo{'key'}`).

3. The answers are

   a. The `%stuff` hash gets four key/value pairs: ‘1’/’one’, ‘2’/’two’, ‘3’/’three’, and ‘4’/’four’. The `qw` function adds quotes around each element.

   b. `@nums` gets the unwound version of the key/value pairs in `%stuff` (key, value, key, value, and so on).

   c. `$foo` gets a code referring to the internal state of the hash.

   d. `$foo` gets the number of elements (keys) in `%stuff`. (`keys %stuff` results in a list, which is evaluated in a scalar context, which then gives the number of elements in that list.)

4. Using a hash in a list context “unwinds” the hash into its component keys and values in some internal order. In a scalar context, the hash returns two numbers indicating the internal structure of the hash.
5. You can’t sort a hash because a hash is unordered. You can, however, extract its keys or its values and then sort that resulting list.
6. The `keys` function gives you a list of all the keys in the hash; the `values` function does the same thing with the values. The `each` function returns a list of a key/value pair in the hash; calling each multiple times eventually gives you all the elements in that hash.
7. `split` breaks a string up into two or more elements in a list. `split` is commonly used when the input you get isn’t a single thing that can be assigned directly to a variable.

Exercises

1. This exercise is harder than it looks. When all the data gets entered on one line, split that line into a list. This makes some things easier and some things harder. On the one hand, you can move the processing of the data out of the `while` loop—it can all happen later on, after the data has been entered, rather than as the data is being entered.

   On the other hand, because the data includes spaces you will run afoul of the error checking because a space is a nondigit character. The easiest way around this is to split the line inside the `while` loop and do the error checking on each individual element in the list.

Here's how I accomplished this script. I've included only the important parts of the stats script, from the while loop up until where the print statements start:

```
while () {
    print 'Enter your numbers, all on one line, separated by spaces: ';
    chomp ($input = <STDIN>);

    if ($input eq '') {
        print "Please enter some input.\n";
        next;
    }

    @nums = split(' ', $input);   # split into nums

    foreach $key (@nums) {
        if ($key =~ /\D/) {
            print "$key contains a non-digit character. ";
            print "Please enter your input again.\n";
            @nums = ();
            next;
        }
    }

    if (@nums) { last; }
}

$count = @nums;                 # get the count

foreach $num (@nums) {          # count freqs, sum
    $freq{$num}++;
    $sum += $num;
}

@nums = sort { $a <=> $b } @nums;
$avg = $sum / $count;
$med = $nums[$count /2];
```

Here's the part that starts with the `while` loop up until the part that prints the results:

```
while () {
    print 'Enter your numbers, all on one line, separated by spaces: ';
    chomp ($input = <STDIN>);

    if ($input eq '') {
        print "Please enter some input.\n";
        next;
    }
```

```
    @nums = split(' ', $input);   # split into nums

    foreach $key (@nums) {
        if ($key =~ /\D/) {
            print "$key contains a non-digit character.";
            print "Please enter your input again.\n";
            @nums = ();
            next;
        }
    }

    if (@nums) { last; }
}

$count = @nums;                  # get the count

foreach $num (@nums) {           # count freqs, sum
    $freq{$num}++;
    $sum += $num;
}
```

2. Here's one answer:

```
#!/usr/local/bin/perl -w

$in = '' ; # temporary input
@sent = (); # sentence
$words = 0; # num words
@reversed = (); # reversed version

print 'Enter a sentence: ';
chomp($in = <STDIN>);
print 'Number of characters in the sentence: ';
print length $in;

@sent = split(' ', $in);
$words = @sent;
print "\nNumber of words in the sentence: $words\n";

@reversed = reverse @sent;
print "Reversed version: \n";
print "@reversed\n";
```

3. Here's one answer:

```
#!/usr/local/bin/perl -w

#in = "";       # temporary input
%names = ();    # hash of names
@raw = ();      # raw words
$fn = "";       # first name
$ln = "";       # last name
```

```
while () {
    print 'Enter a name (first and last): ';
    chomp($in = <STDIN>);
    if ($in eq '') { last; }

    @raw = split(" ", $in);
    if ($#raw == 1) {  # regular case, two names
        $names{$raw[1]} = $raw[0];
    } else {  # build a first name from all names
        $ln = pop @raw; # remove last name
        foreach $name (@raw) { # build up first name
            $fn = $fn . ' ' . $name;
        }
        $names{$ln} = $fn;
    }
    $fn = $ln = "";  # reset each time
}

foreach $lastname (sort keys %names) {
    print "$lastname, $names{$lastname}\n";
}
```

4. Here's one answer that tags each duplicate name with a unique number, and then strips those numbers off when the names are printed:

```
#!/usr/local/bin/perl -w

$in = '';       # temporary input
%names = ();    # hash of names
$fn = '';       # temp firstname
$ln = '';       # temp lastname
$count = 0;      # for nums

while () {
    print 'Enter a name (first and last): ';
    chomp($in = <STDIN>);
    if ($in eq '') { last; }

    ($fn, $ln) = split(' ', $in);

    if (exists $names{$ln}) { # name is already there!
        $ln = $ln . "_" . $count; # tag this name with a number
    }

    $names{$ln} = $fn;
    $count++;
}

foreach $lastname (sort keys %names) {
    if ($lastname =~ /_/) {  # this is a tagged name
        ($ln, undef) = split(/_/, $lastname); #remove number for printing
```

```
        } else { $ln = $lastname }

        print "$ln, $names{$lastname}\n";
    }
```

5. Another solution might be to keep the single last name as the key, and store the first names as a string, adding on the new names to the end of the string, separated by the character of your choice. Then, when printing the list, split apart all the individual first names again. There are many different ways to solve this problem.

WEEK 1

DAY 6

Conditionals and Loops

Finally, we come to conditionals and loops! You've already learned a fair amount about the more popular conditional, `if`, and about `while` loops, so you might have already deduced that conditionals and loops are used to control the execution of blocks of statements in Perl script. Without these structures, your script would run from top to bottom, executing each statement in turn until it got to the end. No testing to see if a value is true, and then branching to a different bit of code; no repeating the execution of a block of statements a number of times. Scripts would be very boring indeed without conditionals and loops. They're so important you had to actually start learning about them two days ago, before we even got to this lesson.

In this lesson, we'll discuss in detail the various conditional and loop constructs you have to work with in Perl, including

- An introduction to block statements
- The `if` and `if...else`, `if...elsif`, and `unless...` conditionals
- The `while`, `do...while`, and `until` loops
- The `foreach` and `for` loops
- Controlling loops with `next`, `last`, `redo`, and labels

In addition, we'll also look at a two other topics that will build on your Perl knowledge, including

- Using `$_` (the default variable) as a shortcut for many operations
- Reading input from files with `<>`

Complex Statements and Blocks

Conditionals and loops are sometimes called *complex statements*. That's because instead of being a single statement like `$x = 5` or `$array[5] = "fifth"` ending with a semicolon, conditionals and loops tend to be more, well, complex. Probably the biggest difference between simple and complex statements, however, is that the latter operate on chunks of Perl code called *blocks*.

A block is, simply, a group of any Perl statements surrounded by curly braces ({}). Inside the block, you can include other statements, other blocks, or anything that can appear outside the block. As with statements in a script, too, the statements inside the block are executed in order. For example, here are two blocks, one that is associated with a `while` loop, and one inside it that is associated with an `if` conditional:

```
while (test) { # start of while block
   statement;
   statement;
   if (test) { # start of if block
      statement;
   } # end of if block
   # ... more statements
}  # end of while loop
```

Note that each closing curly brace ends the nearest enclosing block—the indenting doesn't matter to Perl. In larger scripts, a block might go on for lines and lines and you can easily forget where a closing } is supposed to match to. In this case, an indenting style can really help you figure out where your blocks begin and end. When in doubt, add a comment.

Blocks that are used outside the context of a conditional or a loop are called *bare blocks*, and the statements inside them execute only once. Bare blocks have several uses, particularly when they have labels (more about labels later in this chapter), but for now we'll focus on blocks that are attached to complex statements.

One other feature of blocks is that the last statement in the block doesn't require a semicolon. If it's the only statement in the block, it also doesn't require a semicolon. However, it's probably a good idea to get used to using it anyhow; if you add other statements to that block later, Perl will complain that you forgot the semicolon.

Conditionals

Conditionals are used to execute different bits of code based on the value of a given test. If the test is true, a block of code is executed; if the test is false, either execution continues to the next part of the script, or a different block of code is executed. Unlike loops, each block is executed only once.

`if`, `if...else`, and `if...elsif`

The most common form of conditional is the `if`, and its variant forms `if...else` and `if...elsif`. As you've seen, the `if` statement looks like this:

```
if ( test ) {
   # statements
}
```

The `test` is any expression, evaluated in a boolean scalar context for its truth value. Remember that everything except `""`, `0`, and `undef` is considered true. If the test is true, the block is executed. If it's false, nothing happens and execution continues onto the next statement in the script.

Note that the block after the test (and, in the next two forms, after the `else` and the `elsif`) is always required, even if you only have one statement inside that block. You must always include the curly braces. The block doesn't have to be on different lines, as I showed here; you can format the brackets in any style you prefer. Short `if` statements tend to look neater on one line:

```
if ( $x ) { print "true!" }
```

To execute one block if the test is true and a different block if the test is false, use `if...else`:

```
if ( test ) {
   # statements to execute if test is true
} else {
   # statements to execute if test is false
}
```

A common operation in all languages with `if...else`-like constructs is that there are multiple nested `if`'s and multiple `else`'s, like this:

```
if ( test1 ) {
   # statements1
} else {
   if ( test2 ) {
      # statements2
   } else {
      if ( test3 ) {
```

6

```
        # statements 3
    } else {
        # and so on...}
```

To save a few keystrokes, or to avoid large amounts of indentation, Perl provides a third form of `if` conditional, the `elsif`, to compress these sorts of operations:

```
if ( test1) {
   # statements1
} elsif ( test2 ) {
   # statements2
} elsif ( test3 ) {
   # statements3
} else (
   # else statements
}
```

Note the difference between the nested `if` and separate `if` statements, like this:

```
if ( test1 ) {
   # statements1
}
if ( test2 ) {
   # statements2
}
if ( test3 ) {
   # statements3
}
```

Use separate `if` statements, then, regardless of the outcome of `test1`, `test2` is still tested, and same with `test3`. Every test is independent of every other test. In the case of the nested `if`, if `test1` is true, then the statements in the following block are executed, and then the entire block exits. The remaining tests are never executed—`test2` is only executed if `test1` is false, and `test3` is executed only if both `test1` and `test2` are false.

In some cases, you might want separate, independent `if` statements, but in a lot of cases, you can group your tests in nested ifs instead.

If you're familiar with other languages, you might know `switch` or `case` statements that shorten nested `if`s into a simpler syntax. Perl doesn't have syntax for `switch`, per se (it's probably the only instance you'll find where Perl doesn't provide a syntax to do something you can do in another language). However, there are various ways to use existing Perl constructs to build `switch`-like constructs. We'll go over a couple of these in "Going Deeper," at the end of this lesson.

unless

The unless statement is sort of the reverse of an if. It came about because sometimes an operation is only supposed to occur if a test is false—which means in a standard if...else statement, all the good stuff would go into the else, like this:

```
if ( test ) {
   # do nothing
} else {
   # the good stuff
}
```

That's not really the most optimal way to look at an if. You could, of course, just negate the test (!test or not test), and then switch the blocks and leave off the else. This is a classic case of having to change your thinking to fit the syntax. Perl would prefer that you think the way you want to think, so it gives you alternative syntax. If you want to perform an operation based a test being false, just use unless instead:

```
unless ( test ) {
   # the good stuff
}
```

With the unless here, the statements inside the block are only evaluated if the test is false ("unless this is true, do that") If it's true, execution happily moves onto the next statement. You can also add an else to an unless, if you like (but you can't have an elsif).

Conditional Operator ?..:

Some conditionals are so short that it seems silly to waste all those brackets and words on them. Sometimes, too, it makes sense to embed a conditional inside another expression (something you can't do with an if or an unless because they don't return values). That's what the conditional operator does. Like if...else, it has a test, something to do if the test is true, and something to do if the test is false:

```
test ? true_thing : false_thing;
```

6

Here, the test is evaluated for truth, just as with an if, and if the test is true the true_thing expression is evaluated (and a value returned), otherwise, false_thing is evaluated and returned. Unlike if and unless, true_thing, and false_thing are single expressions, not blocks. So, for example, a quick way to find the maximum of two values might look like this:

```
$max = $x > $y ? $x : $y;
```

This expression tests to see if the value of `$x` is larger than that of `$y`, and if so, it returns `$x`. If the value of `$x` is less than or equal to `$y` it returns `$y`. The return value of the entire conditional expression is then finally assigned to the `$max` variable. That same operation, as an `if...else`, would look like this:

```
if ($x > $y) {
   $max = $x;
} else {
   $max = $y;
}
```

> The conditional operator is sometimes called the *ternary* operator because it has three operands (unary operators have one, binary operators have two; therefore, a ternary operator has three). Will knowing this impress anyone except computer scientists? Probably not.

Using Logical Operators as Conditionals

Back on Day 2, you learned about Perl's logical operators `&&`, `||`, `and`, and `or`, and I mentioned at that time you can construct conditional statements with them. Let's re-examine those operators here so you can get a feel for how this works. Take the following expression:

```
$val = $this || $that;
```

To understand how this expression works, you have to remember two features of logical expressions: short-circuiting, and the fact that logicals return the value of the last thing they evaluated. So, in this case, the left side of the `||` is evaluated for its truth value. One of three things happens:

- If the value of `$this` is anything other than `0` or `""`, it's considered true. Because the `||` operator short-circuits, this means the entire expression exits without even looking at `$that`. It also returns the last thing it did evaluate—the value of `$this`, which then gets assigned to the variable `$val`.
- If the value of `$this` is `0` or `""`, it's considered false. Perl then evaluates `$that`, and if `$that` is true, then the expression exits with a truth value and returns the thing that it evaluated last—`$that`.
- If both `$this` and `$that` are false, the entire expression returns false, and `$val` gets a `0` or `""` value.

> **Note** You could, of course, use the `or` operator in place of the `||`. Either one would work.

Using an `if...else` expression, you could write that expression like this:

```
if ($this) { $val = $this; }
else {$val = $that; }
```

Using a conditional operator, you could write it like this:

```
$val = $this ? $this : $that
```

But both of those take more space and are sort of complex to figure out—or at least more complex than the logical expression, which reads sort of like English: this or that. There, you're done.

As I mentioned on Day 2, probably the most common place you'll see logicals used as conditionals is when you open files, like this:

```
open(FILE, "filename") or die "Can't open\n";
```

But that's a topic for another day (Day 15, "Managing I/O," to be exact).

`while` Loops

The various `if` statements in Perl are all used to control execution by branching to different parts of a script. The second way to control execution is through the use of a loop, where the same block of Perl statements are executed repeatedly, stopping only when some condition is met. Perl has two general sets of loops, both of which do roughly the same thing: `while` loops, which loop until a condition is met, and `for` loops, which loop a certain number of times. Generally, `while`s can be rewritten to emulate `for`s, and vice versa, but conceptually each one seems to lend itself to specific situations better than the other.

We'll start with the `while` loops, of which Perl has three: `while`, `do...while`, and `until`.

`while`

You've already seen the `while` loop, but we'll repeat the description here so you have it all in one place. The basic form of the loop in Perl is the `while`, which takes a test and block, like this:

```
while ( test ) {
   # statements to loop
}
```

In the `while` loop, the test is evaluated, and if it's true, then the statements inside the block are executed. At the end of the block, the test is evaluated again, and if it's still true, then the block is executed again. This process repeats until the test returns false. For example, here's the `while` loop from the cookie script you saw on Day 1:

```
while ( $cookie ne "cookie") {
  print "Give me a cookie: ";
  chomp($cookie = <STDIN>);
}
```

Here, the prompt and input will repeat until the input actually matches the string `"cookie"`. You could read this statement as "while the value of `$cookie` doesn't equal the string `'cookie'`, do these things."

Here's another example from Day 4 that loops through an array using an temporary variable `$i` as the array index:

```
$i = 0;
while ($i <= $#array) {
   print $array[$i++], "\n";
}
```

In this case, the test is whether `$i` is less than the largest index of the `@array` array. Inside the block, we print the current array element, and increment `$i`, so that the loop will only repeat a certain number of times: while `$i` is less than or equal to the largest index in `@array`, actually.

Remember as you write your `while` loops that something has to happen inside the loop to bring the state of the loop closer to exiting. If you forget to increment `$i`, `$i` will never reach a point where the test is true, and the loop will never exit.

Loops that don't exit are called *infinite loops*, and sometimes they're useful to use intentionally. A `while` loop without a test, for example, is an intentional infinite loop. You've seen these in a number of the examples we've done so far. This one's from the various statistics scripts:

```
while () {
  print 'Enter a number: ';
  chomp ($input = <STDIN>);
  if ($input eq '') { last; }

  # more stuff to do
}
```

This loop will read a line of input from the standard input at each pass of the loop, and will never exit based on the test at the top of the `while`—there is no test inside the parentheses after the `while`. But we do test the input in an `if` conditional three lines down, and if the

`$input` doesn't match our test there (if it's equal to the empty string), then the `last;` keyword will forcibly break the loop and go onto the next part of the script. The `last` part is a form of loop control statement, and there are three of them: `last`, `next`, and `redo`. You'll learn about these later in this chapter, in the section, "Controlling Loops."

I could have rewritten this loop so the `while` had a real test, and exited at the appropriate time. For this particular type of example, I found it easier to construct it this way. Perl doesn't enforce a specific kind of mindset for creating loops or conditionals; you can construct your script in the best way based on how you see the problem.

until

Just as the reverse of an `if` is an `unless`, the reverse of a `while` is an `until`. `Until` looks just like a `while`, with a test and a block:

```
until ( test ) {
   #  statements
}
```

The only difference is in the test—in a `while`, the loop executes as long as a test is true. In an `until`, it executes as long as the test is false—"until this test is true, do this stuff." Otherwise, they both behave the same.

do

A third form of `while` loop is called the `do`. With both `while` and `until`, the test is evaluated before the block is executed—so, actually, if the test ends up being false (or true for `unless`), then the block won't get executed and the loop might never do anything. Sometimes you want to execute some block of statements, and then try the test afterwards. That's where `do` comes in. `do` loops are formed differently from `while` and `until` loops; unlike the former, they require semicolons at the end of the statement. `do` loops look like this:

```
do {
   # block to loop
} while (test);
```

Or, with `until`, same idea:

```
do {
   # ...
} until (test);
```

With either of these statements, the statements inside the block are always executed before the test is evaluated. Even if the test returns false (for `while`) or true (for `until`), the block of statements will be executed at least once.

6

One important thing to note about the `do`: `do` in this case is actually a function call pretending to be a loop (that's why you need the semicolon). In most basic cases, it'll perform just like a loop, but if you want to use loop controls inside it (such as `last` or `next`), or include a label, you'll have to use either `while` or `until` instead. More about loop controls and labels later.

An Example: Pick a Number

In this example, we'll play a sort of game where Perl prompts you for a number, picks a random number between 1 and your number, and then has you try to guess which number it's picked, like this:

```
% picknum.pl
Enter top number: 50
Pick a number between 1 and 50: 25
Too high!
Pick a number between 1 and 50: 10
Too low!
Pick a number between 1 and 50: 17
Too high!
Pick a number between 1 and 50: 13
Too high!
Pick a number between 1 and 50: 12
Correct!
Congratulations!  It took you 5 guesses to pick the right number.
%
```

This script makes use of two `while` loops and a number of `if` tests, as well as the `rand` function to pick the number. Listing 6.1 shows the code, our longest script so far.

LISTING 6.1 The `picknum.pl` Script

```
#!/usr/ bin/perl -w

$top = 0;   # topmost number
$num = 0;   # random number
$count = 0; # number of guesses
$guess = ""; # actual guess
$done = "";  # done guessing?

while () {
    print 'Enter top number: ';
    chomp($top = <STDIN>);

    if ($top =~ /\D/) {  # non-numbers, also negative numbers
        if ($top =~ /-\d+/) { # only negative numbers
            print "Positive numbers only\n";
```

LISTING 6.1 continued

```
        } else {
            print "Digits only.\n";
        }
        next;
    } elsif ($top <= 1 ) {
        print "Numbers greater than 1 only.\n";
        next;
    }

    last;
}

srand;
$num = int(rand $top) + 1;

while (!$done) {
    print "Pick a number between 1 and $top: ";
    chomp($guess = <STDIN>);

    if ($guess =~ /\D/) {
        if ($guess =~ /-\d+/) {
            print "Positive numbers only\n";
        } else {
            print "Digits only.\n";
        }
        next;
    } elsif ($guess == 0) {
        print "Numbers greater than 0 only.\n";
    } elsif ($guess < $num) {
        print "Too low!\n";
        $count++;
    } elsif ($guess > $num) {
        print "Too high!\n";
        $count++;
    } else {
        print "\a\aCorrect!  \n";
        $count++;
        $done = 1;
    }
}
print "Congratulations!  It took you $count guesses";
print " to pick the right number.\n";
```

We have four parts to this script: initialization, picking the top number, picking the secret number, and then the guessing process. I'll skip the initialization this time around—you know how to assign scalar variables by now.

Lines 9 through 26 contain a `while` loop for picking the highest number the secret number could be. This is an infinite `while` loop, like you've seen before. In this loop we have two tests: one, to make sure you're entering only digits, and the second to make sure the digits you're entering are greater than 1.

The first test, in lines 13 through 20, is for all entries that are not digits, for example, `a` or `4a`. It will also, however, catch negative numbers—`-4`, for example—because the dash character is considered a nondigit. You could just have one error message for all these cases ("no digits or negative numbers, please"), or we could separate out those cases and provide one error message for negative numbers and one for actual nondigits. That's what we've done here. If the value of `$top` triggers the test in line 13, we then do an additional test in line 14. Does `$top` contain a dash followed by one or more digits? If so, we print the message in line 15. If not, `$top` contains some plain nondigit data, and we print the message in line 17. In either case we need different input, so we call `next` in line 19.

You might wonder, why put the test for the dash in line 14 inside the block for the previous test—why not use a nested if, like this:

```
if ($top =~ /\D/) {  # non-numbers
   print "Digits only.\n";
   next;
} elsif ($top =~ /-\d+/) { # only negative numbers
   print "Positive numbers only\n";
   next;
} elsif ($top == 0) {
...
```

You have to work through the logic of things, here. If you enter an `a` as input, the first test triggers, `Digits only` is printed, `next` is called, and the loop repeats. So far, so good. What happens if you enter as input `-4`? The first test triggers because the dash character is a nondigit. `Digits only` is printed, and the loop repeats. The second test, the one for negative numbers, never gets called at all.

Okay, so you could put the dash test first:

```
if ($top =~ /-\d+/) { # only negative numbers
   print "Positive numbers only\n";
   next;
} elsif ($top =~ /\D/) {  # non-numbers
   print "Digits only.\n";
   next;
}
```

This actually works just fine—the first test traps for negative numbers with the dash, and the second traps for other nondigits with `\D`. So, why not do it this way in `picknum.pl`? You have already seen a number of examples of simple nested `if` statements; the one starting in line 20 is slightly more complex, logic-wise, and demonstrates the sorts of `ifs`-within-`ifs` we'll be working more with as the book progresses.

The second main test in this `while` loop checks to make sure that the digit you've entered is not zero or one. Why do we care? The goal of the problem is to pick a number between 1 and X, where X is your topmost number. You can't have 0 as your topmost number for obvious reasons—its less than 1. You could use 1, technically, although picking a number between 1 and 1 makes for a really boring game. This test makes sure that your topmost number will be at least 2 so that the game holds some interest.

Finally, after these two tests, we presumably have an acceptable top number, and at line 25 we can break out of the infinite `while` loop with a call to `last`.

With a top number in hand, in lines 28 and 29 we generate the secret number between 0 and the top using the `srand` and `rand` built-in functions. The `srand` function, with no arguments, is used to seed the random-number generator with the current time, so that we'll get different numbers each time we run the script (otherwise it would be a very boring game indeed). The `rand` function generates a random number between 0 and an argument, here, our `$top`. We'll truncate that number to an integer, add 1 to it to make sure we don't have zeros and that occasionally a number will be the same as the top, and store that number in `$num` for safekeeping.

Lines 31 through 55 are `while` loops to keep track of the guesses. A couple of things are going on here. The most obvious is a big nested `if` containing a whole lot of tests to see if the guess is the right kind of data, and if so, if it's the right number. But before we get to that, there's also a secondary test here for the loop itself in line 31 that uses a scalar variable called `$done`.

Up until this point when we had input to verify I used an infinite `while` loop, got some input, and if the input was right or if we had the correct amount of input, I just used a `last` to break out of the `while`. This is another way to do the same thing: use a variable to keep track of whether the input is correct or not, and use the status of that variable as the test.

In this case, the variable we're using is `$done`, and at the start of the script its been initialized to 0. As this `while` loop starts at line 31 the test is `!$done` ("not done"), which evaluates to true. Each test inside the `while` loop is tested, and if any of those tests are true, an error message is printed. But then we don't need any `next` or `last` commands; the `while` loop can simply complete normally. At the end of the loop `$done` is still 0; when the `while` loop restarts `!$done` is still false, and the whole thing starts over again.

The only time anything changes is if every test comes out false, if the guess is correct, and the last block in the nested `if` in lines 50 through 54 is executed. Then `$done` is set to 1 in line 53, the loop completes, and starts one more time. This time, however, when `!$done` is tested, it will be false, and the block will not execute at all.

Which method is better—infinite loops and `next/last` statements, or a roving `$done` variable? It's all a matter of style and what looks or reads better to you.

Let's move onto the tests themselves in this big nested `if` in lines 30 through 44. Here we test the value of `$guess` for five things:

- Nondigit characters (lines 35 through 41)
- Negative numbers. This test is part of the nondigit character test in lines 36 and 37
- To make sure the guess is a number greater than 0 (line 42).
- To see if the guess is less than the secret number (line 44), in which case we print, "Too low!"
- To see if the guess is greater than the secret number (line 47), in which case we print, "Too high!"

If the guess is neither too low nor too high and is a valid number, then it must be the right number, so we beep twice (that's what the `\a` escape is for), Perl prints a congratulatory message, and the script exits.

As the user is guessing the numbers, we also keep track of the number of guesses with a `$count` variable. We only want to count a guess if it's a valid number, however, so we only increment `$count` in the three valid number cases. `$count` is then printed at the end as part of the congratulatory message.

Iteration with `foreach` and `for` Loops

`while` loops provide a general way to repeat a block of code—that block will just keep executing until some test is met. The for loop, a second form of loop, is a slightly different approach to the same problem. With `for` loops, the loop is executed a specific number of times, and then stops. This is sometimes called *iteration* because the focus is on the specific number of loops as opposed to the more vague "loop until true" that the `while` provides.

In just about every case, you could write a `while` loop to do iteration, or you could write a `for` loop to do the same thing as a `while`. But some tasks lend themselves better to one form or another, and so we have multiple kinds of loops.

Perl provides two `for` loops: a `foreach` that enables a block to be repeated for each element in a list, and a more general-purpose `for` loop.

`foreach`

You've already seen `foreach` as used to iterate over lists and over the keys in a hash. Here are the specifics of how it's used: The `foreach` loop takes a list as an argument—for example, a range, or a list of keys in a hash—and executes a block of statements for each element in the list. It also takes a temporary scalar variable that gets assigned to each element in the list in turn.

Here's a simple `foreach` loop that prints the number of the counter five times:

```
foreach $loop (1 .. 5) {
   print "loop $loop\n";
}
```

Here the range operator `..` creates a list of numbers 1 to 5, and the `foreach` loop works through that list, assigning each number to the `$loop` variable.

Probably the most common use for `foreach` loops is for iterating over actual lists, for example, to print out the keys and values of a hash, as you learned yesterday:

```
foreach $key (sort keys %hashname) {
   print "Key: $key Value: $hashname{$key}\n";
}
```

You'll note that I haven't initialized the `$key` variable here (or the `$loop` variable, earlier). That's because the variable after the `foreach` and before the list is a local variable to the loop—if it doesn't exist prior to the loop, it'll stop existing after the loop. If it does exist prior to the loop, the `foreach` will just use it as a temporary variable, and then restore its original value when you're done looping. You can think of the `foreach` variable as a sort of scratch variable used solely to store elements, which is then thrown away when the loop's done.

One other important thing to note about the `$key` variable; it does not just contain the value of the current list element, it *is* the actual list element. If you change the value of `$key` inside the block, then you will also be changing that list element, and therefore the list (or array or hash) itself. In programmer parlance: the `$key` variable is *passed by reference*. Here's a short Perl script that demonstrates this:

```
#!/usr/local/bin/perl -w

@ones = (1,1,1,1,1);
$switch = 0;

foreach $key (@ones) {
    if (!$switch) {
        $switch = 1;
        $key = 2;
    } else {$switch = 0};
}

print "@ones\n";
```

Initially in this script the `@ones` array is assigned to `(1,1,1,1,1)`. When the script finishes and the array is printed at the end, the `@ones` array contains `(2 1 2 1 2)`. The `$switch` variable alternates between 0 and 1 with each pass of the loop, so that every other list element is changed. But the line inside the block where `$key` is assigned to 2 is where the list is changed. It's the variable `$key` that is assigned to 2, but `$key` refers to the current list element inside `@ones`, so that list element is changed as well. Even though `$key` changes every time the loop turns, and then vanishes altogether when the loop is complete, the result of changing it still lingers.

If you want to modify the actual value of `$key` without also affecting the list it came from, you can always copy it to a temporary variable:

```
foreach $key (@array) {
   $temp = $key;
   $temp = "blah blah blah";  # will not change the list
   ...
}
```

for

For a more general-purpose iterative loop that isn't necessarily tied to list elements, you can use a `for` loop. Perl borrowed the syntax of this loop from the C language, so if you're familiar with that language this will look the same.

The `for` loop in Perl has four parts:

- An initializer statement
- An ending test
- A change or increment statement
- The loop block

The `for` loop looks like this:

```
for ( init; test; change ) {
   # statements
}
```

Using these statements, then, the `for` loop works like this:

- The first time through, the initializer statement is executed. Often this statement sets a counter such as `$i` or `$j` to 0.
- The test is tested. The test often compares the counter against some value, for example `$i < $#array` or `$i == 0`. If the test is false, the loop exits and none of the statements inside the block are executed.
- If the test is true, the block is executed.

- After all the statements in the block have executed, the change or increment expression is executed. This statement usually brings the loop one iteration closer to completion, for example, to increment or decrement the counter (`$i++`).
- The test is tried again, and again, as the loop repeats.

So, for example, to loop five times you might use a `for` loop like this:

```
for ( $i = 1; $i <= 5; $i++) {
   print "loop $i\n";
}
```

The snippet of code produces this output:

```
loop 1
loop 2
loop 3
loop 4
loop 5
```

You could, of course, have written this loop as a `while`:

```
$i = 1;
while ($i <= 5) {
   print "loop $i\n";
   $i++;
}
```

The two loops would both loop five times, but it might take some searching in the `while` to figure that out and it takes more lines to do it (or at least it does the way I formatted it here). The `for` loop puts it all up front—where to start, where to stop, and the steps to take in between. Whether you use a `for` loop or a `while` loop depends on the situation and what you feel more comfortable with at the time.

Usually, but not always, the `for` loop uses a temporary counter variable (commonly called `$i` or `$j`) to keep track of the iterations. This is very common, but it isn't required. Depending on the iteration you're doing, you can initialize, test, and change anything you want in the top part of the `for`. For example, here's a somewhat pointless `for` loop that creates an array, and then destroys it, backwards, printing the number of remaining and the array itself as it goes:

```
for (@things = (33,44,55,66); @things > 0; pop @things) {
    print scalar @things, " elements left in @things\n";
}
```

I can't imagine what sort of Perl program would need this kind of loop, and because it iterates over a list it would probably make more sense as a `foreach`. The idea to grasp here is that as long as you have the three parts: a start point, an end point, and something to step you between the two, you have a `for` loop.

But wait. You don't even need all three. You can leave off the initialization, the test, the change, or all three, in the top part of the `for`. You still need to include the semicolons between them, however. So, to create an infinite `for` loop, you might leave off the test statement:

```
for ($i = 0; ; $i++) {
   # statements
}
```

Or just this:

```
for (;;) {
   # statements
}
```

The first one initializes the counter and just increments it each time; there's no test so there's no end point. The second doesn't even use a counter or have a test; it just loops. You'll need to do something inside these loops (such as a `last`) to break out of them when an appropriate condition is met.

Want to use multiple counters? You can do that, too; by separating the counter expressions with commas:

```
for ($i=0, $j=1; $i < 10, $j < $total; $i++, $j++ ) {
   # statements
}
```

In this case, the `for` loop will exit if either one of the tests returns false.

Controlling Loops

With both `while` and `for` loops, the tests at the top are there to stop the loop when some sort of condition has been reached. And, in many loops, it'll be the test that stops the loop. When you start working with more complex loops, however, or play with infinite loops as I have in some of the previous examples we've looked at, chances are good there will be some point in the middle of a loop block where you might want to stop looping, stop executing, or somehow control the actual execution of the loop itself. That's where loop controls come in.

Loop controls are simple constructs that are used to change the flow of execution of a loop. You've already seen two of them: `next` and `last`, to restart the loop and to break out of it altogether. In addition, Perl also provides a `redo` control and labels for loops that control which loop to break out of with the other keywords.

> As I mentioned in the section on the `do` loop, you cannot use any loop controls inside `do` loops, or label those loops. Rewrite the loop to use `while`, `until`, `for`, or `foreach` instead.

`last`, `next`, and `redo`

The `last`, `next`, and `redo` keywords are the simplest of loop controls; when one of these occurs inside a `while` or a `for`, Perl will interrupt the normal execution of the loop in some way.

You can use all three of these keywords by themselves, in which case they refer to the innermost loop, or they can be used with labels to refer to specific loops (more about labels later). Here's what happens with each keyword:

- `last` causes the loop to stop looping immediately (like `break` in C). Execution continues onto the next part of the script.
- `next` stops the execution of the current iteration of the loop, goes back to the top, and starts the next iteration with the test. It's like `continue` in C. The `next` keyword is a convenient way of skipping the code in the rest of the block if some condition was met.
- `redo` stops execution of the current loop iteration and goes back to the top again. The difference between `redo` and `next` is that `next` restarts the loop by reevaluating the test (and executing the change statement, for `for` loops); `redo` just restarts the block from the topmost statement without testing or incrementing anything.

So, for example, let's reexamine the first `while` loop in picknum.pl, our number picker game:

```
while () {
    print 'Enter top number: ';
    chomp($top = <STDIN>);

    if ($top =~ /\D/) {  # non-numbers, also negative numbers
        if ($top =~ /-\d+/) { # only negative numbers
            print "Positive numbers only\n";
        } else {
            print "Digits only.\n";
        }
        next;
    } elsif ($top <= 1 ) {
        print "Numbers greater than 1 only.\n";
        next;
    }
    last;
}
```

6

Because the familiar `while` loop in this example is an infinite loop, we have to use some sort of loop control expression to break out of it when some condition has been met—in this case, when an actual number has been met. As you learned, those tests are that its an actual number, and that its greater than 0. In each of these `if` statements, if the number meets that criteria, we use `next` to immediately skip over the rest of the code in the block and go back up to the top of the loop (if there was a test in that `while` loop, we'd have evaluated it again at that point). If the number entered ends up passing both tests, then that number is acceptable, and we can break out of the loop altogether using `last`.

Loop controls are generally only necessary where you're checking for some special-case condition that would interrupt the normal flow of the loop or, in this case, to break out of an infinite loop.

Labeling Loops

Loop controls, by themselves, exit out of the closest enclosing block. Sometimes, however, you might have a situation with multiple nested loops, where some condition might occur that would cause you to want to exit out of several loops, or to jump around inside different nested loops. For just this reason, you can label specific loops, and then use `last`, `next`, and `redo` to jump to those outer loops.

Labels appear at the start of a loop, and are conventionally in all caps. This convention keeps them from getting confused with Perl keywords. Use a colon to separate the label name from the loop:

```
LABEL: while (test) {
   #...
}
```

Then, inside the loop, use `last`, `next`, or `redo` with the name of the label:

```
LABEL: while (test) {
   #...
   while (test2) {
      # ...
      if (test) {
         last LABEL;
      }
   }
}
```

The labels can be anything you want to call them, with two exceptions: `BEGIN` and `END` are reserved labels that are used for package construction and deconstruction. You'll learn more about this on Day 13, "Scope, Modules, and Importing Code."

Here's a simple example without labels. The outer `while` loop controls the repetition of the script itself; tests to see if the variable `$again` is equal to the string `'y'`. The inner `while` loop is an infinite loop that tests the input and repeats until there is correct input (I've deleted the part of the script that processes that input to do whatever this script might be doing).

```
$again = 'y';

while ($again eq 'y') {
    while () {
        print 'Enter the number: ';
        chomp($num = <STDIN>);
        if ($num !~ /\d+/) { # test for strings
            print "No strings.  Numbers only please..\n";
            next;
        }
        # more tests
        last;
    }
    print 'Try another number (y/n)?: ';
    chomp ($again = <STDIN>);
}
```

In this example, the `next` and the `last` command in the inner loop will exit the nearest enclosing loop—the infinite loop where you're entering the number and testing the input for strings. They will not exit out of the outer loop. The only thing that will exit the outer loop is if `$again` gets set to `'n'` at the end of the outer loop (those last two lines prompt for the appropriate answer). Note also that `$again` has to be initialized to `'y'` for the loop to start looping at all.

Say you wanted to add behavior to this simple script so that if you typed `exit` anywhere Perl would exit all the loops and end the script. You might label the outer loop like this:

```
OUTER: while ($again eq 'y') {
   # etc.
}
```

Then, inside both the outer and inner loops, you'd use `last` with the name of the label, like this:

```
OUTER: while ($again eq 'y') {
    while () {
        print 'Enter the number: ';
        chomp($num = <STDIN>);
        if ($num eq "exit" ) { # quit!  exit!  gone!
           last OUTER;
        }
        # etc.
    }
 #  more...
}
```

In this case, if the user typed `exit` at the `'Enter the number'` prompt, the `last` command breaks out all the way to the loop labeled `OUTER`, which in this case is the outer loop.

Note that the label applies to the loop itself, and not to a specific position in the script (in fact, given that a label jumps outside a loop, it actually goes to the next line past that labeled loop, not to the loop itself). Don't think of labeled loops as `goto`s (if you know what a `goto` is); think of them more as handles attached to the loop to which you can jump.

Using the $_ (default) Variable

Congratulations! You now know (just about) everything you need to know about loops in Perl (and anything else you're curious about, you can find out in "Going Deeper.") Let's finish up with two general topics that we'll use quite a lot throughout the rest of this book: the special `$_` variable, and the syntax for reading input from files on the Perl command line.

First, the `$_` variable. This is a special variable in Perl that you can think of as being a default placeholder for scalar values. Lots of different constructs in Perl will use the `$_` if you don't give them a specific scalar variable to deal with; this has the advantage of making your scripts shorter and more efficient—but sometimes it can make them more confusing to read.

One use of the `$_` variable is in `foreach`. Remember that the `foreach` loop takes a temporary variable in which each element of the list is stored. If you leave off that temporary variable, Perl will use `$_` instead. Then, inside the body of the `foreach`, you can refer to `$_` to get to that value:

```
foreach (sort keys %hash) {
   print "Key: $_ Value: $hash{$_}\n";
}
```

Many functions will also use the value of `$_` if you don't give them any arguments—`print` and `chomp` being prime examples. So, for example if you see what appears to be a bare `print` in someone's script, like this:

```
print;
```

Then, mentally add the `$_` on the end of it:

```
print $_;
```

The `$_` variable is very common throughout Perl, so get used to seeing it and remembering the places where it can be used. We'll look more at the `$_` variable in the next section and quite a lot more on Day 9, "Pattern Matching with Regular Expressions."

Input from Files with while Loops and <>

Over the last three days, you've seen a number of examples that read input from the keyboard using <STDIN>. You've also used the standard input file handle in both a scalar and list context, so at this point you should know the difference between input in a scalar context (line by line) and input in a list context (read until end-of-file).

Getting input from the keyboard, however, is pretty tedious for any amount of input more than a few lines. That statistics script we worked on yesterday proves it—entering more than a couple of numbers into the script takes a long time, and if we want to just add to the existing data, we have to reenter it all each time.

Ideally, then, we'd store the data in a separate file, and then read it in each time the script executes. There are actually two ways to do this in Perl: one is to open and read a specific named file from inside your script. I've actually reserved an entire lesson for that, which you'll work through on Day 15, "Working with Files and I/O." There is a quicker and easier way, however, to get data from any random file into your Perl script, which takes advantage of the Perl command line. That's the technique I'm going to teach you today.

The core of this technique involves the Perl input operator (<>). You've been using that operator with <STDIN> to get input from the keyboard using the STDIN file handle. When you use <> without a file handle, however, Perl will get its input from the files you specify on the command line. <> means, effectively, "take all the filenames specified on the command line, open them all, concatenate them all together, and then read them in as if they were one file."

Note

> Technically, Perl gets the filenames to open and read from a special array called @ARGV, which contains the filenames or other values specified on the command line. You could, in fact, set the contents @ARGV yourself. But for now, assume @ARGV contains, and <> operates on, the filenames from the command line. More about @ARGV on Day 15, "Working with Files and I/O."

Here's an example that will read the input files indicated on the command line, line by line, and then print each line in turn:

```
while (defined($in = <>)) {
   print "$in";
}
```

Say you saved that script in a file called echofile.pl. You'd then call it on the command line with the name of the file echo, like this:

```
% echofile.pl afile.txt
```

If you wanted to echo multiple files, just stick all the filenames on the command line:

```
% echofile.pl afile.txt anotherfile.txt filethree.txt
```

Perl will happily open all those files read and print them one after the other.

Note

> If you're using MacPerl, chances are good you don't have a command line and you're feeling somewhat confused. But fear not, you can do the same thing by saving your Perl script as a "droplet." There's a menu in the Save dialog that enables you to do this (click the Type menu to see it). When you save your script as a droplet, you can then drag and drop your files onto your script icon, and MacPerl will launch and read those files into the script.

Let's look at that `while` loop from the inside out so you can figure out what's going on here. The `$in = <>` part will look familiar; that's similar to reading a line from `<STDIN>` in scalar context. And you might remember from Day 4 that the `defined` function returns true or false whether its argument is defined or not (that is, it doesn't contain the undefined value). Here, however, `defined` is used to halt the loop when we get to the end of the file. For each line read using `<>` we'll get a valid value up until the end of the file, and then `<>` returns undefined. `$in` gets undefined as well, and that triggers the defined function to return false, and the `while` loop to stop.

Like `<STDIN>`, the empty angle brackets can be used in either a scalar or a list context. In scalar context, they will read the input files line-by-line; in a list context, each line of the file (or of multiple files) will be an element in the list.

An even shorter version of that `echofiles` script is one that takes advantage of the `$_` variable. You can use `$_` to replace the `$in` variable we used in this script, and then dispense with the temporary variable and the `defined` function altogether, like this:

```
while (<>) {
   print;
}
```

In this case, the `while` loop will read the input files line-by-line, setting the value of the `$_` variable to each line in turn, and stop when `<>` is undefined without you having to test for it.

Note, however, that it's the `while` loop that knows enough to assign each line to `$_` in turn and to test for the end of file—not the `<>` characters. You cannot, for example, do `chomp(<>)`; that function call will not save the current line into `$_`. Only the `while` loop will do that.

This mechanism for getting data into a Perl script is extremely common; in fact, many Perl scripts will have these loops right up at the top of the script to read the input files into an array or hash.

Here's another example of using `<>` and the `$_` variable in place of getting input from the standard input. Yesterday, we worked through a script that prompted the user for a set of names, and then stored those names in an array. The input loop for that script looked like this:

```
while () {
    print 'Enter a name (first and last): ';
    chomp($in = <STDIN>);
    if ($in eq '') { last; }

    ($fn, $ln) = split(' ', $in);
    $names{$ln} = $fn;
}
```

To read those names from an input file, first we can replace the prompt, the call to `<STDIN>` and the test for blank input:

```
while (defined($in = <>)) {
    chomp($in);
    ($fn, $ln) = split(" ", $in);
    $names{$ln} = $fn;
}
```

Then, we could shorten that further to use the default `$_` variable:

```
while (<>) {
    chomp;
    ($fn, $ln) = split(' ');
    $names{$ln} = $fn;
}
```

Here, the `$_` variable is used to store the input from the file in the `while` loop test; `chomp` uses it to remove the newline, and `split` uses it as well to have something to split. You'll find these sorts of shortcuts very common in Perl scripts.

We could shorten the split even further by leaving off the space argument; split with no arguments assumes it will break the string in `$_` on whitespace without any arguments:

```
($fn, $ln) = split;
```

Going Deeper

As with the previous lessons, I still haven't told you everything you might want to know about conditionals and loops. In this section, I'll summarize some of these other features. Feel free to explore these features of the Perl language on your own.

Conditional and Loop Modifiers

The conditionals and loops you learned about in today's lesson are all complex statements—they operate on blocks of other statements, and don't require a semicolon at the end of the line. However, Perl also includes a set of modifiers to simple statements that can be used to form conditional and loop-like expressions. Sometimes these modifiers can provide shorter versions of simple conditionals and loops; other times they can help you express the logic of a statement you're trying to create in Perl that doesn't quite fit into the traditional conditionals or loops.

Each of the modifiers follows a simple statement, just before the semicolon. There are four of them, which mimic the more complex versions: `if`, `unless`, `while`, and `until`. Here are some examples:

```
print "$value" if ($value < 10);
$z = $x / $y if ($y > 0);
$i++ while ($i < 10);
print $value until ($value++ > $maxvalue)
```

In the conditional case, the front part of the statement will only execute if the test is true (or, with `unless`, if it's false). With the `while` and `until` loops, the statement will repeat until the test is false (or true, in the case of `until`).

Note that loops created with `while` and `until` modifiers are not the same as regular `while` and `until` loops; you cannot control them with loop control statements like `next` or `last`, nor can you label them.

The `do` loops you learned about earlier in this lesson are actually forms of loop modifiers. `do` is actually a function that executes a block of code, and you can use `while` and `until` to repeat that block of code some number of times based on a test (you'll learn more about do on Day 13). This is why you cannot use loop controls in `do` loops either.

Using `continue` blocks

The `continue` block is an optional block of statements after a loop that gets executed if the block finished executing, or if the loop was interrupted using `next`. The `continue` block is not executed if the loop was interrupted using `last` or `redo`. After the `continue` block is executed, Perl continues with the next iteration of the loop.

You might use a `continue` block to collect code that would otherwise be repeated for several different loop-exit situations, to change variables in those situations, or do some kind of cleaning up from an error that resulted in the loop exiting in the first place. It looks like this (where the `while` loop here could be a `for` or a `foreach`; any loop will do):

```
while ( test ) {
   # statements
   if (anothertest) {
```

```
        # error!
        next;  # skip down to continue
    }
    # more statements
} continue {
    # cleanup code from error
    # after this is done, go back to top of loop
}
```

Constructing `switch` or `case` Statements

Perl, remarkably, does not have syntax for an explicit `switch` statement. A *switch*, sometimes known as a `case` depending on your favorite language, is a construct that enables you to test a value and get a result in a much more compact, often more efficient, and easier-to-read manner than a whole lot of nested `ifs`. However, with labeled blocks, `do` loops, and logical expressions, you can build something that looks at least a little bit like a switch. Add pattern matching to it, and you get a Perl-like `switch` that works pretty well.

For example, here's a simple switch-like thing in Perl:

```
SWITCH: {
   $a eq "one" && do {
                       $a = 1;
                       last SWITCH;
                     };
   $a eq "two" && do {
                       $a = 2;
                       last SWITCH;
                     };
   $a eq "three" && do {
                       $a = 3;
                       last SWITCH;
                       };
# and so on
}
```

On Day 9, you'll learn a way to make that even shorter with patterns.

6

Summary

Conditionals and loops are the switches and dials of your Perl script. Without them, you can get stuff done, but it'll be the same stuff each time and your script will turn out pretty dull. Conditionals and loops allow you to make decisions and change what your script does based on different input or different situations. Conditional statements are those that branch to different blocks of Perl code depending on whether a test is true or false. You learned about the `if`, the `if...else`, and the `if...elsif` constructs for building conditionals, as well as the conditional operator `?..:`, which can be nested in other expressions, and the use of the logical operators (`&&`, `||`, `and` and `or`) as conditionals.

Next, we moved onto loops: specifically the `while` loops, which repeat a block of statements an unidentified number of times based on a test. There are four loops we covered here: `while`, `until`, `do...while`, and `do...until`.

The second kind of loop is the `for` loop, which also repeats a block of statements, but emphasizes the number of times aspect of the loop much more. You learned about the `foreach` loop for working through elements in a list, and the more general-purpose `for` loop.

You then learned about loop controls, which allow you to stop executing a block and skip to some part of a loop: `next`, `last`, and `redo`, as well as using labels to control jumping around inside nested loops.

And finally, we ended this lesson as we did the previous two: with more notes about input, including using the `<>` syntax to read from files and using the `$_` variable as a shortcut in many popular operations.

After this lesson, you've learned the core of the Perl language, and we'll explore some longer examples tomorrow to finish up the week. But don't stop now—next week's lessons will introduce you to some of the most powerful and exciting features of Perl, including various ways of processing lists and pattern matching.

The functions you learned about in this lesson include

- `do`, a function that behaves like loop with a `while` or `until` at the end of it.
- `rand` generates a random number between 0 and its argument
- `srand` seeds the random number generator used by rand. Without an argument, `srand` uses the time as the seed.

Q&A

Q. It seems to me that `for` loops could be written as `while` loops, and vice versa.

A. Yup, they sure could. If you wanted to strip all the constructs out of Perl that duplicate the behavior of other constructs, this could be one place where either one or the other would work. But there are some problems that are more easily thought of as number-of-times loops, as opposed to repeat-until-done loops. And being able to code the way you think is one of Perl's best features.

Q. I tried to use `continue` to break out of a loop, and Perl spewed errors at me. What did I do wrong?

A. C programmer, eh? You forgot that `continue` isn't used to break out of a loop in Perl (or you skipped that section). The equivalent of `continue` in Perl is `next`. Use `continue` as an optional block of statements to execute at the end of a block (see "Going Deeper.")

Q. I looked at your two examples of reading input from files, the one that uses `$_` and the one that doesn't. The former is shorter, yes, but it's really hard to figure out what's going on if you don't know which operations are using `$_`. I'd rather use actual variables and avoid `$_`. I think it's worth a few extra characters if a script is more readable that way.

A. That's definitely a philosophy to follow, and there are many Perl programmers that do follow that philosophy. And using the `$_` variable willy-nilly to shorten a script can definitely make it much harder to read. But in some cases—reading input from `<>` being one of them—the use of `$_` provides a common idiom in the language that when you get used to seems reasonable and easy to understand. If you have to read or modify other people's Perl scripts, chances are good you'll run into mysterious `$_` behavior at some point.

Be aware of `$_`, use it where it's most appropriate, or avoid it if you feel it hurts readability. That's your choice.

Workshop

The workshop provides quiz questions to help you solidify your understanding of the material covered and exercises to give you experience in using what you've learned. Try and understand the quiz and exercise answers before you go on to tomorrow's lesson.

Quiz

1. What is a block? What can you put inside a block?
2. What's the difference between an `if` and an `unless`?
3. What makes a `while` loop stop looping?
4. Why are `do` loops different from `while` or `until` loops?
5. What are the three parts of the part of the `for` loop in parentheses, and what do they do?
6. Define the differences between `next`, `last`, and `redo`.
7. Name three situations in which the `$_` variable can be used.
8. How does `<>` differ from `<STDIN>`?

Exercises

1. Write a script that prompts you for two numbers. Test to make sure that both numbers entered are actually numbers, and that the second number is not zero. If both numbers meet these requirements, divide the first by the second and print the result.
2. Rewrite #1 to include a test for negative numbers.

3. BUG BUSTER: What's wrong with this script (Hint: there might be more than one error)?

```
if ($val == 4) then { print $val; }
elseif ($val > 4) { print "more than 4"; }
```

4. BUG BUSTER: What's wrong with this script (Hint: there might be more than one error)?

```
for ($i = 0, $i < $max, $i++) {
   $vals[$i] = "";
}
```

5. BUG BUSTER: How about this one?

```
while ($i < $max) {
   $vals[$i] = 0;
}
```

6. Rewrite the `names.pl` script from yesterday to read from a file of names instead of from the standard input.

Answers

Here are the answers to the Workshop questions in the previous section.

Quiz Answers

1. A block is a group of other Perl statements (which can include other blocks) surrounded by curly braces ({}). Blocks are most commonly used in conjunction with conditionals and loops, but can also be used on their own (bare blocks).
2. The difference between and `if` and an `unless` is in the test: an `if` statement executes its block if the test returns true; `unless` executes is block if the test returns false.
3. The `while` loop stops looping when its test returns false. You can also break out of a `while` loop, or any loop, with `last`.
4. `do` loops are different from `while` or `until` loops in several ways. First, their blocks are executed before their tests, which allows you to execute statements at least once (for `while` and `until`, the block might not execute at all). Secondly, because the `do` loop is not actually really a loop (it's a function with a modifier), you cannot use loop controls inside it like `last` or `next`.
5. The three parts of the `for` loop in parentheses are
   - A loop counter initialization expression such as `$i = 0`
   - A test to determine how many times the loop will iterate, for example `$i < $max`
   - An increment expression to bring the loop counter closer to the test, for example, `$i++`.

6. next, last, and redo are all loop control expressions. next will stop executing the current block and start the loop at the top, including executing the test in a for or a while loop. redo is the same as next, except it restarts the block from the first statement in that block without executing the loop control test. last exits the loop altogether without retesting or reexecuting anything.
7. Here are a number of situations that default to the $_ if a variable isn't indicated:
    - while (<>) will read each line into $_ separately
    - chomp will remove the newline from $_
    - print will print $_
    - foreach will use $_ as the temporary variable
8. <> is used to input the contents of files specified on the command line (and as stored in @ARGV). <STDIN> is used to input data from standard input (usually the keyboard).

Exercise Answers

1. Here's one answer:

```
#!/usr/local/bin/perl -w

$num1 = 0;
$num2 = 0;

while () {
    print 'Enter a number: ';
    chomp($num1 = <STDIN>);
    print 'Enter another number: ';
    chomp($num2 = <STDIN>);

    if ($num1 =~ /\D/ or $num2 =~ /\D/ ) {
        print "Numbers only, please.\n";
        next;
    } elsif ( $num2 == 0) {
        print "Second number cannot be 0!\n";
        next;
    } else { last; }
}

print "The result of dividing $num1 by $num2 is ";
printf("%.2f\n", $num1 / $num2 );
```

2. Here's one answer:

```
#!/usr/local/bin/perl -w

$num1 = 0;
$num2 = 0;

while () {
    print 'Enter a number: ';
```

```
    chomp($num1 = <STDIN>);
    print 'Enter another number: ';
    chomp($num2 = <STDIN>);

    if ($num1 =~ /\D/ or $num2 =~ /\D/ ) { # contains non-digit or -
        if ($num1 =~ /-\d+/ or $num2 =~ /-\d+/) {  # contains -
            print "Positive numbers only.\n";
            next;
        } else { # contains non digit, not -
            print "Digits only.\n";
            next;
        }
    } elsif ( $num2 == 0) {
        print "Second number cannot be 0!\n";
        next;
    } else { last; }
}

print "The result of dividing $num1 by $num2 is ";
printf("%.2f\n", $num1 / $num2 );
```

3. There are two errors: `then` is not a Perl keyword; leave it out. And `elseif` is also not a valid Perl keyword; use `elsif` instead.
4. The expressions inside the `for` control expression should be separated with semicolons, not commas.
5. Syntactically, that loop is correct, but there's no way it'll ever exit—there's no increment for `$i` inside the body of the loop.
6. Here's one answer:

```
#!/usr/local/bin/perl -w

%names = ();    # hash of names
$fn = '';       # first name
$ln = '';       # last name

while (<>) {
    chomp;
    ($fn, $ln) = split;
    $names{$ln} = $fn;

}

foreach $lastname (sort keys %names) {
    print "$lastname, $names{$lastname}\n";
}
```

WEEK 1

DAY 7

Exploring a Few Longer Examples

To finish up the week, let's take this day to explore some more examples that make use of the techniques you've learned so far. We won't spend a lot of time on background in this lesson, nor will you have any quizzes or exercises to work through at the end. Consider this a brief pause to look at more bits of code in further detail. We'll have three of these example lessons, one after each six or so lessons, to cement what you've learned.

Today we'll look at three Perl scripts:

- A new version of `stats.pl` with a more complex histogram
- A script to spell numbers
- A script to convert text files into simple Web pages

Statistics with a Better Histogram

Here's yet another version of the statistics program we've been working with throughout the last week. Yesterday's version of the statistics program included a horizontal histogram that looked like this:

```
Frequency of Values:
1   | *****
2   | *************
3   | *******************
4   | ****************
5   | ***********
6   | ****
43  | *
62  | *
```

For this version, we'll print a vertical histogram that looks like this:

```
†††††*
†††††*
†††††*
†††††*
†††††*
†††††*†*
†††††*†*†*
†††††*†*†*†††††††*†††††*†††††*
†††††*†*†*†††*†*†*†††††*†††††*
†††*†*†*†*†††*†*†*†††††*†††††*
†††*†*†*†*†††*†*†*†††††*†††††*
†*†*†*†*†*†*†*†*†*†††††*†††††*††*
†*†*†*†*†*†*†*†*†*††*††*††*††*††*††*
-------------------------------------
†1†2†3†4†5†6†7†8†9†12†23†25†34†37†39†42
```

This form of histogram is actually much harder to produce than a horizontal histogram; this version uses two nested `for` loops and some careful counting for it to come out the right way.

There's one other change to this version of `stats.pl`: it gets its data from a file, rather than making you enter in all the data at a prompt. As with all the scripts that read data from a file, you need to specify a data file for this script to use on the command line, as follows:

```
% statsfinal.pl data.txt
```

The data file, here called `data.txt`, has each of the numbers on individual lines. First, let's look closely at the two parts of this script that are different from the last version: the part that reads in the data file, and the part that prints the histogram.

Listing 7.1 shows the script for our final statistics script. Given how much we've been working with this script up to this point, it should look familiar to you. The parts to concentrate on are the input loop in lines 14 through 21, and the code to generate the new histogram in lines 36 through 49.

LISTING 7.1 The `statsfinal.pl` Script

```
1:  #!/usr/loczl/bin/perl -w
2:
3:  $input = "";  # temporary input
4:  @nums = ();   # array of numbers;
5:  %freq = ();   # hash of number frequencies
6:  $maxfreq = 0; # maximum frequency
7:  $count = 0;   # count of numbers
8:  $sum = 0;     # sum of numbers
9:  $avg = 0;     # average
10: $med = 0;     # median
11: @keys = ();   # temp keys
12: $totalspace = 0; # total space across histogram
13:
14: while (defined ($input = <>)) {
15:     chomp ($input);
16:     $nums[$count] = $input;
17:     $freq{$input}++;
18:     if ($maxfreq < $freq{$input}) { $maxfreq = $freq{$input} }
19:     $count++;
20:     $sum += $input;
21: }
22: @nums = sort { $a <=> $b } @nums;
23:
24: $avg = $sum / $count;
25: $med = $nums[$count /2];
26:
27: print "\nTotal count of numbers: $count\n";
28: print "Total sum of numbers: $sum\n";
29: print "Minimum number: $nums[0]\n";
30: print "Maximum number: $nums[$#nums]\n";
31: printf("Average (mean): %.2f\n", $avg);
32: print "Median: $med\n\n";
33:
34: @keys = sort { $a <=> $b } keys %freq;
35:
36: for ($i = $maxfreq; $i > 0; $i--) {
37:     foreach $num (@keys) {
38:         $space = (length $num);
39:         if ($freq{$num} >= $i) {
40:             print( (" " x $space) . "*");
41:         } else {
42:             print " " x (($space) + 1);
43:         }
```

LISTING 7.1 continued

```
44:         if ($i == $maxfreq) { $totalspace += $space + 1; }
45:     }
46:     print "\n";
47: }
48: print "-" x $totalspace;
49: print "\n @keys\n";
```

Because you've seen the boilerplate code for reading data from files using `<>`, nothing in lines 14 through 21 should be too much of a surprise. Note that we read each line (that is, each number) into the `$input` variable, and then use that value throughout the block.

Why not use `$_`? We could have done that here, but a lot of the statements in this block need an actual variable reference (they don't default to `$_`). Using `$_` for that reference would have made things only very slightly smaller, but would have decreased the readability of the example, and in this case, it was a better idea to err on the side of readability.

> **Note**
>
> A point to remember throughout this book as I explain more and more strange and obscure bits of Perl—just because Perl uses a particular feature doesn't mean you have to use it. Consider the tradeoffs between creating very small code that no one except a Perl wizard can decipher, versus longer, maybe less efficient, but more readable code. Consider it particularly well done if someone else can read your Perl code further down the line.

Anyhow, other than reading the input from a file instead of standard input, much of the `while` block is the same as it was in yesterday's version of this script. The one other difference is the addition in line 18 to calculate the `$maxfreq` value. This value is the maximum frequency of any number—that is, the number of times the most frequent number appears in the data set. We'll use this value later to determine the overall height of the histogram. Here, all we do is compare the current maximum frequency to the current frequency, and change `$maxfreq` if the new one is larger.

Farther down in the script, after we've sorted, summed, and printed, we get to the histogram part of the script, in the daunting set of loops in lines 36 through 49.

Building a horizontal histogram like we did yesterday is much easier than building one vertically. With the horizontal histogram, you can just loop through the keys in the `%freq` hash and print out the appropriate number of asterisks (plus some minor formatting). For the vertical histogram, we need to keep track of the overall layout much more closely, as each line we draw doesn't have any direct relationship to any specific key or value in the hash. Also, we still must keep track of the spaces for formatting.

We'll keep track of the histogram using two loops. The outer loop, a `for` loop, controls the number of lines to print, that is, the overall height from top to bottom. The second loop is a `foreach` loop that moves from left to right within each line, printing either an asterisk or a space. With two nested loops (the `for` and the `foreach`), we can go from left to right and line to line, with both the height and the width of the histogram determined by the actual values in the data.

First, we extract a sorted list of keys out of the `%freq` hash in line 34. This is mostly for convenience and to make the `for` loops coming up at least a little less complex.

Line 36 starts our outer `for` loop. The overall height of the histogram is determined by the most frequent value in the data set. Here's where we make use of that `$maxfreq` variable we calculated when the data is read in. This outer `for` loop starts at the maximum frequency and works down to 0, printing as many lines as it takes.

The inner loop prints each line, looping over the values in the data set (the keys from the `%freq` data set). For each line, we print either a space or a *, depending on whether the given value's frequency should start showing up on the current line. We also keep track of formatting, to add more space for those values that have multiple digits (the spacing for a value of 333 will be different from that for 1).

Line by line, starting at line 38 here's what we're doing:

- In line 38, we calculate the space this column will need, based on the number of digits in the current value.
- Lines 39 and 40 print a * if the * is warranted. The test here is to see if the current value we're looking at is as frequent as our vertical position in the histogram (frequency greater or equal to the current value of `$i`). This way, at the start of the histogram we'll get fewer asterisks, and as we progress downward and `$i` gets lower, more values will need asterisks. Note that the `print` statement in line 40 prints both the asterisk and enough spaces to space it out to the correct width.
- If there's no * to be printed in this line, we print the right amount of filler space: space for the column, plus one extra.
- Line 44 is a puzzler. What's this here for? This line is here to calculate the total width of the histogram, overall, based on the lengths of all the digits in the data set with spaces in between them all. We'll need this in line 48 when we print a divider line, but because we're already in the midst of a loop here, I figured I'd get this calculation now instead of waiting until then. What this loop does is if `$i` is equal to `$maxfreq`—that is, if we're on the very first line of the outer `for` loop—the loop adds the current amount of space to the `$totalspace` variable to get the maximum width.
- And, finally, in line 46, when we're done with a line of data, we print a newline to restart the next line at the appropriate spot.

With the columns of the histogram printed, all we've got left are the labels on the bottom. Here we'll print an appropriate number of hyphens to mimic a horizontal line (using the value we calculated for `$totalspace`), and then print the set of keys, interpolated inside a string, which prints all the elements in `@keys` with spaces between them.

Complicated nested loops such as this are particularly hard to follow, and sometimes a description like the one I just gave you isn't enough. If you're still really bewildered about how this example worked, consider working through it step by step, loop by loop, making sure you understand the current values of all the variables and how they relate to each other.

A Number Speller

This second example isn't particularly useful for the real world, but does show some more complex uses of `if`s, `while`s, and various tests. This script asks you to enter a single-digit number (and has the usual verification tests to make sure you have indeed entered a single-digit number), and then it spells out that number for you—in other words, 2 is *two*, 5 is *five*, and so on. Then, it asks you if you want to enter another number, and if so, it repeats the process. Here's an example:

```
% numspeller.pl
Enter the number you want to spell: foo
No strings.  0 through 9 please..
Enter the number you want to spell: 45
Too big. 0 through 9 please.
Enter the number you want to spell: 6
Number 6 is six
Try another number (y/n)?: foo
y or n, please
Try another number (y/n)?: y
Enter the number you want to spell: 3
Number 3 is three
Try another number (y/n)?: n
```

Listing 7.2 shows the full code.

Listing 7.2 The `numspeller.pl` Script

```
#!/usr/local/bin/perl -w
# numberspeller:  prints out word approximations of numbers
# simple version, only does single-digits

$num = 0;     # raw number
$exit = "";  # whether or not to exit the program.
%numbers = (
    1 => 'one',
```

Listing 7.2 continued

```
 9:       2 => 'two',
10:       3 => 'three',
11:       4 => 'four',
12:       5 => 'five',
13:       6 => 'six',
14:       7 => 'seven',
15:       8 => 'eight',
16:       9 => 'nine',
17:       0 => 'zero'
18: );
19:
20: while ($exit ne "n") {
21:
22:     while () {
23:         print 'Enter the number you want to spell: ';
24:         chomp($num = <STDIN>);
25:         if ($num !~ /\d/ or $num =~ /\D/) { # test for strings
26:             print "No strings.  0 through 9 please.\n";
27:             next;
28:         }
29:         if ($num > 9) { # numbers w/more than 1 digit
30:             print "Too big. 0 through 9 please.\n";
31:             next;
32:         }
33:         if ($num < 0) { # negative numbers
34:             print "No negative numbers.  0 through 9 please.\n";
35:             next;
36:         }
37:         last;
38:     }
39:
40:     print "Number $num is ";
41:     print $numbers{$num};
42:     print "\n";
43:
44:     while () {
45:         print 'Try another number (y/n)?: ';
46:         chomp ($exit = <STDIN>);
47:         $exit = lc $exit;
48:         if ($exit ne 'y' && $exit ne 'n') {
49:             print "y or n, please\n";
50:         }
51:         else { last; }
52:     }
53: }
```

`while`s within `while`s, and `if`s after `if`s. Let's start from the outer loop, and work inward. The first `while` loop, in line 20, includes the bulk of the entire script in its block.

That's because the entire script will repeat, or not, based on the yes/no prompt at the end. At the start, however, we need to run it at least once, so the test in line 8 will return true (note that we carefully initialized the `$exit` variable so that it would).

The second `while` loop, lines 22 through 38, tests our input through the use of three `if`s. The first one checks to make sure you haven't typed any strings using a regular expression; the second one makes sure you haven't typed a number greater than 9 (this version of the script only tests for single-digit numbers); and the third tests for negative numbers. If any of these three tests are true, we use the `next` keyword, which skips the rest of the block and goes back up to the test for the nearest enclosing loop—which in this case is still that infinite `while` loop that started in 10. If the input meets all three criteria—it's not a string, and it's in between 0 and 9, then we call `last`, which breaks out of the nearest `while` loop and goes onto the next statement in the block.

That next statement is line 40, where we print the introductory message. At the beginning of the script set up a hash with a mapping from all the supported digits to their fully spelled out equivalents. Use a simple hash lookup to retrieve the word that corresponds to the digit entered by the user, and print that out. An `if...elsif` type of statement could have been used here to test for each of the possible digits the user could enter, but dealing with the hash is easier.

When our number is printed, we can do it all over again if we want, thanks to the final `while` loop in lines 44 through 52. This one prompts for a `y` or an `n` character in response to the "Try another number" prompt. Note the call to the `lc` function in line 47—if the user types a capital Y or a capital N, we'll still accept that input because the `lc` function will lowercase it before we actually test. That line saves us some extra tests in the body of the `while`.

You'll notice that this chunk of code doesn't actually determine what to do if the reply is `y` or `n`; all it does is verify that it is indeed `y` or `n`. That's because this code doesn't need to do anything. When `$exit` has the appropriate value, the outer `while` loop ends, and we return right back up to the top again to that test in the first `while`. If the reply was `n`, that test returns false and the script exits. Otherwise, we start the body of that outer `while` again, and continue until the user gets bored and types `n` to exit the script.

Text-to-HTML Converter Script

Let's finish up with a slightly more useful script: `webbuild.pl` takes a simple text file as an argument, prompts you for some basic values, and then spits out an HTML version of your text file. It's not a very sophisticated HTML generator—it won't handle embedded boldface or other formatting, it doesn't handle links or images; really, it does little other than stick paragraph tags in the right place, let you specify the foreground and background colors, and give you a simple heading and a link to your e-mail address. But it does give you a basic HTML template to work from.

How It Works

In addition to simply converting text input to HTML, the `webbuild.pl` script prompts you for several other values, including

- The title of the page (`<title>...</title>` in HTML).
- Background and text colors (here I've limited it to the built-in colors supported by HTML, and we'll verify the input to make sure that it's one of those colors). This part also includes some rudimentary online help as well.
- An initial heading (`<h1>...</h1>` in HTML).
- An e-mail address, which will be inserted as a link at the bottom of the final HTML page

Here's what running the `webbuild.pl` script would produce with the some given prompts and output:

```
% webbuild.pl janeeyre.txt
Enter the title to use for your web page: Charlotte Bronte, Jane Eyre, Chapter
One
Enter the background color (? for options): ?
One of:
white, black, red, green, blue,
orange, purple, yellow, aqua, gray,
silver, fuchsia, lime, maroon, navy,
olive, or Return for none
Enter the backgroundcolor (? for options): white
Enter the text color (? for options): black
Enter a heading: Chapter One
Enter your email address: lemay@lne.com
******************************
<html>
<head>
<title>Charlotte Bronte, Jane Eyre, Chapter One</title>
</head>
<body bgcolor="white" text="black">
<h1>Chapter One</h1>
<p>There was no possibility of taking a walk that day. We had been
wandering, indeed, in the leafless shrubbery an hour in the morning;
... more text deleted for space ...
fireside, and with her darlings about her (for the time neither
</p>
<hr>
<address><a href="mailto:lemay@lne.com">lemay@lne.com</a></address>
</body>
</html>
```

7

The resulting HTML file, as the previous output shows, could then be copy-and-pasted into a text editor, saved, and loaded into a Web browser to see the result (Figure 7.1 shows that result).

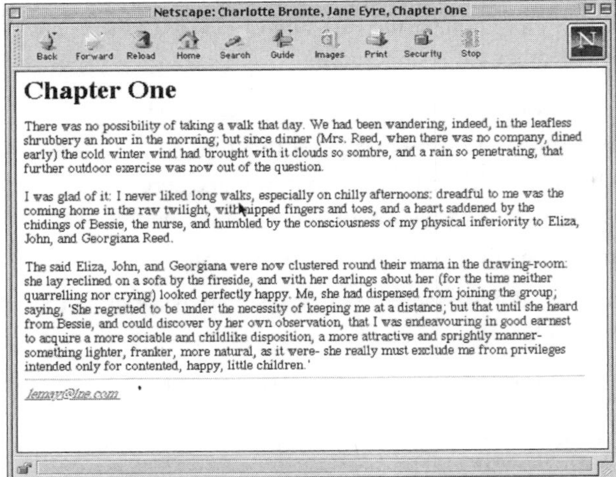

FIGURE 7.1. *The result of the* `webbuild.pl` *script.*

Later in this book (on Day 15, "Managing I/O," specifically), I'll show you a way to output the data to a file, rather than to the screen.

The Input File

One note about the text file you give to `webbuild.pl` to convert: The script assumes the data you give it is a file of paragraphs, with each paragraph separated by a blank line. For example, here are the contents of the file `janeeyre.txt`, which I used for the example output:

```
There was no possibility of taking a walk that day. We had been
wandering, indeed, in the leafless shrubbery an hour in the morning;
but since dinner (Mrs. Reed, when there was no company, dined early)
the cold winter wind had brought with it clouds so sombre, and a
rain so penetrating, that further outdoor exercise was now out of
the question.

I was glad of it: I never liked long walks, especially on chilly
afternoons: dreadful to me was the coming home in the raw twilight,
with nipped fingers and toes, and a heart saddened by the chidings
of Bessie, the nurse, and humbled by the consciousness of my
physical inferiority to Eliza, John, and Georgiana Reed.

The said Eliza, John, and Georgiana were now clustered round
their mama in the drawing-room: she lay reclined on a sofa by the
fireside, and with her darlings about her (for the time neither
```

The Script

Listing 7.3 shows the code for our script.

LISTING 7.3 webbuild.pl

```
#!/usr/local/bin/perl -w
#
# webbuild:  simple text-file conversion to HTML
# *very* simple.  Assumes no funky characters, embedded
# links or boldface, etc.  Blank spaces == paragraph
# breaks.

$title = '';                       # <TITLE>
$bgcolor = '';                     # BGCOLOR
$text = '';                        # TEXT
$head = '';                        # main heading
$mail = '';                        # email address
$paragraph = '';                   # is there currently an open paragraph tag?

print "Enter the title to use for your web page: ";
chomp($title = <STDIN>);

foreach $color ('background', 'text') { # run twice, once for each color
    $in = '';                      # temporary input
    while () {
        print "Enter the $color color (? for options): ";
        chomp($in = <STDIN>);
        $in = lc $in;

        if ($in eq '?') {          # print help
            print "One of: \nwhite, black, red, green, blue,\n";
            print "orange, purple, yellow, aqua, gray,\n";
            print "silver, fuchsia, lime, maroon, navy,\n";
            print "olive, or Return for none\n";
            next;
        } elsif ($in eq '' or
                 $in eq 'white' or
                 $in eq 'black' or
                 $in eq 'red' or
                 $in eq 'blue' or
                 $in eq 'green' or
                 $in eq 'orange' or
                 $in eq 'purple' or
                 $in eq 'yellow' or
                 $in eq 'aqua' or
                 $in eq 'gray' or
                 $in eq 'silver' or
                 $in eq 'fuchsia' or
                 $in eq 'lime' or
                 $in eq 'maroon' or
```

LISTING 7.3 continued

```
                  $in eq 'navy' or
                  $in eq 'olive') { last; }
         else {
             print "that's not a color.\n";
         }
     }

     if ($color eq 'background') {
         $bgcolor = $in;
     } else {
         $text = $in;
     }
}

print "Enter a heading: ";
chomp($head = <STDIN>);

print "Enter your email address: ";
chomp($mail = <STDIN>);

print '*' x 30;

print "\n<html>\n<head>\n<title>$title</title>\n";
print "</head>\n<body";
if ($bgcolor ne '') { print qq( bgcolor="$bgcolor"); }
if ($text ne '') { print qq( text="$text"); }
print ">\n";
print "<h1>$head</h1>\n<p>";
$paragraph = 'y';

while (<>) {
    if ($_ =~ /^\s$/) {
        if ($paragraph eq 'y') {
            print "</p>\n";
            $paragraph = 'n';
        }

        print "<p>\n";
        $paragraph = 'y';
    } else {
        print $_;
    }
}

if ($paragraph eq 'y') {
    print "</p>\n";
}

print qq(<hr>\n<address><a href="mailto:$mail">$mail</a></address>\n);
print "</body>\n</html>\n";
```

There's little that's overly complex, syntax-wise, in this script; it doesn't even use any arrays or hashes (it doesn't need to; there's nothing that really needs storing or processing here). It's just a lot of loops and tests.

There are at least a few points to be made about why I organized the script the way I did, so we can't end this lesson quite yet. Let's start with the large `foreach` loop starting in line 18.

This loop handles the prompt for both the background and text colors. Because both of these prompts behave in exactly the same way, I didn't want to have to repeat the same code for each one (particularly given that there's a really huge `if` test in lines 31 through 47). Later, you'll learn how to put this kind of repetitive code into a subroutine, and then just call the subroutine twice. But for now, because we know a lot about loops at this point, and nothing about subroutines, I opted for a sneaky `foreach` loop.

The loop will run twice, once for the string `'background'` and once for the string `'text'`. We'll use these strings for the prompts, and later to make sure the right value gets assigned to the right variable (`$bgcolor` or `$text`).

Inside the `foreach` loop, we have another loop, an infinite `while` loop, which will repeat each prompt until we get acceptable input (input verification is always a good programming practice). At the prompt, the user has three choices: enter one of the sixteen built-in colors, hit Return (or Enter) to use the default colors, or type `?` for a list of the choices.

The tests in lines 25 through 50 process each of these choices. First, `?`. In response to a question mark, all we have to do is print a helpful message, and then use `next` to drop down to the next iteration of the `while` loop (that is, redisplay the prompt and wait for more data).

The next test (starting in line 30) makes sure we have correct input: either a Return, in which case the input is empty (line 30); or one of the sixteen built-in colors. Note that the tests all test lowercase colors, which would seem overly limiting if the user typed `BLACK` or `Black` or some other odd-combination of upper and lowercase. But fear not; in line 23, we used the `lc` function to lowercase the input, which combines all those case issues into one (but conveniently doesn't affect input of `?`).

If the input matches any of those seventeen cases, we call `last` in line 47 to drop out of the `while` loop (keep in mind that `next` and `last`, minus the presence of labels, refer to the nearest enclosing loop—to the `while`, not to the `foreach`). If the input doesn't match, we drop to the final else case in line 48, print an error message, and restart the `while` loop.

7

The final test in the `foreach` loop determines whether we have a value for the background color or for the text color, and assigns that value to the appropriate variable.

The final part of the script, starting on line 68 and continuing to the end, prints the top part of our HTML file, reads in and converts the text file indicated on the command line to HTML, and finishes up with the last part of the HTML file. Note the tests in line 69 and 70; if there are no values for `$bgcolor` or `$text`, we'll leave off those attributes to the HTML `<body>` tag altogether. (A simpler version would be to just leave them there, as `bgcolor=""` or `text=""`, but that doesn't look as nice in the output).

You'll note also the use of the `qq` function. You learned about `qq` in passing way back in the "Going Deeper" section on Day 2, "Working with Strings and Numbers." The `qq` function is a way of creating a double-quoted string without actually using any double-quotes. I used it here because if I had actually used double-quotes, I would have had to backslash the double-quotes in the string itself. I think it looks better this way.

Lines 74 through 80 read in the input file (using `<>`), and then simply print it all back out again, inserting paragraph tags at the appropriate spots (that is, where there are blank lines). I use the `$paragraph` variable to keep track of whether there's an open `<p>` tag with no corresponding closing tag. If there is, the script prints out a closing `</p>` tag before printing another opening `<p>`. A more robust version of this script would watch for things such as embedded special characters (accents, bullets, and so on) and replace them with the appropriate HTML codes—but that's a task done much easier with pattern matching, so we'll leave it for later.

All that's left is to print the final e-mail link (using an HTML mailto URL and link tags) and finish up the HTML file.

Summary

Often, programming books give you a lot of wordy background, but don't include enough actual code examples for how to do stuff. While I won't claim that this book shirks on the wordy background (you might snicker now), this lesson—and the two to come on Day 14 and Day 21—will offer you some longer bits of code that make use of the techniques you've learned in the previous lessons, put them all together, and maybe even accomplish some sort of useful task (although I'm not certain how often you're going to need to spell a number.)

In today's lesson, we explored three scripts. First, a revision of the familiar stats script, printed a sophisticated histogram using `for` loops and some careful measuring. The second, a number speller, used tests and a hash lookup to print a result. And the third, webbuild, took an input file from the command line and data from the keyboard and converted the contents of the file into something else—in this case, a Web page.

Congratulations on completing the first week of this three-week book. During this week, you've picked up a hefty chunk of the language. From this point on, we'll be building on what you've already learned. Onward to Week 2!

WEEK 2

Doing More

WEEK 2

DAY 8

Manipulating Lists and Strings

We'll start Week 2 with a hodgepodge of things; in today's lesson, we'll look more closely at lists, arrays, hashes, and strings, and the sorts of things you can do to manipulate the data they contain. A lot of what you'll learn about today uses many of Perl's built-in functions, but these functions are useful to have in your repertoire as you learn more about the language itself.

Today we'll explore

- Creating array and hash slices (smaller portions of other arrays and hashes)
- Sorting lists
- Searching lists
- Modifying list contents
- Processing all the elements of a list
- Various string manipulations: `reverse`, finding substrings, extracting substrings

Array and Hash Slices

In addition to all the operations you learned about on Days 4, "Working with Lists and Arrays," and 5, "Working with Hashes," Perl also has a mechanism for copying some subset of elements from the collection. That's called a slice—a subset of an array or a hash that is, in turn, another array or hash.

You take a slice of an array similarly to how you access one element: using brackets. However, there are two significant differences between a slice and a single element. Here are some lines of Perl code that show the syntax for slices:

```
@array = (1,2,3,4,5);
$one = $array[0];      # $one is 1
@slice = @array[0,1,2];  # @slice is (1,2,3)
```

See the differences? In the element access expression `$array[0]`, you use a `$` to refer to the array variable, and a single index number inside the brackets. The result, stored in `$one`, is a single scalar variable. With the slice notation, you use an at sign (`@`) for the array variable, and a list of indexes inside the brackets. With this notation, you end up with a list of three elements in `@slice`.

You can put any expression inside the brackets for a slice, as long as it's a list of indexes. Range operators work exceptionally well here for taking a slice of consecutive numbers:

```
@lowers = @nums[1..100];
```

Note that a very common Perl mistake is to use an array slice with a single index, when what you wanted was a single element:

```
$single = @array[5];
```

This notation won't produce what you're looking for. Here, you're extracting a list of one element from the array `@array`, and then trying to evaluate that list in a scalar context. If you have warnings turned on in your script, Perl will let you know if you're making this mistake.

Hash slices work similarly to array slices, but require different notation:

```
%hashslice = @hash{'this', 'that', 'other'};
```

Note that for a hash slice, the keys you want to extract go into curly brackets, like individual hash keys, but you still use an array variable symbol even though it's a hash. That's because the resulting slice will be a list of the keys and values (in the right order: key, value, key, value, and so on). You can then just assign that slice to a hash variable and turn it into a hash once again. Don't do this:

```
%hashslice = %hash{'this', 'that', 'other'};
```

That'll give you an error (even if you don't have warnings turned on). The rule is, if you want a scalar out of an array or hash, use `$` (scalar notation). If you want a slice, use `@` (array notation).

Sorting Lists

You've already seen how to sort a list, for example, the keys in a hash, using the `sort` function:

```
@keys = sort keys %hash;
```

By default, the `sort` function sorts a list in ASCII order. To sort a list of numbers in numeric order, use `sort` with an extra expression just before the list to be sorted:

```
@keys = sort { $a <=> $b } keys %hash;
```

What does that bit in the middle with the `<=>` operator do? What are `$a` and `$b` for? Up until now, I asked you to just learn that line by heart; here's where I'll explain what all that means.

The extra bit between curly brackets in the `sort` determines how the list is to be sorted, by describing what happens when one element is greater than, less than, or equal to another. Given two arguments (`$a` and `$b`), the expression inside the block should return an integer less than 0 (if the first argument is less than the second), an integer greater than 0 (if the first argument is greater), or 0 (if the two arguments are equal).

Perl, conveniently, has two operators that do just this, making it easy for you to write simple `sort` routines. Why two operators? For the same reason there are two sets of equality and relational operators: one for strings (`cmp`), and one for numbers (`<=>`).

The `cmp` operator works on strings, comparing two arguments and returning -1, 0, or 1 depending on whether the first operand is less than, equal to, or greater than the second. You could write `cmp` the long way something like this:

```
$result = '';
if ($a lt $b ) { $result = -1; }
elsif ($a gt $b { $result = 1; }
else { $result = 0; }
```

The `<=>` operator, sometimes called the spaceship operator for its appearance, does exactly the same comparison, only for numbers.

Which brings us to the `$a` and `$b` part of the `sort` routine. The `$a` and `$b` variables are temporary to the sort (you don't have to declare them, they go away when the sort's done), and contain elements in the list you're sorting. If you were going to write your own `sort` routine inside the block, you would use `$a` and `$b` to refer to the two elements that need to be compared each time.

Because `$a` and `$b` are special to the sort routine, and refer to two elements in the list, be careful about using variables named `$a` and `$b` in your scripts, or of changing the values of `$a` and `$b` inside your `sort` routine. Weird and unexpected results can occur.

The default `sort` routine uses the `cmp` operator to compare values (which is why it sorts in ASCII order). Using `{ $a <=> $b }` compares the values with a numeric comparison, which sorts those values in numeric order.

By default these `sort` routines have sorted lists in ascending order. To sort in the reverse order, simply reverse `$a` and `$b`:

```
@keys = sort { $b <=> $a } keys %hash;
```

You can print a hash, sorted by keys, using a `sort` routine and a `foreach` loop. If you want to do the same thing with the values in the hash, however, things can get a little complicated. If all you need are the values, you can just use the `values` function to get a list of those values, and then sort it. By doing that you lose access to the original keys and there's no way to associate a raw value back to its key. You can, however, sort the keys in value order, and then print out both the key and its value, like this:

```
foreach $key (sort {$things{$a} cmp $things{$b}} keys %things) {
   print "$key, $things{$key}\n";
}
```

Here, the `sort` routine, instead of using raw keys for the values of `$a` and `$b`, sorts the values associated with the keys (`$things{$a}` and `$things{$b}`) instead. The resulting list, which we iterate over using `foreach`, is a list of the keys in the hash sorted by value.

Searching

Sorting's easy; there's a function for it. Searching a list for a particular element—or for a part of an element—isn't quite so straightforward. Searching is one of those things where there is definitely more than one way to do it. Given a list of strings and a search string, you could, for example, simply iterate over the list with a `foreach` loop and test each element against the string, like this:

```
chomp($key = <STDIN>);  # thing to look for
foreach $el (@strings) {
   if ($key eq $el) {
      $found = 1;
   }
}
```

If the thing you were searching for can be a substring of an element in the list, you could use the `index` function to search for the substring in the string. The `index` function returns the position of the substring in the string, if it's found, and -1 otherwise (remember that string positions, like arrays, start from 0):

```
foreach $el (@strings) {
   if ((index $el, $key) >= 0) {   # -1 means not found
      $found = 1;
   }
}
```

A more efficient (and potentially more powerful) version of the substring tests would be to use patterns, which you'll learn more about tomorrow (don't worry about this syntax right now):

```
foreach $el (@strings) {
   if ($el =~ /$key/) {
      $found = 1;
   }
}
```

Despite the differences with the test, all these examples use a number of lines of code. To make things even more efficient, number-of-characters-wise, we can use Perl's built-in `grep` function. Named after the Unix tool of the same name, `grep` is used specifically for searching for things in lists. As with many other Perl features, however, `grep` behaves differently when used either in a list or a scalar context.

In list context, `grep` is used to extract all the elements of a list for which an expression or test is true, and return a new list of those elements. So, for example, here's an example of `grep` that will extract all the elements of the list `@nums` that are greater than 100:

```
@large = grep { $_ > 100 } @nums;
```

Note the use of our friend the `$_` default variable. The `grep` function works by taking each element in the list and assigning it to `$_`, and then evaluating the expression inside the brackets. If the expression is true, that list element "matches" the search and is added to the final list. Otherwise, `grep` moves onto the next element in the `@nums` list until it gets to the end.

You can use any expression you want to inside the brackets. The expression you use, however, should be a test that returns true or false, so that `grep` can build the new list on that criteria.

An alternate way to use `grep` is with a pattern built using a regular expression. We'll learn all about regular expressions tomorrow and the next day, but I'll include an example here (and in the example that follows this section), just to give you a taste:

```
@exes = grep /x/, @words;
```

Instead of a test inside of curly brackets, as with the previous examples, this example uses a pattern. The characters inside the slashes (here, just the character `x`) are the search pattern; in this case, `grep` will find all the elements in the `@words` array that contain the letter `x`, and store those words in the `@exes` array. You can also use a variable inside the search pattern:

```
print "Search for? ";
chomp($key = <STDIN>);
@exes = grep /$key/, @words;
```

The pattern inside the slashes can be any number of characters, and `grep` will search for that set of characters in any element in the list. So, for example, a pattern of `/the/` will match any elements that contain the letters `the` (which includes the word "the" as well as the words "there" or "other"). As you'll learn tomorrow, the pattern can also contain a number of special characters to build much more sophisticated search criteria. Don't forget the comma after the pattern; unlike the syntax with an expression inside brackets, the comma is required after the pattern.

In scalar context, `grep` behaves much the same as in list context, except that instead of returning a list of all the elements that matched, `grep` returns the number of elements that matched (0 means no matches).

The `grep` function works best with lists or arrays, but there's nothing stopping you from using it with hashes, as long as you write your test correctly. For example, this bit of code uses `grep` to find all the hash keys for which *either* the key or its associated value is larger than 100:

```
@largekeys = grep { $_ > 100 or $numhash{$_} > 100 } keys %numhash;
```

In the previous lesson's `webbuild.pl` example, there was a huge `if...elsif` construct that was used to determine whether a color entered by the user was valid. Using the `grep` function, it would be more easily written as:

```
elsif (grep { $in eq $_ } ("white", "black", "red", ...))
```

An Example: More Names

On Day 5, we had a simple example that read in names (first and last), and then split those names into a hash of names keyed by the last name. On Day 6, both in the body of the lesson and in the exercises, we used the `<>` operator to read those names into a hash from an external file. Let's extend the names script here so that it doesn't just read the names into a hash, it also does something with those names. This version of the names script, `morenames.pl`, adds a large `while` loop that gives you a list of four options:

- Sort and print the names list by last name
- Sort and print the names list by first name

- Search for first or last name
- Quit

If you choose any of the options to search or sort the list, the program repeats and allows you to choose another option. The fourth option exits the program. Here's a transcript of how the program might look when run:

```
$ morenames.pl names.txt

1. Sort names by last name
2. Sort names by first name
3. Search for a name
4. Quit

Choose a number: 1
Adams, Douglas
Alexander, Lloyd
Alighieri, Dante
Asimov, Isaac
other names deleted for space

1. Sort names by last name
2. Sort names by first name
3. Search for a name
4. Quit

Choose a number: 2
Albert Camus
Aldous Huxley
Angela Carter
Anne Rice
Anne McCaffrey
Anthony Burgess
other names deleted for space

1. Sort names by last name
2. Sort names by first name
3. Search for a name
4. Quit

Choose a number: 3
Search for what? Will
Names matched:
   William S.  Burroughs
   William Shakespeare

1. Sort names by last name
2. Sort names by first name
3. Search for a name
4. Quit

Choose a number: 4
$
```

Listing 8.1 shows the code for our sorting and searching script:

LISTING 8.1 morenames.pl

```
#!/usr/local/bin/perl -w

%names = ();                        # hash of names
@raw = ();                          # raw words
$fn = "";                           # first name
$in = '';                           # temporary in
@keys = ();                         # temporary keys
@n = ();                            # temporary name
$search = '';                       # thing to search for

while (<>) {
    chomp;
    @raw = split(" ", $_);
    if ($#raw == 1) {  # regular case
        $names{$raw[1]} = $raw[0];
    } else {  # build a first name
        $fn = "";
        for ($i = 0; $i < $#raw; $i++) {
            $fn .= $raw[$i] . " ";
        }
        $names{$raw[$#raw]} = $fn;
    }
}

while () {
    print "\n1. Sort names by last name\n";
    print "2. Sort names by first name\n";
    print "3. Search for a name\n";
    print "4. Quit\n\n";
    print "Choose a number: ";

    if ($in eq '1') {           # sort and print by last name
        foreach $name (sort keys %names) {
            print "$name, $names{$name}\n";
        }

    } elsif ($in eq '2') {      # sort and print by first name
        @keys = sort { $names{$a} cmp $names{$b} } keys %names;
        foreach $name (@keys) {
            print "$names{$name} $name\n";
        }
    } elsif ($in eq '3') {      # find a name (1 or more)
        print "Search for what? ";
        chomp($search = <STDIN>);

        while (@n = each %names) {
```

LISTING 8.1 continued

```
47:             if (grep /$search/, @n) {
48:                 $keys[++$#keys] = $n[0];
49:             }
50:         }
51:
52:         if (@keys) {
53:             print "Names matched: \n";
54:             foreach $name (sort @keys) {
55:                 print "    $names{$name} $name\n";
56:             }
57:         } else {
58:             print "None found.\n";
59:         }
60:
61:         @keys = ();  # undefine @keys for next search
62:     } elsif ($in eq '4') {      # quit
63:        last;
64:     } else {
65:        print "Not a good answer.  1 to 4 please.\n";
66:     }
67: }
```

The basic framework of this script is the large `while` loop that manages the choices, from 1 to 4. After printing the choices and prompting for one, the `while` loop contains a set of statements to test for each answer. If the answer was not 1, 2, 3, or 4 (and we test for the string versions of these numbers, so that an errant letter won't produce warnings), the final `else` in line 64 will handle that and repeat from the top.

The framework itself is just a bunch of tests and not worth a detailed description. What happens at each option is much more interesting. The two sorting options (options 1 and 2, starting in lines 35 and 41, respectively) each use different forms of the `sort` function you've learned about previously in this lesson. The first option, to search for something in the names, uses `grep` to find it.Let's look at the two sorting options first. Our names hash is keyed by last name, so sorting the list by last name is easy. In fact, the `foreach` loop in line 32 through 37 is the same `foreach` loop we used for previous versions of this example.

Sorting by first name, the second option involves sorting the hash by the values, which is more difficult. Fortunately, I just showed you how to do this in the section on sorting, so you can use the technique I showed you there in lines 37 through 41. Build a temporary list of the keys with a `sort` routine that compares the values, and then to use those keys to print out the names in the right order.

Which brings us to the search. We'll start in lines 43 and 44 by prompting for the search key, storing it in the `$search` variable.

At first glance, you might think doing this search is easy—just use the `grep` function with the characters the user entered as the pattern. But the catch here is that we're searching a hash, and there are both keys and values to keep track of.

If all we wanted to search was the last names, we could just use the keys function to extract the keys and search them, like this:

```
@matches = grep /$search/, keys %names;
```

To get at the values, we could use a `foreach` loop to loop through the keys, and then test the pattern against both the key and the value in turn. And there would be nothing wrong with that approach, but in this particular example I wanted to use `grep`, so I took what might look like a rather unusual approach (I prefer to think of it as a *creative* approach). I used the `each` function, which you learned about on Day 5, which gives you a list of a key/value pair. With that list, you can then use `grep`, and if it matches, store the key for printing later.

That's what I'm doing in lines 46 through 50. Let's look at those lines more closely:

```
46: while (@n = each %names) {
47:     if (grep /$search/, @n) {
48:         $keys[++$#keys] = $n[0];
49:     }
50: }
```

The `each` function gives you a two-element list of a key and a value from the hash. Calling `each` multiple times eventually works its way through all the keys and values in the hash. So, in line 54, this `while` loop will iterate as many times as there are key/value pairs in the hash, assigning each pair to the list in `@n`. When there are no more pairs to examine, `@n` will get the empty list `()` and the `while` will stop.

Inside the `while` loop, we use an `if` test and `grep` to test for the search pattern in our simple key/value list. Here we're using `grep` in a scalar context, so if `grep` finds anything, it'll return a nonzero number, and the `if` test will be true. Otherwise, it'll return 0 and we'll skip to the next iteration of the `while`.

Line 55 is where we store the key if `grep` was able to find something that matched the search pattern, by simply appending the key to the end of the `@keys` array. This line is one of those examples of convoluted Perl, so let's look at it more closely:

```
$keys[++$#keys] = $n[0];
```

Remember that `@n` contains two elements, a key and a value. At this point in the script, either the key or the value have matched, so we'll store the key in the `@keys` array (storing the key will give us access to the value, so we don't have to worry about that). `$n[0]` gives us that matched key.

Next step is to assign that value to the end of the `@keys` array. Remember that `$#keys` gives us the highest index position in the array, so `++$#keys` refers to the position just after that last one. Note that the increment is done in prefix notation, so we can increment that element before we assign anything to it. We can then use that new highest index position as the position in which to assign the key.

Whew! This line is one of those examples where you can cram a whole lot of information into a single line, and unless you understand each and every character, it'll take a while to decipher it. Fortunately, if this sort of syntax makes your head spin, there's a much easier way to add an element onto the end of a list, using the `push` function, which we'll look at later in this lesson.

After the list of matched keys has been built, all that's left is to print them. In this case, we'll test first to see if `@keys` has any elements (line 60), and if so, the script sorts and prints them. Otherwise, it prints a helpful message (line 66).

Modifying List Elements

You can always add and remove list, array, and hash elements using the methods I described on Days 4 and 5. But sometimes the standard ways of adding and removing elements from lists can be awkward, hard to read, or inefficient. To help with modifying lists, Perl provides a number of built-in functions, including

- `push` and `pop`: add and remove list elements from the end of a list.
- `shift` and `unshift`: add and remove list elements from the start of a list.
- `splice`: add or remove elements anywhere in a list.

`push` and `pop`

The `push` and `pop` functions allow you to add or remove elements from the end of a list, that is, it affects the highest index positions of that list. Both `push` and `pop` will be familiar functions if you've ever worked with stacks, where the notion is that the first element in is the last element out. If you haven't dealt with stacks before, envision one of those spring-loaded plate dispensers you sometimes see in cafeterias. You add plates to the dispenser (push them onto the stack), but the top plate is always the one you use first (pop them off of the stack). So it is with `push` and `pop` and arrays: pushing adds an element to the end of the list, and popping removes an element from the end of the list.

The `push` function takes two arguments: a list to be modified, and a list of elements to be added. The original list is modified in place, and `push` returns the number of elements in the newly modified list. So, for example, in `morenames.pl` from the previous section, we used this ugly bit of code to add a key to the `@keys` array:

```
$keys[++$#keys] = $n[0];
```

That same bit could be written with `push` like this:

```
push @keys, $n[0];
```

Fewer characters, yes, and also conceptually easier to figure out. Note that the second argument here is a scalar (which is then converted to a list of one element), but the second argument can itself be a list, which lets you combine multiple lists easily like this:

```
push @final, @list1;
```

The `pop` function does the reverse of `push`; it removes the last element from the list or array. The `pop` function takes one argument (the list to change), removes the last element, and returns that element:

```
$last = pop @array;
```

As with `push`, the list is modified in place and will have one less element after the `pop`. A convoluted way of moving elements from one array to another might look like this:

```
while (@old) {
   push @new, pop @old;
}
```

Note that with this bit of code the new array will be in the reverse order because the last element is the first to get pushed onto the new array. A better way of reversing a list is to use the `reverse` function instead, and a better way of moving one list to another is simply to use assignment. You could, however use this mechanism to modify each element as it gets passed from one element to the other:

```
while (@old) {
   push @new, 2 * pop @old;
}
```

`shift` and `unshift`

If `push` and `pop` add or remove elements from the end of the list, wouldn't it be nice to have functions that add or remove elements from the *beginning* of the list? No problem! `shift` and `unshift` do just that, shifting all elements one position up or down (or, as is more commonly envisioned with `shift` and `unshift`, left and right). As with `push` and `pop`, the list is modified in place.

The `shift` function takes a single argument, a list, and removes the first element from that list, moving all the remaining elements down (left) one position. It returns the element it removed. So, for example, this bit of code moves elements from one array to another, but this example doesn't reverse the list in the process:

```
while (@old) {
   push @new, shift @old;
}
```

The `unshift` function is the beginning-of-list equivalent to `push`. It takes two arguments: the list to modify and the list to add. The new list contains the added elements, and then the old elements in the list, shifted as many places upward as there were elements added. The `unshift` function returns the number of elements in the new list:

```
$numusers = unshift @users, @newusers;
```

splice

`push` and `pop` modify the elements at the end of a list, `shift` and `unshift` do the same thing at the beginning. The `splice` function, however, is a much more general-purpose way to add, remove, or replace elements at any position inside the list. `splice` takes up to four arguments:

- The array to be modified
- The point (position, or offset) in that array to add or remove elements after
- The number of elements to remove or replace. If this argument isn't included, `splice` will change every element from the offset forward.
- The list of elements to add to the array, if any.

Let's start with removing elements from an array using `splice`. For each of these examples, let's assume a list of ten elements, 0 to 9:

```
@nums = 0 .. 9;
```

To remove elements 5, 6, and 7, you would use an offset of 5 and a length of 3. There's no list argument because we're not adding anything:

```
splice(@nums, 5, 3);  # results in (0,1,2,3,4,8,9)
```

To remove all elements from position 5 to the end of the list, leave off the length argument:

```
splice(@nums, 5);  # results in (0,1,2,3,4)
```

To replace elements, add a list of the elements to replace to the `splice`. For example, to replace elements 5, 6, and 7 with the elements `"five"`, `"six"`, and `"seven"`, use this code:

```
splice(@nums, 5, 3, qw(five six seven)); # results in (0,1,2,3,4,
                                         # "five","six","seven",8,9)
```

Perl doesn't care whether you're removing the same number of elements as you're adding; it'll just add the elements in the list at the position given by the offset, and move all the other elements out of the way (or shrink the array to fit). So, for example, here's a call to `splice` to delete elements 5, 6, and 7, and add the word `"missing"` in their place:

```
splice(@nums, 5, 3, "missing"); # results in (0,1,2,3,4,"missing",8,9);
```

The new array, in that latter case, will contain only eight elements.

To add elements to the array without also removing elements, use 0 for the length. For example, here's a call to `splice` that adds a couple numbers after element 5:

```
splice(@nums, 5, 0, (5.1, 5.2, 5.3)); # results in
(0,1,2,3,4,5,5.1,5.2,5.3,6.7.8.9)
```

The `splice` function, as with the other list modification functions, modifies the list it's working on in place. It also returns a list of the elements it removed. You can use the latter feature to break up a list into several parts. For example, let's say you had a list of some number of elements, `@rawlist`, that you want broken up into two lists, `@list1` and `@list2`. The first element in `@rawlist` is the number of elements that should be in `@list1`; the second final list will then contain any remaining elements. You might use code similar to this, where the first line extracts the appropriate elements from `@rawlist` and stored them in `@list1`, the second removes the first element (the number of elements) from `@rawlist`, and the third stores the remaining elements in `@list2`.

```
@list1 = splice(@rawlist, 1, $rawlist[0]);
shift @rawlist;
@list2 = @rawlist;
```

Other Ways to Mess with Lists

But wait, that's not all. I've got a couple more functions that are useful for modifying and playing with lists: `reverse`, `join`, and `map`.

`reverse`

The `reverse` function takes each element of a list and turns it blue. Just kidding. `reverse`, as you might expect, reverses the order of the elements in the list:

```
@otherway = reverse @list;
```

Note that if you're sorting a list, or moving elements around using `shift`, `unshift`, `push`, or `pop`, you can use those methods to create reversed lists without having to reverse them using `reverse` (try to avoid moving array elements around more than you have to).

The `reverse` function also works with scalars, in which case it reverses the order of characters in a scalar. We'll come back to this in "Manipulating Strings," later in this chapter.

join

The `split` function splits a string into a list. The `join` function does just the reverse: It combines list elements into a string, with any characters you want in between them. So, for example, if you had split a line of numbers into a list using this `split` command:

```
@list = split(' ', "1 2 3 4 5 6 7 8 9 10");
```

you could put them back into a string, with each number separated by a space, like this:

```
$string = join(' ', @list);
```

Or, you could separate each element with plus signs like this:

```
$string = join('+',@list);
```

Or, with no characters at all:

```
$string = join('',@list);
```

Let's look at a practical application of `join`. If you wanted to turn a list into an HTML list, you could use the following code:

```
print ''<ul><li>'', join(''</li><li>'', @list), ''</li></ul>'';
```

If you're concatenating a lot of strings, it's more efficient to use the join function than to use the `.` operator. Simply include an empty string as the separator, like this:

```
$new_string = join '', ('one', 'two', 'three', 'four');
```

map

Earlier, you learned about `grep`, which is used to extract elements from a list for which an expression or pattern returns true. The `map` function operates in a similar way, except that instead of selecting particular elements from a list, `map` executes a given expression or block on each element in a list, and then collects the results of each expression into a new list.

For example, let's say you had a list of numbers, 1 to 10, and you wanted to build a list of the squares of all those numbers. You could use a `foreach` loop and `push`, like this:

```
foreach $num (1 .. 10) {
   push @squares, (@num**2);
}
```

The same operation in `map` might look like this:

```
@num = (1..10);
@squares = map { $_**2 } @num;
```

Like `grep`, `map` takes each element in the list and assigns it to `$_`. Then, also like `grep`, it evaluates the expression. Unlike `grep`, it stores the result of that expression into the new list, regardless of whether it evaluates to true or not. Depending on how you write the expression, however, you can pass anything you want to the new list, including nothing, some value other than the original list item in `$_`, or even multiple items. Consider `map` to be a filter for each of the list items, in which the result of the filter can be anything you want it to be.The "filter" part of the map can be either a single expression or a block. If you're using a single expression, the value that gets returned at each turn of the map is simply the result of that expression. If you're using a block, the return value is the last expression that gets evaluated inside that block—so make sure you have an expression at the end that returns the value you're looking for. For example, here's a call to `map` that takes a list of numbers. It replaces any negative numbers with zero, and replaces all incidences of the number 5 with two numbers: 3 and 2. I've also formatted this version of `map` so that it's easier to read; there's no requirement for the code in either `map` or `grep` to be all on one line:

```
@final = map {
    if ($_ < 0) {
        0;
    } elsif ($_ == 5) {
        (3,2);
    } else { $_; }
} @nums;
```

This "last thing evaluated" behavior is actually a general rule for how blocks behave. You'll learn more about it when we get to subroutines on Day 11, "Creating and Using Subroutines."

If you want to use an expression rather than a block, you need to include a comma between the two arguments to `map`. If you have an array of strings and you want to remove the line feeds from the end of each of the strings, you can use map as follows:

```
@new = map chomp, @old;
```

There's no rule that says the expression or block has to return a single, scalar value either. If an array is returned, then the entire array will be inserted in the new array where the original element was. Here's an example:

```
@old = ('one two', 'three four');
@new = map { split " "; } @old;
print scalar @new;
```

This snippet will print out the number 4 because the `@new` array now contains four items. Both of the original elements will be split into lists of two items, which will be inserted into the new list that the `map` function generates.

Manipulating Strings

In the bulk of this lesson, we've explored ways you can manipulate lists and list contents with various built-in functions. Perl also has several useful functions for manipulating strings as well (and I summarized a number of these on Day 2). In this section, let's cover a few of these functions, including `reverse`, `index`, `rindex`, and `substr`.

Each of these functions is used to modify strings. In many cases, it might be easier or more efficient to modify strings using other mechanisms—concatenating them using the `.` operator, building them with variable values using variable interpolation, or searching and extracting substrings with patterns (as you'll learn in the next few days). But in many cases, these functions might be conceptually easier to use, particularly if you're used to similar string-manipulation functions from other languages.

`reverse`

You've already seen the `reverse` function, as used with lists, which reverses the order of elements in the list. `reverse`, when used in a scalar context, behaves differently: It reverses all the characters in the number or string.

> **Note**
>
> With a single string like "To be or not to be" or "antidisestablishmentarianism," you'll end up with new strings that simply have all the characters reversed. Note, however, that if the strings you're reversing have newlines at the end, that the reversed strings will have those newlines at the beginning of the string (creating somewhat puzzling results). If you don't want the newline to be reversed, don't forget to `chomp` it first.

The different behaviors of `reverse` in list and scalar context can sometimes be confusing. Take, for example, this bit of code:

```
foreach $string (@list) {
   push @reversed, reverse $string;
}
```

Offhand, that bit of code looks like it takes all the string elements in the `@list` array, reverses each one, and then pushes the result onto the `@reversed` array. But if you run that code, the contents of `@reversed` appear to be exactly the same as the contents of `@list`. Why? The `push` function takes a list as its second argument, so `reverse` is called in a list context, not a scalar context. The string in `$string` is then interpreted as a list of one element, which, when reversed, still contains the one element. The characters inside that element aren't even touched. To fix this, all you need is the `scalar` function:

```
foreach $string (@list) {
   push @reversed, scalar (reverse $string);
}
```

index and rindex

The index and rindex functions are used to find substrings inside other strings. Given two strings (one to look in and one to search for), they return the position of the second string inside the first, or -1 if the substring was not found. Positions are marked between characters, with 0 at the start of the string. So, for example, you could create a grep-like bit of code with index or rindex like this:

```
foreach $str (@list) {
   if ((index $str, $key) != -1) {
      push @final, $str;
}
```

The difference between index and rindex is in where the function starts looking. The index function begins from the start of the string and finds the position of the first occurrence of that string; rindex starts from the end of the string and finds the position of the last occurrence of that string.

Both index and rindex can take an optional third argument, indicating the position inside the string to start looking for the substring. So, for example, if you had already found a match using one call to index, you could call index again and start looking where you left off.

substr

The substr function is shorthand for substring, and can be used to extract characters from or add characters to a string—although it's most common usage is to extract substrings of other strings. The substr takes up to three arguments:

- The string to act on
- The position (offset) of the start of the substring to extract or replace. You can use a negative number to start counting from the end of the string.
- The length of the substring to extract or replace. If the length isn't included, substr will change the substring from the offset to the end of the string.

The substr function returns the characters it removed (it does *not* modify the original string). So, for example, to extract characters 5 through 8 in the string $longstring, and store them in $newstr, use this line:

```
$newstr = substr($longstring, 5, 3);
```

To create a new string that replaces characters or adds characters to another string, use the substr function on the left side of an assignment. The string you use on the right can be larger or smaller than the string you replace; Perl doesn't care:

```
substr($longstring, 5, 3) = "parthenogenesis";
```

If you wanted to search for and replace a substring everywhere in another string, you might use a `while` loop, `index`, and `substr` like this:

```
$str = "This is a test string.  The string we want to change.";
$pos = 0;
$key = 'i';
$repl = "*";

while ($pos < (length $str) and $pos != -1) {
    $pos = index($str, $key, $pos);

    if ($pos != -1 ) {
        substr($str,$pos,length $key) = $repl;
        $pos++;
    }
}
```

Don't become overly attached to this code, however; there are a number of ways to do this sort of operation using much less code. In particular, Perl's regular expressions enable you to compress that entire loop into one line:

```
$str =~ s/$key/$repl/g;
```

Going Deeper

In this lesson, I've shown you how to use many of the more popular functions for modifying or mangling lists and strings. And, in turn, I've only described the more common uses of these functions. If you're interested in more detail about any of these functions, or about any functions I haven't described in this book, see Appendix A or the `perlfunc` man page.

Some of the functions in this chapter have features I didn't talk about, mostly because they involve things you haven't learned yet. For example, the sorting routine for the `sort` function (the part inside the curly brackets) can be replaced with an actual subroutine name, which allows you to use that subroutine in many different places and to write quite sophisticated `sort` routines indeed.

The `pop` and `shift` functions, in turn, can also be used with no arguments. What list they affect depends on where in your script they're used: `pop` and `shift` with no arguments in the main body of the script pops or shifts the `@ARGV` array (containing the arguments to the script); `pop` and `shift` inside a subroutine affect the `@_` argument list to that subroutine (which you'll learn about when we get to Day 11, "Creating and Using Subroutines").

Summary

Learning the Perl language involves learning much more than just the syntax of the core language; the built-in functions provide a lot of the cooler functionality and the power of Perl scripts. Although many of the functions accomplish things in the language that can be better done some other way, others are useful to at least have around for specific cases. The functions you've learned about in this lesson are like that; most everything you've learned here can be done in some other way, although sometimes that other way might be longer, less efficient, or harder to figure out.

Today, then, you learned about the various functions you can use to modify lists and strings, and the ways to use these functions to accomplish simple tasks. You also learned about array and hash slices, which, although they aren't actually functions, give you a method for extracting elements out of a list or hash.

The functions you've learned about today include

- `sort`, for sorting lists
- `grep`, for extracting list elements that match a criteria such as a pattern
- `push` and `pop`, for adding or removing list elements to the end of a list
- `shift` and `unshift`, for adding and removing list elements to the beginning of a list
- `splice`, for adding, removing or replacing elements from anywhere in a list
- `reverse`, to reverse the order of elements in the list, or, in scalar context, for reversing the order of the characters in a string
- `join`, the reverse of `split`, for combining list elements into a string with one or more characters between them
- `map`, for performing some operation on each element of a list and building a new list of the results
- `index` and `rindex`, for finding the position of a given string in another string
- `substr`, for removing, adding, or replacing one string with another

Q&A

Q. Most of the functions you described on this lesson seem to work only with lists. Can I use them with hashes as well?

A. Hashes and lists are interchangeable in the sense that a hash will be unwound into its component parts when used as a list, and then the elements will be paired up into keys and values when the list becomes a hash again. So technically, yes, you can use many of these functions with hashes. The result, however, might not be what you expect and might not be very useful. For example, the `pop` function on a hash will unwind the hash into a list, and then `pop` off the last item in that list (the last key in the hash)—but since you don't know what order the hash's keys will appear in, the result is unpredictable at best. Better to use hash slices or the `delete` function to modify hashes, or use these functions on lists of the keys or values.

Q. I'm trying to use `reverse` on a list of strings. They're not reversing; it's like I never called the function.

A. Are you sure you're using the `reverse` function on a string, and not on a list of one element? A list of one element is still a list, and the `reverse` function will happily `reverse` that list for you—giving you the same string you put into it. Make sure you're calling `reverse` in a scalar context, and if you're not, change the context with a different bit of code or with the `scalar` function.

Q. In a previous lesson, you described the `$"` variable, which is used to set the separator character for list elements. It shows up when you interpolate a list inside a string. How is the `join` function different from this technique?

A. If you're looking at the end result, it's not. Both will provide a way of "flattening" a list into a string with some character in between each of the list elements. The `join` function, however, is more efficient for this purpose because the string in question doesn't have to be interpolated for variables before it's expanded.

Workshop

The workshop provides quiz questions to help you solidify your understanding of the material covered and exercises to give you experience in using what you've learned. Try and understand the quiz and exercise answers before you go on to tomorrow's lesson.

Quiz

1. What is a slice? How does a slice affect the original list?
2. What are the `$a` and `$b` variables used for in `sort` routines?
3. What do the `<=>` and `cmp` operators do? What is the difference between them?
4. The `grep` function takes an expression or a block as its first argument. What is this block used for?
5. How can you use `splice` to add elements to an array? Replace two elements with a list of four elements?
6. How can you return a value from the block in `map`?

Exercises

1. Rewrite the following expressions using `splice`:

```
push @list, 1;
push @list, (2,3,4);
$list[5] = "foo";
shift @list;
```

2. BUG BUSTERS: What's wrong with this code (HINT: there might be multiple errors)?

```
while ($i <= $#list) {
   $str = @novel[$i++];
   push @final, reverse $str;
}
```

3. BUG BUSTERS: How about this code?

```
while ($pos < (length $str) and $pos != -1) {
    $pos = index($str, $key, $pos);

    if ($pos != -1 ) {
        $count++;
    }
}
```

4. Write a version of this expression using a `foreach` loop and `push`:

```
@list2 = grep {$_ < 5 } @list;
```

5. Write a script that prompts you for a string and a character, and then returns the number of times that character occurs in the string. Use the `index` function.
6. Rewrite the script in #5 without using `index` (or patterns, if you already know something of patterns). Hint: try using `grep`.

Answers

Here are the answers to the Workshop questions in the previous section.

Quiz Answers

1. A slice is some subset of the elements in an array or hash. Slices do not affect the original list; they copy the sliced elements into the new list. Compare with elements extracted using `splice`, where the original array or list is permanently changed.
2. The `$a` and `$b` variables in a `sort` routine are local to that routine and refer to two list elements being compared. Use `$a` and `$b` to write your `sort` routines to do what you want.

3. The `<=>` and `cmp` operators take two operands and return -1 if the first is less than the second, 0 if the two are equal, and 1 if the first is larger than the second. Although this behavior might not seem overly useful in ordinary use, these operators work exceptionally well for `sort` routines, which need exactly that kind of output to sort the elements in a list.

   The difference between `<=>` and `cmp` is the same as the difference between `==` and `eq`; the former is used for numbers, the latter for strings.

4. The expression or block as an argument to `grep` is used as a test to determine whether a particular list element (as stored in `$_`) will be saved in the final list `grep` returns. If the expression or block returns true, the list element is saved.

5. Add elements to an array with `splice` by using a length argument (the third argument) of 0. This will remove no elements, and add the new elements at the position specified by the offset:

   ```
   splice(@array, 0, 0, (1,2,3,4); # add (1,2,3,4) at the start of the array
   ```

   To replace two items with four items, use 2 as the length argument, and the items to add as a list:

   ```
   splice(@array, 0, 2, (1,2,3,4); # remove first two elements and replace
   with (1,2,3,4)
   ```

6. To return a value from the block of expressions in `map`, make sure the last thing to be evaluated in the block is the thing you want to return (and therefore to be passed onto the new list).

Exercise Answers

1. Here are the answers:

   ```
   splice(@list, $#list+1, 0, 1);
   splice(@list, $#list+1, 0, (2,3,4));
   splice(@list, 5, 1, "foo");
   splice(@list, 0, 1);
   ```

2. There are multiple bugs and conceptual errors in this snippet of code. The first is in the second line; the array access expression here is actually an array `splice`, so you'll end up with an array of one element instead of an actual string. Perl warnings will catch this one.

   But even if you fix that error, the string will not be reversed, because in the third line `reverse` is being called in a list context, so the string is interpreted as a list of one element. Use the `scalar` function to create a scalar context for `reverse`.

3. At some point inside the loop, you have to increment the current position. Otherwise, the loop will continue to find the same substring at the same position, over and over again, and turn into an infinite loop.

4. Here's one answer:

```
foreach (@list) {
   if ($_ < 5) {
       push @list2, $_;
   }
}
```

5. Here's one answer:

```
#!/usr/bin/perl -w

$str = '';
$key = '';
$pos = 0;
$count = 0;

print "Enter the string to search: ";
chomp($str = <STDIN>);
print "Enter the character to count: ";
chomp($key = <STDIN>);

while ($pos < (length $str) and $pos != -1) {
    $pos = index($str, $key, $pos);

    if ($pos != -1 ) {
        $count++;
        $pos++;
    }
}

print "$key appears in the string $count times.\n";
```

6. Here's one answer:

```
#!/usr/bin/perl -w

$str = '';
$key = '';
$pos = 0;
$count = 0;

print "Enter the string to search: ";
chomp($str = <STDIN>);
print "Enter the character to count: ";
chomp($key = <STDIN>);

@chars = split('',$str);
$count = grep {$_ eq $key} @chars;

print "$key appears in the string $count times.\n";
```

The sneaky part about this example is the line that uses `split` to convert the string into a list of characters. After you have a list using `grep` is easy.

WEEK 2

DAY 9

Pattern Matching with Regular Expressions

As I'm sure you've noticed, I've been gradually introducing regular expressions since nearly the beginning of this book. In this lesson, it's time to focus our full attention on how regular expressions work. Pattern matching is more than just searching for some set of characters in your data; it's a way of looking at data and processing that data in a manner that can be incredibly efficient and amazingly easy to program. Many Perl programmers use regular expressions in nearly every program that they write.

Today, we'll dive deep into regular expressions, why they're useful, how they're built, and how they work. Tomorrow we'll continue the discussion and cover more advanced uses of regular expressions. Today, specifically, you'll learn

- Understanding pattern matching and regular expressions and why you'll find them useful
- Building simple regular expressions with single-character searches and pattern-matching operators

- Matching groups of characters
- Matching multiple instances of characters
- Using patterns in tests and loops

The Whys and Wherefores of Pattern Matching

Pattern matching is the technique of searching a string containing text or binary data for some set of characters based on a specific search pattern. When you search for a string of characters in a file using the Find command in your word processor, or when you use a search engine to look for something on the Web, you're using a simple version of pattern matching: your criteria is "find these characters." In those environments, you can often customize your criteria in particular ways, for example, to search for this or that, to search for this or that but not the other thing, to search for whole words only, or to search only for those words that are 12 points and underlined. As you've seen from the regular expressions I've already explained, pattern matching in Perl, however, can be even more complicated than that. Using Perl, you can define an incredibly specific set of search criteria, and do it in an incredibly small amount of space using a pattern-definition minilanguage called *regular expressions*.

Perl's regular expressions, often called just *regexps* or *REs*, borrow from the regular expressions used in many Unix tools, such as `grep(1)` and `sed(1)`. As with many other features Perl has borrowed from other places, however, Perl includes slight changes and lots of added capabilities. If you're used to using regular expressions, you'll be able to pick up Perl's regular expressions fairly easily because most of the same rules apply (although there are some gotchas to be aware of, particularly if you've used sophisticated regular expressions in the past).

The term *regular expressions* might seem sort of nonsensical. They don't really seem to be expressions, nor is it easy to figure out what's regular about them. Don't get hung up on the term itself; *regular expression* is a term borrowed from mathematics that refers to the actual language with which you write patterns for pattern matching in Perl.

I used the example of the search engine and the Find command earlier to describe the sorts of things that pattern matching can do. It's important for you not to get hung up on thinking that pattern matching is only good for plain old searching. The sorts of things regular expressions can do in Perl include

- Making sure your user has entered the data you're looking for—input validation.
- Verifying that input is in the right specific format, for example, that e-mail addresses have the right components.
- Extracting parts of a file that match a specific criteria (for example, you could extract the headings from a file to build a table of contents, or extract all the links in an HTML file).
- Splitting a string into elements based on different separator fields (and often, complex nested separator fields).
- Finding irregularities in a set of data—multiple spaces that don't belong there, duplicated words, errors in formatting.
- Counting the number of occurrences of a pattern in a string.
- Searching and replacing—find a string that matches a pattern and replace it with some other string.

This is only a partial list, of course—you can apply Perl's regular expressions to all kinds of tasks. Generally, if there's a task for which you'd want to iterate over a string or over your data in another language, that task is probably better solved in Perl using regular expressions. Many of the operations you learned about yesterday for finding bits of strings can be better done with patterns.

Pattern Matching Operators and Expressions

Let me first start with a quick overview of the regular expression information I've already covered. To construct patterns that search a variable for a particular expression, you use two operators: the regular expression operator `m//` and the pattern-match operator `=~`, like this:

```
if ($string =~ m/foo/) {
   # do something...
}
```

As you know, that test simply checks whether the variable `$string` contains `foo`.

For these sorts of patterns, the `m` is optional and can be left off (and usually is). In addition, you can leave off the variable and the `=~` if you want to search the contents of the default variable `$_`. Commonly in Perl, you'll see shorthand pattern matching like this one:

```
if (/^\d+/) { # ...
```

Which is equivalent to

```
if ($_ =~ m/^\d+/)  { # ...
```

You learned a simple case of this yesterday with the `grep` function, which can use patterns to find a string inside the `$_` list element:

```
@foothings = grep /foo/, @strings;
```

That line, in turn, is equivalent to this long form:

```
@foothings = grep { $_ =~ /foo/ } @strings;
```

As we work through today's lesson, you'll learn different ways of using patterns in different contexts and for different reasons. Much of the work of learning pattern matching, however, involves actually learning the regular expression syntax to build patterns, so let's stick with this one situation for now.

Simple Patterns

We'll start with some of the most simple and basic patterns you can create: patterns that match specific sequences of characters, patterns that match only at specific places in a string, or combining patterns using what's called alternation.

Character Sequences

One of the simplest patterns is just a sequence of characters you want to match, like this:

```
/foo/
/this or that/
/   /
/Laura/
/patterns that match specific sequences/
```

All these patterns will match if the data contains those characters in that order. All the characters must match, including spaces. The word `or` in the second pattern doesn't have any special significance (it's not a logical `or`); that pattern will only match if the data contains the string `this or that` somewhere inside it.

Note that characters in patterns can be matched anywhere in a string. Word boundaries are not relevant for these patterns—the pattern `/if/` will match in the string "if wishes were horses" and in the string "there is no difference." The pattern `/if /`, however, because it contains a space, will only match in the first string where the characters `i`, `f`, and the one space occur in that order.

Upper and lowercase are relevant for characters: `/kazoo/` will only match `kazoo` and not `Kazoo` or `KAZOO`. To turn case sensitivety off in a particular search, you can use the `i` option after the pattern itself (the `i` indicates *ignore case*), like this:

```
/kazoo/i # search for any upper and lowercase versions
```

Alternately, you can also create patterns that will search for either upper or lowercase letters, as you'll learn about in the next section.

You can include most alphanumeric characters in patterns, including string escapes for binary data (octal and hex escapes). There are a number of characters that you cannot match without escaping them. These characters are called metacharacters and refer to bits of the pattern language and not to the literal character. These are the metacharacters to watch out for in patterns:

```
^    $
.    +
?    *
{    (
)    \
/    |
[
```

If you want to actually match a metacharacter in a string—for example, search for an actual question mark—you can escape it using a backslash, just as you would in a regular string:

```
/\?/  # matches question mark
```

Matching at Word or Line Boundaries

When you create a pattern to match a sequence of characters, those characters can appear anywhere inside the string and the pattern will still match. But sometimes you want a pattern to match those characters only if they occur at a specific place—for example, match `/if/` only when it's a whole word, or `/kazoo/` only if it occurs at the start of the line (that is, the beginning of the string).

Note

> I'm making an assumption here that the data you're searching is a line of input, where the line is a single string with no embedded newline characters. Given that assumption, the terms *string*, *line*, and *data* are effectively interchangeable. Tomorrow, we'll talk about how patterns deal with newlines.

To match a pattern at a specific position, you use pattern anchors. To anchor a pattern at the start of the string, use ^:

```
/^Kazoo/  # match only if Kazoo occurs at the start of the line
```

To match at the end of the string, use `$`:

```
/end$/  # match only if end occurs at the end of the line
```

Once again, think of the pattern as a sequence of things in which each part of the pattern must match the data you're applying it to. The pattern matching routines in Perl actually begin searching at a position just before the first character, which will match `^`. Then it moves to each character in turn until the end of the line, where `$` matches. If there's a newline at the end of the string, the position marked by `$` is just before that newline character.

So, for example, let's see what happens when you try to match the pattern `/^foo/` to the string "`to be or not to be`" (which, obviously, won't match, but let's try it anyhow). Perl starts at the beginning of the line, which matches the `^` character. That part of the pattern is true. It then tests the first character. The pattern wants to see an `f` there, but it got a `t` instead, so the pattern stops and returns false.

What happens if you try to apply the pattern to the string "`fob`"? The match will get farther—it'll match the start of the line, the `f` and the `o`, but then fail at the `b`. And keep in mind that `/^foo/` will not match in the string "`  foo`"—the `foo` is not at the very start of the line where the pattern expects it to be. It will only match when all four parts of the pattern match the string.

Some interesting but potentially tricky uses of `^` and `$`—can you guess what these patterns will match?

```
/^/
/^1$/
/^$/
```

The first pattern matches any strings that have a start of the line. It would be very weird strings indeed that didn't have the start of a line, so this pattern will match any string data whatsoever, even the empty string.

The second one wants to find the start of the line, the numeral `1`, and then the end of the line. So it'll only match if the string contains `1` and only `1`—it won't match "123" or "foo 1" or even " 1".

The third pattern will only match if the start of the line is immediately followed by the end of the line—that is, if there is no actual data. This pattern will only match an empty line. Keep in mind that because `$` occurs just before the newline character, this last pattern will match both "" and "\n".

Another boundary to match is a word boundary—where a word boundary is considered the position between a word character (a letter, number, or underscore) and some other character such as whitespace or punctuation. A word boundary is indicated using a `\b` escape. So `/\bif\b/` will match only when the whole word "`if`" exists in the string—but not when the characters `i` and `f` appear in the middle of a word (as in "difference."). You can use `\b` to refer to both the start and end of a word; `/\bif/`, for example, will match in both "if I were king" and "that result is iffy," and even in "As if!", but not in "bomb the aquifer" or "the serif is obtuse."

You can also search for a pattern not in a word boundary using the `\B` escape. With this, `/\Bif/` will match only when the characters `i` and `f` occur inside a word and *not* at the start of a word. Table 9.1 contains a list of boundaries.

TABLE 9.1 Boundaries

Boundary Character	*Matches*
^	The beginning of a string or line
$	The end of a string or line
\b	A word boundary
\B	Anything other than a word boundary

Matching Alternatives

Sometimes, when you're building a pattern, you might want to search for more than one pattern in the same string, and then test based on whether all the patterns were found, or perhaps any of the sets of patterns were found. You could, of course, do this with the regular Perl logical expressions for boolean AND (`&&` or `and`) and OR (`||` or `or`) with multiple pattern-matching expressions, something like this:

```
if (($in =~ /this/) || ($in =~ /that/)) { ...
```

Then, if the string contains `/this/` or if it contains `/that/`, the whole test will return true.

In the case of an OR search (match this pattern or that pattern—either one will work), however, there is a regular expression metacharacter you can use: the pipe character (`|`). So, for example, the long `if` test in that example could just be written as

```
if ($in =~ /this|that/) { ...
```

Using the `|` character inside a pattern is officially known as *alternation* because it allows you to match alternate patterns. A true value for the pattern occurs if any of the alternatives match.

Any anchoring characters you use with an alternation character apply only to the pattern on the same side of the pipe. So, for example, the pattern `/^this|that/` means "`this` at the start of the line" or "`that` anywhere," and not "either `this` or `that` at the start of a line." If you wanted the latter form you could use `/^this|^that/`, but a better way is to group your patterns using parentheses:

```
/^(this|that)/
```

For this pattern, Perl first matches the start of the line, and then tries to match all the characters in "`this`." If it can't match "`this`," it'll then back up to the start of the line and try to match "`that`." For a pattern line `/^this|that/`, it'll first try and match everything on the left side of the pipe (start of line, followed by `this`), and if it can't do that, it'll back up and search the entire string for "`that`."

An even better version would be to group only the things that are different between the two patterns, not just the ^ to match the beginning of the line, but also the `th` characters, like this:

```
/^th(is|at)/
```

This last version means that Perl won't even try the alternation unless `th` has already been matched at the start of the line, and then there will be a minimum of backing up to match the pattern. With regular expressions, the less work Perl has to do to match something, the better.

You can use grouping for any kinds of alternation within a pattern. For example, `/(1st|2nd|3rd|4th) time/` will match "1st time," "2nd time," and so on—as long as the data contains one of the alternations inside the parentheses and the string " time" (note the space).

Matching Groups of Characters

So far, so good? The regular expressions we've been building so far shouldn't strike you as being that complex, particularly if you look at each pattern in the way Perl does, character by character and alternate by alternate, taking grouping into effect. Now we're going to start looking at some of the shortcuts that regular expressions provide for describing and grouping various kinds of characters.

Character Classes

Say you had a string, and you wanted to match one of five words in that string: `pet`, `get`, `met`, `set`, and `bet`. You could do this:

```
/pet|get|met|set|bet/
```

That would work. Perl would search through the whole string for `pet`, then search through the whole string for `get`, then do the same thing for `met`, and so on. A shorter way—both for number of characters for you to type and for Perl—would be to group characters so that we don't duplicate the `et` part each time:

```
/(p|g|m|s|b)et/
```

In this case, Perl searches through the entire string for `p`, `g`, `m`, `s`, or `b`, and if it finds one of those, it'll try to match `et` just after it. Much more efficient!

This sort of pattern—where you have lots of alternates of single characters, is such a common case that there's regular expression syntax for it. The set of alternating characters is called a *character class*, and you enclose it inside brackets. So, for example, that same pet/get/met pattern would look like this using a character class:

```
/[pgmsb]et/
```

That's a savings of at least a couple of characters, and it's even slightly easier to read. Perl will do the same thing as the alternation character, in this case it'll look for any of the characters inside the character class before testing any of the characters outside it.

The rules for the characters that can appear inside a character class are different from those that can appear outside of one—most of the metacharacters become plain ordinary characters inside a character class (the exception being a right-bracket, which needs to be escaped for obvious reasons, a caret (^), which can't appear first, or a hyphen, which has a special meaning inside a character class). So, for example, a pattern to match on punctuation at the end of a sentence (punctuation after a word boundary and before two spaces) might look like this:

```
/[.!?]  /
```

Although `.` and `?` have special meanings outside the character class, here they're plain old characters.

Ranges

What if you wanted to match, say, all the lowercase characters `a` through `f` (as you might in a hexadecimal number, for example). You could do

```
/[abcdef]/
```

Looks like a job for a range, doesn't it? You can do ranges inside character classes, but you don't use the range operator `..` that you learned about on Day 4. Regular expressions use a hyphen for ranges instead (which is why you have to backslash it if you actually want to match a hyphen). So, for example, lowercase `a` through `f` looks like this:

```
/[a-f]/
```

You can use any range of numbers or characters, as in `/[0-9]/`, `/[a-z]/`, or `/[A-Z]/`. You can even combine them: `/[0-9a-z]/` will match the same thing as `/[0123456789abcdefghijklmnopqrstuvwxyz]/`.

Negated Character Classes

Brackets define a class of characters to match in a pattern. You can also define a set of characters *not* to match using negated character classes—just make sure the first character in your character class is a caret (`^`). So, for example, to match anything that isn't an `A` or a `B`, use

```
/[^AB]/
```

Note that the caret inside a character class is not the same as the caret outside one. The former is used to create a negated character class, and the latter is used to mean the beginning of a line.

If you want to actually search for the caret character inside a character class, you're welcome to—just make sure it's not the first character or escape it (it might be best just to escape it either way to cut down on the rules you have to keep track of):

```
/[\^?.%]/   # search for ^, ?, ., %
```

You will most likely end up using a lot of negated character classes in your regular expressions, so keep this syntax in mind. Note one subtlety: Negated character classes don't negate the entire value of the pattern. If `/[12]/` means "return true if the data contains 1 or 2," `/[^12]/` does not mean "return true if the data *doesn't* contain 1 or 2." If that were the case, you'd get a match even if the string in question was empty. What negated character classes really mean is "match any character that's not these characters." There must be at least one actual character to match for a negated character class to work.

Special Classes

If character class ranges are still too much for you to type, you can use the character classes that were introduced in Chapter 5. You'll see these a lot in regular expressions, particularly those that match numbers in specific formats. Note that these special codes don't need to be enclosed between brackets; you can use them all by themselves to refer to that class of characters.

Table 9.2 shows the list of special character class codes:

TABLE 9.2 Character Class Codes

Code	*Equivalent Character Class*	*What It Means*
`\d`	`[0-9]`	Any digit
`\D`	`[^0-9]`	Any character not a digit
`\w`	`[0-9a-zA-z_]`	Any "word character"
`\W`	`[^0-9a-zA-z_]`	Any character not a word character
`\s`	`[ \t\n\r\f]`	whitespace (space, tab, newline, carriage return, form feed)
`\S`	`[^ \t\n\r\f]`	Any nonwhitespace character

Word characters (`\w` and `\W`) are a bit mystifying—why is an underscore considered a word character, but punctuation isn't? In reality, word characters have little to do with words, but are the valid characters you can use in variable names: numbers, letters, and underscores. Any other characters are not considered word characters.

You can use these character codes anywhere you need a specific type of character. For example, the `\d` code to refers to any digit. With `\d`, you could create patterns that match any three digits `/\d\d\d/`, or, perhaps, any three digits, a dash, and any four digits, to represent a phone number such as 555-1212: `/\d\d\d-\d\d\d\d/`. All this repetition isn't necessarily the best way to go, however, as you'll learn in a bit when we cover quantifiers.

Matching Any Character with . (Dot)

The broadest possible character class you can get is to match based on any character whatsoever. For that, you'd use the dot character (.). So, for example, the following pattern will match lines that contain one character and one character only:

```
/^.$/
```

You'll use the dot more often in patterns with quantifiers (which you'll learn about next), but the dot can be used to indicate fields of a certain width, for example:

```
/^..:/
```

This pattern will match only if the line starts with two characters and a colon.

More about the dot operator after we pause for an example.

Matching Multiple Instances of Characters

Ready for more? The second group of regular expression syntax to explore is quantifiers. The patterns you've seen up to now refer to individual things or groups of individual things, but quantifiers enable you to indicate multiple instances of things—or potentially no things. These regular expression metacharacters are called quantifiers because they indicate some quantity of characters or groups of characters in the pattern you're looking for.

Perl's regular expressions include three quantifier metacharacters: `?`, `*`, and `+`. Each refers to some multiple of the character or group that appears just before it in the pattern.

Optional Characters with `?`

Let's start with `?`, which matches a sequence that may or may not have the character immediately preceding it (that is, it matches zero or one instance of that character). So, for example, take this pattern:

```
/be?ar/
```

The question mark in that pattern refers to the character preceding it (`e`). This pattern would match with the string "step up to the bar" and with the string "grin and bear it"—because both "bar" and "bear" will match this pattern. The string you're searching must have the `b`, the `a`, and the `r`, but the `e` is optional.

Once again, think in terms of how the string is processed. The `b` is matched first. Then the next character is tested. If it's an `e`, no problem, we move on to the next character both in the string and in the pattern (the `a`). If it's not an `e`, that's still no problem, we move onto the next character in the pattern to see if it matches instead.

You can create groups of optional characters with parentheses:

```
/bamboo(zle)?/
```

The parentheses make that whole group of characters (`zle`) optional—this pattern will match both `bamboo` or `bamboozle`. The thing just before the `?` is the optional thing, be it a single character or a group.

Why bother creating a pattern like this? It would seem that the (`zle`) part of this pattern is irrelevant, and that just plain `/bamboo/` would work just as well, with fewer characters. In these easy cases, where we're just trying to find out whether something matches, yes or no, it doesn't matter. Tomorrow, when you learn how to extract the thing that matched and create more complex patterns, the distinction will be more important.

You can also use character classes with `?`:

```
/thing \d?/
```

This pattern will match the strings "thing 1," "thing 9," and so on, but will also match "thing " (note the space). Any character in the character class can appear either zero or one time for the pattern to match.

Matching Multiple Characters with *

A second form of multiplier is the `*`, which works similarly to the `?` except that `*` allows zero or any number of the preceding character to appear—not just zero or one instance as `?` does. Take this pattern:

```
/xy*z/
```

In this pattern, the x and the z are required, but the y can appear any number of times including not at all. This pattern will match `xyz`, `xyyz`, `xyyyyyyyyyyyyyyyyyz`, or just plain old `xz` without the y.

As with `?`, you can use groups or character classes before the `*`. One use of `*` is to use it with the dot character—which means that any number of any characters could appear at that position:

```
/this.*/
```

This pattern matches the strings "thisthat," "this is not my sweater. The blue one with the flowers is mine," or even just "this"—remember, the character at the end doesn't have to exist for there to be a match.

A common mistake is to forget that `*` stands for "zero or more instances," and to use it like this:

```
if (/^[0-9]*$/) {
    # contains numbers
}
```

The intent here is to create a pattern that matches only if the input contains numbers and only numbers. And this pattern will indeed match "7," "1540," "15443," and so on. But it'll also match the empty string—because the `*` means that no numbers whatsoever will also produce a match. Usually, when you want to require something to appear at least once, you want to use `+` instead of `*`.

Note also that "match zero or more numbers," as that example would imply, does not mean that it will match *any* string that happens to have zero numbers—it won't match the string "`lederhosen`," for example. Matching zero or more numbers does not imply any other matches; if you want it to match characters other than numbers, you'll need to include those characters in the pattern. With regular expressions, you have to be very specific about what you want to match.

Requiring at Least One Instance with +

The + metacharacter works identically to *, with one significant difference; instead of allowing zero or more instances of the given character or group, requires that character or group to appear at least once ("one or more instances."). So, given a pattern like the one we used for *:

```
/xy+z/
```

This pattern will match "xyz," "xyyz," "xyyyyyyyyyyz," but it will not match "xz." The y must appear at least once.

As with * and ?, you can use groups and character classes with +.

Restricting the Number of Instances

For both * and + the given character or group can appear any number of times—there is no upper limit (characters with ? can appear only once). But what if you want to match a specific number of instances? What if the pattern you're looking for does require a lower or upper limit, and any more or less than that won't match? You can use the optional curly bracket metacharacters to set limits on the quantity, like this:

```
/\d{1,4} /
```

This pattern matches if the data includes one digit, two digits, three digits, or four digits, any of them followed by a space; it won't match any more digits than that, nor will it match if there aren't any digits whatsoever. The first number inside the brackets is the minimum number of instances to match; the second is the maximum. Or you can match an exact number by just including the number itself:

```
/a{5}b/
```

This pattern will only match if it can find five a's in a row followed by one b—no more, no less. It's exactly equivalent to /aaaaab/. A less specific use of {} for an exact number of instances might be something like this:

```
/\$\d+\.\d{2}/
```

Can you work through this pattern and figure out what it matches? It uses a number of escaped characters, so it might be confusing. First, it matches a dollar sign (\$), then one or more decimals (\d+), then it matches a decimal point (.), and finally, it matches only if that pattern is followed by two digits and no more. Put it all together and this pattern matches monetary input—$45.23 would match just fine, as would $0.45 or $15.00, but $.45 and $34.2 would not. This pattern requires at least one number on the left side of the decimal, and exactly two numbers on the right.

Back to the curly brackets. You can set a lower bound on the match, but not an upper bound, by leaving off the maximum number but keeping the comma:

```
/ba{4,}t/
```

This pattern matches `b`, at least four instances of the letter `a`, and then `t`. Three instances of `a` in a row won't match, but twenty `a`'s will.

Note that you could represent `+`, `*`, and `?` in curly bracket format:

```
/x{0,1}/  # same as /x?/
/x{0,}/   # same as /x*/
/x{1,}/   # same as /x+/
```


An Example: A Guessing Program

Back in Lesson 6, there was an example program that implemented a number guessing game. In this example, we're going to turn things around and let the program try to guess what you entered. This program illustrates how you can use regular expressions to break down strings and figure out what they are.

The structure of the program is simple. It consists of an infinite while loop that continues to iterate until the `last` function is called. If the user enters 'q' on a line by itself, then the program will exit. Otherwise, it applies a number of regular expressions to the user's input to try to determine what sort of data was entered. If the input does not match any of the expressions, then a message indicating that no match was found is printed, and the program solicits more input.

The most interesting part of this program is the regular expressions themselves—the logic you've seen in several other examples in this book. Let's break each of them down so you can get an idea of how these regular expressions are used.

The first expression is simple, it checks to see whether the input is just male or female:

```
if ($value =~/^(male|female)$/i) {
    print "$value looks like a gender.\n";
    next;
}
```

First, I use one convention in this expression that holds true for all of the expressions in this example. The expression being tested begins with ^ and ends with $, indicating that the expression must match the entire string. This is true of all of the expressions in the program. We're not trying to extract data from the middle of strings, but rather to test entire strings to see whether they conform to a standard. This expression is simple, it checks to see whether the string contains "male" or "female," and uses the i switch to make the search case insensitive.

The next search is a bit more complex—it's used to search for a street address. It searches for a number, followed by a space, followed by a capital letter, followed any number of word characters or white space characters. Here's the expression:

```
if ($value =~ /^\d+\s[A-Z][\w\s]*$/) {
    print "$value looks like a street address.\n";
    next;
}
```

It will match things like `105 Locust`, as well as more complex strings like `10 South Street Plaza`. However, it will not match `10B West Main`, or even `2105 westheimer` (because the first letter is not capitalized). Breaking this down, we see several individual expressions. First, `\d+` is used to match at least one digit. Then, `\s` is used to match exactly one white space character. Next is `[A-Z]`, a character range that matches one capitalized letter. Finally any combination of whitespace or word characters is matched using `[\w\s]*`), which accounts for any sort of weird endings in the address (except incorrect use of punctuation).

The next snippet of code checks to see whether the value being evaluated is an e-mail address. Here it is:

```
if ($value =~ /^[\w.]+@\w[\w.-]+\w\.[A-Za-z]{2,4}$/) {
        print "$value looks like an email address.\n";
        next;
    }
```

Let's look at how this regular expression breaks down. First, I check for one or more word characters, or a period, followed by an @ sign. It then searches for a word character, followed by any number of word characters and periods, followed by a single word character, followed by a period, followed by two to four letters. This expression isn't perfect, but more often than not, it can tell the difference between a valid email address and something that isn't a valid email address. Let's look at why I used each expression after the at sign. First, the expression starts by searching for a single word character, which represents the beginning of the domain name. It ends with two to four letters, which represent the top level domain name. Before that is the period which separates the top level domain name from the rest of the domain name, and before that is the word character which is required at the end of the domain name (prior to the top level domain name). In the middle, any sequence of word characters, hyphens, and periods is allowed.

The next expression matches a typical city, state, and zip code:

```
if ($value =~ /^[A-Z][a-z]+,\s[A-Z]{2}\s{1,2}\d{5}$/) {
    print "$value looks like a city, state, and zip code.\n";
    next;
}
```

This expression is probably a bit more comprehensible than the e-mail address expression. It searches for a capital letter followed by some sequence of lowercase letters, which represent the city name. It then looks for a comma, followed by a white space character, which separate the city from the state. It then checks for two uppercase letters, which represent a state abbreviation. For greater accuracy, I could have included all 50 state abbreviations in an expression like:

```
(AK|AR|LA|TX|...)
```

One or two spaces can follow the state abbreviation, and then the program checks for a five digit number representing a Zip code. The next expression is the most complex, in fact, it spans two lines:

```
if ($value =~ /^\W{0,1}\d{3}\W{0,1}\s{0,1}
    \W{0,1}\s{0,1}\d{3}\s{0,1}\W{0,1}\s{0,1}\d{4}$/x) {
    print "$value looks like a telephone number.\n";
    next;
}
```

This expression is used to match phone numbers. It tries to account for a number of ways of formatting phone numbers—everything from `8005551212` to `(800) 555-1212`. It will even match something like `800/555/1212`. The key here is flexibility. The main thing is that it searches for 10 digits formatted in any way that could be taken to represent a telephone number. The complexity in this expression revolves around all of the optional characters.

First, I search for 0 or 1 non-word characters, so I can catch something like an opening parenthesis. Then I search for 3 digits, representing the area code. I follow that by searching for another nonword character, possibly representing a closing parenthesis. Then there's an optional white space character, which could separate the area code from the exchange. That's followed by an optional nonword character, followed by another optional white space character. The purpose here is to allow things like `800 - 555 - 1212`. Then, I match 3 digits representing the exchange. After that, I again match an optional space, an optional nonword character, and another optional space, finishing with a four digit number representing the extension. This is a /x expression, which means that white space is ignored so that it can span multiple lines.

The rest of the script is just a wrapper that loops and allows the user to enter values and have them tested. The full source listing is in Listing 9.1.

LISTING 9.1 The Source Code for the `values.pl` Script

```
#!/usr/local/bin/perl

print "Enter a value and this program will try to guess what type of\n";
print "value it is. Enter 'q' by itself on a line to quit.\n";
```

LISTING 9.1 continued

```
while () {
    print "Enter a value: ";
    chomp($value = <STDIN>);

    if ($value =~ /^$/) {
        print "Please enter a value.\n";
        next;
    }

    last if ($value =~ /^q$/i);

    if ($value =~/^(male|female)$/i) {
        print "$value looks like a gender.\n";
        next;
    }

    if ($value =~ /^\d+\s[A-Z][\w\s]*$/) {
        print "$value looks like a street address.\n";
        next;
    }

    if ($value =~ /^[\w.]+@\w[\w.-]+\w\.[A-Za-z]{2,4}$/) {
        print "$value looks like an email address.\n";
        next;
    }

    if ($value =~ /^[A-Z][a-z]+,\s[A-Z]{2}\s{1,2}\d{5}$/) {
        print "$value looks like a city, state, and zip code.\n";
        next;
    }

    if ($value =~ /^\W{0,1}\d{3}\W{0,1}\s{0,1}
                \W{0,1}\s{0,1}\d{3}\s{0,1}\W{0,1}\s{0,1}\d{4}$/x) {
        print "$value looks like a telephone number.\n";
        next;
    }

    if ($value =~ /^perl$/i) {
        print "$value looks like the name of a programming language.\n";
        next;
    }

    print "I couldn't figure out what that value is.\n";
}
```

More About Building Patterns

We started this lesson with a basic overview of how to use patterns in your Perl scripts using an if test and the =~ operator—or, if you're searching in $_, you can leave off the =~ part altogether. Now that you know something of constructing patterns with regular expression syntax, let's return to Perl, and look at some different ways of using patterns in your Perl scripts, including interpolating variables into patterns and using patterns in loops.

Patterns and Variables

In all the examples so far, we've used patterns as hard-coded sets of characters in the test of a Perl script. But what if you want to match different things based on some sort of input? How do you change the search pattern on the fly?

Easy. Patterns, like quotes, can contain variables, and the value of the variable is substituted into the pattern:

```
$pattern = "^\d{3}\$";
if (/$pattern/) { ...
```

The variable in question can contain a string with any kind of pattern, including metacharacters. You can use this technique to combine patterns in different ways, or to search for patterns based on input. For example, here's a simple script that prompts you for both a pattern and some data to search, and then returns true or false if there's a match:

```
#!/usr/bin/perl -w

print 'Enter the pattern: ';
chomp($pat = <STDIN>);

print 'Enter the string: ';
chomp($in = <STDIN>);

if ($in =~ /$pat/) { print "true\n"; }
else { print "false\n"; }
```

You might find this script (or one like it) useful yourself, as you learn more about regular expressions.

Patterns and Loops

One way of using patterns in Perl scripts is to use them as tests, as we have up to this point. In this context (a scalar boolean context), they evaluate to true or false based on whether the pattern matches the data. Another way to use a pattern is as the test in a loop, with the /g option at the end of the pattern, like this:

```
while (/pattern/g) {
  # loop
}
```

The /g option is used to match all the patterns in the given string (here, `$_`, but you can use the `=~` operator to match somewhere else). In an if test, the /g option won't matter, case the test will return true at the first match it finds. In the case of `while` (or a for loop), however, the /g will cause the test to return true each time the pattern occurs in the string—and the statements in the block will execute that number of times as well.

> We're still talking about using patterns in a scalar context, here; the /g just causes interesting things to happen in loops. We'll get to using patterns in list context tomorrow.

Another Example: Counting

Here's an example of a script that makes use of that patterns-in-loops feature I just mentioned to work through a file (or any numbers of files) and count the incidences of some pattern in that file. With this script you could, for example, count the number of times your name occurs in a file, or find out how many hits to your Web site came from America Online (`aol.com`). I ran it on a draft of this lesson and found that I've used the word *pattern* 184 times so far.

Listing 9.2 shows this simple script:

LISTING 9.2 `count.pl`

```
#!/usr/bin/perl -w

$pat = ""; # thing to search for
$count = 0; # number of times it occurs

print 'Search for what? ';
chomp($pat = <STDIN>);
while (<>) {
    while (/$pat/g) {
        $count++;
    }
}

print "Found /$pat/ $count times.\n";
```

As with all the scripts we've built that cycle through files using `<>`, you'll have to call this one on the command line with the name of a file:

```
% count.pl logfile
Search for what? aol.com
Found /aol.com/ 3456 times.
%
```

Nothing in Listing 9.2 should look overly surprising, although there are a few points to note. Remember that using `while` with the file input characters (<>) sets each line of input to the default variable `$_`. Because patterns will also match with that value by default, we don't need a temporary variable to hold each line of input. The first `while` loop (line 8), then, reads each line from the input files. The second `while` loop searches that single line of input repeatedly and increments `$count` each time it finds the pattern in each line. This way, we can get the total number of instances of the given pattern, both inside each line and for all the lines in the input.

One other important thing to note about this script is if you have it search for a phrase instead of a single word—for example, find all instances of both a first and last name—then there is a possibility that that phrase could fall across multiple lines. This script will miss those instances because neither line will completely match the pattern. Tomorrow, you'll learn how to search for a pattern that can fall on multiple lines.

Pattern Precedence

Back in Day 2, you might remember we had a little chart that showed the precedence of the various operators, and allowed you to figure out which parts of an expression would evaluate first in a larger expression. Metacharacters in patterns have the same sort of precedence rules, so you can figure out which characters or groups of characters those metacharacters refer to. Table 9.3 shows that precedence, where characters closer to the top of the table group tighter than those lower down.

TABLE 9.3 Pattern Metacharacter Precedence

Character	*Meaning*
`( )`	grouping and memory
`? + * { }`	quantifiers
`x \x $ ^ (?= ) (?!)`	characters, anchors, look-ahead
`|`	alternation

As with expressions, you can group characters with `()` to force them to be evaluated as a sequence.

You haven't learned about all these metacharacters yet. Tomorrow, we'll explore more of them.

Going Deeper

In this lesson, I've given you the basics of regular expressions so you can get started, and tomorrow you'll learn even more uses of regular expressions. For more information about any of these things, the `perlre` man page can be quite enlightening. For this section, let's look at a few other features I haven't discussed elsewhere in this lesson.

More Uses of Patterns

At the start of this lesson, you learned about the `=~` for matching patterns to scalar variables other than `$_`. In addition to `=~`, you can also use `!~`, like this:

```
$thing !~ = /pattern/;
```

`!~` is the logical not version of `=~`; in other words, it will return true only if the pattern is NOT found in `$thing`.

Another useful function for patterns is the `pos` function, which works similarly to the `index` function, except with patterns. You can use the `this` function to find out the exact position inside the pattern where a match was made using `m//g`, or to start a pattern-match at a specific position in a string. The `pos` function takes a scalar value (often a variable) as an argument, and returns the offset of the character *after* the last character of the match. For example:

```
$find = "123 345 456 346";
while ($find =~ /3/g) {
   @positions = (@positions, pos $find);
}
```

This code snippet builds an array of all the positions inside the string `$find` where the number 3 appears (3, 5, 13) in this case.

For more information on the `pos` function, see the `perlfunc` man page.

Pattern Delimiters and Escapes

All the patterns we've seen so far began and ended with slashes, with everything in between the characters or metacharacters to match. The slashes are themselves metacharacters, which means that if you want to actually search for a slash, you must backslash it. This can be problematic for patterns that actually contain lots of slashes—for example, Unix path names, which are all separated by slashes. You can easily end up with a pattern that looks something like this:

```
/\/usr(\/local)*\/bin\//;
```

That's rather difficult to read (more so than many other regular expressions). Fortunately, Perl has a way around this: you don't have to use `//` to surround a pattern—you can use any nonalphanumeric character you want to. The only catch is that if you use a different character you must include the `m` on the `m//` expression (you can also replace the delimiters for substitution, but you have to use the `s///` for that anyhow). You'll also have to escape uses of those delimiters inside the pattern itself. For example, the previous expression could be written like this:

```
m%/usr(/local)*/bin/%;
```

Alternately, if you're creating a search pattern for a number of nonalphanumeric characters that are also pattern metacharacters, you might end up blackslashing an awful lot of those characters, making the pattern difficult to read. Using the `\Q` escape you can essentially turn off pattern processing for a set of characters, and the use `\E` to turn them back on again. For example, if you were searching for a pattern containing the characters `{(^*)}` (for whatever reason), this pattern would search for those literal characters:

```
/\Q{(^*)}\E/;
```

Using `\Q` to turn off pattern processing is also useful for variable interpolation inside patterns, to prevent unusual results in search pattern input:

```
/From:\s*\Q$from\E/;
```

Summary

Pattern matching and regular expressions are, arguably, Perl's most powerful feature. Whereas other languages might provide regular expression libraries or functions, pattern matching is intrinsic to Perl's operation and tightly bound to many other aspects of the language. Perl without regular expressions is just another funny-looking language. Perl with regular expressions is incredibly useful.

Today you learned all about patterns: building them, using them, saving bits of them, and putting them together with other parts of Perl. You learned about the various metacharacters you can use inside regular expressions: metacharacters for anchoring a pattern (^, $, \B, \b), for creating a character class (`[]` and `[^]`), for alternating between different patterns (|), and for matching multiples of characters (`+`, `*`, `?`).

With that language for creating patterns, you can then apply those patterns to strings using the `m//` expression. By default, patterns affect the string stored in the `$_` variable, unless you use the `=~` operator to apply the pattern to any variable.

Tomorrow, we'll expand on what you've learned here, building on the patterns you've already learned with additional patterns and more and better ways to use those patterns.

Q&A

Q. What's the difference between `m//` and just `//`?

A. Nothing, really. The `m` is optional, unless you're using a different character for the pattern delimiter. They both do the same thing.

Q. Alternation produces a logical OR situation in the pattern. How do I do a logical AND?

A. The easiest way is simply to use multiple patterns and the `&&` or `and` operators, like this:

```
/pat1/ && /pat2/;
```

If you know the order in which the two patterns will appear, you can just do something like this:

```
/pat1.*pat2/
```

Q. I have a pattern that searches for numbers: `/\d*/`. It matches for numbers, all right, but it also matches for all other strings. What am I doing wrong?

A. You're using `*` when you mean `+`. Remember that `*` means "zero or more instances." That means if your string has no numbers whatsoever, it'll still match—you've got zero instances. `+` is used for at least one instance.

Workshop

The workshop provides quiz questions to help you solidify your understanding of the material covered and exercises to give you experience in using what you've learned. Try and understand the quiz and exercise answers before you go on to tomorrow's lesson.

Quiz

1. Define the terms *pattern matching* and *regular expressions*.
2. What sort of tasks is pattern matching useful for? Name three.
3. What do each of the following patterns do?

```
/ice\s*cream/
/\d\d\d/
/^\d+$/
/ab?c[,.:]d/
/xy|yz+/
/[\d\s]{2,3}/
/"[^"]"/
```

4. Assume that `$_` contains the value `123 kazoo kazoo 456`. What is the result of the following expressions?

```
if (/kaz/) {  # true or false?
while (/kaz/g) {  # what happens?
```

```
if (/^\d+/) {  # true or false?
if (/^\d?\s/) {  # true or false?
if (/\d{4}/) {  # true or false?
```

Exercises

1. Write patterns to match the following things:

- First words in a sentence (that is, words with initial capital letters following some kind of punctuation and white space)
- Percentages (any decimals followed by a percent sign)
- Any number (with or without a decimal point, positive or negative)

2. BUG BUSTER: What's wrong with this code?

```
print 'Enter a string: ';
chomp($input = <STDIN>);
print 'Search for what? ';
chomp($pat = <STDIN>);

if (/$pat/) {
   # pattern found, handle it
}
```

3. BUG BUSTER: How about this one?

```
print 'Search for what? ';
chomp($pat = <STDIN>);
while (<>) {
    while (/$pat/) {
        $count++;
    }
}
```

4. Yesterday, we created a script called `morenames.pl` that let you sort a list of names and search for different parts. The searching part used a rather convoluted mechanism of `each` and `grep` to find the pattern. Rewrite that part of the script to use patterns instead.

Answers

Here are the answers to the Workshop questions in the previous section.

Quiz Answers

1. *pattern matching* is the concept on Perl of writing a pattern which is then applied to a string or a set of data. *Regular expressions* are the language you use to write patterns.

2. There are many uses of pattern matching—you are limited only by your imagination. A few of them include

   a. Input validation

   b. Counting the number of things in a string

   c. Extracting data from a string based on certain criteria

   d. Splitting a string into different elements

   e. Replacing a specific pattern with some other string

   f. Finding regular (or irregular) patterns in a data set

3. The answers are as follows:

   a. This pattern matches the characters "ice" and "cream," separated by zero or more whitespace characters.

   b. This pattern matches three digits in a row

   c. This pattern matches one or more digits on a line by themselves with no other characters or whitespace.

   d. This pattern matches 'a', and optional 'b', a c, one of a comma, period, or colon, and a 'd'. "ac.d" will match, as will "acb,d", but not "abcd"

   e. This pattern will match either 'xy' or 'y' with one or more 'z's.

   f. This pattern will match either a digit or a whitespace character appearing at least two but no more than three times.

   g. This pattern matches all the characters in between opening and closing quotes.

4. The answers are

   a. True

   b. The loop repeats for every instance of 'kaz' in the string (twice, in this case).

   c. True. The pattern matches one or more digits at the start of a line.

   d. False. This pattern matches 0 or one digits at the start of the line, followed by whitespace. It doesn't match the three digits we have in this string.

   e. False. This pattern matches four digits in a row; we only have three digits here.

Exercise Answers

1. As with all Perl, there are different ways of doing different things. Here are some possible solutions:

```
/[.!?"]\s+[A-Z]\w+\b/
/d+%/
/[+-]\d+\.?\d+/
/([a-zA-z]{3})\s*\1/
```

2. There's a mismatch between where the pattern is trying to match and where the actual data is. The pattern in the `if` statement is trying to match the pattern against `$_`, but as per the second line, the actual input is in `$input`. Use this if test instead:

   ```
   if ($input =~ /$pat/) {
   ```

3. This one's sneaky, because there's nothing syntactically wrong with this statement. The second `while` loop, the one with the pattern in it, will look for the pattern in `$_`, which is correct. But the test is a simple true and false test: Does that pattern exist? The first line that has that pattern in it will register as true, and then `$count` will get incremented. But then the test will occur again, and it'll still be true, and the counter will get incremented again, and again, infinitely. There's nothing here to stop the loop from iterating.

   The `/g` option to the pattern in that `while` loop is what sets up the special case where the `while` loop will loop only as many times as the pattern was matched in the string, and then stop. If you're using patterns inside loops, don't forget the `/g`.

4. The only part that needs to change are the lines that build the `@keys` array (the ones that use `grep` to search for the pattern). Here we'll use a `foreach` loop and a test in both the key and value. We'll also add the `/i` option to make it not case sensitive, and also reset the `@keys` list to the empty list so that it doesn't build up between searches. Here's the new version of option 3:

   ```
   } elsif ($in eq '3') {      # find a name (1 or more)

      print "Search for what? ";
      chomp($search = <STDIN>);

      @keys = ();
      foreach (keys %names) {
          if (/$search/i or $names{$_} =~ /$search/i) {
              push @keys, $_;
          }
      }

      if (@keys) {
          print "Names matched: \n";
          foreach $name (sort @keys) {
              print "   $names{$name} $name\n";
          }
      } else {
          print "None found.\n";
      }
   }
   ```

WEEK 2

DAY 10

Doing More with Regular Expressions

Yesterday, we explored the basics of regular expressions. You learned about the basic metacharacters and the ways you can use them to find patterns in strings. Today, in part two of our regular expression saga, we'll build on that background and explore other more complex ways in which regular expressions can be used. The things you'll learn about today include

- Extracting what was matched by a regular expression
- Notes on using patterns in scalar and list context
- Using patterns for search and replace
- More about using the `split` function
- Matching patterns over multiple lines

Extracting Matches

Using patterns in a boolean scalar context, as tests for conditionals or loops, you can find out whether your pattern will match some part of a string. You can only get one of the two answers to that question: yes or no. Although this is useful for validating input, or for collating instances of patterns in a string, it's only half the story. Yes or no are fine answers, but even more useful is the capability to find out exactly what bit of data matched the pattern, and then reuse that data later in the pattern, or to build a list of all the matches that were found.

Whether the thing you match with a pattern is useful or not, of course, depends on the pattern. If your pattern is /abc/, the thing that pattern matches is "`abc`", and you knew that ahead of time. If, however, your pattern is something like `/\+.*/` (find a `+`, then any number of characters), then the thing that gets matched could be any set of characters—anything in your data that happens to occur after a `+` sign. Being able to get at the actual thing that gets matches is an important feature of regular expressions.

Perl has a number of ways to access matches, and different uses for those matches when you have them. When you have a match, you can refer back to that match later in the pattern, save that match into a scalar variable, or collect a list of all the matches. We'll do all those things in this section.

Using Parentheses for Backreferences

Yesterday, you learned how to use parentheses to group together bits of a pattern, and also how to use parentheses to change the precedence of how a pattern is matched. The third and most important use of parentheses is to save a match, and then refer back to that match later to build a much more complex regular expression. This mechanism of saving matches is often called using *backreferences* in regular expression parlance.

Here's an example. Say you were looking for lines that begin and end with the same word. You don't care what the word is, just that they begin and end with the same one. You could do this with two pattern tests, a loop, and a couple `ifs`. But a better way to do it is to test for the first word at the start of the line, save that value, and then test for that same word at the end of the line. Here's how you would do that:

```
/^(\S+)\s.*\1$/
```

Let's break it down character by character. The first character is a caret (`^`), which refers to the start of a line. Next is a parenthesis, which starts a pattern we will save for later. `\S` is a nonwhitespace character, and `\S+` refers to one or more nonwhitespace characters. The closing parenthesis ends the part that will be saved. With me so far? That pattern inside the parentheses will look for some set of characters followed by whitespace at the start of the line.

Moving on, we have a single whitespace character (\s), zero or more characters of any type (`.*`), `\1`, and then an end-of-line (`$`). What's `\1`? That's a reference to the thing we matched in the parentheses; `\1` says "put the thing you found in the first set of parentheses here." So whatever we matched inside those parentheses will then appear later on in the pattern—and therefore must appear at the end of the line for the entire pattern to return true. All parts of the pattern must be true, not just the one inside parentheses.

So, for example, let's say you had a line like this one:

```
"Perl is the best language for quick scripting.
If you want to get your job done, use Perl."
```

(OK, that's two lines. Pretend it's a single line inside a variable like `$_`). Will this match the pattern above? Let's see. The pattern first tests for the beginning of the line, then any non-whitespace characters, ending with a single whitespace character. What we have: the word `Perl` and the space matches just fine (note, however, that the final whitespace character occurs outside the parentheses, so it won't get saved). The next part of the pattern (.+) will suck up any intervening characters to the end of the line, and then we'll look for a whitespace character and another instance of what we matched earlier. Remember, `\1` becomes the match, so we'll match the word "`Perl`". After matching "`Perl`" the pattern next wants the end of the line with `$`—but no! We're not at the end of the line! We've got a period there! And because of that punctuation, the entire pattern will return false.

10

We could fix that, of course. You could include punctuation by changing the pattern to look like this:

```
/^(\S+)\s.+\s\1[.!?"]$/
```

The most important part, however, is the fact that `\1` refers to the thing that matched in parentheses. The pattern will only be successful if the thing that matched in the parentheses also appears at the same place in the string where you have the `\1` reference to that match.

You might be wondering about the significance of `\1`. It's called `\1` because there's only one pattern saved in parentheses. You can have any number of saved matches in a pattern, all surrounded by parentheses, and refer to each one to using `\1`, `\2`, `\3` and so on, with the numbers matching up left to right. The numbers are assigned based on the *opening* parenthesis—which means that you don't have to end one saved match before starting another one. You can nest the patterns to match, and the numbers will refer to the thing matched by each one.

Be careful with parentheses—whether you use them as groups for changing precedence or you use them for saving matches—Perl will still save the values. You can prevent a parenthesized match from being saved using the special form `(?:`*`pattern`*`)` instead of just `(`*`pattern`*`)`. More about this in "Going Deeper."

Saved Match Variables

Backreferences allow you to refer to a match in a subpattern in that same pattern. There's also a way to refer to those subpatterns outside the pattern. In addition to backreferences referred to by `\1`, `\2` and so on, Perl will assign scalar variables `$1`, `$2`, and so on to the values matched by those subpatterns. This mechanism can be incredibly useful for extracting bits out of strings or out of data. For example, here's a bit that pulls the first word out of a string:

```
if (/^(\S+)\s/) {
   print "first word: $1\n";
}
```

Here, if Perl can match the pattern (if it can find the start of the line and some number of non-whitespace characters followed by a whitespace character), then it'll print "`first word:` " and the match that it found. If the data doesn't have a first word (for example, if it's an empty string, or if there is no whitespace whatsoever in the string), then nothing will get printed because the test will return false. Remember, the whole pattern has to match for the pattern to return true, not just the part in parentheses.

One other important note about the match variables: their values are local to the block, read-only, and very transient. The next time you try to match anything, their original values will disappear. Those values will also vanish when a block ends. In other words, if you want to keep the values of these variables to use later, or if you want to change the values of those variables, you should save them off to some other variable or put them in a list. Match variables are for temporary storage only.

Matches and Context

Up until now, we've seen patterns used only in scalar context, primarily in a boolean test. The two rules for using patterns in a scalar boolean context are

- A test like `/abc/` will return 1 (true) if the pattern was found in the given string (`$_` if no variable, or `=~` for anything else), and false otherwise. This is most useful in conditionals.
- A `/g` option after the pattern allows iteration over the string; the pattern will return 1 (true) each time the pattern is matched, and then false at the end of the string. This is most useful in while loops.

In both instances, parentheses inside the pattern will fill the match variables `$1`, `$2`, `$3`, and so on, and you can then use those values inside the conditional and loop block or up until the next pattern math.

If you use a pattern in a list context, the rules are different (surprise, surprise):

- A pattern containing parenthesized subpatterns to save will return a list of the first subpatterns that matched (`$1`, `$2`, `$3`, and so on, as well as the individual variables themselves). If there are no parenthesized patterns in the pattern, the list `(1)` is returned (that's a list of one element: the number 1).
- A `/g` option after the pattern returns a list of all the subpatterns that matched throughout the string.
- If the pattern doesn't match at all, the result is an empty list `()`.

Because patterns in list context return matches as a list, you could use patterns to split your data into elements. Here's another way of splitting a first and last name into their component parts:

```
($fn, $ln) = /^(\w+)\s+(\S+)$/
```

10

A Note About Greed

On Day 2 we had a short discussion about truth, and now we're going to talk about greed. Perhaps later in the book we can discuss justice and envy.

Humor aside, one tricky feature of extracting patterns has to do with how the quantifier metacharacters behave in respect to what they match. The metacharacters `+`, `*`, and {} are called greedy metacharacters, because given a chance, they will match as many characters as they can up to and including all the characters up to the end the line.

Normal behavior for a pattern is that if a match is to be returned (that is, if the pattern is being used in a list context), it'll return the first match it finds. Take, for example, this expression:

```
@x = /(\d\d\d)/;
```

Now say the data contained in `$_` looks like this:

```
"3443 32 784 234 123 78932"
```

The `@x` array ends up being a list of one element, the first element in the list that matches three digits, which in this case is (`344`). The pattern always stops at the first possible match.

The `*`, `+` and {} quantifiers, however, change the rule. For example, let's use that same data, and try and match this pattern:

```
/(\d*)/;
```

Because `*` is defined as "zero or more of the preceding character," you might think that the pattern will stop when it satisfies that condition—that is, after it's read a single appropriate character, which in the case of our number data would return (3). Although that number satisfies the pattern, the `*` is a greedy quantifier, which means it will keep matching characters until it is unable to. The result of matching that pattern with the string of numbers is (`3443`)—the `*` quantifier here kept sucking up numbers until it hit the space. Space isn't a number, so that's as far as it could go.

Here's an even more problematic example:

```
/'(.*)'/
```

At first glance, this pattern would appear to match (and fill `$1`) with characters in between quotes. However, if you tried this pattern on this string:

```
"She said, 'I don't want to eat that bug,'  and then she hit me."
```

Because the `.*` sequence is greedy, it'll match and return all the characters in between the single-quotes ('I don't want to eat that bug,') the single-quote after the comma, and then continue to match all the characters to the end of the line. Then, because it didn't get to match the quote mark, Perl will keep backing up and trying different characters until it finds the quote mark. You'll get the result you expect, but Perl will spend a lot of time backtracking to find it. And, to make things even worse, if you have multiple quotes in the string, when Perl backtracks, it'll match the first one it finds. Take this string:

```
"'I despise you,' she said, throwing a pot at me. 'I wish you were dead.'";
```

Trying to match that same pattern to this string, `$1` will end up containing this string:

```
 I despise you,' she said, throwing a pot at me.  'I wish you were dead.
```

Assuming you were originally trying to match the contents of the first quote with that pattern (just the words `I despise you`), that's definitely not what you wanted.

Quantifiers initially appear to be a clever way of filling the space between two patterns. Because of their greedy behavior, however, in many cases they are totally inappropriate for that use, and you'll get frustrated trying to get them to work in that way. The better solution—both for making sure you only match what you want and to keep Perl from spinning its wheels —is to use a negated character class instead of a quantifier. Instead of thinking of the problem as "all the characters in between the opening and closing quotes," think of that problem as "an opening quote, then some number of characters that aren't a quote, then the closing quote." Implementing that pattern in a regular expression looks like this:

```
/"([^"]+)"/
```

It's a few more characters, and a little more difficult to sort out, but this pattern is guaranteed to return the characters in between quotes, not to greedily eat all he characters past the closing quote, and not to require any backtracking. As you might imagine, dealing with the greediness of expressions is a common problem. In fact, it's so common that there's another built-in way to deal with greed. To make a quantifier nongreedy, you can just include a question mark after it. Take a look at this expression:

```
/"(.*?)"/
```

The question mark indicates that the smallest possible match should be made, not the greediest. It's a bit more readable than the character negation example used previously.

Note

> One thing you'll find is that question marks have a variety of uses in the world of regular expressions. You've already seen two, and you'll see more in the "Going Deeper" section of this chapter. Whenever you see one, be careful to make sure you understand how it's being used in context.

An Example: Extracting Attributes from HTML Tags

Here's a quick example that illustrates how to use expressions to extract data from a document and how greediness works. This program simply extracts all the HTML tags from a document, prints out their names, and then prints out all their attributes and the values assigned to those attributes. It assumes that the attributes all have values, and that those values are enclosed in quotation marks (single or double).

First, let's go straight to the source code for the script. It's in Listing 10.1.

LISTING 10.1 The `extractattrs.pl` Script

```
#!/usr/bin/perl

while (<>)
{
    while (/<(\w+)(.*?)>/g)
    {
        print "Tag: $1\n";

        my $attrs = $2;

        while ($attrs =~ /(\w+)=('|")(.+?)\2/g)
        {
```

LISTING 10.1 continued

```
                print "Attribute: $1\n";
                print "Value: $3\n";
            }
        }
    }
```

This script is really simple. It iterates over the files that are passed in on the command line, searching for HTML tags. Let's look at the first regular expression in the file:

```
/<(\w+)(.*?)>/g
```

This expression is applied to each line in the file. On the outside of the expression I have `<` and `>` to match tags. Inside the angle brackets, I start with an expression that matches any number of word characters and extracts the tag name. The second expression matches everything else between the angle brackets. This expression is marked as non-greedy so if there are multiple tags on the line they will match the closing angle bracket in the tag I'm currently processing, not the closing angle bracket for the last tag on the line. Everything between the tag name and the closing angle bracket is grouped so that I can process it separately. This expression won't match closing tags because the tag must start with word characters, not `/`.

After the tag information has been extracted the tag name is printed and stored in `$1`. Then, I have another inner while loop that iterates over the information stored in the remainder of the tag. Let's look at that expression:

```
/(\w+)=('|")(.+?)\2/g
```

This expression extracts attributes from the rest of the data in the tag. More specifically, it extracts attributes with values that are enclosed in single or double quotation marks. (If the HTML document is XHTML-compliant, this will catch all the attributes.)

Let's look at the expression in detail. First, it matches some number of word characters, and stores them in the first backreference. Then, it matches an equal sign, then either a single or double quotation mark. Then, a nongreedy expression matches any string of characters (and stores them in backreference three), until it hits the value of backreference two, which contains the quotation mark used to open the value of the expression. This expression matches attributes such as `color="blue"` or `size='3'`, but not `height=15`, or `nowrap`, or `colspan='2"`. The script then prints out the name and value of the attributes in the tag.

Using Patterns for Search and Replace

One of the niftiest uses of regular expressions involves not just searching for a pattern or extracting matches into lists or variables or whatever, but also replacing that pattern with some other string. This is equivalent to a search and replace in your favorite word processor or editor—only with all the power and flexibility that regular expressions give you.

To search for a pattern and then replace it with some other pattern, use this syntax:

```
s/pattern/replacement/
```

For this syntax the *pattern* is some form of regular expression; *replacement* is the string that will replace the match. A missing replacement will delete the match from the string. For example:

```
s/\s+/ /   # replace one or more whitespace characters with a single space
```

10

As with regular patterns, this syntax will search and replace the string in `$_` by default. Use the `=~` operator to search a different location.

The search-and-replace syntax, as shown, will replace only the first match, and return 1. With the `/g` option (`g` stands for global) on the end, Perl will replace all instances of the pattern in the string with the replacement:

```
s/--/—/g # replace two dashes -- with an em dash code —
```

Also, as with regular patterns, you can use the `/i` option at the end to perform a search that's not case sensitive (although the replacement will not match case, so be careful):

```
s/a/b/gi;  # replace [Aa] with b, globally
```

Feel free to use parentheses and match variables inside search-and-replace patterns; they work just fine here:

```
s/^(\S+\b)/=$1=/g  # put = signs around first word
s//^(\S+)(\s.*)(\S+)$/$3†$2†$1/ # swap first and last words
```

Fans of sed will think that it's better to use `\1`, `\2`, and so on in the replacement part of the search and replace. Although this will work in Perl (basically by Perl replacing those references with variables for you), you should really get out of the habit—officially, in Perl, the replacement part of the `s///` expression is a plain old double-quoted string, and `\1` means a different thing in that context.

More About `split`

Remember the `split` function, from Day 5, Working with Hashes?" We were using `split` to divide up names into first and last name lists, like this:

```
($fn, $ln) = split(" ", $in);
```

At the time, I explained that using `split` with a space in quotes was actually a special case that would only work on data in which fields were separated by whitespace. To use `split` for data separated by any other characters, or needing any kind of sophisticated processing to find the elements, you'll use `split` with a regular expression as the pattern to match on:

```
($fn, $ln) = split(/\s+/, $in);  # split on whitespace
@nums = split(//, $num);         # split 123 into (1,2,3)
@fields = split(/\s*,\s*/, $in); # split comma-separated fields,
                                 # with or without whitespace around the comma
```

The first example here, which splits on one or more whitespace characters, is equivalent to the behavior of `split` with a quoted space, and also equivalent to using `split` without any pattern whatsoever. (The quoted space syntax is borrowed from the Unix tool awk, which has that same string-splitting behavior).

You can also tell `split` to limit the number of chunks to split the data into using a number as the third argument:

```
($ln, $fn, $data{$ln}) = split(/,/ $in, 3);
```

This example would be useful for data that might look like this:

```
Jones,Tom,brown,blue,64,32
```

That `split` command will split the data around a comma into a last name, a first name, and everything else, for a total of three elements. The assignment will put the last and first names into scalar variables, and everything else into a hash keyed by last name.

Normally, the parts of the string that are stored in the final list don't include anything matched by the pattern. If you include parentheses in the pattern, however, than anything matched in the pattern inside those parentheses will *also* be included in the final list, with each match its own list element. So, for example, say you had a string like this one:

```
1:34:96:54:0
```

Splitting on the colon (with a pattern of `/:/`) will give you a list of everything that doesn't match the colon. But a pattern of `/(:)/` will give you a list that looks like this, splitting on both things not included in the pattern and things that match the parenthesized parts of the pattern:

```
1, ':', 34, ':', 96, ':', 54, ':', 0
```

Between `split` and regular pattern matching, you should be able to extract data out of strings just about any way you want to. Use patterns and backreferences to extract the things you want, and `split` to break the string up into its elements based on the parts you *don't* want. With the right sets of patterns and understanding the format of the input data, you should be able to handle data in most any format with only a few simple lines of code—something that would be much more difficult to do in a language like C.

Matching Patterns over Multiple Lines

Up to this point we've been assuming that all the pattern matching you've been doing is for individual lines (strings), read from a file, or from the keyboard. The assumption, then, is that the string you'll be searching has no embedded line feeds or carriage returns, and that the anchors for beginning and end of line refer to the beginning and end of the string itself. For the `while (<>)` code we've been writing up to this point, that's a sensible assumption to make.

Quite often, however, you might want to match a pattern across lines, particularly if the input you're working with is composed of sentences and paragraphs, where the line boundaries are arbitrary based on the current test formatting. If you want to, for example, search for all instances of the term "Exegetic Frobulator 5000" in a Web page, you want to be able to find the phrases that cross line boundaries as well as the ones that exist in total in each logical line.

You have to do two things to do this. First, you have to modify your input routines so they will read all the input into a single string, rather than process it line by line. That'll give you one enormous string with newline or carriage return characters in place. Secondly, depending on the pattern you're working with, you might have to tell Perl to manage newlines in different ways.

Storing Multiple Lines of Input

You can read your entire input into a single string in a number of ways. You could use `<>` in a list context, like this:

```
@input = <>;
```

That particular line could potentially be dangerous, for example, if your input is very, very large, it could suck up all the available memory in your system trying to read all that input into memory. There's also no way to get it to stop in the middle. A less aggressive approach for reading paragraph-based data in particular is to set the special `$/` variable. If you set `$/` to a null string (`$/ = "";`), Perl will read in paragraphs of text, including new lines, and stop when it gets to two or more newlines in a row. (The assumption here is that your input data has one or more empty lines between paragraphs):

```
$/ = "";
while (<>) {   # read a para, not a line
   # $_ will contain the entire paragraph, not just a line
}
```

A third way to read multiple lines into a single string is to use nested `whiles` and append lines to an input string until you reach a certain delimiter. For strictly coded HTML files, for example, a paragraph ends with a `</P>` tag, so you could read all the input up until that point:

```
while (<>) {
   if (/(.*)<\/P>/) {
      $in.=$1
   } else {
      $in.=$_
   }
}
```

Handling Input with Newlines

After you have multiline input in a string to be searched, be it stored in `$_` or in a scalar variable, you can go ahead and search that data for patterns across multiple lines. Be aware of several things regarding pattern matches with embedded newlines:

- The `\s` character class includes newlines and carriage returns as whitespace, so a pattern such as `/George\s+Washington/` will match with no problem regardless of whether the words George Washington are on a single line or on separate lines.
- The `^` and `$` anchoring characters refer to beginning of string or end of string—not to embedded newlines. If you want to treat `^` and `$` as beginning and end of line in a string that contains multiple lines, you can use the `/m` option.
- The dot (`.`) metacharacter will NOT match newlines by default. You can change this behavior using the `/s` option.

That last point is the tricky one. Take this pattern, which uses the `.*` quantifier to extract a whole line after an initial "From:" heading:

```
/From: (.*)/
```

That pattern will search for the characters "From:", and then fill $1 with the rest of the line. Normally, with a string that ends at the end of the line, this would work fine. If the string goes onto multiple lines, however, this pattern will match only up to the first newline (`\n`). The dot character, by default, does not match newlines.

You could get around this by changing the pattern to be one or more words or white-space, avoiding the use of dot altogether, but that's a lot of extra work. What you want is the `/s` option at the end of your pattern, which tells Perl to allow dot to include `\n` as a character. Using `/s` does not change any other pattern-matching behavior—`^` and `$` continue to behave as beginning and end of string, respectively.

If your regular expression contains the `^` or `$` characters, you might want to treat strings differently if they stretch over multiple lines. By default, `^` and `$` refer to the beginning and end of the string, and ignore newlines altogether. If you use the `/m` option, however, `^` will refer to either the beginning of a string *or* the beginning of a line (the position just after a `\n`), and `$` will refer to the end of the string or the end of the line (the position just before the `\n`). In other words, if your string contains four lines of text, `^` will match four times, and similarly for `$`. Here's an example:

```
while (/^(\w}/mg) {
   print "$1\n";
}
```


This `while` loop prints the first word of each line in `$_`, regardless of whether the input contains a single line or multiple lines.

If you use the `/m` option, and you really do want to test for the beginning or end of the string, `^` and `$` will no longer work for you in that respect. But fear not, Perl provides `\A` and `\z` to refer to the beginning and end of the string, regardless of the state of `/m`.

You can use both the `/s` and `/m` options together, of course, and they will coexist happily. Just keep in mind that `/s` effects how dot behaves, and `/m` effects `^` and `$`, and you should be fine. Beyond that, embedded newlines in strings are no problem for pattern matching.

A Summary of Options and Escapes

Throughout this lesson, I've been mentioning various options you can use with patterns, as well as a number of the special escapes that you can use inside patterns.

Table 10.1 shows the options you can tag onto the end of the pattern matching expression (`m//` or just `//`) as well as those that can be used with the substitution expression (`s///`).

Note

> I haven't described all these options in this lesson. You'll learn about some of these in "Going Deeper," later in this chapter, but you might also want to check out the `perlre` man page for more information on any options that look interesting.

TABLE 10.1 Pattern Matching and Substitution Options

Option	*Use*
`g`	Match all occurrences (not just one)
`i`	Match both upper and lowercase
`m`	Use `^` and `$` for newlines
`o`	Interpolate pattern once (for better efficiency)
`s`	Dot (`.`) includes newlines
`x`	Extend regular expressions (can include comments and whitespace)
`e`	Evaluate replacement as a Perl expression (`s///` substitution only)

Table 10.2 contains the special escapes that can be used inside regular expressions, in addition to the usual string escapes such as `\t` and `\n`, and backslashes used to turn metacharacters into regular characters.

TABLE 10.2 Pattern Matching Escapes

Escape	*Use*
`\A`	Beginning of string
`\Z`	End of string
`\w`	Word character
`\W`	Non-word character
`\b`	Word boundary
`\B`	Non-word boundary
`\s`	Whitespace character
`\S`	Non-whitespace character
`\d`	Digit
`\D`	Non-digit
`\Q`	Escape all special characters
`\E`	End `\Q` sequence

An Example: Image Extractor

Let's finish up with an example of a pretty hefty regular expression (two of them, actually), used inside a Perl script. This script takes an HTML file as input, ranges over the file and looks for embedded images (using the `<img>` tag in HTML). It then prints a list of the images in that page, printing a list of the various attributes of that image (its location, width or height, text alternative, and so on). The output of the script will look something like this:

```
---------------
Image:  title.gif
   HSPACE: 4
   VPSACE: 4
   ALT: *
---------------
Image: smbullet.gif
   ALT: *
---------------
Image:  rib_bar_wh.gif
   BORDER: 0
   HSPACE: 4
   WIDTH; 50
   HEIGHT: 50
   ALT: --
```


If you're not familiar with HTML, the `<img>` tag can be embedded anywhere inside an HTML file, looks something like this:

```
<img src="imgfile.gif" width="50" height="50" alt="penguins">
```

There are a couple of tricky things about this tag, however, that make this task more difficult than it would initially appear: The tag itself can appear in upper or lowercase, and it can be spread over multiple lines. The attributes (the key/value pairs after the `img` part) can also be in any case, have space around the equal sign, and may or may not be quoted. The values can have spaces (but must be quoted if they do). Only one attribute is required—the `src` attribute—but there are a number of other attributes, and any of them can appear in any order. In an the example where I extracted attributes from HTML tags, nearly all these factors were ignored for the sake of convenience. This example will handle them properly.

All these choices make for a much more complex regular expression than just grabbing everything between the opening and closing tags. In fact, for this particular script I've split up the task into two regular expressions: one to find and extract the `img` tag out of the file, and one to extract and parse each individual attribute.

Listing 10.2 shows the code for this script. Try looking it over now to get a feel for how it works, but don't worry too much about grasping the pattern right now:

LISTING 10.2 The `img.pl` Script

```
#!/usr/local/bin/perl -w

$/ = "";      # paragraph input mode
$raw = "";    # raw attributes
```

LISTING 10.2 continued

```
5:  %atts = ();  # attributes
6:
7:  while (<>) {
8:      while (/<img\s(.+?)>/igs ) {
9:          $raw = $1;
10:         while ($raw =~ /(\w+)\s*=\s*(("|')(.*?)\3|(\w*)\s*)/igs) {
11:            if (defined $4) {
12:               $atts{ lc($1) } = $4;
13:            } else { $atts{ lc($1)} = $2; }
14:         }
15:         if ($raw =~ /ismap/i) {
16:             $atts{'ismap'}= "Yes";
17:         }
18:
19:         print '-' x 15;
20:         print "\nImage:  $atts{'src'}\n";
21:         foreach $key ("width", "height",
22:                       "border", "vspace", "hspace",
23:                       "align", "alt", "lowsrc", "ismap") {
24:            if (exists($atts{$key})) {
25:               $atts{$key} =~ s/\s*\n/ /g;
26:               print "   $key: $atts{$key}\n";
27:            }
28:         }
29:         %atts = ();
30:     }
31: }
```

This script has two main sections: a section to extract the data from the input, and a section to print out a report of what we found.

The first section uses a number of nested `while` loops to range over the HTML file: line 7 to loop over all the input, line 8 to find each instance of the image tag in the input, and line 10 to loop over each attribute in the `<img>` tag and store it into a hash called `%atts`, keyed by attribute name. This is very similar to the mechanism used in the example that extracted attributes from HTML tags.

With the `%atts` hash built, all we have to do is print out the values. Because I wanted them printed in a specific order, with the `foreach` loop in 21, I indicated the keys I wanted to find in a specific order.

But the focus of this script is the regular expressions in lines 8 and 10, so let's look at those two patterns in detail. Line 8 looks like this:

```
while (/<img\s(.+?)>/igs ) {
```

Working through that regular expression, character to character, we look for the characters `<img` (the opening part of the tag), a whitespace character, and then all the characters until a `>` is reached. Note that I use a nongreedy expression here so only the contents of the current tags will match the `.+` qualifier.

Note the parentheses around the ".+?" expression—that's the part we're interested in (which contains the attributes for the image), and that's the part of this pattern that will be extracted and saved for later use inside the body of this loop.

Note also the options at the end of the pattern: `/i` for a search that's not case sensitive (searching for both `<img...>` and `<IMG...>`), and `/g` for a global search (we'll get one pass of the `while` loop for each instance of `<img` in the loop). The `/s` is used to have the `.` match any line breaks that are encountered inside the parts of the tag it matches.

Inside the body of that loop, we can save the attribute list into the `$raw` variable (line 9). We have to do this because the values of `$1`, `$2`, `$3`, and so on are all transient—they'll get reset at the next pattern match. That brings us to line 10 and the truly gnarly regular expression we've got there:

```
while ($raw =~ /(\w+)\s*=\s*(("|')(.*?)\3|(\w*)\s*)/igs) {
```

Four important parts of this regular expression are outlined in Figure 10.1.

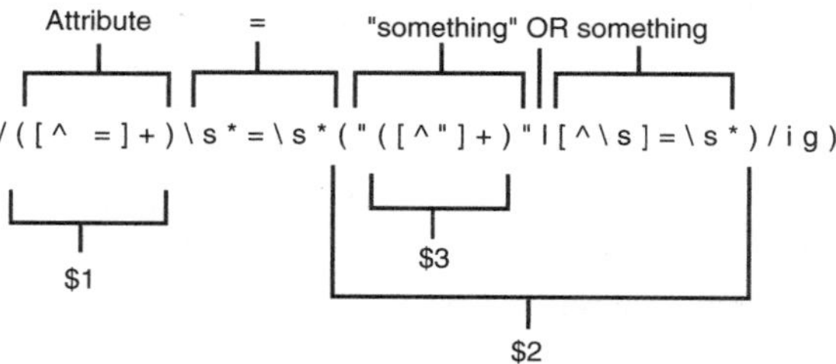

FIGURE 10.1.
Regular expression parts for `img.pl`.

The parts are further explained as follows:

- The attribute name, some set of characters that are neither a space nor an equal sign. We'll save this off into `$1`.
- An equal sign with optional whitespace on either side of it.
- One of two formats of value: This first one is a single or double quotation mark, followed by some number of characters, followed by another quotation mark of the same type as the first. This covers the quoted attributes (for example, `alt="some alternative text"`). The value here is saved into `$4`.
- Some number of word characters followed by optional whitespace. This covers the nonquoted value case (`height=100`). The value here is saved into `$5`.

Note the placement of parentheses for the values, and remember the rule for match variables: the numbers are assigned based on the opening parentheses. So `$2` ends up being the complete value, but `$4` will be the value minus the quotes—if the value had quotes in the first place.

We cover either case in line 11 through 14, where we test to see if `$4`is set. If it is, our value has quotes, and we'll store the nonquoted part into the `%atts` hash. If `$4` isn't defined, our values aren't quoted, and we can store `$2` into `%atts` instead. Note, here we also use the `lc` function to put our attribute names in uppercase before storing them.

Lines 15 through 17 cover a special case for the `<img>` tag—the `ismap` attribute doesn't take a value and indicates whether the image is an image map (that is, you can click different areas on the image and get different results). This form of image maps isn't commonly used in HTML anymore (it's been superseded by another tag), but we'll include it here to be complete. We have to make this one a special case because the expression in line 10 won't match it.

So after all those loops and patterns, we end up with a hash that stores all the attributes of the `<img>` tag we found. All that's left is to print those values. The loop in line 21 loops through all possible values for the `<img>` tag, in the order they'll be printed. But each `<img>` we find in the file can have a subset of those attributes—all of which are optional, except for `src`, so we have to test in line 24 to make sure the attribute actually exists before printing it. The `exists` function tests a hash to see if a key exists and returns true or false.

One other unusual line is 25, where we do a quick search and replace of the value. This is to cover the case where the attribute might have been split over several lines—that value will have an embedded newline character, and we don't want that to be printed out in the final table. This little regular expression will look for optional whitespace followed by a newline character, and then replace it with a single space.

And finally, in line 29 we clear the attributes hash for the next go-around and the next `<img>` tag.

This script, while short, shows the sort of task for which Perl works exceptionally well: finding sophisticated patterns in text, and then printing them back out again in sophisticated reports. This same task in C would most likely take much longer than 30 lines to code.

Hints for Building Regular Expressions

Depending on the complexity of your data or what you need to do with it; formulating a regular expression can either be very easy or need several iterations to get right. Here are some hints to help you get along with patterns:

- Know your data. Try and get a feel for the different ways that your pattern can appear, and to come up with a set of consistent rules before starting to write your pattern.
- Use multiple regular expressions if you need to. Sometimes it's easier to break the task into several smaller chunks than trying to get everything done at once.
- Develop your regular expressions incrementally. If you need a complex expression, generally it's easier to start by writing the first part of the expression, testing it, and then adding pieces one at a time and testing them as you move on. That way, you know immediately where the problem is if you suddenly stop matching things that the expression is supposed to match.
- Don't forget `split`. Some tasks work better using `split` (removing everything except for a pattern) than they do with plain matches. And vice versa.
- Use parentheses to extract what you need (and only what you need). If you don't need the quote marks in a match, put the parentheses inside the quotation marks. Only save what you want, and you'll save yourself time removing the parts you don't want later.
- Remember that `*` and `?` refer to "zero or more" and "zero or one" characters. This means that if the character doesn't exist at all the pattern might still match. If your pattern requires at least one instance of a character, use `+` instead of `*` or `?`.
- Don't forget alternation. The pipe (`|`) character can come in handy for very complex patterns that might have several alternative complex cases to work with.
- Consider not using a regular expression at all for the task you're trying to accomplish. Regular expressions are incredibly powerful but there is a performance hit to using them, particularly for easy things like simple tests.
- Don't obsess. Regular expressions can be incredibly powerful, but can also drive a person absolutely insane when they don't work. If a regular expression just doesn't seem to be working, stop, take a break, and think about it in a different way.

Going Deeper

Regular expressions are one of those things that you could write a whole book about and still not cover the extent to which they can be used. In the last two lessons, I've given you the basics of how to build and how to use regular expressions in your own programs. There are still many more features haven't been discussed, however, including many more metacharacters and regular expression forms specific to Perl. In this section I'll give you an overview of some of these other forms.

For more information about any aspect of regular expressions in Perl, the `perlre` man page can be quite enlightening. If you find yourself enjoying working with regular expressions, consider the book *Mastering Regular Expressions*, (Friedl, O'Reilly & Associates), which covers regular expressions of all kinds, Perl and otherwise, in an amazing amount of detail.

More Metacharacters, Variables, and Options

The metacharacters I described in previous two lessons are most of the basic set of characters you can find in most regular expression flavors (not just those in Perl). Perl includes a number of extra metacharacters, variables, and options that provide different ways of creating complex patterns (or of processing the patterns that match).

Metacharacters

The first of these are nongreedy versions of the quantifiers `*`, `+`, and `?`. As you learned throughout the lesson, these quantifiers are greedy—they'll match any characters far beyond what you expect, sometimes to the detriment of figuring out how the pattern actually works. As I've used throughout the chapter, Perl also provides a second set of quantifiers which are nongreedy (sometimes called lazy quantifiers): `*?`, `+?`, and `??`. These quantifiers match the minimal number of characters needed to match the pattern, rather than the maximum like the regular quantifiers. Don't forget to use negated character classes when necessary. The lazy quantifiers are less efficient than a negated character class.

- The `(?:`*`pattern`*`)` construct is a variant on the use of parentheses to group patterns and save the results in the match variables `$1`, `$2`, `$3`, and so on. You can use parentheses to group an expression, but the result will get saved whether you want it to be or not. Using `(?:pattern)` instead, the expression will be grouped and evaluated as a unit, but the result will not be saved. It provides a slight performance advantage over regular parentheses where you don't care about the result.
- The (`?o`) construct enables you to nest pattern-matching options inside the pattern itself, for example, to make only some parts of the expression not case sensitive. The `o` part of the construct can be any valid pattern-matching option.

Look-ahead is a feature in Perl's regular expressions that enables Perl to peek ahead in a string and see if a pattern will match without changing the position in the string or adding anything to the parenthetical part of the pattern. It's sort of like saying "if the next part of this pattern contains X, then this part matches" without actually going anywhere. Use `(?=`*`pattern`*`)` to create a positive-lookahead pattern (if *pattern* matches in future bits of the string, the previous part of the pattern also matches). The reverse is a negative-lookahead pattern, `(?!`*`pattern`*`)`, and works only if the *pattern* cannot match anything.

Special Variables

In addition to the match variables `$1`, `$2`, and so on, Perl also includes the variables `$'`, `$&` and `` $` ``, which provide context for the text matches by the pattern. `$'` refers to the text leading up to the match, `$&` is the text that was matched, and `` $` `` is the text after the match (note the backquote; that's a different character from quote '). Unlike the transient match variables, these variables will hold their values until the next successful match and regardless of whether or not the original string was changed. Using any of these variables is a significant performance hit, so consider avoiding them when at all possible.

The `$+` variable indicates the highest number of match variables that were defined; for example, if both `$1` and `$2` were filled, but not `$3`, `$+` will be set to 2.

Options

You've learned about most of the options available to Perl regular expressions (both `m//` and `s///`) throughout the body of this lesson. Two not touched on are `/x`, for extended regular expressions, and `/o`, to avoid compiling the same regular expression over and over again.

The `/x` option enables you to add whitespace and comments to a regular expression, for better readability. Normally, if you add spaces to a pattern, those spaces are considered part of the pattern itself. The `/x` option ignores all spaces and newlines, as well as allowing comments on individual lines of the regular expression. So, for example, that regular expression in our `<img>` extractor script, which looked like this in the script:

```
while ($raw =~ /(\w+)\s*=\s*(("|')(.*?)\3|(\w*)\s*)/igs) {
```

Might be rewritten to look like this:

```
while ($raw =~ /([^ =]+)      # find the attribute name
                \s*=\s*       # find the equals, with or without whitespace
                ("([^"]+)"|   # find and extract quoted values
                [^\s]+\s*)    # or find non-quoted values
                /igx) {
```

The use of extended regular expressions can help quite a bit to improve the readability of a regular expression.

And, finally the `/o` option is used to optimize how Perl compiles and reads a regular expression interpolated via a scalar variable. Take the following code snippet:

```
while (<>) {
   if (/$pattern/) {
     ...
   }
}
```

In this snippet, the pattern stored in `$pattern` is interpolated and compiled into a real pattern that Perl can understand. The problem is that because this pattern is inside a `while` loop, that same process will occur each and every time the loop comes around. By including the `/o` at the end of the pattern, you're telling Perl the pattern won't change, and so it'll compile it once and reuse the same pattern each time:

```
if (/$pattern/o) {  # compile once
```

For information on all these metacharacters, variables, and options, see the `perlre` man page.

Summary

In today's lesson, you learned more about using regular expressions, building on the basics you learned about yesterday. Today, we talked about extracting matches from a pattern-matching operation using parentheses, and using backreferences and match variables to save matches and refer back to them later.

As part of that discussion, you also learned about pattern matching in different contexts (scalar contexts return true or false, lists return lists of matches), about the greedy behavior of the quantifier metacharacters, and more about the `split` function. If you made it this far, through both these lessons, you now know enough about regular expressions to match just about any pattern in any set of data.

Q&A

Q. You've discussed efficiency a lot in this chapter, but as far as I can see, all my programs run in the blink of an eye. Is efficiency really worth worrying about?

A. It depends. When you're using Perl to process example data, efficiency probably doesn't make a difference. When your Perl program has to process a 5 gigabyte Web log, it's worthwhile to cash in on any time savings that coding for efficiency can afford you. Perl is a language that's perfect for batch processing, and in the world of batch processing, every millisecond often counts.

Q. I have a bit of code that uses a two-step process to extract something out of a string. The first pattern puts a substring into `$1`, and then the second pattern searches `$1` for a different pattern. The second pattern never matches, and printing `$1` shows that it's empty. But if it was empty, the second pattern shouldn't have even been tried in the first place. What's going on here?

A. It sounds like you're trying something like this:

```
if ($string =~ /some long pattern with a {subpattern} in it/) {
   if ($1 =~ /some second pattern/) {
```

```
        # process second pattern
    }
}
```

Unfortunately, you can't do that. The `$1` variable (or any other variable) is incredibly temporary. Each time you use a regular expression, Perl resets all the match variables. So, for this particular example, the first line does match and fills `$1` with the contents of the parentheses. However, the minute you try another pattern-match (in the second line), the value of `$1` disappears, which means that second pattern can never match.

The secret here is simply to make sure you put the values of any match variables somewhere else if you want to use them again. In this particular case, just adding a temporary variable and searching it instead will work just fine:

```
if ($string =~ /some long pattern with a {subpattern} in it/) {
    $tmp = $1;
    if ($tmp =~ /some second pattern/) {
        # process second pattern
    }
}
```


Q. I've seen some scripts that set a `$*` variable to 1 to do multiline matching, similarly to the way you described the `/m` option. What's `$*`, and should I be using it?

A. In earlier versions of Perl, you set the `$*` to tell Perl to change the meaning of `^` and `$`. In current versions of Perl, you should be using `/m` instead; `$*` is only there for backwards compatibility.

Workshop

The workshop provides quiz questions to help you solidify your understanding of the material covered and exercises to give you experience in using what you've learned. Try and understand the quiz and exercise answers before you go on to tomorrow's lesson.

Quiz

1. Assume that `$_` contains the value "123 kazoo kazoo 456". What is the result of the following expressions?

```
@matches = /(\b[^\d]+)\b/g;
@matches = /\b[^\d]+\b/;
s/\d{3}/xxx/;
s/\d{3}/xxx/g;
$matches = s/\d{3}/xxx/g;
if (/\d+(.*)\d+/) { print $1;}
@matches = split(/z/);
@matches = split/" "/,$_, 3;
```

2. What is the rule for how backreferences and match variables are numbered?
3. How long do the values of match variables stay around?
4. How can you stop the greedy behavior of the quantifiers + and *?
5. What do the following options do?

```
/g
/i
/o
/s
```

Exercises

1. BUG BUSTER: What's wrong with this bit of code?

```
while (<>) {
   $input =~ /pat\s/path /;
}
```

2. BUG BUSTER: What's wrong with this bit of code?

```
@matches = /\b[^\d]+\b/;
```

3. Write a script to find duplicated words ("the the" or "any any") in its input and to replace them with one instance of that same word. Watch out for words duplicated over multiple lines.
4. Write a script to expand acronyms in its input (for example, to replace the letters "HTML" with "HTML (HyperText Markup Language). Use the following acronyms and meanings to replace:

```
HTML (HyperText Markup Language)
ICBM (InterContinental Ballistic Missile)
EEPROM (Electrically-erasable programmable read-only memory)
SCUBA (self-contained underwater breathing apparatus)
FAQ (Frequently Asked Questions)
```

5. Modify the img.pl script to extract and report about links instead of images. Hint: Links look something like this:

```
<a href="url_to_link_to">test to underline for the link</a>
```

Links can also contain attributes for name, rel, rev, target and title.

Make sure you report on both the contents of the link tag and the text in between the opening and closing tags.

Answers

Here are the answers to the Workshop questions in the previous section.

Quiz Answers

1. The answers are

   a. ("kazoo", "kazoo")

   b. (1). A pattern in a list context without parenthesized parts of the pattern or with /g will return (1) if the pattern matched.

   c. The string will be changed to "xxx kazoo kazoo 456"

   d. The string will be changed to " xxx kazoo kazoo xxx"

   e. The `$matches` variable will be set to 2 (the number of changes made).

   f. " kazoo kazoo 45" (watch out for those greedy quantifiers).

   g. ("123 ka", "oo ka" "oo 456")

   h. ("123", "kazoo", "kazoo 456")

2. Backreferences and match variables are numbered based on opening parentheses. Parenthesized patterns can be nested inside each other.
3. Match variables are extremely transient; their values only stay set until the next pattern match or until the end of a block.
4. Two ways: the most efficient way is to avoid using greedy quantifiers with the dot (.) character and use negated characters classes instead; the other way is to use the nongreedy versions of those quantifiers (`+?` and `*?`).
5. The answers are

   a. The `/g` option means "global"; it applies the pattern to the entire string (as opposed to stopping after the first match). Different things happen depending on context.

   b. The `/i` option creates a search that's not case sensitive search. Upper and lower-case letters become irrelevant.

   c. The `/o` option means "compile the pattern only once." It's most useful for optimizations on patterns with embedded variables.

   d. The `/s` option allows the dot (.) character to match newlines.

Exercise Answers

1. There's two parts to that pattern (a pattern and a replacement), but no leading 's' If you leave out the s in front, `$input` is never assigned a value. The fixed version looks like this:

```
while (<>) {
   $input =~ s/pat\s/path /;
}
```

2. Trick question! There's nothing actually wrong with that bit of code, although it probably doesn't do what you expect. A pattern in a list context without parenthesized subpatterns will result in the value (1) if the pattern matches. To save a list of the matches you need to include parentheses somewhere in the pattern.

3. Here's one version:

```
#!/usr/bin/perl -w
# find and extract links
# doesn't handle link text with embedded HTML

$/ = "";      # paragraph input mode
$raw = "";    # raw attributes
$linktext = ""; # link text
%atts = ();   # attributes

while (<>) {
    while (/<a\s([^>]+)>([^<]+)<\/a>/ig) {
        $raw = $1;
        $linktext = $2;
        $linktext =~ s/[\s]*\n/ /g;
        while ($raw =~ /([^\s=]+)\s*=\s*("([^"]+)"|[^\s]+\s*)/ig) {
           if (defined $3) {
              $atts{ lc($1) } = $3;
           } else { $atts{ lc($1)} = $2; }
        }
        print '-' x 15;
        print "\nLink text: $linktext\n";
        foreach $key ("href", "name", "title",
                      "rel", "rev", "target") {
             if (exists($atts{$key})) {
                $atts{$key} =~ s/[\s]*\n/ /g;
                print "   $key: $atts{$key}\n";
             }
        }
        %atts = ();
    }
}
```

WEEK 2

DAY 11

Creating and Using Subroutines

We'll finish up your lesson on the core of the Perl language today with a discussion of subroutines, functions, and local variables. With subroutines you can collect bits of commonly used code into a single operation, and then perform that operation at different times in your script—the same way you use the built-in Perl functions.

The specific things you'll learn about include

- The differences between user-defined subroutines and Perl's standard functions
- How to define and call simple subroutines
- Using variables local to subroutine definitions
- Returning values from subroutines
- Passing arguments to subroutines
- Using subroutines in different contexts

Subroutines Versus Functions

A function, in general, is a chunk of code that performs some operation on some form of data. You call, or invoke, a function by naming it and giving it arguments somewhere in your Perl script. Perl then transfers execution to the function definition, performs the operations in that function, and then returns to where the execution left off when the function is done. This is true of any kind of function.

In previous lessons, we've been working a lot with Perl's built-in functions such as `print`, `sort`, `keys`, `chomp`, and so on. These are functions that are defined by the standard Perl library that you can use anywhere in your Perl programs. Another set of functions are available to you using additional Perl modules or libraries, written by other Perl programmers, that you load in at the start of your script—you learned more about those on Day 3, "Scope, Modules and Importing Code."

A third set of functions are those that you define yourself using a subroutine definition in Perl. In common practice, the terms *function* and *subroutine* are entirely equivalent—some programmers call subroutines *user-defined functions* to differentiate them from the built-in set; in other contexts, there's no distinction to be made. Throughout this lesson, and throughout this book, I'll refer to the functions that you define in your own programs (or modules, later on), as subroutines, and those that you get elsewhere—from the standard Perl distribution or from optional modules—as functions.

Why would you need a subroutine? Any time you're reusing more than a few lines of code in your Perl scripts, that's a good reason to put that code into a subroutine. You could also use subroutines to portion different parts of your script into chunks, perhaps to split up a complex problem into easier bites, or because it's more readable to refer to a certain operation by name (`remove_newlines`, say, or `find_max`) rather than to simply include the code itself. Creating a script as a set of subroutines also makes it easier to isolate programming problems. You can write and test and debug a single subroutine by itself, and be assured when you integrate that subroutine into your larger script that that subroutine will behave as you expect. Whether or not you use subroutines for different problems in your Perl scripts is a matter of programming style; use subroutines any time it will make your life easier as a programmer or your scripts easier to read and understand.

Defining and Calling Basic Subroutines

The most basic subroutine is one that takes no arguments, uses no local variables, and returns no value. Although this kind of subroutine might not seem terribly useful, it's a good place to start learning about them. So, we'll start with that kind of subroutine in this section and build from there. In this section, you learn the drill for defining and calling subroutines in your Perl scripts.

An Example of a Subroutine

Let's take a really simple example of a subroutine. Remember the temperature script from Day 2, which prompted you for a temperature in Fahrenheit, and then converted that temperature to Celsius? We included the actual calculation right in the middle of the script, but it could have been included in a subroutine, like this:

```
#!/usr/ bin/perl -w

print 'Enter a temperature in Farenheight: ';
chomp ($fahr = <STDIN>);
&f2c();
print "$fahr degrees Fahrenheight is equivalent to ";
printf("%d degrees Celsius\n", $cel);

sub f2c {
    $cel = ($fahr - 32) * 5 / 9;
}
```

Look over that example carefully, and see how the subroutine works. Perl executes the script line-by-line starting from the first line, as it always does, but when it gets to a reference to a subroutine (here, `&f2c()`), it switches execution to the subroutine definition (the last couple of lines in the script), executes the block there, and then returns to where it left off. In this case, that means that after the temperature is read from the keyboard, Perl switches to the `&f2c()` subroutine to convert the value to a Celsius value, and then prints out the value it found.

11

Note

By saying *switches execution,* I don't mean Perl actually jumps to that specific line of the script. Perl actually loads the entire script first and keeps track of all subroutine definitions before the script actually begins running, so it actually does just switch execution to the subroutine definition and switch back afterwards.

Defining Subroutines

From this simple example, you can probably infer the basic syntax for a subroutine definition:

```
sub subroutinename {
   statements;
   ...
}
```

A subroutine definition starts with the word `sub`, followed by the name of the subroutine, followed by a block. The block, as with the blocks you used with conditionals and loops, is a set of Perl statements surrounded by curly brackets ({}). Here's an example:

```
sub getnumber {
   print 'Enter a number: ';
   chomp($number = <STDIN>);
}
```

As with all other named things in Perl that start with odd characters, subroutine names can be made up of any number of alphanumeric characters and underscores. Uppercase and lowercase are different from each other, and subroutine names do not conflict with any other scalar, array, or hash variable names.

Subroutine definitions can appear at the start of your script, at the end, somewhere in the middle, or even inside other blocks. Anywhere a regular statement can appear, you can stick a subroutine definition. Generally, however, to make your programs easier to read and to understand, you should group them together either at the start or end of your script.

Calling Subroutines

The most basic way to call a subroutine (or, to use the technical term, to *invoke* a subroutine) is with an ampersand (`&`) followed by the name of the subroutine, followed by parentheses `()`:

```
&f2c();  # convert Fahrenheit to Celsius
&getnumber();
```

Arguments you want to pass to the subroutine are included inside the parentheses, but we'll get to that later (in "Creating Subroutines with Arguments").

The ampersand (`&`) is entirely optional in this case; you can call your subroutines with or without it. Some programmers find it preferable to include the ampersand because it makes it easier to differentiate between the built-in functions and those that they define themselves (or import from modules), but if you end up reading other people's Perl code, you'll see the nonampersand version quite a bit. I'll be using the ampersand syntax throughout the examples in this book to call subroutines.

Note

> The one place where the `&` is not optional is if you are referring to the subroutine indirectly, rather than calling it, for example, if you were using `defined` to find out if the subroutine had been defined or not.
>
> Also, in some cases the parentheses are also optional (specifically, when the subroutine has been predefined with a declaration earlier in the script or in an imported module). You'll learn more about declaring subroutines in "Going Deeper;" in this lesson I'll use the parentheses in each case to prevent confusion.

You don't have to call a subroutine from the main body of your script; you can call a subroutine from inside another subroutine, and another subroutine from inside that one. In fact, you can go as deep into subroutine calls as you want to—unlike some other languages, there are no limits (other than your system memory) to how deeply you can nest subroutine calls. Variable scope can cause issues with the arguments passed to nested subroutine calls—I'll discuss those issues in a bit.

An Example: Son of Stats

Just for kicks, I took the final version of the statistics script we've been working with throughout this week, and "subroutinified" it. I broke the script up into its component parts, and put each of them into a subroutine. The actual body of the script, then, does nothing but call individual subroutines. There's no change in behavior to the script itself; just in how it's organized. Listing 11.1 shows the result:

LISTING 11.1 The `statssubbed.pl` Script

```
#!/usr/local/bin/perl -w

&initvars();
&getinput();
&printresults();

sub initvars {
    $input = "";    # temporary input
    @nums = ();     # array of numbers;
    %freq = ();     # hash of number frequencies
    $maxfreq = 0;   # maximum frequency
    $count = 0;     # count of numbers
    $sum = 0;       # sum of numbers
    $avg = 0;       # average
    $med = 0;       # median
    @keys = ();     # temp keys
    $totalspace = 0; # total space across histogram
}

sub getinput {
    while (defined ($input = <>)) {
        chomp ($input);
        $nums[$count] = $input;
        $freq{$input}++;
        if ($maxfreq < $freq{$input}) { $maxfreq = $freq{$input} }
        $count++;
        $sum += $input;
    }

```

LISTING 11.1 continued

```
30: }
31:
32: sub printresults {
33:     @nums = sort { $a <=> $b } @nums;
34:
35:     $avg = $sum / $count;
36:     $med = $nums[$count /2];
37:
38:     print "\nTotal count of numbers: $count\n";
39:     print "Total sum of numbers: $sum\n";
40:     print "Minimum number: $nums[0]\n";
41:     print "Maximum number: $nums[$#nums]\n";
42:     printf("Average (mean): %.2f\n", $avg);
43:     print "Median: $med\n\n";
44:     &printhist();
45: }
46:
47: sub printhist {
48:     @keys = sort { $a <=> $b } keys %freq;
49:
50:     for ($i = $maxfreq; $i > 0; $i--) {
51:         foreach $num (@keys) {
52:             $space = (length $num);
53:             if ($freq{$num} >= $i) {
54:                 print( (" " x $space) . "*");
55:             } else {
56:                 print " " x (($space) + 1);
57:             }
58:             if ($i == $maxfreq) { $totalspace += $space + 1; }
59:         }
60:         print "\n";
61:     }
62:     print "-" x $totalspace;
63:     print "\n @keys\n";
64: }
```

Because this version of the stats script doesn't do anything functionally different from the one before it, there's only a couple of things to note here:

- The only part of this script that doesn't live inside a subroutine definition are the lines 3 through 5, which call subroutines to initialize variables, to get the input from a file of numbers, and to calculate the results.
- You may note that there are four subroutine definitions in this script, but only three subroutine calls at the top of the script. That's because the `&printresults()` subroutine calls the `&printhist()` subroutine at the end of its block.

Returning Values from Subroutines

Calling a subroutine by itself on one line is one way of splitting the execution of a script to a subroutine, but more useful is a subroutine that returns a value. With return values, you can nest subroutine calls inside expressions, use them as arguments to other subroutines, or as parts of other Perl statements (depending on whether the return value is appropriate, of course).

By default, the return value of a Perl script is the last thing that was evaluated in the block that defines the subroutine. So, for example, here's a short Perl script to read in two numbers and add them together:

```
$sum = &sumnums();
print "Result: $sum\n";

sub sumnums {
    print 'Enter a number: ';
    chomp($num1 = <STDIN>);
    print 'Enter another number: ';
    chomp($num2 = <STDIN>);
    $num1 + $num2;
}
```


The fact that subroutines can return values is important for the first line in that example; the value of the `$sum` variable will only be set as a result of the `&sumnum()` subroutine being called. Inside the subroutine, the last line where the two numbers `$num1` and `$num2` are added together is the value that is returned from the subroutine, the value that gets assigned to `$sum`, and the value that gets printed as the result. The reason the sum of `$num1` and `$num2` is returned is that unless you explicitly tell Perl what to return, it returns the value of the last expression in the subroutine. For example, 42 would be returned if the last line of the subroutine was 42. The catch to this behavior is that although the last statement in the block is often the return value for the subroutine, that's not always the case. Remember, the rule is that the last thing evaluated is the return value for the subroutine—and that might not be the last statement in the block. With loops such as `while` loops or `for` loops, the last thing evaluated might be the test. Or with loop controls, it might be the loop control itself.

Because the return value of a subroutine isn't always readily apparent, it's a much better idea to create a subroutine that explicitly returns a value using `return`. `return`, which is actually a function, takes any expression as an argument and returns the value of that expression. So the last line of that `&sumnums()` subroutine might look like this:

```
return $num1 + $num2;
```

Want to return multiple values from a subroutine? No problem. Just put them in a list and return them that way (and then, in the main part of your script that called the subroutine in the first place, make sure you deal with that returned list in some way). For example, this snippet calls a subroutine that processes an array of values. That subroutine returns a list of three values which can then be assigned (using list assignments in parallel) to the variables `$max`, `$min`, and `$count`.

```
($max, $min, $count) = &process(@foo);
# ...
sub foo {
    # ...
   return ($value1, $value2, $value3);
}
```

What if you want to pass two or more discrete lists of elements out of a subroutine? That you can't do. The `return` function with a list argument flattens all sublists, expands all hashes, and returns a single list of elements. If you want discrete arrays or lists on the outside of a subroutine, you'll need to figure out a way of splitting that list into its component lists after the subroutine is done. This is not a problem specific to return values; Perl also uses this single-list method of getting arguments into a subroutine as well (more about that later).

Using Local Variables in Subroutines

Structuring a Perl script to use subroutines that refer to the same global variables as the code outside the subroutines is essentially an exercise in code formatting. The subroutines in this case don't give you much intrinsic value in terms of efficiency or effective script design. Subroutines are much better designed and used as self-contained units that have their own variables and that deal only with data passed to that subroutine through arguments and passed back through return values. This makes them easier to manage, easier to reuse, and easier to debug. We'll work towards that goal as this lesson progresses, but we'll start here with a discussion of local variables.

The vast majority of the variables we've been looking at up to this point—scalar, list, and array variables—have been global variables, that is, they're available to all parts of the script, and continue to exist as long as the script runs. We've seen a few minor exceptions—the element variable in a `foreach` loop or the match variables in regular expressions, for example—but for the most part we've been looking solely at variables as having global scope.

Local variables, in the context of a subroutine, are variables that spring into existence when the subroutine is called, are available solely to that subroutine, and then disappear when the subroutine is finished. Other than the fact that they're local, they look just like other variables and contain the same sort of data.

Perl actually has two different ways of creating two different kinds of local variables. We'll cover one way (the easiest one) here, and deal with the other and the specific differences between the two on Day 13, "Scope, Modules, and Importing Code."

To create a local variable for a subroutine, use the `my` modifier before you initialize or use the variable for the first time:

```
my $x = 1;   # $x is now local
```

The `my` modifier only applies to a single variable. If you want to create multiple local variables you have to enclose them in parentheses, like this:

```
my ($a, $b, $c);    # three locals, all undefined.
```

In the previous section we created a subroutine that prompted for two numbers and summed them. In that example the two number variables, `$num1` and `$num2` were global variables. We can make a single-line change to make those variables local variables:


```
$sum = &sumnums();
print "Result: $sum\n";

sub sumnums {
   my ($num1, $num2);
   print 'Enter a number: ';
   chomp($num1 = <STDIN>);
   print 'Enter another number: ';
   chomp($num2 = <STDIN>);
   return $num1 + $num2;
}
```

In this version, the line `my ($num1, $num2)` creates variables that are local to the subroutine. They are available to the subroutine as temporary placeholders for the numbers, but are not visible outside the boundaries of that subroutine.

What happens if you create a `my` variable that has the same name as a previously used global variable? Perl has no problem with this; the new variables created by `my` will hide the global variables with the same name. Then, when the subroutine is done, the `my` variables will go away and the global variables will be visible (and usable) again. Because this can often be very confusing to debug, it's generally a good idea to give your local variables different names from global variables, or to simply avoid the use of global variables altogether.

> You can get to the values of global variables from inside a subroutine that declares my variables of the same name by putting your code into a package, and then referring to the package name and the global variable name. But I won't discuss that here; see Day 13 for details.

Here's an example that demonstrates how this works:

```
#!/usr/ bin/perl -w

$value = 0;
print "before callsub, \$value is $value\n";
&callsub();
print "after callsub, \$value is $value\n";

sub callsub {
    my ($value);
    $value++;
    print "inside callsub, \$value is $value\n";
}
```

If you run this example, you'll get the following output:

```
before callsub, $value is 0
inside callsub, $value is 1
after callsub, $value is 0
```

Note here that the `my` variable `$value` is a new variable, local to the subroutine. Changing its value has no effect on the global variable once the subroutine is complete.

The one other catch to watch out for with `my` variables is that they are truly local to the subroutine definition itself. If you nest subroutine calls—call one subroutine from another subroutine—the `my` variables defined in the first subroutine will not be available to the second subroutine, and vice versa. This is different from many other languages, where local variables cascade to nested subroutines. With `my` variables, you can only use them inside the same subroutine definition and nowhere else in the script.

Note

> For the computer scientists in the audience, this means that `my` variables have lexical scope, rather than dynamic scope. They only exist inside the lexical block in which they are defined. There is more about this later in the book when we get to scope.

Passing Values into Subroutines

When you've got local variables to store values specific to a subroutine, and return values to send data out from the subroutine, the only part of the subroutine left is getting information into it. For that you use arguments, just as you do for the built-in Perl functions.

Passing Arguments

Let's start with how arguments get passed into subroutines. Perl has an extremely loose notion of subroutine arguments. Whereas in other languages you have to be very specific when you write your subroutines to make sure you indicate how many and what type of arguments your subroutine will take, Perl doesn't care. When you call a subroutine in Perl, any and all arguments you give it are combined or expanded into a single list of values. For scalar arguments, this is no big deal:

```
&mysub(1,2,3);
```

The `&mysub()` subroutine in this case will get a list of three numeric values. Watch out for lists, though:

```
&mysub(@list, @anotherlist);
```

11

In this case, both `@list` and `@anotherlist` are expanded into their component values and combined into one list. It's that single list that ends up inside the body of the subroutine. Your original arrays lose their identities when passed into a subroutine. This behavior is identical to the behavior when you assign multiple lists to a single array, as described on Day 4, "Working with Lists and Arrays."

A similar thing happens with hashes; the hash is expanded into its keys and values (following the usual hash rules), combined with any other list arguments, and passed into the subroutine as a flat list.

But what if you really want your arguments to consist of multiple arrays or hashes? Perl's argument-passing behavior doesn't make this easy, but there are a number of ways to work around it. One way is to store your arrays or hashes as global variables and just refer to them in the body of your subroutines. Another way is to reconstruct the arrays inside the subroutine using a clever hack (for example, including the count of the first array as an argument to the subroutine). A third way, and arguably the best one, is to pass the arguments to the subroutine as references, which retains the construction of the original arrays or hashes inside the subroutine. You'll learn about references later on in this book on Day 19, "Working with References."

Handling Arguments Inside Subroutines

Okay, so arguments are passed into a subroutine as a single list of values. How do you then get to those arguments from inside the body of your subroutine?

The list of arguments passed to your subroutine is stored in the special local variable `@_`. You can access elements of that array, or split those values into individual values using the standard array access and assignment expressions. The `@_` variable is a local variable to the subroutine; if you set a `@_` global variable, its values are hidden inside the subroutine, and if you call another subroutine from inside a subroutine, that second subroutine will get its own version of `@_`.

Here's an example of a subroutine that adds together its two arguments (and a line of code showing how it's called:

```
&addthem(2,3);

sub addthem {
   return $_[0] + $_[1];
}
```

The two arguments to the subroutine—here `2` and `3`—are put into the list stored in the `@_` variable. Then you can just use `$_[0]` and `$_[1]` access forms to get to those values. Keep in mind that just as `$foo[0]` and `$foo` refer to different things, so are `$_[0]` and `$_` different (the first one is the first element in the argument list; the second is the special default variable).

Note that this subroutine is kind of limited (brain-dead might be a better term)—it only adds together its first two arguments, no matter how many you give it. Because you cannot control how many arguments you can get inside a subroutine, you have to be careful that you only call the subroutine with the right number of arguments, test the number or type of arguments you get, or write the subroutine generally enough to be able to handle multiple arguments. We might modify the above subroutine to add all its arguments together, regardless of the number, like this:

```
sub addthem {
   my $sum = 0;
   foreach $i (@_) {
      $sum += $i;
   }
   return $sum;
}
```

Note

Recent versions of Perl (after 5.003) do actually provide a way to define a subroutine to only take specific numbers and types of arguments. Given that this feature is quite new, it's probably not something you want to rely on in your own scripts. More about subroutine prototypes in the "Going Deeper" section.

Perl doesn't have a way of explicitly naming incoming arguments, but one common trick is to split out the array of arguments into local variables as a first step, like this, where this subroutine expects three arguments:

```
sub foo {
   my($max, $min, $inc) = @_;
   ...
}
```

You can then refer to those arguments using mnemonic local variable names rather than having to keep track of their positions in the array all the time. Another (very common) way of doing this same thing is to use `shift`. Conveniently, `shift` with no arguments inside a subroutine will extract the first element from `@_` (`pop` will do the same thing to the last element):


```
sub foo {
   my $max = shift;
   my $min = shift;
   my $inc = shift;
   ...
}
```

A Note on Arguments Passed by Reference

The argument list that you get inside your subroutine via `@_` are implicit references to the values that were passed in from outside. That means that if you pass in a list of strings, and inside the body of your subroutine, modify those strings (by altering the contents of the `@_` array itself), then the strings will remain modified outside the body of the subroutine as well. As I mentioned earlier, however, arrays and hashes do not maintain their integrity inside the subroutine, nor can you modify a number. And, if you assign the argument list `@_` to a local variable, those values will all be copied and cease to be references. Because Perl's notion of pass by reference is rather vague, it's not commonly used as such; using actual references to pass in arrays or hashes of values is a much more direct way of approaching the problem.

Subroutines and Context

Argument passing, subroutine definition, return values—these are the features of function definitions in any language. But, because this is Perl, there are always wrinkles. You already saw one of those wrinkles with the fact that individual arrays and hashes lose their identities when they're passed into subroutines as arguments. Another wrinkle is the issue of context.

Given that subroutines can be called in either a scalar or list context, and that they can return either a scalar or a list, context is a relevant issue to subroutine development. Or at least it's a relevant issue to keep in mind as you use your subroutines: be careful not to call subroutines that return lists in a scalar context, unless you're aware of the result and know how lists behave in that particular context.

There are the occasions, however, when you want to write a subroutine that will behave differently based on the context in which it was called (a very Perl-like thing to do). That's where the built-in `wantarray` function comes in. You use `wantarray` to find out the context in which your subroutine was called in. `wantarray` returns true if your subroutine was called in a list context; false if it was called in a scalar context (a more proper name might be "wantlist," but it is called `wantarray` for historical reasons). So, for example, you might test for the context of your subroutine before returning a value, and then do the right thing based on that context, like this:

```
sub arrayorlist {
    # blah blah
    if (wantarray()) {
        return @listhing;
    } else { return $scalarthing }
}
```

Be careful with this feature, however. Keep in mind that just as functions that do different things based on context can be confusing (and may sometimes require a check of the documentation to figure out what they do), subroutines that do different things based on context can be doubly confusing. In many cases it's better to just return an appropriate value for the subroutine itself, and then deal with that value appropriately in the statement that called the subroutine in the first place.

Another Example: Stats with a Menu

Let's modify the stats example once more in this lesson to take advantage of just about everything you've learned so far in this book. I've modified stats such that instead of reading the values, printing everything, and then exiting, the script prints a menu of operations. You have a choice of the sort of operations you want to perform on the numbers in the data set.

Unlike the `names.pl` script from Day 8, however, which used a large `while` loop and a number of `if` tests to handle the menu, this one uses subroutines. In addition, it moves a lot of the calculations we performed in earlier versions of this script into the subroutine that actually uses those calculations, so that only the work that needs to be done gets done.

Because this script is rather long, instead of showing you the whole thing, and then analyzing it, I'm going to walk through each important part and show you bits of the overall code to point out what I did when I wrote this version of the stats script. At the end of this section, in Listing 11.2, I'll show you all the code.

Let's start with the main body of code in this script. Previous versions of stats used a rather large set of global variables, which we defined and initialized at the start of the script. This version uses only two: the array of numbers for the input, and a variable to keep track of whether to quit the script or not. All the other variables are `my` variables, local to the various subroutines that need them.

The script starts with a call to a subroutine called `&getinput()`. This subroutine, which we'll look at in a bit, reads in the input from the input files and stores it in the `@nums` array. This version of `&getinput()` is significantly smaller than the one we've used in previous versions of stats—this one simply reads in the numbers. It doesn't keep track of frequencies, sums, or anything else, and it uses the `$_` variable instead of a temporary input variable. It does, however, include the line that sorts the numbers in the final `@nums` array, and it discards any lines of input that contain characters other than numbers.

11

```
sub getinput {
    while (<>) {
        chomp;
        next if (/\D/);
        push @nums, $_;
    }
    @nums = sort { $a <=> $b } @nums;
}
```

After reading the input, the core of this menu-driven version of stats is a `while` loop that prints the menu and executes different subroutines based on the part of the menu that was selected. That `while` loop looks like this:

```
&getinput();
while ($choice !~ /q/i) {
    $choice = &printmenu();
    SWITCH: {
        $choice =~ /^1/ && do { &printdata(); last SWITCH; };
        $choice =~ /^2/ && do { &countsum(); last SWITCH; };
        $choice =~ /^3/ && do { &maxmin(); last SWITCH; };
        $choice =~ /^4/ && do { &meanmed(); last SWITCH; };
        $choice =~ /^5/ && do { &printhist(); last SWITCH; };
    }
}
```

Look! A switch! This is one way to accomplish a switch-like statement in Perl, using pattern matching, `do` statements, and a label. For each value of `$choice`, 1 to 5, this statement will call the right subroutine and then call `last` to fall through the labeled block. Note that the labeled block isn't a loop, but you can still use `last` to exit out of it.

The value of `$choice` gets set via the `&printmenu()` subroutine (we'll look at that one in a bit). Note that the `while` loop here keeps printing the menu and repeating operations until the `&printmenu()` subroutine returns the value 'q' (or 'Q'), in which case the `while` loop stops, and the script exits.

The `&printmenu()` subroutine simply prints the menu of options, accepts input, verifies it, and then returns that value:

```
sub printmenu {
    my $in = "";
    print "Please choose one (or Q to quit): \n";
    print "1. Print data set\n";
    print "2. Print count and sum of numbers\n";
    print "3. Print maximum and minimum numbers\n";
    print "4. Print mean and median numbers\n";
    print "5. Print a histogram of the frequencies.\n";
    while () {
        print "\nYour choice --> ";
        chomp($in = <STDIN>);
        if ($in =~ /^\d$/ || $in =~ /^q$/i) {
            return $in;
        } else {
            print "Not a choice.  1-5 or Q, please,\n";
        }
    }
}
```

Let's work down the list of choices the menu gives us. The first choice is simply to print out the data set, which uses the `&printdata()` subroutine. `&printdata()` looks like this:

```
sub printdata {
    my $i = 1;
    print "Data Set: \n";
    foreach my $num (@nums) {
        print "$num ";
        if ($i == 10) {
            print "\n";
            $i = 1;
        } else { $i++; }
    }
    print "\n\n";
}
```

This subroutine simply iterates over the array of numbers and prints them. But there's one catch: it prints them ten per line for better formatting. That's what that `$i` variable does; it simply keeps track of how many numbers have been printed, and prints a new line after ten of them.

Note one other point—even though the `$num` variable is implicitly local to the `foreach` loop, you still have to declare it as `my` variable in order to get past `use strict` (which is at the beginning of this script even though I didn't show it to you).

The second menu choice prints the count and sum of the data set. The `&countsum()` subroutine looks like this:

```
sub countsum {
    print "Number of elements: ", scalar(@nums), "\n";
    print "Sum of elements: ", &sumnums(), "\n\n";
}
```

This subroutine, in turn, calls the `&sumnums()` to generate a sum of all the elements:

```
sub sumnums {
    my $sum = 0;
    foreach my $num  (@nums) {
        $sum += $num;
    }
    return $sum;
}
```

11

In previous versions of this stats script, we simply generated the sum as part of reading in the input from the file. In this example, we've postponed generating that sum until now. You could make the argument that this is less efficient—particularly since the average uses the sum as well—but it does allow us to put off some of the data processing until it's actually required.

Our third choice is the maximum and minimum value in the data set. We don't actually have to calculate these at all; because the data set is sorted, the minimum and maximum values are the first and last elements of the `@nums` array, respectively:

```
sub maxmin {
    print "Maximum number: $nums[0]\n";
    print "Minimum number: $nums[$#nums]\n\n";
}
```

Fourth choice is the mean and median values, which we can get as we did in previous stats scripts:

```
sub meanmed {
    printf("Average (mean): %.2f\n", &sumnums() / scalar(@nums));
    print "Median: $nums[@nums / 2]\n\n";
}
```

Which brings us to the last subroutine in this script, `&printhist()`, which calculates and prints the histogram of the values. As with previous versions, this part of the script is the most complex. This version, however, collects everything relating to the histogram into this one place, instead having bits of it spread all over the script. That means more local variables for this subroutine than for others, and more processing of the data that has to take place before we can print anything. But it also means that the data input isn't slowed down calculating values that won't be used until later, if at all, and there isn't a hash of the frequencies hanging around and taking up space as the script runs. Here's the `&printhist()` subroutine:

```
sub printhist {
    my %freq = ();
    my $maxfreq = 0;
    my @keys = ();
    my $space = 0;
    my $totalspace = 0;
    my $num;

    # build frequency hash, set maxfreq
    foreach $num (@nums) {
        $freq{$num}++;
        if ($maxfreq < $freq{$num}) { $maxfreq = $freq{$num} }
    }

    # print hash
    @keys = sort { $a <=> $b } keys %freq;
    for (my $i = $maxfreq; $i > 0; $i--) {
        foreach $num (@keys) {
            $space = (length $num);
            if ($freq{$num} >= $i) {
                print( (" " x $space) . "*");
            } else {
                print " " x (($space) + 1);
            }
            if ($i == $maxfreq) { $totalspace += $space + 1; }
        }
        print "\n";
    }
    print "-" x $totalspace;
    print "\n @keys\n\n";
}
```

A careful look will show that beyond collecting all the frequency processing into this one subroutine, little else has changed. Putting it into a subroutine simply makes the process and its data more self-contained.

Listing 11.2 shows the full script (all the individual parts put together):

LISTING 11.2 The `statsmenu.pl` Script

```
#!/usr/ bin/perl -w
use strict;

my @nums = (); # array of numbers;
my $choice = "";

# main script
&getinput();
while ($choice !~ /q/i) {
    $choice = &printmenu();
  SWITCH: {
        $choice =~ /^1/ && do { &printdata(); last SWITCH; };
        $choice =~ /^2/ && do { &countsum(); last SWITCH; };
        $choice =~ /^3/ && do { &maxmin(); last SWITCH; };
        $choice =~ /^4/ && do { &meanmed(); last SWITCH; };
        $choice =~ /^5/ && do { &printhist(); last SWITCH; };
  }
}

# read in the input from the files, sort it once its done
sub getinput {
    while (<>) {
        chomp;
        next if (/\D/);
        push @nums, $_;
    }
    @nums = sort { $a <=> $b } @nums;
}
# our happy menu to be repeated until Q
sub printmenu {
    my $in = "";
    print "Please choose one (or Q to quit): \n";
    print "1. Print data set\n";
    print "2. Print count and sum of numbers\n";
    print "3. Print maximum and minimum numbers\n";
    print "4. Print mean and median numbers\n";
    print "5. Print a histogram of the frequencies.\n";
    while () {
        print "\nYour choice --> ";
        chomp($in = <STDIN>);
        if ($in =~ /^\d$/ || $in =~ /^q$/i) {
            return $in;
        } else {
            print "Not a choice.  1-5 or Q, please,\n";
        }
    }
}

# print out the data set, ten numbers per line
```

LISTING 11.2 continued

```
sub printdata {
    my $i = 1;
    print "Data Set: \n";
    foreach my $num (@nums) {
        print "$num ";
        if ($i == 10) {
            print "\n";
            $i = 1;
        } else { $i++; }
    }
    print "\n\n";
}

# print the number of elements and the sum
sub countsum {
    print "Number of elements: ", scalar(@nums), "\n";
    print "Sum of elements: ", &sumnums(), "\n\n";
}

# find the sum
sub sumnums {
    my $sum = 0;
    foreach my $num  (@nums) {
        $sum += $num;
    }
    return $sum;
}

# print the max and minimum values
sub maxmin {
    print "Maximum number: $nums[0]\n";
    print "Minimum number: $nums[$#nums]\n\n";
}

# print the mean and median
sub meanmed {
    printf("Average (mean): %.2f\n", &sumnums() / scalar(@nums));
    print "Median: $nums[@nums / 2]\n\n";
}

# print the histogram.  Build hash of frequencies & prints.
sub printhist {
    my %freq = ();
    my $maxfreq = 0;
    my @keys = ();
    my $space = 0;
    my $totalspace = 0;
    my $num;

    # build frequency hash, set maxfreq
```

LISTING 11.2 continued

```
        foreach $num (@nums) {
            $freq{$num}++;
            if ($maxfreq < $freq{$num}) { $maxfreq = $freq{$num} }
        }

        # print hash
        @keys = sort { $a <=> $b } keys %freq;
        for (my $i = $maxfreq; $i > 0; $i--) {
            foreach $num (@keys) {
                $space = (length $num);
                if ($freq{$num} >= $i) {
                    print( (" " x $space) . "*");
                } else {
                    print " " x (($space) + 1);
                }
                if ($i == $maxfreq) { $totalspace += $space + 1; }
            }
            print "\n";
        }
        print "-" x $totalspace;
        print "\n @keys\n\n";
    }
```


Going Deeper

Subroutines are fairly basic concepts that don't involve a large amount of depth in Perl. Nonetheless, there are a few concepts that aren't discussed in this lesson, which are summarized here.

The definitive description of Perl subroutines, because `my` is an operator, more information about it can also be found in the `perlfunc` man pages (although we'll also talk more about it on Day 13). See those pages for further details on any of the concepts described in this section.

Local Variables in Blocks

I've made a point of referring to local variables in this section as being defined inside subroutines, and local only as far as those subroutines are running. In reality, local variables can be defined to be local to *any* enclosing block, not just to subroutines. You can use local variables inside conditionals, loops or labeled blocks, and those local variables will follow the same rules as they do in subroutines as far as hiding global variables of the same name and of being only available to the subroutine in which they are defined. Most of the time, however, local variables make the most sense when they are applied to subroutines and not to other blocks.

Leaving Off the Parentheses for Arguments

When you call built-in functions in Perl, you can call them with their arguments in parentheses, or leave off the parentheses if Perl can figure out where your arguments begin and end. You can actually do the same thing with subroutines, if you want to, but only if these two rules are met:

- You also call the subroutine without the leading `&` (with the leading `&` and Perl will try to use `@_` instead)
- Perl has already seen a declaration or definition of that subroutine previously in the script

Perl, for the most part, is not particular about where in a script a subroutine is defined, as opposed to where it is called (some languages require you to define a subroutine further up in the file from where you call it). Leaving off the parentheses for the arguments is the one exception.

One way to get around this is to predeclare a subroutine at the top of your script, similarly to how you'd declare all your global variables before using them. To do this, just leave off the block part of the subroutine definition:

```
sub mysubroutine;
```

With the subroutine declared, you can then call it with arguments with or without parentheses. Don't forget to actually define that subroutine later in your script, however.

Note that common practice among Perl programmers is to include the parentheses, even if it's possible to leave them off. Parentheses make your subroutines easier to read, less error-prone, and more consistent with other programming languages, so consider using this feature sparingly.

Using @_ to Pass Arguments to Subroutines

You've seen how the `@_` variable contains the argument list to any subroutine, and is implicitly local to that that subroutine. You can, however, also use `@_` inside or outside a subroutine to redefine a set of arguments for the subroutine call.

For example, if you set `@_` to a list of elements in the main body of your Perl script, then call a predeclared subroutine with no arguments, Perl will use the values in that array as the arguments to that subroutine. Here's a simple example:

```
@_ = ("this", "that", "other things");
&mysubroutine;   # no specific args, use @_
```

In this case, because the subroutine `&mysubroutine()` was called without ending parentheses, Perl will use the contents of `@_` as the arguments to that subroutine. This could be useful for calling ten different subroutines with all the same arguments, for example.

This works for calling nested subroutines as well; you can use the current contents of any `@_` variable as the arguments to a nested subroutine. Note that calling a subroutine with any arguments whatsoever, including an empty set of parentheses, overrides the use of `@_`. Note also that you must have predeclared the subroutine for this to work.

Anonymous Subroutines

Anonymous subroutines are subroutines without names, and they operate sort of like pointers to functions in C. You use anonymous subroutines to create references to a subroutine, and the use Perl's references capabilities to gain access to that subroutine later.

We'll discuss anonymous subroutines more in Day 19, "Working with References."

Using Subroutine Prototypes

Prototypes are one of those newer features that have snuck into Perl in the minor releases. Added to Perl as of version 5.003, subroutine prototypes enable your subroutines to look and behave just like regular built-in functions—that is, to determine the type of arguments they can accept rather than just stuffing them all into a list.

Subroutine prototypes only effect subroutines called without a leading `&`; you can call that same subroutine with a `&`, but the prototype will be ignored. In this way you can call a subroutine like a function or call it like a subroutine depending on your mood or for any other reason.

To declare or define a subroutine with a prototype, use one of the following:

```
sub subname (prototype);    # predeclaration
sub subname (prototype) {
   ...
}
```

The *subname* is, of course, the name of the subroutine. The prototype contains special characters referring to the number and type of arguments:

- `$` refers to a scalar variable, `@` to an array, `%` to a hash. `@` and `%` indicate list context and must appear last in the argument list (because they eat up the remaining arguments).
- Semicolons separate required arguments from optional arguments.
- Backslashed characters require arguments that start with that actual character.

So, for example, a subroutine with a prototype of `($$)` would expect two scalar variables as arguments. One with `($$;@)` would require two scalars, and have an optional list. One with `(\@)` requires a single list variable argument starting with `@`.

While subroutine prototypes might seem nifty, the fact that they are only available in newer versions of Perl might be problematic because you must be assured that the system you run your scripts on will have at least Per 5.003 installed. If you are only running your scripts on your own system this isn't a problem. If they're intended for wider use, it might be, although there is a way to figure this out at runtime which was described on Day 8, "Manipulating Lists and Strings.")

For more information on subroutine prototypes, see the `perlsub` man page.

The `caller` Function

One function I didn't mention in the body of this lesson is `caller`. The `caller` function is used to print out information about where a subroutine was called from (which can be sometimes useful for debugging). For more information, see the `perlfunc` man page.

Summary

A subroutine is a way of collecting together commonly used code or of portioning a larger script into smaller bits. Today you learned all about defining, calling, and returning values from subroutines, including delving into some of the issues of local and global variables.

Subroutines are defined using the `sub` keyword, the name of a subroutine, and a block containing the definition of the subroutine itself. Inside that block, you can define `my` variables that have a scope local to that subroutine, use the special `@_` variable to get to the arguments that were passed into the subroutine, and use the `return` function to return a value (or list of values) from that subroutine. If the context in which the subroutine was called is relevant, the `wantarray` function will tell you how your subroutine was called.

When you call subroutines, you use the name of the subroutine with an option `&` at the beginning, and with the arguments to the subroutine inside parentheses. Perl passes all the arguments to the subroutine as a flat array of all the values of its arguments, expanding any nested arrays and copying all the values into the local variable `@_`.

Q&A

Q. How are subroutines different from functions?

A. They're not; they both refer to the same conceptual things. In this lesson I simply decided to make the distinction so there would not be any confusion about calling built-in functions versus functions you define yourself.

Note that subroutines you define are, in fact, different from the built-in functions; subroutines don't control the number or type of arguments they can receive (at least, not without prototypes), and the rules of whether you can leave off the parentheses for subroutines are different. Future versions of Perl are working toward making programmer-defined subroutines and built-in subroutines closer in behavior.

Q. Subroutine calls with `&` look really weird to me. Can I just leave off the `&`?

A. Yes, the `&` is entirely optional. Include it or leave it off—it's your choice.

Q. I want to pass two arrays into a subroutine and get two arrays out. But the two arrays get squashed into one list on the way in and on the way out. How can I keep the two arrays discrete?

A. The best way to do this is to use references, but you won't learn about those until Day 19. Another way is to modify global variables inside the subroutine, rather than passing the array data in via an argument list. Yet another way is to compress the arrays into single scalar values (using delimiters), and then expanding them back into arrays inside your subroutine.

Q. But global variables are evil and bad.

A. Well, that depends on who you talk to. In Perl, sometimes the best solution to a problem involves a global variable, and if you're careful (declaring globals with `my`, for example, and making sure you limit the use of those variables), you can get around the disadvantages of global variables.

Q. So I can't figure it out, are Perl subroutines pass-by-value or pass-by-reference?

A. They're pass-by-reference as far as the values in the argument list are concerned. Change a value inside the `@_` array (for example, modify a string), and that value will change outside as well. However, multiple arrays will get squashed into a single flat list, so you could consider arrays to be pass-by-value. And, if you assign the `@_` argument list to one or more local variables, those values will be copied and any changes will not be reflected outside the subroutine.

Workshop

The workshop provides quiz questions to help you solidify your understanding of the material covered and exercises to give you experience in using what you've learned. Try and understand the quiz and exercise answers before you go on to tomorrow's lesson.

Quiz

1. Name two reasons why subroutines are useful.
2. Show how to call a subroutine.
3. Show how to define a subroutine.

4. Does it matter whether or not a subroutine is defined before it's called? Where in your Perl script should subroutine definitions appear?
5. If you don't include an explicit call to `return` in your script, what value does a subroutine return?
6. Is the argument that gets returned from the subroutine with `return` a scalar or a list value?
7. In which parts of a Perl script are variables declared using `my` available?
8. What happens when you declare a `my` local variable with the same name as a global variable?
9. What happens to a hash you pass into a subroutine?
10. What is `@_` used for? Where is it available?
11. How do you name parameters in a Perl subroutine?
12. What does `wantarray` do? Why would you want to use it?

Exercises

1. Write a subroutine that does nothing but print its arguments, one argument per line, with each line numbered.
2. Write a subroutine that takes a string as an argument and returns the string in reverse order by words.
3. Write a subroutine that takes a list of numbers and squares them all, returning the list of squares. If there are elements in the string that are not numbers, delete them from the final list.
4. BUG BUSTER: What's wrong with this script?

```
@int = &intersection(@list1, @list2);

sub intersection {
   my (@1, @2) = @_;
   my @final = ();
   OUTER: foreach my $el1 (@one) {
      foreach my $el2 (@two) {
         if ($el1 eq $el2) {
             @final = (@final, $el1);
             next OUTER;
         }
      }
   }
   return @final;
}
```

5. BUG BUSTER: How about this one?

```
$numtimes = &search(@input, $key);

sub search {
   my (@in, $key) = @_;
   my $count = 0;
   foreach my $str (@in) {
       while ($str =~ /$key/og) {
           $count++;
       }
   }
   return $count;
}
```

6. Write a subroutine that, when used in a scalar context, reads in a single line of input and reverses it (character by character this time). When used in a list context, reads in multiple lines of input into a list and reverses all the lines (last line first, and so on—the individual strings don't have to be reversed).
7. Take the image extractor script we wrote yesterday and turn it into a script that uses subroutines.

Answers

Here are the answers to the Workshop questions in the previous section.

Quiz Answers

1. Subroutines are useful for a number of reasons:
   - They help break up a large script into smaller bits to help manage complexity
   - Procedures in subroutines can be referred to by name to make scripts more readable
   - Subroutines can define local variables that are more efficient, easier to manage and control than globals
   - If you use the same code repeatedly throughout your programs, you can put that code into a subroutine, and then just reuse it
   - Smaller chunks of scripts can be more easily developed and debugged
2. Call a subroutine using one of these forms:

```
&thisubroutine();    # both % and parens
&thissubroutine(1,2); # with arguments
thissubroutine(1,2);  # & is optional
```

3. Define a subroutine like this:

```
sub name {
   # body of subroutine
}
```

4. For most instances, you can call a subroutine before defining it, and vice versa. Perl is not particular about predefining subroutines.

   You can define a subroutine anywhere a regular Perl statement can go, although, typically, subroutines are defined in a group at the beginning or end of a Perl script.

5. Without an explicit `return`, subroutines return the last value that was evaluated in the block.
6. Trick question! `Return` can be used to return either a scalar or a list, depending on what you want to return.
7. My variables are only available to code inside the nearest enclosing block and not to any nested subroutines.
8. Variables declared with `my` that have the same names as global variables will hide the value of the global. Once the subroutine or other block is finished executing, the original value of the global will be restored.
9. When you pass any list into a subroutine, it is flattened into a single list of scalar values. In the case of hashes, this means unwinding the hash into its component keys and values (the same way a hash is handled in any general list context).
10. `@_` refers to the argument list of the current subroutine. It's most commonly used inside a subroutine definition, although you can also define is as a global variable (see "Going Deeper").
11. Perl does not have formal named parameters. You can extract elements from the argument list `@_` and assign them to local variables in the body of your subroutine (although once assigned to local values, they cease to be references to the same values outside that subroutine).
12. The `wantarray` function allows you to find out the context in which your subroutine was called (scalar or list) to provide different behavior or return a sensible result.

Exercise Answers

1. Here's one answer:

```
sub printargs {
    my $line = 1;
    foreach my $arg (@_) {
        print "$line. $arg\n";
        $line++;
    }
}
```

2. Here's one answer:

```
sub reverstring {
    my @str = split(/\s+/, $_[0]);
    return join(" ", reverse @str);
}
```

3. Here's one answer:

```
sub squares {
    my @final = ();
    foreach my $el (@_) {
        if ($el !~ /\D+/) {
            @final = (@final, $el**2);
        }
    }
    return @final;
}
```

4. The fallacy in this script is assuming that the two lists, `@list1` and `@list2`, will remain as two lists inside the body of the subroutine. Because Perl combines all list arguments into a single list, you cannot retain individual lists inside the body of the subroutine. Consider using globals instead.

5. The problem with this script results because of the order of the arguments. The list and scalar arguments are flattened into a single list on their way into the subroutine. The failure results with the line that assigns the local variables `@in` and `$key` to the argument list in `@_`; because `@in` is a list it will copy all the elements in `@_`, and leave none left for `$key`. By simply reversing the order of the arguments (put the key first, then the list), you'll get around this problem.

6. Here's one answer:

```
sub rev {
    my $in = "";
    if (wantarray()) {  # list context
        my @inlist = ();
        while () {
            print 'Enter input: ';
            $in = <STDIN>;
            if ($in ne "\n") {
                @inlist = ($in, @inlist); # reverse order
            }
            else { last; }
        }
        return @inlist;
    }
    else {  # scalar context
        print 'Enter input: ';
        chomp($in = <STDIN>);
        return reverse $in;
    }
}
```

7. Here's one approach:

```
#!/usr/local/bin/perl -w

$/ = "";     # paragraph input mode

while (<>) {
    while (/<IMG\s([^>]+)>/ig) {
        &processimg($1);
    }
}

sub processimg {
    my $raw = $_[0];
    my %atts = ();

    while ($raw =~ /([^\s=]+)\s*=\s*("([^"]+)"|[^\s]+\s*)/ig) {
        if (defined $3) {
            $atts{ uc($1) } = $3;
        } else { $atts{ uc($1)} = $2; }
    }
    if ($raw =~ /ISMAP/i) {
        $atts{'ISMAP'}= "Yes";
    }
    &printatts(%atts);
}

sub printatts {
    my %atts = @_;

    print '-' x 15;
    print "\nImage:  $atts{'SRC'}\n";
    foreach my $key ("WIDTH", "HEIGHT",
                     "BORDER", "VSPACE", "HSPACE",
                     "ALIGN", "ALT", "LOWSRC", "ISMAP") {
        if (exists($atts{$key})) {
            $atts{$key} =~ s/[\s]*\n/ /g;
            print "    $key: $atts{$key}\n";
        }
    }
}
```

WEEK 2

DAY 12

Debugging Perl

No matter how good a programmer you are, chances are fairly high that any script over a few lines long is going to have some bugs. Some of those bugs are easy to figure out—syntax errors, infinite loops, or complaints from Perl because of `-w`. Others are much subtler, producing incomprehensible results or no results at all.

You could figure out what's going on at each point in your script by using several `print` statements to determine the current values of variables and see if loops and conditionals are actually getting executed. But there is an easier way—particularly for larger scripts. Perl comes with a source-level debugger that lets you step through your script, watch it as it executes, and print out the various values of variables throughout the script's execution. The debugger can help you track down subtle problems in your code far more quickly than `print` statements can.

In this chapter, we'll look at how to use the Perl debugger. In particular, we'll

- Explore a quick example of how you might commonly use the debugger
- Learn how to start and run the debugger
- Trace the execution of your program

- Step through the execution of your script
- List the source in various ways
- Print out the values of variables
- Set breakpoints for halting execution at specific places

Using the Debugger: A Simple Example

Probably the best way to see how Perl's debugger works is to show you an example of a typical use of the debugger. For this example, we'll step through the execution of a simple script that contains subroutines—the names script from Day 6, which reads in a list of names, prompts you for something to search for, and returns the names that match that search key.

When you run a script with the Perl debugger turned on, you'll end up inside the debugger itself, which looks something like this:

```
% perl -d  statssubbed.pl statsdata.txt

Loading DB routines from perl5db.pl version 1.01
Emacs support available.

Enter h or `h h' for help.

main::(statssubbed.pl:3):       &initvars();
  DB<1>
```

Don't worry about starting the debugger yet; you'll learn how to do that after we do a little walkthrough.

The debugger prints out two lines of output at each step. That `DB<1>` on the second line is the debugger prompt; you'll type in various commands at this prompt. The number `1` means this is the first command; you can repeat commands by referring to the command number.

The first line provides information about where the debugger is in the script. The number in the information lineshows the line number of the line of code that will be executed next. The part on the left refers to the current package, name of the file, and the line number. The part on the right is the actual line of code, including any comments for that line.

To execute a line of code, use either the `s` or `n` commands. The `s` command is more exhaustive; it will step into subroutines. The `n` command only steps through lines of code at the top level of your script; it'll execute subroutines silently (in other words, it executes them without allowing you to step through them). When you've used either `s` or `n`, you can repeat that command by just pressing Return (or Enter) at each prompt:

```
main::(statssubbed.pl:3):       &initvars();
  DB<1> s
main::initvars(statssubbed.pl:8):              $input = "";  # temporary input
  DB<1>
main::initvars(statssubbed.pl:9):              @nums = ();   # array of numbers;
  DB<1>
main::initvars(statssubbed.pl:10):             %freq = ();   # hash of number frequ
encies
  DB<1>
```

Note in this example how when the script execution moves to the `&initvars()` subroutine (immediately, in the case of this script) that the information on the left side of the output shows the name of that subroutine. This way, you always know where within your script you are. But in case you forget, or can't place the position based on the one line, you can use the `l` command to list some lines:

```
DB<1> l
10==>       %freq = ();   # hash of number frequencies
11:         $maxfreq = 0; # maximum frequency
12:         $count = 0;   # count of numbers
13:         $sum = 0;     # sum of numbers
14:         $avg = 0;     # average
15:         $med = 0;     # median
16:         @keys = ();   # temp keys
17:         $totalspace = 0; # total space across histogram
18      }
19
```


The `l` command will list ten lines after the current line; you can also use `-` to print lines before the current line. Multiple uses of `l` and `-` will move back and forth in the script's source code. Keep in mind that this just prints the lines so you can get some context for where you are in the script—`l` and `-` don't actually execute anything.

As you step through the code, you can print out the value of any variable—any scalar, array, hash, and so on, using the `x` command. In this next example, the `&getinput()` subroutine has just read a line from the data input file, stored it in the `$input` variable, and chomped the newline off the end of it. At `DB<5>` we print the value of `$index`, and print the current values of `@nums` (the array indexes are on the left, and the actual elements on the right). Keep in mind that the line of code displayed (line 23 in the source) is displayed *before* it is run, so the value of `$input` will not yet be in `@nums`.

```
main::getinput(statssubbed.pl:21):          while (defined ($input = <>)) {
  DB<5> s
main::getinput(statssubbed.pl:22):              chomp ($input);
  DB<5>
main::getinput(statssubbed.pl:23):              $nums[$count] = $input;
  DB<5> x $input
0  5
DB<6> x @nums
0  1
1  4
2  3
3  4
DB<7>
```

You can also use the `x` command to execute bits of Perl code; in the following case, to find the number of elements in `@raw`, or to show the first element:

```
DB<3> x scalar(@nums)
0  4
  DB<4> x $raw[0]
0  1
```

Stepping through the script using `n` or `s` enables you to see each line in excruciating detail, but sometimes it's more detail than you want. If you're inside a subroutine, you can use the `r` command to stop stepping through that subroutine, execute the rest of it, and return to the place where that subroutine was called (which, in the case of nested subroutines, may be still another subroutine).

To stop stepping through the script at any time, use the `c` command (*c* for continue). Perl then runs the rest of the script with no intervening stops (unless you've put them into your script itself, for example, to read some input).

In addition to stepping through the execution of a script line by line, you can also control execution of your script with breakpoints. A *breakpoint* is a mark at a line of code or the beginning of a subroutine. Using `c` will run the script until the breakpoint, and then stop. At the breakpoint, you can use `n` or `s` to step through lines of code, use `x` to print variables, or use `c` to continue to the next breakpoint.

For example, take the `statsmenu.pl` script we created yesterday, which organized the stats script into several subroutines. The `&countsum()` subroutine prints out the count and the sum of the data, calling the `&sumnums()` subroutine to get the latter value. To set a breakpoint at the `&sumnums()` subroutine, use the `b` command with the name of that subroutine, then `c` to execute the script up to that breakpoint:

```
# perl -d statsmenu.pl statsdata.txt
```

```
Loading DB routines from perl5db.pl version 1.01
Emacs support available.

Enter h or `h h' for help.

main::(statsmenu.pl:3): @nums = (); # array of numbers;
  DB<1> b sumnums
  DB<2> c
Please choose one (or Q to quit):
1. Print data set
2. Print count and sum of numbers
3. Print maximum and minimum numbers
4. Print mean and median numbers
5. Print a histogram of the frequencies.

Your choice --> 2
Number of elements: 70
main::sumnums(statsmenu.pl:72):      my $sum = 0;
  DB<2>
```

Can't remember the name of a subroutine? You can use the `S` command to print all the available subroutines. `S main` in particular will show you the subroutines you've defined (although there may be some extra Perl subroutines listed in there as well). Take a look at the following example.

```
DB<7> S main
main::BEGIN
main::countsum
main::getinput
main::maxmin
main::meanmed
main::printdata
main::printhist
main::printmenu
main::sumnums
  DB<8>
```

The `main` part is in reference to the `main` package, which is where all your variables and subroutines live by default. We'll explore more about packages tomorrow on Day 13.

If you want to set a breakpoint at a particular line, you can find the line using `l` to list the script, and then just use that line number with the `b` command:

```
DB<3> l
38:         print "5. Print a histogram of the frequencies.\n";
39:         while () {
40:             print "\nYour choice --> ";
```

```
41:             chomp($in = <STDIN>);
42:             if ($in =~ /^\d$/ || $in =~ /^q$/i) {
43:                 return $in;
44              } else {
45:                 print "Not a choice.  1-5 or Q, please,\n";
46              }
47          }
DB<3> b 43
```

One other neat feature of the debugger is the ability to trace the execution of the script as it's running. The `s` and `n` commands step through each statement one at a time, but sometimes it's useful to see a printout of each statement as it executes even if you aren't stepping through each one. The `t` command will turn tracing on or off, toggling between the two. Here's a trace from the `&printdata()` subroutine, with a breakpoint set at the top of the `foreach` loop:

```
  DB<1> b 54
  DB<2> t
    Trace = on
  DB<2> c
Please choose one (or Q to quit):
1. Print data set
2. Print count and sum of numbers
3. Print maximum and minimum numbers
4. Print mean and median numbers
5. Print a histogram of the frequencies.

Your choice --> 1
Data Set:
1 main::printdata(statsmenu.pl:54):         foreach $num (@nums) {
DB<2> c
main::printdata(statsmenu.pl:55):               print "$num ";
1 main::printdata(statsmenu.pl:56):             if ($i == 10) {
main::printdata(statsmenu.pl:59):               } else { $i++; }
main::printdata(statsmenu.pl:54):           foreach $num (@nums) {
  DB<2>
```

Note here that tracing prints not only the script's output (note the `1` at the start of the line in the middle of the output after the `c` command), but it also prints each script line as it's being executed. If we typed `c` here again, we'd get another loop of the `foreach`, and that same output all over again.

To quit the debugger, use the `q` command (not `quit`, just `q`).

```
DB<18> q
%
```

With that walkthrough under your belt, you should now have a basic idea of how the debugger works. For the rest of this section, I'll show you more detail on the specific commands.

Starting and Running the Debugger

Perl's built-in debugger is run from the command line using the `-d` option. If you've been running your Perl scripts on Unix or Windows NT using just the name of the script, you'll need to call Perl explicitly, with the name of the script and any filename arguments after that. In other words, if you usually call a script like this:

```
% myscript.pl names.txt
```

Call it like this for the debugger:

```
% perl -d myscript.pl names.txt
```

Alternately, if you think you'll be using the debugger a lot for a particularly gnarly script, you can add the `-d` option to the shebang line in the script itself:

```
#!/usr/ bin/perl -wd
```

Note

Don't forget to remove it again when you're done debugging.

To turn on the debugger in MacPerl, choose Perl Debugger from the Script menu, and then save your script and run it as usual. If you're going to use the script as a droplet (to accept files as input), don't forget the save the script as a droplet.

Note that before the debugger can run, your script has to be free of syntax errors or warnings. You'll have to fix those fatal errors before you can start debugging your script. But you'd have to do this anyway, so it shouldn't be too much of a burden.

To get help at any time as the debugger is running, use the `h` command, which will print out a list of possible commands. If it scrolls by too quickly you can use the `|h` command instead (which will pause between pages). You can also get help on any command using `h` with an argument; all the commands that match the argument will be printed, as shown here:

```
DB<3> h c
c [line|sub]    Continue; optionally inserts a one-time-only breakpoint
                at the specified position.
command         Execute as a perl statement in current package.
  DB<4>
```

12

Each debugger command has an associated number (in the previous example, the command "h c" was command number 3). You can refer back to any previous command using an exclamation point and the command number:

```
DB<4> !3
```

You can review the last few commands using `H` and number with a minus sign in front of it:

```
  DB<13> H -3
13: H-3
12: b sumnums
11: x @nums
  DB<14>
```

To quit the debugger, use the `q` command. In addition, if the execution of your Perl script is complete, you can use `R` to restart the execution. Note that `R` might not work depending on the environment and command-line arguments you used for that script.

Tracing Execution

Tracing allows you to see each line of your script as Perl executes it. If a line is executed multiple times, for example, as a loop, Perl will show it in the trace multiple times. For very complex scripts, this can often be more output than you need, but with breakpoints in place it might be helpful to see the actual order of execution that Perl takes through your script.

To toggle between trace modes in your Perl script, use the `t` command. If tracing is off, `t` will turn it on and vice versa. For example, this output shows the result of executing a loop with trace turned off and with trace turned on (the breakpoint has been set at line 54, a `foreach` loop).

```
main::printdata(statsmenu.pl:54):          foreach $num (@nums) {
  DB<4> c
2 main::printdata(statsmenu.pl:54):          foreach $num (@nums) {
  DB<4> t
Trace = on
  DB<4> c
main::printdata(statsmenu.pl:55):                print "$num ";
2 main::printdata(statsmenu.pl:56):              if ($i == 10) {
main::printdata(statsmenu.pl:59):                } else { $i++; }
main::printdata(statsmenu.pl:54):            foreach $num (@nums) {
```

Turning tracing on shows you your script as it's executing. A stack trace shows you where you've already been—in the case of nested subroutines, it'll show you the subroutine that called the one you're currently executing, the one that called that subroutine, and so on, all the way back to the top level of your script. Use the `T` command to show the stack trace, as follows:

```
DB<4> T
@ = main::sumnums() called from file `statsmenu.pl' line 68
$ = main::countsum() called from file `statsmenu.pl' line 13
  DB<4>
```

The characters at the beginning of those lines show the context in which the subroutine was called—for example, the first line of this stack trace shows that the `&sumnums()` subroutine (the current routine) was called in a list context (the `@` at the beginning of the line indicates that), from inside the `&countsum()` routine. The `&countsum()` routine in turn was called from the main body of the script, in a scalar context (the `$` at the beginning of the line shows that).

Stepping Through the Script

To step through the code to your script one statement at a time, use either the `s` or `n` commands. Return (or Enter) will repeat the previous `s` or `n`. At each step, Perl displays the line of code it will execute next (not the one it just executed):

```
  DB<1> s
main::getinput(statsmenu.pl:25):                 $nums[$count] = $_;
  DB<1>
```

The difference between the `s` and `n` commands is that `s` will descend into subroutine definitions. The `n` command stays at the same level, executing the subroutines without stepping through them.

To stop stepping through a subroutine, execute the remainder of that subroutine, and return to the statement where the subroutine was originally called, use the `r` command.

To stop stepping through the code altogether, use the `c` command.

Listing the Source

You can list the current source code being run, with line numbers, to get an idea of the context of the current line of code or to find a specific line at which to set a breakpoint.

To list the next ten lines of code from the current line down, use the `l` command:

```
 DB<15> l
75==>               $sum += $num;
76              }
77:             return $sum;
78          }
79
80          # print the max and minimum values
81          sub maxmin {
82:             print "Maximum number: $nums[0]\n";
83:             print "Minimum number: $nums[$#nums]\n\n";
84          }
  DB<15>
```

Additional calls of l will continue to show the next couple of lines. You can also use l with a line number to display just that line, with a range of numbers (1-4, for example) to display those particular lines, or with a subroutine name to list the first ten lines of that subroutine.

To back up a few lines in the display, use the - command. As with l for moving forward in the source, multiple uses of - will continue to move back.

The w command will show a window around the current line (or the line number, if you specify one): a few lines before and a few lines after. An arrow (==>) will show the current line position:

```
DB<3> w
20      # read in the input from the files, sort it once its done
21:     sub getinput {
22:         my $count = 0;
23==>       while (<>) {
24:             chomp;
25:             $nums[$count] = $_;
26:             $count++;
27          }
28:         @nums = sort { $a <=> $b } @nums;
29      }
```

To search for a particular line in the source, use the pattern matching expression. /key/, for example, will find the first instance of the word key. Use ?pattern? to search backwards in the file.

One last useful listing command is S; the S command will show all the subroutines available in the script. Most of those subroutines will be internal to Perl or to the debugger itself, but S with a package name (such as main) will only print those in that package, as shown here:

```
DB<20> S main
main::BEGIN
main::getpat
main::readnames
main::searchpat
```

> **Note** The S command accepts a regular expression as its argument. Any subroutines with names (including package names) containing main will be listed when you use the command S main. You can use any Perl regular expression to create more complex patterns to filter the subroutine list. Regular expressions were discussed on Days 9 and 10.

More about packages tomorrow.

Printing Variables

Scrolling around in the source for your file is all well and good, but it helps to be able to figure out what Perl is doing while it's running your script. To print out the values of variables, use one of the following commands:

The `X` command will print out all the variables in the current package. Because many of these variables are special to Perl (including special variables such as @_, $_, and $1), the list can be fairly long. `X` with the name of a variable will print all the variables that match that name. Note that you should use just the name itself, and not include the `$`, `@`, or `%` character. `X foo` prints the values of all the variables named `foo`, (`$foo`, `@foo`, and `%foo`).

The `V` command is identical to `X`, except that it assumes the first argument is the name of a package and prints the variables in that package. This won't be of much use until you start using packages, but I mention it here for completeness.

Caution

When you provide a variable name to the `x` command, you must include the character that specifies its type ($, @, or %). When you provide a list of variable names to the `X` command, the type identifier must be left off.

The one problem with `X` is that it seems to be unable to recognize local variables inside subroutines. For printing the values of local variables, or to execute small bits of Perl code that will result in values of interest, use the `x` command, as follows:

```
DB<3> x $input
0  'Dante Alighieri'
```

Printing arrays or hashes shows the contents of that array or hash. The output of `X` and `V` is slightly easier to read than that of `x`, particularly for hashes. Here's how a hash looks using `X`:

```
DB<4> X %names
%names = (
   'Adams' => 'Douglas'
   'Alexander' => 'Lloyd'
   'Alighieri' => 'Dante'
   'Asimov' => 'Isaac'
   'Barker' => 'Clive'
   'Bradbury' => 'Ray'
   'Bronte' => 'Emily'
)
```

12

Setting Breakpoints

Setting breakpoints inside a script allows you specify points in the script where the debugger will pause and allow you to use the other commands to figure out where a problem is occurring. Breakpoints are particularly useful in large scripts where you don't want to step over every single line. You can set as many breakpoints in your script as you need to, and then use the stepping or variable printing commands to work through the problem. Use `c` to continue execution past the breakpoint.

To set a breakpoint, use the `b` command. With the name of a subroutine, the breakpoint will be set at the first statement inside that subroutine; with a line number, the breakpoint will be set at that line number. With no argument, `b` will set a breakpoint at the current line. Breakpoints show up as a lowercase `b` in the source listings (there's one here at line 33):

```
DB<19> w 33
30      }
31
32      sub searchpat {
33:b        my $key = $_[0];
34:         my $found = 0;
35:         foreach $ln (sort keys %names) {
36==>           if ($ln =~ /$key/o || $names{$ln} =~ /$key/o) {
37:                 print "$ln, $names{$ln}\n";
38:                 $found = 1;
39              }
```

The `L` command is used to print all the breakpoints you have set at any given time, like in the following:

```
DB<22> L
namessub.pl:
 9:          my @raw = ();  # raw list of names
   break if (1)
 33:         my $key = $_[0];
   break if (1)
```

You can delete a breakpoint using either a line number or a subroutine name using the `d` command. Use `D` to delete all set breakpoints.

```
DB<22> d 9
DB<23> L
namessub.pl:
 33:         my $key = $_[0];
   break if (1)
```

Other Commands

So far, I've only shown you the commands that will help you get started with the debugger and that you're likely to use the most. In addition to the commands here, Perl also allows you to set conditional breakpoints, to change the values of variables, to perform actions at particular lines and, in fact, to enter entire Perl scripts and watch them execute interactively. As you learn more about the Perl debugger, you'll definitely want to make active use of the `h` command, and to refer to the perldebug man page when necessary.

One Other Thing

The debugger will help you figure out problems in your code. However, judicious use of the `-w` option can help you prevent many problems before you even start running your script (or having to resort to the debugger to figure out what's going wrong). Don't forget to use `-w` when you can.

Perl Debugger Command Reference

Table 12.1 contains a list of all the debugger commands mentioned in this chapter. They're the ones you'll probably use most often, but the commands in the table represent a subset of all of the debugger commands available. For the full list of debugger commands, see the `perldebug` chapter of the Perl documentation.

TABLE 12.1 Debugger Command Reference

Command	*Purpose*
`s`	Step into the next statement. If the next statement is a subroutine call, it steps into the subroutine.
`n`	Next statement. If the statement contains subroutine calls, they are executed silently, and the debugger stops at the beginning of the next statement.
`l`	List the next set of lines in the program.
`l` *`min+incr`*	List `incr + 1` lines starting at line *min*.
`l` *`min-max`*	List lines *min* through *max*. (For example, `l 10-20`.)
`l` *`line`*	List a single line.
`l` *`subroutine`*	List the first set of lines in *subroutine*.
`-`	List the previous set of lines.
`x` *`expr`*	Evaluates the expression supplied in list context and prints the results.
`c`	Continue. Execute the statements that follow until a breakpoint is reached.
`c` *`line`*	Continue, inserting a one-time breakpoint at *line*.
`c` *`subroutine`*	Continue, inserting a one-time breakpoint at *subroutine*.
`b` *`line`*	Set a breakpoint at *line*.
`b` *`subroutine`*	Set a breakpoint at *subroutine*.

12

TABLE 12.1 continued

Command	*Purpose*
`d`	Delete breakpoint at the line about to be executed.
`d` *`line`*	Delete the breakpoint at *line*.
`D`	Delete all breakpoints.
`L`	List all breakpoints.
`S`	Show all subroutine names.
`S` *`regex`*	Show all subroutine names matching *regex*.
`t`	Toggle tracing.
`q`	Stop execution of the program and exit the debugger.
`h`	Help.
`|h`	Help, filtered through the pager.
`H`	Show the commands run in the current debugging session.
`H` *`-number`*	Show the last *number* commands.
`R`	Restart the debugging session (start the program being debugged over from the beginning).
`T`	Produce a backtrace for the current statement.
`w`	List the lines of code surrounding the current line.
`w` *`line`*	List the lines of code surrounding *line*.
/pattern/	Search forward in the program for lines matching *pattern*.
?pattern?	Search backward in the program for lines matching *pattern*.
`V`	Display all of the variables in the package `main`.
`V` *`vars`*	Display *vars* in the package `main`. *vars* is a list of variable names, separated by spaces (make sure to leave off the type identifier).
`V` *`package`*	Display all of the variables in *package*.
`V` *`package vars`*	Display *vars* in *package*.
`X`	Display variables in the current package.
`X` *`vars`*	Display the listed variables, if they're members of the current package.

Using a Graphical Debugger

Unless you use the debugger frequently, it can be difficult to keep track of all of the commands that are associated with it. For that reason, you might prefer to use a graphical debugger to debug your programs. ActiveState created the graphical debugger, and is part of a commercial product called the Perl Dev Kit. The price for the package varies based on what sort of user you are. You can find out about it at `http://www.activestate.com/`.

When you install the graphical debugger, it starts automatically when you run a Perl script in debug mode in place of the command-line debugger. There's a screen shot of the debugger in figure 12.1.

FIGURE 12.1

The ActiveState Perl Debugger.

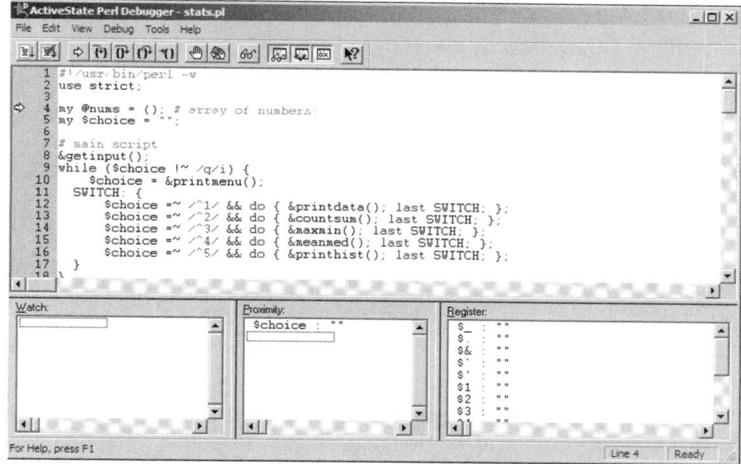

The primary advantage of the graphical debugger is that it presents a lot of information in the interface. Rather than using debugger commands to view snippets of code, see the contents of variables, and list breakpoints, you can see all of the information directly in the debugger window.

The window consists of four panes. The top pane contains the source code to the script being debugged. Not only can you see the full source of the script in this pane, you can also see which will be executed next, and which lines have breakpoints assigned to them.

The pane in the lower-left corner is the watch list. You can add watches for any expression you like. For example, if you want to keep track of the value of an array called `@foo`, you can simply add it to the watch list by selecting it in the source code, right clicking it, and selecting `Copy to Watch`.

The pane in the bottom middle is the Proximity list. It displays the values of all variables referenced in lines of source code near the one currently being executed. Oftentimes you won't even need to bother with the watch list because the variable you're interested in will be listed in the Proximity list.

The final pane is the Register list. It keeps track of the variables that Perl maintains on its own. The special variables like $_ and $1 through $5 are displayed in this listing.

Aside from the data display, the main advantages of the debugger are that you don't have to remember all of the debugger commands to make it work. There are menu items and buttons on the toolbar for all the frequently used debugger commands, so the casual user will find it easier to debug their programs using the graphical interface. Unfortunately, the debugger does not use the same keyboard commands as the command-line debugger, so hardcore debugger users might still prefer the command-line debugger to the graphical version.

Going Deeper

I've discussed essentially all the most important debugger commands in this chapter, but not the complete set. If you begin using the debugger quite a lot, you might want to check the `perldebug` man page or the debugger's online help for more of the options.

Using Different Debuggers

Perl allows you to customize the behavior of the debugger, or to plug in an entirely different debugger system if you like. The `-d` switch, when used with a colon and the name of a module, will use that module as the debugger. For example, the `Devel::DProf` module, available from CPAN, provides profiling for your Perl scripts (testing how long it takes to run each subroutine, to figure out the inefficiencies in your code). When installed, you can call it like this:

```
% perl -d:DProf thescript.pl
```

In addition, the perl5db.pl file contains the actual code for the debugger; you can copy and modify that file to change the behavior of the debugger. For more information, see the `perldbug` man page, or the documentation that comes with the `DProf` module.

Running Perl Interactively

The debugger can be used to run Perl in a sort of interactive mode to test commands and see their output right away. And you don't even need an actual script to do it. Here's a simple command that will load the debugger without a script to debug:

```
# perl -d -e1
```

Actually, you have given Perl a script to execute, a script of one character: 1. The `-e` option is used to run Perl scripts directly on the command line. We'll come back to this at the end of the book, on Day 20, "Odds and Ends."

Common Pitfalls and FAQs

Throughout the last twelve days I've tried to point out common mistakes that new Perl programmers (and even experienced programmers) make in various topics. The Perl documentation also contains a list of common pitfalls, and many more, in the `perltraps` man page. A quick perusal of that page can provide interesting hints for solving problems in difficult code.

The Perl documentation also contains an extensive set of FAQ files (Frequently Asked Questions). Before pulling your hair out over a particular problem, check the FAQs. Start from the `perlfaq` man page and work from there.

Summary

Today you learned not so much about Perl itself, but about Perl's associated command-line debugger. You learned how to start and run the debugger, how to step through each line of your script, list the source, set breakpoints, trace the execution, and find out information about different parts of your script as they're running.

With the debugger there's few problems you can't figure out, and you can usually figure them out faster this way than trying to use print statements everywhere.

Q&A

Q. I use emacs. Is there any way to tie the Perl debugger into emacs?

A. Yup. The `cperl-mode.el` file has a ton of stuff for tying Perl into emacs. You can find this file in the standard Perl distribution in the `emacs` directory.

Workshop

The workshop provides quiz questions to help you solidify your understanding of the material covered and exercises to give you experience in using what you've learned. Try and understand the quiz and exercise answers before you go on to tomorrow's lesson.

Quiz

1. What is a debugger for? Why is it more useful than, say, `-w` or `print`?
2. How do you start the Perl debugger?
3. Name three ways of listing bits of code inside the debugger.
4. How do you print the values of variables in the debugger?
5. How is tracing execution different from stepping through each line of code?
6. How are the `x` and `v` commands for printing variables different?

Exercises

Type the following script:

```
#!/usr/local/bin/perl -w

my @foo = (2,5,3,7,4,3,4,3,2,3,9);

foreach $thing (0..10) {
    &timesit($thing, $foo[$thing]);
}

sub timesit {
    my ($num, $val) = @_;
    print "$num times $val is ", $num * $val, "\n";
}
```

Run the debugger on it. Perform the following debugger operations:

1. Turn on tracing using the `t` command. Type `c` to see the result.
2. Type `R` to restart running the script. Use `n` to step through the script. When you get inside the foreach loop, print the values of `$thing` a number of times.
3. Type `R` to restart the script again. Use `s` to step through the script. Print the values of `$num` and `$val` from inside the `×it()` subroutine. Use `r` to return from inside the `×it()` subroutine.
4. Type `R` to restart the script. Set a breakpoint at the `×it()` subroutine using the `b` command. Type `L` to view the breakpoint. Type `c` to run until the breakpoint is hit. Use `d` to delete the breakpoint.
5. BUG BUSTER: Use the debugger to find the bugs in this script:

```
#!/usr/local/bin/perl -w

@foo = (2,5,3,7,4,3,4,3,2,9);

while ($i < $#foo) {
    &timesit($i, $foo[$i]);
}

sub timesit {
    my ($num, $val) = @_;
    print "$num times $val is ", $num * $val, "\n";
}
```

Answers

Here are the answers to the Workshop questions in the previous section.

Quiz Answers

1. The `-w` command in Perl is there to help you fix (or avoid) syntax mistakes or poor-coding practices. The Perl debugger is there to help you with all other problems: arrays not getting built or not getting printed, values not getting matched, script logic not running the way you expect it to. Using `print` statements will produce some of the same effect, but it'll take longer and often be more difficult to figure out the problem. With the debugger you can also change values of variables and execute different bits of code at different times while your script is running—something you cannot do with a simple print statement.
2. Start the Perl debugger by running `perl` on the command line with the `-d` option followed by the name of your script and any script arguments. In MacPerl, choose Perl Debugger from the Script menu.
3. There are several ways of listing code in the debugger:
    - Use the `l` command to show succeeding chunks of code
    - Use `l` with a line number to show that line number
    - Use `l` with a range of line numbers to show those lines
    - Use `-` to show the preceding chunks of code
    - Use `w` to show a few lines before and a few lines after the current line
4. Print values of global and package variables using the `X` command with a variable name (minus the `$`, `@`, or `%`). Use the `x` command to print other variables and execute other Perl expressions (such as `$hash{'key'}`).
5. Turning on tracing shows each line of code as it's being executed, whether you are stepping through the execution or not. Stepping through the code shows each line as it's about to be executed. Stepping through code using the `n` command skips over subroutines (they get executed, but their contents are not displayed).
6. The `X` command prints the variables for the current package (main). The `V` command prints variables in any given package (something you'll need later when you work with packages).
7. A breakpoint is a marker somewhere in your Perl code. When you run the code in the debugger, Perl runs until it finds a breakpoint, and then stops. You can then step through the code from there, print values of variables, or continue to the next time the breakpoint is hit.

12

Exercise Answers

1–4. There are no answers to these exercises; they demonstrate the use of the debugger.

5. There are two bugs in the script:
   - `$i` is never initialized, which means that the `×it()` subroutine will get initialization errors when it tries to print the value of `$num`.
   - `$i` is never incremented, which means it will be `0` each time and go into an infinite loop.

WEEK 2

DAY 13

Scope, Modules, and Importing Code

In today's lesson, we'll discuss issues concerning space and time (to complement our earlier discussions of truth and greed). By space, I'm referring to variable *namespace*: how variable names are managed across local and global scope, and how packages can be used to manage global variables across programs. Related to space is the capability to import code from modules into your scripts, either at compile time or runtime (thus covering the *time* part of today's lesson). Today we'll explore

- The problem with global variables and various ways of controlling those variables
- More about local variables; going beyond `my` and subroutines
- Importing and using external code with modules and pragmas
- Using modules from the standard library and from CPAN

Global Variables and Packages

Variable scope, in general, refers to the availability and existence of a variable in your script. A *global scope*, then, refers to a variable that is available to all parts of your script and exists as long as your script is running. *Local scope*, in turn, refers to a variable that has some limited scope and might pop in and out of existence depending on what part of your Perl script is currently executing.

We'll start this chapter with a look at global variables and global scope. In the next section we'll turn to local scope.

The Problem with Globals

Throughout this book, we've been using global variables (and global scope) in most of the examples, with the exception of the occasional local variable in a subroutine. There's a good reason for this: Global variables are easy to create and easy to use. Any variable that is not explicitly declared with `my` (or, as you'll learn soon, `local`) automatically becomes a global variable, regardless of the context in which you use it, and is available at any point in that script.

This makes simple scripts easy to write. But as your scripts become larger and larger, the use of global variables becomes more and more problematic. There are more variables to keep track of and more variables taking up space as your script runs. Global variables that mysteriously appear deep in the body of a script can be difficult to debug—which part of the script is updating this variable at what time? Do you even remember what that global variable does?

As you develop larger scripts that use global variables, there's also a significant danger that you will accidentally use a name for a variable that already exists somewhere else in your script. Although this problem can make it more difficult to debug your scripts, it's a particularly difficult problem if you have to incorporate your scripts into someone else's code, or if you want to create reusable Perl libraries. The risk of clashing variable names across multiple bodies of code becomes a very real and very painful problem.

The best way to control the potential of name clashes with promiscuous global variables is to not use them. Organize all your scripts in subroutines, and declare all your variables local to those subroutines. Data that needs to be shared between subroutines can be passed from subroutine to subroutine via arguments. Many software developers argue that all programs—no matter how small, no matter how specialized the purpose—should be written this way, that the avoidance of global variables is Good Software Design.

In real life, however, everyone uses the occasional global variable, particularly in situations where every part of the script must access the same stored data in a list or other structure. Which brings us to another method for organizing and managing global variables: packages.

What's a Package?

A *package* is a way to bundle up your global variables so they aren't really global anymore—they're only global inside a given package. In other words, each package defines its own variable name space. Packages enable you to control which global variables are available to other packages, thereby avoiding the problems of clashing variable names across different bits of code.

Chances are good you'll only need to develop your own packages if you're creating Perl modules or libraries or classes in object-oriented Perl programming—all topics that are too advanced for this book. Even if you don't develop your own, packages are all around you as you write and run your Perl scripts, whether you know it or not. With that in mind, having at least a passing understanding of how packages work will help you not only understand how Perl looks at variables and name spaces in your own scripts, but also how importing code from modules works as well. And it'll help in the event that your code grows to the point where it does become a library or a module later. Learn the rules now, and it'll be that much easier later.

How Packages and Variables Work

The core concept of the package is that every line of Perl is compiled in the current package, which can be the default package or one you define yourself. Each package has a set of variable names (called a *symbol table*) that determines whether a variable is available for Perl to use and what the value of that variable currently is. The symbol table contains all the names you could possibly use in your script—scalars, arrays, hashes, and subroutines.

If you refer to a variable name—say, `$x`—in your script, Perl will try to find that variable in the current package's symbol table. If you tell Perl to switch packages, it will look up `$x` in the new package. You can also refer to a variable by its complete package name, which tells Perl which symbol table to look in for the variable and its value. Package names contain both the name of the package, two colons, and the name of the variable. The special character indicating whether the variable is a scalar, a list, or a hash, or so on, is still included at the start of the package.

So, for example, `$main::x` would be used to refer to the scalar variable `$x` stored in the `main` package, whereas `$x` would refer to the scalar variable `$x` in the current package, which may or may not be the same variable stored in the package `main`. They have the same variable name but because they live in different packages, they have different values (or they might not exist at all in other packages).

Main is the default package that you've been using all along, although you haven't been aware of it. When you create and use global variables in scripts that do not define an explicit package, you're actually creating variables that belong to the main package (you might have seen this come up in the error messages you get when you make a mistake—some of them refer to "Name main::foo used only once..."). All this time, whenever I've been referring to global variables, I've actually been slightly dishonest: Global variables are actually package variables belonging to the package main.

Note that the existence of global variables in packages doesn't make them any less difficult to manage if you use lots of them. A hundred global variables defined in main are going to be just as difficult to use as a hundred global variables defined in a new package called mypackage. Using local variables and passing data between subroutines is still good-programming practice for your own bit of the Perl world.

To create a new package, or switch between packages, use the package function:

```
package mypack;  # define or switch to a package other than main
```

Package definitions have a scope similar to that of local variables: Package definitions inside a subroutine or block compile all the code inside that subroutine or block as part of that new package, and then revert to the enclosing package. Calling package at the start of a script defines a new package for that entire script.

As I said earlier, you'll define your own packages most often when you're writing code libraries or modules of your own. The most important things to understand about packages are

- Every variable name and value is stored in a symbol table for the current package.
- You can refer to a variable name as either a plain variable name for the current package, or with a complete package name. This determines which symbol table Perl checks for the variable's value.
- The default package is package main.

A Simple Package Example

Here's a simple example of a program that uses packages. Its only purpose is to demonstrate how packages affect variable scope. In this program, I create three packages, and demonstrate how the scope of global variables is affected by those package declarations. The source code is in Listing 13.1.

LISTING 13.1 A Program that Demonstrates the Use of Packages

```
#!/usr/ bin/perl -w

package foo;
print "Package foo ...\n";

$bar = 'bar';

package red;
print "Package red ...\n";

$blue = 'blue';

print "Value of \$bar: $bar\n";
print "Value of \$blue: $blue\n";
print "Value of \$foo::bar: $foo::bar\n";
```

Let's look at the source code. First, create a package called `foo`, and initialize a variable in it, `$bar`. Then, initialize a second package, called `red`. In it, initialize a new variable called `$blue`, and print out the values of `$bar`, `$blue`, and `$foo::bar`. When the value of $bar is printed, nothing is displayed because there is no variable called `$bar` in the current package. On the other hand, `$blue`'s value is printed out as you would expect, because it is native to the current package. Finally, when `$bar` is qualified with a package name, the value is printed correctly. By using the full-package qualifier, the value can be retrieved from the other package.

Under ordinary circumstances, you probably wouldn't create more than one package in a single program like I did in this case. However, by presenting the code in this way, you can see how packages can be used to encapsulate variables so they don't get in the way of variable names that you can use elsewhere in your code.

Using Non-Package Global Variables

One way of creating well-mannered globals is to create packages. However, there is one other trick that is very common for creating globals: Declare your globals as local to your own script.

If you declare your global variables with the `my` modifier, as you do local variables inside subroutines, then those global variables won't belong to any package, not even `main`. They'll still be global to your script, and available to all parts of that script (including subroutines), but they won't conflict with any other variables inside actual packages, including those declared in package `main`. Global variables declared with `my` also have a slight performance advantage because Perl doesn't have to access the package's symbol table each time the variable is referenced.

There's one case where you don't want to use non-package globals, and that's if you're writing scripts to run in Apache's `mod_perl` environment. Because of the way `mod_perl` works, if you do so, the main body of your script will run as though it's an anonymous subroutine, and your global variables won't be visible to the other subroutines in your program.

Because of these advantages of using non-package globals, it's recommended Perl practice to do this for all but the simplest of Perl scripts. To make use of it in your own scripts, simply include the `my` modifier when you declare your global variables, the same way you do for the locals:

```
my %names = (); # global hash for the names
```

Perl also includes a special feature to help you make sure you're using all your variables properly, as either local variables inside subroutines, or as non-package variables if they're global. Add the line `use strict` at the top of your script to turn on this feature, like this:

```
#!/usr/local/bin/perl -w
use strict;

my $x = '';  # OK
@foo = ();   # will cause script to exit

# remainder of your script
```

With `use strict` in place, when you run your script Perl will complain about stray global variables and exit. Technically, `use strict` will complain about any variables that are not declared with `my`, referenced using package names, or imported from elsewhere. Consider it an even stricter version of the variable warnings you get with `-w`.

There's one odd side effect of the `use strict` command worth mentioning: It will complain about the placeholder variable in a `foreach` loop, for instance, `$key` in this example:

```
foreach $key (keys %names) {
   ...
}
```

Technically, this is because the `foreach` variable, which is implicitly local, is actually a global variable pretending to be a local. It's still only available to the `foreach`, and behaves as if it were local, but internally it's declared differently (you'll learn about the two different kinds of local variables later in this lesson, in "Local Variables with `my` and `local`.") To fix the complaint from `use strict`, simply put a `my` in front of the variable name:

```
foreach my $key (keys %names) {
   ...
}
```

Throughout the rest of this book, all the examples will use `use strict` and declare global variables as `my` variables.

Local Scope and Variables

A local variable, as you learned on Day 11, "Creating and Using Subroutines," is one that is only available to a certain part of a script. After that part of the script is finished executing, the variable ceases to exist. Local variables also have a limited availability to other parts of a script. They might be private to just the scope in which they were defined, or they might only be available to those parts of the script that are running at the same time as the part of the script that defined the variable.

Local Variables and Local Scope

On Day 11, we looked at local variables, defined with `my`, inside subroutines. A subroutine defines a local scope, and the local variable is available to all the code defined inside that subroutine.

A subroutine isn't the only thing that can create a local scope, however. Any block surrounded by brackets defines a local scope, and any local variables defined within that block will cease to exist at the end of the block. This enables you to define local variables inside loops or conditionals, or even inside bare blocks, if there's some portion of code that will benefit from a new local scope.

All the following snippets of code define a local scope. Each declaration of the variable `$s` is local to that enclosing block, and each `$x` is different from all the other versions of `$x`. Note, in particular, the use of a local variable in the `foreach` loop; here the variable is local to the entire loop, not to each iteration. `$x` will be incremented five times, as you'd expect:

```
if ($foo) {      # conditional
    my $x = 0;
    print "X in conditional: $x\n";
    $x++;
}

foreach (1..5) {  # loop
    my $x += $_;
    print "X in loop: $x\n";
}

{                # bare block
    my $x = 0;
    print "X in bare block: $x\n";
    $x++;
}
```

13

One other rule of variables and scope to always keep in mind: Local variables with the same name as global variables hide the values of the global variable of the same name. The value of the local variable is used throughout the current local scope, and then the original global and its original value will be restored at the end of that scope.

Although this is a convenient feature, it can also be terribly confusing. Generally it's a good idea to avoid naming your locals the same name as your globals unless you've got good reasons for doing so.

Alternately, you can always refer to a global variable using its complete package name, even from inside a local scope. This technique assumes you did not use `use strict` or declare your globals with `my`:

```
$foo = 0;  # global
{
   my $foo = 1;         # local
   print "$foo\n";      # prints 1
   print "$main::foo\n";  # prints 0
}
print "$foo\n";         # prints 0
```

Local Variables with `my` and `local`

In addition to the local variables defined with `my`, there are also local variables defined with `local`. The `local` modifier is used the same way as the `my` modifier, with one or more variable names:

```
local ($x, $y);
```

What's the difference? The most obvious difference between `my` local variables and `local` local variables is that the scope for `local` local variables is determined by the execution of the script, not by how the code is laid out. A `my` variable is only available to the code up until the nearest enclosing block or subroutine definition; if you call another subroutine from within that one, the second subroutine won't have access to those variables. Local variables declared with `local` are available to the code inside that block and subroutine *and* to nested subroutines called from that same subroutine. That variable definition will cascade to any nested subroutines, in much the same way that global variables are available everywhere. `Local` local variables are available from that subroutine and all the subroutines it calls as well.

Note

In technical terms, `my` variables are *lexically scoped*, and `local` variables are *dynamically scoped*. But you don't have to know those terms unless you're a computer scientist, or you're trying to impress other computer scientists.

I've put an example of how the scope differences between `my` and `local` variables work in the section "Going Deeper," if you're interested in looking more at `local` versus `my`. For the most part, however, local variables are best defined with `my`, and not `local`; `my` variables follow the more common definition of *local scope* in other languages and are easier to use and manage.

Using Perl Modules

Half of learning how to script Perl successfully is knowing how to write the code. The other half is knowing when NOT to write the code. Or, to be more exact, knowing when to take advantage of the built-in Perl functions or when to use libraries and modules that other people have written to make your programming life easier.

If you've got a given task to do in Perl that sounds kind of complex but that might also be something other programmers might have done in the past, chances are really good that someone else has beaten you to it. And, in the Perl tradition, he may very well have packaged their code in a module or a library and made it available for public downloading. If it's a really common task, that module might even be part of the standard Perl distribution. Much of the time, all you have to do to make use of these libraries is import them into your own Perl scripts, add some code to customize them for your particular situation, and that's it. You're done.

Throughout many of the lessons in the remainder of this book, we'll be looking at a number of modules that you have available to you as part of the standard Perl distribution, as part of the distribution for your particular platform, or as downloadable files from the Comprehensive Perl Archive Network. In this section, then, you'll learn the basics: what a module is, and how to import and use modules in your own scripts.

Some Terminology

But first, some terminology. I've been bandying about the terms *function*, *library*, *module*, and *package*, and it's worth noting what all these terms mean.

A built-in function, as I've noted before, is a function that comes with Perl and is available for you to use in your script. You don't need to do anything special to call a built-in function; you can call it anytime you want to.

A Perl *library* is a collection of Perl code intended for reuse in other scripts. Old-style Perl libraries were nothing more than this, and were used in other Perl scripts by importing them with the `require` operator. More recently, the term library has come to be equivalent to a Perl module, with old-style libraries and `require` falling out of favor. More about importing code with `require` later in this lesson.

A Perl *module* is a collection of reusable Perl code. Perl modules define their own packages, and have a set of variables defined by that package. To use a module, you import that module into your script with the `use` operator, and then you can (usually) refer to the subroutines (and, sometimes, variables) in that module as you would any other subroutines (or variables). Some modules are object-oriented, which means using them in slightly different ways, but the basic procedure is the same.

In addition, there are also *pragmas*, which are special kinds of Perl modules that affect both how Perl compiles and runs a script (whereas most Perl modules only affect its actual execution). Otherwise, they behave the same. `use strict` is an example of the use of a pragma. We'll look at pragmas later in this lesson in the section entitled "Using Pragmas."

Getting Modules

Where are these modules found? If you have Perl, you already have a number of modules to play with and you don't need to do anything further. The *standard Perl library* is the collection of modules, pragmas, and scripts that are distributed with the standard Perl distribution. Different versions of Perl for different platforms might have a different standard library—the Windows version of Perl, for example, has a set of modules for accessing capabilities specific to Windows machines. Although you have to explicitly import these modules to use them, you don't have to download them or install them.

The "official" set of library modules is fully described in the `perlmod` man page, and includes modules for the following:

- Interfaces to databases
- Simple networking
- Language extensions, module and platform-specific development support, dynamic module and function loading
- Text processing
- Object-oriented programming
- Advanced math
- File, directory, and command-line argument handling
- Error management
- Time
- Locale (for creating international scripts)

For the Windows version of Perl, there are standard `Win32` modules for Windows extensions, including the following:

- `Win32::Process`: Creation and use of Windows processes
- `Win32::OLE`: For OLE automation
- `Win32::Registry`: Access to the Windows Registry
- `Win32::Service`: Management of Windows services
- `Win32::NetAdmin`: Remotely create users and groups

MacPerl includes `Mac` modules for accessing the Mac Toolbox, including AppleEvents, dialogs, files, fonts, movies, Internet Config, QuickDraw, and speech recognition (whew!). We'll explore many of the `Mac` and `Win32` modules on Day 18, "Perl and the Operating System."

In addition to the standard Perl library, there is the *Comprehensive Perl Archive Network*, otherwise known as CPAN. CPAN is a collection of Perl modules, scripts, documentation, and other tools relating to Perl. Perl programmers all over the world write modules and submit them to CPAN. To use the modules from the CPAN, you'll need to download and install those modules into your Perl distribution; sometimes you'll also need to compile them with a C compiler. Let's start in this section, using the modules you've already installed; we'll look more at CPAN later in this lesson.

Importing Modules

To gain access to the code stored in any module from your script, you *import* that module using the `use` operator and the name of that module:

```
use CGI;

use Math::BigInt;

use strict;
```

The `use` operator imports the subroutine and variable names defined and exported by that module into the current package so that you can use them as though you had defined them yourself (in other words, that module has a package, which defines a symbol table; importing that module loads that symbol table into your script's current symbol table).

13

Module names can take on many forms—a single name refers to a single module, for example, `CGI`, `strict`, `POSIX`, or `Env`. A name with two or more parts separated by double-colons refers to parts of larger modules (to be exact, they refer to packages defined inside other packages). So, for example, `Math::BigInt` refers to the `BigInt` part of the `Math` module, or `Win32::Process` refers to the `Process` part of the `Win32` module. Module names conventionally start with an initial capital letter.

When you use the `use` operator to import a module's code into your script, Perl searches for that module's file in a special set of directories called the `@INC` array. `@INC` is a Perl special variable that contains any directories specified on the Perl command line with the `-I` option, followed by the standard Perl library directories (`/usr/lib/perl5` and various subdirectories on Unix, `perl\lib` on Windows, `MacPerl:lib` on Macintosh), followed by `.` to represent the current directory. The final contents of `@INC` will vary from system to system, and different versions of Perl might have different values for `@INC` by default. On my system, a Linux machine running Perl 5.005_02, the contents of `@INC` are

```
/usr/lib/perl5/5.00502/i486-linux
/usr/lib/perl5/5.00502
/usr/lib/perl5/site_perl/5.005/i486-linux
/usr/lib/perl5/site_perl/5.005
.
```

If you want to import a module that's stored in some other directory, you can use the `lib` pragma at the start of your script to indicate that directory in your script:

```
use lib '/home/mystuff/perl/lib/';
use Mymodule;
```

Perl module files have the same names as the modules themselves, and have the extension `.pm`. Many modules contain just plain Perl code with some extra framework to make them behave like modules, so if you're curious about how they work you can go ahead and look at the code. Other modules, however, contain or make use of compiled code specific to the platform on which they run, and are not quite as educational to look at.

These latter modules use what are called Perl extensions, sometimes called XSUBS, which enable you to tie compiled C libraries into Perl modules. Working with extensions is way too advanced for this book, but I'll provide some pointers to more information on Day 20, "Odds and Ends."

Using Modules

Using `use` enables you to import a module. Now what? Well, now you can use the code that module contains. How you actually do that depends on whether the module you're using is a plain module or an object-oriented one (you can find out from the documentation for that module whether it's object-oriented or not).

For example, take the module `Carp`, part of the standard Perl library. The `Carp` module provides the `carp`, `croak`, and `confess` subroutines for generating error messages, similar to how the built-in functions `warn` and `die` behave. By importing the `Carp` module, the three subroutine names are imported into the current package, and you gain access to those subroutines as if they were built-in functions or subroutines you defined yourself:

```
use Carp;
open(OUT, ">outfile" || croak "Can't open outfile\n";
```

The carp and croak subroutines, by the way, are analogous to warn and die in that they are used to print an error message (and then exit, in the case of die and croak). The difference is that if they're used inside a module, the carp subroutines are better at reporting where an error occurred. In the case where a script imports a module that has a subroutine that calls carp, carp will report the package and line number of the enclosing script, not the line number inside of the module itself (which would not be very useful for debugging). We'll come back to carp when we look at CGI scripts on Day 16, "Using Perl for CGI Scripting."

Object-Oriented Modules

Some modules are object oriented. Object-oriented programming involves designing systems so that the components are treated as "objects" that comprise both the data associated with them, and the code used to perform actions associated with the object. The description of what an object looks like is referred to as a class, and you deal with objects by creating instances of those classes. For example, in the object-oriented world, you might have a class called Date, which contains the current date and time, and methods that convert the date and time to alternate calendars, or allow you to display the date in various formats. You could create an instance of Date containing the current date and time, and call a method of the date class called convert_to_julian to get the Julian version of the date. Perl implements the idea of classes and instances of those classes, the means by which it does so are described on Day 20. Modules are often written in an object-oriented manner, here's what you need to know to use them.

13

In object-oriented programming parlance, functions and subroutines are called methods, and they're executed in a different way than normal functions. So, for modules you import that are object-oriented, you'd use special syntax to get at that code (your script itself doesn't have to also be object-oriented, so don't worry about that. You can mix and match object-oriented Perl with regular Perl). Here's an example from the CGI module, which we'll look at in more detail on Day 16:

```
use CGI;
my $x = new CGI;
my $name = $x->param("myname");
print $x->header();
```

```
print $x->start_html("Hello!");
print "<H2>Hello $name!\n";
print $x->end_html();
```

Weird-looking, isn't it? If you're familiar with object-oriented programming, what's going on here is that you're creating a new CGI object, storing the reference to that object in the `$x` variable, and then calling methods using the `->` notation.

If you're not familiar with object-oriented programming, this is going to seem odd. Here's the short version:

- The line `my $x = new CGI;` creates a new CGI object and stores a reference to it in the variable `$x`. `$x` isn't a normal scalar like an array or a string; it's a reference to a special CGI *object*.
- To call subroutines defined by the module, otherwise known as a method, you use the variable holding the object, the `->` operator, and the name of the subroutine. So the line `$x->header()` calls the `header()` subroutine, defined in the object stored in `$x`.

Follow this same notation for other subroutines in that same module, and you'll be fine. We'll get back to references and object orientation later Day 19, "Working with References."

Modules from the Inside Out

If the documentation for the module you're using is insufficient, you can discover which variables and subroutines from the module are available to your program by doing a bit of investigative work. When someone writes a module, they have to list the variables and subroutines (both of which are considered symbols in a module) that are exported to Perl programs that use the module.

There are two key variables in a module that indicate which symbols (variables and subroutines) are available to programs that import the module, `@EXPORT` and `@EXPORT_OK`. The symbols listed in `@EXPORT` are available to the importing module automatically. The symbols listed in `@EXPORT_OK` are available for import, but are not imported automatically when you import the module. I'll explain how to import them in the next section. These two variables are your first clues to how an undocumented module works.

Let's look at the `Carp` module, which I discussed earlier. You can examine the `@EXPORT` and `@EXPORT_OK` variables to see which symbols are exported. In the case of `Carp`, you can also just read the documentation by typing `perldoc Carp`, but that's not the point of this exercise.

```
@EXPORT = qw(confess croak carp);
@EXPORT_OK = qw(cluck verbose);
```

As you can see from those two variables, there are three symbols that are imported automatically with this module, and two that are optional imports. One thing you'll need to look out for is symbols that are not variables or methods that you can use, but instead are flags that control how the module is used in your program. Flags will only appear in the `@EXPORT_OK` variable. If a symbol is imported automatically, it doesn't work very well as a flag that only takes effect when it is imported manually. The only way to tell flags from other optionally exported symbols is by examining the source code of the module.

The exported symbols make up the public interface of the module. Using the package qualifier, you can always access global variables and subroutines within the module if you choose to do so, but keep in mind that accessing the internal structure of the module in a way that the author did not intend can cause results that you didn't plan for. Generally speaking, it's better to use a module in the way the author intended.

Importing Symbols by Hand

Importing a module using `use` brings in the variables and subroutine names defined and exported by the module in question. The words *and exported* in the preceding sentence are important—some modules export all their variables, some export only a subset, and others export none at all. With `use`, you gain access to all the code in the module, but not necessarily as if you had defined it yourself. Sometimes you'll have to do some extra work to gain access to the parts of the module you want to use.

If a module you're using doesn't export any variables or subroutine names, you'll find out soon enough—when you try and use those names, you'll get undefined errors from Perl. There are two ways to gain access to the features of that module:

- You can refer to those variables or subroutines using the full-package name.
- You can import those symbols (variable or subroutine names) by hand, in the `use` statement.

With the first method, all you need to do to access a module's variables or subroutines is add the package name to those variables or subroutines. This is especially useful if you've got variables or subroutines of the same name in your own code and you don't want those names to clash:

```
# call additup, defined in Mymodule module
$result = &Mymodule::additup(@vals);

# change value of the $total variable (defined in Mymodule)
$Mymodule::total = $result;
```

Note that if the package name itself contains two colons, you just add the whole thing before the variable name:

```
$Text::Wrap::columns = 5;
```

The second method, importing all the symbols you need, is easier if you intend to call a module's subroutines a lot in your own code; importing them means you don't have to include the package name each time. To import any name from a module into the current package, add those names to the end of the `use` command. A common way to do this is to use the `qw` function, which enables you to leave off the quotes and add new symbols easily:

```
use MyModule qw(oneSub, twoSub, threeSub);
```

Note that these are symbol names, not variable names. There are no special letters before these names, and all the variables in the module with that name will be imported (the symbol `foo` will import `$foo, @foo, &foo,` and so on). To import specific variables, you can use the variable characters:

```
use MyModule qw($count);
```

Some modules are defined so that they have a set of variables that are imported by default, and a set that are only imported by request (if you look at the code, the hash `%EXPORT` commonly defines exported symbols by default; `%EXPORT_OK` defines the optional symbols). The easiest way to import both these things is to issue two calls to `use`: one for the defaults, and one for any optional symbols:

```
use Mymodule;    # import all default names
use Mymodule qw(this, that);   # import this and that as well
```

Import Tags

Some of the larger modules enable you to import only a subset of their features, for greater efficiency. These modules use what are called *import tags*. If you have a module that uses import tags, you can find out which tags a module supports by checking the documentation of that module. Alternately, the `%EXPORT_TAGS` hash in the source code will show you which tags you can use (tags are exported from the module, and imported into your code).

To import a subset of a module, add the tag to the end of the `use` statement:

```
use CGI qw(:standard);
```

Once again, `qw` is the quote word function; although you could just quote the import tag itself; this format is more commonly used and enables you easily to add more tags if you need them.

How a module behaves—if it uses import tags, or if it has variables or subroutines that must be imported by hand—is defined by the module itself, and (hopefully) documented. You might try running `perldoc` on the module to extract any online documentation the author of that module provided, or check the readme files that came with the module to make sure you're using it right.

Using Pragmas

The line `use strict` for restricting global variables to the current script is an example of a special kind of module called a pragma. A *pragma* is a module that affects how Perl behaves at both compile time and runtime (as opposed to regular modules, which provide code for Perl just at runtime). The `strict` pragma, in particular, tells Perl to be strict in its parsing of your code, and to disallow various unsafe constructs.

The notions of *compile-time* and *runtime* might initially seem odd if you remember back to Day One, where I noted that Perl isn't a compiled language like C or Java. In those languages, you run a compiler to convert your source code into bytecode or an executable file; then you execute that new file to actually run the program. With Perl, the script is your executable. There's no intermediate compiled step.

In reality, I fibbed a little on Day One. Perl does indeed compile its source code, just as C and Java do. But then it goes ahead and runs the result; there is no intermediate executable file hanging around.

What this means is that there are tasks that Perl does during compile time (as the script is compiled), and tasks that happen during runtime (as the result is executing). At compile-time, Perl checks for syntax and verifies that everything it needs to run that script is available. At runtime, the script actually executes and operates on the data you give it. As you grow more advanced in your knowledge of Perl, you'll learn that when some operations happen is as important as whether they happen at all.

But back to pragmas. As I mentioned, a pragma is a bit of imported code that affects how Perl operates both during compile time and runtime. Unlike most imported code in modules and libraries, which only affect a script's runtime behavior, pragmas can change the whole look and feel of your code and how Perl looks at it.

Perl has very few pragmas in its standard library (unlike modules, of which there are dozens). Pragmas are conventionally spelled in all lowercase letters, to differentiate them from modules. You use pragmas just like you do modules, with the `use` operator:

```
#!/usr/local/bin/perl -w
use strict;
use diagnostics;
```

Each of the pragmas can be used at the top of your script to affect the entire script. They can also be used inside a block, in which case they only change the behavior of that enclosing block. At the end of the block the normal script behavior resumes.

Some of the more useful Perl pragmas include `strict` and `diagnostics`. You can find a more complete listing of available pragmas in the `perlmod` man page under the section "Pragmatic Modules."

`strict`

The `strict` pragma that you've seen already, restricts various unsafe constructs in your scripts. The `strict` pragma watches for misplaced global variables, barewords (unquoted strings with no definitions in the language or defined as subroutines), and symbolic references (which we'll look at in greater detail on Day 19). You can control only some of these unsafe constructs by including the strings `'vars'`, `'subs'`, or `'refs'` after the `use strict`, like this:

```
use strict 'vars';
```

You can turn off strictness for various blocks of code using the `no strict` command (and with optional `'vars'`, `'subs'`, and `'refs'`, if necessary). The `no strict` applies only to the end of the enclosing block (subroutine, conditional, loop, or bare block), and then Perl reverts to the usual amount of strictness.

`diagnostics`

The `diagnostics` pragma is used to turn on Perl verbose warnings. It works similarly to the `-w` switch; however, it can be used to limit diagnostic warnings and messages to specific parts of your script enclosed in blocks. You cannot turn off `diagnostics` at the compile phase of your script (as you can with `strict` using `no strict`), but you can control runtime warning using the `enable` and `disable` subroutines:

```
use diagnostics;
#
# various bits of code

disable diagnostics;
# code that usually produces run-time warnings
enable diagnostics;

# continue on as usual...
```

The `English` Module

The `English` module is worth mentioning specifically because, like the pragmas, it offers a way to change how Perl interprets your script, but unlike the pragmas, it operates at runtime, and you can't limit its scope to a block. The `English` module is used to make Perl less terse in its built-in special variable names. Although true Perl wizards can gleefully litter their scripts with variables like `$_`, `$"`, `$\_`, and so on, most mere mortals have trouble keeping all but the most common special variables straight. That's where `use English` can help, by aliasing various longer variable names to the shorter versions.

For example, the variable `$,` is known as the output field separator, and it's used to separate items in `print` statements. With `use English`, you can still refer to the variable as `$,` if you like, or you can also use the names `$OUTPUT_FIELD_SEPARATOR` or `$OFS`. All three will work equally well.

You can find a list of Perl's special variables and all their names (both using the `English` module and not) in the `perlvar` man page.

An Example: Using the `Text::Wrap` Module

Here's a small example that uses a module from the standard library: the `Text:Wrap` module, which, given a very long string, will wrap that string into multiple lines of a given length, and with an optional indentation character to include for each line.

This particular example formats an input file to be 80 or so characters wide and indents it in a format familiar to you if you're used to e-mail—it puts a > symbol at the start of each line. The file to be quoted is assumed to be broken up into multiple paragraphs with a blank line between each one. So, for example, if the input file looks like this (a single long string; the end of lines here are not actual ends of lines in the input):

```
The event on which this fiction is founded has been supposed, by Dr. Darwin, and
some of the
physiological writers of Germany, as not of impossible occurrence. I shall not
be supposed as
according the remotest degree of serious faith to such an imagination; yet, in
assuming it as the
basis of a work of fancy, I have not considered myself as merely weaving a
series of supernatural
terrors. The event on which the interest of the story depends is exempt from the
disadvantages of
a mere tale of spectres or enchantment. It was recommended by the novelty of the
situations which
it develops; and, however impossible as a physical fact, affords a point of view
to the imagination
for the delineating of human passions more comprehensive and commanding than any
which the
ordinary relations of existing events can yield.
```

The output will look like this:

```
> The event on which this fiction is founded has been supposed, by Dr.
> Darwin, and some of the physiological writers of Germany, as not of
> impossible occurrence. I shall not be supposed as according the remotest
> degree of serious faith to such an imagination; yet, in assuming it as
> the basis of a work of fancy, I have not considered myself as merely
> weaving a series of supernatural terrors. The event on which the interest
> of the story depends is exempt from the disadvantages of a mere tale of
```

13

```
> spectres or enchantment. It was recommended by the novelty of the
> situations which it develops; and, however impossible as a physical
> fact, affords a point of view to the imagination for the delineating of
> human passions more comprehensive and commanding than any which the
> ordinary relations of existing events can yield.
```

Listing 13.1 shows the code for the script to do this.

LISTING 13.1 The `wrapit.pl` Script

```
1:  #!/usr/ bin/perl -w
2:  use strict;
3:
4:  use Text::Wrap;                   # import module
5:  my $indent = "> ";                # indent character
6:
7:  while (<>) {
8:      print wrap($indent, $indent, $_);
9 : }
```

As you can see, this is not very much code at all, and it's much easier than writing the same procedure using raw Perl code. The important parts of this script are

- Line 4, where we import the `Text::Wrap` module.
- Line 5, which defines the indent character (here `>`, although it could be any set of indentation characters you want).
- Line 8, where we call the `wrap` function to actually wrap the test. The `wrap` function, defined in the `Text::Wrap` module, takes three arguments: the character to indent the first line with, the character to indent each successive line with, and the string to wrap. In this case, we wanted to indent all the lines with the same character, so we called `wrap` with `$indent` specified twice.

By default, the `Text::Wrap` function wraps to 76 characters wide. You can change this value using the `$columns` variable, although that variable is not imported from the module by default. You'll have to import that variable explicitly or use its full package name to be able to make use of it:

```
use Text::Wrap qw($columns);   # import $columns
$columns = 50;                 # set it
```

Using Modules from CPAN (The Comprehensive Perl Archive Network)

If the modules in the standard Perl library don't have enough capabilities—and often, they don't—there is also CPAN. The Comprehensive Perl Archive Network, as I mentioned earlier, is a massive collection of publicly available modules for Perl; covering just about every topic you can imagine. Want a module to handle encrypting data? CPAN's got it. Need to send e-mail? CPAN's got a module to do that. Want to read in and process an entire HTML file? Not a problem. No matter what it is you want to do, it's a good idea to check CPAN first to see if someone has already done it for you. There's no point in reinventing the wheel when you can use someone else's code. That's the advantage of having a Perl community to rely on.

A Note of Caution

There are two drawbacks to the CPAN modules. The first is that you have to download, build, and install modules before you can use them, which means a bit more work involved than just inserting a `use module` line in your script. Some modules might require you to compile them, which means you'll need a working C compiler installed on your computer.

The second problem with modules on CPAN is that most of them are developed for use with Unix Perl. If you're using Windows or MacPerl, the module you want to use might not be available for that platform. This is changing as time goes on, however, and more and more modules are being developed cross-platform. Windows support, in particular, is becoming more and more widespread. There's even a special tool, PPM, for installing and managing Windows-specific CPAN modules for the ActiveState version of Perl for Windows (we'll look at PPM later in this lesson in the section entitled "Installing CPAN Modules on Windows Using PPM.") If you're not sure if a particular module is available for your platform, you'll need to check the documentation for that module—or be prepared to port it yourself.

13

Acquiring Modules from CPAN

The CPAN modules are stored on the CPAN Web site or one of its mirrors. If you start at `http://www.cpan.org/`you'll find out what CPAN contains, how to get the files, and how to find out if a particular module is available on your platform. There's also a module search engine available so you can figure out quickly if there is a module to do what you want.

Some modules come in bundles to reduce dependencies between different modules (there's nothing more irritating than trying to run a script, which needs one module, only to find after downloading that module that it requires another module, which then requires a third module, and so on down the line). Module bundles usually start with the word "lib"—for example, the `libwww` group of modules includes a whole set of modules for handling things relating to the World Wide Web. If the module you want is contained in a bundle available on CPAN, it's usually a good idea to download the whole bundle instead of the individual module, just to be safe.

Say you've found a module that you want to use. Usually, you'll download that module, uncompress or unarchive it using the tools for your platform (usually `gzip` and `tar` for Unix, `WinZip` for Windows, Stuffit for Mac). On Unix many modules include a makefile to install everything in the right spots (type `perl Makefile.PL` to get the process started). On Windows and the Mac, if there are not specific directions for installing the files on your platform you can sometimes just copy the `.pm` module files into the appropriate spots in your Perl hierarchy. The `perlmodinstall` man page part of the Perl installation offers many specific suggestions for getting modules decompressed and installed. The process, however, can be different for each module, so follow what the README files say to make sure everything is installed correctly.

Some modules have parts written in C that might require you to have a C compiler installed on your machine. If you don't have a C compiler, you might be able to use the module without these extra parts, depending on the module. Again, check the documentation that comes with the module.

If you're on Unix, and you're installing modules that have compiled parts, make sure that the C compiler you use to compile the modules is the same compiler you used to compile Perl in the first place (with network-mounted file systems this isn't as unusual a case as it sounds). You can run into difficult-to-solve incompatibilities with modules compiled in different environments than those with which Perl was compiled.

After you're done dearchiving, building, compiling, and installing, you should have a number of files installed into the right locations in your Perl hierarchy. You might want to explore the various directories in your `@INC` array to make sure they're there.

Installing CPAN Modules on Windows Using PPM

The Perl Package Manager, or PPM, is a tool that comes with the ActiveState version of Perl for Windows that makes installing and managing CPAN modules on Windows much, much easier. With PPM, you don't have to worry whether a particular module is supported on Windows, or figure out how to compile or install it using arcane Unix-based tools. PPM enables you to install, update, and remove individual already-built modules from inside a single program.

> A *package*, per the Perl Package Manager, is a collection of one or more modules and supporting files. It's different from a Perl namespace package.

To use PPM, you must be connected to the Internet. The PPM script gets its packages from a repository on the ActiveState Web site. To start PPM, simply type **ppm** from inside a command shell:

```
c:\> ppm
PPM interactive shell (0.9.5) - type 'help' for available commands
PPM>
```

At the PPM prompt, you have several choices, including

- help, to print a list of choices
- search, to show which packages you have available to install
- query, to show the packages you already have installed
- install, to install a specific package
- verify, to make sure all your packages are up to date
- remove, to remove a specific package

You can find out more about PPM from the PPM Web page (part of ActiveState's Perl for Windows installation), or at
`http://www.activestate.com/activeperl/docs/ppm.html.`

Using Modules from CPAN

After you have a module from CPAN installed—either by downloading and installing it yourself, using PPM, or even by copying files manually to your Perl installation—that module is available to your scripts. You can then import it with `use` and use its capabilities as if it were any other module. You'll need to check its documentation to see if it's a regular or object-oriented module, or to see if it uses import tags, but other than the fact that they need to be installed first, the CPAN modules typically behave the same as those in the standard library.

13

Going Deeper

I've covered a lot of ground in this chapter, from packages to modules to importing, to how Perl actually looks at code at various times. Much of what I've discussed in this chapter is the tip of the iceberg. Packages and modules, in particular, could fill up entire books of their own, and the short description of object orientation is barely even enough to get started.

We'll go a little deeper into a few of these topics later in this book. Other topics, however, including developing your own packages and just about everything to do with creating modules, are best left to the advanced Perl programmer, and as such are outside the scope of this book. After finishing the 21 days of this course, consider exploring modules and packages with the text in the online man pages and FAQs.

There are a few topics that I can describe in this section, however, that relate more closely to the topics we've discussed in this lesson.

Typeglobs

Typeglobs is a strange name that involves being able to refer to multiple types of variables by a single name (the term *typeglob* is borrowed from Unix, where referring to multiple files using file.* or some such character is called file *globbing*). Typeglobbing refers to the symbol table entries of a given package.

The typeglob expression `*foo` refers to any variable with the name `foo`—`$foo`, `@foo`, `&foo`, and so on. Normally, these variables are distinct; typeglobbing is a way of lumping them all together.

In earlier versions of Perl, typeglobbing was used to pass arrays into subroutines by reference. You could use a typeglob to alias a local variable to a global array, and then any changes you made to the local array would be reflected outside the global array, like this:

```
@foo = (1,2,3);
&removethrees(*foo);

sub removethrees {
   my *list = @_;
   foreach my $x @list {
      if ($x == 3) { undef $x }
   }
   return @list;
}
```

In this example, all the changes made to the local list in `@list` are reflected in the list `@foo`, because `@list` has been set up as an alias for `@foo`.

Typeglobs for passing arrays into subroutines have been essentially replaced by the newer reference feature; references not only enable you to pass individual arrays into subroutines by reference, but also enable you to maintain the integrity of multiple arrays. Use references instead of typeglobs for this purpose (more about references on Day 19).

One Other Difference Between `local` and `my`

The most obvious difference between variables defined with `my` and those defined with `local` is that of lexical and dynamic scope, as I noted in the body of this lesson. The other difference is how Perl manages those variables:

- `local` local variables are actually global variables in disguise. When you create a local variable, if a global of the same name exists, Perl saves the value of that global and reinitializes the same variable (and its same location in the symbol table) to the new local value. The value of the global is restored at the end of the local variable's scope.
- `my` local variables are entirely new variables that are not stored in the symbol table. They are wholly private to the block or subroutine in which they're stored. This makes them slightly faster to use than `local` local variables because they don't require a symbol table lookup.

Neither of these differences really change how you would use `local` or `my` in your own scripts (`local` local variables are relevant when it comes to using typeglobs, but that's a detail outside the scope of this book). In most cases, use `my` where you want a local variable and you'll do just fine.

An Example of `local` Versus `my`

In the section on local variables defined using either `local` or `my`, I promised an example of how this works if the difference was totally befuddling. Listing 13.2 shows a script to make things clearer (or perhaps just completely dark).

LISTING 13.2 A Scope Script

```
#!/usr/ bin/perl -w

$global = " global available here\n";

&subA();
print "Main script:\n";
foreach $var ($global, $mylocal, $locallocal) {
    if (defined $var) {
        print $var;
    }
}

sub subA {
    my $mylocal = " mylocal available here\n";
    local $locallocal = " local local available here\n";
    print "SubA:\n";
    foreach $var ($global, $mylocal, $locallocal) {
```

LISTING 13.2 continued

```
18:         if (defined $var) {
19:             print $var;
20:         }
21:     }
22:     &subB();
23: }
24:
25: sub subB {
26:     print "SubB: \n";
27:     foreach $var ($global, $mylocal, $locallocal) {
28:         if (defined $var) {
29:             print $var;
30:         }
31:     }
32: }
```

This script uses three variables: `$global`, `$mylocal`, and `$locallocal`, and declares them all appropriately. For each subroutine, and then once again at the end of the script, the values of those variables are printed if they exist and if they have a proper value. Try to follow the flow of this script and predict what will get printed when.

Here's the actual output:

```
SubA:
 global available here
 mylocal available here
 local local available here
SubB:
 global available here
 local local available here
Main script:
 global available here
```

Was it what you expected? Let's work through it. This script starts at the top and calls `&SubA()`, which calls `&SubB()`, and then prints some variables. In the subroutine `&SubA()`, we declare both `$mylocal` and `$locallocal` with the `my` and `local` modifiers, respectively, in lines 14 and 15. Both those variables, plus the `$global`, will then be available inside the boundaries of that subroutine, so all three values will be printed.

In line 22, `&subA()` calls `&SubB()`, and here we just print the variables that we have available. The global will be there because global variables are available to all parts of a script. But `$mylocal` is not there—the `my` modifier makes that local variable only available to that subroutine and not to other parts of the script. The `$locallocal` variable definition, however, is available to subroutines further down than the one in which it was defined.

After `&SubB()` is finished, execution pops back up to `&subA()`, and then back up to the main part of the script where we try printing those same values again. Here only the global will be available, and only the global will get printed.

Package Initialization and Finalization with BEGIN and END

One aspect of packages worth mentioning before we move on are the subroutines `BEGIN` and `END`, which are used to initialize a script before it runs, and to finalize a script after it's done running. These subroutines are most commonly used inside complex Perl libraries and modules, and as constructors and destructors for object-oriented classes.

The `BEGIN` subroutine is executed just as soon as it's found, during compile time, before the rest of the script is parsed. Use `BEGIN` for any code that you want to run at compile-time, for example, importing symbols for module definitions that will later be exported to other code, or to include other code that is required by the module.

`END`, on the other hand, is executed as the Perl script finishes executing, either if the script executed correctly or if there was an error that caused it to execute prematurely (including `die`). Use `END` to clean up after your script. You can change the status value that is returned to the Unix shell after your script exits using `END`, for example.

You can find out more about `BEGIN` and `END` in the `perlmod` man page.

Importing Code with require

In this lesson, I showed you how to import code from modules using the `use` function. The `use` function, in short, imports code from another source at compile time, and imports various symbols into the current package. The `require` function, on the other hand, is used to include code from other sources at runtime (in fact, `use` is equivalent to calling `require` inside a `BEGIN` subroutine and importing that file's variables into the current namespace).

13

In earlier versions of Perl, `require` was used as the general-purpose import mechanism. You stuck your subroutine or global variable definitions in a separate file, and then included that file in another script using `require`, like this:

```
require 'foo.pl';
```

Perl looks for the given file to be imported in the directories stored in `@INC`. In addition, it keeps track of which files have already been imported, so it won't reimport code that's already been loaded. If the included file, however, defines its own package, then `require` will not import that package's variables into the current package (not even `main`), and you'll have to refer to those variables using the complete package name. Also, you have to be careful when you use `require`; because the `require` occurs at runtime, you must make sure the `require` happens before you actually call or use anything defined in that imported file.

This mechanism for importing code from one file to another still works just fine in current versions of Perl, and you can use it to build your own simple libraries of subroutine definitions. However, the new mechanisms of packages and modules provide better features and more control over what gets imported when. For serious library development, consider learning more about the development packages, modules, and `use`.

One other cool use of `require` is with a Perl version number, in which case if the script is being run with an earlier version of Perl, it will immediately exit with an error. Use this mechanism for making sure the version of Perl that's being run has the features you use in your script—for example, features that only exist in Perl 5, or more advanced features that might only exist in 5.005 or higher:

```
require 5.005;
```

See the `perlfunc` man page for further information on `require`.

Summary

Today's lesson has covered a few topics that might be considered somewhat esoteric, but will become more important as the remainder of this book unfolds. The first half of this lesson discussed aspects of variables and scope, including what a global variable means when there are packages to restrict it from being truly global, and making sure your global variables are local to a script by defining them with `my`.

Then, we turned to local variables, and you learned more about the use of `my` variables inside blocks and subroutines, as well as defining local variables with `local`.

Given all these choices for declaring and using different variables, it's confusing to know what's right. Among Perl programmers, there are general rules and practices that are commonly used for dealing with variables and scope:

- Don't declare raw global variables. Declare all global variables using `my`, and use `use strict` to make sure you're doing it right.
- Use `my` variables over `local` unless you have specific reasons for doing so. `Local` local variables suffer from many of the same reusability and debugging problems that global variables do, and confuse what's an otherwise clean distinction between the concepts of *local* and *global*.

- Try to avoid using local variables that have the same name as globals unless you have a good reason for doing so

In the second half of the lesson, we looked at the `use` function, and how to use it to turn on pragmas—hints to Perl for how to compile and run your scripts—and to import and use code contained in modules either in the standard library or from CPAN. The module part of this lesson was potentially the most important thing you'll learn today; we'll be using modules throughout the rest of this book.

The functions and other commands we explored today include:

- `package`, to switch between different packages
- `my`, to define a local variable or a non-package version of a global variable
- `use strict`, to make sure you're not using any stray global variables
- `local`, another way of defining local variables (use `my` instead)
- `use`, in general, to import a pragma or module

Q&A

Q. How is declaring global variables with `my` any advantage over using regular global variables if I'm writing self-contained scripts to do very simple things?

A. If the only scripts you write are smaller, self-contained scripts, then you don't really need to use `use strict` or make sure your variables are declared using `my`. You'd use `my` globals if there was a chance for your code being incorporated into someone else's code, even accidentally. Because quite a lot of code has a chance of being used in ways contrary to how you intended it to be used, the use of `my` globals and `use strict` is considered a defensive move and good-programming practice. But it is not required.

Q. Most languages use either lexical or dynamic scope, but not both. Why does Perl confuse things and provide multiple kinds of local scopes?

A. It's mostly historical. Earlier versions of Perl provided a dynamic scope for variables with the `local` operator. The `my` operator was added later to provide a more distinct lexical local scope; `local` stays around for backward compatibility with earlier scripts.

If the difference seems hopelessly confusing, just use `my` variables and assume they are private to any given subroutine, and you'll be fine.

Q. I've got an older script that someone wrote that starts out with a lot of `'require thislibrary.pl'` lines. Should I change those to use `use` instead?

A. Actually, no. The `require` operator was the old way of incorporating library code into Perl scripts, and it's likely that the library you're importing (`thislibrary.pl` in your example) isn't written as a module, and won't work well with `use`. Unless you're intending to rewrite the entire script—and potentially rewrite all the libraries as well—you can go ahead and continue to use `require`.

Q. I've got a module called `Mail` which is supposed to give me access to subroutines for sending and receiving mail: `send_mail()` and `rec_mail()`. I've imported the module with `use`, but I keep getting undefined errors for those two subroutines.

A. Sounds like the module doesn't explicitly import those subroutine names. You have two choices: You can import them yourself, or you can call those subroutines using the full package names:

```
use Mail;  # import defaults, if any
use Mail qw(send_mail rec_mail);  # import subroutines
send_mail();
# OR
&Mail::send_mail();  # call subroutine with full package name
```

Workshop

The workshop provides quiz questions to help you solidify your understanding of the material covered and exercises to give you experience in using what you've learned. Try to understand the quiz and exercise answers before you go on to tomorrow's lesson.

Quiz

1. What is a package? Why are packages useful?
2. How do you call a variable by its full package name?
3. Can you use `my` with global variables? Why would you want to do this?
4. What does the line `use strict` do? Why would you want to use it?
5. What are the differences between libraries, modules, packages, and pragmas?
6. What is the CPAN? Where is it?
7. What is the `@INC` array used for?
8. How do you import a module into your script? What does that give you?
9. What is an import tag and why would you use it?
10. How do you call a subroutine you've imported from a module? How do you call a subroutine from an object-oriented module?

Exercises

1. Define a subroutine that takes a single argument, a string, and builds a new string with each of the characters separated by another globally defined value (such as ":"). Return the new string. The catch: Use the same variable name for the local variable that holds the new string, and the global variable that stores the separator character. HINT: Don't use `use strict` or `my` globals.
2. BUG BUSTER: What's wrong with this script?

```
use This:That;                    # import module
while (<>) {
    print theother($_);
}
```

3. Modify the `wrapit.pl` script to prompt you for the column width, and then wrap the input text to that width.
4. Consider the `Config` module, part of the standard Perl library. This module is used to store configuration information about the current version of Perl. Using the documentation that comes with `Config` (which you can get to via the `perldoc` program, the Shuck application in MacPerl, or via the `perlmod` man page), write a script that prints out the various values available in `Config`. NOTE: The `Config` module does not automatically import any subroutine names.

Answers

Here are the answers to the Workshop questions in the previous section.

Quiz Answers

1. Packages are used to, well, package sets of global variables in a single unit, such that those units can be combined without one unit's variables tromping over another's. Packages work best for scripts that are made up of lots of parts that must work in harmony, or for modules of reusable library code.
2. The full package name for any variable or subroutine consists of the variable symbol (`$` for scalars, `@` for arrays, `%` for hashes, `&` for subroutine calls), the package name, two colons, and the variable name, for example, `$AModule::avariable` or `&Amodule::asubroutine()`.
3. Declaring global variables with `my` prevents them from being declared in the `main` package, which makes them slightly more efficient for value lookup and assignment, as well as making your script more well-behaved should it ever be incorporated into a package or combined with other scripts.

4. `use strict` is a special Perl directive that makes sure all the variables in your script are local variables or assigned to a particular package. At this point in your Perl knowledge, it's most useful for catching random global variables and making sure your scripts are self-contained as far as variable declarations go.
5. Libraries are collections of Perl code intended to be reused. Libraries can use packages to manage variable names inside that library. A module is a library that uses a package and has the same filename as that package. Modules include code that allows that module to be reused easily in other scripts. A pragma is a special kind of module that affects Perl's operation during both compile time and runtime.
6. CPAN stands for Comprehensive Perl Archive Network; it's a collection of user-contributed modules, scripts, documentation, and utilities for use by anyone programming in Perl. CPAN is available at several sites around the world; you can find a site local to you starting at `http://www.cpan.org/`.
7. The `@INC` array defines the directories in which Perl will look for modules and code imported into your scripts using `use`.
8. Import a module into your script using `use` with the name of the module and an optional list of variables or import tags. Importing a module gives you access to the variables and subroutines defined by that module.
9. An import tag defines a subset of variables and subroutines in the module to be imported into your own script. Import tags are defined by the module developer and documented in the documentation for that module.
10. Subroutines imported from modules can be called just like regular subroutines, using the name of the subroutine with parentheses surrounding any arguments.

    In object-oriented modules, you must create a new object before you can call subroutines. With a new object stored in a scalar variable, you'd then call a subroutine using the `$var->sub()` syntax, where `$var` is the name of the variable holding the object and `sub` is the name of the subroutine. Subroutines defined inside objects are called methods.

Exercise Answers

1. The secret is to use a real global, stored in the package `main`, and then refer to it by its full package name in the body of the subroutine. Note that this doesn't work with global variables defined by `my` because they do not belong to any package.

```
#!/usr/local/bin/perl -w

$x = ":";                # separator character (global)
print &splitit("defenestration"), "\n";
```

```
sub splitit {
    my $string = $_[0];
    my $x = '';                    # new string (global);

    $x = join $main::x, (split //,$string);
    return $x;
}
```

2. There's only one colon in that module name; modules with two names always have two colons.
3. Changing `wrapit.pl` is a simple question of modifying the `$columns` variable. This variable isn't imported into your script by default, so you'll have to explicitly import it yourself.

```
#!/usr/local/bin/perl -w
use strict;

use Text::Wrap;                   # import module defaults
use Text::Wrap qw($columns);      # also import $columns
$\ = "";                          # Paragraph mode
my $indent = "> ";                        # indent character

print 'Enter a width: ';
chomp($columns = <STDIN>);

while (<>) {
    print wrap($indent, $indent, $_);
}
```

4. The subroutine `myconfig()` will do this for you. Because this subroutine is not imported by default, you'll have to call it with its full package name (or import it explicitly):

```
#!/usr/local/bin/perl -w
use strict;
use Config;

print Config::myconfig();
```

DAY 14

Exploring a Few Longer Examples

To finish up the week, let's explore a couple longer, more useful examples that make use of the techniques you've learned so far in the book. We won't spend a lot of time on background in this lesson, nor will you have any quizzes or exercises to work through at the end. Consider this a brief pause to look at code in detail. This is the second of three example lessons, one after each six or so lessons, to cement what you've learned.

Today we'll look at two longer Perl scripts:

- An address-book script that stores names and addresses in a simple text database format. Our Perl script will allow you to search for addresses in the database using simply logical AND and OR tests
- A Web log file analyzer. This script takes the standard Web server log format (called the *common log format*) and generates various statistics about how the Web site is being used.

A Searchable Address Book (`address.pl`)

Our first script today consists of two parts:

- A simple address book file, containing names, addresses, and phone numbers
- A Perl script that prompts you for things to search for, and then prints out any matching addresses

This script makes use of just about everything you've learned so far this week: scalar and hash data, conditionals, loops, input and output, subroutines, local variables, and pattern matching. There's even a function call here and there to make things interesting. And so, without further ado, let's dive in.

How It Works

The `address.pl` script is called with a single argument: the address file, called `address.txt`. Call it on the command line as you have other Perl scripts:

```
% address.pl address.txt
```

The first thing the address book script does is prompt you for what you want to search:

```
Search for what? Johnson
```

The search pattern you give to `address.pl` can be in several different forms:

- Single words, such as the `Johnson` in the preceding example.
- Multiple words (`John Maggie Alice`). Any addresses that match any of those words will be printed (equivalent to an OR search).
- Multiple words separated by AND or OR (in upper or lowercase). Boolean searches behave as logical operators do in Perl, and are tested left to right. (Note that AND searches only make sense when matched inside a single address; they will not match across multiple addresses the way OR searches will.)
- Multiple words surrounded by quotes (`"this that"`) are treated as a single search pattern. Spaces are relevant in this case.
- Pattern-matching characters are accepted and processed as regular expressions (don't include the `//` around the patterns).

So, for example, in my sample `address.txt` file, the search for the word `Johnson` returned this output:

```
*********************
Paul Johnson
212 345 9492
234 33rd St Apt 12C, NY, NY 10023
http://www.foo.org/users/don/paul.html
*********************
```

```
Alice Johnson
(502) 348 2387
(502) 348 2341
*********************
Mary Johnson
(408) 342 0999
(408) 323 2342
mj@asd.net
http://www.mjproductions.com
*********************
```

> **Note:** In generating this sample address file, I made up all names, addresses, phone numbers, and Web pages. Any similarity between this data and any persons living or dead is coincidental.

The Address File

The core of the address book (and something you'll have to generate yourself if you want to use this script) is a file of addresses in a specific format that Perl can understand. You could consider this a simple text database, and write Perl scripts to add and delete records (addresses) to or from that database.

The format of the address book file looks like this, generically:

```
Name: Name
Phone: number
Fax: number
Address: address
Email: email address
URL: Web URL
---
```

For example:

```
Name: Paul Johnson
Phone: 212 345 9492
Address: 234 33rd St Apt 12C, NY, NY 10023
URL: http://www.foo.org/users/don/paul.html
---
```

Each record has a list of fields (Name, Phone, Fax, Address, E-mail, and URL, although not all of them are required), and ends with three dashes. The field names (`Name`, `Phone`, `URL`, and so on) are separated from their values with a colon and a space. The values do not have to be in any specific format. Although you can include other field names in the database, and search keys will search those extra fields, those fields will be ignored in the final printed output (but if you had to have an extra field, say, for a pager number, you could always modify the script. Perl is easy that way).

14

You can have as many addresses in the `address.txt` file as you like; the larger the address book, the longer it will take to find matching records, as each address is checked from start to finish in turn. Unless you have four or five million friends, you probably won't notice Perl working very hard.

Inside the Script

The `address.pl` script reads in the `address.txt` file, one address at a time, and then processes the search pattern for each of those addresses. The topmost part of the script is a `while` loop that does just this, which in turn works through five other subroutines to handle more complex parts of the script.

Let's start with this topmost part of the script. At this top level, we define three global variables:

- `%rec`, which will hold the current address record, indexed by field name.
- `$search`, the search pattern you enter at the prompt.
- `$bigmatch`, whether a record was found anywhere in the address file that matched the search pattern (there are also local variables for whether the current record matches, but we'll get to those soon enough.

Step one in this outer part of the script is to prompt for the search pattern and store it in `$search`:

```
$search = &getpattern();         # prompt for pattern
```

The `&getpattern()` subroutine is the basic "read the input/chomp it/return the result" code you've seen all too often in this book so far:

```
sub getpattern {
    my $in = '';  # input
    print 'Search for what? ';
    chomp($in = <STDIN>);
    return $in;
}
```

Step two in the outer script is an infinite `while` loop that reads in a record, processes the search pattern, and prints it if it matches. That `while` loop looks like this:

```
while () {                        # range over address file
    my %rec = &read_addr();
    if (%rec) {           # got a record
        &perform_search($search, %rec);
    } else {              # end of address file, finish up
        if (!$bigmatch) {
            print "Nothing found.\n";
        } else { print "*********************\n"; }
        last;             # exit, we're done
    }
```

Inside the `while` loop, we call `&read_addr()` to read in a record, and if a record was found, we search for it by calling `&perform_search()`. At the end of the address file, if the `$bigmatch` variable is 0, that means no matches were found, and we can print a helpful message. At any rate, at the end of the address file, we call `last` to exit from the loop and finish the script.

Reading the Address

The `&read_addr()` subroutine is used to read in an address record. Listing 14.1 shows the contents of `&read_addr()`.

LISTING 14.1 The `&read_addr()` Subroutine

```
sub read_addr {
    my %curr = ();              # current record
    my $key = '';               # temp key
    my $val = '';               # temp value

    while (<>) {                # stop if we get to EOF
        chomp;
        if (!/^---/) {      # record seperator
            ($key, $val) = split(/: /,$_,2);
            $curr{$key} = $val;
        }
        else { last; }
    }
    return %curr;
}
```

In past examples of using a `while` loop with `<>`, we've read in and processed the entire file at once. This `while` loop is a little different; this one reads chunks of the file, and stops when it reaches a record separator (in this case, the string `'---'`). I use a regular expression that matches any lines that don't begin with `'---'`. The next time the `&read_addr()` subroutine is called, the `while` loop picks up where it left off in the address file. Perl has no problem with this stopping and restarting the input, and it makes it particularly convenient for reading and processing sections of a file as we have here.

That said, what this subroutine does is read in a line. If the line does not begin with `'---'`, then it's the inside of a record, and that line gets split into the field name (`Name:`, `Phone:`, and so on) and the value. The call to the `split` function in line 9 is where this takes place; note that the 2 argument at the end of `split` means we'll only end up with two things overall. With the field name (`$key`) and the value (`$val`), you can start building up the hash for this address.

If the line that gets read is the end-of-record marker, then the `if` statement in line 8 drops to the `else` part in line 12, and the last command exits the loop. The result of this subroutine is a hash containing all the lines in the address, indexed by the field name.

Performing the Search

At this point in the script's execution, you have a search pattern, stored in the `$search` variable, and an address stored in the `%rec` variable. The next step is to move to the next part of our big `while` loop at the top of the script, where if `%rec` is defined (an address exists), then we call the `&perform_search()` subroutine to actually see if the pattern in `$search` can be matched to the address in `%rec`.

The `&perform_search()` subroutine is shown in Listing 14.2.

LISTING 14.2 The `&perform_search()` subroutine

```
sub perform_search {
    my ($str, %rec) = @_;
    my $matched = 0;            # overall match
    my $i = 0;                  # position inside pattern
    my $thing = '';             # temporary word

    my @things = $str =~ /("[^"]+"|\S+)/g;  # split into search items

    while ($i <= $#things) {
        $thing = $things[$i];    # search item, AND or OR
        if ($thing =~ /^or$/i) { # OR case
            if (!$matched) {     # no match yet, look at next thing
                $matched = &isitthere($things[$i+1], %rec);
            }
            $i += 2;             # skip OR and next thing
        }
        elsif ($thing =~ /^and$/i) { # AND case
            if ($matched) {      # got a match, need to check other side
                $matched = &isitthere($things[$i+1], %rec);
            }
            $i += 2;             # skip AND and next thing
        }
        elsif (!$matched) {      # no match yet
            $matched = &isitthere($thing, %rec);
            $i++;                # next!
        }
        else { $i++; }           # $match is found, move onto next thing
    }

    if ($matched) {              # all keys done, did we match?
        $bigmatch = 1;  # yes, we found something
        print_addr(%rec);       # print the record then
    }
}
```

That's one large subroutine, and quite complex, but it's not as awful as it looks. Starting from the top, then, this subroutine takes two arguments: the search pattern and the address hash. Note that because those values are stored in global variables, it's not necessary to pass these along into the subroutine via arguments; we could have referred to those global variables in the body of this subroutine. This strategy, however, makes the subroutine more self-contained in that the only data it deals with is that which it gets explicitly. You could, for example, copy and paste this subroutine into another search script without having to worry about renaming any variables.

The first real operation we do in this subroutine is in line 7, where we split the search pattern into its component parts. Remember that the search pattern can appear in many different ways, including nested quoted strings, ANDs and ORs, or just a list of keywords. Line 7 extracts each element from the search pattern and stores all the search "things" in the array `@things` (note that the regular expression has the `g` option at the end, and is evaluated in a list context—meaning the `@things` list will contain all the possible matches captured by the parentheses. What does that particular pattern match? There are two groups of patterns, separated by alternation (`|`). The first is this one:

```
"[^"]+"
```

Which, if you remember your patterns, is a double-quote, followed by one or more characters that are not a double-quote, followed by another closing quote. This pattern will match quoted strings in the search pattern such as `"John Smith"` or `"San Francisco"` and treat them as a single search element. This could also be written as `"*+?"`, the question mark indicating that this is a nongreedy expression (thereby stopping at the first " it finds, rather than the final one.

The second part of the pattern is simply one or more characters that are not whitespace (`\s`). This part of the pattern matches any single words, such as AND or OR, or single keywords. Between these two patterns, a long complex pattern such as `"San Jose" OR "San Francisco" AND John` will break into the list `("San Jose", OR, "San Francisco", AND, John)`.

With all our search objects in a list, the hard part is to work through that list, search the address when necessary, and deal with the logical expressions. This all takes place in the big `while` loop that starts in line 9, which keeps a placeholder variable `$i` for the current position in the pattern, and loops over the pattern until the end. Throughout the `while` loop, the `$matched` variable keeps track of whether any particular part of the pattern has matched the record. We start with a 0—false—for no match yet.

Inside the `while` loop, we start in line 10 by setting the variable `$thing` to the current part of the pattern we're examining, just as a shorthand. Then, there are four major tests:

- If the current thing is an OR, then we're in the middle of two tests, one of which has already occurred and returned either true or false depending on the value of `$matched`. If `$matched` was true, then the thing on the left side was a match, and there's no point to actually trying the thing on the right (yes, it's a short-circuiting OR). If the thing on the left didn't match, the `$matched` variable will be 0, and we have to test the thing on the right. That's what line 13 does; it calls the `&isitthere()` subroutine to actually search for a search pattern, giving it an argument of the right side of the OR (the next thing in the `@things` array) and the record itself (`%rec`).

  Whether there was a match or not, this test handles both the OR itself and the pattern on the right of the OR, so we can skip two elements forward in the `@things` array. Line 15 increments the `$i` counter to do just that.
- If the current thing is an AND, we trigger the test in line 17. This section operates in much the same way as the OR did, with one exception; it short-circuits in the other way. Remember, given a test `x AND y`, if `x` is false then the entire expression is false. If `x` is true, you still have to test to see if `y` is also true. That's how this test works; if the `$matched` variable is true, then the left side of the AND was true, and we call `&isitthere()` to test the right side. Otherwise, we do nothing, and in either case we just skip the AND and the right side of the AND (`$i+=2`, line 21) and move on.
- At line 23, we've covered ANDs and ORs, so the thing we're looking at must be an actual search pattern. It could be a single search pattern, or it could be one of many search patterns contained in a string. Doesn't matter; each one can be treated individually. But we only need to actually search for it if we haven't already found a match (remember, multiple searches are treated as OR tests, so if one matches we're all set for the others). So, in line 23, if we haven't found a match, we search for that thing using `&isitthere()`.
- The final case covers a `$thing` that's an actual search key, and `$matched` is true. We don't need to actually do anything here because the match has already been made. So, increment the position in the pattern by one and restart the loop.

If you can follow all of that, you've made it through the hardest part of this script, by far. If it's still confusing you, try working through various search patterns, with single search elements, elements separated with ANDs and ORs, and patterns with multiple search keys. Watch the values of `$i` and `$matched` as the loop progresses (when you learn how to use the Perl debugger, this will be easy, but you can do it on paper by hand as well).

So what happens in the mysterious `&isitthere()` subroutine that gets called throughout that big `while` loop? That's where the actual searching takes place, given a pattern and the record. I'm not going to show you the contents of `&isitthere()` itself (you can see it in the full code printout in Listing 14.3), other than to note that it simply loops through the contents of the address hash and compares the pattern to each line using a regular expression. If it matches, the subroutine returns 1, and returns 0 if it doesn't match.

In the last part of the subroutine, all the parts of the pattern have been read, some amount of searching has taken place, and now we know whether the pattern matched the record or not. In lines 30 through 33, we test to see if a match was made, and if it was we set the `$bigmatch` variable (we found at least one address that matched), and call `&print_addr()` to print the actual address.

Printing the Record

It's all downhill from here. The last subroutine in the file is one that's only called if a match was made. The `&print_addr()` subroutine simply loops over the record hash and prints out the values to display the address record:

```
sub print_addr {
    my %record = @_;
    print "*********************\n";
    foreach my $key (qw(Name Phone Fax Address Email URL)) {
        if (defined($record{$key})) {
            print "$record{$key}\n";
        }
    }
}
```

The only interesting part of this subroutine is the list of keys in the `foreach` loop. I've listed the specific keys here in this order (and quoted them using the `qw` function) so that the output will print in a specific order. The keys in a hash are not stored in any reliable order, so I have to take measures like this one. It also lets us print only the lines that were actually available—the call to `defined` inside the `foreach` loop makes sure that only those fields that existed in the record get printed.

The Code

Got it? No? Sometimes seeing all the code at once can help. Listing 14.3 shows the full code for `address.pl`. If you've downloaded the source from this book's Web site at `http://www.typerl.com`, the code there has many more comments to help you figure out what's going on.

As I mentioned yesterday in the section on my variables, some versions of Perl might have difficulties with this script's use of `my` variables and `foreach` loops. To get around this problem, simply predeclare the `foreach` variable before using it, like this:

```
my $key = 0;
foreach $key (qw(Name Phone Fax Address Email URL)) { ...
```

LISTING 14.3 The Code for `address.pl`

```
#!/usr/bin/perl -w
use strict;

my $bigmatch = 0;                   # was anything found?
my $search = '';                    # thing to search for

$search = &getpattern();            # prompt for pattern

while () {                          # range over address file
    my %rec = &read_addr();
    if (%rec) {         # got a record
        &perform_search($search, %rec);
    } else {            # end of address file, finish up
        if (!$bigmatch) {
            print "Nothing found.\n";
        } else { print "*********************\n"; }
        last;           # exit, we're done
    }
}

sub getpattern {
    my $in = '';  # input
    print 'Search for what? ';
    chomp($in = <STDIN>);
    return $in;
}

sub read_addr {
    my %curr = ();                  # current record
    my $key = '';                   # temp key
    my $val = '';                   # temp value

    while (<>) {                    # stop if we get to EOF
        chomp;
        if (!/^---/) {      # record seperator
            ($key, $val) = split(/: /,$_,2);
            $curr{$key} = $val;
        }
        else { last; }
```

LISTING 14.3 continued

```
    }
    return %curr;
}

sub perform_search {
    my ($str, %rec) = @_;
    my $matched = 0;               # overall match
    my $i = 0;                     # position inside pattern
    my $thing = '';                # temporary word

    my @things = $str =~ /("[^"]+"|\S+)/g;  # split into search items

    while ($i <= $#things) {
        $thing = $things[$i];      # search item, AND or OR
        if ($thing =~ /^or$/i) { # OR case
            if (!$matched) {       # no match yet, look at next thing
                $matched = &isitthere($things[$i+1], %rec);
            }
            $i += 2;               # skip OR and next thing
        }
        elsif ($thing =~ /^and$/i) { # AND case
            if ($matched) {        # got a match, need to check other side
                $matched = &isitthere($things[$i+1], %rec);
            }
            $i += 2;               # skip AND and next thing
        }
        elsif (!$matched) {        # no match yet
            $matched = &isitthere($thing, %rec);
            $i++;                  # next!
        }
        else { $i++; }             # $match is found, move onto next thing
    }

    if ($matched) {                # all keys done, did we match?
        $bigmatch = 1;             # yes, we found something
        print_addr(%rec);          # print the record then
    }
}

sub isitthere {                    # simple test
    my ($pat, %rec) = @_;
    foreach my $line (values %rec) {
        if ($line =~ /$pat/) {
            return 1;
        }
    }
    return 0;
}
```

14

LISTING 14.3 continued

```
sub print_addr {
    my %record = @_;
    print "*********************\n";
    foreach my $key (qw(Name Phone Fax Address Email URL)) {
        if (defined($record{$key})) {
            print "$record{$key}\n";
        }
    }
}
```

A Web Log Processor (`weblog.pl`)

The second example script is one that takes a log file, as generated by Web servers, and generates statistics about the information contained in that log file. Most Web servers keep files of this sort, which keep track of how many accesses ("hits") have been made to a Web site, the files that were requested, the sites that requested them, and other information.

Many log file-analyzer programs already exist on the Web (and there are usually programs that come with the Web server), so this example isn't breaking any new ground. The statistics it generates are fairly simple, although this script could be easily modified to include just about any information that you'd like to include. It's a good starting point for processing Web logs, or a model to follow for processing log files from any other programs.

How It Works

The `weblog.pl` script is called with one argument: a log file. On many Web servers, these files are commonly called `access_log`, and follow what is known as the *common log format*. The script processes for a while (it'll print the date of the logs it's working on so you know it's still working), and then prints some results. Here's an example of the sort of output you can get (this example is from the logs on my own Web server, `www.lne.com`):

```
% weblog.pl access_log
Processing log....
Processing 09/Apr/1998
Processing 10/Apr/1998
Processing 11/Apr/1998
Processing 12/Apr/1998
Web log file Results:
Total Number of Hits: 55789
Total failed hits: 1803 (3.23%)
(sucessful) HTML files: 18264 (33.83%)
Number of unique hosts: 5911
Number of unique domains: 2121
```

```
Most popular files:
  /Web/index.html (2456 hits)
  /lemay/index.html (1711 hits)
  /Web/Title.gif (1685 hits)
  /Web/HTML3.2/3.2thm.gif (1669 hits)
  /Web/JavaProf/javaprof_thm.gif (1662 hits)
Most popular hosts:
  202.185.174.4 (487 hits)
  vader.integrinautics.com (440 hits)
  linea15.secsa.podernet.com.mx (437 hits)
  lobby.itmin.com (284 hits)
  pyx.net (256 hits)
Most popular domains:
  mindspring.com (3160 hits)
  aol.com (1808 hits)
  uu.net (792 hits)
  grid.net (684 hits)
  compuserve.com (565 hits)
```

This particular output shows only the top 5 files, hosts, and domains, to save space here. You can configure the script to print out any number of those statistics.

The difference between a host and a domain might not be readily apparent; a host is the full host name of the system that accessed the Web server, which might include dynamically assigned addresses and proxy servers. The host `dialup124.servers.foo.com` will be a different host from `dialup567.servers.foo.com`. The domain, on the other hand, is a larger group of hosts, usually consisting of two or three parts. `foo.com` is a domain, as is `aol.com` or `demon.co.uk`. The domain listings tend to collapse separate entries for hosts into major groups—all the hosts under `aol.com`'s purview will show up as hits from `aol.com` in the domain list.

Note also that a single hit can be an HTML page, an image, a form submission, or any other file. There are usually significantly more raw hits than there are actual page accesses. This script points those out by keeping track of HTML hits separately from the total number of hits.

What a Web Log Looks Like

Because the `weblog.pl` script processes Web log files, it helps to know what those log files look like. Web log files are stored with one hit per line, and each line in what's called common log format (common because it's common to various Web servers). Most Web servers generate their log files in this format, or can be configured to do so (many servers use a superset of the common log format with more information in it). A line in a common log format log file might look something like this (here I'm showing it to you on two lines; actually, it only appears on one in real life):

```
proxy2bh.powerup.com.au - - [03/Apr/1998:00:09:02 -0800]
"GET /lemay/ HTTP/1.0" 200 4621
```

The various elements of each line in the log file are

- The host name accessing the server (here `proxy2bh.powerup.com.au`).
- The username of the person accessing the page discovered through ident (a Unix program used to identify users), or through the user signing into your site. These two parts usually show up as two dashes (`-  -`) when the username cannot be determined.
- The date and time the hit was made, in square brackets.
- Inside quotes, the action for the hit (actually a Web server action): `GET` is to get a file or submit a form, `POST` is to submit a form in a different way, `HEAD` is to get header information about a file.
- After the action, the filename (or directory) that was requested, here `/lemay/`.
- The version number of the protocol, here `HTTP/1.0`.
- The return code for the hit; 200 is successful, 404 is "not found," and so on.
- The number of bytes transferred.

Not all these elements of the log file are interesting to a statistics generator script, of course, and a lot of them won't make any sense to you unless you know how Web servers work. But a few, such as the host, the date, the filename, and the return code, can be extracted and processed for each line of the file.

Building the Script

The path of execution for this script is easier to follow than the one for the `address.pl` script; there are basically only two major steps—process the log and generate the statistics. We do have a number of subroutines along the way to help, however.

In fact, all of the code for this script is contained in subroutines. The body of the code consists of a bunch of global variables and two subroutine calls: `&process_log()` and `&print_results()`.

The global variables are used to store the various statistics and information about parts of the log file. Because many of these statistics are hashes, using local variables and passing around the data would become complicated. In this case, keeping the data global makes it easier to manage. The global data we keep track of includes

- The number of hits, number of failed hits, and number of hits to HTML pages
- A hash to store the various host names, and the number of times those hosts appear in the log
- A hash to do the same for the various files in the log

In addition, two other global variables are worth mentioning:

- The `$topthings` variable stores a number indicating how many entries you want to print for the "most popular" parts of the statistics. In the example output I showed you, `$topthings` was set to 5, which gives us some nice short output. Setting it to 20 will print the top 20 files, hosts, and domains.
- The `$default` variable should be set to the default HTML file for your Web server, often called `index.html` or `home.html`. This is the file that serves as the main file for a directory when the user doesn't ask for a specific file. Usually it's `index.html`.

These two variables determine how the script itself will behave. Although we could have put these variables deep inside the program, putting them up here, right up front, enables you or someone else using your script to change the overall behavior of the script in one place without having to search for the right variable to change. It's one of those "good programming practices" that make sense, no matter which programming language you're using.

Processing the Log

The first part of the `weblog.pl` script is the `&process_log()` subroutine, which loops over each line in the script, and stores various statistics about that line. I'm not going to show you every line of this subroutine, but I will point out the important parts. You can see the complete code in Listing 14.7 at the end of this section.

The core of the `&process_log()` subroutine is yet another `while (<>)` loop, to read each line of the input at a time. Unlike `address.pl`, this script doesn't pause anywhere; it just reads in the file from start to finish.

The first thing we do to process each line is to split the line into its component parts and store those parts in a hash keyed by the part name (`'site'`, `'file'`, and so on). There's a separate subroutine to do the splitting, called `&splitline()`. Listing 14.4 shows this subroutine.

LISTING 14.4 The `&splitline()` Subroutine

```
sub splitline {
    my $in = $_[0];
    my %line = ();
    if ($in =~ /^([^\s]+)\s              # site
               ([\w-]+\s[\w-]+)\s        # users
               \[([^\]]+)\]\s            # date
                \"(\w+)\s                # protocol
               (\/[^\s]*)\s              # file
               ([^"]+)\"\s               # HTTP version
```

LISTING 14.4 continued

```
10:                 (\d{3})\s                # return code
11:                 ([\d-]+)                 # bytes transferred
12:      /x) {
13:         $line{'site'} = $1;
14:         $line{'date'} = $3;
15:         $line{'file'} = $5;
16:         $line{'code'} = $7;
17:         return %line;
18:      } else { return (); }
19: }
```

The first thing that probably catches your eye about that subroutine is that enormous monster of a regular expression smack in the middle (lines 4 through 11). It's so ugly it needs six lines! And comments! This regular expression is in a form called *extended regular expressions*; if you read the "Going Deeper" section on Day 5, "Working with Hashes," I described these there. But here's a quick review: Say you have a particularly ugly regular expression like the one in this example (here I've put it on two lines because it doesn't fit on one line!):

```
if ($in =~ /^([^\s]+)\s([\w-]+\s[\w-]+)\s\[([^\]]+)\]\s\"(\w+)
\(\/[^\s]*)\s([^"]+)\"\s(\d{3})\s([\d-]+)/)
```

Chances are good you won't be able to make heads or tails of that expression without a lot of patient dissecting or very strong tranquilizers. And debugging it won't be much fun either. But if you put the `/x` option on the end of the expression (as we have in line 12), then you can spread that regular expression apart into sections or onto separate lines, and comment it as you would lines of Perl code. All whitespace in the pattern is ignored; if you want to match for whitespace in the text, you'll have to use `\s`. All the `/x` option does is make a regular expression easier to read and debug.

This particular `regex` assumes the common log format I described earlier. Specifically:

- Line 4 matches the site (host) name. The site always appears at the start of the line, and consists of some nonwhitespace characters followed by a space (a `\s` here so that extended patterns work).
- Line 5 matches the user fields (two of them). The users consist of one or more alphanumeric characters or a dash separated by and followed by whitespace. Note the dashes inside the character classes; the `\w` class does not include dashes.
- Line 6 matches the date, which is one or more characters or whitespace in between brackets (`[]`).
- Line 7 matches the protocol (`GET`, `HEAD`, and so on), by starting the string with a quote and following it by one or more characters (the closing quote is after the HTTP version in line 9).

- Line 8 matches the file. It always starts with a slash (/), followed by zero or more other characters and ending with whitespace.
- Line 9 matches the HTTP version, which includes any remaining characters before the closing quote.
- Line 10 matches the return code, which is always three digits long followed by whitespace (it would be less specific to just use `\d+` here, but this is a chance to show off the use of the {3} pattern.
- Line 11 finishes up the pattern with the number of bytes transferred, which is any number of digits. If no bytes were transferred—for example, the hit resulted in an error—this field will be a dash. The pattern covers that as well.

Each element of this regex is stored in a parenthesized expression (and a match variable), with the extra brackets or quotes removed. After the match has occurred, we can put the various matched bits into a hash. Note that we only use about half of the actual matches in the hash; we only need to store what we're actually going to use. But if you extend this example to include statistics on other parts of the hit, all you have to do is add lines to add those matches to the hash. You don't have to muck with the regular expression to get more information.

With the line split into its component parts, we return from the `&splitline()` subroutine back up to the main `&process_log()` routine. The next part of this subroutine checks for failed hits. If a line in the Web log didn't match the pattern—and some don't—then the `&splitline()` subroutine will return null. That's considered a failed hit, so we add it to the count of failed hits, and then skip to the end of the loop to process the next line:

```
if (!%hit) {  # malformed line in web log
   $failhits++;
    next;
}
```

The next part of the script is a convenience for the person running the script. Processing a log file of any size takes a long time, and sometimes it can be hard to tell whether Perl is still working on the log file, or if the system has hung and it's never going to return anything. This part of the script prints a processing message with the date of the lines being processed, printing a new message each time a day's hits are complete and showing Perl's progress through the file:

```
$dateshort = &getday($hit{'date'});
if ($currdate ne $dateshort) {
    print "Processing $dateshort\n";
    $currdate = $dateshort;
}
```

Here, the subroutine `&getday()` is simply a short routine that grabs the month and the day out of the date field using a pattern so they can be compared to the date being processed (I'm not going to show you `&getday()`; you can see it in the full code if you're curious). If they're different, a message is printed and the `$currdate` variable is updated.

In addition to lines in the log file that don't match the log format, also considered failed hits are those that matched the pattern, but didn't result in an actual file being returned (misspellings in URLs or files that have moved will cause these kinds of hits, for example). These hits are recorded in the log with error codes that start with 4, for example, the 404 you've probably seen on the Web. The return code was one of the things we saved from the line, so testing that is a simple pattern match:

```
if ($hit{'code'} =~ /^4/) { # 404, 403, etc. (errors)
    $failhits++;
```

The `else` part of this `if` test handles all other hits—that is, the successful ones that actually returned HTML files or images. Those hits will have return codes of 200 or 304:

```
} elsif ($hit{'code'} =~ /200|302|304/) {   # deal only with successes
```

Web servers are set up to deliver a default file, usually `index.html`, when a site requests a URL that ends in a directory name. This means that a request for `/web/` and a request for `/web/index.html` actually refer to the same file, but they show up as different entries in the log file, which means our script will process them as different files. To collapse directories and default files, we have a couple of lines that test to see if the file requested ends with a slash, and if so, to add the default filename on the end of it. The default file, as I noted earlier, is defined by the `$default` variable:

```
if ($hit{'file'} =~ /\/$/) { # slashes map to $default
    $hit{'file'} .= $default;
}
```

With that done, now we can finish up the processing by incrementing the `$htmlhits` variable if the file is an HTML file and updating the hashes for the site and for the file:

```
if ($hit{'file'} =~ /\.html?$/) { # .htm or .html
    $htmlhits++;
}

$hosts{ $hit{'site'} }++;
$files{ $hit{'file'} }++;
```

At this point, we're now at the end of the `while` loop, and the loop starts over again with the next line in the file. The loop continues until all the lines are processed, and then we move onto the printing part of the script.

Printing the Results

The `&process_log()` subroutine processes the log file line by line, and calls the `&splitline()` and `&getday()` subroutines to help. The second part of the `weblog.pl` script is the `&print_results()` subroutine, and it has a few other subroutines to help it as well. Much of `print_results()`, however, is as it sounds: a bunch of `print` statements to print out the various statistics.

First, the script checks to make sure that the log file wasn't empty (using the `$totalhits` variable). If the file was empty, then the script prints an error message and exits. The next few lines print out the total number of hits, total number of failed hits, and total number of HTML hits. The latter are also shown as a percentage of total hits, with HTML hits a total of successful hits. We can get these values with a little math and a `printf`:

```
print "Web log file Results:\n";
print "Total Number of Hits: $totalhits\n";
print "Total failed hits: $failhits (";
printf('%.2f', $failhits / $totalhits * 100);
print "%)\n";
print "(sucessful) HTML files: $htmlhits (";
printf('%.2f', $htmlhits / ($totalhits - $failhits) * 100);
print "%)\n";
```

Next up: total number of hosts. We can get this value by extracting the keys of the `%hosts` hash into a list, and then evaluate that list in a scalar context (using the `scalar` function):

```
print 'Number of unique hosts: ';
print scalar(keys %hosts);
print "\n";
```

To get the number of unique domains, we need to process the `%hosts` hash to compress the hosts into their smaller domains, and build a new hash (`%domains`) that has the new count of all the hits for each domain. We'll use a subroutine called `&getdomains()` for that, which I'll discuss in the next section; assume we've done it, that we have our domains `%hash`. We can do the same `scalar` trick with the keys to that hash to get the number of unique domains:

```
my %domains = &getdomains(keys %hosts);
print 'Number of unique domains: ';
print scalar(keys %domains);
print "\n";
```

14

The last three things that get printed are the most popular files, hosts, and domains. There's a subroutine to get these values as well, called `&gettop()`, which sorts each hash by its values (the number of times each thing appeared in a hit), and then builds an array of descriptive strings with the keys and values in the hash. The array will contain only the top five or ten things (or whatever the value of `$topthings` is). More about the `&gettop()` subroutine in a bit.

Each of those arrays gets printed to the output to finish up. Here's the one for files:

```
print "Most popular files: \n";
foreach my $file (&gettop(%files)) {
    print "  $file\n";
}
```

The `&getdomains()` Subroutine

We're not done yet. We still have to cover the helper subroutines for printing the statistics: `&getdomains()`, to extract the domains from the `%hosts` hash and recalculate the stats, and `gettop()`, to take a hash of keys and frequencies and return the most popular elements. The `&getdomains()` subroutine is shown in Listing 14.5.

LISTING 14.5 The `&getdomains()` Subroutine

```
sub getdomains {
    my %domains = ();
    my ($sd,$d,$tld);       # secondary domain, domain, top-level domain
    foreach my $host (@_) {
        my $dom = '';
        if($host =~ /(([^.]+)\.)?([^.]+)\.([^.]+)$/ ) {
            if (!defined($1)) { # only two domains (i.e. aol.com)
                ($d,$tld) = ($3, $4);
            } else {            # a usual domain x.y.com etc
                ($sd, $d, $tld) = ($2, $3, $4);
            }
            if ($tld =~ /\D+/) { # ignore raw IPs
                if ($tld =~ /com|edu|net|gov|mil|org$/i) { # US TLDs
                    $dom = "$d.$tld";
                } else { $dom = "$sd.$d.$tld"; }
                $domains{$dom} += $hosts{$host};
            }
        } else { print "Malformed: $host\n"; }
    }
    return %domains;
}
```

This is less complex than it looks. A few basic assumptions are made about the makeup of a host name: in particular, that each host name has a number of parts separated by periods, and that the domain consists of either the right-most two or three parts, depending on the name itself. In this subroutine, then, we'll reduce each host into its actual domain, and then use that domain name as the index to a new hash, storing all the original hits from the full hosts into the new domain-based hash.

The core of this subroutine is the `foreach` loop starting in line 4. The argument that gets passed to this subroutine is an array of all the host names from the `%hosts` array, and we'll loop over each host name in turn to make sure we covered them all.

The first part of that `foreach` loop is the long scary-looking regular expression in line 6. All this pattern does is grab the last two parts of the host name, and the last three if it can (some host names only have two parts; this regex will handle those, too). Lines 7 through 11 then check to see how many parts we got (2 or 3), and assign the variables `$sd`, `$d`, and `$tld` to those parts (`$sd` stands for secondary domain, `$d` stands for domain, and `$tld` stands for top-level domain, if you want to keep them straight).

The second part of the loop determines whether we'll use two or three parts of the host as the actual domain (and ignores any hosts made up of IP numbers rather than actual domain names in line 12). The purely arbitrary rule I used for determining whether a domain has two or three parts is this: If the top-level domain (that is, the right-most part of the host name) is a US domain such as `.com`, `.edu`, and so on (full list in line 13), then the domain only has two parts. This covers `aol.com`, `mit.edu`, `whitehouse.gov`, and so on. If the top-level domain is anything else, it's probably a country-specific domain such as `.uk`, `.au`, `.mx`, and so on. Those domains typically use three parts to refer to a site, for example, `citygate.co.uk` or `monash.edu.au`. Two parts would not be enough granularity (`edu.au` refers to all universities in Australia, not to a specific place called `edu`).

This is what lines 13 through 15 deal with; building up the domain name from two or three parts and storing it in the string `$dom`. After we've built the domain name, we can then use it as the key in the new hash, and bring over the hits we had for the original host in line 16. By the time the domain hash is done, all the hits in the host's hash should be accounted for in the domain's hash as well, and we can return that hash back to the `print_results` subroutine.

One last bit: line 28 is a bit of error checking for this subroutine. If the pattern matching expression in 6 doesn't match, then we've got a very weird host name indeed, and we'll print a message to that effect. Generally speaking, however, that message should never be reached because a malformed host name in the log file usually means a malformed host name on the host itself, and the Internet makes that difficult to do.

The `&gettop()` Subroutine

One last subroutine to cover, and then we can put this week to bed and you can go have a beer and celebrate finishing two thirds of this book. This last subroutine, `&gettop()`, takes a hash, sorts it by value, and then trims off the top `x` elements, where `x` is determined by the `$topthings` variable. The subroutine returns an array of strings, where each string contains the key and value for the top `x` elements in form that can be easily printed by the `&print_results()` subroutine that called this one in the first place. Listing 14.6 shows this subroutine.

LISTING 14.6 The `&gettop()` Subroutine

```
sub gettop {
    my %hash = @_;
    my $i = 1;
    my @topkeys = ();
    foreach my $key (sort { $hash{$b} <=> $hash{$a} } keys %hash) {
        if ($i <= $topthings) {
            push @topkeys, "$key ($hash{$key} hits)";
            $i++;
        }
    }
    return @topkeys;
}
```

The Code

Listing 14.7 contains the complete code for the `weblog.pl` script.

Once again, watch out for the `my` variables inside `foreach` loops in certain versions of Perl. See the note just before Listing 14.3 for details.

LISTING 14.7 The Code for `weblog.pl`

```
#!/usr/bin/perl -w
use strict;

my $default = 'index.html';     # change to be your default HTML file
my $topthings = 30;             # number of files, sites, etc to report
my $totalhits = 0;
my $failhits = 0;
my $htmlhits = 0;
my %hosts= ();
my %files = ();

&process_log();
&print_results();

sub process_log {
    my %hit = ();
    my $currdate = '';
    my $dateshort = '';
    print "Processing log....\n";
    while (<>) {
        chomp;
        %hit = splitline($_);
        $totalhits++;
```

Listing 14.7 continued

```

        # watch out for malformed lines
        if (!%hit) {  # malformed line in web log
            $failhits++;
            next;
        }

        $dateshort = &getday($hit{'date'});
        if ($currdate ne $dateshort) {
            print "Processing $dateshort\n";
            $currdate = $dateshort;
        }

        # watch 404s
        if ($hit{'code'} =~ /^4/) { # 404, 403, etc. (errors)
            $failhits++;
        # other files
        } elsif ($hit{'code'} =~ /200|304/) {   # deal only with sucesses
            if ($hit{'file'} =~ /\/$/) { # slashes map to $default
                $hit{'file'} .= $default;
            }

            if ($hit{'file'} =~ /\.html?$/) { # .htm or .html
                $htmlhits++;
            }

            $hosts{ $hit{'site'} }++;
            $files{ $hit{'file'} }++;
        }
    }
}

sub splitline {
    my $in = $_[0];
    my %line = ();
    if ($in =~ /^([^\s]+)\s             # site
                ([\w-]+\s[\w-]+)\s      # users
                \[([^\]]+)\]\s          # date
                 \"(\w+)\s              # protocol
                (\/[^\s]*)\s            # file
                ([^"]+)\"\s             # HTTP version
                (\d{3})\s               # return code
                ([\d-]+)                # bytes transferred
        /x) {
        # we only care about some of the values
        # (every other one, coincidentally)
        $line{'site'} = $1;
        $line{'date'} = $3;
        $line{'file'} = $5;
        $line{'code'} = $7;
```

14

Listing 14.7 continued

```
       return %line;
    } else { return (); }
}

sub getday {
    my $date;
    if ($_[0] =~ /([^:]+):/) {
        $date = $1;
        return $date;
    } else {
        return $_[0];
    }
}

sub print_results {
    if ($totalhits == 0) {
        print "The log file is empty.\n";
        exit;
    }

    print "Web log file Results:\n";
    print "Total Number of Hits: $totalhits\n";
    print "Total failed hits: $failhits (";
    printf('%.2f', $failhits / $totalhits * 100);
    print "%)\n";

    print "(sucessful) HTML files: $htmlhits (";
    printf('%.2f', $htmlhits / ($totalhits - $failhits) * 100);
    print "%)\n";

    print 'Number of unique hosts: ';
    print scalar(keys %hosts);
    print "\n";

    my %domains = &getdomains(keys %hosts);
    print 'Number of unique domains: ';
    print scalar(keys %domains);
    print "\n";

    print "Most popular files: \n";
    foreach my $file (&gettop(%files)) {
       print "  $file\n";
    }
    print "Most popular hosts: \n";
    foreach my $host (&gettop(%hosts)) {
       print "  $host\n";
    }

    print "Most popular domains: \n";
```

LISTING 14.7 continued

```
    foreach my $dom (&gettop(%domains)) {
       print "  $dom\n";
    }
}

sub getdomains {
    my %domains = ();
    my ($sd,$d,$tld);        # secondary domain, domain, top-level domain
    foreach my $host (@_) {
        my $dom = '';
        if($host =~ /(([^.]+)\.)?([^.]+)\.([^.]+)$/ ) {
            if (!defined($1)) { # only two domains (i.e. aol.com)
                ($d,$tld) = ($3, $4);
            } else {            # a usual domain x.y.com etc
                ($sd, $d, $tld) = ($2, $3, $4);
            }
            if ($tld =~ /\D+/) { # ignore raw IPs
                if ($tld =~ /com|edu|net|gov|mil|org$/i) { # US TLDs
                    $dom = "$d.$tld";
                } else { $dom = "$sd.$d.$tld"; }
                $domains{$dom} += $hosts{$host};
            }
        } else { print "Malformed: $host\n"; }
    }
    return %domains;
}

sub gettop {
    my %hash = @_;
    my $i = 1;
    my @topkeys = ();
    foreach my $key (sort { $hash{$b} <=> $hash{$a} } keys %hash) {
        if ($i <= $topthings) {
            push @topkeys, "$key ($hash{$key} hits)";
            $i++;
        }
    }
    return @topkeys;
}
```

Summary

Often programming books give you a lot of wordy background, but don't give you enough actual code examples for how to do stuff. Although I won't claim that this book shirks on the wordy background (you may snicker now), these example sections offer you some longer bits of code that accomplish real things and show how a real-world script is put together.

In today's lesson, we explored two longer scripts. The first is a simple searchable address file, which used a text-based database of names and addresses. The script to process that file enabled you to process a reasonably complex search pattern, including nesting logical expressions and grouping words and phrases via quotes. You could extend this example to cover just about any situation that calls for a complex search over parts of a data file; for example, to filter mail messages out of a mail folder based on some criteria, or to search for specific comic books in a collection of comics. Any text file can serve as a simple database, and this script can search it as long as it's modified to handle the data in that database.

The second example was a log file analyzer that processes Web log files and prints statistics about those files. Raw Web log files tend to be sort of daunting to look at; this script provided some basic summary information about what's actually going on with the Web site. Along the way, it used some complex regular expressions and a whole lot of hashes to store the raw data. You could extend this example to generate other statistics (for example, to generate histograms of the number of hits per day or per hour, or to keep track of image or other files in addition to HTML files). Or, you could modify it to cover other log files (mail logs, FTP logs, whatever logs you have lying around).

Congratulations on completing the second week of this three-week book. After this week, you've picked up a substantial part of the language, and you should be able to accomplish quite a few tasks in Perl. From this point on we'll be building on what you've already learned. Onward to Week 3!

WEEK 3

Advanced Perl

15

16

17

18

19

20

21

WEEK 3

DAY 15

Working with Files and I/O

Throughout the first two weeks of this book, I introduced you to input and output (otherwise known as I/O) a little at a time. You've learned about standard input and output using `<STDIN>` and `print`, and about file input using the command line, the `<>` operator, and a `while` loop to automatically assign each line to the `$_` variable.

In today's lesson, we'll expand on what you already know about input and output in greater detail, as well as touch more on script argument lists and getting data and options into your script. Today, we'll explore

- All about file handles: creating them, reading input from them, writing output to them
- Simple file tests for finding out information about a particular file
- Working with script arguments and `@ARGV`
- Using the `Getopt` module for managing switches

Input and Output with File Handles

Way back on Day 2, "Working with Strings and Numbers," you learned just a bit about file handles, as part of the information on standard input and output. At that time, I explained that `STDIN` and `STDOUT` are a special kind of file handle that refer to nonfile-based input and output streams–the keyboard and the screen, for example. And, conveniently, much of what you've learned already is going to apply just as well to file handles that refer to actual files.

In this section, you'll learn how to tame the wily file handles: creating them with the `open` function, reading from them, writing or appending to them, and closing them when you're done. Along the way, we'll review what you've learned so far about input and output.

Creating File Handles with `open`

To read input from a source, or to write output to a destination, you need to use a file handle. A file handle is commonly associated with a specific file on a disk that you're reading or writing from. It can also refer to a network connection (a socket), to a pipe (a sort of connection between standard output and standard input we'll look at on Day 18, "Perl and the Operating System"), or even to and from a specific hardware device. The file handle simply just makes all those things consistent so you can do the same things regardless of where the data is coming from or going to.

Perl provides three default file handles, two of which you've already seen: `STDIN`, `STDOUT` and `STDERR`. The first two are for standard input and output (the keyboard and the screen, typically). `STDERR` is the standard error, and is used for error messages and other asides that aren't part of the actual script output. You'll commonly see `STDERR` messages printed to the screen just like `STDOUT`; it's only programs that specifically make use of standard output (programs on the other side of pipes in Unix, for example) that will notice the difference.

You don't have to do anything to open or initialize these file handles; you can just go ahead and use them (as we have been throughout last week's lessons).

To read from or write to a file, you must first create a file handle for that operation with the `open` function. The `open` function opens a file for reading (input) or for writing (output), and associates a file handle name of your choosing to that file. Note that reading from and writing to a file are separate operations, and you'll need a file handle for each one.

The `open` function takes two arguments: the name of a file handle, and the file to open (which includes a special code indicating opening the file for reading or writing). Here are a few examples:

```
open(FILE, 'myfile');

open(CONFIG, '.scriptconfig');

open(LOG, '>/home/www/logfile');
```

The name of the file handle is anything you want it to be. File handles are, by convention, all uppercase, and contain letters, numbers, or underscores. Unlike variables, they must start with a letter.

The second argument is the name of the file on the disk that will be attached to your file handle. A plain filename with no path information will be read from the current directory (either the one your script is being run from, or from some other directory if you've changed it). You learn more about navigating directories on Day 17, "Managing Files and Directories."

If you're going to use path names other than single files, be careful—the path notation varies from platform to platform. On Unix, paths are delineated with forward slashes, as in the last one of the preceding examples.

For Windows systems, standard DOS notation, with backslashes in between directory names, works fine as long as you use single quotes to surround the path. Remember that backslashes indicate special characters in Perl, so you might end up creating a bizarre path with no relation to reality. If you do use double-quoted string, you must backslash each backslash to escape it properly.

```
open(FILE, 'c:\tempfiles\numbers');  # correct

# eeek! contains a tab and a newline (\t, \n)
open(FILE, "c:\tempfiles\numbers");


open(FILE "c:\\tempfiles\\numbers"); # correct
```

Because most modern Windows systems can handle directory pathnames with forward slashes, you might want to use those instead, for better portability to Unix systems (if you care) and to improve the readability of your scripts.

On the Mac, the directory separator is a colon, and absolute path names start with the disk or volume name (hard disk, CD-ROM, mounted disk, and so on). If you're concerned about portability to other systems, you'll need to make a note of it and convert your path names later. A couple examples of Mac syntax are

```
open(FILE, "My Hard Disk:Perl Stuff:config");

open(BOOKMARKS, "HD:System Folder:Preferences:Netscape:Bookmarks.html");
```

In each of these cases, we've been opening a file handle for reading input into the script. This is the default. If you want to write output back to a file, you still need a file handle and you still use `open` to get it, but you use it with a special character ahead of the filename:

```
open(OUT, ">output");
```

The `>` character indicates that this file handle is to be opened for writing. The given file is opened and any current contents, if they exist, are deleted (you can test to see if a file exists before you open it for writing to avoid this behavior; more about file tests later on in "Managing Files.")

What if you want to read input from a file, do something with it, and then write the same file back? You'll have to open two file handles: one to read in the input, and then another later on to reopen the file for writing. Reading and writing are different processes and require different file handles.

Actually, there is a code for both reading and writing to the same file: `"+>`*`filename`*`"`. You might use this if you wanted to treat a file as a database, where instead of reading in the whole thing, you store it on disk, and then read and write to that file as you read or change data. This book will stick with reading and writing simple text files, in which case it's less confusing and easier to manage the data if you use two separate file handles: one to read the data into memory, and one to write the data back out again.

You can also open a file for appending—where the current contents of the file are retained, and when you print to the output file handle, your output is appended to the end of that file. To do this, use the `>>` special characters in your call to `open`:

```
open(FILE, ">>logfile");
```

The `die` Function

The `open` function is nearly always called in conjunction with a logical `or` and a call to `die` on the other side, like this:

```
open(FILE, "thefile") or die "Can't findfile";
```

The call to `die` isn't required, but it occurs so frequently in Perl code that the combination is almost boilerplate. If you don't do something like this, chances are good that if anyone else sees your code, they're going to ask you why you didn't.

"Open this file or die!" is the implied threat of this statement, and that's usually precisely what you want. The `open` command could potentially fail—for example, if you're opening the file for reading and it doesn't exist, if the disk is behaving weirdly and can't open the file, or for whatever other strange reason. Usually, you don't want your script to plow ahead if something has gone horribly wrong and it can't find anything to read. Fortunately, the `open` function returns `undef` if it could not open the file (and `1` if it could), so you can check the result and decide what to do.

Sometimes "what to do" can vary depending on the script. Commonly, however, you just want to exit the script with an error message. That's what the `die` function does: it immediately exits the entire Perl script, and prints its argument (a string message) to the `STDERR` file handle (the screen, typically).

If you put a newline character at the end of the message, Perl will print that message as it exits. If you leave off the newline, Perl will print an additional bit of information: `at script.pl line` *nn*. The `script.pl` will be the name of your script, and line *nn* will be the actual line number in which the `die` occurred. This can be useful for debugging your script later.

One other clever use of `die`: The Perl special variable `$!` contains the most recent operating system error (if your OS will generate one). By putting the `$!` variable inside the string to `die`, your error message can sometimes be more helpful than just "Can't open file." For example, this version of die:

```
die "Can't open file: $!\n";
```

might result in the message "Can't open file: Permission denied" if the reason the file can't be opened is because the user doesn't have the right access to that file. Use of `$!` is generally a good idea if you're calling `die` in response to some sort of system error.

Although `die` is commonly used on the other side of a call to `open`, don't think it's only useful there. You can use `die` (and its nonfatal equivalent, `warn`) anywhere in your script where you want to stop executing the script (or print a warning message). See the `perlfunc` man page for more information on how to use `die` and `warn`.

Reading Input from a File Handle

So you've got a file handle. It's attached to a file you've opened for reading. To read input from a file handle, use the `<>` (input) operator with the name of that file handle, like this:

```
$line = <FILE>;
```

Looks familiar, right? You've been doing the same thing with STDIN to get a line of input from the keyboard. That's what's so cool about file handles—you use exactly the same procedures to read from a file as you do to read from the keyboard or to read from a network connection to a server. Perl doesn't care. It's exactly the same procedure, and everything you've already learned applies.

In scalar context, the input operator reads a single line of input up until the newline:

```
$line = <STDIN>;
if (<FILE>) { print "more input..." };
```

One special case of using the input operator in a scalar context is to use it inside the test of a while loop. This has the effect of looping through the input one line at a time, assigning each line to the $_ variable, and stopping only when the end of the input is reached:

```
while (<FILE>) { .
   # ... process each line of the file in $_
}
```

You've seen this same notation a lot with empty input operators. The empty input operators <> are, themselves, a special case in Perl. As you've learned, you use the empty input operators to get input from files contained on the script's command line. What Perl does for those files is open them all for you and send their contents to you in order via the STDIN file handle. You don't have to do anything special to handle them. Of course, you could open and read each file yourself, but the use of <> in a while loop is an extremely handy shortcut.

In list context, the input operators behave as if the entire input was being read in at once, with each line in the input assigned to an element in the list. Watch out for the input operator in a list context, as it might not always do what you expect it to. Here are some examples:

```
@input = <FILE>;  # read the entire file into @input;

$input = <FILE>;  # read the first line of file into $input

($input) = <FILE>; # read the first line of file into $input,
                   # throw the rest of FILE away (yikes!)
print <FILE>;     # print the entire contents of <FILE> to the screen
```

Writing Output to a File Handle

To write output to a file handle, you'll commonly use the print or printf functions. By default, the print (and printf) functions print to the file handle STDOUT. To print to a different file handle, for example, to write a line to a file, first open the file handle for writing, as follows:

```
open(FILE, ">$myfile") or die "Can't find $myfile\n";
```

And then use `print` with a file handle argument to put data into that file:

```
print FILE "$line\n";
```

The `printf` and `sprintf` functions work similarly; include the file handle to print to before the formatting string and the values as shown here:

```
printf(FILE "%d responses have been tabulated\n", $total / $count);
```

One very important part of `print` and `printf` that you need to be aware of: There is no comma between the file handle and the list of things to print. This comes under the heading of most common Perl mistakes (and will be caught if you have Perl warnings turned on). The file handle argument is entirely separate from the second argument, which is a list of elements separated by commas.

Reading and Writing Binary Files

Throughout this book, we've been reading and writing text data. But not all the files you work with in Perl are in text format; many of them may be binary files. If you're using Perl on Unix or the Mac, the difference won't matter; Unix and MacPerl can handle both text and binary files just fine. If you're using Windows, however, you'll get garbled results if you try to process a binary file in a normal Perl script.

Fortunately, there's an easy work-around: The `binmode` function takes a single file handle as an argument, and will process that file handle (read from it or write to it) in binary mode:

```
open(FILE, "myfile.exe ") or die "Can't open myfile: $!\n";
binmode FILE;
while (<FILE>) { # read in binary mode...
```

For the sake of portability, it's a good idea to just go ahead and use `binmode` whenever you're dealing with binary programs. It never hurts anything, and if your program ever winds up being used on a system that requires the use of `binmode`, it will just work without modification.

Closing a File Handle

When you're done reading from or writing to a file handle, you need to close it. Actually, you often don't have to close it yourself; when your script finishes executing, Perl closes all your file handles for you. And if you call `open` multiple times on the same file handle (for example, to open a file handle for writing after you're done reading from it), Perl will close that file handle automatically before opening it again. However, it's considered good programming practice to close your file handles after you're done with them; that way they won't take up any more space in your script.

To close a file handle, use the `close` function, like this:

```
close FILE;
```

An Example: Extract Subjects and Save Them

E-mail mailboxes are one of those formats that Perl is really good at managing because each message follows a very specific format (based on the protocol RFC822), and all are collected in a plain-text file. If you want to range over a mailbox and do something to messages that fits a specific criteria, then Perl is your language.For this example, however, let's do something really simple. The script in Listing 15.1 takes a mailbox as an argument on the script command line, reads in each message, extracts all the Subject lines, and writes a file called `subjects` in the same directory containing that list of subjects. If the file `subjects` already exist, this script will overwrite it (we'll learn in the next few sections how to test to see if the file exists and complain if it does).

Listing 15.1 shows the (very simple) code.

LISTING 15.1 The `subject.pl` Script

```
1:  #!/usr/local/bin/perl -w
2:  use strict;
3:
4:  open(OUTFILE, ">subjects.txt") or die "Can't open subjects file: $!\n";
5:
6:  while (<>) {
7:      if (/^Subject:/) {
8:          print OUTFILE $_;
9:      }
10: }
11: close OUTFILE;
```

A short script almost not worth pointing out as an example, you might think. But that's just the point—reading from and writing to files uses the same techniques you've used all along for standard input and output. There are two things to watch for here. First, line 4 opens the file `subjects` for writing (note the `>` character at the start of the filename). Second is line 8, where we print to that same `OUTFILE` file handle, rather than to standard output.

This script has no visual output, although if you run it on a file of mail, and then examine the `subjects.txt` file, you'll see lines like this (I ran this particular example on a file of "commercial mail," otherwise known as spam–hence the strange subjects):

```
Subject: FREE SOFTWARE TURN$ COMPUTER$ INTO CA$H MACHINE$!!
Subject: IBM 33.6 PCMCIA Modem $89.00
Subject: 48 MILLION Email Leads $195 + BONUSES
Subject: Re: E-ALERT: URGENT BUY RECOMMENDATION
Subject: Make $2,000 - $5,000 per week -NOT MLM
Subject: Email your AD to 57 MILLION People for ONLY $99
Subject: SHY?..................................
Subject: You Could Earn $100 Every Time the Phone Rings!!
```

File Tests

Opening files for reading and writing is all well and good when you know something about the files you're working with—for example, that they're all there, or that you're not about to overwrite something important. But sometimes in Perl you want to be able to check the properties of a file before you open it, or handle a file differently depending on the various properties of that file.

Perl has a (rather large) set of tests for the various properties of files: to see if they exist, that they have data in them, that they're a certain kind of file, or that it's a certain age. (1996 was a very good year for binary files, wasn't it?) These tests all look like switches (`-e`, `-R`, `-o`, and so on), but don't confuse them with actual switches (the reason they look like this is because they're borrowed from Unix shell scripting, and they look like that there).

Table 15.1 shows some of the more useful file tests. The `perlfunc` man page, in the entry for `-X`, contains the complete set (although you might note that not all the options are appropriate for all platforms).

Each of these tests can take a filename or a file handle as an argument; either will work (although if you're testing to see whether or not a file exists, you'll probably want to test the filename before calling `open` on it).

TABLE 15.1 File Tests

Operator	*Test*
`-d`	Returns 1 if the file is a directory, 0 if not.
`-e`	Returns 1 if the file exists, 0 if not.
`-f`	Returns 1 if the file is a plain file (as opposed to a directory, a link, or a network connection), 0 if not.
`-l`	Returns 1 if the file is a link (Unix only), 0 if not.

TABLE 15.1 continued

Operator	Test
`-r`	Returns 1 if the file is readable, 0 if not.
`-s`	Returns the size of the file in bytes.
`-t`	Returns 1 if the file handle is open to `STDIN` (or some other `tty` on Unix), 0 if not.
`-w`	Is the file writable (by user or group on Unix)?
`-x`	Returns 1 if the file is executable, 0 if not.
`-z`	Returns 1 if the file exists, but is empty, 0 if not.
`-A`	Returns the number of seconds that have elapsed since the file was last accessed.
`-B`	Returns 1 if the file is a binary file, 0 if not.
`-M`	Returns the number of seconds that have elapsed since the file was last modified.
`-T`	Returns 1 if the file is a plain text file, 0 if not.

Each test returns either true (`1`) or false (`""`), except for `-e`, which returns `undef` if the file doesn't exist, `-s`, which returns the number of bytes (characters) in the file, and the time operators `-M` and `-A`, which return the number of seconds since the file was modified or accessed, respectively.

So, for example, let's say you wanted to modify the `subject.pl` script such that if the `subjects.txt` file exists, you'd prompt the user to make sure they want to overwrite it. Instead of the plain call to `open` we had, you could test to see if the file exists, and if it does, make sure the user wants to overwrite it. Study the following code:

```
if (-e 'subjects.txt') {
    print 'File exists.  Overwrite (Y/N)? ';
    chomp ($_ = <STDIN>);
    while (/[^yn]/i) {
        print 'Y or N, please: ';
        chomp ($_ = <STDIN>);
    }
    if (/n/i) { die "subjects file already exists; exiting.\n"; }
}
```

Here you see another use of the `die` function, this time away from the `open` function. If the user answers `n` to the overwrite question, you could simply exit the script; the `die` function is an explicit end and prints a message to that effect.

A File Test Example

Here's an example program that uses the file tests described above. It accepts two strings as arguments, followed by a file or list of files. It replaces any occurrences of the first string in the file with the second string. Before it modifies any file, though, it performs a number of tests on it to make sure that performing the search and replace is okay. Let's skip straight to the source code, which is in Listing 15.2

LISTING 15.2 The `sr.pl` Search and Replace Program

```
#!/usr/bin/perl

use strict;

if (@ARGV < 3)
{
    print "Usage: sr.pl old_string new_string file(s)\n";
    exit;
}

my $old = shift @ARGV;
my $new = shift @ARGV;

my $filename;

foreach $filename (@ARGV)
{
    print "Processing $filename ...\n";

    # If the file does not exist, move along.
    unless (-e $filename)
    {
        print "Skipping $filename, it does not exist.\n";
        next;
    }

    # If the file is a directory, move along.
    if (-d $filename)
    {
        print "Skipping $filename, it's a directory.\n";
        next;
    }


    # If the file is not readable, move along.
    unless (-r $filename)
    {
        print "Skipping $filename, it's not readable.\n";
        next;
```

LISTING 15.2 continued

```
40:     }
41:
42:     # If the file is not writable, move along.
43:     unless (-w $filename)
44:     {
45:         print "Skipping $filename, it's not writable.\n";
46:         next;
47:     }
48:
49:     # If the file is not a text file, move along.
50:     if (-B $filename)
51:     {
52:         print "Skipping $filename, it's a binary file.\n";
53:         next;
54:     }
55:
56:     my $backup_filename = $filename . "~";
57:
58:     # If the backup file already exists, raise an error
59:     if (-e $backup_filename)
60:     {
61:         print "Skipping $filename, backup file $backup_filename exists.\n";
62:         next;
63:     }
64:
65:     rename $filename, $backup_filename;
66:
67:     open (IN, "< $backup_filename")
68:         or die "Can't open $backup_filename";
69:
70:     open (OUT, "> $filename")
71:         or die "Can't write to $filename";
72:
73:     while (<IN>)
74:     {
75:         s/$old/$new/g;
76:         print OUT;
77:     }
78:
79:     close IN;
80:     close OUT;
81: }
```

First things first, on lines 5 through 9, check to see whether the user called the script properly. If he didn't include at least three arguments, print a message indicating the proper usage of the script. On lines 11 and 12, extract the string to search for and the string to replace it with from `@ARGV`. Any further arguments are assumed to be the names of files that will be searched.

Loop over the remaining arguments to the array, treating them as filenames. Five tests are performed on each argument before even trying to deal with it as a file. If the file does not exist, is a directory, is not readable or writable, or is a binary file, it is skipped. These tests assure that a file is not processed and fails, or that a binary file or directory is not corrupted by processing it without checking out what it is first.

If any of these tests fail, a message is printed indicating that something went wrong, and use `next` to stop processing the current filename and move to the next one. If the tests all succeed, append to the file's name to create the name of the backup file that the script will produce. If the backup file exists, go ahead and skip the file so that the user's work isn't inadvertently destroyed.

If the backup file doesn't exist everything is okay for the script to proceed. First, rename the file to the backup file name that was generated. Then, open the backup file for input and the original filename for output. On line 73, start looping over the contents of the backup file, replacing the old string with the new one, and printing out those lines to the output file, which has the name of the file that we're currently processing.

In the end, the original file is saved as the file named in the variable `$backup_file`, and `$filename` contains the results of the processed file.

Working with `@ARGV` and Script Arguments

One aspect of running Perl scripts that I've sort of sidestepped over the last few days is that of dealing with command-line arguments. Yesterday we talked a bit about Perl's own switches (`-e`, `-w`) and so on, but what if you want to actually pass switches or arguments to your own scripts—how do you handle those? That's what we'll discuss in this section: script arguments in general, and handling script switches.

Anatomy of the `@ARGV`

When you call a Perl script with arguments beyond the name of the script, those arguments are stored in the special global list `@ARGV` (on the Mac, for droplets, `@ARGV` will be the filenames that were dropped onto the droplet). You can process this array the same way you would any other list in your Perl script. For example, here's a snippet that will just print out the arguments the script was called with, one on each line:

```
foreach my $arg (@ARGV) {
   print "$arg\n";
}
```

If your script uses a construct such as `while (<>)`, Perl will use the contents of the `@ARGV` list as the filenames to open and read (if there are no files in `@ARGV`, Perl will try to read from the standard input). Multiple files are all opened and read sequentially, as if they were all one big file.

If you want more control over the contents of the files you're reading into a script, you could examine the contents of `@ARGV` to find the filenames to open and read. Processing `@ARGV` is also useful if you're looking for a specific number of arguments—for example, one configuration file and one data file. If you just want to process the contents of any number of files, it's handy to use the `<>` shortcut. If you want to specifically have a set of arguments, and control the processing of each one, read the files from `@ARGV` and process them individually.

Unlike C and Unix's `argv`, Perl's `@ARGV` contains only the arguments, not the name of the script itself (`$ARGV[0]` will contain the first argument). To get the name of the script, you can use the special variable `$0` instead.

Script Switches and Fun with Getopt

One use of the script command line is to pass switches to a script. Switches are arguments that start with a dash (`-a`, `-b`, `-c`), and are usually used to control the behavior of that script. Sometimes switches are single letters (`-s`), sometimes they're grouped (`-abc`), and sometimes they have an associated value or argument (`-o outfile.txt`).

You can call a script with any switches you want; those switches will end up as elements of the `@ARGV` array just as any other arguments do. If you were using `<>` to process `@ARGV`, you'll want to get rid of those switches before reading any data—otherwise, Perl will assume that your `-s` switch is the name of a file. To process and remove those switches littering `@ARGV`, you *could* laboriously go through the array and figure out which elements were options, which ones were options with associated arguments, and finally end up with a list of actual filenames after you were done doing all that. Or you could use the Getopt module to do all that for you.

The Getopt module, part of the standard module library that comes with Perl, manages script switches. There are actually two modules: `Getopt::Std`, which processes single-character switches (`-a`, `-d`, `-o`*file*, and so on); and `Getopt::Long`, which allows just about any kind of options, including multicharacter options (`-sde`) and GNU-style double-hyphen options (`--help`, `--size`, and so on).

In this section, I describe the `Getopt::Std` module, for handling simple options. If you want to handle more complex options via the `Getopt::Long` module, you are welcome to explore that module's documentation for yourself (see the `perlmod` manual page for details).

To use the `Getopt::Std` module, you import it in your script as you do all modules:

```
use Getopt::Std;
```

Importing `Getopt::Std` gives you two functions: `getopt` and `getopts`. These functions are used to extract the switches from your `@ARGV` array and set scalar variables in your script for each of those switches.

getopts

Let's start with `getopts`, which defines and processes single-character switches with or without values. The `getopts` function takes a single string argument containing the single-character switches that your script will accept. Arguments that take values must be followed by a colon (:). Uppercase and lowercase are significant and represent different switches. For example:

```
getopts('abc');
```

The argument here, `'abc'`, processes `-a`, `-b` or `-c` switches, in any order, with no associated values. Those switches can be grouped: `-ab` or `-abc` will work just as well as the individual switches will. Here's another:

```
getopts('ab:c');
```

In this example, the `-b` switch can take a value, which must appear on the Perl command line immediately after that switch, like this:

```
% myscript.pl -b 10
```

The space after the switch itself isn't required: `-b10` works as well as `-b 10`. You can also nest these switches as long as the value appears after the switch itself, like this:

```
% myscript.pl -acb10 # OK
% myscript.pl -abc10 # wrong
```

Note

If you want to pass regular arguments to your script that look like switches, you can include the argument `--` to indicate that the items that follow are arguments, not switches. For example, if you wanted to pass the argument `-whatever` to your script, you could call it

```
% myscript.pl -acb10 -- -whatever
```

For each switch defined in `getopts`, the `getopts` function creates a scalar variable switch with the name `$opt_x`, where `x` is the letter of the switch (in the example above, `getopts` would create three variables for `$opt_a`, `$opt_b`, and `$opt_c`). The initial value of each scalar variable is undefined. Then, if that switch was included in the arguments to the script (in @ARGV), getopts sets the value of its associated variable to 1. If the switch required a value, getopts assigns the value on @ARGV to the scalar variable for that option. The switch, and its associated value, are then deleted from @ARGV. After getopts finishes processing, your @ARGV will either be empty, or will contain any remaining filename arguments which you can then read with file handles or with <>.

After getopts is done, you'll end up with a variable for each switch that will either have a value of 0 (that switch wasn't used), 1 (that switched was used), or have some value (that switch was used with the given value). You can then test for those values and have your script do different things based on the switches it was called with, as shown here:

```
if ($opt_a) {  # -a was used
   ...
}
if ($opt_b) {  # -b was used
  ...
}
```

So, for example, if your script was called like this:

```
% script.pl -a
```

then getopts('abc') will set $opt_a to 1. If it was called like this:

```
% script.pl -a -R
```

then $opt_a will be set to 1, and the -R switch will be quietly deleted with no variable set. If you called it like this:

```
% script.pl -ab10
```

and called getopts like this:

```
getopts('ab:c');
```

then $opt_a will be set to 1, and $opt_b will be set to 10.

Note that if you're using use strict Perl will complain about the $opt_ variables suddenly popping into existence. You can get around this by predeclaring those variables with use vars, like this:

```
use vars qw($opt_a $opt_b $opt_c);
```

or, you can use the our keyword, as follows:

```
our ($opt_a, $opt_b, $opt_c);
```

Error Processing with getopts

Note that getopts reads your @ARGV in order, and stops processing when it gets to an element that does not start with a dash (-) or that isn't a value for a preceding option. This means that when you call your Perl script, you should put the options first and the bare arguments last, otherwise you may end up with unprocessed options or errors trying to read files that aren't files. You may want to write your script to make sure @ARGV is empty after getopts is done, or that its remaining arguments do not start with a dash.

The switches defined by getopts are expected to be the *only* switches that your script will accept. If you call a script with a switch not defined in the argument to getopts, getopts will print an error ("Unknown option"), delete that option from @ARGV, and return false. You can use this behavior to make sure your script is being called correctly, and exit with a message if it's not. Just put the call to getopts inside an if statement, as follows:

```
if (! getopts('ab:c')) {
   die "Usage: myscript -a -b file -c \n";
}
```

Note also that if getopts stops processing your switches in the middle because of an error, any switch variables that were set beforehand will still have their values, and may contain bad values. Depending on how robust you'd like your argument checking to be, you might want to check those values if getopts returns false (or exit altogether).

getopt

The getopt function works just like getopts, in that it takes a string argument with the switches, and it assigns $opt_ variables to each of those arguments and removes them from @ARGV as it goes. However, getopt differs from getopts in three significant respects:

- The argument to getopt is a string containing the switches that must have associated values.
- getopt does not require you to define arguments without values beforehand. It allows any single-letter options, and creates an $opt_ variable for each one.
- getopt does not return a (useful) value, and does not print errors for unexpected options.

Say, for example, you have a call to getopt like this:

```
getopt('abc');
```

This function assumes that your script will be called with any of three switches, -a, -b, or -c, each one with a value. If the script is called with switches that don't have values, getopt will not complain; it happily assigns the next element in @ARGV to the variable for that switch—even if that next element is another switch or a filename that you might have wanted to read as a file. It's up to you to figure out if the values are appropriate, or if the script was called with the wrong set of arguments.

Essentially, the core difference between `getopt` and `getopts` is that `getopt` doesn't require you to declare your options, but also makes it more difficult to handle errors. I prefer `getopts` for most cases, to avoid having to do a lot of value testing.

Another Example

Here's a simple example (in Listing 15.3) that processes a file in various ways depending on the switches that you use with that script.

LISTING 15.3 The `switches.pl` Script

```
#!/usr/bin/perl -w
use strict;
use Getopt::Std;
use vars qw($opt_r $opt_l $opt_s $opt_n);

if (! getopts('rlsn')) {
    die "Usage: switches.pl -rlsn\n";
}

my @file = <>;

if ($opt_s) {
    @file = sort @file;
}

if ($opt_n) {
    @file = sort {$a <=> $b} @file;
}

if ($opt_r) {
    @file = reverse @file;
}

my $i = 1;
foreach my $line (@file) {
    if ($opt_l) {
        print "$i: $line";
        $i++;
    } else {
        print $line;
    }
}
```

This script uses single switches only, with no values (note the call to `getopts` in line 7; there are no colons after any of those options. Those switches are `-r`, to reverse the contents of the file; `-s`, to sort the lines of the file; `-n` to sort the lines numerically; and `-l` to print line numbers. You can combine options on the command line, although some multiple options don't make sense (`-sn` sorts the file, and then resorts it numerically).

Line 4 predeclares our variables, so they won't suddenly spring into existence when `getopts` creates them (and cause `use strict` to complain).

The test in lines 6 through 8 make sure the script is being called with the right options. If a stray option slipped through (for example, an `-a` or `-x`), then the script exits with a usage message.

Finally, the various if statements test for the existence of the `$opt_r`, `$opt_l`, `$opt_s`, and `$opt_n` variables, and performs different operations depending on which options were called on the command line. Any arguments that aren't switches remain in `@ARGV` after `getopts` is done, and are read into the script via the `<>` operator in line 10.

Going Deeper

In this lesson, I've given you the basics of I/O and of managing file systems; the lessons you learn here should apply to all your basic Perl programs that need to use files and command-line arguments. On Day 17 we'll explore how to handle aspects of the file system itself. In this lesson's Going Deeper, I'll try and point you to a number of other places to look for more information and details about advanced input and output and handling filesystem features.

All the built-in Perl functions, as I've noted before, are documented in the `perlfunc` man page. Also of some use may be the FAQ on files and formats contained in the `perlfaq` man page.

More About `open` and File Handles

A few other shortcuts and features of the `open` function:

You can leave off the filename to the `open` function if, and only if, a scalar variable with the same name as the file handle has already been set to the file to be opened. For example:

```
$FILE = "myfile.txt";
open(FILE) or die "Can't open $FILE: $!\n";
```

This can be useful for filenames that need to be opened or reopened; you can set a variable at the start of your script, and then reuse that filename over and over again.

Contrary to what I claimed earlier in this chapter, you can open a file both for reading and writing using the `+>` special character in front of the filename:

```
open(FILE, "+>thefile") or die "Can't open file: $!\n";
```

Because this can often be confusing, however, I prefer to use separate file handles and to read and write as separate operations.

Filenames that start with pipes (`|`) operate as if the filename was a command, and the output will be piped to that command via the command shell for your system.

For many more details about the various uses of `open`, see the `perlfunc` man page.

Various Other File-Related Functions

Table 15.2 shows several file-related built-in functions that I have not described in this lesson.

TABLE 15.2 More I/O Functions

Function	*What It Does*
`eof`	Returns true if next line input will be at the end of file
`eof()`	Different function than `eof`; this version detects end of the last file for files input using `<>`
`lstat`	Displays information about links
`pack`	Outputs data into a binary structure
`select`	Changes the default file handle for output (if lots of print statements will be directed to the same filehandle, it's usually easier just to `select` it)
`stat`	Prints various bits of information about a file or file handle
`truncate`	Truncates (delete the contents of) a file or file handle
`unpack`	Inputs data from a binary structure

Expert-Level I/O

The input and output techniques described in this chapter provide simple, line-oriented buffered input and output from and to file handles and standard input, output, and error. If you're interested in doing more low-level sophisticated forms of input and output, explore the various other I/O functions Perl provides for you, as listed in Table 15.3.

TABLE 15.3 More I/O Functions

Function	*What It Does*
`fcntl`	File control (the Unix `fctrl(2)` function)
`flock`	Lock file (Unix `flock(2)` function)
`getc`	Get next byte
`ioctl`	TTY control (The Unix `ioctl(2)` system call)
`read`	Input a specific number of bytes `(fread(2))`
`rewinddir`	Set the current (input) position to the beginning of the directory handle
`seek`	Position the file pointer at a specific location in a file (same as `fseek()` in C)
`seekdir`	Same as seek for directory handles
`select`	Make file descriptors ready for reading (same as the `select(2)` command on Unix. Not to be confused with `select` on a file handle for setting the default file handle.
`syscall`	Call a Unix system call (`syscall(2)`)
`sysopen`	Open a file handle with a mode and permissions
`sysread`	Read a certain number of bytes using `read(2)`
`syswrite`	Write a certain number of bytes to the file handle with `write(2)`
`tell`	Return the current file pointer position
`telldir`	Same as tell for directory handles.
`write`	Write a formatted record to an output file handle (see Day 20, "Odds and Ends.") `write` is not the opposite of `read`

In addition, the `POSIX` module provides a number of features for handling more sophisticated I/O (but, alas, only works on Unix). See the `perlmod` man page for more information about `POSIX`.

DBM Files

Perl provides built-in and module behavior for reading and writing files from and to Berkeley Unix DBM (database) files. These files can be smaller and faster to deal with than flat text-based databases. For more information about DBM, see the `DB_File` module, the `tie` function, and the various `Tie` modules (`Tie::Hash`, `Tie::Scalar`, and so on).

CPAN also provides a number of modules for dealing with databases—both those you write yourself, as well as interfaces to and drivers for various commercial databases such as Oracle and Sybase. For the latter, the DBD (Database Drivers) and DBI (Database Interface) packages by the Perl Database Initiative come highly recommended.

Timestamps

Files and directories can both contain timestamps, that is, indications of when that file was created, modified, or just accessed. You can test a file for its timestamp using the `-M` (modification), `-A` (access), and `-C` (inode change, Unix only) file tests, get more information about timestamps via the `stat` function, or change the timestamp of a file using the `utime` function. The behavior of these tests and functions might vary from platform to platform.

All times are in seconds elapsed since a certain date; that date is January 1, 1970 for Unix and Windows and January 1, 1904 on the Macintosh. The functions `time`, `gmtime`, `localtime`, and the `Time::Local` modules might also be of interest for decoding and changing timestamps.

Summary

In this chapter, we've reviewed and expanded on all the information you've learned about input and output so far in this book, taking what you already knew about reading from standard input and writing to standard output and using those same techniques to read and write from files.

Files and file handles were the focus of the start of this chapter, and you learned about using the `open` function to open a file and create a file handle to read from or write to that file. As an adjunct to `open` you also learned about `die`, a function that exits the script and prints an error message to the standard error file handle as it goes.

In the next part of the lesson, we talked about script arguments and switches: what happens when you call a script with arguments (they get put into `@ARGV`) and what you can do to process those arguments. If those arguments includes switches, the best way to process them is with the `Getopt::Std` module, which lets you define and process, switches to your script, and then tests for the existence of those switches using special variables.

The functions you learned about in this chapter include

- `open`, for creating file handles
- `die`, for exiting the script with an error message
- `binmode`, for setting a file handle to binary mode
- `close`, to close a file handle
- `getopts`, part of the Getopt module, for declaring and processing arguments
- `getopt`, also part of the Getopt module, for handling arguments

Q&A

Q. I'm trying to open a file for writing, but `die` keeps getting triggered and I can't figure out why. The directory is writable, the file doesn't exist–there's no reason why things should be going wrong.

A. Did you remember to put the `>` character at the start of your filename? You need that character to tell Perl that the file is to be written to–otherwise it'll assume the file is to be read from, and if it can't find the file it won't be able to open it.

The `open` function should work most of the time; it should only fail under unusual circumstances. If it's consistently failing for you, consider double-checking your use of `open`.

Q. I want to use a subroutine to open my file, and then pass the file handle around to other subroutines. But when I try this is doesn't work. Why?

A. Well, you can't. You can do sneaky things with typeglobs to pass symbol names between subroutines, but that's a kludge with its own set of problems. The best way to pass file handles around is to use the `FileHandle` module, create a file handle as an object, and then pass that object between subroutines.

But, since we haven't learned much about objects, you might (for now) want to just create your file handle globally and refer to them inside subroutines instead. (We'll explore objects on Day 19, "Working with References.")

Q. I'm trying to read a simple text-based database file in Perl. I know what the format for the file is, and I know how to decode it into something I can use, but the input I'm getting is really garbled. What's going on here?

A. Are you on a Windows system? Is the database file in a binary format. Use the `binmode` function to make sure Perl is reading your file handle in binary format.

Workshop

The workshop provides quiz questions to help you solidify your understanding of the material covered and exercises to give you experience in using what you've learned. Try and understand the quiz and exercise answers before you go on to tomorrow's lesson.

Quiz

1. What's a file handle? What are the `STDIN`, `STDOUT`, and `STDERR` file handles used for?
2. What are the differences between creating file handles for reading, writing, or appending?
3. What's the `die` function used for? Why should you bother using it with `open`?

4. How do you read input from a file handle? Describe how input behaves in a scalar context, in a scalar context inside a `while` loop test, and in a list context.
5. How do you send output to a file handle?
6. What do the following file tests test for?

```
-e
-x
-f
-M
-z
```

7. What is `@ARGV` used for? What does it contain?
8. What's the difference between `getopt` and `getopts`?
9. What switches do the following calls to `getopts` allow?

```
getopts('xyz:');
getopts('x:y:z');
getopts('xXy');
getopts('xyz');
getopt('xyz');
```

Exercises

1. Write a script that merges two files (specified on the command line) with their lines intertwined (one line from file 1, one line from file 2, another line from file 1, and so on). Write the resulting data to a file called `merged`.
2. Write a script that merges the two files only if the filename extensions are the same, and use that same filename extension for the final merged file. If the extensions are different, exit the script with an error message. (Hint: use regular expressions to find the filename extensions).
3. Write a script that merges two files and takes a single option: `-o`, which bypasses the error message from the previous exercise and merges the file anyhow (the extension of the final file is up to you).
4. Write a script that takes a single-string argument and any of four switches, `-u`, `-s`, `-r`, and `-c`. `-u` returns the string in uppercase, `-s` removes all punctuation and whitespace (s stands for "squash"), `-r` reverses the string, and `-c` counts the number of characters. Make sure you can combine the options for different effects.
5. BUG BUSTERS: This script is called like this:

```
myscript.pl -sz inputfile
```

What's wrong with this script? (Hint: The test for `$opt_z` will not return true).

```
use strict;
use Getopt::Std;
```

```
use vars qw($opt_s $opt_z);
getopt('sz');

if ($opt_z) {
   # ...
}
```

Answers

Here are the answers to the Workshop questions in the previous section.

Quiz Answers

1. A file handle is used by Perl to read data from or write data to some source or destination (which could be a file, the keyboard, the screen, a network connection, or another script). The `STDIN`, `STDOUT`, and `STDERR` file handles refer to standard input, standard output, and standard error, respectively. You create file handles to any other files using the `open` function.
2. Use special characters in the filename to be opened to indicate whether that file will be opened for reading, writing, or appending. The default is to open a file for reading.
3. The `die` function exits the script gracefully with a (supposedly) helpful error message. It's most commonly used in conjunction with `open` because if something so unusual happened that the file couldn't be opened, generally you don't want your script to continue running. Good programming practice says *always* check your return values for `open` and call `die` if it didn't work.
4. Read input from a file handle using the input operator `<>` and the name of the file handle. In scalar context, the input operator reads one line at a time. Inside a `while` loop, it assigns each line to the `$_` variable. In a list context, all the input to end of file is read.
5. Send output to a file handle using the `print` function and the name of the file handle. Note that there is no comma between the file handle and the thing to print.
6. `-e` test to see if the file exists

   `-x` tests to see if the file is executable (usually only relevant on Unix)

   `-f` tests to see if the file is a plain file (and not a directory, a link or anything else)

   `-M` tests the modification date of the file

   `-z` tests to see if the file exists and is empty

7. The `@ARGV` array variable stores all the arguments and switches the script was called with.

8. The `getopt` function defines switches with values, and can accept any other options. The `getopts` declares the possible options for the script and if they have values or not. The other difference is that `getopts` returns a false value if there were errors processing the command-line switches; `getopt` doesn't return any useful value.

9. `getopts('xyz:')` allows the switches `-x`, `-y`, and `-z` with a value.

   `getopts('x:y:z')` allows `-x` and `-y`, each with values, and `-z` without a value.

   `getopts('xXy')` allows `-x` and `-X` (they are separate switches) and `-y`, none with values.

   `getopts('xyz')` allows `-x`, `-y` and `-z`, none with values.

   `getopt('xyz')` allows `-x`, `-y` and `-z`, each one with required values, as well as any other single-character switches.

Exercise Answers

1. Here's one answer:

```
#!/usr/ bin/perl -w
use strict;

my ($file1, $file2) = @ARGV;

open(FILE1, $file1) or die "Can't open $file1: $!\n";
open(FILE2, $file2) or die "Can't open $file2: $!\n";
open(MERGE, ">merged") or die "Can't open merged file: $!\n";

my $line1 = <FILE1>;
my $line2 = <FILE2>;
while (defined($line1) || defined($line2)) {
    if (defined($line1)) {
        print MERGE $line1;
        $line1 = <FILE1>;
    }
    if (defined($line2)) {
        print MERGE $line2;
        $line2 = <FILE2>;
    }
}
```

2. Here's one answer:

```
#!/usr/bin/perl -w
use strict;

my ($file1, $file2) = @ARGV;
my $ext;
```

```
if ($file1 =~ /\.(\w+)$/) {
    $ext = $1;
    if ($file2 !~ /\.$ext$/) {
        die "Extensions do not match.\n";
    }
}

open(FILE1, $file1) or die "Can't open $file1: $!\n";
open(FILE2, $file2) or die "Can't open $file2: $!\n";
open(MERGE, ">merged.$ext") or die "Can't open merged file: $!\n";

my $line1 = <FILE1>;
my $line2 = <FILE2>;
while (defined($line1) || defined($line2)) {
    if (defined($line1)) {
        print MERGE $line1;
        $line1 = <FILE1>;
    }
    if (defined($line2)) {
        print MERGE $line2;
        $line2 = <FILE2>;
    }
}
```

3. Here's one answer:

```
#!/usr/bin/perl -w
use strict;
use Getopt::Std;
use vars qw($opt_o);
getopts('o');

my ($file1, $file2) = @ARGV;
my $ext;

if ($file1 =~ /\.(\w+)$/) {
    $ext = $1;
    if ($file2 !~ /\.$ext$/) {
        if (!$opt_o) {
            die "Extensions do not match.\n";
        }
    }
}

open(FILE1, $file1) or die "Can't open $file1: $!\n";
open(FILE2, $file2) or die "Can't open $file2: $!\n";
open(MERGE, ">merged.$ext") or die "Can't open merged file: $!\n";

my $line1 = <FILE1>;
my $line2 = <FILE2>;
while (defined($line1) || defined($line2)) {
```

```
        if (defined($line1)) {
            print MERGE $line1;
            $line1 = <FILE1>;
        }
        if (defined($line2)) {
            print MERGE $line2;
            $line2 = <FILE2>;
        }
    }
```

4. Here's one way:

```
#!/usr/bin/perl -w
use strict;
use Getopt::Std;
use vars qw($opt_s $opt_r $opt_u $opt_c);
getopts('sruc');

my $str = $ARGV[0];

if ($opt_s) {
    $str =~ s/[\s.,;:!?'"]//g;
}

if ($opt_r) {
   $str = reverse $str;
}

if ($opt_u) {
   $str = uc $str;
}

if ($opt_c) {
   $str = length $str;
}

print "$str\n";
```

5. The script snippet uses the `getopt` function. This function (as opposed to `getopts`, assumes all the switches will have values associated with them. So when the script is called with the switch `-sz`, `getopt` assumes that you're using the `-s` switch, and that its value is `z`. The `-z` switch never registers to `getopt`. Use the `getopts` function instead to make sure both `$opt_s` and `$opt_z` are set.

WEEK 2

DAY 16

Using Perl for CGI Scripting

In recent years one of the most common uses of Perl has been for creating CGI scripts. CGI, short for the Common Gateway Interface, refers to programs and scripts that live on a Web server and run in response to input from a browser—form submissions, complex links, some image maps—just about anything that isn't a plain ordinary file involves some sort of CGI script.

Because of Perl's popularity as a CGI language, I would be remiss if I did not give you a short introduction to CGI using Perl. Today we'll use what you already know about Perl in the context of creating CGI scripts on the Web. Today, you'll learn

- Some notes about CGI, before we start
- How the CGI process works, from browser to server and back again
- Creating a short CGI script, from start to finish
- An introduction to the `CGI.pm` module
- Working with data from HTML forms
- Printing the output
- Debugging the script

Before You Start

To write CGI scripts in Perl, you'll need three things:

- A Web server that supports Perl and an understanding of how to install CGI scripts on that server
- The `CGI.pm` module, which should have come with your Perl distribution (more about this later)
- A basic understanding of HTML

You don't *specifically* need the `CGI.pm` module to write CGI scripts in Perl. There are other utility scripts to help you do CGI, or you could hand-write all of the underlying code yourself. But that would mean a lot of work for you, and it's much, much easier just to use `CGI.pm`. Everyone else is doing it; why not join us?

Because of the wide variety of Web servers for different platforms and the differences between them, the space isn't available to get into a discussion of getting your Web server set up for CGI. There are extensive help files on the Web, however, including

- The basic CGI documentation at `http://hoohoo.ncsa.uiuc.edu/cgi/`, which applies mostly to Unix-based servers.
- The Perl CGI FAQ at `http://www.perl.com/pub/a/doc/FAQs/cgi/perl-cgi-faq.html`.
- "The Idiot's Guide to Solving CGI Problems" at `http://www.perl.com/language/CPAN/doc/FAQs/cgi/idiots-guide`.html.

You should also refer to the documentation that came with your Web server. If you plan to do a lot of work with CGI, you might consider *Sams Teach Yourself CGI Programming in a 24 Hours* for more help and more examples beyond what is offered here.

If you don't have at least a passing background in HTML, much of the rest of this lesson may be difficult to follow. Again, consider boning up with the multitude of HTML tutorials on the Web, or with *Sams Teach Yourself Web Publishing with HTML and XHTML in 21 Days*.

How CGI Works

Let's start with some conceptual background about CGI and how it fits into the relationship between a Web browser and a Web server.

CGI, as mentioned, stands for Common Gateway Interface. Common because the same process is used for many different kinds of Web servers, and gateway because the scripts at one time commonly served as a gateway between the Web server itself and some larger program—for example, a database or a search engine. These days, CGI has lost much of its original precise meaning, and now refers simply to a script or program that runs in response to input from a Web browser.

There are a lot of different things you can do with a CGI script and different ways to write one. For the purposes of this lesson, we'll focus on one typical use: CGI scripts to handle data received as part of an HTML form. Figure 16.1 shows a typical flowchart for how things work when a user with a Web browser requests a form, fills it out, and submits it:

FIGURE 16.1.
The CGI process.

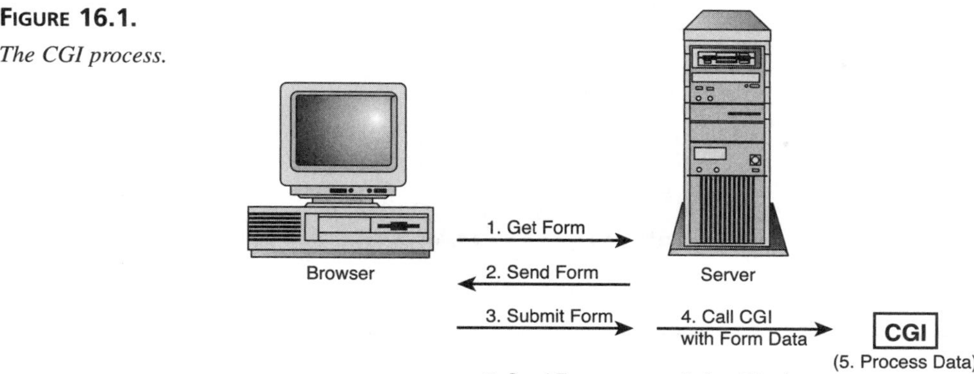

Here's what's going on at each step:

- The user, running a Web browser, requests a page with a form on it.
- The server sends the form. The form itself may be a CGI script that generates the HTML for the form, or just a plain old HTML file.
- The user fills out the form and clicks the submit button.
- The browser packages up the form data and sends it to the Web server.
- The Web server passes the data to the CGI script.
- The CGI script decodes the data, processes it in some way, and returns a response (typically another HTML file).
- The server sends the response to the browser

This is obviously not all that complicated, but you should understand where the CGI script fits into the process so you know where the data is coming from and where its going. This will be important later.

Building a CGI Script, From Form to Response

The best way to learn how to code CGI is to go ahead and do it, so let's do it. In this section we'll create a really simple CGI script—the equivalent of Hello, World—using a basic HTML form, Perl for the CGI script, and the `CGI.pm` module to help put it all together. I'll give you the HTML form to work from, but we'll build up the script itself line by line.

The Form

Listing 16.1 shows the HTML code for a simple HTML form that asks you for your name. Figure 16.2 shows what this form looks like in a Web browser.

LISTING 16.1 The *`name.html`* File

```
1:  <html>
2:  <head>
3:  <title>Tell Me Your Name</title>
4:  </head>
5:  <body>
6:  <form action="/cgi-bin/name.pl">
7:  <p>Enter your Name: <input name="name" /></p>
8:  <p><input type="submit" value="Submit me!"></p>
9:  </form>
10: </body>
11: </html>
```

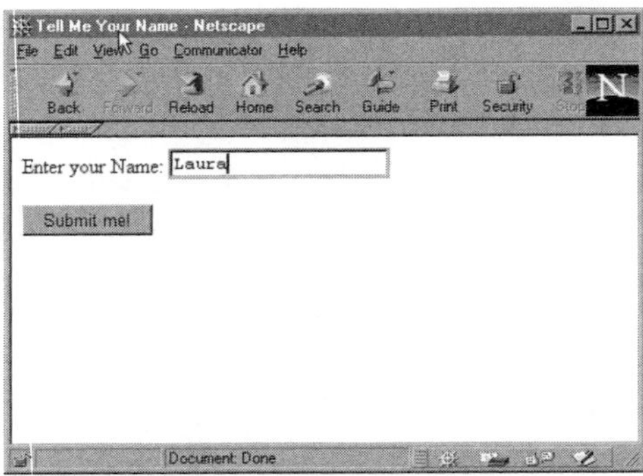

FIGURE 16.2.
Hello!

There are two important parts to note about this bit of HTML:

- In Line 6, the `action` attribute points to the CGI script that will process this form when it's submitted to the server. Here, that script is called `name.pl`, and it's stored in the server's `cgi-bin` directory (the usual place for CGI scripts to be stored, although it might be different for your server, or you might need permission to put your scripts there). You'll need to substitute the path to your version of the script when you write it in the next section.

Some Web servers might also require you to rename your scripts with a .cgi extension for those scripts to be recognized as CGI scripts. This differs from server to server, so check your documentation.

- Line 7 defines a text field form element (in the `<input>` tag). Note that the `name` attribute gives this element a name. This will also be important when you build the CGI script for this form.

Creating the Script

Now let's create a Perl script to process the data we get back from that CGI script. Although writing a CGI script in Perl is similar in many ways to writing an ordinary command-line Perl script, there are several important differences relating to the fact that your script is called by the Web server, not by you. You won't get any command-line options or filename arguments. All the data you get into the script will come from the Web server (or you'll read it in yourself from files on the disk). The output you write will have to be in a specific format—usually HTML.

Fortunately, the `CGI.pm` module, written by Lincoln Stein and available as part of the standard Perl installation, is there to make CGI scripting easier and to cover up a lot of the oddities.

Let's start with the top couple of lines of our CGI script:

```
#!/usr/local/bin/perl -w
use strict;
use CGI qw(:standard);
```

The shebang line and `use strict` you already know, and the third `use CGI` line shouldn't be much of a surprise either. The `:standard` tag, as you learned on Day 13, "Scope Models and Importing Code," imports a subset of the CGI module, rather than importing the whole thing. In the case of `CGI.pm`, the `:standard` tag will probably be the one you use most often. (It exports most of the commonly used subroutines in the module into the namespace of your script.)

Most CGI scripts have two main parts: the initial part reads and processes any data you got from the form or from the Web browser, and the second outputs a response, usually in HTML form. In this example, because there isn't any real processing to do, we can skip directly to the output part.

The first thing you need to output is a special header to the Web server indicating the kind of file you're sending back. If you send back an HTML file, the type is `text/html`. If you send back a plain text file, it's `text/plain`. Send back an image, and it's `image/gif`. These file types are all standardized as part of the MIME specification, and if you get into serious CGI scripting you'll need to learn at least some of these. The most common type, however, is `text/html`. `CGI.pm` provides a basic subroutine, `print_header()`, for printing out the appropriate header for that type:

```
print header();
```

After the header, all the output you print will be in HTML format. You can either print raw HTML tags or use `CGI.pm`'s Perl subroutines for generating HTML, or you can use a combination of both. Because I know HTML fairly well, I like to use the `CGI.pm` subroutines where it will save me some typing, and regular `print` statements for everything else. Here's the remainder of our simple CGI script:

```
print start_html('Hello!');
print "<h1>Hello, ", param('name'), "!</h1>\n";
print end_html;
```

The first line calls `CGI.pm`'s `start_html()` subroutine, which prints the top part of an HTML file (the `<html>`,`<head>`,`<title>`, and `<body>` tags). The string argument to `start_html()` is the title of the page. There are also other arguments you can give this subroutine to set the background color, keywords, and other features of the header (more about that in the next section).

The second line is a regular `print` statement, which prints an HTML heading (`<h1>` tag) to say hello. In between the opening and closing tags, however, is the interesting part. The `param()` subroutine, part of `CGI.pm`, is how you get to the information that your user entered into the form. You use `param()` with the name of the form element (from the `name` attribute of the element's HTML tag), and it returns the value the user entered for that element. By calling `param('name')` here, we get the string the user entered into the one text field on our form, and we can use that value to generate the response.

The third line is another `CGI.pm` subroutine that simply prints out the closing bits of HTML (`</body>` and `</html>`), finishing up the response. Here's the complete script, all put together:

```
#!/usr/local/bin/perl -w
use strict;
use CGI qw(:standard);

print header;
print start_html('Hello!');
print "<h1>Hello, ", param('name'), "!</h1>\n";
print end_html;
```

You might have noticed that we're not doing anything special as far as output is concerned; we're just using simple `print` statements. And yet, the output doesn't go to the screen; it goes back to the browser. A CGI script is a prime example of how standard input and output don't necessarily have to be the keyboard or the screen. CGI scripts do read their input from the standard input, and output to the standard output. Except in this case the standard input and output is the Web server. You don't have to do anything special to deal with that server; the standard ways work just fine.

So what is the output? If the user entered "Fred" into the form, the output of the CGI script will look like this, with the header and the HTML data in place:

```
Content-Type: text/html; charset=ISO-8859-1

<?xml version="1.0" encoding="utf-8"?>
<!DOCTYPE html
   PUBLIC "-//W3C//DTD XHTML Basic 1.0//EN"
   "http://www.w3.org/TR/xhtml-basic/xhtml-basic10.dtd">
<html xmlns="http://www.w3.org/1999/xhtml" lang="en-
US"><head><title>Hello!</title>
</head><body><h1>Hello, Fred!</h1>
</body></html>
```

That data will get passed over the standard output to the Web server, which in turn will pass it back to the Web browser that Fred is running.

Testing the Script

Before actually installing the script on your Web server, it's helpful to be able to test it to make sure you haven't made any obvious errors. Using `CGI.pm`, you can run a CGI script from the command line to test it, like this:

```
% name.pl
(offline mode: enter name=value pairs on standard input)
```

After that line, you can enter sample form input as a name=value pair. For example, for the Hello form the name is "name" and the value would be a sample name (like "Fred"), so you'd type:

```
name=Fred
```

You don't have to include quotes unless the input has spaces in it. After you've entered your name and value pairs, hit Ctrl-D (Ctrl-Z on Windows) to end the standard input. The script will then run as if it had received that input from the form, and output the result to the screen.

Alternatively, you can also enter the names and values as arguments to the script's command line:

```
% name.pl name=Fred
```

The script will then use those name=value pairs as the input, and not prompt you for more.

When you've verified your CGI script works as you expect, the final step is to install it on your Web server. Installation might involve putting the script in a special directory called `cgi-bin`, renaming it with a `.cgi` extension, or indicating by some other method to the Web server that your script is a CGI script. (Again, this varies from server to server, so see the docs that came with your server to figure it out). You may also need to make sure the script is executable or to give it special user permissions. And, finally, you'll need to modify the original HTML file to point to the actual location of the script.

With all that out of the way, you should then be able to bring up the HTML for the form, fill in a name, click the Submit button, and have the CGI script give you a response. Figure 16.3 shows the response as a Web page.

FIGURE 16.3.

Hello, the response.

Developing CGI Scripts with `CGI.pm`

The core of any CGI script is the `CGI.pm` module. While you can write CGI scripts using raw Perl, or using various other CGI libraries out there, `CGI.pm` is available as part of the Perl distribution, is well-supported and robust, runs across platforms, and gives you just about any feature you might want as you work with CGI. Working without it will make your CGI-scripting life much harder.

In the preceding section, I showed you a really simple example of using `CGI.pm`. Let's explore the features of this module in more detail in this section, so you know the sorts of things you can do with it.

Using CGI.pm

To use CGI.pm in your Perl scripts, you import it like you do any module. CGI.pm has several import tags you can use, including the following:

- :cgi imports features of CGI protocol itself, including param()
- :html2 imports features to help generate HTML 2 tags including start_html() and end_html()
- :form imports features for generating form elements
- :standard imports all the features from :cgi, :html2, and :form.
- :html3 imports features from HTML 3.0
- :netscape imports features from Netscape's version of HTML
- :html imports all the features from :html2, :html3, and :netscape.
- :all imports everything

CGI.pm is implemented such that you can use it in an object-oriented way (using a CGI object and calling methods defined for that object), or by calling plain subroutines. If you use any of the preceding import tags, you'll have those subroutine names available to you in your script. If you just use CGI without any import tags, it's assumed you'll be using the object-oriented version of CGI.

Processing Form Input

The most significant feature that CGI.pm gives you is that it handles the CGI-encoded form input that the Web browser sends to the Web server and the server passes on to the script. This input comes from the browser in a special encoded form, sometimes on the standard input and sometimes as keyword arguments, with nonalphanumeric characters encoded in hex. If you were writing a raw CGI processor you'd have to deal with all that decoding yourself (and it's not pretty). By using CGI.pm you can avoid all that stuff and deal solely with the actual input values, which is what you really care about.

The input you get from a form is composed of key/value pairs, where the key is the name of the form element (as indicated by the name attribute in HTML), and the value is the actual thing the user typed, selected, or chose from the form when it was submitted. The value you actually get depends on the form element—some values are a string, as with text fields; others might be simply yes or no, as with check boxes. Pop-up menus and scrolling lists created with the HTML <select> tag (or check box groups) might have multiple values.

The `CGI.pm` module stores these keys and values in a parameter array. To get at them you use the `param()` subroutine. Without any arguments, `param()` returns a list of keys in the parameter array (the names of all the form elements). This is mostly useful to see whether the form was filled out in the case where the CGI script generates both the initial HTML page and the result. You could also call `param()` without any arguments if you were printing out all the keys and values on the form for debugging purposes, like this:

```
foreach $key (param()) {
   print "$key has the value ", param($key), "\n";
}
```

Note that the order of the parameters in the array is the same order in which the browser sent them, originally, which in many cases will be the same order in which they appear on the page. However, that behavior isn't guaranteed, so you're safest referring to each form element explicitly if you're concerned about order.

The `param()` subroutine with a form element name as an argument returns the value of that form element, or `undef` if there's no submitted value for that form element. This is probably the way you'll use `param()` most often in your own CGI scripts. The key you use as the argument to `param()` must match the name of the form elements in the HTML file exactly—to get to the value of a text field defined `<INPUT NAME="foozle">` you'd use `param('foozle')`. Most of the time you'll get back a single scalar value, but some form elements that allow multiple selections will return a list of all the possible selections. It's up to you to handle the different values you get from a form in the CGI script.

Generating HTML

The bulk of a CGI script is often taken up mostly by generating the HTML for the response. The scripts we write for handling CGI will probably have more `print` statements than any other scripts we've written so far.

To generate HTML output, you simply print lines of output to the standard output as you would in any other script. You have a number of options for doing this:

- Using individual `print` statements
- Using "here" documents
- Using shortcut subroutines from `CGI.pm`

Output with `print`

The first way is simply to use `print` with the bit of HTML to output, as you've been doing all along, like this:

```
print "<html><head><title>This is a Web page</title></head>\n";
print "<body bgcolor=\"white\">\n";
# and so on
```

Output with Here Documents

While `print` statements work fine, they can get somewhat unwieldy, particularly when you have a lot of print and you have to deal with nested quotation marks (as with the "white" value in the preceding example). If you have a block of HTML to print pretty much verbatim, you can use a Perl feature called a here document. Awkward name, but what it means is simply "print everything up to *here*." A here document looks something like this:

```
print <<EOF;
These lines will be printed
as they appear here, without the need
for fancy print statements, "escaped quotes,"
or special newline characters.  Just like this.
EOF
```

That bit of Perl code results in the following output:

```
These lines will be printed
as they appear here, without the need
for fancy print statements, "escaped quotes,"
or special newline characters.  Just like this.
```

In other words, the text outputs pretty much exactly the same way the text appears in the script. The initial `print` line in the here document determines how far to read and print before stopping, using a special code that can be either a word that has no other meaning in the language, or a quoted string. Here I used `EOF`, which is a nice, short, common phrase and easy to pick out from the rest of the script.

The quotes you use around that word, if any, determine how the text inside the here document is processed. A single word, like the EOF we used above, allows variable interpolation as if the text inside the here document were a double-quoted string. The same is true if you use a double-quoted word ("EOF"). A single-quoted word ('EOF') suppresses variable interpolation just as it does in a regular single-quoted string.

The end of the here document is that same word or string that started the here document, minus the quotes, on a line by itself with no leading trailing characters or whitespace. After the ending tag you can start another here document, go back to `print`, or use any other lines of Perl code that you like.

For more information on using here documents, see the `perldata` man page.

Output with `CGI.pm` Subroutines

The third way to generate HTML in a CGI script is to use `CGI.pm`'s subroutines for doing so. Most HTML tags have equivalent Perl subroutines in `CGI.pm`, and the `CGI.pm` subroutines have the advantage of letting you insert variable references (through double-quoted strings) and to generate things like form elements quickly. In addition, `CGI.pm` has the `start_html()` and `end_html()` subroutines to print the top and bottom of an HTML file, respectively. All the HTML generation subroutines return strings; you'll need to use them with a `print` to actually print them.

Some subroutines generate one-sided tags that take no arguments (`p()` and `hr()`, for example, which generate `<p>` and `<hr>` tags, respectively). Others create opening and closing tags, in which case they take one or more string arguments for the text in between the opening and closing tags. You can nest subroutines inside other subroutines:

```
h1('This is a heading');      # <H1>This is a heading</H1>
b('Bold');                    # <B>Bold</n>
# <b>some bold and some <i>italic</i></b>
b('some bold and some', i('italic'));
ol(
  li('item one),
  li('item two'),
  li('item three'),
);
```

If the HTML tag takes attributes inside the tag itself, indicate those using curly brackets `{}` and the name and value of the attribute separated using `=>` (as with hashes):

```
a({href=>"index.html", name=>"foo"}, "Home Page");
# <a href="index.html" name="foo">Home Page</a>
```

Most every HTML tag you can use in an HTML file is available as a subroutine, although different tags might be available at different times depending which group of subroutines you import in your `use CGI` line. `CGI.pm` has a particularly robust set of subroutines for generating other form elements. I won't go through all of them here; if you're interested, see the documentation for `CGI.pm`.

Debugging the Result

You've already seen, in the Hello example, one of the ways to debug your scripts before you install them by entering your CGI input as name=value pairs either on the script command line or as standard input. This mechanism can be invaluable in fixing the smaller errors that creep up as you're writing your CGI scripts. By running the script from the command line you can also use the Perl debugger to make sure your script is running right before you install it.

There comes a time, however, when you need to install the CGI script and run it in place to make sure that it's working right. When it's installed, however, it can be difficult to debug because errors tend to get reported to the browser with unhelpful messages like `Server Error 500`, or to the error logs without any kind of identifier or timestamp to figure out which errors are yours.

That's where the `CGI::Carp` module comes in. `CGI::Carp` comes with `CGI.pm`, although as with the latter module it should also be part of your standard Perl distribution (make sure you look for it in the CGI subdirectory of Perl's lib directory; there's also a regular Carp module that's related, but not the same thing). Carp is used to generate error messages for CGI scripts, which can be useful for debugging those scripts. In particular, the `fatalsToBrowser` keyword can be very useful for debugging because it prints any Perl errors in the CGI script as an HTML response, which are then displayed in response to the form submission in the browser that called the form in the first place. To echo these errors to the browser, include a `use` line at the top of your script like this:

16

```
use CGI::Carp qw(fatalsToBrowser);
```

Even if you don't use `fatalsToBrowser`, the `CGI::Carp` module provides new definitions of the `warn()` and `die()` functions (and adds the `croak()`, `carp()`, and `confess()` subroutines) such that errors are printed with sensible identifiers and appear in the errors logs for your Web server. (See the documentation for the standard `Carp` module for information on `croak()`, `carp()`, and `confess()`). `CGI::Carp` is quite useful for debugging your CGI scripts in place.

An Example: Survey

Our Hello World example earlier might have given you a taste of how CGI scripts work, but it was too simple to be of much use. Here's a much more complex script that handles a Web-based survey. The script keeps track of all the survey for the data, handling the input from the current form and generating tables of results based on all the data submitted so far. Figure 16.4 shows our simple survey.

FIGURE 16.4.

A simple Web survey.

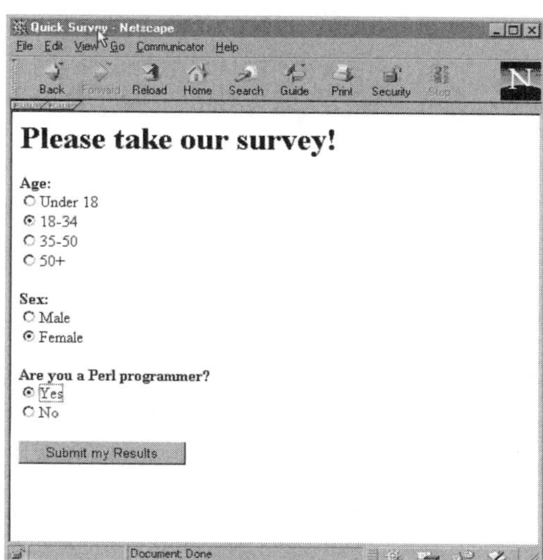

After filling out the survey, the CGI script processes the input, adds it to the data already received, and generates a set of tables, shown in Figure 16.5.

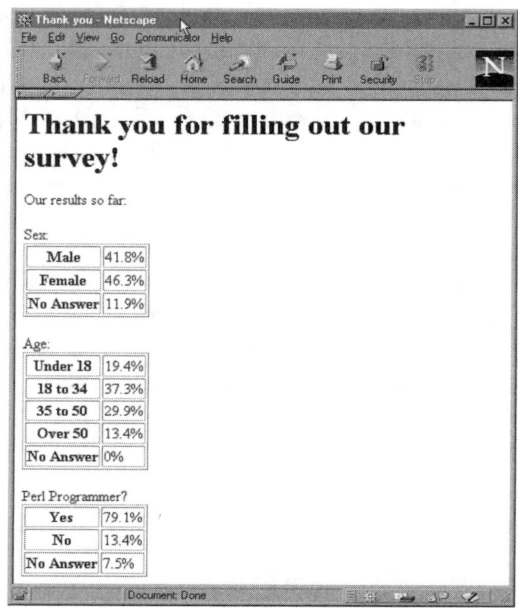

FIGURE 16.5. *The Web survey results*

All the data from the survey is stored in a separate file on the Web server. You'll open, read, and write that data file as part of the CGI script to process the form.

The Form

Let's start with the HTML for the form, just to point out the values that you'll be working with in the CGI script. Listing 16.2 shows that HTML code:

LISTING 16.2 *survey.html*

```
<html>
<head>
    <title>Quick Survey</title>
</head>
<body>
<h1>Please take our survey!</h1>
<form action="/cgi-bin/survey.pl">
<p><strong>Age: </strong><br />
<input type="radio" name="age" value="under18" />Under 18<br />
<input type="radio" name="age" value="18to34" />18-34<br />
```

LISTING 16.2 continued

```
<input type="radio" name="age" value="35to50" />35-50<br />
<input type="radio" name="age" value="50plus" />50+
</p>
<p><strong>Sex: </strong><br />
<input type="radio" name="sex" value="male" />Male<br />
<input type="radio" name="sex" value="female" />Female
</p>
<p><strong>Are you a Perl programmer? </strong><br />
<input type="radio" name="perl" value="yes">Yes<br />
<input type="radio" name="perl" value="no">No
<p><input type="submit" value="Submit my Results" /></p>
</form>
</body>
</html>
```

There are only a few important things to note about this HTML code. Here, instead of a text field like we had in the last example, we're using groups of radio buttons. Note that each group has the same name (for example, all four radio buttons in the age group are named "age"). This prevents more than one button from being selected at one time. It also means that when you get the input from your script, only one value from each group will appear. You'll have to test for the existence of each one to find out which one was selected.

The Script

The CGI script to process this form accomplishes four main things:

- It opens and reads the survey data file into a hash.
- It processes the input from the form, adding the new data to the old data.
- It writes out the new data to the file again.
- It generates HTML for the output, containing tables generated from the current survey data.

Listing 16.3 shows the code for our CGI script, called `survey.pl`.

LISTING 16.3 The *survey.pl* Script

```
#!/usr/local/bin/perl -w
use strict;
use CGI qw(:standard);

my $results = 'survey_results.txt';
my %data = ();
```

LISTING 16.3 continued

```
my $thing = '';
my $val = 0;

open(RESULTS, $results) or die "Can't open results file: $!";
while (<RESULTS>) {
    ($thing, $val) = split(' ');
    $data{$thing} = $val;
}
close(RESULTS);

# overall total
$data{total}++;
# handle age
if (!param('age')) { $data{age_na}++ }
else {
    if (param('age') eq 'under18') { $data{age_under18}++; }
    elsif (param('age') eq '18to34') { $data{age_18to34}++; }
    elsif (param('age') eq '35to50') { $data{age_35to50}++; }
    elsif (param('age') eq '50plus') { $data{age_50plus}++; }
}

# handle sex
if (!param('sex')) { $data{sex_na}++ }
else {
    if (param('sex') eq 'male') { $data{sex_m}++; }
    elsif (param('sex') eq 'female') { $data{sex_f}++; }
}

# perl
if (!param('perl')) { $data{perl_na}++ }
else {
    if (param('perl') eq 'yes') { $data{perl_y}++; }
    elsif (param('perl') eq 'no') { $data{perl_n}++; }
}

open(RESULTS, ">$results") or die "Can't write to results file: $!";
foreach $thing (keys %data) {
    print RESULTS "$thing $data{$thing}\n";
}
close(RESULTS);

print header;
print start_html('Thank you');
print <<EOF;
<h1>Thank you for filling out our survey!</h1>
<p>Our results so far:
<p>Sex:
<table border="1"><tr><th>Male</th><td>
EOF

```

LISTING 16.3 continued

```
57: print &percent('sex_m'), "</td></tr>\n";
58: print "<tr><th>Female</th><td>\n";
59: print &percent('sex_f'), "</td></tr>\n";
60: print "<tr><th>No Answer</th><td>\n";
61: print &percent('sex_na'), "</td></tr>\n";
62: print "</table>\n";
63:
64: print "<p>Age:\n";
65: print "<table border=\"1\"><tr><th>Under 18</th><td>\n";
66: print &percent('age_under18'), "</td></tr>\n";
67: print "<tr><th>18 to 34</th><td>\n";
68: print &percent('age_18to34'), "</td></tr>\n";
69: print "<tr><th>35 to 50</th><td>\n";
70: print &percent('age_35to50'), "</td></tr>\n";
71: print "<tr><th>Over 50</th><td>\n";
72: print &percent('age_50plus'), "</td></tr>\n";
73: print "<tr><th>No Answer</th><td>\n";
74: print &percent('age_na'), "</td></tr>\n";
75: print "</table>\n";
76: print "<p>Perl Programmer?\n";
77: print "<table border=\"1\"><tr><th>Yes</th><td>\n";
78: print &percent('perl_y'), "</td></tr>\n";
79: print "<tr><th>No</th><td>\n";
80: print &percent('perl_n'), "</td></tr>\n";
81: print "<tr><th>No Answer</th><td>\n";
82: print &percent('perl_na'), "</td></tr>\n";
83: print "</table>\n";
84:
85: print end_html;
86:
87: sub percent {
88:     if (defined $data{$_[0]}) {
89:         return sprintf("%.1f%%", $data{$_[0]} / $data{total} * 100);
90:     }
91:     else { return '0%'; }
92: }
```

I'm not going to go through this script line by line because much of this is code you've seen in a similar form before (and a whole lot of it is just `print` statements). Here are some of the important parts to note, however.

The name of the survey data file is stored in the `$results` variable in line 10. Here, that file is assumed to be in the same directory as the CGI script itself; you'll need to set the pathname to the appropriate location for your script. That file consists of a set of data keys for each choice in the survey, as well as "na" keys for no answer. Each key has a value for the number of "votes" submitted. Lines 10 through 15 open and read that data file into the `%data` hash, closing it again immediately afterward.

> The results file—here, located in the same directory as the CGI script—must be writeable by the Web server. On Unix, that means the file must have the right permissions so that the user or group ID the Web server runs under (usually `nobody`) can write to it. On Windows that means your security must also be set accordingly. If you run into "can't write to results file" errors when you run this script under a Web server (that didn't happen when you ran it with regular Perl), check your file permissions.

Lines 17 through 41 process the input from the form in groups, corresponding to each group of radio buttons in the HTML file (age, sex, and perl). Note that for each group, you have to test to see if there was no answer (in which case, there won't be a key for that group in the `param()` array `CGI.pm` gives you). If there was a vote, we'll increment the value of that key in the data hash. We also keep track of the overall total (line 16), which we'll need to calculate the percentages for the final output.

After we're done processing the data, we can write out the new data file to that same file, one data key and value per line, separated by a space. The actual order of the keys doesn't matter because they'll just be re-read by the script again into a hash. A simple `foreach` loop in lines 44 and 45 will print the new values to the results file (which we reopened for writing in line 43).

The second half of the script prints the output to the survey so the user can get a response from the survey. Starting from line 49 we print the output starting with the header (line 49), the beginning of the HTML file (line 50), and some boilerplate HTML printed with a here document in lines 51 through 56.

Line 58 is where things start getting interesting. The rest of the HTML file consists of tables that show the current results of the survey. Much of the printing here involves the HTML code for the tables, but the final percentages are calculated using a help subroutine we defined called `&percent()`. The `&percent()` routine, defined in lines 89 through 94, generates a percent string based on the value it's given divided by the total number of responses. It also makes sure that the given data key actually has a value (if it's zero, it won't even appear in the `%data` hash). And, finally it formats the percentage with one decimal point and a percent sign using the `sprintf` function (note that because of the `sprintf` formatting codes, if you want to print an actual percent sign, you have to type it as `%%`).

Going Deeper

As I mentioned at the beginning of this lesson, I could easily go on for pages and pages and chapters and chapters about all the different aspects of CGI. Documenting all of `CGI.pm` itself would give us a much larger lesson than I've got here. There are a few other features of `CGI.pm` I'd like to mention, however. All of these features are documented in the documentation for `CGI.pm` (`perldoc CGI` will show it to you), as well as in the Web page at `http://stein.cshl.org/WWW/software/CGI/`.

If you need further details about CGI itself, feel free to visit the Web pages or to read the book I mentioned at the beginning of this lesson. The Usenet newsgroup `comp.infosystems.www.authoring.cgi` can also provide assistance in getting your CGI scripts to work on different platforms.

Using CGI Variables

When your CGI script gets called, along with the data from the browser, the Web server also provides several values in its environment that relate to the script itself, to the Web server, and to the system running the browser that submitted the form in the first place. On Unix systems, these are environment variables that you can access from inside your Perl script using the `%ENV` hash. Other Web servers may have different ways of passing in these variables. However, `CGI.pm` provides subroutines to access these variables in a way that works across platforms and Web servers. You aren't required to use any of these subroutines in your CGI scripts, but you might find the data useful.

Table 10.1 shows the CGI variable subroutines for `CGI.pm`.

TABLE 10.1 CGI Variable Subroutines

Subroutine	*What it Gives You*
`accept()`	A list of MIME types the browser will accept.
`auth_type()`	The authentication type (usually `'basic'`).
`path_info()`	Path information encoded into the script URL (if used).
`path_translated()`	Same as `path_info()` expanded into a full pathname.
`query_string()`	Arguments to the CGI script tagged on to the URL.
`raw_cookie()`	Returns raw cookie information. Use the `cookie()` subroutines to manage this information.
`referer()`	The URL of the page that called this script (note the incorrect spelling).
`remote_addr()`	The IP address of the host that called this script (the browser's host).
`remote_ident()`	The user's ID, but only if the system is running `ident` (not common).
`remote_host()`	The name of the host that called this script.

TABLE 10.1 continued

Subroutine	*What it Gives You*
`remote_user()`	The name of the user that called this script (usually only set if the user has logged in using authentication).
`request_method()`	The Web server method the script was called with (for example, `GET` or `POST`).
`script_name()`	The name of the script.
`server_name()`	The host name of the Web server that called this script.
`server_software()`	The name and version of the Web server software.
`virtual_host()`	For servers that support virtual hosts, the name of the virtual host that is running this script.
`server_port()`	The network port the server is using (usually 80).
`user_agent()`	The browser name and version that called this script, for example `Mozilla/4.x (Win95)`.
`user_name()`	The name of the user who called this script (almost never set).

`POST` Versus `GET`

CGI scripts can be called by a browser in one of two forms: `POST` and `GET`. `GET` submissions encode the form elements into the URL itself; `POST` sends the form elements over the standard input. `GET` can also be used to submit a form without actually having a form—for example, you could have a link in which the URL contained the hard-coded form elements to submit.

Inside your CGI script, `CGI.pm` will process both these kinds of methods and store them in the parameters array, so you don't have to worry about which method was used to submit the script. If you really want to get the parameters from the URL, use `url_param()` instead of `param()`.

Redirection

Sometimes the result of a CGI script isn't a raw HTML file, but rather a pointer to an existing HTML file on this server or elsewhere. `CGI.pm` supports this result with the `redirect()` subroutine:

```
print redirect('http://www.anotherserver.com/anotherfile.html');
```

The redirect tells the user's browser to retrieve a specific page on the Web, rather than to display any HTML. Because a CGI script that uses redirect doesn't create a new Web page, you should not combine a redirect and any HTML code in the output from a CGI script.

Cookies and File Upload

`CGI.pm` also enables you to manage cookie values and to handle files that get uploaded via the file upload feature of HTML forms. For managing cookies, see the `cookie()` subroutine in `CGI.pm`. File upload works similarly to ordinary form elements; the `param()` subroutine is used to return the filename that was entered in the form. That filename is also a filehandle that is open and which you can read lines from using the standard Perl mechanisms.

See the `CGI.pm` documentation for information on both these things.

CGI Scripts and Security

Every CGI script is a potential security hole on your Web server. A CGI script runs on your server based on input from any random person out on the Web. Depending on how carefully you write your scripts and how determined someone is, your CGI scripts could offer openings up to and including allowing malicious users to break into your system and irreparably damage it.

The best way to prevent a problem is to understand it and take steps to avoid it. A great starting point is at the World Wide Web security FAQ at `http://www-genome.wi.mit.edu/WWW/faqs/www-security-faq.html`. Perl also includes a feature, called *taint mode*, which prevents you from using nonsecure data in a way that could do harm to your system. More about taint mode on Day 20, "Odds and Ends."

Embedding Perl in Web Servers

Each time a Perl CGI script is called from a Web server, Perl is called to execute that script. For very busy Web servers, running lots and lots of CGI scripts can mean running many copies of Perl at once, and a considerable load for the machine acting as the Web server. To help with performance, many Web servers provide a mechanism for embedding the Perl interpreter inside the Web server itself, so that scripts that run on Web servers no longer run as actual CGI scripts. Instead, they run as if they were Web server libraries, reducing the overhead and startup time for each script. In many cases, you don't even have to modify your CGI scripts to get them to work under this system.

Different Web servers on different platforms provide different mechanisms for doing this. You'll need to check the documentation that comes with your Web server to see if Perl-based CGI scripts can be embedded, and if so, where to get the tools or modules to embed them.

If you're using an ISAPI-based Web server on Windows (such as IIS), you'll need the Perl for ISAPI package (sometimes called PerlIIS). This package is part of ActiveState's version of Perl for Windows, and is installed with that package. You can also get it separately from ActiveState's Web site at `http://www.activestate.com`.

If you're using the open source Apache Web server, `mod_perl` is an Apache module that embeds the Perl interpreter in the Apache Web server. While the most obvious feature this gives you is better CGI performance, it also allows you access, with Perl, to all of Apache's internal extension APIs, allowing almost infinite customization of the Web server itself. Find out more about the Apache Web server at `http://www.apache.org`, and the Apache/Perl Integration Project, the developers of `mod_perl`, at `http://perl.apache.org`.

If you want to run CGI scripts under `mod_perl`, you should use the `Apache::Registry` module, which is designed for porting scripts that use CGI.pm to the `mod_perl` environment. You can read the documentation for the module at `http://www.perldoc.com/cpan/Apache/Registry.html`.

Summary

Not everything to do with Perl has to involve long and involved scripts with lots of subroutines. Sometimes the most useful things in Perl can be done using modules with a little glue code to get the result you want. CGI is a terrific example of this; the `CGI.pm` module covers up most of the gritty parts of CGI scripting and makes it easy to get the values from a form or other CGI submission and return an HTML file as the result.

Today you learned something about using Perl for CGI, including how CGI works from the browser to the server to the script and back again; how `CGI.pm` can be imported and used in your script, and how to use its various features to make your life with CGI more pleasant. We also explored a couple of CGI examples: a survey form that keeps track of the survey data in an external file, and a color-generation script that is its own form and which maintains the current form values each time the form is regenerated. I can't guarantee that this lesson has given you everything you need to create CGI scripts (because it hasn't), but hopefully it's given you a starting point from which you can work.

The subroutines you've learned about in this lesson are all part of the `CGI.pm` module, and include

- `param()` gets the parameters that were given to the CGI script, usually as part of a form submission. `param()` with no arguments returns a list of the keys (form element names) available; `param()` with a key argument returns the value for that key.

- `print header()` prints the CGI header for the output. The `print_header()` subroutine without any arguments assumes the output will be in HTML format.
- `start_html()` returns the top part of an HTML page, including the `<html>`, `<head>`, `<title>` and `<body>` tags. Different arguments to the `start_html()` tag will generate different values for the HTML (for example, a single string argument will set the title of the page.
- `end_html()` generates closing `</body>` and `</html>` tags for the output.

Q&A

Q. I've seen a number of CGI scripts written in Perl that don't use `CGI.pm`; they use other libraries like `cgi-lib.pl`. Are those bad scripts that should be fixed?

A. Not necessarily. There are a number of libraries floating around the Web for managing CGI scripts with Perl; `cgi-lib.pl` is one of the more popular ones. There's nothing wrong with using those other libraries. I chose to use `CGI.pm` for this lesson because it's become the standard for using Perl with CGI, it's a well-behaved module and follows the standard module conventions, it's object-oriented if you choose to use it that way and, most importantly, it's available as part of the standard Perl distribution. This gives it significant advantages over other libraries.

If you have a script that uses `cgi-lib.pl`, but you don't actually have the `cgi-lib.pl` library, you can use `CGI.pm` to emulate it. You just replace these lines:

```
require "cgi-lib.pl";
ReadParse();
```

with these:

```
use CGI qw(:cgi-lib);
ReadParse();
```

Q. My CGI scripts work from the command line, but don't work when I try them from a Web page. What am I doing wrong?

A. With all the different platforms and Web servers out there, there's no one single answer to this question. Is the script executable? Is the place where you put your script an "official" CGI location according to your server (usually a special `cgi-bin` directory or something like it)? Does your script have the right permissions (Web servers run CGI scripts as a special user with limited permissions)? Are you sure you even have a Web server running on your machine?

The list of Web sites I gave you earlier in the lesson have ideas and suggestions for debugging CGI scripts.

Q. My Web site is stored on a Unix machine. I can run CGI scripts there. But I'd like to write and debug my CGI scripts on my Windows machine at home so I don't have to be logged in all the time. Can I do this?

A. Through the wonder of cross-platform Perl and the `CGI.pm` module, you certainly can. You'll need a Web server running on your Windows system—hopefully one similar or identical to the one running on your Unix machine—but then you can install and debug and run CGI scripts locally all you want. (There's a version of Apache available for Windows, you can download it at `http://httpd.apache.org`.) Watch out for differences in paths to files, and differences in how different servers deal with CGI. Try to keep things simple, and you should need little work to get your scripts to run on Unix.

Q. I modified the survey file to be used with a guestbook-like script, which allows people to post comments to a Web page. But I'm having problems where if multiple people post to the Web page at once, sometimes the file gets written to before the other one is done, and the comments get lost or weird things happen. What's going on here?

A. The survey example here demonstrates basic CGI scripting in the technical sense; for real production Web sites you'll need to go a little deeper (I recommend the Web sites I mentioned earlier, or another book). In particular, if you've got an external file that will potentially be written to by multiple users at once—as any CGI script might—you'll want to "lock" the file before writing to it, and then release the lock after you're done. This could be as easy as creating another temporary file, called, for example, `survey.lock`. In your script, before actually writing to the survey results file, you would:

- Check to see if the lock file exists. If it does, someone else is writing to the file. Wait a little bit (check out the sleep function for this) and try again.
- When the file is free, set the lock file yourself.
- Write the data.
- Unlock the file.

Workshop

The workshop provides quiz questions to help you solidify your understanding of the material covered and exercises to give you experience in using what you've learned. Try to understand the quiz and exercise answers before you go on to tomorrow's lesson.

16

Quiz

1. What does CGI stand for? What's it used for?
2. What does the `CGI.pm` module give you? How do you get it and use it?
3. Why would you want to run a CGI script on the command line before trying to run it via a Web page?
4. How do you use the `param()` subroutine?
5. List three ways to print HTML code as output for your CGI script.
6. Why is a here document sometimes more useful than `print`?

Exercises

1. Write a CGI script that prints the form elements it was submitted with as a bulleted list. HINT: bulleted lists in HTML look like this:

```
<ul>
<li>One item</li>
<li>Two items</li>
<li>Three items</li>
</ul>
```

   Another hint: `param()` without any arguments gives you a list of all the form element names the script was submitted with.

2. BUG BUSTER: What's wrong with this bit of script?

```
if (!param()) { $data{sex_na}++ }
else {
    if (param() eq 'male') { $data{sex_m}++; }
    elsif (param() eq 'female') { $data{sex_f}++; }
}
```

3. Write a CGI script that prints a simple HTML page (a hello world is fine) but also keeps track of how many times the page has been accessed and prints that value on the page as well.
4. Write a CGI script to implement a very simple guestbook-like feature that allows users to post one-line comments to a Web page. Keep track of all past postings. You can assume the existence of an HTML form with two elements: a text field called mail for the e-mail address of the poster, and a text field called comment for comments.

Answers

Here are the answers to the Workshop questions in the previous section.

Quiz Answers

1. CGI stands for Common Gateway Interface, and refers to programs that run on the Web server in response to requests from a Web browser (commonly from a form on an HTML page).
2. The `CGI.pm` module provides behavior for writing, running, and debugging CGI scripts. It provides a number of subroutines for managing input to and output from those scripts as well as other utility subroutines for just about any aspect of CGI you can think of.

   The `CGI.pm` module is shipped with most current versions of Perl. If it is not already available as part of your Perl distribution, you can download and install it from the URL mentioned earlier in this lesson.

   To use the CGI module, you import it like you do any other module: with `use` and an import tag such as `:standard` or `:all`.
3. Running a CGI script from the command line is usually easier to find the smaller syntax or basic errors you might have made without needing to install the script on the Web server, connect to the Internet, and so on. By running the script on the command line and giving it sample data, you can test your script before actually putting it online.
4. The `param()` subroutine is used to find out the values of any form elements on the Web page that called this script. Without any arguments, `param()` returns a list of keys referring to the names of the form elements. With a key argument (a string), `param()` returns the value associated with that form element.
5. You can print HTML code using one of these methods:
   - Use regular `print` statements. Watch out for embedded quotes!
   - Here document
   - Various subroutines via the `CGI.pm` module.
6. Here documents provide a way to print a block of text verbatim: all newlines and quotes are printed verbatim. Here documents provide a way for you to avoid a lot of repetitive `print` statements or escaped quotation marks.

16

Exercise Answers

1. Here's one way to do it:

```
#!/usr /bin/perl -w
use strict;
use CGI qw(:standard);

my @keys = param();

print header;
print start_html('Hello!');
print "<h1>Key/Value Pairs</h1>\n";
print "<ul>\n";

foreach my $name (@keys) {
    print "<li>$name = ", param($name), "</li>\n";
}
print "</ul>\n";

print end_html;
```

2. The `param()` subroutine is called without any arguments. In some cases—such as the one in Exercise 1—this may be exactly what you want to do. In this case, however, because the tests are looking for string values, `param()` should probably be called with some sort of string argument to extract a value from the form parameters.
3. Here's one way to do it (don't forget to create `count.txt` beforehand):

```
#!/usr /bin/perl -w
use strict;
use CGI qw(:standard);

my $countfile = 'count.txt';
my $count = '';

open(COUNT, $countfile) or die "Can't open counter file: $!";
while (<COUNT>) {
    $count = $_;
}
close(COUNT);

$count++;

open(COUNT, ">$countfile") or die "Can't write to counter file: $!";
print COUNT $count;
close(COUNT);

print header;
print start_html('Hello!');
print "<h1>Hello, World</h1>\n";
print "<p>This page has been visited $count times.</p>\n";

print end_html;
```

4. Here's one (particularly simple) way of doing it. This script assumes a file of past comments, one per line, with the e-mail address first.

```
#!/usr/ bin/perl -w
use strict;
use CGI qw(:standard);

my $guestbook = 'guest.txt';
my $mail = '';                    # email address
my $comment = '';                 # comments

open(GUEST, $guestbook) or die "Can't open guestbook file: $!";

print header;
print start_html('Comments');
print "<H1>Comments</H1>\n";
print "<P>Comments about this Web site!\n";
print "<HR>\n";

while (<GUEST>) {
      chomp();
     ($mail, $comment) = split(' ',$_,2);
     if ($mail) {
         if (!$comment) { $comment = "nothing\n"; }
         else {  print "<p><n>$mail says:</b> $comment</p>"; }
     }
}

$mail = param('mail');
$comment = param('comment');
print "<p><b>$mail says:</b> $comment</p>\n";

open(GUEST, ">>$guestbook") or die "Can't open guestbook file: $!";
print GUEST "$mail $comment\n";

print end_html;
```

DAY 17

Managing Files and Directories

On Day 15, we covered dealing with reading and writing files inside a Perl script. In today's lesson, we'll look at several other aspects of managing files—in particular, dealing with various aspects of the file system itself from inside your scripts. Here's what you learn about today:

- Managing files: removing, renaming, copying and linking them, and changing permissions
- Managing directories: navigating, creating, and removing them
- Getting the contents of directories with file "globs" (a way to indicate groups of files quickly), and using directory handles.

Managing Files

In addition to simply reading from and writing to files, you can also manage them from inside Perl, just as you might from a command line or in a file manager: you can rename them, delete them, change their permissions, or create links to them. Each of these tasks makes use of several Perl built-in functions. In this section, you get an overview of each of these.

Renaming Files

To rename a file from one name to another, keeping its contents intact, use the `rename` function with two arguments: the old name of the file and the new name:

```
rename myfile, myfile.bak;
```

If a file with the same name as the new file already exists, Perl will overwrite it. If you're used to Unix, this won't be a problem. If you're a Windows or Mac user, beware! There are no checks to make sure you're not overwriting an existing file. You might want to test to make sure that the new file doesn't exist (with one of the file tests, such as `-e`) before you rename it.

The `rename` function returns `1` or `0` (true or false) depending on whether the rename was successful or not. You (or the user running the script) must have the right file permissions to rename the file.

Creating and Following Links

The Unix version of Perl also provides two functions for creating links between files: `link` and `symlink`, which create hard and symbolic links, respectively (similar to the Unix command `ln(1)`). *Hard links* are used to create a file with more than one name; if you remove any of those names (including the original file), the file continues to exist as long as there are multiple names for it. *Symbolic links* are pointers to other files; if you remove the link, the file continues to exist, but if you remove the original file, the symbolic link will no longer point to anything useful. Some Unix systems might not support symbolic links.

Use either the `link` or `symlink` functions with two arguments: the name of the original file to link to, and the name of the new link. Take this example:

```
link file1, file2;
```

Both functions return `1` (true) or `0` (false) depending on whether they were successful or not.

Both hard and symbolically linked files are transparent to Perl; if you use `open` with a filename that is actually a link, the original file will be opened instead. You can test to see if a given file is a symbolic link with the `-l` file test, and then follow that link to its original location with the `readlink` function:

```
if (-l $file) {  # file is a link
   $realfile = readlink $file;   # get the real file
}
```

Note that `readlink` returns the location of the real file as a relative path to the symbolic link, which means you might need to expand that path into a full path, or change directories to the place where the symbolic link is able to use the original file's path name. Changing directories is covered later in this chapter.

Using Perl for Windows? Neither hard nor symbolic links are available in Perl for Windows. You can use the `Win32::Shortcut` module to create Windows Explorer shortcuts on Windows.

Removing Files and Links

You're done with a file, you're sure you don't need it anymore. How do you get rid of it? Use the `unlink` function (despite its name, it's used to remove *both* links and files). It works much like the Unix command `rm` or the DOS command `del`; it does not move the file to a trashcan or recycle bin like Windows or the Mac. When the file is removed, it's really removed. Be careful or you can easily delete files you actually wanted to be there.

`unlink` takes a list argument, which can be a single file or a list of files. It returns the number of files it deleted:

```
unlink temp, config, foo;
```

Be aware that on some systems—Unix being the most obvious—Perl has no qualms about deleting read-only files, so watch what you're doing (the state of being read-only actually determines whether the *contents* of the file can be changed, not whether or not that filename can be moved or deleted).

The `unlink` function, when used on a hard link, removes that link. Other hard links to the file will continue to exist. On a symbolic link, you'll remove the link, but not the original file. You can use `readlink` to follow any symbolic links. Note that removing a file that has other symbolic links to it causes those symbolic links to point to nothing.

You cannot use `unlink` to remove directories; you'll learn how to remove directories in the section "Managing and Navigating Directories."

Other Operations

I'm going to lump a number of other file-related functions together here, because these operations tend to vary from platform to platform (or not to exist at all on Windows or Mac). Table 17.1 shows some of the other file-management functions available on Unix systems, all of which correspond to actual Unix commands. If you're interested in running any of the functions listed in Table 17.1, check the documentation for your particular version of Perl to see if these functions are supported (or if the capabilities are supported through other means such as platform-specific modules.)

For more information on any of these functions, see the `perlfunc` man page.

17

TABLE 17.1 Other File Management Functions

Function	*What It Means*
`chmod`	Change the permissions for the file (read, write, execute, for world, group or owner). Windows and Mac have limited versions of this command that only accept permissions of 0666 (read and write) and 0444 (read only or locked).
`chown`	Change the owner of the file (Unix only).
`fileno`	Return the file descriptor number for the file.
`utime`	Change the timestamp for a file.

For managing file permissions and attributes on Windows and Windows NT, consider the `Win32::File` and `Win32::FileSecurity` modules, which allow you to check and modify file attributes and NT user permissions.

Managing and Navigating Directories

Just as you can work with files inside Perl as you might in a shell or command line, you can also navigate around your file system and manage directories (or folders, depending on your OS loyalties). You can find out the current directory, change the current directory, list the contents of that directory or some subset of its files, and create or remove the directories themselves. This section explains some of the nuances of performing these operations with Perl.

Navigating Directories

Each Perl script has a notion of a current working directory, that is, the directory from which the script was called (if you're used to working with command line–based systems, this is no surprise to you).To change the current directory from inside a Perl script, use the `chdir` function:

```
chdir "images";
```

As with the directory names in the `open` function, watch out for path names and different systems. Relative paths, as in this example, are fine. This example changes the current working directory to the `images` directory, which resides in the same directory in which the script was originally called (whew!).

Is it possible to actually find out what directory you're currently in? Yes, but it varies depending on the system on which you're running. In Unix, the back-quote operator can execute the Unix `pwd` command to find out the current directory (you'll learn more about back-quotes on Day 18, "Perl and the OS"):

```
$curr =`pwd`;
```

On Windows, the `Win32::GetCWD` function will give you the current working directory. However, the best way to find out the current working directory–and the method that will work across platforms–is to use the `Cwd` module, part of the standard library. The `Cwd` module gives you a `cwd` function, which returns the current working directory (in fact, `cwd` actually executes `` `pwd` `` on Unix, so you're safe there as well):

```
use Cwd;
$cuur = cwd();
```

Listing Files

Perl provides two ways to get a list of files in a directory. The first, *file globbing*, gives you a list of specific files matching a pattern. The second method, using the `opendir` and `readdir` functions, allows you to get a complete list of all files in a directory.

File Globbing

The somewhat bizarrely named technique called file globbing enables you to get a list of files in the current directory that match a certain, simple pattern. If you've used a command-line system, and you've ever listed files using a pattern such as `*.txt` or `*foo*`, then you've done file globbing (although you might not have known it was called that).

Note The term *glob*, in case you haven't guessed, is borrowed from Unix. Never use a simple word when a weird one works just as well.

File globbing allows you to indicate a set of filenames using a *. Don't confuse file globbing with regular expressions–here, the * simply stands for any character (zero or more), and it's the only special character you can use. The result of a file glob is all the filenames in the current directory that match the pattern: *.html will return all the filenames that end with a `.html` extension, *foo* will return all the files with `foo` in their names, and so on. You could then use those filenames to perform operations on each file in turn.

Perl has two ways of creating file globs: the `<>` operator, which looks like the input operator but isn't, and the `glob` function.

To operator (file globbing)> (file globbing)> use the `<>` operator for file globs, put the pattern inside the brackets:

```
@files = <*.pl>;
```

This expression, using `<>` in a list context, returns a list of all the files with a `.pl` extension. If you use `<>` as a glob in a scalar context, you get each filename in turn, just like with input (and if you stick it inside a `while` loop, each filename will get assigned to `$_`, just like input as well).

So, for example, this snippet will print out a list of all the files in the current directory that end with a .txt extension:

```
while (<*.txt>) {
   print $_, "\n";
}
```

Don't confuse the `<>` operator for globbing with the `<>` operator for input–they might look the same, but they behave differently. The latter needs a file handle as an argument and reads the contents of that input file; the former returns the plain filename strings that match the pattern in the current directory.

Because it's so easy to confuse the use of `<>` for globbing and for input, there is also the `glob` function, which makes globbing more apparent and less open to confusion:

```
@files = glob '*.pl';
```

The result is the same; you end up with a list of files that end with the `.pl` extension (or one at a time, in scalar context). The latter form is preferable to the former in modern Perl scripts.

Directory Listings

The second way to get a listing of files in a directory is through directory handles, which look and behave sort of like file handles, but only apply to directories. Reading with directory handles gives you a list of all the files in a directory, including hidden files starting with a dot (which file globs won't give you), as well as `.` and `..` for the current and parent directories on Unix and Windows.

Just as you open and close file handles, so do you open and close directory handles using the `opendir` and `closedir` functions. The `opendir` function takes two arguments: the name of a directory handle—of your choosing—and the directory to open:

```
opendir(DIR, ".") or die "Can't open directory: $!\n";
```

As with the `open` function, you should always check the result and fail gracefully with the `die` function (the `$!` variable is helpful here as well).

The directory file handle (here `DIR`) follows all the same rules as a file handle in terms of naming. Directory file handles are also entirely separate from file handles–you could give both the same name and they would not conflict.

When the file handle is open, use `readdir` to read from it. As with the input operator `<>`, `readdir` returns a single filename in scalar context, and a list of all the filenames in list context. So, for example, this snippet will open the current directory (on Unix and Windows, use `":"` on Mac instead), and print a directory listing:

```
opendir(CURR, ".") or die "can't open directory: $!\n";
while (defined($file = readdir(CURR))) {
   print "$file\n";
}
```

Note that unlike the input operator `<>`, `readdir` does not assign anything automatically to the `$_` variable. You can do that yourself inside the `while` loop or just use a temporary variable (as I've done here).

`Readdir` gives you a list of all the files and subdirectories in the directory. If you want to screen out specific files (hidden files, `.` or `..`), you'll have to do that yourself with a regular expression test.

When you're finished with the directory handle, close it using the `closedir` function:

```
closedir(CURR);
```


Making and Removing Directories

You can also create new directories and remove unused directories from inside Perl using the `mkdir` and `rmdir` functions.

The `mkdir` function takes two arguments: a directory (folder) name, and a set of permissions. On Unix, the permissions refer to the standard permission bits from the `chmod` command in octal format (0 plus three numbers 0 through 7). On Windows and the Mac, the permissions argument is required but not useful; use `0777` as the permissions argument and you'll be fine:

```
mkdir temp, 0777;
```

> `0777` is an octal number that refers to Unix permission bits for read, write, and execute permissions for world, group, and owner. Windows uses different forms of file and directory permissions, and doesn't use the permissions argument to `mkdir` (although you'll need to put something in there, anyhow. `0777` is a good general purpose answer).

The `mkdir` function creates the given directory in the script's current working directory. You can create directories in different locations using full path names, by changing the current directory first, or if you want to get really fancy, check out the `File::Path` module, part of the standard library, which enables you to create or remove whole subsets of directories.

To remove a directory, use rmdir:

```
rmdir temp;
```

The directory must be empty (contain no files) for you to remove it.

An Example: Creating Links

Here's a useful example I tend to use a lot in real life: Given a directory full of files that are either GIF or JPEG images (that is, they have .gif, .jpeg, or .jpg extensions), this script will generate an HTML file, called `index.html`, which contains nothing but links to each of the files. This is a good way to get a whole lot of images up on the Web really quickly without having to spend a lot of time creating HTML files (or it at least provides a basic file you can then edit to make it read better).

The script I wrote for this task uses file handles to open and write to the index.html file, directory handles to read the contents of the current directory, and file tests and regular expressions to match the files we're actually looking for. Listing 17.1 shows the result.

LISTING 17.1 The `imagegen.pl` Script

```
#!/usr/ bin/perl -w
use strict;
use Cwd;

open(OUT, ">index.html") or die "Can't open index file: $!\n";
&printhead();
&processfiles();
&printtail();

sub printhead {
    my $curr = cwd();
    print OUT "<html>\n<head>\n";
    print OUT "<title>Image files in directory $curr</title>\n";
    print OUT "</head>\n<body>\n";
    print OUT "<h1>Image Files</h1>\n";
    print OUT "<p>";
}

sub processfiles {
    opendir(CURRDIR, '.') or die "Can't open directory ($!), exiting.\n";
    my $file = "";

    while (defined($file = readdir(CURRDIR))) {
        if (-f $file and $file =~ /(\.gif|\.jpe?g)$/) {
            print OUT  "<a href=\"$file\">$file</a><br />\n";
        }
```

LISTING 17.1 continued

```
27:     }
28:     closedir(CURRDIR)
29: }
30:
31: sub printtail {
32:     print OUT "</p></body></html>\n";
33:     close(OUT);
34: }sub printtail {
    print OUT "</p></body></html>\n";
    close(OUT);
}
```


We start by opening the output file (index.html) in line 5. Note the `>` character, which indicates an output file handle.

The `&printhead()` subroutine, in lines 10 through 17, simply prints out the top part of an HTML file. The only tricky part is the use of the current working directory in the title of the page, which we get using the `cwd()` function (as imported from the `Cwd` module in line 3). I didn't bother using a "here" document to print out the HTML code; that would have ended up being even more lines than are already here.

The `&processfiles()` subroutine (lines 19 through 29) is where the real work goes on. Here, we open the current directory in line 20, and then loop over each filename in that directory in the `while` loop in lines 23 through 26. The test in line 24 checks to see if the file is an actual file and not a directory (the `-f` test), and uses a regular expression to only operate on image files (those that have a `.gif`, `.jpg`, or `.jpeg` extension). If the current file is indeed an image file, we print out a link to that file in line 25, using the filename as the actual link text.

Note that using the filename as the link text doesn't make for very descriptive links–you could end up with a set of links that say "image1.gif," "image2.gif," "image3.gif," and so on. Not very descriptive, but it's a start. After the script runs you could edit the HTML to create more descriptive links ("nice sunset," "Easter parade," "Bill behaving foolishly," and so on).

To finish up the script we call the `&printtail()` subroutine, which simply prints the end of the HTML file and closes the output file handle.

Going Deeper

In addition to the functions I've described in this lesson and on Day 15, all of which are described in the `perlfunc` man page, there are also quite a few modules in the standard module library for managing files and file handles.

Many of these modules are simply object-oriented wrappers for the standard file operations; others are especially useful for covering up or getting around cross-platform issues. Still others simply provide convenience functions for managing files and directories.

I've mentioned a number of these modules previously in this chapter—`Getopt` and `Cwd` in particular. Table 17.2 shows the more complete list; for details on any of these modules, see the `perlmod` man page.

TABLE 17.2 File-Related Modules

Module Name	*What it Does*
`Cwd`	Finds out the current working directory in a safe, cross-platform way
`DirHandle`	An object-oriented wrapper for manipulating directory handles
`File::Basename`	Allows you to parse file and directory path names in a cross-platform manner
`File::CheckTree`	Performs multiple file tests on a group of files
`File::Copy`	Copies files or file handles
`File::Find`	Similar to the Unix find command, traverses a directory tree to find a specific file that matches a specific pattern
`File::Path`	Creates or removes multiple directories or directory trees
`FileCache`	Some systems might not let you have large numbers of files open at once; this gets around that limit.
`FileHandle`	An object-oriented wrapper for manipulating file handles
`Getopt::Long`	Manages script arguments (complicated POSIX syntax)
`Getopt::Std`	Manages script arguments (simpler single-character syntax)
`SelectSaver`	Saves and restores file handles (used with the `select` function. We'll look at `select` on Day 20, "Odds and Ends"

Summary

No Perl script is an island. At some point, chances are good your script is going to need to peek outside at the world of the file system, particularly if your script reads and writes extensively from files. On Day 15, you learned how to read and write the contents of the files themselves; today, we covered how to handle the bigger issues of file and directory management from inside Perl scripts.

We started with files: renaming them, linking them, and moving them as you might outside your script with a command line or iconic file manager.

If you can manage files, you must be able to manage directories. And so, in the second half of this lesson, we discussed creating and removing directories, printing and changing the current working directory from inside the Perl script, and reading lists of the files inside a directory (either through the use of file globs or by reading from a directory handle.

Q&A

Q. I'm on Unix. I was testing a script that reads from a file, and then deletes it. Because I didn't want it to actually delete the file until I was done debugging the script, I removed write permission from the file. But Perl went ahead and deleted it anyhow. Why?

A. Setting the permissions on a file determines whether you can read or write the contents of that file. The filename—and whether that file can be renamed, moved, or changed—is controlled by the permissions of the enclosing directory. To actually prevent Perl from deleting files, remove write permission from the directory the file is in. Or, even better, comment out your `unlink` command until you've got the rest of the script debugged.

17

Q. You've described how to rename a file, how to link to one, and how to remove it. How do you copy a file?

A. You could just open both the file to copy from and the file to copy to, and then read lines from one and print them to the other. Or you could use back-quotes to call the system copy command (as you'll learn on Day 18). Or you could use the `File::Copy` module, which gives you a copy function for copying files or file handles from a source to a destination.

Workshop

The workshop provides quiz questions to help you solidify your understanding of the material covered and exercises to give you experience in using what you've learned. Try and understand the quiz and exercise answers before you go on to tomorrow's lesson.

Quiz

1. What's the difference between a hard link and a symbolic link? What happens if you remove the file that you've linked to with either one?
2. What's the difference between `` `pwd` `` and `cwd()`? Why would you want to use one over the other?
3. What is a file glob? Why are they useful?
4. What's the difference between a file glob of `<*>` and the list of files you get with `readdir()`?

5. What are the differences between file handles and directory handles?
6. What does the permissions argument to `mkdir` do?

Exercises

1. Write a script that reads in a list of files from the current directory and prints them in alphabetical order. If there are directories, print those names with a slash (/) following them.
2. BUG BUSTER: This script is supposed to remove all the files and directories from the current directory. It doesn't. Why not?

```
while (<foo*>) {
   unlink $_;
}
```

3. BUG BUSTER: How about this one?

```
#!/usr/ bin/perl -w

opendir(DIR, '.') or die "can't open directory ($!), exiting.\n";
while (readdir(DIR)) {
  print "$_\n";
}
closedir(DIR);
```

4. Write a script that gives you a menu with five choices: create a file, rename a file, delete a file, list all files, or quit. For the choice to create a file, prompt the user for a filename and create that file (it can be empty) in the current directory. For the rename and delete operations, prompt for the old file to rename or delete; also for rename, prompt for the new name of the file and rename it. For the choice to list all files, do just that. SUGGESTION: You don't have to bother with handling directories. EXTRA CREDIT: Do error checking on all filenames to make sure you're not creating a file that already exists, or deleting/renaming a file that doesn't exist.

Answers

Here are the answers to the Workshop questions in the previous section.

Quiz Answers

1. Hard links provide a way for a single file to have multiple filenames. Removing one instance of the filename—be it the original or the link—leaves all other hard links intact. The file is only actually removed when all the links to it are also removed. Symbolic links also provide a way for a single file to have multiple names, except that the original file is separate from the links. Removing the links has no effect on the file; removing the original file makes any existing links point to nothing.

Note that only Unix systems differentiate between hard and symbolic links, and some Unix systems don't even have symbolic links. Aliases on the Mac or shortcuts on Windows are analogous to symbolic links.

2. The `` `pwd` `` command makes use of back quotes and the pwd command in Unix. While some versions of Perl work around this function on other systems, for a more portable version use the `Cwd` module and the `cwd()` function. Note: you'll have to import `Cwd` (`use Cwd`) before you can use it.
3. A file glob is a way of getting a list of files that match a certain pattern. `*.pl`, for example, is a glob that returns all the files in a directory with a `.pl` extension. Globs are useful for grabbing and reading a set of files without having to open the file handle, read the list, and process only those files that match a pattern.
4. A file glob of `<*>` returns all the files in a directory, but it does not include hidden files, files that start with a `.`, or the `.` and `..` directories. Directory handles return all these things.
5. File handles are used to read and write the contents of files (or to the screen, or to a network connection, and so on). Directory handles are used to read lists of files from directories. Both file handles and directory handles use their own variables, and the names do not clash.
6. The argument to mkdir determines the permissions that directory will have. On Unix, those permissions follow the usual format of read, write, and execute access for owner, group and all; on Mac and Windows, the permissions argument isn't useful, but you have to include it anyway (use `0777` and everything will work fine).

17

Exercise Answers

1. Here's one answer:

```
#!/usr/ bin/perl -w
use strict;
use Cwd;

my $curr = cwd();
opendir(CURRDIR, $curr) or die "can't open directory ($!), exiting.\n";

my @files = readdir(CURRDIR);
closedir(CURRDIR);

foreach my $file (sort @files) {
    if (-d $file) {
        print "$file/\n";
    }
    else { print "$file\n"; }
}
```

2. The `unlink` function is only used to remove files. Use `rmdir` to remove directories. If the goal, per the description, is to remove all the files and directories in the directory, you'll need to test each filename to see if it's a file or directory and call the appropriate function.

3. The bug lies in the test for the `while` loop; the assumption here is that `readdir` inside of a `while` loop assigns the next directory entry to `$_`, the same way that reading a line of input from a file handle does. This is not true. For `readdir` you must explicitly assign the next directory entry to a variable, like this:

   ```
   while (defined($in = readdir(DIR))) { ... }
   ```

4. Here's one example. Pay particular attention to the `&getfilename()` subroutine, which handles error checking to make sure the file that was entered doesn't already exist (for creating a new file) or does actually exist (renaming or deleting a file).

```
#!/usr/ bin/perl -w
use strict;

my $choice = '';
my @files = &getfiles();

while ($choice !~ /q/i) {
    $choice = &printmenu();
  SWITCH: {
        $choice =~ /^1/ && do { &createfile(); last SWITCH; };
        $choice =~ /^2/ && do { &renamefile(); last SWITCH; };
        $choice =~ /^3/ && do { &deletefile(); last SWITCH; };
        $choice =~ /^4/ && do { &listfiles(); last SWITCH; };
        $choice =~ /^5/ && do { &printhist(); last SWITCH; };
  }
}

sub printmenu {
    my $in = "";
    print "Please choose one (or Q to quit): \n";
    print "1. Create a file\n";
    print "2. Rename a file\n";
    print "3. Delete a file\n";
    print "4. List all files\n";
    while () {
        print "\nYour choice --> ";
        chomp($in = <STDIN>);
        if ($in =~ /^[1234]$/ || $in =~ /^q$/i) {
            return $in;
        } else {
            print "Not a choice.  1<\!->4 or Q, please,\n";
        }
    }
}
```

```
sub createfile {
    my $file = &getfilename(1);

    if (open(FILE, ">$file")) {
        print "File $file created.\n\n";
        @files = &getfiles();
        close(FILE);
    } else {
        warn "Cannot open $file ($!).\n";
    }
}

sub renamefile {
    my $file = &getfilename();
    my $in = '';

    print "Please enter the new filename: ";
    chomp($in = <STDIN>);

    if (rename $file,$in) {
        print "File $file renamed to $in.\n";
        @files = &getfiles();
    } else {
        warn "Cannot rename $file ($!).\n";
    }
}

sub deletefile {
    my $file = &getfilename();

    if (unlink $file) {
        print "File $file removed.\n";
        @files = &getfiles();
    } else {
        warn "Cannot delete $file ($!).\n";
    }
}

sub getfilename {
    my $in = '';

    # call with no args to make sure the file exists
    my $new = 0;

    # call with an arg to make sure the file *doesn't* exist
    if (@_) {
       $new = 1;
    }

    while (!$in) {
        print "Please enter a filename (? for list): ";
```

```
        chomp($in = <STDIN>);
        if ($in eq '?') {
            &listfiles();
            $in = '';
        } elsif ((grep /^$in$/, @files) && $new) {
            # file exists, not a new file, OK
            # file exists, new file: error
            print "File ($in) already exists.\n";
            $in = '';
        } elsif ((!grep /^$in$/, @files) && !$new) {
            # file doesn't exist, new file, OK
            # file doesn't exist, not a new file: error
            print "File ($in) not found.\n";
            $in = '';
        }
    }

    return $in;
}



sub getfiles {
    my $in = '';
    opendir(CURRDIR, '.') or die "can't open directory ($!), exiting.\n";
    @files = readdir(CURRDIR);
    closedir(CURRDIR);
    return @files;
}

sub listfiles {
    foreach my $file (@files) {
        if (-f $file) { print "$file\n"; }
    }
    print "\n";
}
```

WEEK 3

DAY 18

Perl and the Operating System

Throughout this book I've been focusing on those features of Perl that behave the same whether you're running your scripts on a Unix system, under Windows, or on a Mac (or at least I've been letting you know about the differences where they exist). Fortunately, as far as the core language is concerned, there aren't too many issues surrounding writing cross-platform scripts; a hash is a hash is a hash, regardless of where you're looking at it.

There are other features of Perl, however, that are not portable. Some of these are historical—because Perl was developed for Unix, many of its built-in features relate to features of Unix that simply don't exist on other platforms. Other features are contained in platform-specific modules, and relate to features of those platforms, like the Windows Registry. If you're certain your scripts will only run on a single platform, you can take advantage of these features to solve platform-specific problems. Or, if you've been given a script to port from one platform to another, it'll help if you know which features are specific to which platform.

In this lesson we'll look at some of the features of Perl available to specific platforms, both in the built-in language and in some of the modules. In particular, today we'll explore

- Unix features such as back quotes and the `system` function
- Creating Unix processes with `fork` and `exec`
- Functions for handling various Unix system files
- Windows compatibility with Unix features
- Using the Win32 group of modules, including the `Win32::Process` and `Win32::Registry` modules

Unix Features in Perl

Perl's Unix heritage shows in many of its built-in features, which are borrowed directly from Unix tools such as shells, or relate specifically to the management of various Unix files. In this part of the lesson, then, we'll look at the features in Perl useful on Unix systems, including

- Working with environment variables
- Using the `system` function to run other programs
- Running other programs and capturing their output with backquotes
- Creating and managing new processes with `fork`, `wait`, and `exec`
- Some functions for managing Unix user and group information

Note that with the exception of processes, many of these features might also be available in versions of Perl for other systems, with different or more limited behavior. So, even if you're working on Windows, you might want to at least scan this section before skipping down to the part that relates to your own platform.

> If you're a Mac OS X user, you should pay attention to the Unix information in this lesson. Mac OS X is based on BSD Unix, and so the version of Perl that it uses is the Unix version.

Environment Variables

Perl scripts, like shell scripts, inherit their environment (the current execution path, username, shell, and so on) from the shell in which they were started (or from the user ID that runs them). And, if you run other programs or spawn processes from inside your Perl script, they will get their environment from your script in turn. When you run Perl scripts from the command line, these variables might not have much interest for you. But Perl scripts that run in other environments might have additional variables relating to that environment, or might have different values for those variables than what you expect. CGI scripts, for example, have a number of environment variables relating to various CGI-related features, as you learned on Day 16.

Perl stores all its environment variables in a special hash called `%ENV`, where the keys are the names of the variables, and the values are those values. Environment variables are commonly in uppercase. So, for example, to print the execution path for your script, you'd use a line like this:

```
print "Path: $ENV{PATH}\n";
```

You can print out all the environment variables and values using a regular `foreach` loop:

```
foreach $key (keys %ENV) {
   print "$key -> $ENV{$key}\n";
}
```

Running Unix Programs with `system`

Want to run some other Unix command from inside a Perl script? No problem. Just use the `system` function to do it, like this:

```
system('ls');
```

In this case, `system` will simply run the `ls` command, listing the contents of the current directory to the standard output. To include options to the command you want to run, just include them inside the string argument. Anything you can type at a shell command (and that is available through the current execution path), you can include as an argument to `system`.

```
system("find t -name '*.t' -print | xargs chmod +x &");
system('ls -l *.pl');
```

If you use a double-quoted string as the argument to `system`, Perl will interpolate variables before it passes the string on to the shell:

```
system("grep $thing $file | sort | uniq >newfile.txt");
```

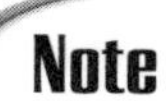

Be very careful when passing data you have not personally verified to the shell (for example, data some user entered from the keyboard). Malicious users could give you data that, when passed through to the shell unchecked, could damage or allow unauthorized access to your system. At the very least, verify incoming data before passing it to the shell. Alternatively, a mechanism in Perl called taint mode allows you to control and manage potentially insecure (tainted) data. See the `perlsec` man page for more information.

The return value of the `system` function is the return value of the command itself from the shell: 0 for success and 1 or greater for failure. Note that this is the reverse of the standard values Perl uses for true and false, so if you want to check for errors that might result from calling `system`, you'll want to use an `and` logical instead of an `or`:

```
system('who') and die "Cannot execute who\n";
```

When `system` runs, Perl passes the string argument to a shell (usually `/bin/sh`) to expand any shell metacharacters (for example, variables or filename globs), and that shell then executes the command. If you don't have any shell metacharacters, you can make the process more efficient by passing `system` a list of arguments, instead of a single string. The first element of the list should be the name of the command to run, and any other elements should be the various arguments to that command:

```
system("grep $thing $file");  # starts a shell
system("grep", "$thing", "$file");   # bypasses the shell, slightly more
efficient
```

Perl will also make this optimization for you if your string argument is simple enough—that is, if it doesn't contain any special characters that the shell must process before actually exiting the program (for example, shell variables or filename globs).

In either case—a single string argument or a list—the system function will end up spawning new subprocesses to handle each of the commands in its argument. Each new process inherits its current environment variables from the values in `%ENV`, and shares its standard input, output, and error with the Perl script. Perl will wait for the command to complete before continuing on with the script (unless the command has a `&` at the end of it, which will run that command in the background, just as it would in the shell).

Don't be too quick to use the `system` function. Because `system` spawns a separate process for each of the commands it runs (and sometimes a process for the shell that runs those commands as well), all those extra processes can mean a lot of overhead for your Perl script. Usually it's better to do a task with a bit of code inside your Perl script than to spawn a Unix shell to do the same thing. More portable, too.

Input with Backquotes

You've already seen how to get input into a script through the use of standard input and via file handles. The third way is through the use of backquotes (``), a common paradigm used in Unix shells.

Backquotes work similarly to `system` in that they run a Unix command inside a Perl script. The difference is in the output. Commands run with `system` simply print their output to the standard output. When you use backquotes to run a Unix command, the output of that command is captured either as a string or as a list of strings, depending on the context in which you use the backquotes.

For example, take the `ls` command, which prints out a listing of the directory:

```
$ls = `ls`;
```

Here, the backquotes execute the `ls` command in a Unix shell, and the output of that command (the standard output) is assigned the scalar variable `$ls`. In scalar context (as with this example), the resulting output is stored as a single string; in list context each line of output becomes a list element.

As with `system`, any command you can give to a Unix shell you can include as a backquoted command, and that command runs in its own process, inherits its environment from `%ENV`, and shares standard input, output, and error. The contents of the backquoted string are also variable-interpolated by Perl as double-quoted strings are. The return status of the command is stored in the special variable `$?`. As with `system`, that return status is 0 if successful, or 1 or greater if it failed.

Using Processes: `fork`, `wait`, and `exec`

When you run a Perl script, it runs as its own Unix process. For many simple scripts, one process might be all you need, particularly if your script runs mostly in a linear start-to-finish way. If you create more complex scripts, where different parts of the script need to do different things all at the same time, then you'll want to create another process and run that part of the script independently. That's what the `fork` function is used for. When you have a new process, you can keep track of its process ID (PID), wait for it to complete, or run another program in that process. You'll learn about all these things in this section.

Note

Creating new processes, and managing how they behave, is the one feature of Unix Perl that's nearly impossible to duplicate on other systems. So while creating new processes can give you a good amount of power over your Perl scripts, if your scripts are portable you'll want to avoid these features or think about how to work around them on other platforms.

Threads, a new experimental feature in Perl 5.005, promise to help with the problems of porting process-based scripts across platforms. Threads offer quite a lot of the multiprocessing-like behavior of Unix processes, while also being more lightweight and portable across all platforms. As of this writing, however, threads are extremely new and very experimental.

How Processes Work

Multiple processes are used to run different parts of your script concurrently. When you start your script, a process is created. When you create a new process from inside a script, that new process will run on its own, in its own memory space, until it's done or until you stop it from running. From your script you can spawn as many processes as you need, up to the limits of your system.

Why would you need multiple processes? When you want different bits of your program to run at once, or for multiple copies of your program to run at the same time. One common use for processes is for creating network-based servers, which wait for a connection from a client, and then process that connection in some way. With a server that uses a single process, when the connection comes in the server "wakes up" and processes that connection (parsing the input, looking up values in databases, returning files—whatever). But if your server is busy processing one connection and another connection arrives in the meantime, that second connection will just have to wait. If you've got a busy server you can end up with a whole queue of connections waiting for the server to finish and move on to the next connection.

If you create a server that uses processes, however, you can have a main body of the script that does nothing but wait for connections, and a second part that does nothing but process those connections. Then, if the main server gets a connection, it can spawn a new process, hand off the connection to that new process, and then the parent is free to go back to listening for new connections. The second process, in turn, handles the input from that connection, and then exits (dies) when it's done. It can repeat this procedure for every new connection, allowing each one to be dealt with in parallel rather than serially.

Network servers make a good example for explaining why processes are useful, but you don't need a network to use them. Any time you want to run different parts of your script in parallel, or separate some processing-intensive part of your script from the main body, processes can help you.

If you're familiar with threads in a language like Java, you might think you understand processes already. But beware. Unlike threads, any running process is completely independent of any other process. The parent and child processes run independently of each other. There is no shared memory, no shared variables, and no simple way to communicate information from one process to another. To communicate between processes you'll need to set up a mechanism called inter-process communication (IPC). The space isn't available to talk about IPC in this book, but I'll give you some pointers in "Going Deeper" at the end of the lesson.

Using `fork` and `exit`

To create a new process in your Perl script, you use the `fork` function. `fork`, which takes no arguments, creates a new second process in addition to the process for the original script. Each new process is a clone of the first, with all the same values of the same variables (although it doesn't share those with the parent; they're different memory locations altogether). The child continues running the same script, in parallel, to the end, using the same environment and the same standard input and output as the parent. From the point of the `fork` onward, it's as if you had started two copies of the same script.

Running the same identical script, however, is not usually why you create a new process. Usually you want the new process (known as the child) to execute something different from the first process (the parent). The most common way to use `fork`, then, is with an `if` conditional, which tests for the return value of the `fork` function. `fork` returns a different value depending on whether the current process is the parent or the child. In the parent, the return result is the PID (process ID) of the new process. In the child, the return result is 0 (if the `fork` didn't happen, for whatever reason, the return value is `undef`). By testing for this return value, you can run different bits of code in the child than you do in the parent.

The core boilerplate for creating processes often looks something like this:

```
if (defined($pid = fork)) {  # fork worked
   if ($pid) {               # pid is some number, this is the parent
      &parent();
   } else {                    # pid is 0.  this is the child.
      &child();
   }
} else {                       # fork didn't work, try again or fail
   die "Fork didn't work...\n";
}
```

In this example, the first line calls `fork` and stores the result in the variable `$pid` (the variable name `$pid` is almost universally used for process IDs, but you can call it anything you want, of course). That result can be one of three things: a process ID, 0, or `undef`. The call to `defined` in that first line checks for a successful result; otherwise we drop down to the outer `else` and exit with an error.

If the `fork` doesn't occur because of some error, the current error message (or error number, depending on how you use it) will be stored in the global system variable `$!`. Because many `fork` errors tend to be transient (an overloaded system might not have new processes available at the moment, some Perl programmers test for a value of `$!` that contains the string `"No more Processes"`, wait a while, and then try forking again.

The successful result can either be 0 or some number representing the process ID (PID) of the new process; each result tells the script which process it is. Here two mythical subroutines, `&parent()` and `&child()`, are called to execute different parts of the script depending on whether the script is executing as the parent or as the child.

Here's a simple example (in Listing 18.1) of a script that forks three child processes, printing messages from the parent and from each child. The end of the script prints the message `"End"`:

LISTING 18.1 `processes.pl`

```
#!/usr/bin/perl -w
use strict;

my $pid = undef;

foreach my $i (1..3) {
    if (defined($pid = fork)) {
        if ($pid) { #parent
            print "Parent: forked child $i ($pid)\n";
        } else {    #child
            print "Child $i: running\n";
            last;
        }
    }
}

print "End...\n";
```

The output of this script will look something like this (you might get different results on your own system:

```
# processes.pl
Parent: forked child 1 (8577)
Parent: forked child 2 (8578)
Parent: forked child 3 (8579)
End...
#
Child 1: running
End...
Child 2: running
Child 3: running
End...
End...
```

That's some weird output. All the output from each process is intermingled, and what's that extra prompt doing in the middle? Why are there four "End..." statements?

The answer to all these questions lies in how each process executes and what it prints at what time. Let's start by looking solely at what happens in the parent:

- Fork a new process in line 7. In the parent, `$pid` gets the process id of that new process.
- Test for a nonzero value of `$pid`, and print a message for each process that gets forked (lines 8 and 9).
- Repeat these steps two more times for each turn of the `foreach` loop.
- Print "End...".
- Exit (printing the system prompt).

All that occurs fairly rapidly, so the output from the parent happens fairly quickly. Now let's look at any of the three children, whose execution starts just after the `fork`:

- Test for the value of `$pid` in line 8. `$pid` for each of the children is 0, so the test in line 8 is false and we drop to line 10. Print the message in line 11.
- Exit the `foreach` immediately with `last`. Without a `last` here the child would go ahead and repeat the loop as many times as remain (remember, the child starts from the exact same point as the `fork` left off. It's a clone of the parent).
- Print "End...".
- Exit. No system prompt, because it was the parent that created the child.

The output from all the processes is intermingled as each one prints to the standard output. Each child process, however, does take some time to start up before it runs, which is why the output of the parent is printed and the parent exits before some of the children even start. Note also that the line that prints the "End..." is printed regardless of whether a parent or a child is running; because the child has all the same code as the parent when it runs, it will happily continue past the block that it's supposed to run and continue on.

Depending on your situation, you might not want any of this behavior. You might want the parent to exit only after the child is done, or the child to stop running when it's done with its specific block of code. Or you might want the parent to wait for one child to finish before you start up another child. All this involves process management, which we'll explore in the next section.

Process Management with `exit` and `wait` (and Sometimes `kill`)

Starting up a child process with `fork`, and then letting it run is kind of like letting an actual child of say, age 4, run wild in a public place. You'll get results, but they might not be exactly what you (or the people around you) want. That's what process control is for. Two functions, `exit` and `wait`, help you keep control of your processes.

Let's look at `exit` first. The `exit` function, most simply, stops running the current script at the point where it is called. It's sort of like the `die` function, in that respect, except that `die` exits with a failed status (on Unix) and prints an error message. `exit` simply ends the program with an option status argument (0 for success, 1 for failed).

Exit is most commonly used to stop a child from executing more of the parent's code than it's supposed to. Put an `exit` at the end of the block of the child's code, and the child will run only that far and then stop. So, for example, in the little `processes.pl` script we looked at in that last section, let's replace the call to `last` with a call to `exit`, like this:

```
...
} else {    #child
    print "Child $i: running\n";
    exit;
}
```

With this modification, the child will print its message, and then exit altogether. It won't restart the `foreach` loop, and it also won't ever print the "End…". The parent, which is executing the other branch of the `if`, executes the "End…" after the loop is complete. The output of this version of the script will look like this:

```
# procexit.pl
Parent: forked child 1 (11828)
Parent: forked child 2 (11829)
Parent: forked child 3 (11830)
End...
#
Child 1: running
Child 2: running
Child 3: running
```

As with the previous example, the output from the parent and the child is intermingled, and the parent completes before the children do.

For further control over when each child runs and when the parent exits, use the `wait` or `waitpid` functions. Both `wait` and `waitpid` do the same thing: they cause the current process (often the parent) to stop executing until the child is finished. This prevents mingling of the output, keeps the parent from exiting too soon and, in more complicated scripts than this one, prevents your script from leaving "zombie" processes (child processes that have finished executing but are still hanging around the system taking up processing space).

The difference in `wait` and `waitpid` is that `wait` takes no arguments, and waits for any child to return. If you spawn five processes, and then call `wait`, the `wait` will return a successful result when any of the five child processes exits. The `waitpid` function, on the other hand, takes a process ID argument, and waits for that specific child process to finish (remember, the parent gets the PID of the child as the return to the `fork` function).

Both wait and waitpid return the PID of the child that exited, or -1 if there are no child processes currently running.

Let's return once again to our process example, where we spawn three children in a foreach loop. For exit we changed the behavior of the children. Now let's change the behavior of the parent by adding a call to wait, and another message inside the parent part of the conditional:

```
if ($pid) { #parent
  print "Parent : forked child $i ($pid)\n";
  wait;
  print "Parent: child $i ($pid) complete\n";
} else { ....
```

In the parent code for the previous example, the parent simply printed the first message, and then the foreach loop would repeat, spawning three children in quick succession. In this version, the child is created, the parent prints the first message, and then waits for that child to complete. Then it prints the second message. Each turn of the loop occurs only after the current child is done and has exited. The output of this version of the script looks like this:

```
# procwait.pl
Parent : forked child 1 (11876)
Child 1: running
Parent: child 1 (11876) complete
Parent : forked child 2 (11877)
Child 2: running
Parent: child 2 (11877) complete
Parent : forked child 3 (11878)
Child 3: running
Parent: child 3 (11878) complete
End...
#
```

Note here that execution is very regular: each child is forked, runs, and exits before the next process starts. And the parent stays in execution until the third child is done, exiting only at the end.

The fact that this example runs each child serially, one after the other, makes it sort of silly to have processes at all (particularly given that each process takes time to start up and takes up extra processing space on your system). Because the wait function is so flexible, however, you don't have to wait for the most recently spawned child to finish before spawning another one—you could spawn five processes, and then later on in your script call wait five times to clean up all the processes. We'll look this later in this lesson when we explore a larger example.

There's one last function worth mentioning in reference to controlling processes: the kill function, which sends a kill signal to a process. To use kill, you'll need to know something about signals. For the sake of space I'm not going to talk about signals in this chapter, but see "Going Deeper" and the perlfunc man pages for a few pointers.

Running Something Else in a Process with exec

When you create a new process with `fork`, that process creates a clone of the current script and continues processing from there. Sometimes, however, when you create a new process, you want that process to stop what it's doing altogether and to run some other program instead. That's where `exec` comes in.

The `exec` function causes the current process to stop running the current script, and to run something else. The "something else" is usually some other program or script, given as the argument to `exec`, something like this:

```
exec("grep $who /etc/passwd");
```

The arguments to `exec` follow the same rules as with `system`; if you use a single string argument, Perl passes that argument to the shell first. With a list of arguments you can bypass the shell process. In fact, the similarities between `exec` and `system` are not coincidental—the `system` function is, actually, a `fork` and an `exec` put together.

When Perl encounters an `exec`, that's the end of that script. The `exec` shifts control to the new program being `exec`'ed; no other lines in the script will be executed.

Other Unix-Related Functions

In addition to the functions mentioned throughout this section, Perl's set of built-in functions includes a number of other process-related functions and smaller utility functions for getting information about various parts of the system. Because these functions apply specifically to Unix system files or features, most of these functions are not available on other systems (although the developers porting Perl to those systems might attempt to create rudimentary equivalents for the behavior of these functions).

Table 18.1 shows a summary of many of these functions. For more information on any of these, see Appendix A, "Perl Functions," or the `perlfunc` man page.

TABLE 18.1 Unix-Related Functions

Function	*What it Does*
`alarm`	Send a SIGALRM signal to a process
`chroot`	Change the root directory for the current process
`getgrent,`	Look up or set `setgrent`,values from `endgrent` /etc/groups
`getgrgid`	Look up a group file entry in /etc/groups
`getgrnam`	Look up a group file entry by name in /etc/groups
`getpgrp`	Get the process group name for a process
`getppid`	Get the process ID of the parent process (if the current script is running in a child process)

TABLE 18.1 continued

Function	*What it Does*
`getpriority`	Return the current priority for a process, process group, or user
`getpwent`, `setpwent`, `endpwent`	Look up or set values from /etc/passwd
`getpwnam`	Look up a user by name in /etc/passwd
`getpwuid`	Look up a user by user ID (UID) in /etc/passwd
`setpgrp`	Set the process group for a process

Perl for Windows

Perl for Windows supports most of the core set of Unix features, as well as a number of extensions for Win32 features. If you've installed the ActiveState version of Perl for Windows, you'll get the Win32 modules as part of that package. If you compile Perl for Windows yourself, you'll need to get the `libwin32` package yourself from CPAN (see `http://www.perl.com/CPAN-local/modules/by-module/Win32/` for the latest version). Otherwise, the functionality is the same.

Earlier versions of Perl for Windows were much less coordinated as far as which modules and features were available in which package. If you're using a version of Perl earlier than 5.6.1 (or ActiveState's Perl earlier than Build 631), you should upgrade to make sure you have the newest and best version.

Compatibility with Unix

With a few notable exceptions, most Unix-like Perl features will work on Windows, although how they are used is different. The biggest notable exception is `fork` and its related functions, which was not supported at all before version 5.6.1 of Perl. Version 5.6.1 provided a support for `fork` under Windows on an experimental basis. For more information, see the `perlfork` man page. You can run another program from inside a Perl script using `system`, `exec`, backquotes, of one of the Win 32 extensions (more about those later).

The `system` function, `exec`, and backquotes work on Perl for Windows. The "shell" for these commands is cmd.exe for Windows NT, or command.com for Windows 95. Commands and argument lists that you give to these commands must follow Windows conventions, including pathnames and file globbing.

Keep in mind, of course, that if you're porting a Unix script to Windows, and that Unix script uses Unix utilities in `system` or backquotes, that you'll need to find the Windows equivalents of those same utilities; simply having support for `system` and backquotes is not enough.

> The Cygwin project provides probably the most complete set of Unix tools for Windows. It includes Windows versions of most familiar shell commands, along with the bash shell itself. You can find out more about Cygwin, and download the installation program at `http://sources.redhat.com/cygwin/`.

Functions that relate to specific Unix features (such as those listed in Table 18.1) are unlikely to work on Perl for Windows. Other functions that do not work are specialized functions I haven't bothered to mention in this book relate to interprocess communication or low-level networking. In general, most of the common Perl functions you'll use will be available in Perl for Windows. You can find a complete list of unimplemented functions in the FAQ for Perl for Win32 at `http://aspn.activestate.com/ASPN/Reference/Products/ActivePerl/faq/Windows/ActivePerl-Winfaq5.html` (look in the section on "Implementation Quirks").

Built-in Win32 Subroutines

The extensions to Perl for managing Windows features come in two parts: a set of built-in Win32 subroutines, and a number of additional Win32 modules for more sophisticated techniques (such as `Win32::Registry` or `Win32::Process`). The Win32 subroutines provide easy access to system information, as well as a number of smaller utility routines. If you are running Perl for Windows, you don't need to import any of the Win32 modules to use these subroutines. Table 18.2 contains a list of several of the Win32 subroutines available in Perl for Windows.

For more information on any of these subroutines, you might want to check the Win32 man page. I also found Philippe Le Berre's pages at `http://www.le-berre.com/` to be especially helpful.

TABLE 18.2 Built-in Win32 Subroutines

Subroutine	*What it Does*
`Win32::DomainName`	Returns the Microsoft Network domain.
`Win32::FormatMessage`	Takes the error returned by `GetLastError` *`errorcode`* and turns it into a descriptive string.
`Win32::FsType`	The filesystem type (FAT or NTFS).

TABLE 18.2 continued

Subroutine	*What it Does*
`Win32::GetCwd`	Gets the current directory.
`Win32::GetLastError`	If the last Win32 subroutine failed, this subroutine will give you the reason why (format the result of this with `FormatMessage`).
`Win32::GetNextAvailDrive`	Gets the drive letter of the next available drive, for example, "E:".
`Win32::GetOSVersion`	Returns an array representing the OS version and number: (`$string`, `$major`, `$minor`, `$build`, `$id`), where the `$string` is an arbitrary string, `$major` and `$minor` are version numbers, `$build` is the build number, and `$is` is 0 for a generic Win32, 1 for Windows 95, or 2 for Windows NT.
`Win32::GetShortPathName`	Given a long filename ("thisisareallylongfilename.textfile"), returns the 8.3 version (THISI~1.TXT).
`Win32::GetTickCount`	The number of ticks (milliseconds) that have elapsed since Windows was started.
`Win32::IsWin95`	True if you're on Windows 95.
`Win32::IsWinNT`	True if you're on Windows NT.
`Win32::LoginName`	The username of the user running the script.
`Win32::NodeName`	The Microsoft Network node name for the current machine.
`Win32::SetCwd` *`newdir`*	Changes the current directory.
`Win32::Sleep milliseconds`	Sleep for the given number of milliseconds.
`Win32::Spawn`	Spawn a new process (see the following section, "Win32 Processes").

18

`Win32::MsgBox`

The basic Win32 subroutines give you access to basic Windows features and system information from inside Perl. Installing the libwin32 modules (or using ActiveState's version of Perl for Windows) gives you access to the Win32 modules, with which you can access a lot more of the advanced Windows features. One nifty feature in the Win32 modules is the `Win32::MsgBox` subroutine, which can be used to pop-up rudimentary modal dialog boxes from inside your Perl scripts. `Win32::MsgBox` takes up to three arguments: the text to put in the dialog itself, a code representing the icon in the dialog and some combination of buttons, and the test to put in the title bar of the dialog. For example, the following code will show the dialog on the left side of Figure 18.1:

```
Win32::MsgBox("I can't do that!");
```

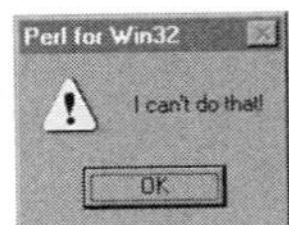

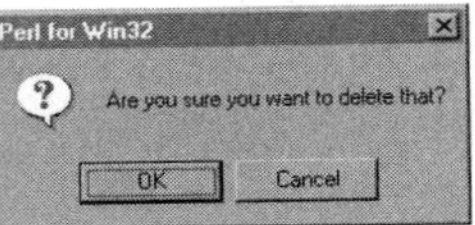

FIGURE 18.1
Dialogs.

This one shows a dialog with two buttons, OK and Cancel, and a Question icon (as shown on the right side of Figure 18.1):

```
Win32::MsgBox("Are you sure you want to delete that?", 33);
```

The second argument represents the codes for the number of buttons and the type of icon. Table 18.3 shows the choices for number of buttons.

TABLE 18.3 Button Codes

Code	*Result*
0	OK
1	OK and Cancel
2	Abort, Retry, Ignore
3	Yes, No, and Cancel
4	Yes and No
5	Retry and Cancel

Table 18.4 shows the choices for the icon.

TABLE 18.4 Icon Codes

Code	*Result*
16	Hand
32	Question (?)
48	Exclamation point (!)
64	Asterisk (*)

To get the second argument for `Win32::MsgBox`, just pick a choice from each table and add the numbers together. So an exclamation icon (48) with Yes and No buttons (4) would result in a code of 52.

The return value of `Win32::MsgBox` is based on the buttons you used in the dialog and what the user actually clicked. Table 18.5 shows the possible return values.

TABLE 18.5 Button Codes

Code	*Button Clicked*
1	OK
2	Cancel
3	Abort
4	Retry
5	Ignore
6	Yes
7	No

Win32 Processes

If you don't feel comfortable using the experimental version of the `fork` subroutine for Windows provided in Perl 5.6.1, or you're using an earlier version of Perl, you won't be able to write programs that fork new processes while running. However, you can start new processes that run separate programs (the equivalent for a `fork` followed by an `exec`). The easiest way to do this is to use either `system` or backquotes, or to halt the current script with an `exec`. An alternative way is the use either `Win32::Spawn` or the `Win32::Process` module.

`Win32::Spawn` is part of the basic Win32 subroutines, and enables you to start up another process in a really simple way. The `Win32::Process` module, on the other hand, is more recent, more robust, uses proper module conventions, but is somewhat more difficult to understand.

To create a new process with `Win32::Spawn`, you'll need three arguments: the full pathname to the command to run in the new process, the arguments to that command (including the command name again), and a variable to hold the process ID of the new process. Here's an example that starts up Notepad on Windows NT with a temporary file in `"C:\tempfile.txt"`. It also traps errors:

```
my $command = "c:\\windows\\notepad.exe ";
my $args = "notepad.exe c:\\tempfile";
my $pid = 0;

Win32::Spawn($command, $args, $pid) || &error();
print "Spawned!  The new PID is $pid.";

sub error {
    my $errmsg = Win32::FormatMessage(Win32::GetLastError());
    die "Error: $errmsg\n";
}
```

One annoying side effect of `Win32::Spawn` is that the new process—in this case, Notepad—comes up minimized, so it appears as if nothing is happening. The original Perl script also continues executing (or, in this case, finishes executing) as the new process is running.

The `Win32::Process` module handles processes in a much more sensible way. However, it's more complex, and it's set up to be object oriented, which means some slightly different syntax (but you learned the basics on Day 13, "Scope, Modules, and Importing Code," so you should be okay).

Creating a `Win32::Process` object is vaguely similar to using `Win32::Spawn`. You'll still need a command and a list or arguments, but you'll also need some other stuff. To create a `Win32::Process` object, first make sure you import `Win32::Process`:

```
use Win32::Process;
```

Then call the `Create` method to create your new process object (you'll need a variable to hold it):

```
#!c:/perl/bin/perl

my $command = "c:\\windows\\notepad.exe ";
my $args = "notepad.exe c:\\tempfile";
my $proc; # process object

Win32::Process::Create($process,
     $command,
     $args,
     0,
     DETACHED_PROCESS,
     '.') || die &error();
```

(I've left off the definition for the error subroutine here to save space.)

The arguments to `Win32::Process` are

- A variable to hold a reference to the new process object.
- The command to run.
- The arguments to that command.
- Whether handles are inherited (if you don't know what that means, just use 0).
- One of several options. DETACHED_PROCESS is the most popular, although CREATE_NEW_CONSOLE might also be useful. All the options are listed in the `Win32::Process` man page.
- The temporary directory for this process.

In this case, when the new process is created, Notepad will start up maximized and edit the file in C:\tempfile. But the original Perl script will still continue executing.

To make the parent process wait for the child to finish executing, use the `Wait` method (note the capital W; this isn't the same as Perl's `wait` function). You'll have to call this as an object-oriented method, with the process object first:

```
$proc->Wait(INFINITE);
```

In this case, the parent process will wait indefinitely until the child finishes. You can also give `Wait` an argument of some number of milliseconds to wait before continuing.

In addition to `Wait`, the `Win32::Process` module also includes these methods:

- `Kill`, to kill the new process
- `Suspend`, to temporarily stop the process
- `Resume`, to start a suspended process
- `GetPriorityClass` and `SetPriorityClass`, to look up or change the process's priority
- `GetExitCode`, to find out why a process exited

You can get more information about `Win32::Process` from the documentation that comes with the Win32 modules, or from the online documentation at `http://aspn.activestate.com/ASPN/Reference/`.

Working with the Win32 Registry

The Windows Registry is a warehouse of information about your system, its configuration, and the programs installed on it. The `Win32::Registry` module, an object-oriented module, allows you to read from, modify, and add values to the Windows Registry from inside a Perl script.

> If you're unfamiliar with the Windows Registry, chances are good you should not be playing with it from inside Perl. You can make your system unusable by messing with the Registry and changing things that are not intended to be changed. You can use the Windows program `regedit` to examine and modify the Windows Registry.

The Windows Registry consists of a number of trees of keys and values. At the topmost level, the Registry contains several subtrees, including HKEY_LOCAL_MACHINE for information about the configuration of the local machine, or HKEY_CURRENT_USER for information about the currently logged-in user. Depending on whether you're running Windows NT or Windows 95, you'll have a different set of subtrees. Inside each subtree are a number of sets of keys and values, like hashes, only nested (a key can map to a whole other hash tree).

When you import the `Win32::Registry` module (with use `Win32::Registry`), you get a registry key object for each of the topmost subtrees, for example $HEKY_LOCAL_MACHINE. Using the various `Win32::Registry` methods, you can open, traverse, and manage any part of the Windows Registry.

Unfortunately, to get the most use out of the `Win32::Registry` module, you need to know something of references to handle the nested-hash nature of the Registry keys. For now, then, Table 18.6 shows several of the `Win32::Registry` methods and their arguments; after going on to the lesson on references these will be more meaningful.

To start working with any part of the Registry, you must first use `Open` with of the major subkey objects, like this (don't forget to use `Win32::Registry` at the top of your script):

```
use Win32::Registry;
my $reg = "SOFTWARE";
my ($regobj, @keys);
$HKEY_LOCAL_MACHINE->Open($reg,$regobj)|| die "Can't open registry\n";
```

Then, you can call the various Registry methods on that new Registry object:

```
$regobj->GetKeys(\@keys);
$regobj->Close();
```

TABLE 18.6 `Win32::Registry` Methods

Method	*What it Does*
`Close`	Closes the currently open key.
`Create` *`keyname,keyref`*	Creates a new key with the name *keyname*. *keyref* will contain a reference to the new key.
`DeleteKey` *`keyname`*	Deletes the key *keyname.*
`DeleteValue` *`valname`*	Deletes the value *valname.*
`GetKeys` *`listref`*	Returns a list of the keys in the current key. *listref* is a reference to a list.
`GetValues` *`hashref`*	Returns a hash of the keys and values in the current key. The keys in this hash are nested lists. *hashref* is a reference to a hash.
`Open` *`obj, objref`*	Opens a key. *obj* is the key to open, *objref* is a reference to the object that will hold that key.
`Save` *`filename`*	Saves the currently open key to *filename*
`SetValue`	Change the value of *keyname* to *value*.
`keyname``,REG_SZ,`*`value`*	The second argument must be REG_SZ.
`Load` *`keyname, filename`*	Imports the keys and values in *filename* into *keyname.*

For more information on `Win32::Registry`, the documentation that comes with the Win32 modules is helpful. You might also want to check out Phillipe Le Berre's How To Guide at `http://www.le-berre.com/perl/main.htm`, which has lots of examples and notes on using `Win32::Registry`.

Other Win32 Modules

The Win32 modules, shipped with Active State's Perl and gathered in the `libwin32` bundle, contain lots and lots of modules for handling various aspects of Windows operations—by only describing `Win32::Process` and `Win32::Registry` I've only touched the surface. And in addition to those "standard" Win32 modules, more and more is being written and included on CPAN. If you do lots of work with Windows, and intend to do more work with Perl on that platform, look into these modules for many more features to work with. Table 18.7 contains a summary of the standard Win32 modules; see CPAN for even more.

TABLE 18.7 Win32 Modules

Module	*What it Does*
`Win32::AuthenticateUser`	Enables you to authenticate Windows users using domains.
`Win32::ChangeNotify`	Provides access to Windows change-notification objects.
`Win32::Clipboard`	Enables you to interact with the Windows clipboard.
`Win32::Console`	Functions for Windows console and character mode.
`Win32::Event`	Provides access to Win32 event objects.
`Win32::EventLog`	Provides access to the Windows event log.
`Win32::File`	Manages file attributes.
`Win32::FileSecurity`	Manages NTFS file security.
`Win32::Internet`	Wrapper for WININET.DLL.
`Win32::IPC`	Inter-Process Communication: allows you to synchronize and communicate between Process, ChangeNotify, Semaphore, and Mutex.
`Win32::Mutex`	Provides access to Windows Mutex objects.
`Win32::NetAdmin`	Administers users and groups (Windows NT only).
`Win32::NetResource`	Administers system resources (printers, servers, and so on) (Windows NT only).
`Win32::ODBC`	Provides access to ODBC databases from Perl.
`Win32::OLE`	Provides access to OLE automation.

TABLE 18.7 continued

`Win32::PerfLib`	Provides access to the Windows Performance Counter.
`Win32::Pipe`	Enables you to use named pipes from Perl.
`Win32::Process`	Creates and manages Windows processes
`Win32::Registry`	Works with the Windows registry.
`Win32::Semaphore`	Provides access to Windows Semaphore objects.
`Win32::Service`	Enables you to administer services.
`Win32::Sound`	Provides access to Windows sounds.
`Win32::TieRegistry`	Enables you to access the registry via tied hashes.

Going Deeper

Whole books have been written on using the various platform-specific bits of Perl (or for avoiding them). To keep this chapter to the minimum, I've skipped over a number of features that you might want to explore on your own when you're done with this book.

Pipes

Probably the biggest feature that was not talked about in this book is the use of pipes. A pipe is sort of a channel from which you can read data, and to which you can send data. The pipe can connect to the standard input and output of your script and some other program, or it can also connect to a device such as a printer, or a network connection such as a socket.

On Unix, you can open a pipe as if it were just another file handle, and read and write to it that way. The pipe can be to another program, or to another process running the same program. You can also use named pipes that might exist on your system. The `perlipc` man page contains more information about using pipes.

On Windows, you can use regular pipes with `open` as on Unix to other processes running on the system. For named pipes, look for the `Win32::Pipe` module.

Signals

Signals are a Unix feature that let you trap various errors and messages and handle them in some sensible way. The `%SIG` hash contains references to various signal handlers. Signals only work in Unix; see the `perlipc` man page for more information.

Basic Networking

The Unix version of Perl has a number of built-in functions for handling low-level networking commands and sockets. Most of these functions are unsupported on other platforms, superseded by various platform-specific networking modules. If you're a real network fiend, feel free to visit the `perlipc` man page for plenty of information on sockets and network programming.

If you just want to, say, retrieve a Web page from the Internet, there are modules that will do that for you without you needing to know anything about what a TCP is. I'll discuss those on Day 20, "Odds and Ends."

Creating User Interfaces with Perl

Creating a graphical user interface (GUI) in Perl isn't easy, and it's not very cross-platform. But it is possible.

One of the best ways to create GUIs in Perl is with the Tk package. Tk is a simple way of creating and managing user interface widgets, originally associated with the TCL language, but now available for Perl as well. Tk is available for both Unix and Windows, and has a platform-specific look for each one. Perl/Tk has an FAQ at `http://www.faqs.org/faqs/by-newsgroup/comp/comp.lang.perl.tk.html`.

The `Win32::OLE` module can enable you to create interfaces in Visual Basic, and then control them with OLE automation. See `Win32::OLE`.

Summary

Someday, Perl will be a seamless cross-platform language in which you can write a script to do just about anything, and it will work on any platform with a Perl environment. That day isn't here yet. And some would argue that the goal of total cross-platform compatibility isn't all that great an idea when there are so many differences between platforms and so many cool platform-specific things to play with.

Today, we stopped looking at Perl as a language that works exactly the same across platforms and explored a few of the differences, including environment variables, running programs, and forking processes on Unix, and creating and working with processes and the Registry on Windows. Along the way, I pointed out differences between the ports and other dark corners of each port to explore.

Q&A

Q. I have a script that calls several programs via `system`. I want to run this script via Unix `cron` job. It runs fine when I run it on the command line, but when I install it I get errors that such-and-such command cannot be found. What's going on here?

A. Probably an execution path problem. Remember that each Perl script inherits the execution path (that is, the `PATH` environment variable) from the shell or user ID that is currently running the script. When a script is intended to be run by some other process—for example, a CGI script or a cron job—it gets a different or limited execution path than what you expect. In this case, the cron user ID probably has a very limited execution path, and the system function cannot find the programs it needs. To avoid this problem, you can always use full pathnames to all executable programs you call from `system`, or you could set the PATH variable yourself inside the Perl script through the `%ENV` hash.

Q. I have a script that forks multiple processes. I have a single global variable and I want to be able to increment that variable globally across all the child processes. This isn't working. Why?

A. All processes created with `fork` are totally independent of all the other processes. That includes all the variables defined by the parent; the child gets a copy of all those variables, and has no access back to the parent's version.

To communicate between processes, you'll have to set up a mechanism for inter-process communication (IPC). See "Going Deeper" for some suggestions on IPC.

Q. When I fork child processes, the output from the children is all mixed up with the output from the parent. How can I separate them?

A. You can't. There's only one standard output, and that output is shared between all the children. If you absolutely have to have separate output from each process, you could do something like store each process's output to a temporary file, and then print each file in turn.

Q. I have a Perl script that was written on Unix. It uses `system` and the Unix program `sendmail` all over the place. How can I adapt this program for other systems?

A. Sending mail is awfully convenient on Unix; just call the mail program and ship off the message. Unfortunately, it's not that easy on other platforms. If you're on Windows, the Perl for Win32 FAQ lists alternative methods for sending mail. Alternately, the `Net::SMTP` (at CPAN) package might also provide some help in getting mail to work across platforms.

Q. I want to be able to find out what platform I'm on, so I can be sure my script will only run on one platform.

A. The `Config` module can help you with that. The `'osname'` key in the `%Config` hash contains the platform you're running on. So, for example, to make sure you're running on Windows, you could use something like this:

```
use Config;
if ( $Config{'osname'} !~ /Win/i ) {
  die "Hey!  This is a Win32 script.  You can't run it here.\n";
}
```

Workshop

The workshop provides quiz questions to help you solidify your understanding of the material covered and exercises to give you experience in using what you've learned. Try to understand the quiz and exercise answers before you go on to tomorrow's lesson.

Quiz

1. What is `%ENV` used for? Why is it useful?
2. What's the difference between using `system` and backquotes?
3. Why would you want to use multiple processes in your Perl script?
4. What does `fork` do?
5. What's the difference between `system` and `exec`?
6. Can Win32 processes be used interchangeably with `fork`?

Exercises

1. (Unix only) Create a script that takes a single number as an argument. `Fork` that number of child processes, and make sure the parent waits for each to finish. Each process should:
    - Generate a random number between 1 and 100,000.
    - Sum all the numbers between 1 and that random number.
    - Print the result.
2. (Unix only) Modify the `img.pl` script from Day 10 (the one that printed information about the images in an HTML file) such that the output is e-mailed to you instead of displayed on the screen. HINT: this command will send a message:

    ```
    mail yourmail@yoursite.com < bodyofmessage
    ```
3. (Windows only) Create a script that takes a directory listing (using the `dir` command) and prints only the filenames, one per line (you don't have to sort them).

Answers

Here are the answers to the Workshop questions in the previous section.

Quiz Answers

1. The `%ENV` hash holds the variable names and values for the script's environment. On Unix and Windows, the values in this hash can be useful for finding out information about the system environment (or for changing it and passing it on to other processes). On the Mac `%ENV` doesn't serve any useful purpose.
2. The `system` command runs some other program or script from inside your Perl script and sends the output to the standard output. Backquotes also run an external program, but they capture the input to a scalar or list value (depending on context).
3. Multiple processes are useful for portioning different parts of your script that might need to be run simultaneously, or for splitting up the work your script needs to do.
4. The `fork` function creates a new process, a clone of the original process. Both the new processes continue executing the script at the point where the `fork` occurred.
5. `system` and `exec` are closely related; both are used to execute an external program. The difference is that `system` does a `fork` first; `exec` stops running the current script in the current process and runs the external program instead.
6. `Win32::Process` and `fork` are not interchangeable. The `fork` function ties very strongly to processes on Unix; `Win32::Process` is more analogous to a `fork` followed immediately to an `exec`.

Exercise Answers

1. Here's one answer:

```
#!/usr/local/bin/perl -w
use strict;

if (@ARGV > 1) {
    die "Only one argument, please.\n";
}
 elsif ($ARGV[0] !~ /^\d+/) {
    die "Argument should be a number.\n";
}

my $pid;
my $procs = pop;

foreach my $i (1..$procs) {
    if (defined($pid = fork)) {
        if ($pid) { #parent
            print "Parent: forked child $i\n";
        } else {    #child
```

```
                srand;
                my $top = int(rand 100000);
                my $sum;
                for (1..$top) {
                    $sum += $_;
                }
                print "Finished child $i:  Sum of $top is $sum\n";
                exit;
            }
        }
}

while ($procs > 0) {
    wait;
    $procs--;
}
```

2. All you need are three changes. First, create and open a temporary file:

```
my $tmp = "tempfile.$$";                # temporary file;
open(TMP, ">$tmp") || die "Can't open temporary file $tmp\n";
```

Second, make sure all print statements write to that file:

```
if (exists($atts{$key})) {
   $atts{$key} =~ s/[\s]*\n/ /g;
   print TMP "   $key: $atts{$key}\n";
}
```

Finally, use `system` to mail the temporary file and remove it:

```
close TMP;
my $me = "youremail@yoursite.com";
system("mail $me <$tmp");
unlink $tmp
```

3. Here's one way to do it (start the `substr` function from character 44 if you're on Windows 95):

```
#!c:/perl/bin/perl -w
use strict;

my @list = `dir`;

foreach (@list) {
   if (/^\w/) {
      print substr($_,39);
   }
}
```

18

DAY 19

Working with References

For the last several chapters, we've been looking at a number of aspects of Perl that you might consider auxiliary to the core language itself. For instance, working with various functions in the standard library for managing filesystems or processes, importing code from modules, and then using those modules to accomplish various tasks, or working with the Perl debugger. Today, as we reach the final few lessons in this book, we'll return to the core language with a discussion of references. References are a way of indirectly pointing to other bits of data in Perl. They allow you to manage data in more advanced and often more efficient ways than handling the data itself. In today's lesson, we'll explore these topics:

- What references are, and the advantages they give you
- Creating and using references to scalars, arrays, and hashes
- Using references in subroutines for arguments and return values
- Creating nested data structures (multidimensional arrays, arrays of hashes, and so on)
- Clever ways to avoid using references

What Is a Reference?

A *reference* is a form of data in Perl that indirectly points to some other bit of data. The reference itself is a scalar, like a number or string—it can be assigned to a scalar variable, printed, added to, tested to see if it's true or false, stored in a list, or passed to a subroutine, just as numbers and strings can. In addition to its scalar-like behavior, however, the reference also refers, or points to, the location of some other bit of data. To find out what the reference points to, you *dereference* the reference—fancy terminology for essentially following the pointer to the thing it points to.

If you actually want more fancy terminology in your life, the thing the reference points to is called the *referent*. You dereference the reference to get to the referent. Me, I prefer regular words like "the thing it points to."

References in Perl are similar to pointers or references in other languages, and have the same advantages. But, if you're not used to other languages, you might wonder, "What's the point? Why would you want to deal with a reference when you could deal with the data itself?" The answer is that by indirectly referring to data, you can do more advanced things with that data—for example, pass large amounts of data by reference into and out of subroutines, or create multidimensional arrays. References also allow more advanced uses of data, including creating object-oriented structures in Perl. We'll look at a number of these uses as the lesson progresses.

There's one other technical point to make before we move on to actual code. What I'm referring to in this chapter as references are known in technical Perl circles as *hard* references. Perl also has another form of reference called a *symbolic reference*. Although there are perfectly good reasons for using symbolic references, hard references are more useful in general, so for the bulk of this chapter we'll stick to those. I'll talk more about symbolic references in "Going Deeper" at the end of this lesson.

The Basics: A General Overview of How to Use References

Let's look at a few simple examples of creating and using references so you can get a feel for the technique. Perl actually has a number of ways of working with references, but here we'll focus on the easiest and most popular mechanisms, and explore the others in a later section ("Other Ways of Using References").

Creating a Reference

Start with something you've seen a gazillion times before in this book: A plain old scalar variable that contains a string.

```
$str = "This is a string."
```

This is an ordinary scalar variable, holding ordinary scalar data. There's some location in memory that stores that string, which you can get to through the `$str` variable name. If you assigned something else to `$str`, the memory location would have different contents and there would be a different value for `$str`. All this is the basic stuff you've been doing all along.

Now let's create a reference to that data. To create a reference, you need the actual memory location of the data in question (a scalar, an array, a hash, or a subroutine). To get at that memory location, you use the backslash (\) operator and a variable name:

```
$strref = \$str;
```

The backslash operator gets the memory location of the data stored in `$str` and creates a reference to that location. That reference then gets assigned to the scalar variable `$strref` (remember, references are a form of scalar data).

Note

> The backslash operator is very similar to the address (&) operator in C. Both are used to access the actual memory location of a piece of data.

19

At no point here do the actual contents of `$str`—the string "This is a string."—come into play. The reference doesn't care about the contents of `$str`, just its location. And `$str` remains a scalar variable containing a string; the reference's existence doesn't change anything about that either. (See Figure 19.1.)

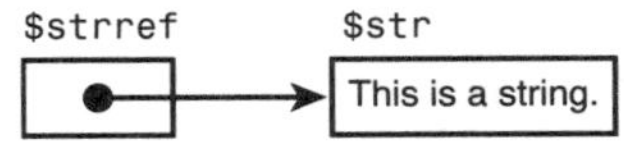

FIGURE 19.1
A variable, a string, and a reference.

This example created a reference to a string. But you can also create references to arrays, hashes, or subroutines—anything that has a memory location in Perl. For example, here's a reference to an array:

```
@array = (1..10);
$arrayref = \@array;
```

And here's one for a hash:

```
%hash = (
   'red' => '0 0 255',
   'green' => '0 255 0',
   'blue' => '255 0 0; );
$hashref = \%hash;
```

As with the reference to a scalar value, the array and hash in these examples remain arrays and hashes stored in the `@array` and `%hash` variables, respectively. And the array and hash references in `$arrayref` and `$hashref` are bits of scalar data, regardless of the data they point to. The most important thing to remember here is that the reference itself is a scalar. The thing it points to can be any kind of data.

You can also create references to subroutines. Because this is an advanced topic, and not as commonly used as references to scalars, arrays, and hashes, we'll look at references to subroutines and how they're used in this lesson's "Going Deeper" section.

Printing and Using References

So now you've created a reference with the backslash operator and stored it in a scalar variable. What do these references look like? They're scalars, and as such can be used anywhere a scalar can, and as with numbers and strings they behave differently based on context.

A reference used as a string indicates the data it refers to (a scalar, an array, a hash, and so on), and a hexadecimal number representing the internal memory location the reference points to. So, for example, if you did this:

```
print "$strref\n";
```

You'd get something like this:

```
SCALAR(0x807f61c)
```

The equivalent for `$arrayref` and `$hashref` would look like this:

```
ARRAY(0x807f664)
```

```
HASH(0x807f645)
```

Using a reference in a numeric context gives you the same hexadecimal number that you get when you use the reference in a string context, representing the memory location of the thing the reference points to. The numbers in both the string and number representations of the reference will vary depending on when you run the script and the memory that's free for Perl to use at that time. You wouldn't want to rely on those numbers; just consider that to be an internal representation of where the reference points.

Other uses of references? You can assign them to scalar variables, as we have here, use them as list elements, or store them in arrays and hashes (although they cannot be used as hash keys—more about this later). A reference, when used as a test, will always be true. But the most typical thing you do with references is to dereference them to gain access to the data they point to.

Dereferencing References

When you dereference a reference, you get at the data that reference points to. You could also think of it as following the reference, or accessing the location the reference refers to. But the term *dereference* is what is most commonly used.

There are a number of ways to dereference a reference, but the easiest way is to substitute the reference's scalar variable where a plain variable name would be expected, like this:

```
$originalstr = $$strref;
```

Two dollar signs? Yes. A single dollar sign is just the scalar variable `$strref`, which gives you the reference itself. The double dollar sign says "give me the thing that `$strref` points to." In this case, the thing that `$strref` points to was the original string "This is a string." You could think of two dollar signs as putting the reference—`$strref`–in place of the actual name of the variable you want to access.

To follow an array reference and gain access to the array itself, you'd do the same thing with an `@` sign instead, and the `$arrayref` goes where the name of the array would be

```
@firstlist = @$arrayref;
```

The contents of `@firstlist` will now be that initial array we created and that `$arrayref` pointed to (actually, it'll be a copy of all the elements of that array).

Need to gain access to an actual array element from a reference? No problem. It's the same rule, just put the variable holding the reference where the name of the array would be

```
$first = $$arrayref[0];
```

Same rule for getting the topmost index number of an array:

```
$index = $#$arrayref;
```

Hashes work similarly:

```
%newhash = %$hashref;  # copy what $hashref points to
```

```
$value = $$hashref{red};  # get the value for the key "red"

@keys = keys %$hashref;   # extract keys
```

Changing Referenced-To Data

Here's the tricky part of references: changing the data that the reference points to. Say you've got your `$strref` as before, but then you change the value of `$str` later:

```
$str = "This is a string."
$strref = \$str;
...
$str = "This is a different string."
```

What happens to the reference `$strref`? It continues to exist. It continues to point to that same memory location named by `$str`. If you dereference it, you'll now get the new string:

```
print "$$strref\n";   # results in "This is a different string."
```

The reference itself doesn't care about the contents of the thing it points to, just the location. You can merrily change the contents all you want—the reference will just keep pointing to that same spot. Each time you dereference it, you'll get the thing contained at that location.

Note that this is different from regular variable assignment, which copies the contents of one memory location to another. References always continue to point to the same locations, and the contents can be changed out from under that reference. Take, for example, these statements:

```
@array1 = qw(ready set go);
@array2 = @array1;
$arrayref = \@array1;
push @array1, "stop";

$, = ' ';  # set the array element delimeter
print "@array1\n";
print "@array2\n";
print "@$arrayref\n";
```

Can you guess what will get printed in each of the three print statements? The contents of `@array1` were created in the first statement, and then changed in the fourth, so the printout of `@array1` will be this:

```
ready set go stop
```

`@array2` was assigned to the contents of `@array1` in the second line. With list assignment, the array on the right is expanded into its component elements, and then those elements are assigned to the array on the left. So, `@array2` gets a copy of `@array1` at that time and will print like this:

```
ready set go
```

Modifying `@array2` has no effect on `@array1`; they are now separate arrays with separate contents.

The reference to `@array1` in `$arrayref`, however, will be the same as the current contents of `@array1` because the reference points to the same memory location as `@array1` does. Printing that dereference, then, will result in this:

```
ready set go stop
```

Using References with Subroutine Arguments and Return Values

So far, you've got a basic idea of how references work. There's still lots more detail to explain about creating and using references, but let's stop for a moment and do something practical. On Day 11, "Creating and Using Subroutines," when we talked about subroutines, I mentioned that lists and subroutines tend to be somewhat awkward without references. Let's revisit that topic and explore how references can make subroutine list arguments and return values much easier to manage.

Subroutine Arguments

As you already know, Perl has a very basic capability to pass arguments into and out of subroutines. All list arguments into a subroutine are flattened into a single list and stored in `@_`. Return values, as well, are returned as a single scalar or flattened list of scalars. Although this makes simple arguments easy to process, subroutines that take several lists as arguments can become problematic, as those lists lose their identities on their way into the subroutine. As noted on Day 11, you can work around this limitation in a variety of ways, including storing lists in global array or hash variables (avoiding argument passing altogether), or passing along information about the lists themselves (such as the length) as an argument, which allows you to reconstruct the list inside the subroutine itself.

19

The most sensible way—and often the most efficient—to get around Perl's list-flattening behavior with subroutines is to avoid passing actual list contents into subroutines altogether. Pass in references instead, and then dereference the references inside the subroutine to get at the contents of those lists.

Here's an example, borrowed from an earlier exercise, of a subroutine that takes two arrays as arguments and returns a list of all the elements that are common between them (the intersection of the two arrays). The length of the first array is passed in as the first argument, so we can reconstruct the two arrays inside the subroutine. Here we do it with a call to `splice` (remember that `shift` inside a subroutine, with no arguments, shifts `@_`):

```
sub inter {
  my @first = splice(@_,0,shift);
  my @final = ();
  my ($el, $el2);

  foreach $el (@first) {
      foreach $el2 (@_) {
          if (defined $el2 && $el eq $el2) {
              push @final,$el2;
              undef $el2;
              last;
          }
      }
  }
  return @final;
}
```

We'd call this subroutine with a length and two arrays as arguments:

```
@one = (1..10);
@two = (8..15);
@three = inter(scalar(@one),@one,@two);
```

You could argue that this example isn't too awful; it's only two arrays, after all, and a splice takes care of splitting up the elements. But what if you had more than two arrays as arguments? That would be a lot of splitting. And if any of the arrays were particularly huge, that would mean a lot of copying elements before you even started actually processing any elements. Not very efficient.

Let's rewrite that subroutine to use references. Instead of passing the actual arrays into the subroutine, pass references to those arrays. Then assign those references to variables inside the subroutine and dereference them to get the contents. Our new subroutine might look like this:

```
sub inter {
    my ($first, $second) = @_;
    my @final = ();
    my ($el, $el2);

    foreach $el (@$first) {
        foreach $el2 (@$second) {
            if (defined $el2 && $el eq $el2) {
                push @final,$el2;
                undef $el2;
                last;
            }
        }
    }
    return @final;
}
```

You'd call this subroutine with only two arguments, two references to arrays:

```
@one = (1..10);
$oneref = \@one;
@two = (8..14);
$tworef = \@two;
@three =  inter($oneref,$tworef);
```

There are only two differences between this subroutine and the one before it: The first line that manages the argument list (line 2), and the references to the lists inside both nested `foreach` loops (lines 6 and 7). In the reference version, we don't need to splice elements from a single argument list; the argument list only has two elements: the two scalar references. So we can replace the splice with an ordinary scalar assignment to two local variables.

With the references in hand, we move on to the `foreach` loops that test each element. Here, we don't have local arrays at all, all we have are references. To get at the array contents, we dereference the references using `@$first` and `@$second`, and access the array contents from there.

With this subroutine, each array retains its original contents and makeup. If you pass in references to hashes, those hashes remain hashes and are not flattened into lists. And there's also no copying of the list data from one place to another as there is with passing regular lists. It's more efficient and it's often easier to manage and to understand, particularly with subroutines with complex arguments.

Passing References Back from Subroutines

The converse of passing lists to subroutines is returning lists back from subroutines using the `return` operator. By default, `return` can return either a single scalar or a list, and will flatten multiple lists into a single list.

To return multiple items from a subroutine, and keep the integrity of lists and hashes, simply return references to those structures instead of the contents themselves, just as you did with passing list data into the subroutine:

```
sub foo {
   my @templist;
   my %temphash;
   ...

   my $tempref = \@templist;
   my $temphashref = \%temphash;
   return ($tempref, $temphashref);
}
```

This might initially seem wrong, given that the variables in this example, `@templist` and `%temphash`, are local variables, and will vanish after the subroutine is done executing. If the variables go away, what do the references have left to point to? The secret here is that even though the variable *name* goes away when it goes out of scope (when the subroutine finishes executing), the data it contained still exists, and the reference continues to point to it. In fact, dereferencing that reference will now be the *only* way to continue to get access to that data. This behavior affects how Perl stores and reclaims memory while your script is running; we'll look at that notion in the section "A Note About Memory and Garbage Collection."

An Example

Here's an example that illustrates how useful references can be in dealing with lists that are passed to subroutines as arguments and returned by subroutines. The program is basically a shell for a subroutine that accepts an arbitrary number of lists, sorts them numerically, and returns all the sorted lists. It also provides a sneak preview of a topic that will be discussed later in this chapter—nested data structures. The source code for the program is in Listing 19.1.

LISTING 19.1 The Source Code for `args.pl`

```
#!/usr/ bin/perl

my @one = (55, 11, 33, 22, 44);
my @two = (8, 4, 7, 3, 1);
my @three = (100, 700, 200);

my @sorted_arrays = sort_arrays(\@one, \@two, \@three);

foreach my $ref (@sorted_arrays)
{
    foreach my $num (@$ref)
    {
        print $num, " ";
    }
    print "\n";
}

sub sort_arrays
{
    my @new_arrays = ();

    foreach my $ref (@_)
    {
```

LISTING 19.1 continued

```
        my @sorted = sort {$a <=> $b} @$ref;
        push @new_arrays, \@sorted;
    }

    return @new_arrays;
}
```

Three arrays were created on lines three through five, all of which will be passed to the subroutine at the same time. They each contain lists of numbers, which will be sorted by the subroutine. On line seven the subroutine is called `sort_arrays`, and the results are assigned to the variable `@sorted_arrays`. The subroutine returns a list of references to the newly sorted arrays, and accepts a list of references to lists as its argument. As you can see, its argument list contains references to the three arrays that were just created.

The `foreach` loop that starts on line nine prints out the newly sorted arrays. It iterates over the list of references, assigning each of the individual references to a variable called `$ref`. There's also an inner `foreach` loop, which dereferences `$ref` and processes the individual elements in the arrays passed back by the subroutine. This is your first look at a nested data structure—a list of lists. The `@sorted_arrays` variable is a list of references, each of which points to a list that was created when the `sort_arrays` subroutine was executed. When those references are dereferenced, we're able to iterate over the individual values in those lists using the `foreach` loop. Inside the `foreach` loop, just print out each element individually, and when the inner `foreach` loop finishes, print out a line feed to separate the lists.

19

Now let's look at `sort_arrays`, which begins on line 18. First, declare a new list variable called `new_arrays`. This is where we are going to stick the sorted arrays that the subroutine will return. On line 22, begin another `foreach` loop. This one processes all the arguments to the subroutine. Each argument is a reference to a list, and is assigned to the variable `$ref`. On line 24, dereference `$ref` and pass it to the `sort` function, assigning the results to a list called `@sorted`. Then, push a reference to `@sorted` onto the `@new_arrays` variable. What results is the nested data structure that I talked about previously, a list of lists. Then return that list from the subroutine.

Finally, use a `foreach` loop to process each of the references in the list. Because each reference points to another list, inside the body of the loop, use another `foreach` loop to process the elements in the list referenced by the current element in the outer loop. Print out those elements, and print a newline to separate each list following the inner `foreach` loop.

Other Ways of Using References

Both using the backslash operator to create a reference and putting the reference where a name would be expected to dereference that reference are two common ways of creating and using references. But there are lots of other ways for doing the same things, some of which give you new and complex abilities, and others that provide more readable ways of doing the same thing. In this section, we'll look at some of the other ways to create and use references, as well as explore some of the other issues surrounding references.

Dereferencing List Reference Elements

If you have a reference to a list, one of the more common things you'll want to do with that reference is to get access to the individual elements inside that list—to print them, to sort them, to slice them, and so on. One way to do that is to use the basic syntax you learned about at the start of this lesson, and that we used in the previous example:

```
print "Minimum number: $$ref[0]\n";
```

This particular line prints the first element of the array pointed to by the reference `$ref`. If you were going to do the same thing to a hash, you'd use hash syntax, and replace the hash name with the reference:

```
print "John's last name: $$ref{john}\n";
```

There's another way to gain access to the list and hash elements pointed to by a reference, one that in many cases (particularly with complex data structures and object-oriented objects) is slightly easier to read. Use the reference, the arrow operator (`->`), and an array subscript to gain access to list elements pointed to by references:

```
$first =  $listref->[0];
```

Note that in this expression there is only one dollar sign. This expression dereferences the list reference in the variable `$listref`, and returns the 0th element of that list. It is precisely the same as using the standard dereferencing mechanism:

```
$first = $$listref[0];
```

To use this syntax with hashes, use the hash reference, the arrow operator `->`,, and the hash key in brackets:

```
$value = $hashref->{$key};
```

This form is just the same as the standard way:

```
$value = $$hashref{$key};
```

> **Note**
>
> Don't confuse the arrow operator `->` with the hash pair operator `=>`. The former is used to dereference a reference; the latter is the same as a comma and is used to make initializing the contents of hashes easier to read.

We'll come back to this syntax in the section on "Creating Nested Data Structures with References."

References with Blocks

A third way of dereferencing references is similar to that of basic references; instead of using a reference variable name in place of a regular variable name, you use a block (inside curly brackets) in place of a regular variable name. The block, when evaluated, should return a reference. So, for example, say you had a reference to a list:

```
$listref = \@list;
```

You could get at the third element of that list using regular dereferencing:

```
$third = $$listref[3];
```

Or, through arrow notation:

```
$third = $listref->[3];
```

Or, with a block:

```
$third = ${$listref}[3];
```

19

To get the contents or last index of a list through a reference you might use regular dereferencing:

```
@list = @$listref;
$index = $#$listref;
```

Or a block:

```
@list = @{$listref};
$index = $#{$listref};
```

This particular block doesn't have much of a point, given that all it does is evaluate the `$listref` variable, and you could do that just as easily and with fewer characters using a regular dereference. But you could, for example, have called a subroutine inside the block that returned a reference, used an `if` conditional to choose one reference or another, or put any other expression inside that block. It doesn't have to be a simple variable.

Block dereferencing also allows you to build up some very complex dereferences for very complex structures that use those references. We'll look at this in more detail in the section on "Accessing Elements in Nested Data Structures."

The `ref` Function

Say you've got a reference stored in a scalar variable. You'd like to know what kind of data that reference actually points to, so you don't end up trying to multiply lists or get elements out of strings. Perl has a built-in function to do just that called `ref`.

The `ref` function takes a scalar for an argument. If the scalar isn't a reference, that is, if it's a string or a number, then `ref` returns a null string. Otherwise, it returns a string indicating the kind of data the reference points to. Table 19.1 shows the possible values.

TABLE 19.1 Possible Return Values of `ref` Function

Return Value	*Means the Reference Points To*
REF	Another reference
SCALAR	A scalar value
ARRAY	An array
HASH	A hash
CODE	A subroutine
GLOB	A typeglob
"" (null string)	Not a reference

> We'll look at references to subroutines and typeglobs in the "Going Deeper" section of this lesson.

The `ref` function is most commonly used to test references for their type:

```
if (ref($ref) eq "ARRAY") {
   foreach $key (@$ref) {
      ...
   }
} elsif (ref($ref eq "HASH") {
   foreach $key (keys %$ref) {
      ...
   }
}
```

A Note About Memory and Garbage Collection

One internal side effect of using references concerns the amount of memory that Perl uses up as it runs your script and creates various bits of data. Normally, when your script runs, Perl sets aside bits of memory for your data automatically, and then reclaims the memory when you're done with it. The process of reclaiming the memory—called *garbage collection*—is different from many other languages, such as C, where you must allocate and free memory on your own.

Perl uses what's called a reference-counting garbage collector. That means for each bit of data, Perl keeps track of the number of references to that data—including the variable name that holds it. If you create a reference to that bit of data, then Perl increments the reference count by 1. If you move the reference to something else, or if a local variable that holds a bit of data disappears at the end of the block or a subroutine, Perl decrements the reference count. When the reference count goes to 0—there are no variables referring to that data, nor any references that point to it—then Perl reclaims the memory that was held by that data.

Normally, this all works automatically and you don't have to do anything about it in your scripts. However, there is a case with references that you have to be careful about: the problem of circular references.

Take these two references:

```
sub silly {
   my ($ref1, $ref2);
   $ref1 = \$ref2;
   $ref2 = \$ref1;
   # .. do silly things
}
```


In this example, the reference in `$ref1` points to the thing `$ref2` points to, and `$ref2` points to the thing `$ref1` points to. This is called a circular reference. The difficulty here is when the subroutine is done executing, the local variable names `$ref1` and `$ref2` disappear, but the data that each one contains still has at least one reference pointing to it, so the memory those references hold cannot be reclaimed. And without the variable names, or a returned reference to one or the other of the references, you can't even get to the data inside that subroutine. It's just going to sit there. And each time that subroutine runs while your script executes, you'll end up with more and more bits of unclaimable memory until Perl takes up all the memory on your system (or your script stops executing).

Circular references are bad things. Although this particular example might seem silly and easy to catch, with complex data structures containing references pointing all over the place, it is possible to accidentally create a circular reference where you don't intend one to be. Consider "cleaning up" any references you use in blocks or subroutines (`undef` them or assign them to something like 0 or '') to make sure they don't become unclaimed memory.

Creating Nested Data Structures with References

Subroutines are not the only place where references come in handy. The other significant feature that becomes possible with references is complex data structures such as multidimensional arrays. In this section we'll look at constructing complex data structures with nested arrays and hashes using references and anonymous data. Later in the lesson, in "Accessing Elements in Nested Data Structures," we'll look at getting data back out of the nested data structures you've just created.

What Is a Nested Data Structure?

Normally in Perl, lists, arrays, and hashes are flat, one dimensional, containing nothing but scalars. Combine multiple lists, and they all get squished down to a single one. Hashes are effectively just lists with a different way of organizing the data inside them. Although this makes creating and using collections of data really easy, it's also quite limiting when you're trying to represent larger or more complex data sets efficiently.

Say, for example, that your data consists of information about people: first name, last name, age, height, and names of all that person's children. How would you represent this data? First and last names are easy: create a hash, keyed by last name, and with the first names as the values for those keys. Heights—well, you might create a second hash, also keyed by last name, for the heights. But then there's the names of children. Perhaps a third hash, keyed by last name, with the values being strings representing the names of the children, separated by colons, and then split on-the-fly when you want to use them? As you can see, when the data gets complex, you end up creating too many flat lists to keep track of it all, or creating funny workarounds with strings to get around the inability to store lists inside other lists.

That's where references come in. It's true a list is a flat collection of scalars. But a reference is a scalar—and a reference can point to another list. And that list, in turn, can contain references to other lists. Get it? References allow you to nest lists inside other lists, arrays inside arrays, hashes inside arrays, arrays as values for hashes, and so on. We'll call all these things—any combination of lists, arrays, and hashes—*nested data structures*.

Using Anonymous Data

Although references are crucial for creating nested data structures, there's one other thing you need to know that will make building nested data structures easier: anonymous data. The term *anonymous* means without a name. Anonymous data in Perl, specifically, refers to data (usually arrays and hashes, but also subroutines) that you can only access through a reference—that data does not also have an associated variable name.

As with the last section, in this section we'll look specifically at arrays and hashes. We'll cover anonymous subroutines and the references to them in "Going Deeper," at the end of this lesson.

We've already seen anonymous data earlier in this chapter, when we created arrays inside subroutines, and then returned references to those arrays. After the subroutine exits, the original local variable that held the data disappears, and the only way to get at the data is through a reference. That data is then anonymous.

Anonymous data is useful for nested data structures because if you're going to create a list of lists, then the only variable name you need is the one that holds the outside list (and you don't even really need that one). You don't need separate variables for all the data inside the lists; references will work just fine.

You could create anonymous data for nested data structures using local variables inside subroutines or blocks. In some ways, when you're filling structures with data you read from files or from standard input, it's easier to do so that way. But there's another way to create anonymous data, and that's with actual Perl syntax: brackets (`[]`) or curly brackets (`{}`).

Say you wanted to create a reference to an array. The normal way would be as we've seen it:

```
@array = ( 1..10 );
$arrayref = \@array;
```

But this isn't anonymous; the array is stored in the variable `@array`. To create that same array anonymously, you'd initialize that list inside brackets, instead of parentheses. The result is a reference, which you can then store:

```
$listref = [ 1..10 ];
```

This array is accessible through the reference. You would dereference it the way you would any array, but not through a variable name. It's anonymous data.

You can do the same thing with anonymous hashes, where curly brackets create a reference to an anonymous hash:

```
$hashref = {
   'Taylor' => 12,
   'Ashley' => 11,
   'Jason'  => 12,
   'Brenadan' => 13,
}
```

Note that the elements inside the hash must still be in pairs, and will be combined into keys and values just as regular hashes are.

> The brackets and curly brackets here should not be confused with the array indexes (`$array[0]`) and hash lookups (`$hash{key}`). The characters are the same so that you can remember that brackets go with array and curly brackets with hashes, but they do entirely different things.

Array and hash brackets construct an array or hash in memory, and then return a reference to that memory location. Anything that you can put inside an array or a hash, you can put inside anonymous array or hash brackets. That includes array and hash variables, although these two lines do *not* produce the same result:

```
$arrayref = \@array;

$arrayref = [ @array ];
```

The difference between these two is that the first reference points to the actual memory location of the `@array` variable. The second one produces a new array, copying all the elements of `@array`, and then creates a reference to that new memory location. You could consider it as simply creating a reference to a copy of `@array`. This will be an important trick to know later when we create data structures inside loops.

Creating Data Structures with Anonymous Data

With anonymous data and references, creating nested data structures is a simple matter of putting it all together. In this section, we'll look at three kinds of nested data structures: arrays of arrays, hashes of arrays, and hashes of hashes.

Arrays of Arrays

Let's start with something simple: an array of arrays, or a *multidimensional array* (see Figure 19.2). You might use an array of arrays to create a sort of two-dimensional field such as a chessboard (where each square on the "board" has a position somewhere inside a row, and the larger array stores all the rows).

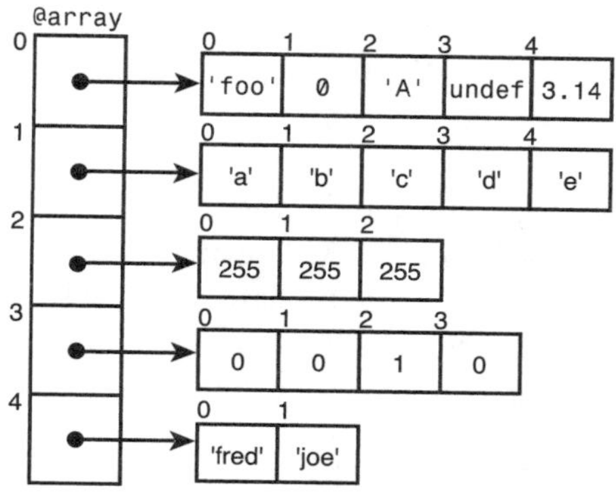

FIGURE 19.2
An array of arrays.

> **Note**
>
> If you're used to C's true multidimensional arrays, note that Perl's multidimensional arrays are more like arrays of pointers and are not truly multidimensional.

To create an array of arrays, use anonymous array syntax for the inner arrays, and regular list syntax for the outer (this array of arrays represents the red, green, and blue values for various shades of gray):

```
@greys = (
    [ 0, 0, 0 ],
    [ 63, 63, 63 ],
    [ 127, 127, 127 ],
    [ 191, 191, 191 ],
    [ 255, 255, 255],
);
```

Here, the arrays with the numbers are inside brackets, which creates references to those arrays. Then the larger array, inside parentheses, creates a simple array of those references. Be careful not to do this:

```
@greys = [
    [ 0, 0, 0 ],
    [ 63, 63, 63 ],
    ...
];
```

The brackets around the outer array will create a reference to an array, not a regular array. Perhaps that is what you want, but in that case you wouldn't assign it to an array variable. Use a scalar variable to hold the reference instead.

To access data within one of the inner arrays, the following notation is used:

```
print $greys[1]->[2];
```

Hashes of Arrays

A hash of arrays is a nested data structure in which a hash, with normal keys, has values that are references to arrays (see Figure 19.3). You might use a hash of arrays to keep track of a list of people and their children, where the hash would be keyed by the people's names, and the values would be lists of their children's names. Or a movie theater might keep a hash of movie names and their associated show times.

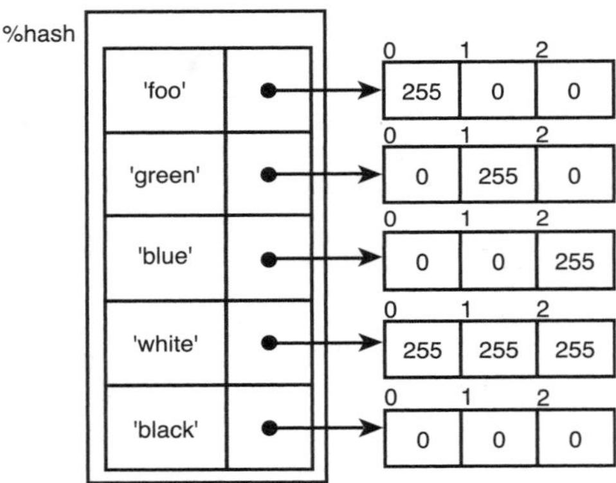

FIGURE 19.3
Hashes of arrays.

To create a hash of arrays, use hash syntax for the outer hash, normal strings as the keys, and anonymous arrays as the values (this one keeps track of a schedule of activities at a summer camp):

```
%schedule = (
   'monday' => [ 'archery', 'soccer', 'dance' ],
   'tuesday' => [ 'basketweave', 'swimming', 'canoeing' ],
   'wednesday' => [ 'nature walk', 'soccer', 'dance' ],
   'thursday' => [ 'free time', 'swimming', 'canoeing' ],
   'friday' => [ 'archery', 'soccer', 'hike' ],
);
```

Once again, watch out for the placement of brackets and parentheses. Here, the inner brackets create the anonymous arrays. The outer parentheses create a list that is then converted into a hash when it's assigned to the `%schedule` variable. Using curly brackets ({}) around the entire list would create a reference to an anonymous hash.

To access the data in one of the arrays inside the hash, use the following notation:

```
print $schedule{'monday'}->[1];
```

Note that in a hash of arrays, only the values can be arrays. The hash keys must be strings, and, in fact, Perl assumes they will be strings and converts anything else (numbers and references) to strings. Be careful when you build nested hashes to make sure your keys are strings.

Hashes of Hashes

How complex would you like to get? Hashes of hashes allow you to create very complex data structures. In a hash of hashes, the outer hash has regular keys and values that in turn store other hashes (see Figure 19.4). You could then look up specific keys and "subkeys" in each of the hashes. For example, a hash of hashes could collect a classroom full of children and the grades they were getting in each subject. Have the children's last names be the keys, and the values would be another hash containing, for example, first name, date of birth, and then the grades for each class.

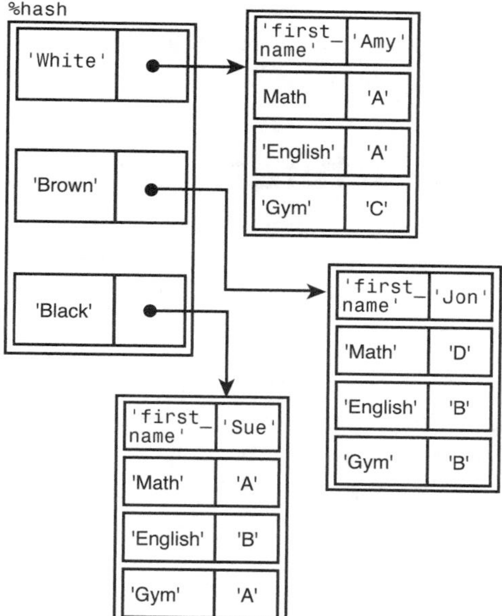

FIGURE 19.4
Hashes of hashes.

Hashes of hashes get anonymous hash syntax for the insides, and regular list syntax for the outside:

```
%people = (
   'Jones' => {
      'name' => 'Alison',
      'age' => 15,
      'pet' => 'dog',
   },
```

```
   'Smith' => {
      'name' => 'Tom',
      'age' => 18,
      'pet' => 'fish',
   },
);
```

To retrieve data from one of the inner hashes, you could use the following code:

```
print $people{'Smith'}->{'pet'}, "\n";
```

Other Structures

I've shown you three simple and common nested data structures in this section: arrays of arrays, hashes of arrays, and hashes of hashes. But you can combine arrays and hashes with references and anonymous data in just about any way you'd like, depending on the data you're working with and the best way to organize that data. You can also nest your data further down than I did here, to create, for example, a hash of a hash in which the keys are in turn arrays, and those array elements are hashes, and so on. There's no limit to how deeply you can nest your data structures, so if it seems appropriate, go ahead and do it.

Building Data Structures with Existing Data

The examples of creating nested data structures with anonymous data work great when you already know exactly what data that structure is going to contain ahead of time. But in real life, these sorts of structures tend to get built from data that might be read in from a file or entered via the keyboard.

In that case, sometimes you'll end up combining anonymous data with references to regular variables. As long as you end up with references in the right spot, there's no harm in using whatever mechanism works best for building your data structure. For example, let's say that you had a file that contained a matrix of numbers that looked something like this:

```
3 4 2 4 2 3
5 3 2 4 5 4
7 6 3 2 8 3
3 4 7 8 3 4
```

You want to read that file into an array of arrays, with each row its own array, and a larger array to store the individual rows. You might accomplish that with a loop that looks something like this:

```
while (<>) {
   chomp;
   push @matrix, [ split ];
}
```

That loop would read each line, chomp off its newline with `chomp`, split it into elements with split, create an anonymous array of those elements with brackets, and then finally push the reference to that array onto a larger array.

You might think that this example would be more readable if we split the elements into a list first, and then stored a reference to that list instead, like this:

```
my @list = ();
while (<>) {
   chomp;
   @list = split;
   push @matrix, \@list;
}
```

But there's a big catch to this example (a catch lots of programmers make the first time they try this). Given input like the preceding matrix, with this loop you'd end up with an array of arrays that looked like this:

```
3 4 7 8 3 4
3 4 7 8 3 4
3 4 7 8 3 4
3 4 7 8 3 4
```

Can you guess why? The problem is with the variable name and, later, the reference to it. With each turn of the loop, although the *contents* of the variable `@list` change, the memory location stays the same. Each time you read a line, you're pushing a reference to the *same* memory location. The array you end up with is an array of four references, and each one points to exactly the same place.

One solution to this mistake—and it's a common one, so watch out for it—is to create a reference to a copy of the array's data, not to the array itself. This way, a new location is created in memory each time the loop executes, so you end up with references to different places. You can do this simply by putting anonymous array brackets around your array variable:


```
my @list = ();
while (<>) {
   chomp;
   @list = split;
   push @matrix, [ @list ];
}
```

Watch out with hashes that you do the same thing with an anonymous hash (in this case, putting an anonymous hash into an array of hashes):

```
push @arrayofhashes, { %hash };
```

The other solution to this problem is to use a `my` variable inside the loop itself. Because the `my` variable will be created from scratch at each turn of the loop, the references will point to different bits of memory each time:

```
while (<>) {
   chomp;
   my @list = split;
   push @matrix, \@list ;
}
```

Accessing Elements in Nested Data Structures

Building nested data structures is one thing; getting elements out of them is another. With references inside arrays pointed to by other references, getting at an actual element can be a chore, particularly in complex structures. Fortunately, Perl has syntax to help.

Say you have a matrix (array of arrays) of numbers like the one we used in the last section:

```
@nums = (
   [ 3, 4, 2, 4, 2, 3 ],
   [ 5, 3, 2, 4, 5, 4 ],
   [ 7, 6, 3, 2, 8, 3 ],
   [ 3, 4, 7, 8, 3, 4, ],
);
```

Now let's say you wanted to access the fourth element of the third row. You could use standard array access to get to the third row:

```
$nums[2]
```

But that would give you a reference, not the data that reference points to (remember, you only get the data pointed to by a reference by explicitly referencing it). To dereference the reference and give you an actual element, you could do this (the fourth element of the array pointed to the reference in `$nums[2]`):

```
$nums[2]->[3]
```

Or this (`$nums[2]` gives you a reference which is dereferenced inside the block):

```
${ $nums[2] }[3];
```

Either one of these would work, but neither is particularly readable. Perl provides a shorthand syntax for multidimensional arrays that makes this easier: Using the standard arrow deferencing syntax, you can leave off the `->` characters, like this:

```
$nums[2][3];
```

That's much easier to figure out, and analogous to multidimensional array access in other languages (like C, for instance).

The situation is different if, instead of an actual array in `@nums`, all you had was a reference to an array of arrays. Then there are two references to dereference, and you'd use syntax like this (where `$numref` is the reference to the array of arrays):

```
$numref->[2][2];
```

Nested hashes of arrays and hashes of hashes work analogously, using curly brackets for the hash keys and brackets for the array indexes:

```
$hash{joe}[5]; # sixth element of array accessed
               # by the key 'joe' in the hash %hash

$hashref->{joe}[5] # same thing, if $hashref contains a reference

$hash{Jones}{age}; # age value for the Jones record in the hash %hash

$hashref->{Jones}{age}; # samething, $hashref is reference
```

If all these nested subscripts and keys are too disturbing, there's nothing wrong with creating a temporary copy of the reference to an internal array or hash, and then dereferencing that reference in a more simple way:

```
# same as $nums[0][5]
my $tempref = $nums[0]; # get reference to first row of nums
print $$tempref[5];  # print fifth element
```

Need to take a slice of a nested array? You'd use normal slice syntax for that, with the references in the appropriate spots. You'll also need to use block dereferencing in this case, and you'll end up with something ugly like this (this one extracts elements 2 through 5 in the second array in `@nums`:

19

```
@elements = @{ $nums[1] }[2..5];
```

Because this notation can quickly become really ugly, it might be easier to pull references into temporary variables and take slices of those, or to create loops that extract individual elements from a nested array. If you want to take vertical slices (one element from some number of nested "rows") or rectangular slices (some number of elements across, another number of elements down), then you'll have to create a loop to do that.

Another Example: A Database of Artists and Their Works

Nested data structures work best for representing complex sets of data and allow you to do various things with that data. In this example, then, we'll look at a database of artists, some information about those artists, and their various works. To save space, we'll keep this example short. All this example does is

- Read the artist data from a file into a complex nested data structure
- Prompt for a search string
- Print the data for that particular artist, given that search string

The data we'll look at in this example consists of an artist's first and last names, their birth and death dates, and a list of titles of their works. The artist's data is stored in an external file consisting of two lines per artist:

```
Monet,Claude,1840,1926
Woman With a Parasol:Field of Poppies:Camille at the Window:Water Lillies
```

The first line consists of the artist's personal data, separated by commas. The second line is the artist's works, separated by colons. The data file (which I've called `artists.txt`) contains a number of artists in this format.

The structure we'll read this information into is a hash of hashes with a nested array. The topmost hash is keyed by artist's last name. The extra artist data is a nested hash with the keys "FN," "BD," "DD," and "works." The value of the `works` key is, in turn, an array consisting of all the titles. Figure 19.5 shows how a single record (artist) of this structure might look and where each part of the data fits into that structure.

Listing 19.2 shows the code for this simple example. Before reading down to the discussion of this code, look carefully at the lines inside the `while` loop in the `&read_input()` subroutine (lines 21 through 35), and the dereferences in the `&process()` subroutine (lines 53 and 55).

LISTING 19.2 The `artists.pl` Script

```
1:  #!/usr/ bin/perl -w
2:  use strict;
3:
4:  my $artdb = "artists.txt";              # name of artists database
5:  my %artists = ();                      # hash of artists, keyed by last name
6:
7:  &read_input();
8:  &process();
9:
10: sub read_input {
11:     my $in = '';                # temp input line
12:     my ($fn,$ln,$bd,$dd);       # last name, first name
13:                                 # date of birth, date of death
14:     my %artist = ();            # temp artist hash
15:
```

LISTING 19.2 continued

```
    open(FILE, $artdb) or die "Cannot open artist's database ($artdb): $!\n";

    while () {
        # name and dates on first line
        chomp($in = <FILE>);
        if ($in) {
            ($ln,$fn,$bd,$dd) = split(',',$in);
            $artist{FN} = $fn;
            $artist{BD} = $bd;
            $artist{DD} = $dd;

            chomp($in = <FILE>); # list of works in second line
            if ($in) {
                my @works = split(':',$in);
                $artist{works} = \@works;
            } else { print "no works";}

            # add a reference to the artist hash in the bigger
            # artists hash
            $artists{$ln} = { %artist };

        } else { last; }        # end of DB
    }

}

sub process {
    my $input = '';
    my $matched = 0;

    print "Enter an Artist's Name: ";
    chomp($input = <>);

    foreach (keys %artists) {
        if (/$input/i  and !$matched) {
            $matched = 1;
            my $ref = $artists{$_};
            print "$_, $ref->{FN} $ref->{BD}-$ref->{DD}\n";
            my $work = '';
            foreach $work (@{$ref->{works}}) {
                print "   $work\n";
            }
        }
    }
    if (!$matched) {
        print "Artist $input not found.\n";
    }
}
```

You may note that in this example I did exactly the reverse of the last example: I'm using a global variable to hold the global artists database, rather than keeping all variables local. How you organize your data and variables is your choice; in this case I'm using a global variable because the dereferences are complicated enough without adding another level of reference at the topmost level.

One other kind of odd thing I did in this example is to hard-code the name of the artists database into the script, rather than indicating the name of the database file on the command line. Once again, this is a question of programmer choice and how the script will be used; either way will work equally well (note, however, that I put the filename of the artists database right at the top of the script so it can be easily changed if necessary).

Let's look first at the `&read_input()` subroutine, which reads the artists database and fills our nested data structure with that data. The way I've approached this task is to create a temporary hash for the current artist, to fill up that hash with the data, and then to put that temporary hash into the larger hash with a reference.

We start in line 18 with a loop that reads in the artists database file, two lines at a time. The loop will be exited when there's no more data (as determined by the test in line 21). We'll start with the first line of data, which contains the artist's name and date information:

```
Monet,Claude,1840,1926
```

Line 22 splits this data into its component parts, and lines 23 and 25 put that data into a temporary hash (called `%artist`, not to be confused with the larger `%artists` hash).

Line 27 reads the second line of each artist's data, the list of works:

```
Woman With a Parasol:Field of Poppies:Camille at the Window:Water Lillies
```

In line 29, we split this line into list elements, based on a ":" separator character, and then store that list into the `@works` temporary array. In line 30 we add a reference to that array to the temporary `%artist` hash with the key "works." Note that each time the `while` loop executes, we'll end up with a new `@works` temporary array (declared with `my`), so we'll avoid the problem of referencing the same memory location each time.

With the individual artist's data built, we can add that record to the larger artist's hash with the last name as the key. Line 35 does just that. Note in this instance that because we use the same `%artist` hash for each turn of the loop, we'll use an anonymous hash constructor and a copy of the `%artist` hash to make sure the reference points to a different memory location each time.

If `&read_input()` puts data into the nested hash, then `&process()` subroutine gets that data out again. Here we'll use a simple search on the artist's last name and print the matching record. The output that gets printed looks like this:

```
Enter an Artist's Name: Monet
Monet, Claude 1840-1926
   Woman With a Parasol
   Field of Poppies
   Camille at the Window
   Water Lillies
   The Artist's Garden at Giverny
```

The most important parts of this subroutine are the parts that dereference the references to get at the important data in lines 52 through 56. But let's back up a bit and start from line 49, the `foreach` loop. In this loop, because we don't have an actual loop variable, Perl will store each key (each artist's last name) in the `$_` variable.

Line 50 is our core test: We use a pattern-match here with the input and the current key to see if a match was made. And, because we're only interested in the first match for this example, we'll also keep track of a `$matched` variable to see if we've already found a match.

Assuming a match was indeed found, we move to line 52. Here we'll create a temporary variable to hold the reference to the artist's data record—as in the stats example, not entirely necessary, but it makes it easier to manage references this way. In this case, because `$_` holds the matched key, we can use a simple hash lookup to get the reference.

With the reference in hand, we can dereference it to gain access to the contents of the hash. In line 53 we print the basic data: the last name (`$_`), the first name (the value of the key "FN" in the hash), the date of birth ("BD"), and date of death ("DD").

Lines 54 through 56 are used to print each of the artist's works on separate lines. The only odd part of these lines is the reference in the `foreach` loop. Let's look at that one in detail:

```
@{$ref->{works}}
```

Remember that what we have in `$ref` is a reference to a hash. The expression `$ref->{works}` dereferences that reference, and returns the value indicated by the key "works." But that value is also a reference, this time a reference to an array. To dereference that reference, and end up with an actual array for the `foreach` loop to iterate over, you need the block syntax for dereferencing: `@{}`.

Figuring out references and how to get at the actual data you want can be a complex process. It helps to start from the outer data structure and work inward, using blocks where necessary and temporary variables where it's helpful. Examining different referencing expressions in the Perl debugger or with print statements can also go a long way toward helping create the right dereferences.

Avoiding the Use of References

Just because you can use references doesn't mean you have to. For one thing, understanding references can be tricky. For another, references were not available until Perl 5, so seasoned programmers might be used to doing things other ways.

Let's say you want to pass two arrays to a subroutine. One way is to create references to them and call the subroutine, like this:

```
@colors = ('red', 'green', 'blue');
@shapes = ('circle', 'square', 'triangle);
$colors_ref = \@colors;
$shapes_ref = \@shapes;
&some_subroutine($colors_ref, $shapes_ref);
```

There's an alternative approach, too. If you like, you can turn the arrays into regular strings with a known delimiter, and use them instead of references. For example, here's an approach you could use to pass the two arrays in separately without using references:

```
@colors = ('red', 'green', 'blue');
@shapes = ('circle', 'square', 'triangle');
$colors_str = join ',', @colors;
$shapes_str = join ',', @shapes;
&some_subroutine($colors_str, $shapes_str);

sub some_subroutine
{
   my @colors = split /,/, $_[0];
   my @shapes = split /,/, $_[1];
}
```

To maintain the identity of my arrays, I used the `join` function to turn them into comma-delimited strings before passing them to the subroutine. Inside my subroutine, I use the `split` function to extract the values from the strings and turn them back into arrays. As you can see, this is a bit more tedious than simply passing in two references, but it can make life easier.

You might also use such a technique when you're dealing with nested data structures, such as an array of arrays or a hash of arrays. Converting your arrays into strings and using them as elements in an array or values in a hash can be a bit more tedious than just using anonymous arrays, but can also be easier to understand. Here's a simple example that uses arrays nested in a hash.

```
@items = ('can', 'bucket', 'needle');
%stuff = ();
$stuff{'items'} = join ',', @items;
@temp = split /,/, @stuff{'items'};
print @temp[1];
```

As you can see, you can just put the comma-delimited list into the hash as a value rather than putting in a reference to an anonymous array (or a regular array). This allows you to avoid using references, but again at the cost of additional tedium when it comes to extracting the values from the data structure.

This technique is worth knowing about for two reasons. One is that if you don't use references often, it can be easy to forget how they work. The second is that there's a good chance that if you ever work on scripts written by other people, you'll see techniques similar to these. Until Perl 5 was released, the only way to create complex data structures was to use collapse arrays and hashes into strings and extract them when you wanted to use them.

If you're writing new code, you probably ought to bite the bullet and use references. They might seem confusing at first, but the more you use them, the more you'll get the hang of it.

Going Deeper

The creation and use of references is probably one of the more complex aspects of Perl (arguably surpassed only by object-oriented programming, which we'll look at tomorrow). In today's lesson I've introduced you to the basics of references and the places where you'll most commonly use them. But as with most Perl topics, there's plenty of other features I haven't covered that relate to references, including symbolic references (a whole other form of reference), and references to subroutines, typeglobs, and filehandles.

For more information on references, check out the `perlref` man page. If you do more work with nested data structures, the man pages `perldsc` (data structures cookbook) and `perllol` (lists of lists) provide further detail and examples.

Shorthand References to Scalars

Need to create a lot of scalar references at once? Here's an easy way to do it:

```
@listofrefs = \($thing1, $thing2, $thing3, $thing4);
```

Here you'll end up with a list of references in `@listofrefs`. It's a shorthand for something doing this:

```
@listofrefs = (\$thing1, \$thing2, \$thing3, \$thing4);
```

Symbolic References

As I mentioned in passing earlier in this lesson, Perl actually defines two kinds of references: hard references and symbolic references. The references I've used throughout this lesson are hard references that are actual bits of scalar data that can be manipulated like scalars or dereferenced to get to the data they refer to.

Symbolic references are different: a symbolic reference is simply a string. If you try to dereference that string, the string is interpreted to be the name of a variable, and if that variable exists, you get the value of that variable. So, for example:

```
$foo = 1;          # variable $foo contains 1
$symref = "foo";  # string
$$symref = "I am a variable"; # sets the variable $foo
print "synbolic reference: $symref\n";    # results in "foo"
print "Foo: $foo\n";  # results in "I am a variable"
print "dereferenced: $$symref\n";   # prints $foo, results in "I am a variable"
```

As you can see, you can use symbolic references as if they were real references, but they're just strings that name variables. The difference is subtle and confusing, particularly if you mix hard and symbolic references. You can accidentally dereference a string when you meant to dereference a scalar, and end up with it being difficult to debug problems. For this reason, Perl provides a `strict` pragma to restrict the use of references to hard references:

```
use strict 'refs';
```

Setting this pragma at the top of your script will prevent you from using symbolic references. You'll also get this effect if you use a regular `use strict` at the top of your script as well.

References to Typeglobs and Filehandles

Two types of references I didn't mention in the body of this lesson were references to typeglobs, which in turn allow references to filehandles. A typeglob, as I've mentioned in passing previously in this book, is a way of referring to multiple types of variables that share the same name (it holds an actual symbol table entry). Typeglobs are not as commonly used in Perl as they were in the past (they used to be how you passed references to lists into subroutines before there were references), but they do provide a mechanism for creating references to filehandles, which allows you to pass filehandles into and out of subroutines, or to create local filehandles, if you feel the need to do so.

To create a reference to a filehandle, use a typeglob with the name of the filehandle and the backslash operator (\):

```
$fh = \*MYFILE;
```

To create a local filehandle, use the `local` operator (not `my`) and a filehandle typeglob:

```
local *MYFILE;
```

See the `perldata` man page (the section on typeglobs and filehandles) for details.

References to Subroutines

Much more useful than references to filehandles are references to subroutines. Given that a subroutine's definition is stored in memory just as an array or hash is, you can create references to subroutines just as you can references to other bits of data. By dereferencing the reference to a subroutine, you call that subroutine.

References to subroutines allow you to change the definition of a subroutine on-the-fly, or to choose between several different subroutines depending on the situation. They also allow advanced features in Perl such as object-oriented programming and closures (anonymous subroutines whose local variables "stick" based on the time and scope in which they were defined, even if they're called in a different scope).

To create a reference to a subroutine, you can use the backslash operator with the name of a predefined subroutine:

```
$subref = \&mysub;
```

You can also create an anonymous subroutine by simply leaving off the name of the subroutine when you define it:

```
$subref = sub { reverse @_;};
```

Dereference a subroutine using regular reference syntax or with a block. When you dereference a subroutine, you call it, so don't forget to include arguments:

```
@result = &$subref(1..10);
```

For more details on references to subroutines, and of closures, see the `perlref` man page.

Summary

The last major feature of Perl we had left to cover in this book were references, and today you got a good introduction to creating and using references in various contexts.

A reference is a bit of scalar data that points to another piece of data: another scalar, an array, a hash, or a subroutine. Because a reference is a scalar, you can pass it to subroutines, store it in variables, treat it as a string or a number, test it for its truth value, or include it inside another array. To create a reference, you can use one of two methods:

- Use the backslash operator (\) with a variable
- Use one of the anonymous constructors to create a reference to an array, a hash, or a subroutine

To gain access to the thing the reference points to, you dereference that reference. You can dereference references in one of three ways:

- Place the reference variable where a regular variable name might go, for example `$$ref`, `@$ref`, or `$$ref[0]`.
- Place a block expression (which evaluates to a reference) where a variable name might go, for example `@{$ref[0]}`.
- Use "arrow notation," particularly for references to lists (`$ref->[0]` or `$ref->{key}`). For nested arrays and hashes, you can include multiple subscripts without needing intervening arrows, (`$ref->[0][4]`, or `$ref[0]{key}`).

In addition to the basics of creating and using references, we also looked at two of the most common uses of references: as subroutine arguments (for retaining the structure of arrays and hashes inside subroutines), and for creating nested data structures such as arrays of arrays and arrays of hashes. Finally, you also learned about the `ref` function, which returns a string indicating the kind of data the reference contains.

Congratulations! Today you've completed the bulk of the hard work of this book. Tomorrow we'll explore some of the other Perl features we haven't looked at in this chapter, and then finish up on Day 21, "Exploring a Few Longer Examples," with some examples that make use of everything you've learned in this book.

Q&A

Q. Can you create references to references?

A. Sure! All you have to do is use the backslash operator to get the memory location of that reference. Keep in mind that if you create references to references, you'll need to dereference them twice to get to the data at the end of the chain.

Q. I'm trying to fill an array of arrays from a bunch of data in a file. I read the data into an simple array, and the add that array to a larger array. But at the end, the whole array has nothing but the last values I added. What am I doing wrong?

A. Sounds like you're doing something like this:

```
while (<>) {
    @input = split $_;
    @bigarray = \@input;
}
```

The problem is that each time you create a reference to `@input`, you're pointing to exactly the same location each time. The contents of `@input` change with each turn of the loop, but the location is the same. Each reference then points to the same location and has the value of the last thing you put in there. To get around this problem, either:

- Declare your temporary input variable as a my variable inside the loop itself. This will create a new memory location each time.
- Use an anonymous array constructor with the `@input` variable (that is, `[ @input ]`). This will create a reference to a copy of the contents of input, creating a new memory location each time.

Q. I created an array of arrays. I printed it with a simple `print "@myarray\n";`. But all I got was this:

```
ARRAY(0x807f048) ARRAY(0x808a06c) ARRAY(0x808a0cc)
```

What am I doing wrong?

A. You can't use variable interpolation with arrays of arrays. What your print command is doing is printing the top-level of the array—which is essentially three references. The ARRAY(...) stuff is the printable string representation of those references. To print a nested array (or any nested data structure) you'll have to use one or more `foreach` loops and dereference the references yourself. Here's an example of what you're actually looking for:

```
foreach (@myarray) {
  print "( @$_ )\n";
}
```

19

Workshop

The workshop provides quiz questions to help you solidify your understanding of the material covered and exercises to give you experience in using what you've learned. Try to understand the quiz and exercise answers before you go on to tomorrow's lesson.

Quiz

1. What's a reference? What advantages do they give you?
2. Show two ways of creating a reference to an array.
3. Show two methods for gaining access to an element of an array through a reference.
4. What happens to a reference if you change the data that reference points to?
5. What happens when you print a reference? Add four to it? Test to see if it's true?

6. Assume you have a reference in `$ref` that can refer to a scalar, an array, a hash, or to some nested data structure. What do the following dereferences result in (assume the reference points to the data most appropriate for each example)?

```
$$ref;
$$ref[0];
$ref->[0];
@$ref;
$#$ref;
$ref->[0][5];
@{$ref->{key}}
```

Exercises

1. Create a subroutine that takes any arbitrary number of references to arrays, reverses each of those arrays, and returns them in the same order it received them. Be sure to test whether the references you get are indeed references to arrays.
2. BUG BUSTER: What's wrong with this snippet of code (Hint: there's more than one error)?

```
%hash = {
 key => [ 1.. 10 ],
 key2 => [ 100 ..110 ],
};
$ref = \%hash;
foreach (keys %$ref) {
   print "$$ref{$_}\n";
}
```

3. Write a subroutine that takes a rectangular slice of a multidimensional array. Your subroutine should take five arguments: a reference to the array to slice, the indexes of the element to start with (row and element), and the number of rows and number of elements to slice. So, for example, if you had a reference to a multidimensional array that looked like this stored in the variable `$listref`:

```
[ 3, 4, 2, 4, 2, 3 ]
[ 5, 3, 2, 4, 5, 4 ]
[ 7, 6, 3, 2, 8, 3 ]
[ 3, 4, 7, 8, 3, 4 ]
```

And if you called your subroutine (`&rect()`) to start at 0,0 and slice a 3×3 element square, like this:

```
&rect($listref,0,0,3,3);
```

Your result should be

```
3 4 2
5 3 2
7 6 3
```

4. Write a simple version of the game Battleship. Use a 5×5 grid (numbers for the rows, letters for the columns), choose one "cell" at random, and then allow the user to choose a cell to hit. Print out the current state of the board, with choices marked, in between guesses. Here's a sample:

```
Enter the coordinates of your choice (eg A4): C4
Miss!  Try again.

   A B C D E
   ---------
1| 0 0 0 0 0
2| 0 0 0 0 0
3| 0 0 0 0 0
4| 0 0 X 0 0
5| 0 0 0 0 0

Enter the coordinates of your choice (eg A4): B3
Miss!  Try again.

   A B C D E
   ---------
1| 0 0 0 0 0
2| 0 0 0 0 0
3| 0 X 0 0 0
4| 0 0 X 0 0
5| 0 0 0 0 0

Enter the coordinates of your choice (eg A4): E1
Congratulations!  You sank the battleship!
```


Answers

Here are the answers to the Workshop questions in the previous section.

Quiz Answers

1. A reference is a bit of scalar data that allows you to refer to some other bit of data in an indirect way. References allow you to pass subroutine arguments by reference (retaining the structure of multiple arrays and hashes), return discrete multiple lists, as well as create and manage nested data structures such as lists of lists.
2. You can create a reference to an array using the backslash operator:

```
$ref = \@array;
```

Or with an anonymous array constructor:

```
$ref = [ 1 ..100 ];
```

3. You can dereference a reference to an array to get access to its elements by substituting the reference where the array name is expected:

   ```
   $thing = $$ref[0];
   ```

   Or using arrow notation:

   ```
   $thing = $ref->[0];
   ```

4. Changing the data a reference points to has no effect on the reference itself. The reference points to that data's location in memory, not to the data itself.
5. A reference is a scalar, and will behave like a scalar in scalar context, according to these rules:
   - A reference as a string prints the type of data the reference points to (SCALAR, ARRAY, HASH, and so on) and a hexadecimal number representing the memory location that data is located in
   - A reference as a number is that same memory location number. Adding four to it gets you that same number plus four (not a very meaningful number)
   - All references are true
6. The answers are as follows:

   a. Assuming `$ref` is a reference to a scalar, returns a scalar

   b. Assuming `$ref` is a reference to an array, returns the first element of that array

   c. Same as b

   d. Assuming `$ref` is a reference to an array, returns the contents of that array (or the number of elements, in scalar context)

   e. Assuming `$ref` is a reference to an array, returns the last index in that array

   f. Assuming `$ref` is a reference to a multidimensional array, returns the sixth element in the first row

   g. Assuming `$ref` is a reference to a hash of arrays, returns the contents of the array that is the value of the key "key."

Exercise Answers

1. Here's one answer:

   ```
   sub reverseall {
       my $listref;
       foreach $listref (@_) {
           if (ref($listref) eq 'ARRAY') {
               my @templist = reverse @$listref;
               $listref = \@templist;
           } else {
               print "$listref is not a list\n";
   ```

```
            }
        }
        return @_;
    }
```

2. There are two errors in this snippet. The first is in the definition of the hash; the curly brackets around the hash definition ({}) produce a reference to a hash, not a regular hash. Use parentheses for that, like this:

```
%hash = (
 key => [ 1.. 10 ],
 key2 => [ 100 ..110],
);
```

The second error is in the print statement. This print will successfully dereference `$ref` and print each value in the hash, but each value is in turn a reference, and you'll end up with a printout that looks like this:

```
ARRAY(0x807f670)
ARRAY(0x807f7a8)
```

To print the actual values of those arrays, you need to dereference those references as well. You could do that with some complex dereferences like this:

```
print "@{ $$ref{$_} }\n";
```

Although judicious use of temporary references would make that easier to read:

```
my $arrayref = $$ref{$_};
print "@$arrayref\n";
```

3. Here's one answer (this one does no error-reporting for slices that are too wide or too tall for the data; it slices as much as it can):

```
sub rect {
    my $ref = shift;
    my ($c1,$c2,$width,$height) = @_;
    my @finalarray = ();
    my @slice = ();
    my $rowref;

    for (; $height > 0; $height--) { # do the rows
        my $c = $c2;
        if ($$ref[$c1]) {       # catch too-tall heights
            $rowref = $$ref[$c1];
        } else {next;}

        for (my $w = $width; $w > 0; $w--) {  # do the columns
            if ($$rowref[$c]) { # catch too-wide widths
                push @slice, $$rowref[$c];
                $c++;
            }
        }
```

19

```
        push @finalarray, [ @slice ];
        @slice = ();             # reset the slice for next time
        $c1++;
    }
    return \@finalarray;
}
```

4. Here's one example. The "board" is a nested array of arrays:

```
#!/usr/ bin/perl -w
use strict;

my @board = (
          [ 0, 0, 0, 0, 0 ],
          [ 0, 0, 0, 0, 0 ],
          [ 0, 0, 0, 0, 0 ],
          [ 0, 0, 0, 0, 0 ],
          [ 0, 0, 0, 0, 0 ],
          );
my $hit = 0;
my @coords = &init();

while () {
    &print_board();
    my @choice = &get_coords();

    if (&compare_coords(@choice,@coords)) {
        print "Congratulations!  You sank the battleship!\n";
        last;
    } else {
        print "Miss!  Try again.\n";
        &mark_board(@choice);
    }
}

sub init {
    srand;
    my $num1 = int(rand 5);
    my $num2 = int(rand 5);
    return ($num1, $num2);
}

sub print_board {
    $, = ' ';
    print "\n   A B C D E \n";
    print "   --------- \n";
    my $i = 1;
    foreach (@board) {
        print "$i| @$_ \n";
        $i++;
    }
```

```
    print "\n";
}

sub get_coords {
    my ($c1, $c2);
    my $coords;
    while () {
        print "Enter the coordinates of your choice (eg A4): ";
        chomp($coords = <>);
        ($c1,$c2) = split('',$coords);
        $c1 = uc $c1;

        if ($c1 !~ /[ABCDE]/i) {
            print "Invalid letter coordinate.  A - E, please.\n";
            next;
        } elsif ($c2 !~ /[1-5]/) {
            print "Invalid number coordinate.  1- 5 please.\n";
            next;
        } else { last; }
    }
    ($c1 eq 'A') and $c1 = 0;
    ($c1 eq 'B') and $c1 = 1;
    ($c1 eq 'C') and $c1 = 2;
    ($c1 eq 'D') and $c1 = 3;
    ($c1 eq 'E') and $c1 = 4;
    $c2--;

    return ($c1, $c2);
}


sub compare_coords {
    my ($c1,$c2,$d1,$d2) = @_;
    if ($c1 == $d1 and $c2 == $d2) { return 1; }
    else { return 0; }
}

sub mark_board {
    my ($c2,$c1) = @_;
    $board[$c1][$c2] = 'X';
}
```

WEEK 3

DAY 20

Odds and Ends

As this book draws to a close, you've now learned, or at least explored, the bulk of the Perl language as it exists today. But, as with every individual subject in Perl, there are other things to do and other ways to do them that I have not explored in this book.

This lesson, then, is the "Going Deeper" for the whole book. In this lesson we'll look at a number of topics that are either too complex or too tangential to have been explored earlier. Those topics include the following:

- One-liner scripts called on the Perl command line
- An introduction to object-oriented programming in Perl
- Sockets and simple networking
- POD Files (Plain Old Documentation)
- Evaluating code on-the-fly
- International Perl scripts
- Checking for security holes with Perl's "taint mode"
- Using PerlScript on Windows
- What's coming up in Perl 6

Perl One-Liners

When you write a Perl script, much of the time you'll write it as you have throughout this book—putting the script into a file, and then using the Perl interpreter to run that script. But sometimes there might be a task that's just really simple, or there might be something that you only need to do once (or very infrequently). For these kinds of tasks, it's almost a waste of time to start up an editor to write an actual script. For just this reason there are Perl one-liners.

Perl one-liners are scripts that you type directly on the Perl command line. They aren't saved anywhere; if you get them wrong you'll have to type them again.

To create a Perl one-liner, use the `-e` option, followed by the script inside quotes, like this:

```
% perl -e 'print "this is a one-liner\n";'
this is a one-liner
%
```

In Windows, you'll have to use double-quotes around the entire script, and back-slash the quotes for the strings, like this:

```
C:\> perl -e "print \"this is a windows one-liner\n\";"
```

If your script contains multiple statements, put them all on the single line (in most Unix shells, you can continue a single command onto multiple lines by putting a backslash (\) at the end of a line). Remember, Perl doesn't care much about whitespace, so you could theoretically create an incredibly complex Perl one-liner, and Perl would have no problem executing it (in fact, this is a boast you'll commonly hear from Perl programmers—"I can do that in one line!"—of course, you can do anything in Perl in one line, as long as that line is long enough).

Here are a couple example Perl one-liners. To reverse all the lines in a file

```
% perl -e 'print reverse <>;' filename.txt
```

To print all the lines in a file, with line numbers

```
% perl -e '$i=1;while(<>){print "$i: $_";$i++}' filename.txt
```

To remove all leading whitespace from each line in a file

```
% perl -e 'while(<>){s/^\s+//g;print;}' filename.txt
```

To print a file all in uppercase

```
% perl -e 'while(<>){print uc  $_;}'
```

Because these sorts of scripts commonly use `while` loops with `<>` and some form of print, Perl has a shortcut for that. The `-p` option allows you to omit the `while (<>)` part. It will also print `$_` for each line. So, for example, that uppercase example could be written like this instead (whether this example is better or not is up to you):

```
% perl -p -e '$_ = uc $_;' test.txt
```

This is equivalent to the code

```
while (<>) {
   $_ = uc $_;
   print;
}
```

You can also collapse the options into a single dash, as long as the `e` comes last:

```
% perl -pe '$_ = uc $_;' test.txt
```

Note

`-p` isn't the only Perl option designed to optimize your typing in one-liners. The `-n` option does the same thing as `-p`, minus the `print` part (all it gives you is the `while (<>)` loop). The `-l` option, when used with either `-p` or `-n`, will automatically chomp the newlines off of each line for you, and then put it back when you print the line. (Or, to be more specific, it sets the value of the `$\` variable, the output record separator, to be `$/`, the input record separator, usually a newline.) You can also give `-l` an octal argument representing the character you want to use as the output record separator.

Finally, Perl one-liners can be extremely powerful when used in conjunction with the `-i` option. For example, say you had written a novel and had it stored in a series of files ending with a `.txt` extension. You want to change all instances of the name "Steve" with the name "Fred." Here's a Perl one-liner that modifies all the original files and creates a backup copy of each:

```
% perl -p -i.bak -e 's/Steve/Fred/g' *.txt
```

The `-i` option changes your original files in place, so that the new versions will have the same filenames as the originals. The old versions of the files (the ones with Steve in them) will be saved off to filenames with the extension `.txt.bak`. This way, if you find that it wasn't Steve you wanted to change, it was Albert, you can get your original files back. Be careful when you use this Perl command—try it on a single file without modifying it, first, to make sure your one-liner works right. Otherwise you could end up moving a lot of `.bak` files back to where they belong!

Object-Oriented Programming

One of the major topics I didn't cover in this book is the use of Perl for object-oriented programming, or OOP (if this was *Sams Teach Yourself Perl in 25 and a Half Days*, we might have been able to cover it). Fortunately, Perl makes object-orientation easy by using familiar Perl features such as packages, subroutines, and references to implement an object-oriented programming environment. This way, if you know something about OOP, you can start programming right away by following only a few rules. If you don't know object-oriented programming, you have some basic background to catch up on, but then you won't have any other major new language features of Perl to learn to be able to use OOP skills right away.

Getting Started and Learning More

If you're unfamiliar with object-oriented programming but want to do some, your best first step is to learn about the basic concepts. Object-oriented programming is simply a different way of looking at the same programming problem. Everything you've learned so far in this book about syntax and good programming practice still applies; the difference is how your whole larger script is organized and how it behaves.

The central notion behind object-oriented programming is that instead of your script being a collection of sequentially executed statements and subroutines, it is a collection of objects that interact with each other in some predefined way. Each object has a defined appearance or state (variables, or properties in OOP jargon) and a defined set of behaviors (subroutines, called methods in OOP parlance). Objects get this template of behavior and state from a class definition. That class definition, in turn, often automatically inherits (uses) features from one or more other classes. When you build an object-oriented script, you use Perl to create one or more of your own classes, which import and use classes and objects from other sources (usually modules). When your Perl script runs, runtime objects are created from the various classes that modify each other's variables and call each other's subroutines to produce some result at the end.

If that previous paragraph scared the living daylights out of you, don't panic. Perl makes it easy to learn about OOP slowly, to use only some features of OOP without having to learn about everything at once. And there are lots of OOP tutorials out there to help you grasp the concepts and the theory. The following are some good places to start:

- The definitive text for writing object-oriented programs in Perl is Damian Conway's *Object Oriented Perl*, which is published by Manning. It's not an easy read, but if you're serious about object-oriented Perl, it's the book to get.
- The `perltoot` (object-oriented tutorial) man page comes with Perl and offers a basic tutorial and Perl background for object-oriented programming. From there,

the `perlobj` (Perl Objects) and `perlbot` ("bag of tricks") man pages will fill in the gaps.

- Many books that deal with other OOP languages such as Java or C++ might offer basic OOP background chapters, if you've already got those books lying around or if you can borrow one from a friend. I wrote one for *Sams Teach Yourself Java in 21 Days* that may be of use. OOP concepts can usually be applied from one language to another.

If you're still boggled, don't panic. Although OOP is considered the wave of the future by many, if you're comfortable working in plain-old Perl and no one at a job is demanding that you learn OOP, there's nothing wrong with sticking to what you know. There's more than one way to do it.

The Basics (for Those Who Already Know OOP)

So you know what an object is, how it relates to a class, and you're familiar with the terms instance variable, method, inheritance, constructors, destructors, and encapsulation. Let's apply that terminology to Perl.

Using Classes, Objects, and Object References

In Perl, a class is a package, and the namespace defined by the package defines the encapsulation and scope for that class. Variables defined in that package are class (static) variables; instance variables are typically created by using a reference to a hash, keyed by instance variable name. Class and instance methods are both defined by using subroutines; the only difference between a method and a regular subroutine is that a method assumes its first argument will be a classname (for class methods) or an object reference (for instance methods).

An object reference? Indeed. This is the one bit of new Perl information you need to know to use OOP in Perl. An object in Perl is effectively a reference to some data structure (typically an anonymous empty hash) that has been specially marked so that it behaves as an object and knows to which class it belongs. To mark something as an object, you use the built-in `bless` function. The `bless` function returns a reference to an object that you can then assign to a scalar variable the way you would any reference.

20

Typically, you'll use `bless` in the constructor for your class. That constructor is simply a subroutine conventionally called `new`. The `bless` function takes two arguments: the thing for which you want to create an object reference and the name of a class. A simple class definition, then, might look something like the following:

```
package MyClass;
sub new {
   my $classname = shift;
```

```
    my $self = {};
    return bless $self, $classname;
}
```

Here, the new class method is assumed to be called with one argument, a classname. Inside new we create an empty anonymous hash, `bless` it with the current classname, and return that reference. Note that this is a class method, and class methods always have the name of the class as their first argument.

Note

You can also use `bless` with a single argument (the thing to `bless`), and Perl will use the name of the current class for the second argument. However, because of the way Perl operates on inherited methods, using the single-argument `bless` can result in wrong results if some other class inherits your constructor. It's generally a good idea to get into the habit of using the two-argument version of `bless` and to get the classname from the argument list for the method.

To create and use an object (from this class or from any other class), you'd call the new method with the package (class) name. You can do it in the same file as your class definition, as long as you switch to package main first:

```
package main;
$obj = new MyClass;
```

The scalar variable `$obj` then contains a reference to the object defined by the class `MyClass`. Alternately, you can use an alternate syntax with `->` to call the new constructor:

```
$obj = MyClass->new();
```

The two different ways of calling `new` are exactly the same; however, if your new constructor requires arguments other than the classname, it's often easier to use the latter format:

```
$obj = MyClass->new(12, 240, 15);
```

To call methods defined in your new object, you'd simply dereference the object reference. The `->` syntax works particularly well here:

```
$obj->aSubroutine('foo','bar');
```

Alternately, you can use a more standard function call syntax for methods, where the classname or an object reference must be the first argument to that method:

```
aSubroutine $obj, 'foo', 'bar';
```

In this case, because the first argument is an object reference, Perl will dereference the reference for you and call the right method.

You can also call a method as if it were a function inside a package (`Myclass::aSubroutine()`), but don't do that unless you know what you're doing. You're subverting the OOP-ness of the class when you do that, and you lose the ability to get at a method definition available through inheritance. More about defining and calling references in the next section, "Instance Variables."

Instance Variables

When you create an object by using this example, you use an anonymous hash as the "thing" to be blessed into an object. Why a hash? Because you can use that hash to store and access instance variables, and you'll get a new version of those variables each time. This is how all internal object state is stored in Perl objects.

> **Note**
>
> Some OOP languages make a distinction between instance variables and class variables (the latter is sometimes called *static* data). Perl does not have class variables per se. Although you can always create package global variables to represent class variables (and access them through normal package syntax (`$MyClass::myclassvar`), those variables are not inherited and can be accessed or changed without restriction by any user of your class. Try to work around the use of class variables by using instance variables instead.

Generally, a class's instance variables are defined and initialized in the constructor for your class. In fact, you might want to pass arguments to `new` that represent the initial values of that class:

```
#!/usr/bin/perl -w

package Rectangle;
sub new {
   my ($classname, $w, $h) = @_;
   my $self = {};
   $self->{Width} = $w;
   $self->{Height} = $h;
   return bless $self, $classname
}
sub area {
   my $self = shift;
   return $self->{Width} * $self->{Height};
}

package main;
```

```
$sq = new Rectangle (12, 20);
print "Area: ", $sq->area(), "\n";
```

In this example, we used a class constructor that takes two extra arguments—a width and a height—with which it constructs the rectangle object, storing those values in the object's hash keyed by the strings `Width` and `Height`. We also created an `area` method that multiplies the current values of those instance variables and returns the result.

Generally, Perl's model for instance variables is that to access or modify the values of those variables, you create and use methods to do so rather than modifying those values yourself through direct assignment. This has advantages for inheritance, and some would argue provides more of a "pure" object-oriented interface to your class or object. You can, however access instance variables by using regular dereferencing syntax:

```
# non OOPy variable access
print "Width: $sq->{Width}\n";
print "Height: $sq->{Height}\n";
```

Inheritance

Similar to any respectable object-oriented programming language, Perl provides class inheritance to allow classes to automatically make use of and expand on the definitions of other classes. If class B inherits behavior from class A, class A is called the superclass or base class. Class B, in turn, is called the derived class or subclass.

To indicate that a class inherits from some other class, use the special array `@ISA`. The `@ISA` array indicates in which classes to search for method definitions if a definition for a method being called does not exist in the current class. So, for example, if you had a superclass called `Feline`, a subclass called `Lion` might look like this:

```
package Lion;
@ISA = qw( Feline );
...
```

The call to `qw` here isn't really needed when a class inherits from only one superclass, but it does make it easy to add more superclasses later, for multiple inheritance:

```
package HouseCat;
@ISA = qw( Feline Pet );
...
```

When a method is invoked on a particular object and no definition of that method is found in the current class definition, Perl looks for a method definition in each of the listed superclasses, depth first, in the `@ISA` array. In other words, the method `eat`, invoked on the `HouseCat` class, would first look for a definition in `HouseCat` itself, then in `Feline`, and then in all the superclasses of `Feline`, if any, and in those classes' superclasses, before looking for that definition in `Pet`. The first definition found is the one that will be used.

Perl only provides method inheritance. For "inherited" instance variables you can use inherited constructor methods to build a single hash of instance variables, which is made up of all the superclasses' instance variables plus any defined for the current class (the `perlobj` man page includes an example of this).

Defining Methods

There are three general conceptual ways to look at defining a method:

- New methods specific to the current class
- Methods that override methods defined in superclasses
- Methods that expand on or add to the behavior of a superclasses' methods

Regular methods that don't make use of inheritance are defined as regular subroutines inside the class (package) definition. The only assumption you need to make concerns the first argument to that subroutine, which determines whether the method is a class or instance method.

For instance methods, the first argument is an object reference. Typically, the first thing you do in these methods is extract that reference from the argument list and store it in a scalar variable (`$self` is a very common variable name, but you can call it anything you like):

```
sub myMethod {
   my $self = shift;
...
}
```

For class methods, the first argument is simply the name of the class—just a string, nothing special. Again, generally you'll want to extract and save it in a scalar variable.

What about methods that could be class or instance methods, depending on their argument? You'll need a way to test that argument inside the body of the method to see if it's an object or a class. The `ref` function works well this way:

```
sub classOrInstance {
  my $arg = shift;
  if (ref($arg)) {
     print "Argument is an object\n";
  } else {
     print "Argument is a class name\n";
  }
}
```

Note that the `ref` function, given an object reference as an argument, returns the name of the class of which the object is an instance.

Invoking methods defined in the current class will execute that method—even if there's a method of the same name further up in the inheritance chain. This is how you define methods that override existing methods—just define it and you're done.

If you want to add to the behavior of some superclass's method rather than override it altogether, a special package called `SUPER` tells Perl to search for a method definition in the classes defined by `@ISA`:

```
sub calculate {
   my $self = shift;
   my $sum = $self->SUPER::calculate(); # do superclass first

   foreach (@_) {
      $sum += $_;
   }
   return $sum;
}
```

> **Note**
>
> One common use of `SUPER` is in inherited constructors (new methods). With `SUPER`, you can create a constructor that runs up the chain of inheritance to make sure the current object has all the instance variables and default state of those variables that it needs.

You've already seen how to create constructor methods by using `bless`; you can also create destructor methods, which are executed after all references to the object have gone away and it's just about to be garbage collected. To create a destructor method, define a subroutine called `DESTROY` in your class:

```
sub DESTROY {
   print "Destroying object\n";
   ...
}
```

Autoloaded Methods

One nifty feature of Perl's method invocation is that of autoloaded methods. Autoloaded methods are sort of the methods of last resort—if you invoke a method on an object and Perl cannot find any existing definition for that method, it will attempt to call a method called `AUTOLOAD` instead. The package variable `$AUTOLOAD` will contain the name of the method that was called (including the original classname from which it was called); you can then use that information to do something for otherwise unknown methods. The `perlobj` man page shows a great example of using autoloaded methods as accessor methods for instance variables without having to define separate methods for each one. Here's a simple example of an autoloaded method to handle this sort of behavior:

```
package HouseCat;
@ISA = qw( Feline, Pet );

sub new {
  my $classname = shift;
  return bless {}, $classname;
}

sub AUTOLOAD {
   my ($self,$arg) = @_;
   my $name = $AUTOLOAD;

   my $name =~ s/.*://;  # get rid of package part
   if ($arg) {  # set value
      $self->{$name} = $arg;
      return $arg;
   } else {     # no arg, return value
      return $self->{$name};
   }
}

package main;
my $cat = new HouseCat;
$cat->color("Grey");
print "My cat is " . $cat->color() . "\n";
```

In this example, the `HouseCat` class doesn't have a `color` method (and we're assuming that none of its superclasses has one either). When the `color` method is called, Perl calls `AUTOLOAD` instead. For this definition of `AUTOLOAD`, we get the name of the method that was called through the `$AUTOLOAD` variable, strip off the package name at the beginning, and then use that method name as an instance variable name. If the method was called with an argument, we'll set that instance variable; otherwise we'll just print the current value (it's up to the caller to manage undefined instance variables). You could just as easily use this `AUTOLOAD` method for any instance variable—name, age, temperament, favorite_food, and so on.

20

Note

> `AUTOLOAD` methods aren't technically the methods of last resort; in addition to `AUTOLOAD` there is also the `UNIVERSAL` class. `UNIVERSAL` is used as sort of a global superclass; you can define your last-resort methods there.

An Example: Using Object-Oriented Modules

Perl's sense of OOP is that much of it is optional; you can use only a little OOP, or go whole hog and OOP everything in sight if you want. It all depends on whatever's easiest, and how much of an OOP fanatic you are.

In many cases, the easiest way to use Perl's OOP in your scripts is to make use of the various CPAN modules in an object-oriented way, but not necessarily to structure your own scripts as a set of objects. Let's re-examine the work we did on Day 16, "Using Perl for CGI Scripting," with CGI scripts and the CGI module. This module is written so that its subroutines can be used as ordinary subroutines or as object-oriented methods. Let's take an exercise we did at the end of that lesson—Exercise #1, a CGI script that does nothing but print the keys and values that were submitted to it—and use the CGI module in an object-oriented way.

Listing 20.1 shows the original script.

LISTING 20.1 pairs1.pl

```
 1: #!/usr/bin/perl -w
 2: use strict;
 3: use CGI qw(:standard);
 4:
 5: my @keys = param();
 6:
 7: print header;
 8: print start_html('Hello!');
 9: print "<H1>Key/Value Pairs</H1>\n";
10: print "<UL\n";
11:
12: foreach my $name (@keys) {
13:     print "<LI>$name = ", param($name), "\n";
14: }
15: print "</UL>\n";
16:
17: print end_html;
```

We use four of the CGI module's subroutines in this script: `param` (lines 5 and 13), which gives us both the full list of available keys and the values of specific keys; `header` (line 7), which prints a CGI header; `start_html` (line 8), which prints the top part of an HTML file; and `end_html` (line 17), which prints the tail end of an HTML file. In this previous example, we used these subroutines as regular subroutines.

But the CGI module can also be used as an object-oriented class. Create an instance of that class, and you can use those subroutines as if they were methods (because, well, they are). All this involves is one extra line of code and some slightly different syntax for the subroutines. I also removed the "standard" flag when I imported the CGI module because it's not necessary to import the standard methods when using it in object-oriented mode.) Listing 20.2 shows the result.

LISTING 20.2 An Object-Oriented `pairs1.pl`

```
 1: #!/usr/bin/perl -w
 2: use strict;
 3: use CGI;
 4:
 5: my $obj = CGI->new();
 6: my @keys = $obj->param();
 7:
 8: print $obj->header();
 9: print $obj->start_html('Hello!');
10: print "<H1>Key/Value Pairs</H1>\n";
11: print "<UL\n";
12:
13: foreach my $name (@keys) {
14:     print "<LI>$name = ", $obj->param($name), "\n";
15: }
16: print "</UL>\n";
17:
18: print $obj->end_html();
```

See the differences? There are effectively only two:

- Line 5 is where we instantiate our CGI object and store a reference to it in the `$obj` variable. Following Perl conventions, the object constructor for the CGI class is called `new`.
- All our subroutines—`param`, `start_html`, `header`, and `end_html`—are called as object methods by using dereferencing syntax (the object, `->`, and the name of the method).

The end result? Exactly the same thing as the non-OOP version. The CGI module is written to work equally well as a regular collection of subroutines and as an object-oriented class.

Note that this example isn't a pure OOP program; we haven't created any of our own classes here. A "true" OOP script would put the bulk of the code into its own class, using the CGI module there, and then do little in the main package other than instantiate our class and call a method or two to get it running. This is one of the neat things about OOP in Perl—you can use only as much object-oriented programming as you need to. Unlike more strict OOP languages, you don't have to objectify the things that don't seem to fit into objects.

Sockets

Unix was built from the ground up with networking in mind, and Perl shows its Unix roots by providing robust support for networking code. Perl includes a number of built-in functions for dealing with sockets (listed in Table 20.1), which behave similarly to their C counterparts. If you're familiar with socket-based programming, these functions should look familiar to you. You might also want to use the `Socket` module, which gives you access to the common structure definitions from C's `socket.h`.

Some caveats about the use of sockets in Perl, however. The first is that some of the Perl socket features are available only on Unix; on some Windows or Macintoshes you'll need to use Win32 or MacPerl equivalents, making your scripts much less portable. The second caveat is that unless you're implementing some form of nonstandard networking protocol, chances are very good that there's a module that already exists to do what you want to do with sockets. There's no reason to implement any part of a Web server or Web browser; there are modules that will do that, and all you have to do is use them. I'll discuss the LWP (a popular Web library for Perl) library a bit later in this chapter, and we'll use it extensively in the next lesson.

Before you write any program by hand that implements a well-known protocol, be sure to check out CPAN. You might want to look specifically at modules in the `Net` package, most of the non-Web networking modules are subpackages of that package.

Let's look at some example code that demonstrates how to use sockets. Listing 20.3 is the source code for a simple TCP client that uses a socket to connect to a Web server. What it amounts to is the world's simplest Web browser.

LISTING 20.3 A Program That Uses a Socket to Connect to a Web Server

```
#!/usr/bin/perl

use Socket;

my ($hostname, $file, $port, $iaddr, $paddr, $proto, $line);
```

LISTING 20.3 continued

```
$host = "www.perl.org";
$file = "/pub/a/language/info/software.html";

$iaddr = (gethostbyname($host))[4];
$port = 80;
$paddr = sockaddr_in($port, $iaddr);
$proto = getprotobyname( 'tcp' );

socket(SOCK, AF_INET, SOCK_STREAM, $proto)
    or die "socket: $!";

# Connect our socket to the server socket.
connect( SOCK, $paddr )
    or die "connect: $!";

# For flush on socket file handle after every
# write.
select(SOCK);
$| = 1;
select(STDOUT);

# Send get request to server.
print SOCK "GET $file HTTP/1.0\n\n";

# Print out the contents of the page
while (<SOCK>)
{
    print;
}

close(SOCK);
```

This script is very straightforward, the name of the server to connect to, and the name of the file to retrieve are hard coded. The script simply connects to the server, requests the file specified, and then prints out the data that's returned—the HTML that makes up the Web page. Let's break down the script line by line.

On line 3 import the `Socket` module, which imports a bunch of symbols into the script. I'll indicate later when I use things from the `Socket` module. On line 5, a number of variables are declared using the `my` function so that they're local to my script. It's not necessary, but it is a good programming practice.

On lines 7 and 8, the hostname of the server to which I'll be connecting, and the filename I want to retrieve from the server are defined. From this point forward we get into real socket programming. On line 10 the `gethostbyname` function (passing in the hostname I defined earlier as an argument) is used to retrieve the address of the server and assign it to the `$iaddr` variable. There's a little bit going on here that needs explaining.

The `gethostbyname` function returns a list. I'm only interested in the fifth element in the list, which is the first address associated with that hostname. The format of the address is four bytes, so if you print it out, you could very well end up with control characters or something weird from the higher end of the ASCII character set. The important thing is that the socket code uses this format to connect to the remote host.

On line 12, the `sockaddr_in` function is used, which is provided by the `Socket` module, and returns a `SOCKADDR_IN` structure when passed a port number and four-byte address. On line 13, the built-in function `getprotobyname` is used to retrieve the number associated with the TCP protocol.

At this point, I've prepared all the information I need to create a socket connection. The next step is to actually create the socket. To do so, the `socket` function is used, which is another Perl built-in. It accepts four arguments—the filehandle to assign to the socket, the domain, the type of socket to create, and the protocol to use. The second and third arguments are constants provided by the `Socket` module. As you can see, the fourth argument is the `$proto` variable that was set earlier.

The next step is to connect to the remote machine, using the built-in `connect` function. The filehandle is passed in to the socket and the address (stored in `$paddr`) that I want to connect to. Assuming that the script is still executing, I'm now connected to the Web server.

On lines 30–32, the `SOCK` filehandle is selected, set `$|` to 1, turning off buffering of output, and then select `STDOUT` so that everything printed will go to standard out by default. The reason buffering is turned off is so that I'm only sending a bit of output to the socket, and the Web server won't start returning data until it receives the HTTP command I'm sending.

On line 35, you'll find the actual HTTP `GET` command that retrieves the filename specified from the Web server. As soon as the server receives two consecutive carriage returns, it sends the requested Web page over the socket. On lines 38–41, just iterate over the lines of output received over the socket, and print them out to the screen. That's all there is to it.

Table 20.1 shows the built-in functions for sockets; see the `perlfunc` man page for details on any of these functions.

TABLE 20.1 Socket Functions

Function	*What it Does*
`accept`	In a network server, accept a socket connection from a client. Same as `accept(2)`.
`bind`	Binds an address to an already-open socket file handle. Same as `bind(2)`.
`connect`	In a network client, connects to a server that is waiting for connections. Same as `connect(2)`.
`getpeername`	Returns the socket address at the other end of a connection.
`getsockname`	Returns the socket address at this end of a connection.
`getsockopt`	Returns values of socket options.
`listen`	In a server, tells the system to listen for and queue socket connections to this socket. Same as `listen(2)`.
`recv`	Receive a message on a socket. Same as `recv(2)`.
`send`	Send a message on a socket. Same as `send(2)`.
`setsockopt`	Sets the socket options.
`shutdown`	Close a socket, with some control options. You could also use `close()`.
`socket`	Open a socket and associate it with a file handle.
`socketpair`	Open a pair of unnamed sockets. Same as `socketpair(2)`.

POD (Plain Old Documentation) Files

POD, short for Plain Old Documentation, is a simple formatting language for creating documentation to go along with your Perl scripts or modules. Commonly, you'll embed that documentation inside your script file itself; that way you can keep both the script and the documentation together and not have to keep track of each separately (Perl will happily ignore the POD content when it executes your scripts).

20

To view the POD content of your script (or to view POD files containing nothing but POD content), you can use the `perldoc` script (part of the Perl distribution) to display that text on your screen, or you can use a translator to convert the POD files into something else—for example, `pod2text` for text files, `pod2html` for HTML, `pod2man` for `nroff`-formatted man pages, or `pod2latex` for LaTeX formatting. Throughout this book you've probably been using `perldoc`—and therefore POD files—to view the various bits of Perl documentation online.

POD is not a fully featured text-formatting language such as `troff`, TeX, or even HTML. If you want to create lots of heavily formatted documentation for your scripts, you'd be better off using something else and keeping your document files separate from your scripts. But POD files generally can be read on different platforms and with different systems or can be converted to other more common formats on-the-fly.

You can find examples of POD text in just about any publicly available script or module from the Perl distribution and from CPAN. More details than those in this section can also be found in the `perldoc` man page.

Creating POD Files

POD-formatted text consists of command paragraphs and regular paragraphs. Command paragraphs describe simple formatting and some text; regular paragraphs contain actual body text. You can also embed character-formatting commands inside regular paragraphs.

Command paragraphs appear on individual lines and begin with an equal sign. Some command paragraphs have associated text, which appears just after the name of that paragraph. The end of the command paragraph is a blank line.

For headings, use the `=head1` and `=head2` command paragraphs, with the text of the heading immediately following the command. These headings are similar to the `<H1>` and `<H2>` tags in HTML or the `.SH` tag in `troff` or `nroff`.

For lists or other indented items, use the `=over`, `=item`, and `=back` commands. Use `=over` to start a list, with an optional number indicating the number of spaces to indent the list. Each list item begins with an `=item` tag, with an optional character indicating the symbol or number to mark each item (you'll have to do numbering yourself; it doesn't happen automatically). And, finally, use `=back` to undo the indent created by the `=over`.

Regular paragraphs are included as simple paragraphs, typed, with no command paragraph to indicate them. Paragraphs that start without initial whitespace are typically reformatted to fit the page width (like `<p>` in HTML); paragraphs with initial indentation are used verbatim (like `<pre>` in HTML). All paragraphs must end with a blank line.

You can embed character-formatting codes and links in paragraphs to emphasize a particular word or to link to something else (commonly another Perl-related man page like `perlfunc` or the like). The following are some of the more common character formats:

- `I<text>` will italicize the word text.
- `B<text>` will boldface the word text.
- `C<text>` uses text as literal code.
- `&escape;` substitutes a special character for the code escape. These are nearly identical to the HTML escape codes for accents and other special characters.

- E<escape> does the same thing as &escape;.
- L<manpage> will create a link (or a textual cross-reference) to a man page, for example, L<perlfunc> links to the perlfunc man page. You can also link to specific sections in the man page itself.

To embed text formatted in some other formatting language—HTML, or troff, for example—use the =for, =begin, and =end commands. Text formatted for specific formatting languages will be output unprocessed by the specific translator (for example, the pod2html translator will copy any formatted HTML directly to the output) and will be ignored otherwise. Use embedded formatting as a way of providing conditional formatting in specific instances.

Embedding POD in Scripts

You can either include POD-formatted text in its own file (conventionally as files ending with a .pod extension), or you can include them inside your script files, making them easy to change and keep updated.

To include POD text inside a script, start it with any POD command (typically =head1, although the =pod command can indicate the start of POD text as well). End all the POD text with =cut. This will tell Perl when to stop and restart parsing the text for actual Perl code.

Although POD text is usually included as a block either at the beginning or end of a script, you can also put it anywhere inside your script, for example, to describe a subroutine's behavior next to the subroutine itself. As long as you start and end your POD text with a command paragraph and =cut, Perl won't have a problem with this.

To include POD text at the end of a file, and when you're using an __END__ marker (as you might be if you're creating modules), make sure you include a blank line after the __END__.

Evaluating Code On-the-Fly

One useful advanced feature of Perl borrowed from other languages is the capability to evaluate a string as a bit of Perl code on-the-fly at a script's runtime. This is accomplished through the use of the eval function, which takes a string or a block as an argument and compiles and runs that bit of Perl code as if it were typed into a file or executed by using a Perl one-liner—all inside another currently running Perl script.

Why is this useful? For a number of reasons. One use is that it allows you to build up sophisticated structures and function calls without needing extensive if-else branches: just compose the thing you want to call by appending strings together, and then call eval to execute that string. It also allows you to read in and execute other files of Perl code from inside a Perl script—similar to how use and require works, but always at your script's runtime (in fact, require is semantically similar to eval with some extra features for handling where to find files and reloading those files). It also allows you to execute code on-the-fly when that's your actual intent—the Perl debugger's code execution feature uses this, for example. Or you could write an interpreter for your own language in Perl by using eval.

The eval feature of Perl is also useful for testing code before actually running it and handling any errors or unusual conditions that result from executing that code. This is a feature other languages often call exceptions. For example, if you were looking for a particular feature of Perl to see if it was available on the current system—for example, fork—you could try a simple example inside an eval, see if it works and, if so, continue on with the script and if not try something else. Exception handling with eval allows for more robust error-checking and handling in your scripts.

For a description of eval, see the perlfunc man page.

Commonly Used Modules

Modules have been discussed on and off throughout this book. Now that the end is here, it's time to discuss a few useful modules that we didn't cover earlier. As has been mentioned several times already, CPAN is huge—these modules are just a selection that are widely used, but that aren't included as part of the Perl distribution.

LWP

LWP, also referred to as libwww-perl, is a massive package that contains a number of individual modules that pertain to basically all things Web-related. It's most frequently used for its built-in HTTP client, but it provides plenty of other Web-related features as well. After you've installed it, you can type perldoc LWP for details.

One module in the LWP package is LWP::Simple, which enables you to easily use the HTTP client features of LWP. More flexible (and difficult to use) modules exist if you have unusual requirements, but if you're just retrieving regular old Web pages (even if you're calling CGI programs or other applications with arguments), LWP::Simple will do the trick.

Let's look at an example of how LWP::Simple is used:

```
#!/usr/bin/perl
use LWP::Simple;
getprint("http://www.typerl.com/");
```

That's the whole script. First, I import the `LWP::Simple` module, then I call the `getprint` function and pass in the URL `http://www.typerl.com/`. As you might have guessed, the script downloads the Web page and prints it out to STDOUT. Of course, there are plenty of other ways to simply print out the source code to a Web page.

If you want to do more to the Web page than just print it out, you can use the `get` function, which retrieves the contents of a page and returns a string. Here's what a script that uses `get` looks like:

```
#!/usr/bin/perl
use LWP::Simple;
my $text = get("http://www.typerl.com/");
```

The function returns `undef` if there's an error, so you can make sure that the request worked. You might want to use some other functions as well. The head function is used to retrieve information from the headers of a request. It can be called as follows:

```
($content_type, $document_length, $modified_time, $expires, $server)
    = head("http://www.typerl.com/");
```

There are also two functions used to copy remote Web pages to local files. `getstore()` simply takes two arguments, a URL and a filename, and copies the contents of the requested into the filename provided. The `mirror` function is a bit more sophisticated. It attempts to fetch and store a file, just like `getstore()`, but before storing the file, it checks to see if the local file already exists. If it does, it only stores the remote file if it has been modified since the file on disk was modified, and only if the content length of the remote file is different from the file stored on disk.

If `LWP::Simple` doesn't fulfill your requirements, the next step is to use the `LWP::UserAgent` module, which offers more flexibility. For information on `LWP::UserAgent`, check out the perldoc for it. You might also find the `lwpcook` Perl documentation useful, it's a cookbook for LWP users.

Sending E-mail with `Net::SMTP`

If you're writing Perl programs with Unix, it's easy to send mail. You just do something like this:

```
open (MAIL, "| mail someone@example.com")
    or die "Can't send email:";
```

Then you can just print out your e-mail message to the `MAIL` filehandle and close it when you're ready to send the message. Unfortunately, if your script will run somewhere other than on a computer running Unix, your calls to the `mail` program won't work. If you want to make sure that your script works correctly across platforms, using `Net::SMTP` is the wiser choice.

`Net::SMTP` sends mail by connecting directly to an SMTP server and transmitting your e-mail message. Because it doesn't use any local program on the computer you're using, it will work from any platform. You just have to know the address of an SMTP server that will allow you to connect and send an e-mail.

`Net::SMTP` is an object-oriented module, here's some example code that demonstrates how it is used:

```
use Net::SMTP;
$smtp = Net::SMTP->new('mailhost');
$smtp->mail('user');
$smtp->to('anybody@example.com');
$smtp->data();
$smtp->datasend("To: postmaster\n");
$smtp->datasend("\n");
$smtp->datasend("A simple test message\n");
$smtp->dataend();
$smtp->quit();
```

Let's look at the example line by line. First, the `Net::SMTP` method is imported so that it can be used. On the next line, the constructor is called to create a new SMTP session. The constructor accepts the hostname (or IP address) of the SMTP server as its argument. Needless to say, the host specified must be running an SMTP server, and you must be authorized to use it for this to work.

Next, the `mail` method is used to initiate the sending of the new message. The argument passed in is the address that will appear in the `From:` field of the e-mail. If you just pass in a username, the hostname of the machine that the script is running on will be appended to the address.

The `to` method is used to specify the recipient (or list of recipients) to which the message will be sent. If you are sending the e-mail to multiple recipients, the argument list should take the following format:

```
$smtp->to('anybody@example.com', 'somebody@example.com',
'everybody@example.com');
```

The `data` method can be used in two ways. In this example, I use the `data` method to indicate that I'm going to start sending the body of the e-mail. Then, the `datasend` method is used to send the actual data and `dataend` to indicate that I'm finished. The alternate approach is to supply a list (or list reference) as an argument to data. The data in the list is used as the body of the e-mail message.

When you've sent your e-mail message, you can use the `quit` method to end your SMTP session.

Handling XML with Perl

At this point, XML is more than just a trend. It's being used as a storage format for documents, an interchange format for sharing data between applications, and a standardized, structured format for things like configuration files. Perl is a perfect match for handling XML data just because of its built-in functionality for dealing with text files. However, because valid XML follows a specific structure, you don't just have to rip apart your XML files using regular expressions and functions such as `split`. Instead, you can use a module designed to handle XML files.

There are a number of XML modules for Perl, including `XML::Parser` and `XML::Simple`, which can be used to parse XML and to create it. There are also a lot of modules that are designed to produce XML output, like a module that turns POD documentation into XML files. For a list of all the XML-related modules, check out CPAN.

Here's a specific example that uses the `XML::Simple` module. First, let's look at our data file, a very simple XML document. Here's the data:

```
<computers>
    <computer name="foo">
        <os>Mac OS X</os>
        <memory>256</memory>
        <address>foo.example.com</address>
        <applications>
            <application>Emacs</application>
            <application>Microsoft Word</application>
            <application>FileMaker</application>
        </applications>
    </computer>
    <computer name="bar">
        <os>Linux</os>
        <memory>256</memory>
        <address>bar.example.com</address>
        <applications>
            <application>vi</application>
            <application>mutt</application>
            <application>Apache</application>
        </applications>
    </computer>
</computers>
```

20

As you can see, the data in the XML document is stored in a tree-like data structure. `XML::Simple` will parse the file and create a nested data structure using hashes and arrays that mirror the data in the XML file. Using the `Data::Dumper` module, we can see the data structure that's created.

Here's the program:

```
#!/usr/bin/perl

use XML::Simple;
use Data::Dumper;

my $computers = XMLin("computers.xml", searchpath=>("."));

print Dumper($computers);
```

First, the `XML::Simple` and `Data::Dumper` modules are imported. Then, the `XMLin()` function is used to parse the XML file. The first argument to `XMLin()` is the name of the file to parse and the second is a hash of options. For a list of all the options, see the perldoc for `XML::Simple`. In this case, I just put the current directory in the search path for XML documents.

The last line of the script runs the data structure generated by `XML::Simple` through data dumper, producing the following:

```
'computer' => {
               'foo' => {
                         'os' => 'Mac OS X',
                         'memory' => '256',
                         'address' => 'foo.example.com',
                         'apps' => {
                                     'app' => [
                                                'Emacs',
                                                'Microsoft Word',
                                                'FileMaker'
                                              ]
                                   }
                       },
               'bar' => {
                         'os' => 'Linux',
                         'memory' => '256',
                         'address' => 'bar.example.com',
                         'apps' => {
                                     'app' => [
                                                'vi',
                                                'mutt',
                                                'Apache'
                                              ]
                                   }
                       }
             }
```

(I cheated a bit and trimmed the output, but for all intents and purposes, it's the same.) Compare the output of `Data::Dumper` to the example XML document. The root level of the document is mapped to the variable `$computers`, which is a reference to a hash. The hash has one element—its key is `computer`. Its value is a reference to another hash, with keys denoted by the `name` attributes of the `computer` elements in the XML file. Each of those hashes has members with keys mapped to children of the `computer` elements. Let's look at one special item. The `apps` element contains a number of `app` elements. Those are stored in an anonymous array, which is referenced by the value of the `app` element.

Let's look at a program that fetches specific data from the data structure:

```
#!/usr/bin/perl

use XML::Simple;

my $computers = XMLin();

print $computers->{computer}->{foo}->{os}, "\n";
print $computers->{computer}->{foo}->{applications}->{application}->[0], "\n";
```

On line 3, the module is imported. On line 5, the `XMLIn()` subroutine is called, which reads in the XML document and assigns the data structure to the variable `$computers`. Because a filename is not specified anywhere in this program, it assumes I want to load an XML file with the same base name as the name of the program. So if the program is called `testxml.pl`, it looks for `testxml.xml`.

The output of this program is

```
Mac OS X
Emacs
```

It's easy to save a data structure to an XML file as well. To convert a data structure into XML, you just use the `XMLout()` function. It returns a string that you can save to a file, or a database field, or anywhere else you choose. Here's the syntax:

```
my $xml = XMLout($computers);
```

Creating International Perl Scripts

20

Internationalization, sometimes called I18N, is the process of generalizing a script or program so that it can be easily moved or translated into a different language or dialect. Localization, L10N, is the process of taking the internationalized version of a script and making it work in a specific language. Some internationalization can be done in core Perl—extracting all the text strings that a script uses, for example, to allow those to be translated without mucking with the core code. Other things—working with character sets other than English's A to Z, using sorting (collating) systems other than simple A to Z, and formatting numbers—can be controlled through the use of Perl's local module.

For more information on using and managing Perl locales to create internationalized (or localized) scripts, see the `perllocale` man page.

Script Security with Taint Checking

Say you wrote a Perl script that was intended to be run by someone you don't know and don't necessarily trust—for example, if you're administering a multiuser Unix machine, or if your script will be used for CGI. Because you don't know the person running that script, that person could theoretically have hostile intentions and attempt to use your script to gain unauthorized access to your system or damage it in some way.

So what can you do to prevent a malicious user from doing any damage through your script? Careful programming can help with that—checking to make sure input doesn't include any sneaky things before passing it to a `system` function call or backquotes, for example. But sometimes it's hard to keep track of what data might be insecure, or hard to remember to make those sorts of checks. That's where taint mode can come in handy.

Taint mode is enabled with the `-T` option to Perl. (It also runs automatically if the user or group ID of the script itself is different from the user or group ID of the person running the script—for example, setuid scripts on Unix systems). When taint mode is enabled, Perl will watch the data that comes into your script—the environment, any command-line arguments, or data from a file handle (including standard input). If you try to use that data to affect anything outside your script, Perl will immediately exit. To actually use that data, you'll have to write your script to modify or extract specific bits of that data, thereby preventing data you don't expect from slipping through.

In other words, taint mode doesn't provide any extra security, but it does force you to write your code with an eye for security. If your scripts might end up running in an insecure environment, taint mode can help you make sure your scripts aren't glaring security holes for your system.

Find out more about taint mode and security in Perl in the `perlsec` man page. For more general issues of security and CGI, check out the WWW security FAQ at `http://www.w3.org/Security/Faq/`.

If you're particularly concerned about the security of your scripts in general, you might also want to check out Penguin, part of CPAN, which provides an environment that allows you to encrypt and digitally sign a piece of code and send it to some other site. At the destination site, Penguin decrypts and checks the trustworthiness of that code before executing it. Even then, Penguin executes the code within tightly controlled confines. You could consider Penguin similar to Java's mechanism for signing applets, and then running them inside a closed, secure "sandbox." See CPAN for more details about Penguin.

PerlScript

PerlScript, part of ActiveState's Perl for Windows package, is an ActiveX scripting engine. PerlScript allows you to add Perl as a scripting language to any ActiveX scripting host—in Internet Explorer, IIS or any Web server, or Microsoft's Windows Scripting Host (WSH), for example.

Microsoft's ActiveX scripting engines natively support VBScript and JavaScript scripting engines. Although those languages are adequate for many purposes, Perl can in many instances provide for features and more power. And if you're used to working with Perl, the capability to continue working in Perl rather than having to switch between languages is a nice advantage.

For the Web, PerlScript enables you to create Perl scripts embedded inside Web pages both on the client (Web browser) and the server side, in much the same way JavaScript and VBScript scripts and Active Server Pages (ASP) behave today.

PerlScript also works with the Windows Scripting Host, which enables you to control various aspects of the Windows system itself through the use of scripts (it's a replacement for old-fashioned DOS batch scripts). Windows Scripting Host has been built into all versions of Windows since Windows 98.

For information on ActiveX scripting in general, check out `http://msdn.microsoft.com/scripting`. For information on PerlScript, see the simple documentation that comes with PerlScript at `http://aspn.activestate.com/ASPN/Reference/`, or Matt Sergeant's excellent Complete Guide to PerlScript at `http://www.fastnetltd.ndirect.co.uk/Perl/Articles/PSIntro.html`.

What's Coming in Perl 6

The next major revision of Perl will be Perl 6. The development team will continue releasing versions of Perl under version number 5 until Perl 6 is released. Perl 6 is going to be a rewrite of Perl from the ground up. In most ways, it will be the same language that Perl 5 is, but everything in the language has been evaluated for inclusion in Perl 6, and lots of new things will be added as well. Unfortunately, there's so much going on with Perl 6 that it can't all be described here, especially because nothing is final until it's released.

The design for Perl 6 started with a request for comments process that yielded 361 RFC documents. The documents are currently being sifted through by Larry Wall and converted into a cohesive design of the next version of the language. The architecture of Perl will be changing fundamentally. Perl 6 will consist of a parser, a compiler, a byte code optimizer, and a virtual machine. This will make Perl 6 significantly more flexible than Perl 5. For example, there can be parsers for multiple languages, which produce syntax trees that can be compiled by the Perl 6 compiler. The compiler will produce byte code for the new Perl 6 runtime engine. Alternate compilers will be able to produce byte code for other runtime engines, like Microsoft .NET or the Java Virtual Machine.

As you can see, the emphasis with Perl 6 will be on creating a more flexible architecture for the language. There will also be plenty of syntax enhancements and features added to make life easier for Perl programmers. Also, thanks to the flexible parser built into Perl 6, Perl 5 programs will run without changes.

Going Deeper

Because this whole chapter is a larger version of the "Going Deeper" sections, there's not much left to talk about here. So instead, a reminder: If you have problems, questions, difficulties, or just curiosities about how any part of Perl behaves—from the basic operators to regular expressions to references to modules—try the Perl documentation (man pages and POD files), and particularly the Perl FAQs—for help and more information. The camel book (*The Perl Programming Language*, which I mentioned in Day 1's "Going Deeper") can often clear up many of the smaller details of how Perl is supposed to behave. If you're still stuck, hit the Web—`www.perl.com`, `www.activestate.com` (for Windows), and many of the other Web sites I've mentioned throughout this book can offer further assistance. Beyond that, there are a number of newsgroups (such as the `comp.perl` hierarchy—`comp.perl.misc`, in particular) and mailing lists where other Perl programmers hang out.

Good luck!

Summary

Today is the tying-up-the-loose-ends day. Today we looked at a number of extra features in Perl, the stuff that wasn't discussed in the previous 19 lessons of this book. It's a bit of a hodgepodge of stuff, including

- Perl one-liners, simple scripts that can be run directly from a command line to accomplish basic tasks without having to create a whole script

- Object-oriented programming in Perl—a combination of references, packages, modules, and subroutines, and some extra stuff to pull it all together
- An overview of network socket programming in Perl
- POD files, Perl's simple method for creating embedded documentation that can be formatted in various other ways (HTML, text, and so on)
- Building and evaluating code on-the-fly with `eval`
- Internationalization and localization with the locale module
- Checking for tainted data to prevent security bugs and holes in your scripts
- Using the PerlScript engine on Windows to incorporate Perl scripts into HTML Web pages or as a replacement for DOS and Windows batch files

Congratulations! We've only got one day left, and that one's full of examples. You've now learned enough of Perl to get quite a lot of exciting things done. Go to it! And don't forget—Perl is a collaborative effort. Make use of the modules in the CPAN, and if you write something that you think others might find useful, consider submitting it to the CPAN yourself.

Q&A

Q My one-liners don't work in MacPerl.

A Make sure in the Edit, Peferences, Scripts dialog that you have "Run Scripts Opened from Finder" selected. If you've chosen "Edit" here your one-liners won't work ("One Liner" is itself a MacPerl script).

Q My one-liners don't work in Windows.

A Notions of quotes are different in the Windows/DOS command line than they are on Unix. You can use both single and double-quotes in Unix; in Windows you can only use double quotes. For one-liners in Windows, make sure that you surround the entire one-line script in double-quotes and that all quotes inside the actual script are back-slashed.

Q My one-liners don't work in Unix.

A They don't? Did you type the script all on one line with no returns? Did you surround the entire script with single-quotes? Did you remember the `-e` option to Perl? If you've checked all these things, make sure the same script works if you put it into a file of its own.

Q From your description, Perl doesn't appear to support the object-oriented programming notions of public and private data. What's to stop someone from using methods in your class that you didn't intend to be part of the public API?

A Nothing. Perl's object-oriented model doesn't enforce any notion of a public or private API; it assumes that you and the programmers who use your classes will behave decently as far as the API is concerned. As the developer of a class, you should be sure to document your API and which of your methods are public (POD is good for this) and assume that if someone is using your class that they'll stick to that API. Conversely, if you're using someone else's class, you should stick to their documented public API and use internal methods or data only at your own risk and if you're sure you know what you're doing.

Q Multiple inheritance is really confusing and error-prone. Why didn't Perl use single inheritance instead?

A What, and limit the power of the language? It should be apparent at this point in the book that Perl doesn't really ever try to limit what the programmer can do. Multiple inheritance may indeed often be confusing and difficult to debug, but it's also incredibly powerful when used in conjunction with a good design (and don't forget, a good design doesn't necessarily involve inheritance). The designers of Perl would rather err on the side of having too much rope to hang yourself than not enough to tie a good knot.

Q Where on earth did the terms I18N and L10N come from?

A There's eighteen letters between the I and the N in the word internationalization (and ten between the L and N in localization). Internationalization and localization are really long words to type. Programmers hate that.

Workshop

The workshop provides quiz questions to help you solidify your understanding of the material covered and exercises to give you experience using what you've learned. Try to understand the quiz and exercise answers before you go on to tomorrow's lesson.

Quiz

1. What do the following Perl switches do (with regard to one-liners):

```
-e
-i
-p
```

2. How are classes, methods, and instance variables represented in Perl?

3. Show two ways to call a method.
4. How are multiply inherited superclasses searched when a method is invoked?
5. What do autoloaded methods do?
6. What are Perl formats used for? What are the two functions that make them work?
7. What is a POD file? Why use POD in your Perl scripts over some other format like HTML?
8. What does the `eval` function do? Why would you want to use it?
9. What is "taint mode" used for? How do you turn it on?

Exercises

1. Write a Perl one-liner that counts all occurrences of the letter "t" in the input and prints the result.
2. Write a Perl one-liner that sums all its input (assume all the input is numeric).
3. Write a Perl one-liner that replaces all instances of three spaces with a tab and saves the result in a file of the same name.
4. BUG BUSTER: What's wrong with this one-liner?

   ```
   perl -p 's/t/T/q';
   ```

5. BUG BUSTER: How about this one (HINT: There's more than one problem)?

   ```
   perl -ne 'print 'line: ', reverse $_;';
   ```

6. EXTRA CREDIT: Write a Perl class called `SimpleClass` that has three instance variables: `a`, `b`, and `c`. Include these methods:
   - A new constructor to create and initialize the `a`, `b`, and `c` variables.
   - Methods to print and change the values of `a`, `b`, and `c`. Implement these however you want.
   - A method to print the sum of a, b, and c. Make sure to test to see if `a`, `b`, and `c` contain numbers; print warnings otherwise.

Answers

Here are the answers to the Workshop questions in the previous section.

Quiz Answers

1. The `-e` option runs a Perl script on the command line (a one-liner).

   The `-i` option edits files in place; that is, the result of the script will be saved back to the original file. Any file extension argument to the `-i` option will be used to save the original version of the file.

The `-p` option surrounds the Perl one-liner with a `while (<>)` loop with a `print` statement at the end. If you want to perform some operation for each line of a file and then print it, use this command to save some typing.

2. Classes are packages in Perl; methods are subroutines that have either a classname or an object reference as their first argument. Instance variables are commonly implemented as hash elements with the name of the variable as the key.

3. You can call methods as if they were regular functions:

   ```
   method $obj,1,2,3;
   ```

   Or, using dereferencing syntax:

   ```
   $obj->method(1,2,3);
   ```

4. Multiply inherited superclasses are searched depth-first; that is, all the superclasses of the first superclass in the list (including any multiply inherited ones, in turn) are searched before the other superclasses in the list are searched.

5. Autoloaded methods are called when a method is called that doesn't have a corresponding method definition in the current class or any of its superclasses. You can use autoloaded methods to group together common methods (such as `get` and `set` variable methods) or to otherwise catch unknown method names.

6. Perl formats are used to format data in a tabular format for text output. The data will be fit automatically to the appropriate width, with each column aligned or filled based on the format you define. To create a format, you use `format` to define the format template and `write` to output the final result.

7. POD stands for Plain Old Documentation; it's a simple way of creating online-accessible documentation for your Perl scripts. POD makes a good general-purpose documentation format that can be easily extracted and converted into some other output format, like HTML or `troff`.

8. The `eval` function is used to evaluate bits of Perl code on-the-fly, during your script's runtime. You might use `eval` to incorporate other scripts into your current script or to test bits of code before actually running them for real.

9. Perl's taint mode is used to protect against errors and omissions in your Perl scripts that could result in insecure code. Insecure code, run in an insecure environment, could result in a malicious user tampering with or damaging your system. Taint mode puts all external data and settings in a special controlled environment and prevents you from accidentally using that data in a way that could be harmful. You turn on taint mode by using the `-T` option to Perl; it'll also automatically run if Perl is run in a situation where the user or group of the person running the script are different from the user or group of the script itself, for example, a CGI script running from a Web server.

Exercise Answers

1. Here's one way to do it:

```
perl -e ' while (<>){while (/t/g){$c++;}};print $c;' file.txt
```

2. Here's one way:

```
perl -e 'while(<>){$sum+=$_;}print "$sum\n";'
```

3. Here's one way:

```
perl -pe -i.bak 's/   /\t/g' ozy.txt
```

4. It's missing the `-e` option.
5. There are two problems with this example: one syntactic, one conceptual. The first is that you cannot nest single quotes inside single quotes. Replace the inner single quotes with double quotes.

   The second problem concerns the `reverse` function. Although this one-liner might appear to print each line in reverse order by character with the word "line" at the start, keep in mind that the `reverse` function behaves differently depending on whether it's used in scalar or list context. Here, because the arguments to print are always a list or combination of lists, `reverse` is called in a list context, which reverses the order of lines in an array. The `$_` argument is then converted to a list, that list of one line is reversed, and then passed onto print. In other words, nothing appears to happen.

   To actually reverse the string, you have to call the `reverse` function in a scalar context. This can be easily remedied with the `scalar` function:

```
perl -ne 'print "line: ", scalar (reverse $_);';
```

   Watch out for the newlines, though. Reversing a line with a newline at the end will print the newline at the beginning. An even better solution is to chomp the string, `reverse` it, and then print it with the newline tacked on again:

```
perl -ne 'chomp;print "line: ", scalar(reverse $_), "\n" ; '
```

   Conveniently, there's a Perl option that'll let you shorten this a little bit: the `-l` option, which pulls the newline off input, and then puts it (or any other end-of-line character you choose) back for you:

```
perl -lne 'print "line: ", scalar(reverse $_);'
```

6. Here's one way to do it (with code to test the result at the end). This version shows three different ways you might consider implementing instance variable access. Note that none of these methods is very robust; none of them check to make sure you're not trying to get or set the values of nonexistent variables (and, in fact, the generic versions will happily add an instance variable other than `a`, `b`, or `c`.)

```
#!/usr/bin/perl -w

package SimpleClass;

sub new {
   my ($classname, $a, $b, $c) = @_;
   my $self = {};
   $self->{a} = $a;
   $self->{b} = $b;
   $self->{c} = $c;
   return bless $self, $classname;
}

# the long way
sub getA {
    my $self = shift;
    return $self->{a};
}
sub setA {
    my $self = shift;
    if (@_) {
        $self->{a} = shift;
    } else {
        warn "no argument; using undef\n";
        $self->{a} = undef;
    }
}

# a more generic way, needs more args.
sub get {
    my ($self, $var) = @_;
    if (!defined $var) {
        print "No variable!\n";
        return undef;
    } elsif (!defined $self->{$var}) {
        print "Variable not defined, or no value.\n";
        return undef;
    } else {
        return $self->{$var};
    }
}
sub set {
    my ($self, $var, $val) = @_;
    if (!defined $var or !defined $val) {
        print "Need both a variable and value argument!";
        return undef;
    } else {
        $self->{$var} = $val;
        return $val;
    }
}
```

```
# a really generic way
sub AUTOLOAD {
    my $self = shift;
    my $var = $AUTOLOAD;
    $var =~ s/.*::Σet//;
    $var = lc $var;

    if (@_) {
        $self->{$var} = shift;
        return $self->{$var};
    } else {
        return $self->{$var};
    }
}

sub sum {
   my $self = shift;
   my $sum = 0;
   foreach ('a','b','c') {
       if (!defined $self->{$_} or $self->{$_} !~ /^\d+/ ) {
           warn "Variable $_ does not contain a number.\n";
       } else { $sum += $self->{$_}; }
   }
   return $sum;
}

package main;
$obj = new SimpleClass (10,20,30);

print "A: ", $obj->getA(), "\n";
$obj->setA("foo");
print "A: ", $obj->getA(), "\n";

print "B: ", $obj->get('b'), "\n";
$obj->set('b', 'bar');
print "B: ", $obj->get('b'), "\n";

print "C: ", $obj->getC(), "\n";  # no such method getC; will autoload
$obj->setC('baz');               # ditto setC
print "C: ", $obj->getC(), "\n";

# reset
print "\nA: 10\n";
$obj = new SimpleClass (10);
print "Sum: ", $obj->sum(), "\n";
print "\nA: 10 B: 5\n";
$obj = new SimpleClass (10,5);
print "Sum: ", $obj->sum(), "\n";
print "\nA: 10 B: 5 C: 5\n";
$obj = new SimpleClass (10,5,5);
print "Sum: ", $obj->sum(), "\n";
```

WEEK 3

DAY 21

Exploring a Few Longer Examples

As with Days 7 and 14, which closed out Weeks 1 and 2 of this book, we'll close Week 3 with another chapter of examples. The two we'll look at cover nearly every aspect of Perl you've learned over the last twenty days. If you can make it through these examples, you'll be just fine with most of the things you might be asked to do with Perl.

Today we'll look at two examples, both of which are CGI scripts:

- A customized stock portfolio manager that keeps track of multiple portfolios and downloads the latest stock prices from Yahoo! Finance whenever you view your portfolio.
- A Web-based To Do list that allows you to add and remove items, mark them as done, prioritize them, and sort them in a variety of ways.

Both of these examples are longer than the ones we've looked at earlier; the latter example more than doubly so. Remember that all the examples from this book are available online at the Teach Yourself Perl Web site at `http://www.typerl.com/`—please don't think you have to type 350 lines of Perl code yourself. Use this chapter to explore what the code does and then, if you want to experiment further, you can download the online versions.

Both of these examples run as CGI scripts. As with the CGI scripts we looked at on Day 16, "Using Perl for CGI Scripting," how these scripts are installed and used might vary from platform to platform and from Web server to Web server. Some servers might require scripts to be installed in a special directory (`cgi-bin`), to have special filename extensions (`.cgi` rather than `.pl`), or to have special permissions. You might also need to set the permissions of the configuration and data files that these scripts use. See the documentation that comes with your Web server or your system administrator for more information on installing and using CGI scripts.

A Stock Portfolio Manager

Let's look at an example program that illustrates just how much time you can save using Perl modules that are already written. The example application is a stock portfolio manager. It maintains any number of portfolios, each of which can contain any number of securities. The portfolio manager downloads the latest share prices for all the stocks in your portfolio from Yahoo! Finance every time you view a portfolio.

First, the program creates a list of portfolios. From that page, you can add a new portfolio or view or delete an existing portfolio. When you view a portfolio, the latest prices for those stocks will be displayed. You can also delete stocks from the portfolio, or add new stocks to the portfolio from that page as well.

One thing this program demonstrates is how you can save yourself a lot of pain and suffering by using modules to take care of a lot of the grunt work in your script. In this example, the CGI modules `LWP::Simple` and `XML::Simple` were used. Both were introduced in earlier lessons. I use the LWP module to download stock prices from the Yahoo! Finance Web site. The CGI module takes care of everyday stuff such as processing query parameters on HTTP requests. All the persistent data is stored in an XML file, which is accessed using the `XML::Simple` module.

The Data File

Let's look at how the data is stored from request to request. Bear in mind that this data file is generated by the `XML::Simple` module from the data structure used in the program. I actually start out by writing the XML file, use the `XML::Simple` to read it in, and then write it back out every time the script runs to be sure to catch any changes that were made. Listing 21.1 contains a data listing.

LISTING 21.1 The Data for the Stock Portfolio Program

```
<opt>
  <portfolio name="red">
    <stock lastfetch="1015292886" lastprice="48.65" company="DU PONT CO"
        name="dd" />
    <stock lastfetch="1015279312" lastprice="17.81" company="YAHOO INC"
        name="yhoo" />
  </portfolio>
  <portfolio name="foo">
    <stock lastfetch="1015280450" lastprice="63.30" company="MICROSOFT CP"
        name="msft" />
    <stock lastfetch="1015280613" lastprice="17.81" company="YAHOO INC"
        name="yhoo" />
    <stock lastfetch="1015280455" lastprice="16.05" company="AT&amp;T CORP"
        name="t" />
  </portfolio>
  <portfolio name="bar">
    <stock lastfetch="1015296403" lastprice="13.67" company="ORACLE CORP"
        name="orcl" />
    <stock lastfetch="1015296404" lastprice="17.81" company="YAHOO INC"
        name="yhoo" />
    <stock lastfetch="1015296404" lastprice="24.29" company="APPLE COMP INC"
        name="aapl" />
    <stock lastfetch="1015296405" lastprice="16.05" company="AT&amp;T CORP"
        name="t" />
  </portfolio>
  <portfolio name="baz">
    <stock lastfetch="1015278274" lastprice="31.85" company="INTEL CORP"
        name="intc" />
  </portfolio>
</opt>
```

When `XML::Simple` reads this file, it turns it into a structure of nested hashes (using references). One of the challenges when reading the program is figuring out how the data in this file maps to the data structure used throughout.

How the Program Works

Let's look at how this program is structured. The first thing to point out is that this program actually responds to many different kinds of requests. It is used to view a list of portfolios, view individual portfolios, and handle the addition and removal of both portfolios and stocks. The program expects a parameter named `c` (for command), which will indicate what sort of action should be taken. If the `c` parameter is not supplied, the program assumes that you want a list of portfolios.

21

Depending on the command sent to the program, other parameters might also be expected. The two optional parameters are the name of the portfolio and the ticker symbol of the stock. For example, if the command is `del` and the `p` parameter (for portfolio) is `foo`, the program knows you want to delete the portfolio named `foo`.

The core of the program is an `if` construct that checks which command was issued, and performs the tasks associated with that command. For example, if the command is `add_stock`, the program performs some basic error checking, calls the `add_stock` subroutine, and then displays the updated portfolio and the add stock form (using the `view_portfolio` and `display_add_stock_form` subroutines).

The commands that the program supports are

- `list`—Lists the portfolios available.
- `view`—Views the stocks in a particular portfolio.
- `del`—Deletes the specified portfolio.
- `del_stock`—Deletes the specified stock from the specified portfolio.
- `add`—Adds a portfolio with the name specified.
- `add_stock`—Adds the stock with the ticker specified to the current portfolio.

Before the conditional statement that drives the program, some modules were imported, some variables were initialized, and the parts of the page were printed out that are consistent regardless of which command was used. The footer of the page was printed out following the conditional statement.

Setting Up

Before I get into the meat of the program, some things have to be set up. This means importing the CGI, `CGI::Carp` (for better error reporting), `XML::Simple`, and `LWP::Simple` modules. Then, some global variables for this package that will be used throughout the script are set up. For example, the URLs for downloading stock information from Yahoo! Finance are hard coded, so that if those URLs change, they can be updated at the top of my program.

Also `$command` is initialized so that if the user fails to supply a command, `list` is used as the default. Probably the biggest job here, though, is reading in my data file. Amazingly, that part seems simple:

```
my $portfolios = XMLin("./portfolio.xml", forcearray => 1);
```

This code reads in a file called `portfolio.xml`, parses the XML data, and produces a reference to a data structure, which is assigned to a variable called `$portfolios`. An argument is passed to the `XMLin()` subroutine, `forcearray`, which basically tells it to treat all data as though it were in an array instead of handling lists of one item differently. This eliminates problems when a portfolio contains only one stock.

Displaying a List of Portfolios with `list_portfolios()`

Most of the `list_portfolios()` subroutine is concerned with printing out HTML, but there's some stuff that's worth inspecting here. For one thing, it introduces the data structure in the XML file. On the first line of the subroutine, a reference to the value in the top-level anonymous hash is created in my datastructure with the key `portfolio`, using this statement:

```
my $hashref = $portfolios->{portfolio};
```

The reference that's returned is to a hash containing all the portfolios in my file. On line 87, the keys in that anonymous hash are looped over, like this:

```
foreach my $port (keys %$hashref)
```

A list of the portfolios is printed out, along with links to view and delete them.

Displaying the Contents of a Single Portfolio Using `view_portfolio()`

This subroutine is a bit more complex. First, I read the argument passed to the subroutine and assign it to `$port`. Then, I create a reference to the hash containing the stocks in the named portfolio, like this:

```
my $hashref = $portfolios->{portfolio}->{$port}->{stock};
```

This reference points to a hash that contains hashes for each stock in the portfolio. The hashes are keyed on the stock's ticker symbol. Each of the stocks are then looped over using a foreach loop (just like the previous subroutine):

```
foreach my $stock_ticker (keys %$hashref)
```

In the body of the loop, the first thing to do is create a reference to the stock currently being processed, like this:

```
my $stock = $hashref->{$stock_ticker};
```

Then, some variables are set up that will be used to display this stock, print out the name of the company, and a delete link. Then, the `get_current_price()` subroutine is called to fetch the current price of the stock from Yahoo! Finance. I'll discuss that subroutine in a bit. After the price is fetched, a couple of temporary variables are set up so that the data can be used to update the record (which I do immediately after):

```
$stock->{lastprice} = $current_price;
$stock->{lastfetch} = time;
```

These two lines update the data structure so that the current price and time will be written to the data file as the previous price and time. At this point, all that's left is to print out the rest of the information about the stock.

Deleting Stocks and Portfolios Using `delete_stock()` and `delete_portfolio()`

When a user clicks on a delete link, the appropriate subroutine is called depending on whether they want to delete a stock or a portfolio. The statement used to delete a portfolio is

```
delete $portfolios->{portfolio}->{$portfolio_name};
```

And here's the statement that deletes a stock:

```
delete $portfolios->{portfolio}->{$portfolio_name}->{stock}->{$ticker};
```

As you can see, these statements simply delete values from hashes in the large data structure. When the data is saved, the changes will automatically be applied to the XML data file.

Adding a Portfolio Using `add_portfolio()`

Adding a portfolio is simple, you just test to make sure that the portfolio name entered doesn't already exist, and add a new empty hash to the data structure, like this:

```
$portfolios->{portfolio}->{$portfolio_name} = {};
```

That's all there is to it. The user can populate the new portfolio. They just have to view it and start adding stocks to it.

Adding a Stock Using `add_stock()`

Okay, here's where the real action is. This subroutine demonstrates how error handling is dealt with, how to access the data structure, and it pulls information down from the Web. I'll go ahead and list the source code for this subroutine so that it can be examined closely:

```
sub add_stock
{
    my $portfolio = shift(@_);
    my $ticker = shift(@_);
    my $stock_name = "";
    my $stock_price = 0;

    if (exists $portfolios->{portfolio}->{$portfolio}->{stock}->{$ticker})
    {
        $errors .= "<li>That stock is already in the portfolio.</li>\n";
        return;
    }

    my $url = $stock_info_url . "$ticker";
    my $content = get($url);

```

```
17:     if (!$content)
18:     {
19:         $errors .= "<li>Couldn't retrieve stock information.</li>\n";
20:         return;
21:     }
22:
23:     if ($content =~ /No such ticker symbol/i)
24:     {
25:         $errors .= "<li>Invalid ticker symbol.</li>\n";
26:         return;
27:     }
28:
29:     if ($content =~ /<td colspan=7><font(.+?)><b>(.+?)\s+<\/b>/i)
30:     {
31:         $stock_name = $2;
32:     }
33:
34:     if ($content =~ /Last Trade<br>(.+?)<b>([\d.]+)<\/b>/i)
35:     {
36:         $stock_price = $2;
37:     }
38:
39:     my $hashref = $portfolios->{portfolio}->{$portfolio}->{stock};
40:
41:     $hashref->{$ticker} = { lastfetch => time, lastprice => $stock_price,
42:         company => $stock_name };
43: }
```

First, on lines 3 through 6, set up some variables. The first two variables take their values from the arguments passed to the subroutine, and the next two are set to default values. I'll get the real values from Yahoo! Finance, assume everything goes as planned.

Next, check to ensure that the stock the user is trying to add isn't already in the portfolio. If it is, add an error message, `$errors`, and return. Next, append the stock ticker to the URL for retrieving information about the stock. Then, use the `get` subroutine (which is part of `LWP::Simple`) to request the page associated with that URL. If the page was requested successfully, the HTML code that makes up the page is assigned to `$content`. Just in case it isn't, a test is done to see whether `$content` evaluates as true, and if it doesn't, raise an error and return.

If it isn't empty, look for a particular string named `No such ticker symbol`. This text only appears on the page if the ticker symbol is invalid. If it's there, they've requested a stock using a ticker symbol that doesn't exist, so raise an error and return.

Now we're ready to start grabbing data using regular expressions. First, grab the stock name, and then the current price. By carefully examining the source code of the page, I wrote the regular expressions used to extract this information (and nothing extraneous) from the page. The catch here is that if Yahoo! changes the appearance of this page, there's a pretty good chance that these regular expressions will stop matching what they're supposed to, and therefore, you'll have to update your script. When you extract information from Web pages like this, that's just something you have to contend with. One bit of advice is that you should use as small an expression as possible, which makes it less likely that someone will come along and break your script.

After these two bits of data have been extracted from the page, access the data structure to insert a new anonymous hash into the portfolio. When the data is written to disk, this new stock will be included.

Getting the Current Stock Price Using `get_current_price()`

I explained `add_stock()` in detail, therefore, I don't have to go into that much detail for this subroutine because it's sort of like `add_stock()`, except simpler. Like the previous subroutine, take the ticker symbol as an argument, append it to the URL where stock quotes are found, and then fetch the page containing the pertinent information. If, for some reason, the page isn't found, I raise an error and return from the subroutine.

What we then have is a large regular expression that extracts the current stock price from the HTML that was returned. This is a different regular expression than was used before. The same one could have been used, but because this is an example program, I wanted to use multiple pages and expressions. After the price has been extracted, it's returned.

Writing the Data Using `write_data()`

One of the last things the program does before exiting is write its data to disk. Transforming the data in `$portfolios` to XML is easy with `XML::Simple`, just use the following subroutine call:

```
my $xml = XMLout($portfolios);
```

After the XML is stored in the variable `$xml`, open a filehandle and write the data out to disk.

The Source Code

Listing 21.2 contains the source code for the `portfolio.cgi` program.

LISTING 21.2 The Stock Portfolio Program

```
#!/usr/local/bin/perl

use strict;
use CGI;
```

LISTING 21.2 continued

```
use CGI::Carp qw(fatalsToBrowser);
use XML::Simple;
use LWP::Simple;

my $portfolios = XMLin("./portfolio.xml", forcearray => 1);
my $command = "list";
my $query = new CGI;
my $quote_url = 'http://finance.yahoo.com/q?d=v1&s=';
my $stock_info_url = 'http://finance.yahoo.com/q?d=t&s=';
my $errors = "";

if ($query->param('c'))
{
    $command = $query->param('c');
}

print $query->header;
print "<html><head><title>portfolio</title></head><body>\n";
print "<h1 align=\"center\">Stock Portfolio</h1>\n";

if ($command eq "list")
{
    &list_portfolios;
    &display_add_form;
}
elsif ($command eq "view")
{
    &view_portfolio($query->param('p'));
    &display_add_stock_form($query->param('p'));
}
elsif ($command eq "del")
{
    &delete_portfolio($query->param('p'));
    &list_portfolios;
    &display_add_form;
}
elsif ($command eq "del_stock")
{
    &delete_stock($query->param('p'), $query->param('s'));
    &view_portfolio($query->param('p'));
    &display_add_stock_form($query->param('p'));
}
elsif ($command eq "add")
{
    if ($query->param('p'))
    {
        &add_portfolio($query->param('p'));
    }
    else
```

LISTING 21.2 continued

```
    {
        $errors .= "<li>You must enter a portfolio name.</li>\n";
    }

    &list_portfolios;
    &display_add_form;
}
elsif ($command eq "add_stock")
{
    if ($query->param('s'))
    {
        &add_stock($query->param('p'), $query->param('s'));
    }
    else
    {
        $errors .= "<li>You must enter a ticker symbol.</li>\n";
    }

    &view_portfolio($query->param('p'));
    &display_add_stock_form($query->param('p'));
}

# Write out the update data file.
&write_data;
print "<p><a href=\"portfolio.pl\">return to portfolio list</a></p>\n";
print "</body></html>\n";

sub list_portfolios
{
    my $hashref = $portfolios->{portfolio};

    print "<div align=\"center\">\n";
    print "<table cellpadding=\"8\">\n";
    foreach my $port (keys %$hashref)
    {
        my $encoded_port = &encode_string($port);
        my $view_link = "portfolio.pl?c=view&amp;p=$encoded_port";
        my $delete_link = "portfolio.pl?c=del&amp;p=$encoded_port";
        print "<tr>\n";
        print "<td><b>$port</b></td>\n";
        print "<td>";
        print "<a href=\"$view_link\">view</a></td>\n";
        print "<td><a href=\"$delete_link\">delete</a></td>\n";
        print "</tr>\n";
    }
    print "</table>\n";
    print "</div>\n";
}

```

LISTING 21.2 continued

```
sub view_portfolio
{
    my $port = shift(@_);

    my $hashref = $portfolios->{portfolio}->{$port}->{stock};

    print "<h3>$port</h3>";
    foreach my $stock_ticker (keys %$hashref)
    {
        my $stock = $hashref->{$stock_ticker};
        my $company_name = $stock->{company};
        my $delete_link = "portfolio.pl?c=del_stock&amp;p=$port";
        $delete_link .= "&s=" . $stock_ticker;

        print "<p>\n";
        print "<table border=\"1\" cellspacing=\"0\" cellpadding=\"5\">\n";
        print "<tr><td colspan=\"2\"><b>", $company_name, "</b>";
        print "<br /><font size=\"1\">";
        print "<a href=\"$delete_link\">delete</a>";
        print "</font>";
        print "</td></tr>\n";

        my $current_price = &get_current_price($stock_ticker);

        my $lastprice = $stock->{lastprice};
        my $lastfetch = $stock->{lastfetch};

        # Move this soon.
        $stock->{lastprice} = $current_price;
        $stock->{lastfetch} = time;

        print "<tr><td>ticker</td>";
        print "<td>", $stock_ticker, "</td></tr>\n";
        print "<tr><td>current price:</td>";
        print "<td>", $current_price, "</td></tr>\n";
        print "<tr><td>last price:</td>";
        print "<td>", $lastprice, "</td></tr>\n";
        print "<tr><td>as of:</td>";
        print "<td>", scalar localtime($lastfetch), "</td></tr>\n";
        print "</table>\n";
        print "</p>\n";
    }
}

sub delete_portfolio
{
    my $portfolio_name = shift(@_);

    delete $portfolios->{portfolio}->{$portfolio_name};
```

LISTING 21.2 continued

```
}

sub delete_stock
{
    my $portfolio_name = shift(@_);
    my $ticker = shift(@_);

    delete $portfolios->{portfolio}->{$portfolio_name}->{stock}->{$ticker};
}

sub get_current_price
{
    my $ticker = shift(@_);
    my $url = $quote_url . "$ticker";
    my $content = get($url);

    if (!$content)
    {
        return "request failed";
    }

    my $current_price = "not found";

    if ($content =~ /<td[^>]*><font[^>]*><a[^>]*>(\w+?)<\/a><\/font><\/td><td[^>]*><font[^>]*>(.+?)<\/font><\/td><td[^>]*><font[^>]*><b>([\d.]+?)<\/b><\/font><\/td>/i)
    {
        $current_price = $3;
    }

    return $current_price;
}

sub add_portfolio
{
    my $portfolio_name = shift(@_);

    if (exists $portfolios->{portfolio}->{$portfolio_name})
    {
        $errors .= "<li>That portfolio name is already in use.</li>\n";
        return;
    }

    $portfolios->{portfolio}->{$portfolio_name} = {};
}

sub add_stock
{
    my $portfolio = shift(@_);
```

LISTING 21.2 continued

```
    my $ticker = shift(@_);
    my $stock_name = "";
    my $stock_price = 0;

    if (exists $portfolios->{portfolio}->{$portfolio}->{stock}->{$ticker})
    {
        $errors .= "<li>That stock is already in the portfolio.</li>\n";
    }

    my $url = $stock_info_url . "$ticker";
    my $content = get($url);

    if (!$content)
    {
        $errors .= "<li>Couldn't retrieve stock information.</li>\n";
        return;
    }

    if ($content =~ /No such ticker symbol/i)
    {
        $errors .= "<li>Invalid ticker symbol.</li>\n";
        return;
    }

    if ($content =~ /<td colspan=7><font(.+?)><b>(.+?)\s+<\/b>/i)
    {
        $stock_name = $2;
    }

    if ($content =~ /Last Trade<br>(.+?)<b>([\d.]+)<\/b>/i)
    {
        $stock_price = $2;
    }

    my $hashref = $portfolios->{portfolio}->{$portfolio}->{stock};

    $hashref->{$ticker} = { lastfetch => time, lastprice => $stock_price,
        company => $stock_name };
}

sub write_data
{
    my $xml = XMLout($portfolios);
    open (FILE, "> portfolio.xml")
        or die "Can't open data file: ";
    print FILE $xml;
    close FILE;
}

```

LISTING 21.2 continued

```
sub display_add_form
{
    print "<h3 align=\"center\">add a new portfolio</h3>\n";
    if ($errors)
    {
        print "<div align=\"center\"><table><tr><td>\n";
        print "Please correct the following error:\n";
        print "<ul>\n", $errors, "</ul>\n";
        print "</td></tr></table>\n";
    }
    print "<form>\n";
    print "<input type=\"hidden\" name=\"c\" value=\"add\">\n";
    print "<div align=\"center\"><table>\n";
    print "<tr><td>portfolio name:</td><td>";
    print "<input type=\"text\" name=\"p\" value=\"\">";
    print "</td></tr>\n";
    print "<tr><td colspan=\"2\"><input type=\"submit\"></td></tr>\n";
    print "</table></div>\n";
    print "</form>\n";
}

sub display_add_stock_form
{
    my $portfolio_name = shift(@_);
    print "<h3 align=\"center\">add a new stock</h3>\n";
    if ($errors)
    {
        print "<div align=\"center\"><table><tr><td>\n";
        print "Please correct the following error:\n";
        print "<ul>\n", $errors, "</ul>\n";
        print "</td></tr></table>\n";
    }
    print "<form>\n";
    print "<input type=\"hidden\" name=\"c\" value=\"add_stock\">\n";
    print "<input type=\"hidden\" name=\"p\" value=\"$portfolio_name\">\n";
    print "<div align=\"center\"><table>\n";
    print "<tr><td>stock ticker symbol:</td><td>";
    print "<input type=\"text\" name=\"s\" value=\"\">";
    print "</td></tr>\n";
    print "<tr><td colspan=\"2\"><input type=\"submit\"></td></tr>\n";
    print "</table></div>\n";
    print "</form>\n";
}

sub encode_string
{
    my $string_to_encode = shift @_;

    $string_to_encode =~ s/\&/%26/g;
```

LISTING 21.2 continued

```
        $string_to_encode =~ s/\+/%2B/g;
        $string_to_encode =~ s/\?/%2B/g;
        $string_to_encode =~ s/ /+/g;

        return $string_to_encode;
}
```

A Web-Based To Do List (`todolist.pl`)

Our second—and final—example, is a simple To Do list application that runs on the Web called `todolist.pl`. You can add, delete, and change list items, sort by date, priority, or descriptions, and mark items as done. Figure 21.3 shows an example of the To Do list at work:

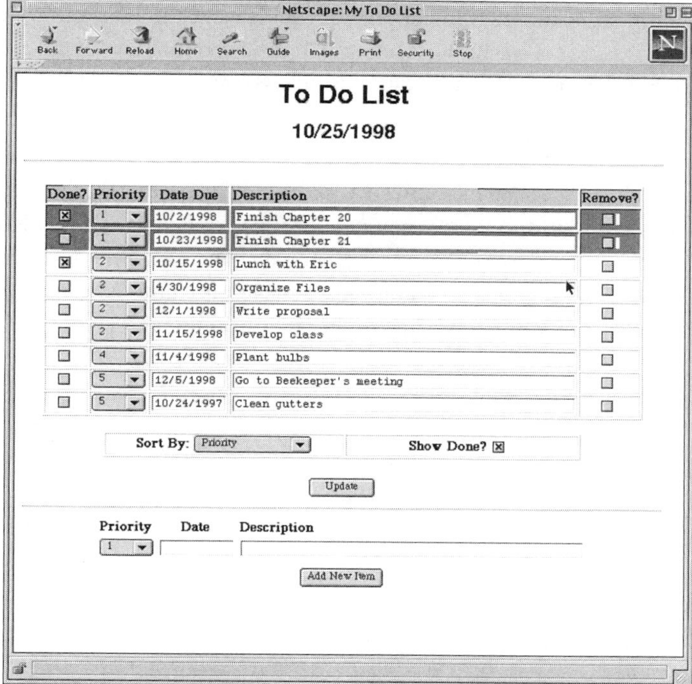

FIGURE 21.1
To Do List Web application.

The To Do list application consists of a large table containing the To Do items. Each item has a check box indicating whether it is done or not, a priority, a due date, and a description. All the data in this table is editable through form elements; the changes are applied when the user chooses the Update button. Also affected with Update is whether an item is to be removed (the check boxes in the right-most column of the table), how to sort the data (the Sort By menu just below the table), and whether to display done items (the Show Done check box under the table as well).

In addition to the table and the display preferences, there is also an area for adding new items to the list. By filling out the boxes in that part of the application and choosing Add Item, new items are added (and all other changes applied as well).

As with the stock portfolio program, the script that runs the To Do list is a CGI script, and runs directly as a URL, no initial form needed. The script generates its own content, including the forms that enable you to change the items in the list and how they are displayed. It's all the same script. The only other part is a data file—`listdata.txt`—which stores the To Do data, and which is read and written by the To Do script.

This script is twice the size of anything we've looked at in this book, so, as with the last example, I'm not going to go over it line by line. The complete script is at the end of this section, in Listing 21.3, and you can get it from the Web site for this book as well (`www.typerl.com`). In this section, I'll describe the flow and general structure of how the script works and, if you're still curious, you can check out the code for yourself.

The Data File

As with most of the examples we've looked at this week, this script has a data file that it reads and writes to that keeps track of the scripts data. The data file for this script, called `listdata.txt`, stores the To Do item data. The `todolist.pl` script reads this file at each iteration and writes new data to it whenever anything is changed. It looks much like the data files you've seen previously in other examples:

```
id=1
desc=Finish Chapter 20
date=3/1/2002
prior=1
done=1
---
id=2
desc=Finish Chapter 21
date=3/14/2002
prior=1
done=0
---
id=3
desc=Lunch with Eric
date=3/16/2002
prior=2
done=1
---
```

Each record is separated in the file by three dashes (---). Each field of the record has a key and a value, separated by an equal sign.

When the CGI script for the To Do list is installed, an initial data file must also be installed somewhere the Web server can read (and write) it. The initial data file can be empty—the script will simply generate a Web page with no items in it—but the file must exist for the script to work.

How the Script Works

The `todolist.pl` is large, but pretty straightforward. There aren't many confusing regular expressions, and the flow from function to function is fairly straightforward. In fact, much of the bulk of the script is taken up by print statements to generate the HTML for the To Do List and its various form elements—and customizing those elements to behave differently in different situations.

The two starting subroutines for the `todolist.pl` script are `&init()` and `&process()`. The `&init()` determines the current date, calls the `&read_data()` subroutine, and prints the top part of the HTML file to be generated by the script. Let's start from there and work down.

Data Initialization with `&init()`

The initialization subroutine is responsible primarily for calling `&read_data()` to open the data file and read each of its elements into a single data structure. That data structure is an array of hashes, with each hash containing the data for each To Do item. The keys in the hash are

- `id`—The unique ID of the item.
- `desc`—The description of the item.
- `date`—The due date for the item. The date is of the format MM/DD/YYYY (this is enforced by the script).
- `prior`—The priority of the item, from 1 (highest) to 5.
- `done`—Whether or not this item is complete.

In addition to these keys, which come from the data file, each item in the list also has an ID. The ID is assigned when the data file is read, from 0 to the number of elements. The ID will be used later to keep track of the various form elements for each list item.

Process the Form and the Data with `&process()`

The `&process()` routine is where the major work of the script takes place. In this subroutine there are two main branches, based on the `param()` function from the `CGI.pm` module. Back on Day 16 you learned about `param()`, and how it can be used to get the values of form elements. Another way of using `param()` is without any arguments, in which case it returns all the names of all the form elements—or, if the script wasn't called with a form, `param()` returns undefined (`undef`). In the `&process()` subroutine, we take advantage of that behavior to produce two different results:

- The first time the script is called, there are no parameters, so we simply display the current To Do list (by using the `&display_all()` subroutine).
- All other times the script is called, there are potential changes to be managed, either changes to how the existing items are or changes and additions to the items. If the Update button was selected, we remove the items to be deleted (the `&remove_selected()` subroutine), update all the data (`&update_data()`), write the data back out to the file (`&write_data()`), and display it over again (`&display_all()`).

  If the Add Items button was pressed, we do all the same steps, except that in between updating the data and writing it out, we call `&add_item()` to add the new To Do Item to the list of items.

As all the updating and adding is happening, we're also checking for formatting errors in the dates. More about that later when we talk about updating the data and adding list items.

Displaying the Data with `&display_all()` and `&display_data()`

The largest part of the To Do list script, number-of-lines-of-code-wise, is contained in the `&display_all()` and `&display_data()` script. These subroutines don't just generate HTML for the data; the data table is also a form, and all the elements need to be generated automatically. In addition, a lot of the HTML that is generated is conditional on various states of the table. Priority 1 items are displayed in red, for example, and the menus for each priority are set to their current values based on the data. So rather than just using an enormous "here" document for this part of the script, we need to work through line by line to generate it.

The `&display_all()` subroutine is the main one that gets called first. It starts the table, prints the headers, sorts the main array based on the current sort order, and then calls `&display_data()` inside a `for` loop to display each element in the To Do list. It also generates the elements below the data itself: the Sort By menu, the Show Done check box, the form elements for adding an item, and both of the buttons to submit the form. Along the way, it also prints and manages warnings if there's an error processing the date. All this involves a lot of conditional statements and prints, as well as a whole lot of lines of HTML.

The &display_data() subroutine has a similar task for each specific element of the To Do list. Each row of the table has five columns, each of which contains a form element. Each element needs a unique name, and many form elements change appearance based on the data they reflect (a check box is checked if an item is done, for example). &display_data() also handles NOT displaying some items—if the Show Done check box is not selected, it won't display any item that is marked Done—but it will generate a hidden form element with some of that item's data so that the updates work right.

As with &display_all(), this involves a lot of if statements and a lot of HTML. The result is a gigantic form with each form element attached to the item to which it refers, and which is already filled in with the current To Do list data. Change any part of that data and, when the form is submitted, those changes will make it back to the original data set.

Updating Changes with &update_data()

Speaking of updating the changes, let's move onto the &update_data() subroutine. This subroutine is called regardless of whether the user chooses the Update or Add Item buttons to make sure that any changes made to the data get made in either case. What &update_data() does is loop through all the form elements on the page—each element for the list items, as well as the Sort By and Show Done form elements—and change the data or global settings to reflect the changes that were made on the Web page.

Let's focus on the data itself. Each part of the HTML form that is generated by &display_data() has a unique name, generated from the name of the field (description, priority, and so on) and that item's ID number. By picking apart those form element names that come back when the form is submitted, we can match each name to each part of the data set, compare the values, and if they differ, update the data set with the new value. Each time the form is submitted, every single element is checked. This isn't the most efficient way to keep track of the data, but it does let us keep everything on one page.

The other thing the &update_data() subroutine does is check for bad dates in the existing data. If you tried to change a date from its normal format ("10/9/1998" or something like that), &update_data() will catch that and report an error, which will then be displayed along with the data set when &display_all() is called.

Adding and Removing items with &add_item() and &remove_selected()

To remove items from the list, you select the check boxes in the Remove column for the data and choose Update. To add an item to the list, you enter its data in the form at the bottom of the page and choose Add Item. In either case, &remove_selected() is called; for the latter case, &add_item() is also called.

The &remove_selected() subroutine is responsible for updating the data to delete any records that have been chosen by the user to be removed. In this case, because all our data is stored in an array of references, removing those items is easy—we just build another array of references, minus the ones we want to delete, and then put that new array back in the old one's variable. Because it's an array of references, all the data referred to by those references stays put and doesn't need to be recopied or reconstructed anywhere. At the end of the subroutine, renumber all the records so that there aren't any gaps that could cause problems when the form is processed.

The &add_item() subroutine is equally easy; with all the data from the form elements, all we need to do is stuff it into a hash and put a reference to that hash in the data array. We also assign this new item a new ID, one larger than the current largest ID.

Other Subroutines: Writing Data and Checking for Errors

All that's left are a few minor supporting subroutines: &write_data() to write the data back out to the listdata.txt file, and two subroutines to manage date formats and comparisons.

The &write_data() subroutine is easy; here all we do is open the listdata.txt file for writing, and then loop over the data set to write out each of the records. Because this subroutine is called once each time the script is run and after any changes have been made to the data, we can be close to certain that the data will never be corrupted or items lost. Note here that the item IDs are not written to the data file with the rest of the data; those IDs are generated when the data is initially read and used only to keep track of form elements, so they don't need to be preserved between calls to the script.

The final two sets of subroutines relate to date management. Dates, as I mentioned earlier, are of the format MM/DD/YYYY. Using a single consistent format is important because it enables the list of items to be sorted by the date—which is a form of numeric sort. To convert the data format into a number that can be compared to some other number, the formatting must be correct. For this reason, whenever a date is changed in the existing data or added to a new item, its format is checked with the &check_date() subroutine and errors are reported if the format doesn't match up or the numbers used are clearly out of bounds (both a large red message at the top of the Web page and by asterisks added to the wrong date itself).

Sorting the list by date happens in the &display_all() subroutine, if the value of the Sort By menu is Date. To convert the dates into something that can be compared against something else, we use the Time::Local module, a built-in module that can be used to convert various parts of a date and time into time format—that is, number of seconds since 1900 (the value returned by the time function). The &date2time() subroutine is used for just this purpose, to split up a correctly formatted date into its elements and return the `time` value. The `&date2time()` subroutine also watches for dates in error format—with leading asterisks—and sorts those values to the top.

The Code

Listing 21.3 contains the (very) complete code for the `todolist.pl` script. Start from the top and read down. The only tricky parts are those that deal with attaching the IDs to the form elements, and handling the data errors (watch for the `&check_date()` subroutine). And, as with all CGI scripts, it helps to have an understanding of HTML and of how forms and CGI.pm interact with each other.

LISTING 21.3 The Code for `todolist.pl`

```
#!/usr/local/bin/perl -w
use strict;
use CGI qw(:standard);
use CGI::Carp qw(fatalsToBrowser);
use Time::Local;

my $listdata = 'listdata.txt';   # data file
my @data = ();                   # array of hashes

# global default settings
my $sortby = 'prior';            # order to sort list
my $showdone = 1;                # show done items?  (1 == yes)

&init();
&process();

sub init {
    # get the current date, put in in MM/DD/YY format
    my ($day,$month,$year) = 0;
    (undef,undef,undef,$day,$month,$year) = localtime(time);
    $month++;                    # months start from 0
    $year += 1900;               # Perl years are years since 1900;
    # this keep us from getting bit by Y2K
    my $date = "$month/$day/$year";
    # open & read data file
    &read_data();

    # start HTML
    print header;
    print start_html('My To Do List');
    print "<h1 align=\"center\"><font face=\"Helvetica,Arial\">";

    print "To Do List</font></h1>\n";
    print "<h2 align=\"center\"><font face=\"Helvetica,Arial\">";
```

LISTING 21.3 continued

```
    print "$date</font></h2>\n";
    print "<hr />\n";
    print "<form method=\"post\">\n";
}

sub process {
    my $dateerror = 0;              # error in date format in old list
    my $newerror = 0;               # error in date format in new item

    # main switching point.  There are 2 choices:
    # no parameters, for displaying defaults
    # any parameters: update, add item if necessary, write and display
    if (!param()) {                 # first time only
        &display_all();
    } else {                        # handle buttons
        &remove_selected();
        $dateerror = &update_data(); # update existing changes, if any

        # add items
        if (defined param('additems')) {
            $newerror = &check_date(param('newdate'));
            if (!$newerror) {
                &add_item();
            }
        }

        &write_data();
        &display_all($dateerror,$newerror);
    }

    print end_html;
}

# read data file into array of hashes
sub read_data {
    open(DATA, $listdata) or die "Can't open data file: $!";
    my %rec = ();
    while (<DATA>) {
        chomp;
        if ($_ =~ /^\#/) {
            next;
        }
        if ($_ ne '---' and $_ ne '') { # build the record
            my ($key, $val) = split(/=/,$_,2);
            $rec{$key} = $val;
        } else {                    # end of record
            push @data, { %rec };
            %rec = ();
        }
```

LISTING 21.3 continued

```
    }
    close(DATA);
}

sub display_all {
    my $olderror = shift;        # has an error occurred?
    my $newerror = shift;

    if ($olderror or $newerror) {
        print "<p><font color=\"red\"><b>Error:  Dates marked with *** ";
        print "not in right format (use MM/DD/YYYY)</b></font></p>\n";
    }

    print "<table width=\"75%\" align=\"center\">\n";
    print "<tr bgcolor=\"silver\"><th>Done?</th><th>Priority</th>";
    print "<th>Date Due</th><th align=\"left\">Description</th>";
    print "<th>Remove?</th></tr>\n";

    # determine sort type (numeric or string) based on $sortby
    my @sdata = ();

    # sort the array of hashes based on value of $sortby
    if ($sortby eq 'date') {        # special date sort
        @sdata = sort {&date2time($a->{'date'}) <=>
                       &date2time($b->{'date'})} @data;
    } else {                        # regular text/priority sort
        @sdata = sort {$a->{$sortby} cmp $b->{$sortby}} @data;
    }

    # print each item in order
    foreach (@sdata) {
        &display_data(%$_);        # pass in record
    }

    print "</table>\n";

    # preference table, with state preserved
    print "<p><table width=\"75%\" align=\"center\">\n";
    print "<tr><td align=\"center\"><b>Sort By:</b>";
    print "<select name=\"sortby\">\n";

    my @sort_options = ('prior', 'date', 'desc');
    my @sort_option_names = ('Priority', 'Date', 'Description');

    for (my $i = 0; $i < @sort_options; $i++)
    {
        # get current val of sortby, show menu
        print "<option value=\"$sort_options[$i]\" ";
        if ($sortby eq $sort_options[$i]) {
```

21

LISTING 21.3 continued

```
            print "selected>";
        } else {
            print ">";
        }
        print "$sort_option_names[$i]</option>\n";
    }

    print "</select></td>\n";

    # get current val of showdone, show check boxn
    print "<td align=\"center\" width=\"50%\"><b>Show Done?<b>\n";
    my $checked = '';
    if ($showdone == 1) {
        $checked = 'checked';
    }
    print "<input type=\"checkbox\" name=\"showdone\" value=\"showdone\"";
    print " $checked /> </td>\n";

    # print submit button and start of add items table
    print <<EOF;
    </tr></table>
    <p><table align=\"center\">
    <tr><td align="center" valign="center">
    <input type="submit" value="   Update    " name="update"></td></tr>
    </table><hr />
    <table align="center">
    <tr><th>Priority</th><th>Date</th><th align="left">Description</th>
EOF
    # print priority menu;
    print "<tr><td><select name=\"newprior\">\n";
    my $i;
    foreach $i (1..5) {                 # priorities 1 to 5
        if ($newerror and param('newprior') == $i) {
            $checked = 'selected';
        }
        print "<option $checked>$i</option>\n";
    }
    print "</select></td>\n";

    # print date and description cells; may be different in case of
    # errors
    my $newdate = '';
    my $newdesc = '';
    print "<td align=\"center\"><input type=\"text\" name=\"newdate\"";
    if ($newerror) {                    # has an error occurred?
        $newdate = "***" . param('newdate');
        $newdesc = param('newdesc');
    }
```

LISTING 21.3 continued

```
    print "value=\"$newdate\" size=\"10\"></td> \n";
    # description cell; preserve old value if error
    print "<td><input type=\"text\" name=\"newdesc\" value=\"$newdesc\"";
    print "size=\"50\"></td></tr></table><table align=\"center\">\n";

    # and finish up
    print <<EOF;
    <tr><td align="center" valign="center">
    <input type="submit" value="Add New Item" name="additems" /></td></tr>
    </table></form>
EOF
}

# display each line of the data.  Data is already sorted; this just
# prints an inidividual record
sub display_data {
    my %rec = @_;                # record to print

    # don't show done items if Show Done is unchecked
    # BUT include their settings anyhow (otherwise its too
    # difficult to figure out what's shown and changed versus
    # what's hidden
    if ($showdone == 0 and $rec{'done'}) {
        print "<input type=\"hidden\" name=\"done", $rec{'id'};
        print "\" />\n";
        next;
    }
    # make 1 priority items print in red
    my $bgcolor = '';              # priority items are red, all others ''
    if ($rec{'prior'} == 1) {
        $bgcolor = "bgcolor=\"red\"";
    }

    # Is it done or not?
    my $checked = '';              # done items are checked
    if ($rec{'done'}) {
        $checked = 'checked="checked"';
    }

    print "<!-- ID: ", $rec{id}, " -->\n";

    print "<tr>\n";                # start row

    # done boxes
    print "<td width=\"10%\" align=\"center\" $bgcolor>";
    print "<input type=\"checkbox\" name=\"done", $rec{'id'};
    print "\" $checked /></td>\n";

```

LISTING 21.3 continued

```
    # priority menus
    print "<td width=\"10%\" align=\"center\" $bgcolor>";
    print "<select name=\"prior", $rec{'id'}, "\">\n";
    my $select = '';
    my $i;
    foreach $i (1..5) {                # priorities 1 to 5
        $checked = '';
        if ($rec{'prior'} == $i) {
            $checked = 'selected';
        }
        print "<option value=\"$i\" $checked>$i</option>\n";
        $select = '';
    }
    print "</select></td>\n";

    # dates
    print "<td $bgcolor width=\"10%\" align=\"checked\">";
    print "<input type=\"text\" size=\"10\" name=\"date", $rec{'id'}, "\" ";
    print "value=\"", $rec{'date'}, "\" /></td>\n";

    # descriptions
    print "<td $bgcolor><input type=\"text\" name=\"desc", $rec{'id'};
    print "\" size=\"50\" value=\"", $rec{'desc'}, "\" /></td>\n";

    # Remove boxes
    print "<td $bgcolor align=\"center\">";
    print "<input type=\"checkbox\" name=\"r", $rec{'id'}, "\" /></td>";

    # end row
    print "</tr>\n\n";
}

# update all values in case changes were made
sub update_data {
    my $error = 0;                # error checking
    # check to see if showdone is selected;
    if (defined param('showdone')) {
        $showdone = 1;
    } else {
        $showdone = 0;
    }

    # get currrent sortby value
    $sortby = param('sortby');

    foreach (@data) {
        my $id = $_->{'id'};        # not the global $id

```

LISTING 21.3 continued

```
        # Entries that are marked done cannot be changed (usability
        # assumption).  So if an entry is marked done, and hasn't
        # been changed to not-done, we can skip checking any of the
        # rest of its data.
        if ($_->{'done'} == 1 && defined param('done' . $id)) {
            next;
        }

        # All newly done items.
        if (defined param('done' . $id)) {
            $_->{'done'} = 1;
        } else {
            $_->{'done'} = 0;
        }
        # dates.  check for weird date
        if (param('date' . $id) ne $_->{'date'}) {
            $error = check_date(param('date' . $id));
            if ($error) {
                $_->{'date'} = "*** " . param('date' . $id);
            } else {
                $_->{'date'} = param('date' . $id);
            }
        }

        # priorities, descriptions, change only if different
        my $thing;
        foreach $thing ('prior', 'desc') {
            if (param($thing . $id) ne $_->{$thing}) {
                $_->{$thing} = param($thing . $id);
            }
        }
    }
    return $error;
}

# remove items by redoing the @data list
sub remove_selected {
    my @newdata = ();
    foreach (@data) {
        my $id = $_->{'id'};        # also not the global id

        if (!defined param('r' . $id)) {
            push @newdata, $_;        # $_ is the reference
        }
    }
    @data = @newdata;                  # get rid of removed items
}

# add a new item.  This is only called if check_date has already said OK
```

LISTING 21.3 continued

```
sub add_item {
    my %newrec = ();

    $newrec{'desc'} = param('newdesc');
    $newrec{'date'} = param('newdate');
    $newrec{'prior'} = param('newprior');
    $newrec{'done'} = 0;

    my $max_id = 0;

    foreach my $datum (@data) {
        if ($datum->{'id'} > $max_id) {
            $max_id = $datum->{'id'};
        }
    }

    $newrec{'id'} = ++$max_id;        # global ID + 1
    push @data, { %newrec };
}

# dates must be in XX/XX/XX format
sub check_date {
    my $date = shift;
    # MM/DD/YYYY, MM and DD can be 0 or 1 char, but YYYY must be four
    # ending whitespace is OK.
    if ($date !~ /^(\d{1,2})\/(\d{1,2})\/(\d{4})\s*$/) {
        return 1;                    # error!
    }
    return 1 if ($1 > 12);
    return 1 if ($2 > 31);

    return 0;                        # OK date
}

# rewrite data file
sub write_data {
    open(DATA, ">$listdata") or die "Can't open list data: $!.";
    foreach (@data) {
        my %rec = %$_;

        foreach ('id', 'desc', 'date','prior','done') {
            print DATA "$_=$rec{$_}\n";
        }
        print DATA "---\n";
    }
    close(DATA);
}

# I use MM/DD/YY format for dates.  To sort by date you need to
```

LISTING 21.3 continued

```
# convert this format back into Perl's seconds-since-1900 format.
# the Time::Local module and the timelocal func do this.
sub date2time {
    my $date = shift;
    if ($date =~ /^\*\*\*/) {          # error formatting, sort to top
        return 0;
    } else {
        my ($m,$d,$y) = split(/\//,$date);
        $m--;                      # months start from 0 in perl's time format
        return timelocal(0,0,0,$d,$m,$y);
    }
}
```

Summary

If you had picked up this book without understanding anything about Perl and looked at the script in Listing 21.3, chances are pretty good you might have had a hard time deciphering it—even if you already knew something about programming languages (Perl is funny that way). After 21 days deep into the language and its idiosyncrasies, reading the code in these examples should be easy—or at least less perplexing.

Today, we finished up the week and the book with the usual longer examples (one longer than the other). The two scripts we looked at in this lesson, the Stock Portfolio manager and the To Do list application, are both CGI scripts that process data from different sources (or multiple sources) and generate HTML as their output. The first is a good example of cobbling together code from various modules on CPAN and your own glue, saving a lot of time in the process. The latter displayed HTML form construction and used a nested data structure to keep track of the data. From these scripts, and the work you've done in the previous 20 chapters, you're now off and running as far as Perl is concerned.

Off you go!

Appendixes

APPENDIX A

Perl Functions

This appendix contains a brief reference, organized in alphabetical order, of all the built-in functions in the Perl language. If you're looking for a function that doesn't exist, there's a good chance that someone has written a module that supports it.

Note that not all the functions in this appendix are supported by all versions of Perl. Day 18, "Perl and the Operating System," contains some background information on which functions might not be available for Windows or the Mac OS. For the ultimate list, see the documentation that comes with your Perl port.

For More Information

Further information on any of these functions can be found in the `perlfunc` man page. As with all Perl documentation, you can access this man page through the `man` command on Unix, the `perldoc` command on Unix or Windows (`perldoc perlfunc` for the whole thing, or `perldoc -f` for individual functions, or the Shuck application if you use MacPerl).

All the documentation for Perl can also be found on the Web at `http://www.perldoc.com`.

In addition to Perl-related man pages, this appendix also frequently refers to other Unix man pages (mostly because Perl makes use of many Unix features).

Unix man pages are organized into numbered chapters. When you see an item listed with a number in parentheses after it, it indicates that the item is found in that chapter in the man pages. For example, fseek(2) is found in Chapter 2 of the Unix manual. To look up `fseek` in Chapter 2, you would use the following Unix command:

```
man 2 fseek
```

Or, on some systems:

```
man -s 2 fseek
```

The command `man man` will help you on the `man` command itself.

Perl Functions, in Alphabetical Order

Here are the Perl functions, listed alphabetically.

abs

```
abs VALUE
```

Returns the absolute value of `VALUE`. `VALUE` can be a number (such as `-7`), or an expression (such as `int(5/2)`).

accept

```
accept NEWSOCKET, GENERICSOCKET
```

`accept` is used to accept an incoming socket connection. If the connection is successful, the packed address is returned, otherwise, `FALSE` is returned. Identical to the `accept(2)` system call.

alarm

```
alarm SECONDS
```

The `alarm` function sends a `SIGALRM` to the program after the number of seconds specified in `SECONDS` has elapsed. Only one timer can be running at a time, so if you call this function and a timer is already running, it will be replaced by the more recent call. Calling this function with an argument of 0 will suspend the current timer without starting a new one. If `SECONDS` is not specified, the value in `$_` is used.

atan2

```
atan2 Y, X
```

Returns the arctangent of Y/X in the range -p to p. Functions for the tangent operation are in the POSIX and `Math::Trig` modules.

bind

```
bind SOCKET, NAME
```

The `bind` function binds a network address to a socket. `NAME` should contain the packed address for that type of socket. If the `bind` function is successful, it returns `TRUE`, otherwise it returns `FALSE`. Identical to the `bind` system call.

binmode

```
binmode FILEHANDLE
```

`binmode` accepts a filehandle as an argument, and indicates that data should be written to (or read from) the filehandle as binary, as opposed to ASCII, data. It has no effect under Unix, but is critical under MS-DOS and other archaic platforms. It should be called after a file is opened, but before any I/O is performed on that file.

bless

```
bless REFERENCE, CLASSNAME
```

`bless` is used in object-oriented Perl programming to assign whatever is referenced by `REFERENCE` to the package named by `CLASSNAME`. If `CLASSNAME` is omitted, `REFERENCE` is assigned to the current package. `bless` returns the reference being blessed. Usually to create an object you `bless` an anonymous hash. For detailed information check out the `perlobj` man page.

caller

```
caller EXPR
caller
```

`caller` returns the context of the current subroutine call. In the scalar context, `caller` returns the package name from which the subroutine was called; in the list context, it returns the package name, filename of the program, and line number from which the call was issued. If `EXPR` is supplied, `caller` also returns extra information used to print a stack trace. `EXPR` indicates how many call frames to go back before the current one. When `EXPR` is supplied, the following list of values is returned:

```
($package, $file, $line, $subname, $hasargs, $wantarray, $evaltext,
$is_require, $hints, $bitmask) = caller(any_func);
```

If called from within the DB package, caller also sets the variable `@DB::args` to the arguments passed to the given stack frame.

chdir

```
chdir EXPR
```

`chdir` accepts an expression as an argument, and attempts to set the current directory to the directory supplied by the expression. If no argument is provided, it attempts to change to the home directory for the current user.

chmod

```
chmod LIST
```

`chmod` is used to change the file permissions for the list of files provided in `LIST`. The first element of `LIST` must be the numerical mode for the files, in octal notation. It should also include the SUID bit. Here's an example of the usage of `chmod`:

```
chmod 0755, @files;
```

Note that the first element of the list is not enclosed within quotation marks, it is a bare number. For more information on file permissions, see the `chmod` man page.

chomp

```
chomp VARIABLE
chomp LIST
chomp
```

`chomp` is a safe version of `chop`, which is described next. It removes any line ending that matches `$/` (the variable that contains the input record separator, usually a newline). If it is called in paragraph mode, it removes all the trailing newlines from a string.

chop

```
chop VARIABLE
chop LIST
chop
```

`chop` is used to remove the last character from a string. Originally it was designed to make it easy to strip the line feed from the end of a string (when you're editing a file line by line, it often makes sense to remove the line feeds from the lines before you start working on them). The problem with `chop` is that it removes the last character from the string regardless of what it is, so if the string ends with a line feed, great, but if it doesn't you lose the last character, which might have been meaningful.

```
while (<INPUT_FILE>) {
#    Note that in this example, $_ is assumed to be the argument to
#    the chomp function.
    chop;
    push (@names);
}
```

If no argument is supplied to `chop`, it removes the last character from `$_`. If a list is supplied, the last character in all the items in the list is removed.

chown

```
chown LIST
```

`chown` is used to set the user and group ownership for files provided in `LIST`. It returns the number of files that were successfully changed. The first two elements of `LIST` must be the numerical uid and gid of the user and group, which will become the owners of the files. Usually, only the `root` user can change the owner of files on a system.

chr

```
chr NUMBER
```

The `chr` function returns the character in the ASCII table associated with the number passed to the function. For example; `chr(80);` returns `R`. The `pack` function can be used to convert multiple characters at the same time.

chroot

```
chroot DIRNAME
```

The `chroot` function does the same thing as the `chroot` system call (see the `chroot(2)` man page for details). Basically, `chroot` tells the program that's currently running, as well as all `exec` calls and subprocesses, to use the directory named in `DIRNAME` as the new root directory. So, paths starting with `/` will begin in `DIRNAME` instead of the actual root directory of the file system. Only the root user can use the `chroot` function.

close

```
close FILEHANDLE
```

The `close` function is used to close a previously opened file handle (whether it is a file or a pipe). It performs the necessary system-level cleanup operations at the system level, and returns true if all those operations are successful. Note that all filehandles are closed automatically when a Perl program exits, so you can often get by with not explicitly closing all the filehandles that you open.

closedir

```
closedir DIRHANDLE
```

`closedir` closes a directory opened using the `opendir` function.

connect

```
connect SOCKET, NAME
```

`connect` attempts to connect to a remote socket. `NAME` should contain the packed address appropriate to the type of socket. The function returns `TRUE` if it is successful or `FALSE` if it isn't. Identical to the `connect` system call.

cos

```
cos EXPR
```

Returns the cosine of `EXPR`. To use the inverse cosine operation, you should use the `POSIX::acos()` function, or the `Math::Trig` module.

crypt

```
crypt PLAINTEXT, SALT
```

The `crypt` function is used to encrypt strings in the same way that passwords are stored in a Unix password file. The function accepts two arguments, the string to be encrypted, and the salt code used to seed the encryption algorithm. The `crypt` function is one-way; there is no known method for decrypting text enciphered using `crypt` (Unix tests passwords by using `crypt` on the password the user enters and testing the encrypted password against it).

dbmclose

```
dbmclose HASH
```

`dbmclose` breaks the binding between `HASH` and the DBM file with which it is associated. It has been superseded by the `untie` function.

dbmopen

```
dbmopen HASH, DBNAME, MODE
```

`dbmopen` binds a dbm, ndbm, sdbm, gdbm, or Berkeley DB file to hash. `HASH` is the name of the hash variable to which the database will be bound, and `DBNAME` is the name of the database file, minus the extension. If `DBNAME` doesn't exist, a new file will be created with permissions specified by `MODE`.

This function has been superseded by `tie`.

defined

```
defined EXPR
```

`defined` is used to identify expressions that return the undefined value (as opposed to 0, newline, or other empty return values). It can be used to determine whether a subroutine exists or a scalar variable is defined. If no `EXPR` is given, `defined` checks to see if `$_` is undefined.

delete

```
delete EXPR
```

The `delete` function is used to remove elements from a hash. To delete a member of a hash, you simply pass the name of the hash and the key you want to remove to the delete function. Here's an example:

```
delete $hash{$key};
```

Note that because you're referring to a single member of the hash, you reference the hash variable in the scalar context (using `$`).

die

```
die LIST
```

`die` accepts a list as its argument. When `die` is called, the program exits returning the value of `$!`, and the list passed to `die` as an argument is printed to standard error. If the list does not end with a newline, the name of the program and the line number where execution halted are appended, along with a newline, to the output of the function.

Here's an example:

```
open (FILE, $file) or die "Can't open $file";
```

will return the following if `$file` can't be opened:

```
Can't open /tmp/file at test_program line 13.
```

do

```
do BLOCK
do SUBROUTINE(LIST)
do EXPR
```

When used with a block of code inside `BLOCK`, `do` executes the statements in a block and returns the value of the last statement in the block. If `do` is used with a loop expression, `BLOCK` is executed before the loop condition is tested for the first time.

do SUBROUTINE is a deprecated way to call a subroutine. do EXPR provides a way to run code in another file. EXPR is treated as the filename for a Perl file, and the code inside is executed. Even though you can use do in this way, you should probably use require or use instead because they are more robust.

dump

```
dump LABEL
```

dump causes Perl to immediately dump core. You can then use the undump program to create a binary that will begin execution by issuing a goto LABEL command.

each

```
each HASH
```

The each function is used to grab values from a hash so that they can be iterated over in a loop. It acts differently depending on whether it is used in the scalar or the list context. Let's look at each.

In the scalar context, the each function returns the key for the next element in the hash. So, you could use it as follows:

```
while ($key = each %hash) {
    $hash{$key}++;
}
```

On the other hand, used in the list context, the each function returns a two-element list that contains the key and the value for the next element in the hash. Let's take a look:

```
while (($key, $value) = each %hash) {
    print "$key = $value\n";
}
```

eof

```
eof FILEHANDLE
eof ()
eof
```

The eof function returns 1 if the next read on FILEHANDLE will return the end of file marker, or if FILEHANDLE is not open. Used without an argument, eof evaluates the last file read. Called with empty parentheses, eof detects the end of the pseudo-file made up of all the files specified on the command line. As the perlfunc man page astutely points out, eof is rarely useful, because Perl returns the undefined value automatically when the end of a file is reached, making it easy to detect file endings without it.

eval

```
eval EXPR
eval BLOCK
```

`eval` is used to execute an expression or block of code as though it were a separate Perl program. It is executed within the context of the Perl program that's running, so when the expression within `eval` finishes executing, all the variables and other persistent values for the larger program are still defined.

The value returned by an `eval` is the value of the last expression evaluated. To explicitly return a particular value, you can use a return statement inside the `eval`. If a syntax or runtime error occurs within the `eval` statement, or a `die` statement is executed, the `eval` statement returns an undefined value, and the variable `$@` contains the error message.

Because fatal errors executed within `eval` statements don't stop execution of the closing program, they can be used to trap errors, or run potentially volatile code.

exec

```
exec LIST
```

The `exec` function executes a system command and never returns, unless the command does not exist. If `LIST` consists of more than one element, `exec` uses the system call `execvp(3)` with the arguments in `LIST`. If the argument contains a single scalar value, the argument is checked for shell metacharacters. If shell metacharacters exist, the argument is executed through `/bin/sh -c`, otherwise, the argument is broken into words and passed on to `execvp`.

exists

```
exists EXPR
```

The `exists` function is used to check whether a particular key is defined within a hash. Whether a value is defined for that key is not checked by the `exists` function, it is strictly used to test keys. Here's an example of the usage:

```
if (exists $hash{$key}) { print "Yes."; }
else { print "No.\n"; }
```

exit

```
exit EXPR
```

The `exit` function evaluates `EXPR` and immediately exits the program. The `die` function is usually a cleaner way to abort execution of a program, because the error information returned can be trapped.

exp

```
exp EXPR
```

Returns *e* to the power of `EXPR`; if `EXPR` is omitted, then `exp($)` is assumed. For regular exponents, use the ** operator.

fcntl

```
fcntl FILEHANDLE, FUNCTION, SCALAR
```

Used to emulate the `fcntl(2)` system call. You can `use Fcntl;` to obtain the function definitions needed to use this function. See the man page for more information on this function. `fcntl` returns a fatal error if it is not implemented on the platform on which it is called.

fileno

```
fileno FILEHANDLE
```

`fileno` returns a file descriptor for a given filehandle. A file descriptor is a small integer identifying the file. It can be used to construct bitmaps for use with `select`. If `FILEHANDLE` is not open, it returns `undefined`.

flock

```
flock FILEHANDLE, OPERATION
```

This function calls the `flock(2)` system call on `FILEHANDLE`. For more information on the operations available, see the `flock(2)` man page. It produces a fatal error on systems that do not support `flock(2)` or some other file-locking mechanism.

fork

```
fork
```

`fork` is used to fork a system call into a separate process. `fork` returns the child PID to the parent process. It is only implemented on Unix-like platforms. All the code inside the block will run in a new process.

format

```
format
```

The `format` function is designed to give Cobol programmers a head start in learning Perl. Actually, it provides a method for creating templates for formatted output. For all the details on generating output using `format`, read the `perlform` man page.

formline

```
formline PICTURE, LIST
```

The `formline` function is used internally by formats. It is used to format `LIST` according to `PICTURE`. For more information, see the `perlform` man page.

getc

```
getc FILEHANDLE
```

`getc` returns the next character from `FILEHANDLE`. If `FILEHANDLE` is omitted, `getc` returns the next character from `STDIN`. `getc` does not allow unbuffered input (in other words, if `STDIN` is the console, `getc` does not get the character until the buffer is flushed with a newline).

getlogin

```
getlogin
```

Returns the current login from `/etc/utmp`, if any. If null, you should use `getpwuid()`.

getpeername

```
getpeername SOCKET
```

`getpeername` returns the packed `sockaddr` address of the other end of the `SOCKET` connection.

getpgrp

```
getpgrp PID
```

`getpgrp` returns the process group for the specified process. Supplying a PID of 0 will return the process group for the current process.

getppid

```
getppid
```

`getppid` returns the process ID for the parent process of the current process.

getpriority

```
getpriority WHICH, WHO
```

`getpriority` returns the priority for a process, process group, or user, assuming the system function `getpriority` is implemented on this machine.

getsockname

```
getsockname SOCKET
```

`getsockname` returns the packed `sockaddr` address of this end of the `SOCKET` connection.

getsockopt

```
getsockopt SOCKET, LEVEL, OPTNAME
```

`getsockopt` returns the requested option, or undefined in the case of an error.

glob

```
glob EXPR
```

The `glob` function returns the value of `EXPR` with filename expansions, similar to those that would occur under a shell. If `EXPR` is omitted, `$_` is assumed to be the argument.

gmtime

```
gmtime EXPR
```

`gmtime` converts a time in the format returned by the `time` function (seconds since Jan. 1, 1970, 00:00), to Greenwich Standard Time (otherwise known as Greenwich Mean Time). The time is returned as a nine-element list. The contents of each element are provided in this example:

```
($sec,$min,$hour,$mday,$mon,$year,$wday,$yday,$isdst) = gmtime(time);
```

Note that all the items are returned in numerical format, and numbers in series (such as month and day of the week) begin with 0 rather than 1. This means that months range from 0 to 11. The year returned is the number of years since 1900, not simply the last two digits of the year, thus avoiding the dreaded year 2000 problem. If you use `gmtime` in the scalar context, it returns the time in `ctime(3)` format, like this:

```
Sat Jun  6 01:56:44 1998
```

goto

```
goto LABEL
goto EXPR
goto &NAME
```

The `goto` function finds the statement labeled with `LABEL`, and continues executing from there. It cannot shift execution to statements within blocks that require initialization, such as subroutines or `foreach` loops. The other two usages of `goto` are rather arcane. `goto EXPR` is used to jump to a label that is specified by `EXPR`, which is scoped dynamically. `goto &name` substitutes a call to the named subroutine for the currently running subroutine, as though it was the one that was called in the first place.

grep

```
grep EXPR, LIST
grep BLOCK LIST
```

The grep function is used to search lists, and return all the elements in that list matching a particular pattern. grep accepts two arguments, an expression and a list. It returns another list containing each of the elements for which the expression was true. Let's look at an example:

```
@newarray = grep /red/, @oldarray;
```

@newarray will contain a list of all the items in @oldarray that contained the string red. If you call grep within the scalar context, it will return the number of items that matched, instead of a list of items that matched.

hex

```
hex EXPR
```

hex reads EXPR as a hexadecimal string and returns the decimal value. If EXPR is omitted, the function reads $_.

import

```
import CLASSNAME LIST
import CLASSNAME
```

import is not a built-in function; instead, it is implemented by modules that want to export names into another module. The import function is called by the use function when a module is loaded into a Perl program.

index

```
index STR, SUBSTR, POSITION
index STR, SUBSTR
```

index is used to locate a substring within a larger string. It accepts three arguments, one of which is optional. The arguments are the string to search, the substring to search for, and the position where the search should begin (optional). index returns the position in the string where the first occurrence of the substring begins. For example, to find the string go within the larger string bingo, you could use the following code index ('bingo', 'go');. To find the second occurrence of go within the string go or no go, you could use the optional third argument to start at position 3 in the string like this: index ('go or no go', 'go', 3);.

int

`int EXPR`

`int` returns the integer portion of a string. Basically, if a string begins with an integer, such as `55 MPH`, `int` will return that integer, in this case, `55`. Strings that don't begin with an integer will return 0 if you have Perl warnings turned on, you'll get a warning any non-numbers in the string.

ioctl

`ioctl FILEHANDLE, FUNCTION, SCALAR`

`ioctl` is used to implement the `ioctl(2)` system call. You will probably need to use

```
require "ioctl.ph";
```

to import the function definitions for `ioctl`. If it doesn't exist, you will need to create your own function definitions based on the system's `ioctl.h` file.

join

`join EXPR, LIST`

The `join` function is the opposite of split, it is used to join the elements of a list into a single string. It takes two arguments, an expression and a list. The contents of the expression are used as the delimiter between the elements in the string that is returned.

keys

`keys HASH`

The `keys` function returns an array containing all the keys in the named hash. It is oftentimes used to sort the keys in a hash before you iterate over them in a loop. Here's a common example:

```
foreach $key (sort (keys %hash)) {
    print $key, " = ", $value, "\n";
}
```

kill

`kill LIST`

`kill` is actually used to send a signal to a list of processes, rather than simply killing them. The first argument in `LIST` must be the signal to send, the rest should be the processes that will receive the signal. To kill processes, you would use this code:

```
kill 1, 100, 102, 110;
```

A

To kill those same processes with extreme prejudice, you would use this code:

```
kill 9, 100, 102, 110;
```

You can supply the signal name inside quotes instead of the signal number if you prefer. See the `signal(5)` man page for more information on signals.

last

```
last LABEL
last
```

The `last` command immediately exits the loop specified by `LABEL`. If no label is specified, the innermost loop exits.

lc

```
lc EXPR
```

The `lc` function converts all the alphabetic characters in a string to lowercase. `lc 'ABC';` returns `abc`. If no expression is provided, the `lc` function acts on `$_`.

lcfirst

```
lcfirst EXPR
```

Returns the value in `EXPR` with the first character lowercased. If `EXPR` is omitted, `$_` is used.

length

```
length EXPR
```

`length` accepts a string as an argument, and returns an integer containing the length of the string in bytes. For example, `length("dog");` returns 3. If `EXPR` is not supplied, `$_` is used.

link

```
link OLDFILE, NEWFILE
```

Creates a hard (as opposed to symbolic) link from `OLDFILE` to `NEWFILE`. To create a symbolic link, use the `symlink` function.

listen

```
listen SOCKET, QUEUESIZE
```

The `listen` function in Perl performs the same function as the `listen` system call. It returns `TRUE` if it succeeds, `FALSE` if it doesn't.

local

```
local EXPR
```

`local` specifies that the variables listed will be local to the currently executing block, loop, subroutine, `eval {}`, or `do`. If more than one variable is passed to `local`, they should be enclosed in parentheses. To restrict the scope of a variable, though, you should probably use `my` instead.

localtime

```
localtime EXPR
```

The `localtime` function is identical to `gmtime`, except that it returns the time converted to the local time zone instead of Greenwich time.

log

```
log EXPR
```

Returns the logarithm (base *e*) of `EXPR`, or `$_` if `EXPR` is not provided.

lstat

```
lstat FILEHANDLE
lstat EXPR
lstat
```

`lstat` is identical to the `stat` function, except that it stats a symbolic link instead of the file the link points to. If `EXPR` is omitted, `lstat` acts on the value in `$_`.

map

```
map BLOCK LIST
map EXPR, LIST
```

`map` provides an alternative to `foreach` for performing an operation on every element in a list. It can take two forms, and you can perform all the operations in a block of code on a list like this:

```
@backwards_words = map {
   lc;
   reverse;
} @words;
```

The previous example reverses and lowercases each element in the array `@words`. The results of `map` are returned in a list context, which is why I assign them to an array. Note that when each element is processed, it is assigned to the `$_` variable, which is why I can use the functions within the code block without arguments. To perform a single operation on each element of a list, `map` is called like this:

```
@newlist = map(uc, @oldlist);
```

Note that when a single operation is used with `map`, a comma is used to separate the function from the list that is being processed.

mkdir

```
mkdir FILENAME, MODE
```

`mkdir` is used to create a new directory, the name of which is specified in `FILENAME`. You should set the permissions for the directory with `MODE`, which should be specified in standard octal format (as a bare number, not within quotation marks), and should include the SUID bit.

msgctl

```
msgctl ID, CMD, ARG
```

`msgctl` calls the `msgctl(2)` system call. This function is available only on machines supporting System V IPC.

msgget

```
msgget KEY, FLAGS
```

Calls the System V IPC function `msgget` and returns the message queue ID, or undefined in the case of an error.

msgrcv

```
msgrcv ID, VAR, SIZE, TYPE, FLAGS
```

Calls the System V ICP function `msgrcv` to receive a message from message queue `ID`, into variable `VAR`, with a maximum size of `SIZE`. Returns `TRUE` if successful or `FALSE` if there's an error.

msgsnd

```
msgsnd ID, MSG, FLAGS
```

Calls the System V IPC function `msgsnd` to send `MSG` to the message queue specified in `ID`. Returns `TRUE` if successful or `FALSE` if there's an error.

my

```
my EXPR
```

`my` is used to scope the listed variables so that they are local to the current block, `eval {}`, subroutine, or imported file. If more than one variable is supplied, they must be placed within parentheses.

next

```
next LABEL
next
```

When the `next` command is encountered within a loop, it skips immediately to the next iteration of that loop.

no

```
no MODULE LIST
```

The `no` module is the opposite of the `use` operator. You can find more information in the `perlobj` man page.

oct

```
oct EXPR
```

`oct` reads `EXPR` as an octal string and returns the decimal value, unless the string starts with 0x, in which case it is interpreted as a hex value. If `EXPR` is omitted, the function reads `$_`.

open

```
open FILEHANDLE, EXPR
```

The `open` function opens the file specified in `EXPR`, and assigns it to `FILEHANDLE`. If `EXPR` is omitted, a variable with the same name as `FILEHANDLE` is assumed to contain the name of the file.

By prepending `<` to the filename you can open it for input. By prepending `>` to the filename you can open it for output. To append data to the output file, instead of overwriting it, you should prepend the filename with `>>`. To open a filehandle using a pipe instead of standard input and output, you can use the pipe character. Placing a `|` before the program name opens a pipe to that program, whereas placing a `|` after the filename opens a pipe from the program to your filehandle.

For more information on the open function, look at Chapter 15, "Working with Files and I/O."

opendir

`opendir DIRHANDLE, EXPR`

The `opendir` function opens the directory specified in `EXPR` for input, and assigns it to `DIRHANDLE`. A list of entries in the directory can then be read from the directory handle. Note that the namespace for directory handles does not overlap with that for filehandles.

ord

`ord EXPR`

Returns the numeric ASCII value of the first character of `EXPR`. If `EXPR` is omitted, `$_` is used.

pack

`pack TEMPLATE, LIST`

`pack` accepts a list of values, packs it into a binary structure, and returns the string containing that structure. The `TEMPLATE` is a list of characters that gives the order and type of the values.

TABLE A.1 `pack` Template Characters

Character	*What It Means*
A	An ascii string, will be space padded.
a	An ascii string, will be null padded.
b	A bit string (ascending bit order, like `vec()`).
B	A bit string (descending bit order).
h	A hex string (low nybble first).
H	A hex string (high nybble first).
c	A signed char value.
C	An unsigned char value.
s	A signed short value.
S	An unsigned short value. (This 'short' is exactly 16 bits, which might differ from what a local C compiler calls "short.")
i	A signed integer value.
I	An unsigned integer value. (This "integer" is at least 32 bits wide. Its exact size depends on what a local C compiler calls "int", and might even be larger than the "long" described in the next item.)
l	A signed long value.

TABLE A.1 continued

Character	What It Means
L	An unsigned long value. (This "long" is exactly 32 bits, which might differ from what a local C compiler calls "long.")
n	A short in "network" (big-endian) order.
N	A long in "network" (big-endian) order.
v	A short in "VAX" (little-endian) order.
V	A long in "VAX" (little-endian) order. (These "shorts" and "longs" are exactly 16 bits and exactly 32 bits, respectively.)
f	A single-precision float in the native format.
d	A double-precision float in the native format.
p	A pointer to a null-terminated string.
P	A pointer to a structure (fixed-length string).
u	A uuencoded string.
w	A BER compressed integer. Its bytes represent an unsigned integer in base 128, most significant digit first, with as few digits as possible. Bit eight (the high bit) is set on each byte except the last.
x	A null byte.
X	Back up a byte.
@	Null fill to absolute position.

Each letter can be followed with a number, which is used as the repeat count for that letter. The `unpack` function can be used to extract items stored in a binary structure.

package

```
package NAMESPACE
```

The `package` function declares that all the variables inside the innermost enclosing block, subroutine, eval, or file, belong to `NAMESPACE`. For more information, see the `permod` man page.

pipe

```
pipe READHANDLE, WRITEHANDLE
```

`pipe` opens a pipe from `READHANDLE` to `WRITEHANDLE`, similar to the system call of the same name.

pop

```
pop ARRAY
```

The pop function removes the last item in an array (shortening it by one element) and returns it as a scalar value. Both push (which will be discussed later) and pop are known as stack functions. If you imagine an array as a stack of trays in a cafeteria, pop is used to remove the top item from that stack.

pos

```
pos SCALAR
```

Returns the location in SCALAR where the last m//g search left off. If SCALAR is not specified, $_ is used.

print

```
print FILEHANDLE LIST
print LIST
print
```

The print function is used to output the data passed to it in the list context to standard output, or if a filehandle is specified, to that filehandle. If the list of data to print is omitted, the contents of $_ are printed by default. Note that there shouldn't be a comma between the filehandle and the actual list of data being printed, so to print some data to the filehandle FILE, you would use the following:

```
print FILE $data;
```

Or, to print a list of data, you could do this:

```
print FILE $data, ' ', $more_data, '\n';
```

printf

```
printf FILEHANDLE LIST
printf LIST
```

printf is used to format output using the conventions set for the sprintf function. Basically, this:

```
printf FILEHANDLE FORMAT, LIST;
```

is identical to:

```
print FILEHANDLE sprintf(FORMAT, LIST);
```

push

```
push ARRAY, LIST
```

push is used to add an element onto the end of an array. When you push a scalar value onto an array, the array is lengthened by one element, and that value is assigned to the last element in the array. Imagining the same stack of trays from the description of the pop function, you can envision the push function as putting a tray onto the top of the stack. You can also push multiple values onto the array by using a list as the argument to the push function.

quotemeta

```
quotemeta EXPR
quotemeta
```

quotemeta returns the value of EXPR, with all the nonalphanumeric characters escaped using backslashes. Uses $_ when EXPR is omitted.

rand

```
rand EXPR
rand
```

The rand function returns a random number between 0 and EXPR. If EXPR is omitted, the function returns a value between 0 and 1 (not including 1). See srand for information on seeding the random number generator.

read

```
read FILEHANDLE, SCALAR, LENGTH, OFFSET
read FILEHANDLE, SCALAR, LENGTH
```

The read function is used to read an arbitrary number of bytes of data from a filehandle into a scalar value. It accepts four arguments; filehandle, scalar, length, and offset (offset is optional). The filehandle argument specifies the filehandle from which to read the data. The scalar argument defines the variable to which the data will be assigned. Length specifies how many bytes of data will be read. Offset is used if you want to read the data from a place other than the beginning of the string. Here's an example, which would read 1024 bytes of data from 2048 bytes into the filehandle FILE, and assign them to the variable $chunk:

```
read FILE, $chunk, 1024, 2048;
```

A

readdir

`readdir DIRHANDLE`

`readdir` is used to read entries from a directory that has been opened using the `opendir` function. When used in the scalar context, it returns the next entry in the directory. In the list context, it returns all the remaining entries in the directory. If all the entries in the directory have already been read, it returns the undefined value.

readlink

`readlink EXPR`

The `readlink` function reads the value of a symbolic link. If symbolic links are not implemented on the platform, it returns a fatal error. If `EXPR` is omitted, the value in `$_` is used.

recv

`recv SOCKET, SCALAR, LEN, FLAGS`

`recv` is used to receive a message on a socket, using a C `recvfrom`. Receives `LEN` bytes into variable `SCALAR` from `SOCKET`. It returns the address of the sender, unless there's an error, in which case it returns undefined. `recv` accepts the same flags as the system call of the same name.

redo

```
redo LABEL
redo
```

`redo` restarts the current loop block, without reevaluating the loop's test condition. If `LABEL` is omitted, `redo` acts on the innermost enclosing block.

ref

`ref EXPR`

`ref` returns `TRUE` if `EXPR` is a reference, `FALSE` otherwise. If `EXPR` is omitted, `$_` is used.

rename

`rename OLDNAME, NEWNAME`

The `rename` function changes the name of the file `OLDNAME` to `NEWNAME`.

require

```
require EXPR
```

`require` is most often used to load an external Perl file into the current program, but more generally speaking, it is used to base some sort of dependency on its argument. If `EXPR` is numeric, that version of Perl is required for the program to run. If no argument is supplied, `$_` is used.

To load a file, you should provide the filename as the argument to `require`. If you provide the filename as a bare word, `.pm` is automatically appended, and `::` will be replaced by `/` to make it easy to load standard modules. The required file must end with a statement that evaluates as true. Customarily, files built to be required end with the `1;` statement.

reset

```
reset EXPR
reset
```

`reset` is used to clear global variables or `??` searches, and is often used at the beginning of a loop, or in the continue block at the end of a loop. `reset` clears the values of all the variables beginning with the character provided in `EXPR`. If called with no arguments, reset clears all `??` searches.

return

```
return EXPR
```

The `return` function suspends execution of an `eval`, subroutine, or `do` FILE, and returns the value of `EXPR`. If no return statement is provided, the value of the last expression evaluated will be returned.

reverse

```
reverse LIST
```

The `reverse` function accepts a scalar value or a list as its argument. For scalar values, it reverses of the order of the characters in the scalar. For example, `reverse "red";` returns `der`. When a list is passed to `reverse`, the order of the items in the list is reversed. `reverse ("red", "green", "blue");` returns `("blue", "green", "red")`.

rewinddir

```
rewinddir DIRHANDLE
```

`rewinddir` resets the directory handle for a directory opened with `readdir` back to the first entry in that directory.

rmdir

```
rmdir FILENAME
```

`rmdir` removes the directory specified by `FILENAME`, if it is empty. If the directory is not empty, or the function fails for some other reason, it returns 1. It returns 0 if it is successful. If `FILENAME` is not provided, the value in `$_` is used.

scalar

```
scalar EXPR
```

Forces the value of `EXPR` to be evaluated in the scalar context, and returns the value of `EXPR`.

seek

```
seek FILEHANDLE, OFFSET, WHENCE
```

`seek` is used to set the position of `FILEHANDLE`. `WHENCE` can be any of the following values; 0 to set the position to `POSITION`, 1 to add `POSITION` to the current position, and 2 to set it to EOF plus `POSITION` (usually a negative number is used here, for obvious reasons).

seekdir

```
seekdir DIRHANDLE, POS
```

`seekdir` sets the position of `DIRHANDLE` for the `readdir` function. `POS` must be a value returned by `telldir`.

select

```
select FILEHANDLE
select
```

Called without arguments, `select` returns the currently selected filehandle. When you provide a filehandle (or an expression that returns a filehandle) to `select`, that filehandle is now the default handle to which output will be sent, in other words, it becomes standard output. So, if you will be printing a number of items to a particular filehandle, it might be easier to `select` that filehandle, and leave the filehandles out of your print statements.

semctl

```
semctl ID, SEMNUM, CMD, ARG
```

`semctl` calls the System V IPC system call `semctl(2)`.

semget

```
semget KEY, NSEMS, SIZE, FLAGS
```

`semget` calls the System V IPC system call `semget(2)`, and returns the semaphore ID, or undefined if there is an error.

semop

```
semop KEY, OPSTRING
```

Calls the System V IPC system call `semop(2)`, which performs semaphore operations like signaling and waiting.

send

```
send SOCKET, MSG, FLAGS, TO
send SOCKET, MSG, FLAGS
```

The `send` function sends a message over a socket. If the socket is not connected, you must specify an address to send to. The function takes the same flags as the `send` system call, and returns the number of characters sent if it is successful, or undefined if it fails.

setpgrp

```
setpgrp PID, PGRP
```

`setpgrp` sets the process group for the specified PID. If 0 is supplied as the PID, the process group is set for the current process. Produces a fatal error if `setpgrp(2)` is not supported by the system.

setpriority

```
setpriority WHICH, WHO, PRIORITY
```

Sets the priority for a process, process group, or user. If `setpriority(2)` is not supported, a fatal error occurs.

setsockopt

```
setsockopt SOCKET, LEVEL, OPTNAME, OPTVAL
```

`setsockopt` is used to set the specified option for a socket. If there is an error, undefined is returned. Use `undef` for `OPTVAL` to set an option without specifying a value for the option.

shift

```
shift ARRAY
shift
```

The `shift` function is the opposite of the `unshift` function, it removes the first element from an array and returns it as a scalar value. The indexes of all the other elements in the array are decreased by one, and the array winds up one element shorter than it was before. `shift` is commonly used to process arguments passed to a user-written function. As you know, arguments are passed to functions through the array `@_`. By using commands such as `$arg = shift @_;`, you can easily make use of function arguments without worrying about their indexes.

shmctl

```
shmctl ID, CMD, ARG
```

`shmctl` calls the System V `shmctl(2)` system call. For more information on all the shared memory functions (which begin with `shm`), see the `perlipc` man page.

shmget

```
shmget KEY, SIZE, FLAGS
```

`shmget` calls the System V `shmget(2)` system call.

shmread

```
shmread ID, VAR, POS, SIZE
```

`shmread` calls the System V `shmread(2)` system call.

shmwrite

```
shmwrite ID, STRING, POS, SIZE
```

`shmwrite` calls the System V `shmwrite(2)` system call.

shutdown

```
shutdown SOCKET, HOW
```

`shutdown` closes a socket connection in the manner specified with `HOW`, which uses the same syntax as the `shutdown` system call.

sin

```
sin EXPR
```

Returns the sine of `EXPR`, or of `$_` if no argument is provided.

sleep

```
sleep EXPR
sleep
```

`sleep` causes the program to sleep for `EXPR` seconds, or if `EXPR` is not specified, to sleep indefinitely. `sleep` can be interrupted using the `SIGALRM` signal. It returns the number of seconds actually slept.

socket

```
socket SOCKET, DOMAIN, TYPE, PROTOCOL
```

The `socket` function is used to open a socket attached to filehandle `SOCKET`. `DOMAIN`, `TYPE`, and `PROTOCOL` are specified in the same way that they are specified for the socket system call. You should use `Socket;` to import the `Socket` module before you call the `socket` function to import the proper definitions.

socketpair

```
socketpair SOCKET1, SOCKET2, DOMAIN, TYPE, PAIR
```

The `socketpair` function creates a pair of unnamed sockets, in the specified domain, of the specified type. A fatal error occurs if this function is unimplemented, if it is successful, it returns `TRUE`.

sort

```
sort SUBNAME LIST
sort BLOCK LIST
sort LIST
```

The `sort` routine is used to sort the entries in a list, and returns the members in the list in the sorted order. There are three ways `sort` can be used; the simplest is to simply invoke `sort` with the list you want to sort as the argument. This returns the list sorted in standard string comparison order.

Another option is to supply a subroutine to compare with the items in the list. The subroutine should return an integer less than, equal to, or greater than zero, depending on how the elements of the list should be ordered (the `<=>` operator, which performs numeric comparisons, and the `cmp` operator, which provides string comparisons are often used in these subroutines).

Although the subroutine method described in the preceding paragraph can be used to sort lists by criteria other than the default, it is more common to simply insert a block of code as the first argument to the function call. You've probably seen the `sort` function used like this:

```
@sortedlist = sort { $a <=> $b } @list;
```

The preceding example sorts `@list` in ascending numerical order and assigns the list returned to the array `@sortedlist`. The items being compared by the sort routine are sent to the code block (or subroutine) as `$a` and `$b`, so the preceding block of code compares the two items using the `<=>` operator. Let's take a look at some other common code blocks used with the sort function:

```
# Sort in lexical order (the same as the default sort)
@sortedlist = sort {$a cmp $b } @list;

# Sort in descending lexical order
@sortedlist = sort { $b cmp $a } @list;

# Sort in numerical order
@sortedlist = sort { $a <=> $b } @list;

# Sort in descending numerical order
@sortedlist = sort { $b <=> $a } @list;
```

splice

```
splice ARRAY, OFFSET, LENGTH, LIST
splice ARRAY, OFFSET, LENGTH
splice ARRAY, OFFSET
```

`splice` is the Swiss Army Knife of array functions; it provides a general purpose for inserting elements into an array, removing elements from an array, or replacing elements in an array with new values. `splice` can be called with up to four arguments, the last two of which are optional. The first argument should be the array you want to splice. The second argument is the offset, the position in the array where the action will take place (to count back from the end of the array, you can use a negative number). The third argument, which is optional, is the number of items you want to remove (if you leave it out, all the items from the offset to the end of the array will be removed). The rest of the arguments are assumed to be a list of items that will be inserted at the offset. That sounds pretty confusing, but an example will make it all clear.

To delete all the elements in the array after the second element (remember that array indexes begin with 0), you could use the following code:

```
splice(@array, 2);
```

To insert a new scalar value between the second and third elements in an array, without removing anything, you would use

```
splice(@array, 2, 0, "new value");
```

To replace the second and third elements in an array with three new elements, you could use the following:

```
splice(@array, 2, 2, "red", "green", "blue");
```

You should note that after an array is spliced, all the elements in the array are reindexed to reflect the changes in the structure. So, in the previous example, all the indexes for the items after the ones we inserted would be incremented by one because we replaced two items with three.

split

```
split /PATTERN/, EXPR, LIMIT
split /PATTERN/, EXPR
split /PATTERN/
split
```

The `split` function is used to break a string into multiple parts and return those parts as a list. It accepts up to three arguments: a pattern on which to split, the string to split up, and a limit on the number of list items returned (optional). If you leave out the string to be split up, the value stored in `$_` will be used. You can also leave out the pattern on which to split up the string, and Perl will use whitespace as the delimiter. The pattern argument is always a regular expression contained within `//`, so to split the string on commas, you would use `/,/` as the pattern. Let's look at some examples:

```
# Empty pattern splits string into individual characters
@letters = split //, "word";
# A space in the pattern splits the sentence
# into individual words
@words = split / /, "this is a sentence";
# This pattern splits on any white space instead of just
# spaces (same as the default)
@words = split /\s/, "this is a sentence";
# The third argument ensures that only the first two items
# extracted from the string will be returned in the list.
($first, $second) = split /\s/, "this is a sentence", 2;
```

sprintf

```
sprintf FORMAT, LIST
```

The Perl `sprintf` function is used to format strings using the conventions established for the C `sprintf` function. Here's a table listing the conversions used with `sprintf`:

TABLE A.2 `sprintf` Formats

Format	*What It Represents*
`%%`	A percent sign
`%c`	A character
`%s`	A string
`%d`	A signed integer, in decimal notation
`%u`	An unsigned integer, in decimal notation

TABLE A.2 continued

Format	*What It Represents*
`%o`	An unsigned integer, in octal notation
`%x`	An unsigned integer, in hexidecimal notation
`%e`	A floating point number, in scientific notation
`%f`	A floating point number, in fixed decimal notation
`%g`	A floating point number, in `%e` or `%f` notation
`%X`	The same as `%x`, but using capital letters for hexidecimal notation
`%E`	The same as `%e`, but using a capital E
`%G`	The same as `%g`, but using a capital E (if applicable)
`%p`	A pointer, prints the memory location of the Perl value in hexadecimal
`%n`	Stores the number of characters output so far in the next variable in the parameter list

For detailed information on the conventions used with `sprintf`, check out the man page for `printf(3)`.

sqrt

`sqrt EXPR`

`sqrt` returns the square root of `EXPR`, or of `$_` if `EXPR` is not supplied.

srand

`srand EXPR`

`srand` seeds Perl's random number generator. If you leave off `EXPR`, `srand(time)` is assumed. You should only use it once in your program.

stat

`stat FILEHANDLE`

The `stat` function gathers some information on the file specified by `FILEHANDLE`, and returns a list containing that information. It can also accept an expression containing a filename instead of an open filehandle. If no argument is provided, the `stat` function uses the value of `$_` as its argument. The data returned by `stat` is in list form, and includes

- The device number of the filesystem
- The file's inode
- The file mode (type and permissions)

- The number of hard links to the file
- The uid and gid of the file's owner
- The device identifier (for special files)
- The size of the file in bytes
- The times since the file was last accessed, last modified, and the inode was changed
- The file's block size
- The number of blocks used

Let's take a look at the values returned by `stat`. This is how you might assign the list returned by `stat` to a group of variables.

```
($dev,$inode,$mode,$uid,$gid,$rdev,
$size,$atime,$mtime,$ctime,$blksize,$blocks) = stat $filename
```

study

```
study SCALAR
study
```

`study` takes extra time to study `SCALAR` (or `$_` if `SCALAR` is omitted), to make future pattern matches on the value more efficient. Whether this saves time or not depends on how many pattern matches you plan on making, and the nature of those matches.

substr

```
substr EXPR, OFFSET, LENGTH, REPLACEMENT
substr EXPR, OFFSET, LENGTH
substr EXPR, OFFSET
```

`substr` is used to extract some characters from a string. It accepts three arguments, the last of which is optional. The arguments are the expression from which characters should be extracted (this can be a scalar value, a variable, or a call to another function), the position to begin extracting characters, and, optionally, the number of characters to extract. So, `substr("foobar", 3, 2);` returns `ba`. Leaving out the length, like this: `substr("foobar", 3);` returns `bar`. You can also use a negative offset value, which will count positions from the end of the string instead of the beginning. Here's an example: `substr("foobar", -4, 2);` returns `ob`.

symlink

```
symlink OLDFILE, NEWFILE
```

The `symlink` function is used to create a symbolic link from `OLDFILE` to `NEWFILE`. `symlink` produces a fatal error if the system doesn't support symbolic links.

A

syscall

```
syscall LIST
```

`syscall` calls the system call specified as the first argument in `LIST`. The remaining items in `LIST` are passed to the system call as arguments.

sysopen

```
sysopen FILEHANDLE, FILENAME, MODE
sysopen FILEHANDLE, FILENAME, MODE, PERMS
```

Opens the file specified by `FILENAME`, associating it with `FILEHANDLE`. If the file does not exist, it is created.

sysread

```
sysread FILEHANDLE, SCALAR, LENGTH, OFFSET
sysread FILEHANDLE, SCALAR, LENGTH
```

Reads `LENGTH` bytes from `FILEHANDLE` into `SCALAR` using the `read(2)` system call. Returns the number of bytes read, or undefined if there is an error. `OFFSET` places the bytes read that many bytes into the string, rather than at the beginning.

sysseek

```
sysseek FILEHANDLE, POSITION, WHENCE
```

Similar to the `seek` function, except that it uses the `lseek(2)` system call rather than the `fseek(2)` call.

system

```
system LIST
```

The `system` function works exactly like `exec LIST`, except that it forks a new process and executes the commands in `LIST` in that process, and then returns.

syswrite

```
syswrite FILEHANDLE, SCALAR, LENGTH, OFFSET
syswrite FILEHANDLE, SCALAR, LENGTH
```

`syswrite` attempts to write `LENGTH` bytes of data from variable `SCALAR` to `FILEHANDLE`, using the `write(2)` system call. It returns the number of bytes written, or undefined in the case of an error.

tell

```
tell FILEHANDLE
```

`tell` returns the current position for the specified filehandle, or if no filehandle is specified, for the last file read.

telldir

```
telldir DIRHANDLE
```

`telldir` returns the current position in the specified directory handle.

tie

```
tie VARIABLE, CLASSNAME, LIST
```

`tie` binds a variable to a package class that will provide the implementation for a variable. `VARIABLE` is the name of the variable to be bound, and `CLASSNAME` is the name of the class implementing objects of the correct type. Any additional arguments are passed to the `new` method of the class.

tied

```
tied VARIABLE
```

`tied` returns a reference to the underlying object of `VARIABLE`, if it is tied to a package. If the variable isn't tied, it returns undefined.

time

```
time
```

The `time` function returns the number of seconds that have elapsed since the time that the system considers the epoch. On most systems, this is 00:00:00 UTC, January 1, 1970; on the MacOs, 00:00:00, January 1, 1904. Most often passed to `localtime` or `gmtime` for formatting.

times

```
times
```

`times` returns a four element array containing the user and system times for the current process, and its children. Here's an example:

```
($user, $system, $cuser, $csystem) = times;
```

truncate

```
truncate FILEHANDLE, LENGTH
truncate EXPR, LENGTH
```

Truncates the file assigned to `FILEHANDLE`, or specified by `EXPR`, to `LENGTH`. If truncate isn't implemented on the system, a fatal error occurs.

uc

```
uc EXPR
```

Just as `lc` converts all the letters in a string to lowercase, `uc` converts all the letters in a string to uppercase.

ucfirst

```
ucfirst EXPR
```

Returns `EXPR` with the first character capitalized.

umask

```
umask EXPR
```

`umask` is used to set the default `umask` for the process. It accepts an octal number (not a string of digits). The `umask` function is useful if your program will be creating a number of files. If `EXPR` is omitted, `umask` returns the current `umask`.

undef

```
undef EXPR
```

`undef` is used to eliminate the value of a variable. It can be used on a scalar variable, an entire array, or an entire hash.

unlink

```
unlink (LIST)
```

`unlink` deletes the files passed to it via `LIST`. It returns the number of files it successfully deletes. If no list is passed to `unlink`, it uses `$_` as its argument.

unpack

```
unpack TEMPLATE, EXPR
```

`unpack` is the reverse of `pack`. It accepts a data structure and translates it into a list, based on `TEMPLATE`. The `TEMPLATE` format is the same as that for `pack`.

unshift

`unshift ARRAY, LIST`

The `unshift` function inserts a scalar value as the first element in an array, moving the indexes of all the other items in the array up by one.

utime

`utime LIST`

`utime` is the Perl equivalent of the Unix `touch` command; it sets the access and modification times for a list of files. The first two arguments must contain the numerical access and modification times for the files. All the arguments after the first two are assumed to be files that should have their access and modification dates changed. The function returns the number of files that were successfully touched.

values

`values HASH`

Returns an array containing the `values` for each of the items in a hash, much like `keys` returns an array of the keys in a hash.

vec

`vec EXPR, OFFSET, BITS`

`vec` treats a string (specified by `EXPR`) as a vector of unsigned integers, and returns the value of the bit field specified by `OFFSET`.

wait

`wait`

`wait` simply waits for a child process to die, and then returns the PID of that process.

waitpid

`waitpid PID, FLAGS`

The `waitpid` function waits for a particular child process (specified by PID) to exit, and then returns the process ID of the dead process.

wantarray

```
wantarray
```

wantarray returns TRUE if the context of the subroutine currently being executed requires a list value. If it was called in the scalar or void context, this function returns FALSE. To avoid executing the entire subroutine, you can use a statement like this to make sure that the subroutine was called in the list context:

```
return unless defined wantarray;
```

warn

```
warn LIST
```

warn is used to print a message to standard error without terminating the program. Other than the fact that the program doesn't stop executing, it is just like the die function.

write

```
write FILEHANDLE
```

The write function is used to output data using a template defined with the format function. For more information, check out the perlform man page.

APPENDIX B

Installing Perl on a Unix System

This appendix explains how to obtain and install Perl for a computer running Unix. Unlike Windows, installing Perl on a Unix computer involves compiling Perl from the source code. Fortunately, thanks to tools such as the Configure program and `make`, this process is pretty straightforward. However, it does mean that certain tools should be present on your computer before you get started. This appendix explains which tools are required to install Perl, and where to get them. It also provides step-by-step instructions on performing the installation.

Do You Need to Install Perl?

Unless you're running on your own personal Unix system where you're the owner and the only person on it, chances are really good that you don't need to install Perl at all. It would be odd if Perl hadn't already installed because it is so useful to Unix system administrators. From your Unix system prompt, try this first:

```
% perl -v
```

If you get a message that says `This is perl, v5.6.0 built for sun4-solaris` or some such, you're set. Stop here, and go directly to Day 1, "An Introduction to Perl," to start working with Perl.

If you get a message that says `perl: command not found`, or if you get the proper version message, but it says something like `This is perl, version 4`, then things are going to be tougher. It means that either Perl isn't installed on your system, or Perl is installed but it's an older version (you want to be running a version of Perl 5 or higher for this book; older versions won't work). Or it could mean that Perl is installed, but it's not in your search path; you might try looking around in `/usr/bin` or `/usr/local/bin`.

If you still can't find Perl and if you're on a Unix machine administered by someone else (that is, a system at work, or a public ISP) your next step is to contact the system administrator or support organization for that system and ask them if they have Perl installed (and if they do, where they put it), or if they've got an old version, to upgrade it. Although you can install Perl on a system that you don't have administrator access to, it's generally a better idea for your administrator to do it for you.

And, finally, if you run your own Unix system—say, a Linux system on a partition of your Windows machine—and you cannot find Perl already installed, then you are your own system administrator, and it's your job to install Perl.

Obtaining Perl

To install Perl on your system, you have three choices:

- Install a vendor package
- Download and install a prebuilt binary version
- Download, compile, and install the source-code version

Installing a Vendor Package

If you're using a free variety of Unix (Linux, FreeBSD, or OpenBSD) your vendor probably supplies a vendor-created package designed for your system. Usually, when you install these operating systems, you have the option of installing Perl along with the rest of the operating system. They also provide tools that enable you to download and install updated packages. For example, Red Hat provides many third-party applications as RPM files. You can use any RPM tool to download and install Perl on your system. Most free Unixes have similar systems.

For more information on these types of packages, see your vendor's Web site. If such a system is available, you'll definitely want to look into installing Perl that way rather than using the following methods. These systems generally make it easy to uninstall and update packages, so it's best to use them when you can.

Getting Binaries

Installing a binary version is the simpler than installing Perl—you don't need to compile anything, just unpack and go. However, binaries are only available for a very few Unix platforms, they tend to lag behind the current version of the Perl source code, and there is a danger of viruses or other nasties being hidden in the binary versions if you don't get them from a reputable source. Building the Perl source code is not difficult, and if you use Unix for any extensive period of time you'll probably end up doing a lot anyhow. Plus, with the source code you'll always end up with the latest and greatest versions. If you can't get a vendor-supplied package, building Perl from source is the preferred method of getting Perl installed on your system.

Another place to look, particularly for Solaris and Linux software, is the archive at `http://ibiblio.org/pub/`, formerly called Sunsite. Check in `http://ibiblio.org/pub/packages/solaris/sparc` for Solaris software, and `http://ibiblio.org/pub/Linux` for Linux.

Different companies and sites have different ways of packaging their binaries; you'll need to follow the directions for each site to discover how to install the Perl binaries on your system. You might find that with tracking down binaries and figuring out how to install them that it was easier to just go the source code route in the first place.

Getting Source (and Related Tools)

To compile and install Perl from the source code, there are several other things you'll need in addition to the Perl code itself: `tar` and `gzip` to unpack the source archive, and a C compiler to compile the source. The Perl installation will also go most smoothly if you have superuser (root) access on the computer on which Perl will be installed. If you're not the system administrator for the computer on which you need to run Perl, you'll probably be better off tracking down the person who is, and asking him to do it.

To expand the Perl archive you'll need `tar` and `gzip`. The `tar` utility is present on almost every Unix machine. Most Unix computers also have `gzip` installed, especially if they're running a free version of Unix such as FreeBSD or Linux. If you don't have these utilities, you'll need to locate them on the Internet, download them, and install them. As with the Perl binaries, it's likely that the vendor of your Unix system can provide you with access to these tools, or if your Unix system came on a CD-ROM they might have been bundled with that CD-ROM. Solaris users can download precompiled `GNUtar` and `gzip` packages from SunSite at `http://metalab.unc.edu/pub/packages/solaris/sparc`.

Second, you'll also need a C compiler. It is likely that the computer you're using will have either `cc` or `gcc` installed (type cc or gcc at a prompt and see what happens). If you can't locate a C compiler on your system, you should contact your system administrator about locating or installing one. Again, C compilers are almost always installed by default with free Unix systems, and are also installed with many popular commercial Unix variants. Solaris users can download precompiled versions of `gcc` at the SunSite URL mentioned previously.

When you're sure that you have all the tools required to successfully install Perl, you can download the Perl source code. The easiest way to get it is to simply point your Web browser to `www.perl.com`, which keeps the latest stable version of Perl at `http://www.perl.com/CPAN/src/stable.tar.gz`.

The `stable.tar.gz` package contains the C source code, which should compile successfully on nearly every Unix platform. As I write this, that's version 5.6.1, and that's the version this book covers. If you're feeling really adventurous, you can download the new experimental developer's version of Perl at `http://www.perl.com/CPAN/src/devel.tar.gz`. The developer's version is currently version 5.7.2 (but has most likely changed by the time you read this). You should only use it if you already know Perl, know what you're doing, want to check out some of the newer features, and are willing to put up with some odd behavior.

All the `.gz` packages are in binary format, so make sure you download them as binary files. If you download them in text format, they won't decompress (if you use a browser to download them, you don't have to worry about this).

Extracting and Compiling Perl

When you've successfully downloaded the Perl source code, extract it from its archive. There are two steps required to extract the Perl archive; decompressing it using `gzip`, and expanding the archive using `tar`. To unzip the file, use the following command:

```
gzip -d latest.tar.gz
```

Then, untar the file using this command:

```
tar xvf latest.tar
```

As the `tar` program runs, a list of all the files being extracted from the archive will be printed on the screen. Don't worry about the output. A directory named `perl5.6.1` or something similar will be created with all the Perl files inside.

Detailed installation instructions can be found in the README and INSTALL files; I'll summarize the process in the following sections.

Running the Configure Program

Before you install Perl, run the `Configure` program to set up the compile-time options. First, `cd` to the Perl directory created when you untarred the archive (usually, perl plus a version number, for example, `perl5.6.1`). Then, remove any existing configuration file using

```
rm -f config.sh
```

(There might not be any existing configuration file, but don't worry about it.) Then run the Configure program like this:

```
sh Configure
```

`Configure` will ask you a lot of questions about the makeup of your system and where things should be installed. If you want to skip most of those questions, you can use `sh Configure -d` instead. This will cause `Configure` to automatically select as many default values as it can, and install Perl in various default locations typical for your platform. These instructions assume you want to run `Configure` the long way.

Note

> Before we start, please be aware that `Configure` is written to configure software for all kinds of complex features of different platforms. Unless you're really very familiar with Unix systems and with C, a lot of the questions it asks might be really confusing or seem to make no sense. Most every question will have a default value, which you can accept by pressing Return or Enter. Generally, you'll do no harm by accepting Configure's default values, so if you don't know what the program is asking, just press Return.
>
> Also, depending on the version of Perl you're installing, some of the following questions may or may not appear in a slightly different order. If things start to get confusing, just accept the defaults and you should be fine.

Setting Up

First, `Configure` ensures that you have some things necessary for the Perl installation, provides you with some instructions on the installation process (you can read them if you want to, but it's not necessary), and then locates some of the utilities used in the installation process.

To speed up the installation process, `Configure` guesses which system you're on so that it can set up some default values. Most likely, it'll guess right, so you can just press Enter and accept the default.

Then, it makes a guess at which operating system you're using. If the defaults are correct, just press Enter for both the name and version.

Depending on your Perl version, you might be asked if you want to build a threading version of Perl. Unless you know what you're doing, you're better off not building one right now because threads are experimental. When you know more about Perl you can go back and recompile it with threads turned on.

Directories and Basic Configuration

The next step, an important one, is to specify under which directory hierarchy Perl will be installed. The default is typically under the `/usr/local` hierarchy; binaries in `/usr/local/bin`, man pages in `/usr/local/man`, and libraries in `/usr/local/lib`. You can change the basic hierarchy where Perl is installed if you choose to do so; for example, to install them under `/usr` with the system files (`/usr/bin/`, `/usr/lib`, `/usr/man`). Just indicate a prefix here; if you want to customize where you put each part of Perl you'll have an opportunity to do that later.

The next directory you need to specify is the location for site-specific and architecture-dependent Perl libraries. If you've accepted the defaults for the other directory locations, accepting the defaults here are almost certainly okay.

Depending on the version of Perl you're installing, the next question might be whether you want Perl to be binary-compatible with Perl's earlier versions. If Perl 5.001 was installed on the machine you are currently installing Perl, you'll need to specify where to put the old architecture-dependent library files. For both these questions, the defaults are fine unless you have reason to change them.

`configure` then checks for secure `setuid` scripts, and you have a choice of whether to do `setuid` emulation. Chances are good that if you don't know what this means, you don't need it. Accept the default.

The next question is which memory models are supported on the machine; for most, it's none. Accept the default.

Compilers and Libraries

`Configure` asks you which compiler to use. It figures out which compiler it would prefer to use, and offers you that as the default.

`Configure` also figures out in which directories to look for libraries. If you know of other directories to search for shared libraries, add them to the list, and remove any directories that should not be searched from the list. The default will probably work here.

`Configure` asks for the file extension for shared libraries. If you don't want to use shared libraries, change the default to none. You probably don't want to change it, however.

Next, `Configure` checks for the presence of some specific libraries on your system. It presents you with a list of shared libraries it will use when it's done. You can add or remove libraries from the list, but the default list will probably work fine.

The `Configure` program then asks some questions about your compiler. If you don't specifically know a good reason to change the defaults, just go ahead and use them.

One of the compiler questions is where you want to store the Perl binaries. By default the choice is the prefix hierarchy you chose, plus the `bin` directory, for example, `/usr/local/bin`. You have the opportunity to change that here.

Documentation and Networking

After all the compiler-related questions are finished, `Configure` asks where you want to place the Perl man files. As with the binaries, the default is the directory prefix plus `man`. You'll only need to change it if you want to put the man page somewhere else on your system. It also asks for the extensions for your man pages; you should accept the default.

`Configure` then tries to determine your host and domain names. If it guesses right, you can accept the defaults. Otherwise, edit its choices and enter the correct values (the host-name is your fully-qualified Internet name for that particular system (for example, `www.typerl.com`); the domain name is the last part of the address (`typerl.com`).

The next question is your e-mail address. Perl will try to get the right e-mail address here, but it will be specific to the machine on which you are installing Perl. You might need to change it to your general e-mail address. (For example, it will probably select `person@somemachine.somedomain.com`, when what you really want is `person@somedomain.com`.)

Perl also wants the e-mail address for the person who will be responsible for administration of Perl on the machine. If it's not you, enter the e-mail address for the person or group who will be responsible here (be nice).

Other Things

Next, Perl wants the value to place in the shebang line of scripts. The default value is almost certainly correct because you've already told `Configure` where the Perl binaries will be installed. (Don't worry if you don't know what a shebang is; you'll learn about that soon enough. Accept the defaults.)

Then, you need to tell Perl where to place publicly executable scripts. Reasons why you might not want to accept the default are provided by `Configure`.

Depending on your Perl version, you might be asked for yet more directory pathnames, this time for library files. Once again, the defaults are probably fine.

The next question is whether you want to use the experimental PerlIO abstraction layer instead of `<stdio.h>`. You probably don't.

`Configure` then checks for the presence of certain system calls, and for other system specific things. It might ask you a few questions along the way. You can probably accept the defaults for all these. Even if Configure seems to have misgivings (my Linux system triggered a few "WHOA THERE" and "Are you sure" messages), accept the defaults and you'll be fine.

The last questions `Configure` asks is which Perl extensions you want to load dynamically and statically. You can probably just accept the default, which is to load them all dynamically.

Perl then gives you a chance to edit the configuration file it just built, `config.sh`, manually. You probably don't need to do so; just press Return.

`Configure` gives you the chance to run `make depend` (go ahead), and then exits.

For detailed instructions on most of the options in the Configure program, you should read the `INSTALL` file in the Perl directory.

Run `make`

The next step after the `Configure` program generates the `config.sh` file is to type `make` in the Perl directory. `make` will compile all the Perl binaries and prepare them for installation.

On some systems, the `ar` program is required to build Perl. Unfortunately, for most users, `ar` is not in their path. If the make fails because it can't find `ar`, you should do a `man ar`, find out where it is located, and add that directory to your `PATH` environment variable (on Solaris systems, `ar` is in `/usr/ccs/bin`). You should then be able to run `make` again and successfully build Perl. It will take a while for the `make` process to work, so you might want to go do something else while it's working.)

Before you install Perl, you should type `make test` in the Perl directory to make sure everything was built correctly. After that's finished, you can `make install` to move all the Perl files to the locations that you specified using `Configure`.

One last question that might be asked is whether you want to link `/usr/bin/perl` to the location where you actually installed Perl. Many scripts assume that Perl will be located in `/usr/bin/perl`, so if you link your Perl binary to `/usr/bin/perl`, it could save you some work down the road.

After `make install` is finished, Perl should be installed and ready to go. This time, if you installed Perl in a standard location in your PATH, then this time if you type

```
% perl -v
```

you should get a version message (`This is perl, version 5....`), and you're all set and ready to learn Perl.

For More Information

Because you're on Unix, Perl was written for you. All core Perl man pages, FAQs, utilities, modules, and documentation were originally written for Unix, so you should be fine starting right off. The central repository of all things Perl is at `www.perl.com`; start from there and work downward. And, of course, there are always the pointers scattered throughout this book.

APPENDIX C

Installing Perl for Windows

This appendix explains how to obtain and install Perl for the Windows platform, sometimes known as Win32 Perl. Perl for Windows will run on Windows NT or Windows 95/98, although it is slightly more robust on Windows NT (I found very little that was different between the two platforms).

With the release of version 5.005 of Perl, Windows support has been incorporated into the core Perl source code tree, and is up to date with the Unix version. Previously, there had been several different versions of Perl for Windows, with each version supporting different features and lagging behind the Unix platform in different ways. The merged 5.005 version made a tremendous difference in stability and support for the Windows platform. If you have installed a previous version of Perl for Windows, I *strongly* suggest you upgrade to the latest version before starting this book.

To install Perl for Windows, you have two choices. You can

- Download the core Perl source code, and compile and build it yourself
- Download a prebuilt version of Perl for Windows, sometimes called ActivePerl, from ActiveState

Going the source code route enables you to be up-to-minute with the latest bug fixes, experimental features, and changes, but you must have a modern C++ compiler (Microsoft's Visual C++, Borland C++, and so on), and you must understand how to build large C projects. Windows 2000 and XP are definitely the better-supported platforms for building Perl yourself. You'll also need to download and install the Win32 modules (`libwin32`) yourself to get access to various Windows features such as OLE and processes.

The other choice is to download the prebuilt binary version of Perl from ActiveState. ActivePerl, as this version is called, contains Perl for Windows, some nice installation scripts, the Win32 Perl modules, PerlScript (an ActiveX scripting engine to replace JavaScript or VBScript inside Internet Explorer), Perl of ISAPI for Perl CGI scripts, and the Perl Package Manager (PPM), which makes installing extra Perl modules much easier.

Because the prebuilt ActiveState version of Perl is probably the better choice for most Windows users, this appendix will primarily cover downloading and installing that version. If you'd prefer to build Perl yourself, I've included a section at the end of this appendix ("Downloading the Perl Source Code") to help you get started. The README files included with the source can help you get started from there.

Downloading Perl for Windows

The first step in installing Perl for Windows on your computer is to download the installation package from ActiveState's Web site.

ActiveState is a company dedicated to building and supporting Perl and its tools on the Windows platform. ActiveState also offers a Perl developer's kit, a GUI-based Perl debugger, and a plug-in for NT-based Web serves that improves CGI performance (although none of these packages are part of the core Perl for Windows package).

Get the latest version of Perl for Windows at `http://www.activestate.com/ActivePerl/download.html`. The first page lists the requirements for installing Perl. Download and install any of the required software, if you lack any, before adding Perl. On the next page, you can download the actual Perl installation file.

Installing Perl for Windows

The Perl installed file you downloaded from ActiveState is an MSI file, which works with Microsoft's built-in installation program (users of Windows 95 or Windows NT 4.0 will have to install Microsoft Installer 2.0 before they can install the MSI file). If you save the file to disk, double-click it to launch and start the installation process. An installation wizard will launch, and you'll need to agree to the Perl license. The next screen enables you to select packages to install and to specify where to install Perl.

The packages you can install are as follows:

- Perl: The core Perl installation.
- Perl ISAPI: Only needed if you've got a IIS Web server and you'll be using Perl to develop CGI scripts for it.
- PerlScript: Only needed if you'll be using the PerlScript ActiveX plug-in.
- Perl Package Manager (PPM): You definitely want this if you're going to use any public modules that aren't included with Perl.
- Example Files: Also useful.

Next screen: Here are those options you learned about earlier in the installation notes. You can have up to four choices:

- Adding Perl to your path
- Associate .pl files with the Perl executable
- Associate .pl files with your IIS or Web site Web servers
- Associate .plx files with IIS and Perl for ISAPI

Unless you have compelling reasons not to, you can go ahead and allow all four of these options when they occur.

The final screen offers you a last chance to confirm that you want to install Perl. You can go back and change your choices, or choose Install to start the actual installation and configuring process.

After the installer finishes installing the files and configuring Perl for Windows, you can view the release notes or exit (the release notes contain lots of information about what's changed since the last release, but probably aren't exceptionally useful if you're installing Perl for the first time).

Now you're ready to get started with Perl. If you look at the directory C:\Perl on your computer (or wherever you chose to install Perl), you'll see several subdirectories:

- `bin`: Contains the executable for Perl and all supporting tools.
- `Docs`: The included Perl documentation.
- `eg`: Examples. Look at the files in this directory for example scripts and various bits of Perl code (most of them are supplied on an as-is basis, and are undocumented, so they won't necessarily be helpful).

- `html`: Online documentation, in HTML format. You can use your favorite browser to read any of these files. Start from the file index.html.
- `lib`: core library files.
- `site`: additional library files supplied by ActiveState.

Running Perl for Windows

To run Perl for Windows, you'll need to start a command prompt window (a DOS Prompt in Windows 95, or a Command Prompt in Windows NT). At the command line, you can make sure Perl's running with the -v option:

```
c:\> perl -v
```

You'll get a message telling you the version of Perl you're running and some other information about your Perl installation. This verifies that Perl has been installed correctly, and that your system can find the Perl executable. From here, you can proceed to Day 1 and start writing Perl scripts.

Downloading the Perl Source Code

If you're looking to live on the cutting edge of Perl for Windows, you'll want to get the Perl source code instead of the binary version. Alternately, if you know something about C code, sometimes having the source around can help you figure out what's going on when your Perl scripts are not behaving the way you want them to. In either of these cases, you'll want to download the actual Perl source code as well as, or instead of, the ActiveState version of Perl.

Perl's source code is available at `http://www.perl.com/pub/a/language/info/software.html`. A number of versions are available to choose from. The latest stable version is always available as `stable.tar.gz` (as I write this, that's version 5.6.1). Alternatively, the experimental development version is at `devel.tar.gz` (that's version 5.7.2 as I write this, but most likely will have changed by the time you're reading it). This book covers the `stable.tar.gz` version.

Perl source code is stored in Unix-format tar archives, compressed with GNU zip. They are binary files, so download them in binary format. After you have the archive stored on your system, WinZip can decompress and unarchive the Perl source files just fine.

The file README.win32 provides detailed documentation for compiling the source into a workable Perl installation.

Getting More Information

Regardless of whether you're using the ActiveState build of Perl for Windows or not, ActiveState's Web site at `www.activestate.com` is a great place to start for help getting started with Perl for Windows. From there you can find the ActivePerl FAQ at `http://aspn.activestate.com/ASPN/Perl`, and the various ActivePerl mailing lists at `http://aspn.activestate.com/ASPN/Perl/Mail`.

ActiveState also offers support for their version of Perl. See `http://www.activestate.com/support/` for details.

And, of course, the standard Perl resources are always available at `www.perl.com`, and pointers are scattered throughout this book.

INDEX

Symbols

B

C

E

F

G

H

J-K

L

N

O

Q

R

S

T

X-Z